LOEB CLASSICAL LIBRARY
FOUNDED BY JAMES LOEB 1911

EDITED BY
JEFFREY HENDERSON

PHILO

SUPPLEMENT I

LCL 380

PHILO

QUESTIONS AND ANSWERS ON GENESIS

TRANSLATED FROM THE ANCIENT ARMENIAN VERSION OF THE ORIGINAL GREEK BY

RALPH MARCUS

HARVARD UNIVERSITY PRESS
CAMBRIDGE, MASSACHUSETTS
LONDON, ENGLAND

First published 1953

ISBN 978-0-674-99418-8

Printed on acid-free paper and bound by
The Maple-Vail Book Manufacturing Group

CONTENTS

PREFACE

Philo's *Quaestiones et Solutiones in Genesin et Exodum* presents a special problem of translation because all but a small portion of the Greek original—less than ten per cent if we disregard the paraphrastic citations in late writers—has been lost and because for the bulk of the work we must depend upon the ancient Armenian version published by Aucher in 1826.[a] This edition is based chiefly upon three mss., all of them from the thirteenth century, and in part upon two others of about the same date. The Armenian version itself seems to have been made in the fifth century.[b]

For various reasons we can be reasonably sure that the Armenian version has faithfully preserved Philo's meaning except in a few cases where the Greek text used by the translator was corrupt or ambiguous or unusually obscure. In the first place, the Armenian language is singularly well designed to reproduce the word-order, word-compounds and many of the idioms of Greek. In the second place, the literalness and consistency of the Armenian version are shown by the correspondences between it and the original Greek in several treatises of Philo which are extant in both languages. The same is true of the correspondences between the Armenian *Quaestiones* and the Greek fragments which are not paraphrastic. A third check on the accuracy of the Armenian version is to be found in the Armenian-Greek equivalents given by Avedikean, Siurmelean and

[a] J. B. Aucher, *Philonis Judaei Paralipomena Armena : libri videlicet quatuor in Genesin, libri duo in Exodum, sermo unus de Sampsone, alter de Jona, tertius de tribus angelis*, etc., Venetiis, MDCCCXXVI.

[b] *Id.* pp. i-ii.

Aucher in their Armenian dictionary published in Venice in 1836 in two large volumes.

With the help of this material I have ventured to reconstruct many of the philosophical and religious terms used by Philo in passages which are no longer extant in Greek. These reconstructions are not all to be regarded as certain but most of them, I think, are probably correct. At the same time I have tried to improve upon Aucher's Latin translation of the Armenian version. A good many of the inaccuracies in his pioneer rendering are really the fault of the ancient Armenian translator. Others result from Aucher's failure to divine the Greek idiom underlying a literal Armenian rendering. In calling attention to Aucher's deficiencies I am in a sense repaying the great debt I owe him for helping me to see the meaning of many a difficult passage. It would be ungrateful of me to let it appear that my knowledge of Armenian remotely approaches his.

To one of my students, Mr. Edward Hobbs, I am indebted for help in reading proof. To my friend Professor H. A. Wolfson, whose book on Philo is a fine contribution to knowledge, I owe several good suggestions about the solution of problems of Greek philosophy.

The firm of R. and R. Clark has, as always, been remarkably accurate in printing.

R. M.

University of Chicago
16 *November* 1951

INTRODUCTION

I

Philo's *Questions and Answers on Genesis and Exodus* is, as its name indicates, a brief commentary in the form of questions and answers on the first two books of the Pentateuch, and in its form resembles Hellenistic (pagan) commentaries on the Homeric poems.

To each question concerning the meaning of a Biblical expression or verse Philo gives a twofold answer ; one refers to the literal meaning (τὸ ῥητόν), and the other to the allegorical meaning (τὸ πρὸς διάνοιαν,[a] τὸ συμβολικόν). The allegorical interpretation may be subdivided into three kinds : the physical (*i.e.* cosmological or theological), the ethical or psychological, and the mystical. Sometimes Philo's comment contains only one kind of allegorical interpretation, sometimes two, and occasionally all three.

Thus Philo's twofold method of interpretation is a forerunner of the fourfold method used by Rabbinic and Patristic commentators. His " literal " interpretation corresponds to the " literal " or " historical " interpretation of the Church Fathers and to the *pešaṭ* of the Rabbis. His " physical " interpretation corresponds to the " allegorical " interpretation of the Church Fathers and to the *remez* of the Rabbis. His " ethical " interpretation corresponds to the " moral " interpretation of the Church Fathers and to the *deraš* of the Rabbis. His mystical interpretation corresponds to the " anagogical " inter-

[a] This is the literal equivalent of Armenian *aṛ i mitsn*, but Philo elsewhere uses τὸ ἐν ὑπονοίαις and other expressions.

pretation of the Church Fathers and to the *sod* of the Rabbis.

In his earlier work,[a] the *Allegoriae* or allegorical commentary on Genesis, which now consists of eighteen treatises in twenty-one books (about ten treatises have been lost, and some of the extant ones are incomplete), Philo allowed himself the luxury of long digressions and comparisons of the verses discussed with other passages in Scripture. The *Quaestiones* sticks more closely to the text and stays within a more limited area of ideas. On the other hand, there appears to be relatively more Pythagorean number-symbolism in the *Quaestiones* than in the *Allegoriae*. Possibly this indicates that Philo became more interested in this rather mechanical form of mysticism as he grew older.

II

Something must now be said about the original extent of the *Quaestiones et Solutiones* and the division into books of the treatises on Genesis and Exodus.

Massebieau and Schürer [b] have called attention to a passage (*QG* iv. 123) in which Philo says, " the principle of these things will be explained when we inquire into the blessings." This may be a reference either to Genesis ch. xlix or to Deuteronomy ch. xxxiii or to both. It is likely, however, that Philo refers only to the passage on blessings in Genesis, since Eusebius knew only of Questions and Answers on Genesis and Exodus (*Hist. Eccl.* ii. 18. 1, 5) and also because the Greek fragments preserved by Byzantine

[a] That the *Quaestiones* is later than the *Allegoriae* is indicated by the fact that in the former Philo occasionally refers to the larger commentary, *e.g.* in *QG* ii. 4, *QE* ii. 34, 113. Schürer (*GJV* iii, 3rd ed. 501) believes that the *Quaestiones* is partly earlier, partly later than the *Allegoriae*. That is possible.

[b] M. L. Massebieau, " Le Classement des œuvres de Philon," *Bibl. de l'École des Hautes Études . . . sciences rel.* 1 (1889), 1-91 ; Emil Schürer, *Geschichte d. jüdischen Volkes*, etc., 3rd ed. (Leipzig, 1898), iii. 497, n. 33.

writers are, with two doubtful exceptions, all ascribed either to Genesis or Exodus.[a] We shall probably be safe in assuming either that Philo never wrote similar commentaries on the last three books of the Pentateuch or that, if he did, they were lost before the time of Eusebius.

As for the original book-divisions of *Quaestiones et Solutiones in Genesin*, it is clear that there were originally six books instead of the four indicated in the Armenian version. This is shown by the fact that some of the Greek fragments are ascribed to books ε′ and ϛ′ of *QG* and that six books are listed for *QG* in a Vienna codex of the *De Opificio Mundi*.[b]

But it is also clear that the Armenian version has preserved all six books of the original treatise. As Wendland [c] and other scholars have pointed out, Book IV of the Armenian *QG* is about as long as Books I, II and III together. It therefore probably contains Books IV, V and VI of the original *QG*. Since the end of Book IV reaches only Gen. xxviii. 9, it seems that Philo did not intend to treat the whole of Genesis.[d]

We can also tell with a fair degree of certainty just where in the present Book IV the beginnings of the original Books V and VI are to be placed. Since the Old Latin version begins with *QG* iv. 154 and since it extends through approximately a third of the book, it is probable that

[a] J. Rendel Harris, *Fragments of Philo Judaeus* (Cambridge, 1886), p. 75, labels two fragments as " from the lost book of Questions on Leviticus," but only one of the two is said in the MS. (Cod. Vat. 1553, cited from Mai) to be ἐκ τῶν ἐν Λευιτικῷ ζητημάτων. See also Schürer, *op. cit.* p. 497, n. 34.

[b] See L. Cohn in Cohn-Wendland, *Philonis Opera*, vol. i (Berlin, 1896), p. xxxvi.

[c] Paul Wendland, *Neu entdeckte Fragmente Philos* (Berlin, 1891), p. 92 ; see also Schürer, *op. cit.* p. 498, n. 35.

[d] In the Armenian version Book I covers Gen. ii. 4-vi. 13 ; Book II covers Gen. vi. 14-x. 9 ; Book III covers Gen. xv. 7-xvii. 27 ; Book IV covers Gen. xviii. 1-xx. 18 and xxiii. 1-xxviii. 9. Thus, beside the omission of single verses in all four books, the following entire chapters are omitted : i, xi-xiv, xxi-xxii, xxix-l.

Book VI of the original treatise corresponded to *QG* iv. 154-245 (end).

As for the beginning of Book V, Wendland [a] would locate it between *QG* iv. 76 and *QG* iv. 99 because this would give a book about one-third the size of the Armenian Book IV and also because *QG* iv. 99 and 104 are ascribed to Book ϵ′ in the Greek fragments. I think, however, that we should place the beginning of Book V at *QG* iv. 71 (on Gen. xxiii. 1), since this section begins with a new episode and also corresponds to the beginning of a new Pentateuch-lection in both the Palestinian triennial cycle (where it is Seder 19b [b]) and the Babylonian annual cycle (where it is Seder 5).

Thus we may suppose that the original book-divisions of the *Quaestiones et Solutiones in Genesin* were as follows :

Original Greek		Armenian Version
Book I	=	Book I
Book II	=	Book II
Book III	=	Book III
Book IV	=	Book IV. 1-70
Book V	=	Book IV. 71-153
Book VI	=	Book IV. 154-245

Somewhat similar but more complicated is the problem of the original extent and the book-divisions of the commentary on Exodus. The Armenian version has two books of unequal size. Book I covers Ex. xii. 2-23 in 25 pages of Aucher's edition, while Book II (aside from the first section on Ex. xx. 25) covers Ex. xxii. 21-xxviii. 34 (with the omission of several verses) in 80 pages. If we suppose that *QE* was divided into books of about the same length as those of *QG*, we must conclude that the present Book I is less than half of an original Book I or Book II, and that the present Book II is either a complete book or else contains parts of several of the original books.

[a] *L.c.*

[b] See Jacob Mann, *The Bible as Read and Preached in the Old Synagogue*, vol. i (Cincinnati, 1940), p. 183.

When we turn to the external evidence, we find further complications. According to Eusebius (*Hist. Eccl.* ii. 18. 5), Philo's commentary on Exodus contained five books, but since he proceeds to mention a work περὶ τῆς σκηνῆς, which seems to be a reference to *QE* Book II, we ought perhaps not to rely too heavily upon his authority. The Vienna codex of *De Opificio Mundi*, mentioned above, lists the books of the *QE* as Books A′ (with a line drawn through it), B′ and E′, leaving it in doubt whether the scribe knew of two books or three. The Greek fragments of *QE* preserved by Byzantine writers are usually ascribed to Books α′ or β′ or τοῦ τελευταίου.[a] If, then, Eusebius was right in counting five books, some of these must have been lost soon after his death. Wendland [b] believes that part of the original Book I has been preserved in the Armenian Book I but doubts that as many as three of the original five books have been lost, while Schürer [c] thinks that our Book I is the original Book II, and our Book II is the original Book V.

III

It may be that a clue to the original extent and book-divisions of *QE* will be furnished by the correspondences between the books of *QG* and the Pentateuch-lessons of the ancient synagogue. We must bear in mind that in Philo's time neither the Hebrew nor the Greek Bible was divided into chapters like those in our printed Bibles, and that these chapter-divisions date from the Middle Ages.[d]

It was natural for Philo to think of his Greek Pentateuch as divided into weekly lessons for reading in the synagogue, just as Origen did two centuries after Philo when he composed homilies on the Church-lessons. Now the Jews of Palestine in Philo's time, or soon after,[e] read the whole

[a] One Greek fragment is said to come from Book δ′, but this is a corruption of α′.

[b] *Op. cit.* p. 103.

[c] *Op. cit.* p. 498, n. 36.

[d] See Henry B. Swete, *An Introduction to the Old Testament in Greek* (Cambridge, 1914), pp. 343-344.

[e] See Mann, *op. cit.* p. 5.

Pentateuch in the course of three years, dividing it into 154 weekly lessons, called in Hebrew *sedarim* (sing. *seder*). Each lesson was, on the average, as long as one of our modern chapters. The Jews of Babylonia, however, read the whole Pentateuch in the course of a single year, dividing it into 54 weekly lessons. Each of these was, on the average, as long as three and a half of our modern chapters.

Unfortunately we do not know whether the Alexandrian Jews followed the Palestinian triennial system or the Babylonian annual system. One might assume the former on the ground of the close relations between Egypt and Palestine, but we must remember that lateral areas are more conservative than the central area of a culture. Moreover, it has been found that in certain points Philo's legal exegesis agrees with the Palestinian exegesis of the pre-Roman period rather than that of his Palestinian contemporaries. It is quite possible, therefore, that the Alexandrian Jews, like the Babylonian Jews, followed an annual system that may have been in use in Palestine also before the Hellenistic or Roman period.

At any rate, we find a remarkable agreement between the coverage of some of the books of Philo's commentary on Genesis (assuming our reconstructions, as given above, to be correct) and of the weekly lessons of the Babylonian annual system.

Books of *QG* (as reconstructed)		Babylonian *sedarim*
Book III on Gen. xv. 7-xvii. 27	~	3. (*lek-leka*) on Gen. xii. 1-xvii. 27.
Book IV on Gen. xviii. 1-xx. 18	~	4. (*wayyiqra*) on Gen. xviii. 1-xxii. 24.
Book V on Gen. xxiii. 1-xxv. 8	~	5. (*ḥayye Śarah*) on Gen. xxiii. 1-xxv. 18.
Book VI on Gen. xxv. 20-xxviii. 9	~	6. (*toledot*) on Gen. xxv. 19-xxviii. 9.

Books I and II together on Gen. ii. 4-x. 9 correspond to a single *seder*, Nr. 2 (*Noaḥ*) on Gen. ii. 9-xi. 32.

These correspondences, while not complete, are close enough, it seems to me, to warrant our supposing that Philo designed each book of his commentary on Genesis to cover a Pentateuchal portion of about the same length as a weekly lesson in the Babylonian annual cycle of 54 *sedarim*, and that each portion in his synagogal Bible began at just about the same place as did a Babylonian *seder*.

If we apply the same comparison to the two books of the commentary on Exodus, we see that Book I, covering Ex. xii. 2-23, corresponds to only part of the Babylonian *seder*, Nr. 15 (*bo'*), on Ex. xi-xiii. 16. Book II (if we ignore the isolated first section) covers Ex. xxii. 21-xxviii. 33. It therefore seems to contain parts of three successive *sedarim*:

18. (*mišpaṭim*) on Ex. xxi. 1-xxiv. 18.
19. (*terumah*) on Ex. xxv. 1-xxvii. 19.
20. (*teṣawweh*) on Ex. xxvii. 20-xxx. 10.

It therefore seems justified to conclude that the present Book II of *QE* contains parts of the lost Books III, IV and V. Book I may preserve part of the lost Book I or the lost Book II. In any case, it is clear that the original treatise did not discuss more than a quarter of the Biblical book.

If the preceding hypothesis is sound (and there is room for doubt), it will serve to determine the original extent and book-divisions of the *Quaestiones et Solutiones in Exodum*, and at the same time will furnish at least some evidence that the Alexandrian Jews in Philo's time followed a system of weekly synagogue-readings of the Pentateuch very much like that used in ancient Babylonia and still in use to-day.

ABBREVIATIONS AND SYMBOLS

Arm. = Armenian version of *Quaestiones*.
Aucher = J. B. Aucher, *Philonis Judaei Paralipomena*, etc. (see Preface), Venice, 1826.
A.V. = Authorized (King James) Version of the Bible.
Colson = F. H. Colson in Loeb Philo, vols. i-ix.
frag. = Greek fragment of *Quaestiones* (see Appendix A).
Früchtel = Ludwig Früchtel, " Griechische Fragmente zu Philons Quaestiones, etc.," *Zeit. f. Alttest. Wiss.*, N.F. 14 (1937), 108-115.
Harris = J. Rendel Harris, *Fragments of Philo Judaeus* Cambridge, 1896.
Heb. = Hebrew Old Testament.
Lewy = Hans Lewy, *Neue Philontexte in der Ueberarbeitung des Ambrosius*, etc., Berlin, 1932.
lit. = literally.
LXX = Septuagint or Greek Old Testament.
OL = Old Latin version of *Quaestiones in Genesin* iv. 154-245 (see Appendix B).
QE = *Quaestiones et Solutiones in Exodum*.
QG = *Quaestiones et Solutiones in Genesin*.
Staehle = Karl Staehle, *Die Zahlenmystik bei Philon von Alexandreia*, Leipzig-Berlin, 1931.
v.l. = *varia lectio*.
vel sim. = *vel simile* (used of some reconstructions of Philo's Greek given in footnotes to translation).
Wendland = Paul Wendland, *Neu entdeckte Fragmente Philos*, Berlin, 1891.
Wolfson = H. A. Wolfson, *Philo*, 2 vols., Cambridge, Mass., 1947.
* placed before section number indicates that part of the section is extant in Greek (see Appendix A).
(.) indicate words supplied by translator.

LIST OF PHILO'S WORKS

SHOWING THEIR DIVISION INTO VOLUMES IN THIS EDITION

VOLUME

I. On the Creation (De Opificio Mundi)
Allegorical Interpretation (Legum Allegoriae)

II. On the Cherubim (De Cherubim)
On the Sacrifices of Abel and Cain (De Sacrificiis Abelis et Caini)
The Worse attacks the Better (Quod Deterius Potiori insidiari solet)
On the Posterity and Exile of Cain (De Posteritate Caini)

III. On the Unchangeableness of God (Quod Deus immutabilis sit)
On Husbandry (De Agricultura)
On Noah's Work as a Planter (De Plantatione)
On Drunkenness (De Ebrietate)
On Sobriety (De Sobrietate)

IV. On the Confusion of Tongues (De Confusione Linguarum)
On the Migration of Abraham (De Migratione Abrahami)
Who is the Heir (Quis Rerum Divinarum Heres)
On the Preliminary Studies (De Congressu quaerendae Eruditionis gratia)

V. On Flight and Finding (De Fuga et Inventione)
On the Change of Names (De Mutatione Nominum)
On Dreams (De Somniis)

VI. On Abraham (De Abrahamo)
On Joseph (De Iosepho)
Moses (De Vita Mosis)

LIST OF PHILO'S WORKS

VOLUME

VII. On the Decalogue (De Decalogo)
On the Special Laws Books I-III (De Specialibus Legibus)

VIII. On the Special Laws Book IV (De Specialibus Legibus)
On the Virtues (De Virtutibus)
On Rewards and Punishments (De Praemiis et Poenis)

IX. Every Good Man is Free (Quod Omnis Probus Liber sit)
On the Contemplative Life (De Vita Contemplativa)
On the Eternity of the World (De Aeternitate Mundi)
Flaccus (In Flaccum)
Hypothetica[1] (Apologia pro Iudaeis)
On Providence[1] (De Providentia)

X. On the Embassy to Gaius (De Legatione ad Gaium)
General Index to Volumes I-X

SUPPLEMENT

I. Questions and Answers on Genesis[2] (Quaestiones et Solutiones in Genesin)

II. Questions and Answers on Exodus[2] (Quaestiones et Solutiones in Exodum)
General Index to Supplements I-II

[1] Only two fragments extant.
[2] Extant only in an Armenian version.

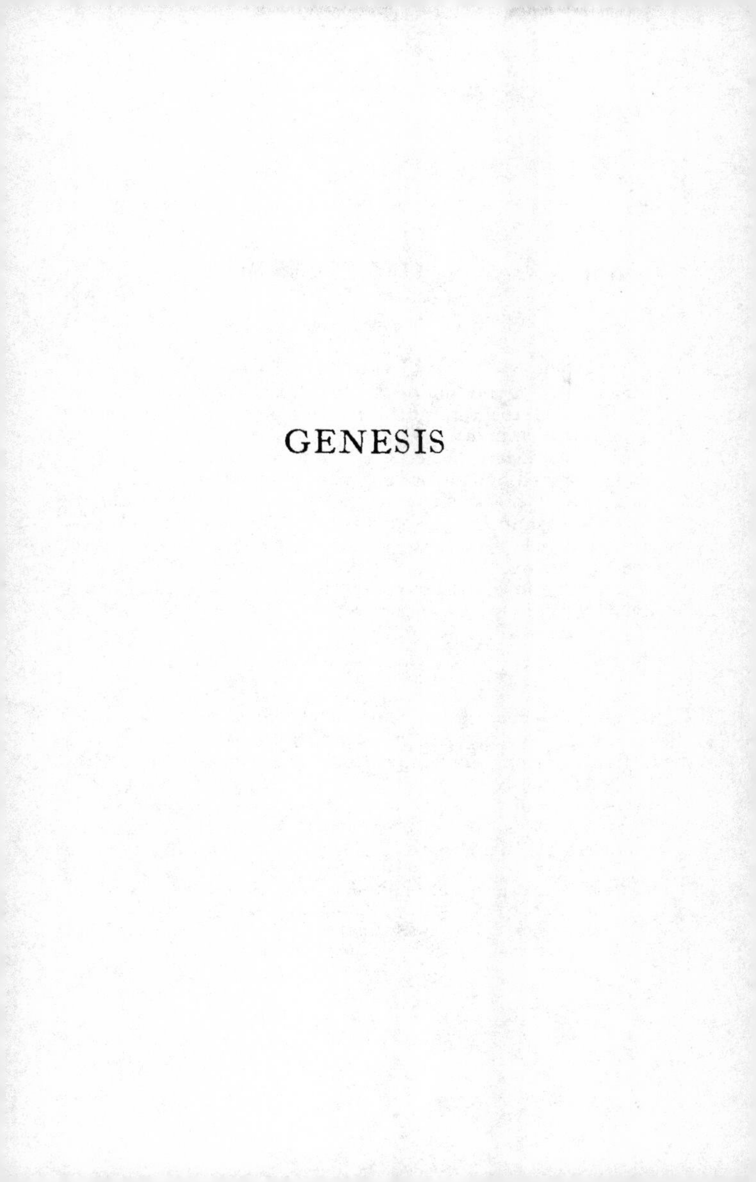

GENESIS

GENESIS

BOOK I

*1. (Gen. ii. 4) Why, when he (Moses) considers and reflects on the creation of the world, does he say, " This is the book of the coming into being of heaven and earth when they came into being " ?

The expression " when they came into being," which is undetermined and uncircumscribed,[a] apparently indicates time. And this evidence confutes those who consider it to be a certain number of years summed under one head, during which the cosmos was to come into being. But the expression, " this is the book of coming into being " is meant to indicate a supposed book [b] which contains the creation of the world and an intimation of the truth about the creation of the world.[c]

2. (Gen. ii. 5) What is the meaning of the words, " And God made every green thing of the field before it came into being on the earth, and every grass before it grew " ?

In these words he alludes to the incorporeal ideas. For the expression, " before it came into being " points to the perfection [d] of every green thing and grass, of plants and trees. And as Scripture says that before they grew on the earth He made plants and grass and the other things,

[a] The Greek frag. has only *ἄριστον* (*l.* *ἀόριστον*).
[b] The Greek frag. has *τοῦ ὑποκειμένου τεύχους*.
[c] The Greek frag. reads differently *ἀναφορα τῶν εἰρημένων περὶ τῆς κοσμοποιίας πρὸς τὰ ἐπ' ἀληθείας γεγονότα*.
[d] *τὸ τέλος*.

it is evident that He made incorporeal and intelligible ideas in accordance with the intelligible nature which these sense-perceptible things on earth were meant to imitate.

3. (Gen. ii. 6) What is the meaning of the words, " a spring went up from the earth and watered all the face of the earth " ?

How is it possible to water all the earth from one spring ? Not only because of its size but also because of the unevenness of mountains and plains. Unless indeed as all the cavalry force of the king is called " the horse," so also " spring " means all the veins of the earth producing potable water, which comes like that from a spring. But well does Scripture also say, not " all (the earth)," but " its face " was watered. Just as in a living being the head is the ruling part,[a] so the good and fertile and principal part of the earth is that which can become fruitbearing, and this is in need of the help given by springs.

4. (Gen. ii. 7) Who is the " moulded "[b] man ? And how does he differ from him who is (made) " in accordance with the image (of God) " ?

The moulded man is the sense-perceptible[c] man and a likeness of the intelligible type.[d] But the man made in accordance with (God's) form[e] is intelligible and incorporeal and a likeness of the archetype, so far as this is visible. And he is a copy of the original seal.[f] And this is the Logos of God, the first principle, the archetypal idea,[g] the pre-measurer[h] of all things. For this reason the man who was moulded as by a potter was formed out of dust and earth, in respect of the body. And he obtained a spirit when God breathed life into his face. And the mixture of his nature was a mixture of the corruptible and incorruptible. For that which is in accordance with form[i]

[a] τὸ ἡγεμονικόν. [b] πλαστός. [c] αἰσθητός.
[d] νοητοῦ τρόπου. [e] εἶδος. [f] σφραγίδος.
[g] ἀρχέτυπος ἰδέα. [h] προμετρητής. [i] εἶδος or ἰδέαν.

is incorruptible, coming from an invisible nature, from that which is simple and pure.

5. (Gen. ii. 7) Why is He said to have breathed life into his face?

First of all, because the face is the principal part of the body. For the rest (of the body) was made like a pedestal, while the face, like a bust, is firmly placed above it. And sense-perception is the principal part of the animal species, and sense-perception is in the face. In the second place, man is admitted to be part not only of the animal order but also of that of rational animals, and the head is the temple of the mind, as some have said.

6. (Gen. ii. 8) Why is God said to have "planted Paradise" and for whom? And what is Paradise?

Of Paradise, so far as the literal meaning is concerned, there is no need to give an explicit interpretation. For it is a dense place full of all kinds of trees. Symbolically, however, it is wisdom [a] or knowledge [b] of the divine and human and of their causes. For it was fitting, after the coming into being of the world, to establish the contemplative life in order that through a vision of the world and the things in it praise of the Father might also be attained. For it is not possible for nature to see nor is it possible without wisdom to praise the creator of all things. And His ideas the Creator planted like trees in the most sovereign thing, the rational soul. But as for the tree of life in the midst (of the garden), it is the knowledge, not only of things on the earth, but also of the eldest and highest cause of all things. For if anyone is able to obtain a clear impression [c] of this, he will be fortunate and blessed and truly immortal. But after the world wisdom came into being, since after the creation of the world Paradise was made in the same manner as the poets say the chorus of

[a] σοφία.
[b] ἐπιστήμη.
[c] σαφεῖαν φαντασίαν.

Muses (was formed), in order to praise the Creator and His work. For just as Plato said,[a] the Creator is the greatest and best of causes, while the world is the most beautiful of created things.

7. (Gen. ii. 8) Why is He said to have planted Paradise in Eden toward the East?

In the first place, because the movement of the world is from East to West; and that from which movement starts is first. Second, that which is in the region of the East is said to be the right side of the world, while that in the region of the West is the left. And so the poet testifies,[b] calling the birds in the region of the East "right," and those which are in the region of the West "on the left side." If they go to the right side, it is to the day and the sun; but if to the left, toward evening and darkness. But the name Eden when translated is certainly a symbol of delicacies, joy and mirth. For all good things and benefits have their origin in this sacred place. In the third place, because it[c] is wisdom and radiance and light.

8. (Gen. ii. 8) Why does He place the moulded man in Paradise, but not the man who was made in His image?

Some, believing Paradise to be a garden, have said that since the moulded man is sense-perceptible, he therefore rightly goes to a sense-perceptible place. But the man made in His image is intelligible and invisible, and is in the class of incorporeal species. But I would say that Paradise should be thought a symbol of wisdom. For the earth-formed man is a mixture, and consists of soul and body, and is in need of teaching and instruction, desiring, in accordance with the laws of philosophy, that he may be happy. But he who was made in His image is in need of nothing, but is self-hearing and self-taught and self-instructed by nature.

[a] *Timaeus* 92 c.

[b] Hom. *Il.* xii. 239, *Od.* xx. 242.

[c] *i.e.* Paradise.

9. (Gen. ii. 9) Why does (Scripture) say that in Paradise was every tree beautiful to look at and good [a] to eat?

Because there are two virtues of trees, to be many-branched and fruitful, of which one is for the pleasure of sight, and the other for the enjoyment of taste. But not ineptly is the word "beautiful" used, for it would be natural [b] that plants should be ever flourishing and ever green, as belonging to the divine Paradise, without suffering the extremity of being leafless. But it did not say that the fruit also was "beautiful" but "good," [a] and this is philosophically said, for men use food not only for pleasure but also for utility, and utility is the outflowing [c] and the distillation of the good.

10. (Gen. ii. 9) What is "the tree of life" and why is it in the midst of Paradise?

Some believe that as plants are corporeal and subject to death, so also some have life and immortality. Wherefore they say that life and death are opposed to each other. And some plants are destructive, and it is necessary to be saved (from their effects).[d] But that this state is healthful they do not know. For generation, as the arguments of philosophers go, is the beginning of corruption. And may it not be that this (*i.e.* the above) is said allegorically? For some say that the tree of life is the earth, for it causes all things to grow for the life of both man and all other things. Wherefore He apportioned a central place to this plant; and the centre of all is the earth. And some say that the tree of life is a name for the seven circles [e] which are in heaven. And some say it is the sun because it is, in a sense, in the midst of the planets and is the cause of the seasons, by which all things are produced. And some have said that the tree of life is the government [f] of the soul. For the soul innervates and strengthens sense-

[a] *καλός*. [b] *εἰκὸς ἂν εἴη*. [c] *ἀπόρροια*.
[d] Arm. obscure, lit. "and of necessity salvation is obtained." [e] *κύκλοι* or *στροφαί*.
[f] *ἡγεμονία* (or *ὑφήγησις*).

perception by directing its energies[a] to what is suitable for it, with the participation[b] of the parts of the body. And the centre, in one meaning, is the chief and head, as is the leader of a chorus. But worthy and excellent men say that the tree of life is the best of the virtues in man, namely piety,[c] through which pre-eminently the mind becomes immortal.

11. (Gen. ii. 9) What is "the tree of knowing the science[d] of good and evil"?

This very clear statement, which in its literal meaning is elusive, it presents to us as an allegory. For, as he intimates, it is prudence,[e] and this is the science of knowing, through which good and beautiful things and bad and ugly things are distinguished; and (the science of knowing) all things which are contrary to each other, of which the one is of a superior order, and the other of an inferior order. Now the wisdom which is in this world is not God but is truly the work of God[f]; it sees nature and studies it. But the wisdom which is in man sees with dim eyes, confusing one thing with another, for it is weak in seeing and understanding purely, simply, clearly each thing by itself alone. Wherefore with man's wisdom a kind of deception is mixed, in the same manner as to the eyes certain shadows are often an impediment to catching sight of unmixed and pure light. For what the eye is to the body, mind and wisdom are to the soul.

12. (Gen. ii. 10) What is the river that went out from Eden, by which Paradise is watered; and four rivers separated, the Pishon,[g] Gihon,[h] Tigris and Euphrates?

[a] ἐνεργείας. [b] κοινωνίᾳ. [c] εὐσέβεια.

[d] τοῦ γιγνώσκειν τὴν ἐπιστήμην (or τῆς γνώσεως τῆς τοῦ ἐπίστασθαι). [e] φρόνησις.

[f] Probably we should correct the Arm. to read "Now the wisdom which is in this world sees (*tesē* for *ē* "is") not God but truly the work (or the true work) of God."

[g] Arm. *Phison* = Gr. Φεισών. [h] Arm. *Gehōn* = Gr. Γηών.

For the sources of the Tigris (Arm. *Dkłat'*) and Euphrates (Arm. *Araçani*) are said to rise in the Armenian mountains. And in that place there is no Paradise, nor are there the two other sources of the river. Unless perhaps Paradise is in some distant place far from our inhabited world, and has a river flowing under the earth, which waters many great veins so that these rising send (water) to other recipient veins, and so become diffused. And as these are forced by the rush of water, the force which is in them makes its way out to the surface, both in the Armenian mountains and elsewhere. And these are the supposed sources, or rather the outflowings of the river; but properly the supposed sources, since divine Scripture, in which the matter of the four rivers is mentioned, is wholly veracious. For the origin is a river and not a source (according to Scripture). Unless perhaps in this passage matters are allegorized, and the four rivers are a symbol of four virtues[a]: of prudence,[b] called Pishon in respect of frugality[c]; of moderation,[d] called Gihon because it labours with regard to food and drink, and produces the various pleasures of the belly and those parts which are below the belly, and this is earthly; of courage,[e] called Tigris, for this checks the affection of anger which rages in us; of justice,[f] called Euphrates, for in nothing do the thoughts of man rejoice and have gladness more than in justice.[g]

13. (Gen. ii. 14) Why does (Scripture) omit to give the location of the Euphrates alone, while it says that the Pishon goes round all the land of Havilah (Arm. and LXX *Evilat*), and the Gihon goes round all the land of Cush (Arm. and LXX *Ethiopia*), and the Tigris flows opposite Assyria (Arm. *Asorestan*)?

The Tigris (*Dkłat'*) is the wildest and most destructive

[a] ἀρετῶν. [b] φρόνησις. [c] φειδώ.
[d] σωφροσύνη. [e] ἀνδρεία. [f] δικαιοσύνη.
[g] In the above passage, paralleled in *Leg. All.* i. 63 ff., Philo plays on the Greek names of the four rivers.

of rivers, as the Babylonians and the Magians testify, who have determined that its nature is somewhat different from (that of) water. However it is likely that (Scripture) has still another reason for keeping silence. For the Euphrates (*Araçani*) is very gentle and life-giving and nourishing, wherefore the wise men of the Hebrews and Assyrians call it " augmenting " and " prospering." For this reason it is known, not from anything else, like the three (other rivers) but by itself. To me it seems that the matter is symbolical and figurative. Since prudence [a] is a faculty [b] of the rational element,[c] in which evil is found, and courage [d] is a faculty of the irascible element,[e] and moderation [f] is a faculty of the concupiscent element,[g] but anger and concupiscence are bestial.[h] Thus (Scripture) refers to the three rivers by the regions through which they flow but the Euphrates (*Araçani*), which is a symbol of justice,[i] is not similarly referred to, since not merely some part of it is assigned to the soul, but it is acquired all at once and becomes a partnership [j] and harmony of the three parts of the soul and of the same number of virtues.

14. (Gen. ii. 15) Why does (God) place the man in Paradise for two things, to work and guard it, when Paradise was not in need of work, for it was complete in all things as having been planted by God, and was not in need of a guardian, for who was there to be harmed ?

These are the two things which a cultivator should keep in mind and achieve, cultivation of the field and guarding of the things in it, for it may be ruined either by idleness or by invasion. But although Paradise was not in need of either of these things, nevertheless it was necessary that he who received the supervision and care of it, (that is) the first man, should be, as it were, a law to husbandmen in all things which it is fitting to labour in. Moreover it was

[a] φρόνησις. [b] ἀρετή. [c] τοῦ λογικοῦ.
[d] ἀνδρεία. [e] τοῦ θυμικοῦ. [f] σωφροσύνη.
[g] τοῦ ἐπιθυμητικοῦ. [h] θηριώδεις.
[i] δικαιοσύνης. [j] ὁμόνοια, κοινωνία, etc.

proper that as it was full of all things, He should leave to the cultivator the superintendence[a] and the work of caring for it, such as watering it, tending it, nurturing it,[b] spading it, digging trenches, and irrigating it with water. And although there was no other man, it was necessary to guard it at least against wild animals, and especially against air and water, for when there is a drought, one must water it abundantly, but when there are rainstorms, one must stop the overflow by making another channel.

15. (Gen. ii. 16) Why does (God) say, when He commands (Adam) to eat of every tree which is in Paradise, " Eat " in the singular number; but, when He forbids eating of the tree which gives knowledge of good and evil, says, in the plural number, " Do not eat, for on the day when ye shall eat, ye shall die " ?

First, because though it extends over many things,[c] the good is one, and not less for this reason,[d] namely that He who gave the benefit is one, as is also the one who received the benefit. This " one " I speak of, not with reference to the number which precedes the number two, but with reference to the unitary power, in accordance with which many things are harmonized and agree and by their concord imitate the one, such as a flock, a herd, a drove, a chorus, an army, a nation, a tribe, a household, a city. For all these, extending over many, are one community and embrace lovingly; but when they are unmixed and have nothing in common, they fall into duality and into a multitude and are divided. For duality is the beginning of division. But two who use the same philosophy as one enjoy an unadulterated and clear virtue which is free of evil. But when good and evil are mixed, they have as their beginning a mixture of death.

[a] *ἐπιμέλειαν.* [b] *τρυφᾶν, μαλακίζειν*, etc. [c] *διὰ πολλῶν.*
[d] The Arm. phrase is obscure to me, as also to Aucher apparently. He renders, " primum, quia unum ex multis factum bonum est; id autem haud exiguum his etiam rationibus . . ."

16. (Gen. ii. 17) What is the meaning of the words, " Ye shall die by the death [a] " ?

The death of worthy men is the beginning of another life. For life is twofold ; one is with corruptible body ; the other is without body (and) incorruptible. So that the evil man dies by death even when he breathes, before he is buried, as though he preserved for himself no spark at all of the true life, and this is excellence of character.[b] The decent and worthy man, however, does not die by death, but after living long, passes away to eternity, that is, he is borne to eternal life.

*17. (Gen. ii. 18) Why does (Scripture) say, " It is not good for man to be alone. Let us make for him a helpmeet like him " ?

By these words it refers to partnership, and that not with all persons but with those who wish to help and bring mutual profit even though they may not be able (to do so). For love is a strengthener of character [c] not more by usefulness than by union and concord, so that to every one of those who come together in the partnership of love the saying of Pythagoras can be applied, that " a lover is indeed another self."

18. (Gen. ii. 19) Why, after first saying, " Let us make a helper for man," does (God) create wild animals and cattle ?

Intemperate [d] and gluttonous people would say that wild animals and fowl, being necessary food, are a help to man. For the eating of meat co-operates with the stomach toward (attaining) health and bodily strength. But I believe that now, because evil is found in him, man has enemies and adversaries in terrestrial animals and fowl. But to the first man, who was altogether adorned with virtue, they were rather like military forces and allies, and a close

[a] θανάτῳ ἀποθανεῖσθε, a reflection of the Hebrew idiom.
[b] καλοκἀγαθία. [c] βεβαίωσις ἠθῶν, *cf.* Greek frag.
[d] ἀκόλαστοι.

friend naturally becomes tractable (?). And with this man alone they became familiar, as was fitting for servants with a master.

19. (Gen. ii. 19) Why are beasts and birds now again created, when their creation [a] was announced [b] earlier in the six-day (creation story)? [c]

Perhaps those things which (were created) in the six days were incorporeal [d] and were symbolically typical species [e] of beasts and birds. But now were produced in actuality [f] their likenesses, [g] sensible [h] (likenesses) of invisible things. [i]

*20. (Gen. ii. 19) Why does (God) bring all the animals to the man that he may give names to them?

Scripture has cleared up the great perplexity of those who are lovers of wisdom by showing that names exist by being given and not by nature, since each is an apt and naturally suitable name through the skilful calculation of a wise man who is pre-eminent in knowledge. And very proper to the mind of the wise man alone, or rather to the first of earth-born creatures, is the giving of names. For it was fitting that the lord of mankind and the king of all earth-born creatures should obtain this great honour also. For as he was the first to see living creatures, so he was the first to be worthy of being lord over all and the first introducer and author of the giving of names. For it would have been vain and foolish to leave them without names or to accept names from some other younger man to the disgrace and degradation of the honour and glory of the older man. We must, however, also suppose that the giving of names was so exact that so soon as he gave the name and the animal heard it, it was affected as if by the phenomenon of a familiar and related name being spoken.

[a] γένεσις. [b] ἀνηγγέλθη. [c] ἐν τῷ ἑξαημέρῳ.
[d] ἀσώματα. [e] δεικτικαὶ καὶ τροπικαὶ ἰδέαι.
[f] ἔργῳ. [g] ὁμοιότητες. [h] αἰσθηταί. [i] ἀοράτων.

*21. (Gen. ii. 19) Why does (Scripture) say, " He led the animals to man to see what he would call them," when God is not in doubt ?

Truly it is alien to the divine power to be in doubt. But it appears that He was not in doubt, since He gave mind to man, especially the first earth-born noble man, in accordance with which he became wise and could naturally reason like a leader and ruler and know how to move and make himself known.[a] And he saw the good origin of his spirit. Moreover through this he also typifies all that is voluntary in us, thus confounding those who say that all things exist by necessity. Or perhaps because mankind was destined to use them, for that reason He granted to man the giving of their names.

22. (Gen. ii. 19) What is the meaning of the words, " Whatever he called a living soul, that was its name " ?

It is necessary to believe that he gave names not only to animals but also to plants and to all other things without life, beginning with the highest genus: and the animal is the highest thing. Scripture contents itself with the best part, not completely illustrating the naming of all things for stupid men. Wherefore the naming of inanimate things, which could not change their places or make use of the affections of the soul,[b] was easy. It was more difficult in the case of animals because of the movements of the body and the various manifestations of the impulses of the soul through the senses and passions from which energies arise. Thus the mind was able to give names to the more difficult and more troublesome genera of animals. Wherefrom it follows that he named (other things) as if they were easy and near at hand.

23. (Gen. ii. 20) What is the meaning of the words, " For Adam there was not found a helper like himself " ?

[a] The Arm. is very obscure and apparently a mistranslation. *Cf.* Greek fragment, in Appendix A in Suppl. II.
[b] παθήματα τῆς ψυχῆς.

Everything helped and co-operated with the founder of mankind, such as earth, rivers, sea, air, light and sky. Also co-operated all the species of fruit and plants and herds of cattle. And wild animals were not ferocious to him. However, none of these was in any way a helper like himself, since they were not human. Thus (Scripture) approves of one man showing himself a succourer and co-operator with another man and showing his complete similarity in body and soul.

*24. (Gen. ii. 21) What is the meaning of the words, " And He cast a trance [a] upon Adam, and made him sleep " ?

Philosophers are at a loss and uncertain how to explain how sleep comes about. But the prophet clearly solved the problem. For sleep in itself is properly [b] a trance, not that which comes about through madness,[c] but that which comes about through the relaxing [d] of the senses and the withdrawal of the reason. For then the senses withdraw from sense-perceptible things, and the intellect withdraws from the senses, not activating the nerves and not giving motion even to those parts which have as their special function the production of energy, being separated from sense-perceptible things.

25. (Gen. ii. 21-22) What is the " side " [e] which He took from the earth-born man ; and why did He mould the side into a woman ?

The literal sense is clear. For by a certain symbolical use of " part " [f] it is called a half of the whole, as both man and woman, being sections of Nature, become equal in one harmony of genus,[g] which is called man. But in the figurative sense, man is a symbol of mind, and his side

[a] ἔκστασιν.
[b] " Properly " is omitted in the Greek frag.
[c] μανίας. [d] ὕφεσιν in the Greek frag.
[e] πλευρά. [f] μέρος.
[g] ἐν μιᾷ τοῦ γένους ἁρμονίᾳ.

is a single sense-faculty. And the sense-perception of a very changeable reason is symbolized by woman. Some speak of prowess [a] and strength as "side," whence they call a fighting athlete with strong sides a powerful man. Accordingly the lawgiver says that woman was made from the side of man, intimating that woman is a half of man's body. For this we also have evidence in the constitution of the body, its common parts,[b] movements, faculties, mental vigour and excellence. For all things are seen as if in double proportion. Inasmuch as the moulding [c] of the male is more perfect than, and double, that of the female, it requires only half the time, namely forty days; whereas the imperfect woman, who is, so to speak, a half-section of man, requires twice as many days, namely eighty. So that there is a change in the doubling of the time of man's nature (or natural growth), in accordance with the peculiarity of woman. For when the nature of the body and soul [d] of something is of double measure, such as man's, then the forming [e] and moulding of that thing is in half-measure. But when the nature of the body and the construction of something is in half-measure, such as woman's, then the moulding and forming of that thing is in double measure.[f]

26. (Gen. ii. 22) Why does Scripture call the likeness [g] of the woman "a building" [h]?

The harmonious coming together [i] of man and woman and their consummation is figuratively a house. And everything which is without a woman is imperfect and homeless.[j] For to man are entrusted the public affairs of state; while to a woman the affairs of the home are proper.

[a] ἀρετήν. [b] κοινωνία. [c] πλάσμα.
[d] ψυχή (or πνεῦμα). [e] τύπωσις.
[f] *i.e.* that material which is imperfect or half-perfect takes twice as long to complete as that which is perfect to start with.
[g] εἰκόνα.
[h] οἰκοδομήν; *cf.* LXX ᾠκοδόμησε.
[i] συναγωγὴ ἁρμονίας *vel sim.* [j] ἄοικος.

The lack [a] of her is ruin,[b] but her being near at hand [c] constitutes household management.[d]

*27. (Gen. ii. 21) Why was not woman, like other animals and man, also formed [e] from earth, instead of the side of man?

First, because woman is not equal in honour with man. Second, because she is not equal in age, but younger. Wherefore those who take wives who have passed their prime are to be criticized for destroying the laws of nature. Third, he wishes that man should take care of [f] woman as of a very necessary [g] part of him; but woman, in return, should serve him [h] as a whole. Fourth, he counsels man figuratively to take care of [i] woman as of a daughter, and woman to honour man as a father. And this is proper; for woman changes her habitation from her family [j] to her husband. Wherefore it is fitting and proper that one who receives something should in return show goodwill to those who have given it, but one (*i.e.* the woman) who has made a change should give to him who has taken her the honour which she showed those who begot her. For man has a wife entrusted to him as a deposit [k] from her parents, but woman (takes a husband) by law.

*28. (Gen. ii. 23) Why does the moulded man, on seeing the woman, say in addition, "This is now bone of my bones and flesh of my flesh; she shall be called woman, for she was taken from her husband" [l]?

He might have said deprecatingly,[m] being dumbfounded

[a] *ἀπορία*. [b] *κατάλυσις*.
[c] *οὐσία τῆς ὁμιλίας* or *ἀγχιστείας*, prob. for original *οὔσης αὐτῆς πλησίον*. [d] *οἰκονομία*. [e] *ἵδρυτο*.
[f] *προκήδεσθαι* or *προνοεῖν*. [g] *ἀναγκαιότερον*.
[h] *ἐκεῖ*, an error for *ἐκείνῳ*. [i] *προκήδεσθαι*.
[j] The Greek frag. has *γονέων*.
[k] *παρακαταθήκην*, as in the Greek frag.
[l] The Arm. has a word-play on *aṙn* "man" and *aṙnem* "to take."
[m] *ὡς παραιτούμενος vel sim.*

at this apparition, " Is it really possible that this wonderful and lovely vision [a] came from bones and formless flesh and things without quality [b]—this most shapely [c] and very charming creature! It is incredible that a similar thing can be. And yet it is credible, for God was the creator and painter." [d] He might have said trustingly,[e] " Truly this is a creature of my bone and my flesh, for she has been separated and put together from these several parts of mine." Moreover he makes mention of bones and flesh very naturally, for the human [f] tent [g] is made of bones, flesh, arteries, veins, nerves, ligaments and the vessels of breathing and of the blood. And the woman is called the power of giving birth [h] with fecundity, and truly so; either because after receiving the seed, she conceives and gives birth, or, as the prophet says, because she came from man, not through spirit nor through seed, like those after him, but by a kind of mediate nature, just as a shoot is taken from a vine for growing another vine.[i]

*29. (Gen. ii. 24) Why does (Scripture) say, " Wherefore man shall leave his father and mother, and cleave to his wife, and they shall be two in one flesh " ?

(Scripture) commands man to act toward his wife with the most extreme exaggeration in partnership,[j] so that he may endure to abandon even his parents. Not as though this is proper, but as though they would not be causes of goodwill [k] to the wife. And most excellent and careful was it not to say that the woman should leave her parents and be joined to her husband—for the audacity [l] (of man) is bolder than the nature of woman—but that for the sake of woman man is to do this. Since with a very ready

[a] εἶδος, ἰδέα, ὅρασις, etc.
[b] ἀποίων. [c] εὐμορφότατος. [d] ζωγράφος.
[e] ὡς ἀναδεχόμενος. [f] Variant " corporeal."
[g] σκηνή.
[h] The Greek must have had a word-play on γυνή and γεννᾶν. [i] The Greek frag. paraphrases.
[j] κοινωνίᾳ. [k] εὐνοίας. [l] παρρησία.

and prompt impulse[a] he is brought to a concord of knowledge.[b] Being possessed [c] and foreseeing the future,[d] he controls and stills his desires,[e] being fitted to his spouse alone as if to a bridle. And especially because he, having the authority of a master,[f] is to be suspected of arrogance. But woman, taking the rank of servant, is shown to be obedient to his life. But when Scripture says that the two are one flesh, it indicates something very tangible and sense-perceptible, in which there is suffering and sensual pleasure, that they may rejoice in, and be pained by, and feel the same things, and, much more, may think the same things.

30. (Gen. ii. 25) Why are both the earth-born man and the woman said to be naked, and were not ashamed?

First, because they were related to the world, and its parts are naked, all showing their own qualities and using their own covering. Second, because of the simplicity of their morals [g] and because they were by nature without arrogance; for not yet had presumption been created. Third, because the pleasant climate of the place was also a quite sufficient covering to them, so that there was neither too much cold nor too much heat for them. Fourth, because of their kinship with the world, they suffered no harm from any of its parts, it being closely related to them.

*31. (Gen. iii. 1) Why does (Scripture) represent the serpent as more cunning [h] than all the beasts?

It is proper to tell the truth, that the serpent is truly more cunning than all the beasts. To me, however, it seems that this was said because of the serpent's inclina-

[a] ἑτοιμωτέρᾳ καὶ προχείρᾳ ὁρμῇ.
[b] ὁμόνοιαν τῆς ἐπιστήμης (or γνώσεως). [c] μαινόμενος.
[d] προνοῶν. [e] ἐγκρατεῖται καὶ συστέλλει τὰς ἐπιθυμίας.
[f] κυρίαν ἔχων ἐξουσίαν.
[g] διὰ τὴν τῶν ἠθῶν ἁπλότητα.
[h] Or "prudent"—φρονιμώτερος.

tion toward passion, of which it is the symbol. And by passion is meant sensual pleasure,[a] for lovers of pleasure are very clever and are skilled in arts[b] and means[c]; they are clever in finding devices,[d] both those which produce pleasure and those which lead to enjoyment of some kind. But it seems to me that since that creature which excelled in cunning was prepared to become the deceiver of man,[e] the argument applies to a very cunning creature, not the whole genus, but this particular serpent alone, for the reason mentioned.

*32. (Gen. iii. 1) Did the serpent speak in the manner of men?

First, it is likely that not even in the beginning of the world's creation were the other animals without a share in speech, but that man excelled in voice (or utterance), being more clear and distinct. Second, when some miraculous deed is prepared, God changes the inner nature. Third, because our souls are filled with many sins and deaf to all utterances except one or another tongue to which they are accustomed; but the souls of the first creatures,[f] as being pure of evil and unmixed, were particularly keen in becoming familiar[g] with every sound. And since they were not provided only with defective senses, such as belong to a miserable bodily frame, but were provided with a very great body and the magnitude of a giant, it was necessary that they should also have more accurate senses,[h] and what is more, philosophical sight and hearing. For not inaptly do some conjecture that they were provided with eyes with which they could see those natures and beings and actions which were in heaven, and with ears to perceive sounds of every kind.

[a] ἡδονή. [b] ἐν τέχναις.
[c] τρόποις or ἐξευρέσεσι. [d] μηχανάς.
[e] The Greek frag. reads differently. [f] τῶν πρώτων.
[g] *əndeloutʻiun* "familiarity" is prob. error for *əndounelout'iun* = "perception." The Greek frag. paraphrases.
[h] ἀκριβεστέρας αἰσθήσεις.

33. (Gen. iii. 1) Why does the serpent speak to the woman and not to the man?

In order that they may be potentially mortal [a] he deceives by trickery and artfulness. And woman is more accustomed to be deceived than man. For his judgment,[b] like his body, is masculine and is capable of dissolving or destroying the designs of deception; but the judgment of woman is more feminine, and because of softness she easily gives way and is taken in by plausible falsehoods which resemble the truth. Accordingly, since in old age the serpent casts off his skin from the top of his head to his tail, by casting it, he reproaches [c] man, for he has exchanged death for immortality. From his bestial nature he is renewed and adjusts himself [d] to different times. Seeing this, she was deceived, though she ought to have looked, as if at an example, at him who practised stratagems and trickery, and to have obtained ageless and unfading life.

34. (Gen. iii. 1) Why does the serpent lie, saying, "God said, Do not eat of any [e] tree of Paradise"? For on the contrary, He said, "From every tree which is in Paradise you may eat except from one."

It is the custom of those who fight to lie artfully in order that they may not be found out. This is what happens now. For it was commanded that every (tree) might be used except one. But he who devises evil stratagems, coming between, says, "The command was given not to eat of any." As a slippery thing and a stumbling-block to the mind, he put forward an ambiguity [f] of words. For the expression "not to eat from all" clearly means "not even from one," which is false. And again it also means

[a] Arm. obscure, lit. = ὑπὲρ τοῦ εἶναι αὐτοὺς δυνάμει θανασίμους. [b] διάνοια, λογισμός. [c] ὀνειδίζει.

[d] ὁμοιοῦται, ἀπεικάζεται, lit. "likens himself."

[e] Lit. "all, every," reflecting the Semitic idiom in which "all" after a negative = "any."

[f] ἀπορίαν, ἀμφισβήτησιν.

" not from every one," by which is to be understood " not from some," which is true. Thus he spoke a falsehood in a very clear manner.

35. (Gen. iii. 3) Why, when the command was given not to eat of one particular tree, did the woman include even approaching it closely, saying, " He said, You shall not eat of that one and not come near it " ?

First, because taste and every sense consists generically [a] in its contact.[b] Second, for the severe punishment of those who have practised this. For if merely approaching was forbidden, would not those who, besides touching the tree, also ate of it and enjoyed it, adding a great wrong to a lesser one, become condemners [c] and punishers of themselves ?

36. (Gen. iii. 5) What is the meaning of the words, " You will be as gods, knowing good and evil " ?

Whence did the serpent know this plural noun " gods ? " For the true God is one, and he now names Him for the first time. It could not have been a prescient quality [d] that foresaw that there was to be among mankind a belief in a multitude of gods, which, as the narrative [e] first proved, came about not through anything rational nor yet through the better irrational creatures, but through the most noxious and vile of beasts and reptiles. For these lurk in the ground, and their dens are in caves and in the hollows of the earth. And it is truly proper [f] to a rational being to consider God to be the one truly existing being,[g] but to a beast to create many gods,[h] and to an irrational creature to create a god who does not exist in truth.[i]

[a] γένει. [b] ὁμιλίᾳ. [c] κατάκριτοι.

[d] προγνωστικὴ δύναμις.

[e] διήγησις, ἱστορία, etc. ; apparently Scripture is meant.

[f] ἴδιον. [g] τὸν ἕνα ὄντως Ὄντα. [h] θεοπλαστεῖν.

[i] Aucher's rendering, " to create many gods and irrational ones," is not justified grammatically.

Moreover he shows cunning in another way; for not only is there in the Deity knowledge of good and evil but also the acceptance[a] and pursuit of good and the aversion to and rejection of evil. But these things he did not reveal, for they were useful; he included a reference only to the knowledge of both contraries, good and evil. In the second place, "as gods" in the plural was now said not without reason but in order that he might show forth the good and evil, and that these gods are of a twofold nature. Accordingly, it is fitting that particular[b] gods should have knowledge of opposites; but the elder cause[c] is superior (to good and evil).

37. (Gen. iii. 6) Why does the woman first touch the tree and eat of its fruit, and afterwards the man also take of it?

According to the literal meaning the priority (of the woman) is mentioned with emphasis.[d] For it was fitting that man should rule over immortality and everything good, but woman over death and everything vile. In the allegorical sense, however, woman is a symbol of sense, and man, of mind. Now of necessity sense comes into contact with the sense-perceptible; and by the participation of sense,[e] things pass into the mind; for sense is moved by objects,[f] while the mind is moved by sense.

38. (Gen. iii. 6) What is the meaning of the words, "And she gave to her husband with her"?

What has just been said is stated because there is almost one and the same time of appearance—at the same time sense-perception is received from objects and the mind is impressed by sense-perception.

[a] τὸ δέχεσθαι or μετοχή. [b] κατὰ μέρος.
[c] ἡ πρεσβυτέρα αἰτία (God).
[d] ἐνεργείᾳ, the precise sense of which is doubtful here.
[e] τῇ τῆς αἰσθήσεως κοινωνίᾳ.
[f] ὑπὸ τῶν ὑποκειμένων κινεῖται.

39. (Gen. iii. 7) What is the meaning of the words, "The eyes of both were opened"?

That they were not created blind is evident from the fact that even all the other beings were created perfect,[a] both animals and plants; and should not man be endowed with the superior parts, such as eyes? Moreover, a little while before he gave earthly[b] names to all animals, and so it is clear that he had first seen them. Or it may be that by eyes Scripture symbolically indicates the vision of the soul, through which alone are perceived all good and bad, noble and shameful things, and all opposites. But if the eye is a separate intelligence,[c] which is called the counsellor[d] of the understanding,[e] there is also a special irrational eye which is called opinion.[f]

40. (Gen. iii. 7) What is the meaning of the words, "For they knew that they were naked"?

It was of this, that is, of their own nakedness, that they first received knowledge by eating of the forbidden fruit. And this was opinion[g] and the beginning of evil, for they had not used any covering, inasmuch as the parts of the universe[h] are immortal and incorruptible[i]; but (now) they needed that which is made by hand and corruptible. And this knowledge was in being naked, not that it was in itself the cause of change[j] but that now a strangeness[k] was conceived by the mind toward the whole world.[l]

*41. (Gen. iii. 7) Why do they sew the leaves of the fig tree as loin-cloths?[m]

First, because the fruit of the fig tree is sweeter and

[a] τέλεια. [b] Lit. "earth-born"—γηγενᾶ.
[c] διάνοια, λογισμός, etc.
[d] νουθέτημα, συμβουλία, παιδεία, etc.
[e] φρονήσεως, ἐπιστήμης, etc. [f] δόξα.
[g] δόξα. [h] τοῦ παντός.
[i] ἄφθαρτα. [j] ἀλλοιότητος or διαφορᾶς.
[k] ἀλλοτρίωσις. [l] κόσμον.
[m] The Arm. Bible has "apron" = LXX περιζώματα.

pleasant to the taste. Accordingly it symbolically indicates those who sew together [a] and weave together [b] many sense pleasures [c] one with another. Wherefore they (the leaves) are girded round the place of the genitals, which are the instrument [d] of greater things.[e] Second, because the fruit of the fig tree is, as I have said, sweeter than that of other trees, and its leaves are rougher.[f] Accordingly (Scripture) wishes to make clear symbolically that although the movement of pleasure seems to be somewhat slippery and smooth, nevertheless in truth it proves to be rough, and it is impossible to feel joy or pleasure without first feeling pain and again feeling additional pain. For it is always a grievous thing to feel pain in the midst of two painful states, one of them being at the beginning, and the other being added.[g]

42. (Gen. iii. 8) What is the meaning of the words. " The sound was heard of God's walking " ? Can there be a noise of words or feet, or does God walk ?

Whatever sensible gods are in heaven—that is, the stars —all move in a circle and proceed in revolutions.[h] But the highest and eldest cause [i] is stable and immobile,[j] as the theory of the ancients holds. For He gives an indication and impression [k] as though He wished to give the appearance [l] of moving ; for though no voice is given forth, prophets hear through a certain power a divine voice sounding what is said to them. Accordingly, as He is heard without speaking, so also He gives the impression of walking without actually walking, indeed without moving at all. And you see that before there was any tasting of evil, (men) were stable, constant, immobile, peaceful and eternal ; similarly and in the same way they believed God

[a] συρράπτουσι. [b] συνυφαίνουσι. [c] ἡδονάς.
[d] ὄργανον. [e] μειζόνων. [f] τραχύτερα.
[g] The Greek frag. paraphrases.
[h] περιφοραῖς or περιόδοις.
[i] πρεσβυτέρα αἰτία. [j] βεβαία καὶ ἀκίνητος.
[k] φαντασίαν, ἐπιφάνειαν. [l] δόξαν.

to be, just as He is in truth. But after they had come into association with deceit, they moved of themselves, and changed from being immobile, and believed that there was alteration and change in Him.

43. (Gen. iii. 8) Why, when they hid themselves from the face of God, was not the woman, who first ate of the forbidden fruit, first mentioned, but the man; for (Scripture) says, " Adam and his wife hid themselves "?

It was the more imperfect and ignoble element, the female, that made a beginning of transgression [a] and lawlessness,[b] while the male made the beginning of reverence and modesty [c] and all good, since he was better and more perfect.

44. (Gen. iii. 8) Why did they hide themselves, not in any other place, but in the midst of the trees of Paradise?

Not all things are done with reflection and wisdom by sinners; but there are times when thieves sit over the theft which they have committed, not seeing the consequence [d] and that that which lies beside them and at their feet is already sought and hunted. So also it now befell. Whereas they ought to have fled far away from the tree whence came their transgression, in the very midst of this place he was caught, so that proof of their lawlessness was more evident and clear, and there was no fleeing. And thus (Scripture) symbolically indicates that every evil person has a refuge in evil, and every sensual person resorts to, and finds rest in, sensuality.

45. (Gen. iii. 9) Why does He, who knows all things, ask Adam, " Where art thou? ", and why does He not also ask the woman?

The things said appear to be not a question but a kind

[a] παραβάσεως. [b] παρανομίας.
[c] αἰσχύνης. [d] τὸ ἀκόλουθον.

of threat and reproach[a]: where art thou now, from what good hast thou removed thyself, O man!; giving up immortality and a blessed life, thou hast gone over to death and unhappiness, in which thou hast been buried. But the woman He did not consider it fitting to question, although she was the beginning of evil and led him (man) into a life of vileness.[b] But this passage also has a more apt[c] allegory. For the sovereign and ruling element[d] in man, having reason,[e] when it listens to anyone, introduces the vice of the female part also, that is, perception.

46. (Gen. iii. 12-13) Why does the man say, "The woman gave me of the tree and I ate," while the woman says, "The serpent did not give it, but deceived me, and I ate"[f]?

What is so stated (literally) contains a sentiment that is to be approved,[g] for woman is of a nature to be deceived rather than to reflect greatly, but man is the opposite here. But according to the deeper meaning,[h] the object of sense-perception[i] deceives and deludes the particular senses of an imperfect being to which it comes; and sense-perception being already infected by its object,[j] passes on the infection to the sovereign and ruling element.[k] So then the mind receives from sense, the giver, that which the latter has suffered. And sense is deceived and deluded by a sense-perceptible object,[l] but the senses of a wise man, like the reflections of his mind, are not to be deceived.

[a] ἀπειλὴ καὶ ἐπιτίμησις. [b] τοῦ φαύλου.

[c] προχειροτέραν.

[d] τὸ ἀρχηγετικὸν καὶ τὸ ἡγεμονικόν. [e] λόγον.

[f] So the Arm. literally; one expects "the woman said not, 'the serpent gave me it,' but, 'the serpent deceived me and I ate.'" The "not" appears to be out of place.

[g] δόξαν ἀποδεκτήν. [h] πρὸς διάνοιαν.

[i] τὸ αἰσθητόν.

[j] ὑπὸ τοῦ ὑποκειμένου.

[k] τῷ ἀρχηγετικῷ καὶ ἡγεμονικῷ (*i.e.* mind).

[l] ὑπὸ τοῦ ὑποκειμένου αἰσθητοῦ.

47. (Gen. iii. 14-17) Why does He first curse the serpent, next the woman, and third the man ?

The arrangement of curses follows the order of the wrongdoing. The serpent was the first to deceive. Second, the woman sinned through him, yielding to deceit. Third the man (sinned), yielding to the woman's desire rather than to the divine commands. However the order also is well suited [a] to allegory ; for the serpent is a symbol of desire,[b] as was shown ; and woman is a symbol of sense, and man of mind. So that desire becomes the evil origin of sins, and this first deceives sense, while sense takes the mind captive.

48. (Gen. iii. 14-15) Why is this curse laid upon the serpent—to move upon its breast and belly, to eat dust and to have enmity toward woman ?

The text is plain, since we have as testimony that which we see. But according to the deeper meaning it is to be allegorically interpreted as follows. Since the serpent is a symbol of desire,[c] he takes the form [d] of lovers of pleasure,[e] for he crawls upon his breast and belly, stuffed with food and drink, and has the insatiable desire of a cormorant,[f] and is intemperate and unbridled in eating flesh.[g] And whatever has to do with food is altogether earthy ; wherefore he is said to eat dust. And desire has a natural enmity toward sense, which (Scripture) symbolically calls woman. And notwithstanding that desires seem to be critical [h] of the senses, they are in reality flatterers who plot evil in the manner of enemies. And it is the custom of adversaries [i] that through that which they bestow as gifts [j] they cause great harm, such as defectiveness of vision to the eyes, and difficulty of hearing to the ears, and insensibility [k] to the other (sense organs) ; and they bring

[a] καλῶς ἔχει. [b] ἐπιθυμίας. [c] ἐπιθυμίας.
[d] σχηματίζει or σχηματοποιεῖ. [e] φιληδόνων.
[f] ἀκορέστῃ τῆς αἰτύας (?) ἐπιθυμίᾳ. [g] σαρκοφαγίᾳ.
[h] φιλαίτιοι. [i] Or "warriors"—πολεμίων.
[j] χαρίζονται. [k] ἀναισθησίαν.

upon the whole body together dissolution and paralysis,[a] taking away all its health [b] and for no good reason [c] newly bringing [d] many bad sicknesses.

49. (Gen. iii. 16) Why does the curse on the woman consist of an increase in sorrow and lamentation and in giving birth in pain and in turning [e] to her husband and being under his rule.[f]

This experience comes to every woman who lives together with [g] a man. It is (meant) not as a curse but as a necessity. But symbolically the senses of man have difficult labours and suffering,[h] being treated badly [i] and scourged by domestic ills.[j] And these are the offspring [k] of sense: seeing, of the organ of sight; hearing, of the organ of hearing; smelling, of the nostrils; tasting, of the organ of taste; contact, of the organ of touch. And since the life of the worthless and evil man is sorrowful and necessitous,[l] it is necessary that whatever is acted upon [m] by sense should be mixed with fear and suffering. But according to the deeper meaning, there takes place a turning of sense to the man, not as to a helper, for it is a subject of no worth,[n] but as to a master,[o] since it prizes force [p] more than righteousness.[q]

50. (Gen. iii. 17) Why does He curse the serpent and the woman by referring directly to them [r] and not do so similarly to the man, instead of placing it [s] on the earth, saying, "Cursed be the earth for thy sake; in sorrow shalt

[a] ἔκλυσιν καὶ παράλυσιν. [b] ὑγίειαν.
[c] εἰκῇ. [d] καινουργοῦντες. [e] ἐπιστροφῇ.
[f] κυριότητι or ἐξουσίᾳ. [g] συμβιῶσα.
[h] χαλεποὺς πόνους καὶ ἀλγήματα.
[i] φαυλιζόμεναι *vel sim.* [j] οἰκονομικαῖς κακίαις.
[k] ἔκγονοι. [l] ἄπορος. [m] ἐνεργεῖται.
[n] ὑποκειμένη καὶ εὐτελής. [o] κύριον.
[p] δυναστείαν or βίαν. [q] δικαιοσύνην.
[r] νεύσας πρὸς αὐτοὺς ἐφ' ἑαυτούς. [s] *i.e.* the curse.

thou eat it ; thistles and thorns it shall grow for thee, and thou shalt eat the grass of the field ; in the sweat of thy brow shalt thou eat thy bread " ?

Since the mind is a divine inbreathing,[a] He does not deem it right to curse it, but He turns the curse against the earth and its cultivation.[b] And the earth is of the same nature [c] as the body of man, of which the mind is the cultivator. When the cultivator is virtuous and worthy, the body also bears its fruits, namely health, keenness of sense,[d] power and beauty. But when he is cruel,[e] the opposite is brought to pass, for his body is cursed, receiving as its cultivator a mind undisciplined and imprudent.[f] And its fruit consists of nothing useful but only of thistles and thorns, sorrow and fear and other ills, while thoughts strike the mind and shoot arrows at it. And the " grass " is symbolically food, for he changes from a rational being to an irrational creature, overlooking [g] the divine foods ; these are those which are granted by philosophy through principles [h] and voluntary laws.[i]

*51. (Gen. iii. 19) What is the meaning of the words, " Until thou return to the earth from which thou wast taken " ? For man was moulded not only from the earth but also from the divine spirit.

First, it is evident that the earth-born creature was compounded out of earth and heaven. And because he did not remain uncorrupted [j] but made light of the commands of God, turning away from the best and most excellent part, namely heaven,[k] he gave himself wholly over to the earth, the denser and heavier element.[l] Second, if he had been desirous of virtue, which makes the soul immortal,[m] he would certainly have obtained heaven as his lot. Since

[a] ἐμφύσησις. [b] γεωργίαν. [c] ὁμοφυής or ὁμοούσιος.
[d] εὐαισθησίαν. [e] δεινός or χαλεπός *vel sim.*
[f] ἀπαίδευτον καὶ ἄφρονα. [g] ὑπερορῶν.
[h] λόγων. [i] ἑκουσίων νόμων. [j] ἄφθαρτος.
[k] The Greek frag. reads differently.
[l] παχυτέρῳ καὶ βαρυτέρῳ στοιχείῳ. [m] ἀθανατίζει τὴν ψυχήν.

he was zealous for pleasure, through which spiritual death is brought about, he again gives himself back to earth; accordingly Scripture says, "Dust thou art, wherefore to dust shalt thou return." Thus earth is the beginning and end of the evil and vile man, but heaven of the virtuous man.

52. (Gen. iii. 20) Why does the earth-born man call his wife "Life" and exclaim, "Thou art the mother of all living things"?

First, he gave the name of Life, which was most suitable [a] to the first created woman, because she was to be the source of all the generations that were to come after them. Second, perhaps because she took the substance of her being [b] not from the earth but from a living being, and from one part of the man, the rib, was given bodily form as a woman, she was called Life; for from a living being she first came into being, and because the first rational creatures were born to her. However it is also possible to understand this metaphorically [c]; for is not sense, which is symbolically woman, rightly called Life? For the living is distinguished from the non-living by sense, through which impressions [d] and impulses [e] come to us, since sense is the cause of these. And in truth sense is the mother of all living things; just as nothing is born without a mother, so there is no living creature without sense.

53. (Gen. iii. 21) Why does God make tunics [f] of skin for Adam and his wife and clothe them?

Some may ridicule the text when they consider the cheapness [g] of the apparel of tunics, as being unworthy of the touch [h] of such a Creator. But a man who has tasted

[a] οἰκειότερον.
[b] τὴν τῆς ὑπάρξεως οὐσίαν or possibly τὴν τῆς οὐσίας σύστασιν.
[c] τροπικῶς. [d] φαντασίαι. [e] ὁρμαί.
[f] χιτῶνας. [g] εὐτέλειαν. [h] ἐφάπτεσθαι.

of wisdom and virtue [a] will surely consider this work suitable to God for the wise instruction [b] of those who labour idly [c] and care little about providing necessities but are mad for wretched glory [d] and give themselves up to amusement, and despise wisdom and virtue. Instead, they love a life of luxury [e] and the skill of the artificer [f] and that which is hostile to the good.[g] And the wretches do not know that contentment with little,[h] which is in need of nothing, is like a relative and neighbour,[i] but luxury [j] is like an enemy, to be driven away and made to live far off. Accordingly, the tunics of skin, if we judge truly, are to be considered a more precious possession [k] than varicoloured dies and purple stuffs. So much, then, for the literal meaning. But according to the deeper meaning,[l] the tunic of skin is symbolically the natural skin of the body.[m] For when God formed the first mind, He called it Adam; then he formed the sense, which He called Life; in the third place, of necessity He made his body also, calling it symbolically a tunic of skin, for it was proper that the mind and sense should be clothed in the body as in a tunic of skin, in order that His handiwork might first appear worthy of the divine power.[n] And could the apparel of the human body be better or more fittingly made by any other power than God? Wherefore, having made their apparel, He straightway clothed them. For in the case of human clothing, there are some who make it and others who put it on. But this natural tunic, that is, the body, was the work of Him who had also made it, and having made it, also clothed them in it.

[a] σοφίας καὶ ἀρετῆς. [b] εἰς παιδείαν σοφίας.
[c] ματαίως. [d] πρὸς ταλαίπωρον δόξαν μαινόμενοι.
[e] βίον λαμπρόν. [f] χειροτεχνίτου.
[g] τὸ μισόκαλον. [h] ὀλιγόδεια.
[i] συγγενὴς καὶ γείτων.
[j] λαμπρότης or πολυτέλεια.
[k] τιμαλφεστέραν κτῆσιν. [l] πρὸς διάνοιαν.
[m] τὸ τοῦ σώματος φυσικὸν δέρμα.
[n] ἄξιον τῆς θείας δυνάμεως.

54. (Gen. iii. 22) To whom does He say, " Behold, Adam is as one of us, to know good and evil " ?

" One of us " indicates plurality.[a] But it must not be thought that He spoke with His powers,[b] which He used as instruments [c] in making the whole universe.[d] Now the word " as " is indicative of an example and likeness and comparison [e] not of a dissimilarity.[f] For the intelligible and sense-perceptible good is known by God in one way and by man in another way.[g] For to the extent that the natures of those who inquire and comprehend [h] differ, as do those things which are accurately grasped and comprehended, to that extent is man's power able to comprehend.[i] And all these things are likenesses and forms and images in man. But in God they are archetypes and models and very brilliant examples of [j] dark things. And the unbegotten and uncreated One [k] and Father mingles and associates with no one. He holds out [l] to sight the glory of His powers.[m]

*55. (Gen. iii. 22) What is the meaning of the words, " Lest perchance he put forth his hand and take of the tree of life and eat and live forever " ? For there is neither doubt [n] nor envy [o] in God.

It is true that the Deity neither doubts nor envies. However, (Scripture) often uses ambiguous [p] terms and names, according as it indicates a principle as if addressed to man.[q] For the highest principles, as I have said, are two: one, that God is not like man; and the

[a] πλῆθος. [b] δυνάμεσι. [c] ὀργάνοις. [d] τὸν κόσμον.
[e] δηλωτικὸν τῶν ὑποδειγμάτων καὶ ὁμοιοτήτων καὶ ἀναλογιῶν.
[f] ἀνομοιότητος. [g] ἄλλως . . . ἄλλως.
[h] τῶν ἐξεταζόντων καὶ καταλαμβανόντων. [i] καταληπτική.
[j] ὑποδείγματα. [k] ὁ ἀγέννητος καὶ ἀγένητος.
[l] προτείνει. [m] τὴν τῶν δυνάμεων δόξαν.
[n] ἐνδοιασμός, as in one Greek frag.
[o] φθόνος *ibid.* [p] ἐνδοιαστικοῖς.
[q] The Greek frag. from John Monachus reads κατ' ἀναφορὰν ἐπὶ τὸ " ὡς ἄνθρωπος " κεφάλαιον.

other, that just as a man disciplines[a] his son, so the Lord God disciplines you. Accordingly, the first principle is a matter of authority,[b] while the second is one of discipline[c] and the first step in training,[d] in order that one may be quite voluntarily and gradually led into it.[e] For the words "lest perchance" are not a sign of doubt in God but an indication[f] of man's being a doubter by nature, and a manifestation of the affection[g] that exists in him. For whenever there comes to someone an appearance of something, there immediately follows an impulse[h] toward the appearance, of which the appearance is the cause.[i] And (so comes) the second uncertainty[j] of one who is in doubt and is drawn here and there in spirit, whether (the appearance) is to be received or not. It is this second "lest perchance" that these words indicate. The Deity, however, is without part[k] in any evil and is not envious of immortality or anything else whatever in the case of the good man. And a sure sign of this is that without being urged by anyone,[l] He created the world as a benefactor,[m] making contentious, disordered, confused and passive substance[n] into something gracious and lovingly mild with a great and harmonious order and array of good things. And the truly existent One[o] planted the tree of life by His lucid understanding.[p] Moreover, He did not use any intermediary to urge Him or exhort Him[q] to give others a share of incorruptibility.[r] Now while (man's) mind was pure and received no impression[s]

[a] *παιδεύει.* [b] *ἐξουσίας.* [c] *παιδείας.*

[d] *τῆς πρώτης εἰς ἐπιτήδευμα ἀγωγῆς.*

[e] *καὶ ἑκούσιος παρεισάγηται.*

[f] *νεῦμα*, but *cf.* Procopius. [g] *πάθος.* [h] *ὁρμή.*

[i] Arm. construction not quite clear.

[j] *ἀπορία.* [k] *ἀμέτοχος.*

[l] *μηδενὸς παρακαλουμένου.* [m] *εὐεργετῶν.*

[n] *ἐρίζουσαν καὶ ἄκοσμον καὶ ἄτακτον καὶ πάσχουσαν οὐσίαν.*

[o] *ὁ ὄντως Ὤν.*

[p] *τῇ λαμπρᾷ (φωτεινῇ) φρονήσει.*

[q] *μεσίτῃ παρακαλοῦντι καὶ προτρέποντι.*

[r] *πρὸς τὴν τῆς ἀφθαρσίας κοινωνίαν.* [s] *φαντασίαν.*

of any evil deed or word, he had secure enjoyment [a] of that which led him to piety,[b] which is unquestioned and true immortality.[c] But after he began to turn to wickedness [d] and to hurl himself down [e] thereto, desiring mortal life, he failed to obtain immortality,[f] for it is unseemly [g] to immortalize [h] evil, and it is unprofitable for him to whom it happens. For the longer the evil and wicked man lives, the more wretched he is and the more greatly harmful both to himself and to others.

56. (Gen. iii. 23) Why does He now call Paradise " delight," [i] when He drives man out of it to till the earth, from which he was taken ?

The difference in agriculture is clear.[j] When he was cultivating wisdom in Paradise, he took care [k] of the cultivation of wisdom as if of trees, nourishing himself on its immortal and beneficial fruits, through which he became immortal. And when he was driven out of the place of wisdom, he was to practise the opposite, (namely) works of ignorance,[l] through which his body is polluted,[m] and his mind is blinded,[n] and being starved of his own food,[o] he wastes away and suffers a miserable death. Wherefore now indeed as a reproach to the foolish man [p] He called Paradise " pleasure " as the antithesis [q] of a painful and terrible life. For in truth a life of wisdom is a delight of spacious joy [r] and an enjoyment most suitable to the rational soul.[s] But a life without wisdom is harsh and

[a] ἄδειαν τῆς ἀπολαύσεως. [b] εὐσέβειαν.
[c] ἀψευδὴς καὶ ἀληθὴς ἀθανασία. [d] τὸ φαῦλον.
[e] ἑαυτὸν καταρρίπτειν. [f] διήμαρτε τῆς ἀθανασίας.
[g] ἀπρεπές. [h] ἀθανατίζειν. [i] τρυφή = Heb. *'ēden*.
[j] ἡ τῆς γεωργίας διαφορὰ σαφής ἐστι.
[k] ἐπεμελεῖτο. [l] τὰ τῆς ἀμαθίας ἔργα.
[m] βεβηλοῦται, μιαίνεται. [n] τυφλοῦται.
[o] πεινῶν τῆς ἑαυτοῦ τροφῆς. [p] εἰς ὄνειδος τοῦ ἄφρονος.
[q] εἰς ἀντίθεσιν. [r] εὐρυχώρου εὐφροσύνης.
[s] οἰκειοτάτῃ τῇ λογικῇ ψυχῇ.

terrible. For even though one is completely deceived by sense-pleasures, both before and after (them) comes suffering.

57. (Gen. iii. 24) Why did He place[a] over against Paradise the cherubim and the fiery[b] sword, which was turning, to guard the way to the tree of life?

The cherubim are symbols of the two primary attributes[c] of God, namely the creative[d] and the kingly,[e] of which one is called God,[f] and the other, the kingly one, is called Lord.[g] And the form of the creative attribute is a benevolent and friendly and beneficent[h] power. But that of the kingly attribute is legislative and punitive.[i] Moreover "fiery sword" is a symbolical name for heaven, for the ether[j] is flamelike and turns round the world.[k] And as all these have undertaken the guarding of Paradise, it is evident that they are overseers of wisdom,[l] like a mirror. For in a certain sense[m] the wisdom of the world was a mirror of the powers of God, in accordance with which it became perfect[n] and this universe is governed and managed.[o] But the road to wisdom is called philosophy, for the creative power is a lover of wisdom[p]; so also the kingly power is a lover of wisdom, and the world too is a lover of wisdom. But there are some who say that the fiery sword is the sun, since by its revolution and turning it reveals the yearly seasons,[q] as if it were the guardian of life and of whatever leads to the life of all things.

[a] κατῴκισε: LXX κατῴκισε . . . καὶ ἔταξε.
[b] πυρίνην: LXX φλογίνην.
[c] τῶν δυοῖν πρώτων δυνάμεων.
[d] τῆς ποιητικῆς. [e] τῆς βασιλικῆς.
[f] θεός. [g] κύριος.
[h] εὐμενὴς καὶ φίλη καὶ εὐεργετική.
[i] νομοθετικὴ καὶ κολαστική. [j] αἰθήρ.
[k] αἰῶνα. [l] ἐπιστάται τῆς σοφίας.
[m] τρόπον τινά. [n] ἐτελειώθη.
[o] κυβερνᾶται καὶ οἰκονομεῖται. [p] φιλοσοφική.
[q] τοὺς ἐτησίους χρόνους.

58. (Gen. iv. 1) Was it correctly said about Cain, " I have acquired [a] a man through God " ? [b]

(Concerning acquisition) a distinction is made between " by someone " [c] or " from someone " [d] and " through something " [e] or " from something," that is, from matter.[f] " Through someone " means through a cause,[g] and " through something " means through an instrument.[h] But the father and creator of the universe [i] is not an instrument but a cause. Accordingly he errs against correct thinking [j] who says that things [k] come into being not by the agency of God [l] but through God.[m]

*59. (Gen. iv. 2) Why does (Scripture) first describe the work of the younger man Abel, saying, " He became a shepherd of flocks, and Cain tilled the ground " ?

Even though the righteous man [n] was younger in time than the wicked one,[o] still he was older in activity.[p] Wherefore now, when their activities are appraised,[q] he is placed first in order. For one of them labours and takes care of living beings [r] even though they are irrational,[s] gladly undertaking the pastoral work which is preparatory [t] to rulership and kingship. But the other occupies himself with earthly and inanimate things.

[a] ἐκτησάμην.

[b] Arm. has instrumental case of θεός: LXX διὰ τοῦ θεοῦ.

[c] Arm. has instrumental case of indef. m. pr.

[d] ἔκ τινος.

[e] Arm. has instrumental case of indef. n. pr.

[f] ἐξ ὕλης.

[g] δι' αἰτίαν, ἐξ αἰτίας.

[h] δι' ὀργάνου, ἐξ ὀργάνου.

[i] πατὴρ καὶ ποιητὴς τοῦ παντός.

[j] ὀρθοῦ λογισμοῦ, λόγου.

[k] τὰ γενόμενα.

[l] Arm. has ablative case of " God."

[m] Arm. has instrumental case of " God."

[n] ὁ δίκαιος in Procopius.

[o] τοῦ φαύλου.

[p] ἐπιτηδεύμασι in Procopius.

[q] Or " tested " ? (δοκιμάζονται): Aucher " conferenda sunt."

[r] ἐμψύχων.

[s] ἀλόγων.

[t] προγυμναστικόν.

*60. (Gen. iv. 3-4). Why did Cain after some days[a] offer firstfruits of offerings,[b] while Abel (brought an offering) from the first-born[c] and fat ones, not after some days?"

Scripture manifests a distinction between the lover of self and the lover of God. For one of them took for himself the fruit of the firstfruits and impiously thought God worthy (only) of the second fruits. For the words "after some days" instead of "immediately" and "from the offerings" instead of "from the firstfruits"[d] indicate great wickedness.[e] But the other offered[f] the first-born and elder animals without any delay at all or rejection by his Father.

*61. (Gen. iv. 4-5) Why does (Scripture), having begun by first mentioning Cain, (now) mention him in second place, for it says, "God looked upon Abel and his offerings,[g] but of Cain and his sacrifice[h] He did not approve"?[i]

First, (Scripture) does not mean that he is first by nature who happens to be the first to be perceived, but he who comes in his time and with sound morals. Second, as there were two persons, good and evil, He turned toward the good man, looking upon him because He is a lover of goodness and virtue,[j] and first seeing him to be more inclined toward that side in the order of nature,[k] He

[a] Arm. obscure: Aucher "post dies primitias fructuum offert," in note "*vel ita*, post dies primitiarum primitias offert," but *cf.* Greek fragments.

[b] Procopius differs: LXX ἀπὸ τῶν καρπῶν τῆς γῆς θυσίαν.

[c] τῶν πρωτοτόκων.

[d] τῶν πρωτοτόκων.

[e] ἀδικίαν, ἀνομίαν.

[f] ἁγιάζων ἦν, ἀνατιθέμενος ἦν.

[g] δῶρα, προσφοράς.

[h] θυσίᾳ.

[i] οὐκ ηὐδόκησε; Aucher suggests *hayeçaw* "looked" for *hačeçaw* "approved." LXX οὐ προσέσχεν.

[j] Aucher translates, "seeing that he (Abel) is a lover of goodness and virtue," but in that case we should expect in the Arm. *zi* "that" for *wasn zi* "because."

[k] τῇ τῆς φύσεως τάξει.

deprecates [a] and turns away from the evil man. Accordingly, most excellently (Scripture) says not that God saw the offerings [b] but that He first saw those who were offering gifts [c] before the gifts themselves, for men look at the quantity of gifts and approve [d] them ; but God looks at the truth of the soul,[e] turning aside [f] from arrogance [g] and flattery.[h]

*62. (Gen. iv. 4-5) What difference is there between a gift [i] and a sacrifice ? [j]

He who slaughters [k] a sacrifice,[l] after dividing it, pours the blood on [m] the altar [n] and takes the flesh home. But he who offers [o] something as a gift [p] offers the whole of it, it seems, to him who receives it. And the lover of self is a divider,[q] as was Cain, while the lover of God is a giver,[r] as was Abel.

*63. (Gen. iv. 5) Whence did Cain know that his sacrifice was not pleasing ? [s]

Perhaps his difficulty was resolved through the cause mentioned in the addition [t] ; for he was grieved [u] and his countenance fell. He therefore took this grief as a sign of having sacrificed something not pleasing. For joy [v] and gladness [w] ought to come to him who sacrifices something purely [x] and blamelessly.[y]

[a] *παραιτεῖται.* [b] *τὰ προσφερόμενα.*
[c] *τοὺς τὰ δῶρα προσφέροντας.* [d] *δοκιμάζουσι.*
[e] *εἰς τὴν τῆς ψυχῆς ἀλήθειαν.* [f] *ἐκκλίνων.*
[g] *ἀλαζονείας, τύφους, ὑπερηφανίας vel sim.*
[h] *κολακείας.* [i] *δῶρον.* [j] *θυσία.*
[k] *θύει, σφάττει.* [l] *θυσίαν.*
[m] Or " around," v.l. " near."
[n] *βωμόν, θυσιαστήριον.* [o] *προσφέρει.*
[p] *ὡς δῶρον.* [q] *ἐπιδιαιρῶν*, as in Greek fragments.
[r] *δωρούμενος*, as in Greek fragments. [s] *ἀρεστή.*
[t] In the second half of verse 5. [u] *ἐλυπήθη.*
[v] *εὐφροσύνη.* [w] *χαρά.*
[x] *καθαρῶς.* [y] *ἀμώμως.*

*64. (Gen. iv. 7) What is the meaning of the words, "Not that thou dost not offer rightly,[a] but that thou dost not divide rightly"?

First of all, correct division and incorrect division are nothing else than order.[b] And through order equally[c] are made the whole world and its parts.[d] Wherefore the creator of the world,[e] when He began to order[f] refractory[g] and unordered[h] and passive[i] substance,[j] made use of cutting[k] and division. For in the midst of the universe,[l] He placed the heavy things[m] and those that naturally bear downwards,[n] (namely) earth and water; but air and fire He placed above, for they ascend through their lightness.[o] But He separated[p] and marked off[q] the pure nature, (namely) heaven, and surrounded and enclosed[r] the universe by it, that it might be invisible[s] to all, containing within itself all things equally.[t] But the fact that animals and plants come into being from moist and dry seeds[u]—what else is this than a cutting and separative division?[v] Accordingly it is necessary to imitate this order in all things in the world and especially in returning thanks for those things for which we are required[w] to make a corresponding[x] return to him who gives them to us. In the second place, to give thanks[y] to God is right in itself[z] specifically,[a] but it is blameworthy that He should not first receive them nor receive the first of the new products. For it is not proper to offer the best things[b] to that which is created, namely oneself,

[a] ὀρθῶς. [b] τάξις. [c] ἴσως.
[d] ὁ κόσμος καὶ τὰ αὐτοῦ μέρη. [e] ὁ τοῦ κόσμου ποιητής.
[f] τάττειν. [g] ἐρίζουσαν. [h] ἄτακτον.
[i] πάσχουσαν. [j] οὐσίαν. [k] τομῇ, διαιρέσει.
[l] τοῦ παντός. [m] τὰ βαρῆ. [n] τὰ φύσει καταφερῆ.
[o] κουφισιν. [p] διεχώρισε. [q] ἀφώρισε.
[r] περιβάλλων συνέκλεισε.
[s] ἀόρατος: Aucher conj. *tesaneli* = ὁρατός.
[t] ἴσως or κοινῇ. [u] ἐξ ὑγρῶν καὶ ξηρῶν σπερμάτων.
[v] διάστημα διακρίσεως. [w] ἐξεταζόμεθα?
[x] ἄλλῳ τρόπῳ? [y] εὐχαριστεῖν.
[z] καθ' ἑαυτό. [a] ἰδίως. [b] τὰ πρεσβεῖα.

and the second best to the All-wise. This is a reprehensible and blameworthy division,[a] showing a certain disorderliness of order.[b]

*65. (Gen. iv. 7) What is the meaning of the words, "Thou hast sinned, be quiet"?[c]

The oracle[d] utters something very useful. For not to sin at all is the greatest good. But he who sins and is abashed and ashamed is kin to this man[e] and, as one might say, is the younger beside the elder. For there are some who rejoice[f] over sins as if over good deeds,[g] thus having a disease[h] that is difficult to cure[i] or rather is incurable.[j]

*66. (Gen. iv. 7) Why does He seem to give the good man into the hand of the evil man, saying, "To thee is his return"?

He does not give him into his hand, but the sense[k] is quite the contrary, for He speaks not of the pious man[l] but of an act already done. And He says to him, "the return[m] and reference[n] of this impiety is to thee.[o] Do not therefore blame necessity,[p] but thine own character,[q] so that in this place He represents it as voluntary.[r] But the words, 'thou shalt rule over him,' again have reference[s] to an act." In the first place thou didst begin to act impiously, and then another wrong[t] follows a great and impious lawlessness.[u] And so He considers and proves[v] that this is the beginning of every voluntary wrongdoing.

[a] *διαίρεσις*. [b] *ἀταξίαν τινὰ τάξεως*, as in John Monachus.
[c] = LXX *ἥμαρτες, ἡσύχασον*. [d] *χρησμός*.
[e] *i.e.* the one who does not sin. [f] *ἀγάλλονται*.
[g] *κατορθώμασι*. [h] *πάθος*. [i] *δυσίατον*. [j] *ἀνίατον*.
[k] *ἀκοή*? [l] *θεοσεβοῦς*. [m] *ἀποστροφή*. [n] *ἀναφορά*.
[o] *πρὸς σέ ἐστιν*. [p] *μὴ τὴν ἀνάγκην αἰτιάσῃς*.
[q] *ἦθος, τρόπον*. [r] *ἑκούσιον*.
[s] *νεῦμα*. [t] *ἀδικία*.
[u] *μεγάλην ἀνομίας ἀσεβίαν*. [v] *ἐλέγχει*.

67. (Gen. iv. 8) Why does he (Cain) kill his brother in the field ?[a]

In order that[b] when once again it is sown or planted, infertility[c] and unfruitfulness[d] may altogether come upon its fruits, and by bringing the murder to mind, may reveal its foulness.[e] For the ground[f] was not to be the same after being forced to drink human blood unnaturally so as also to grow food for him who polluted it with the blood of a foul deed.

*68. (Gen. iv. 9) Why does He who knows all ask the fratricide, " Where is Abel, thy brother ? " ?

He wishes that man himself of his own will shall confess,[g] in order that he may not pretend[h] that all things seem to come about through necessity.[i] For he who killed through necessity would confess[j] that he acted unwillingly ; for that which is not in our power[k] is not to be blamed.[l] But he who sins of his own free will[m] denies it,[n] for sinners are obliged to repent.[o] Accordingly he (Moses) inserts[p] in all parts of his legislation[q] that the Deity is not the cause of evil.

*69. (Gen. iv. 9) Why does he (Cain) reply as if to a man, saying, " I do not know. Am I my brother's keeper ? " ?

It is an atheistic[r] belief not to hold that the divine eye penetrates[s] all things and sees all things at one time, not only what is visible but also what is in recesses, depths and abysses. " Why dost thou not know where thy brother is ? " someone will say. " And how shouldst thou not know this, being the fourth man in the world together

[a] ἐν τῷ πεδίῳ. [b] *v.l.* " lest." [c] ἀφορία.
[d] ἀκαρπία, ἀγονία. [e] βδέλυγμα. [f] τὸ ἔδαφος.
[g] ἐξομολογῆται. [h] προσποιῆται. [i] ἀνάγκῃ.
[j] Construction of Arm. uncertain. [k] Lit. " in us."
[l] ἀνυπαίτιόν ἐστιν. [m] ἑκουσίᾳ γνώμῃ.
[n] ἀπαρνεῖται. [o] τῇ μετανοίᾳ ἔνοχοι.
[p] ὑφαίνει. [q] τῆς νομοθεσίας.
[r] ἄθεος. [s] διήκει.

with thy two parents and thine only brother?" But the reply, "I am not my brother's keeper" is a fine defence![a] And of whom else rather than of thy brother shouldst thou have been a keeper and protector?[b] Thou didst show so much care for violence,[c] injustice,[d] treachery[e] and homicide,[f] which is a great abomination[g] and accursed[h] deed, but didst show contempt for[i] thy brother's safety, as though it were something superfluous.[j]

*70. (Gen. iv. 10) What is the meaning of the words, "The voice of thy brother calls to me from the earth"?

This is most exemplary,[k] for the Deity hears the deserving[l] even though they are dead,[m] knowing that they live an incorporeal life.[n] But from the prayers of evil men He turns away His face even though they enjoy the prime of life,[o] considering that they are dead to true life and bear their body with them like a tomb that they may bury their unhappy soul[p] in it.

71. (Gen. iv. 11) Why does he (Cain) become accursed upon[q] the earth?

The earth is the last[r] of the parts of the universe.[s] Accordingly, if this curses him, it is understandable that appropriate[t] curses will be laid upon him by the other elements[u] as well, namely by springs, rivers, sea, air, winds, fire, light, the sun, the moon, the stars and the whole heaven together.[v] For if inanimate[w] and terrestrial

[a] ἀπολογία. [b] ὑπερασπιστής. [c] βίᾳ. [d] ἀδικίᾳ.

[e] Text uncertain; I conj. *dawačank'* = ἐπιβουλία for Arm. *dawank* = ὁμολογία. [f] ἀνδροφονίᾳ.

[g] βδέλυγμα. [h] κατάρατον. [i] κατεφρόνησας.

[j] περισσόν. [k] δογματικώτατον.

[l] ὁσίων or δικαίων in Greek fragments.

[m] καίπερ τελευτήσαντας. [n] ζωὴν ἀσώματον.

[o] κἂν εὐεξίᾳ χρήσωνται in the Greek fragments.

[p] ταλαίπωρον ψυχήν. [q] ἐν or ἐπί: LXX ἀπό

[r] ἔσχατον or "latest" ὕστατον. [s] τοῦ κόσμου.

[t] ἁρμονικάς, ἀκολούθους. [u] στοιχεῖα.

[v] κοινῇ. [w] ἄψυχος.

nature opposes and revolts [a] against wrongdoing,[b] will not purer natures [c] do so still more? But he with whom the parts of the universe wage war—what hope of salvation [d] will he any longer have? I do not know.

*72. (Gen. iv. 12) What is the meaning of the words, "Groaning and trembling [e] shalt thou be upon the earth"?

This too is a universal principle.[f] For every evildoer has something which immediately awaits him and is to come.[g] For things to come [h] already bring fears,[i] and that which is immediately present causes grief.[j]

*73. (Gen. iv. 13) What is the meaning of the words, "Too great is my guilt [k] to let me go"? [l]

Indeed there is no misfortune of greater hopelessness [m] than God's leaving and abandoning [n] one. For the lack of a ruler [o] is terrible and difficult for depraved men. But to be overlooked [p] by a great king and to be cast out and rejected [q] by the chief authority is an indescribable misfortune.[r]

*74. (Gen. iv. 14) What is the meaning of the words, "Every one who finds me will kill me," inasmuch as there were no other people but his parents?

[a] ἀντιλέγει καὶ στασιάζει.
[b] ἀδικίαν.
[c] καθαρωτέραι φύσεις.
[d] σωτηρίας.
[e] στενάζων καὶ τρέμων: so LXX: Heb. different (A.V. "a fugitive and a vagabond").
[f] λόγιον καθολικώτατον in Procopius.
[g] δεχόμενον καὶ μέλλον.
[h] τὰ μέλλοντα.
[i] φόβους.
[j] λύπας.
[k] αἰτία.
[l] *Cf.* LXX τοῦ ἀφεθῆναί με; Arm. O.T. "for thee to let me go."
[m] μείζονος ἀπορίας.
[n] ἀφιέναι καὶ ἐγκαταλείπειν.
[o] ἀναρχία.
[p] Or "looked down upon"—παροράσθαι or ὑπεροράσθαι.
[q] ἀποβάλλεσθαι.
[r] ἀτυχία.

First of all, he was likely [a] to suffer harm from the parts of the world, which were made for the use [b] and participation [c] of good men but none the less exact punishment from the wicked. Second, because he feared the attacks of beasts and reptiles, for nature produced these for the punishment of unjust men. Third, perhaps one may think of his parents, to whom he first brought new grief and their first misfortune,[d] as they had not known what death is.

75. (Gen. iv. 15) Why shall everyone who slays Cain suffer seven punishments?

Our soul [e] is made and constituted of eight parts: of the rational part,[f] which permits of no division, and of the irrational part,[g] which is naturally [h] divided into seven parts—the five senses,[i] the organ of speech and the organ of reproduction. And these seven parts are the causes of wickedness and are brought to judgment.[j] And death is acceptable [k] to the chief ruler (*i.e.* the mind) in whom evil is.[l] Accordingly whoever kills the mind [m] by mixing in folly [n] instead of sense [o] will cause the dissolution and breaking up [p] of the seven irrational parts. For just as the chief ruler is disposed toward virtue,[q] so also are disposed [r] the parts which are subordinate to him.[s]

*76. (Gen. iv. 15) Why is a sign placed upon the fratricide in order that any who finds him may not kill him, when it

[a] συνέβη αὐτῷ. [b] ὠφέλειαν. [c] κοινωνίαν.

[d] Procopius reads more briefly κοινὸν πένθος.

[e] ψυχή. [f] τὸ λογικόν. [g] τὸ ἄλογον.

[h] πέφυκε. [i] αἰσθήσεις. [j] εἰς κρίσιν. [k] ἀγαπητός.

[l] The Arm. construction is not clear to me; Aucher's rendering is very doubtful, "mors autem principis praesidis (mentis *sc.*) proprie est illa quae in eo sedet malitia." The word "ruler" (*išxan*) is nom., not gen. as Aucher renders.

[m] τὸν νοῦν. [n] ἀφροσύνην. [o] αἴσθησιν.

[p] λύσιν καὶ παράλυσιν. [q] πρὸς ἀρετὴν ἔχει.

[r] ἁρμόζεται. [s] αὐτῷ ὑποτάττεται.

was fitting to do the opposite[a] and give him into the hands (of another) for destruction?

First, one kind of death is the change of nature of the living. But continuous sorrows, unmixed with joy, and violent fears,[b] empty[c] of good hope, bring on[d] many grave and manifold[e] deaths, which are caused by sense.[f] Second, immediately at the outset[g] (Scripture) wishes to describe the law of the incorruptibility of the soul[h] and to refute the false belief[i] of those who think that this bodily life alone is blessed.[j] For behold one of the two (brothers) is guilty[k] of the greatest evils, namely impiety[l] and fratricide, and yet is alive and begets children and founds cities. But he who gave evidence of piety is destroyed by cunning.[m] Not only does the divine word[n] clearly proclaim that it is not the life of sense[o] which is good and that death is not an evil, but also that the life of the body is not even related[p] (to life). But there is another (life) unaging and immortal,[q] which incorporeal souls[r] receive as their lot.[s] For that which was said by the poet about Scylla, "She is not a mortal but an immortal evil,"[t] was said more appropriately about him who lives evilly and enjoys many years of life. Third, although Cain in the first place committed a great fratricide, He offers him an amnesty,[u] imposing a benevolent and kindly law concerning the first (crime) on all judges, not that they may not destroy evil men, but that by hesitating[v] a little and showing patience,[w]

[a] τοὐναντίον.

[b] ἄκρατοι φόβοι. Aucher mistakenly takes Arm. *anapak* (= ἄκρατος) in the sense of "unmixed" ("meri").

[c] ἀμέτοχοι. [d] ἐπάγουσι. [e] πολυτρόπους.

[f] Arm. construction doubtful, but apparently = διδούσης τῆς αἰσθήσεως, *cf.* the Greek frag. [g] εὐθὺς ἐν τῇ ἀρχῇ.

[h] τῆς τῆς ψυχῆς ἀφθαρσίας. [i] ἐξελέγχειν τὴν ψευδοδοξίαν.

[j] μακάριος. [k] ἔνοχος. [l] ἀσεβείας.

[m] ἐπιβουλῇ διαφθείρεται. [n] ὁ τοῦ κυρίου λόγος.

[o] ἡ αἰσθητὴ ζωή. [p] οὐ συγγενής ἐστι.

[q] ἀγήρως καὶ ἀθάνατος. [r] ἀσώματοι ψυχαί.

[s] λαγχάνουσι. [t] *Odyssey* xii. 118. [u] ἀμνηστίαν.

[v] παυόμενοι. [w] μακροθυμοῦντες.

they may cleave to mercy rather than to cruelty. But He most wisely [a] prescribed a canon of gentleness [b] and understanding [c] concerning the first sinner, not killing the homicide but destroying [d] him in another manner. For He did not permit him to be numbered with his father's family,[e] but announces that he is proscribed not only by his parents but also by the whole human race, counting him a genus [f] peculiar and separate from the rational species,[g] like one driven out and a fugitive,[h] and one transformed into the nature of beasts.

*77. (Gen. iv. 23) Why does Lamech after five generations condemn himself [i] for his ancestor Cain's fratricide, for, says Scripture, he said to his wives Ada and Zillah, " A man have I killed to my wound, and a young man to my hurt. If sevenfold punishment shall be exacted for Cain, then for Lamech seventy times seven " ?

In numbers the ones are prior to the tens both in order and in power,[j] for the former are the beginnings and elements and measures.[k] And the tens are younger [l] and are measured, and are second both in order and in power. So that seven is more archetypal and elder [m] than seventy ; but seventy is younger than seven and has the status [n] of that which is generated. These things being determined,[o] the first man who sinned, as one who did not exactly [p] know what it really meant,[q] was more simply [r] punished

[a] πανσόφως.

[b] Arm. here = ἡμερότητος, not οἰκειότητος as Aucher's rendering " familiaritatis " implies.

[c] Or " moderation "—συνέσεως or ἐπιεικείας.

[d] διαφθείρων.

[e] τῇ πατρίᾳ γενεᾷ.

[f] γένος.

[g] τοῦ λογικοῦ εἴδους.

[h] διωκόμενος καὶ φυγάς.

[i] ἑαυτὸν καταγιγνώσκει.

[j] τάξει καὶ δυνάμει.

[k] ἀρχαὶ καὶ στοιχεῖα καὶ μέτρα.

[l] νεώτεραι.

[m] ἀρχετυπικωτέρα καὶ πρεσβυτέρα.

[n] λόγον.

[o] τούτων ὁρισθέντων.

[p] ἀκριβῶς, βεβαίως.

[q] τὸ κύριον.

[r] ἁπλούστερον.

in accordance with the first and doubtful number, I mean one. But the second man, as one who had the first man as an example,[a] and had no excuse, was guilty of voluntary sin. And in not receiving august wisdom[b] through the first simpler punishment, he will suffer this punishment also, and in addition, will receive the second punishment which is in the tens. For just as in the hippodrome it is the horse-trainer who gets both the first and second prize, so also some evil men by rushing toward an unjust victory,[c] carry off a miserable victory,[d] and then they are punished by a double penalty, first by that which is in the ones, and then by that which is in the tens. Wherefore also Cain, who was the first to commit homicide, because he did not know the magnitude of the foul deed,[e] since he had never encountered death, paid the simpler penalty, the seven of the ones. But his imitator, not being able to take refuge in the same defence of ignorance,[f] deserved to suffer a double punishment, the first equal and similar to the other (Cain's), and another, the seven of the tens. For according to the law a sevenfold judgment is given. First, upon[g] the eyes, because they saw what was not fitting; second, upon the ears, because they heard what was not proper; third, upon the nose, which was deceived by smoke and steam; fourth, upon (the organ of) taste, which was a servant of the belly's pleasure; fifth, upon (the organs of) touch, to which by the collaboration[h] of the former senses in overcoming the soul[i] are also brought in addition other separate[j] acts, such as the seizure of cities and the capture of men and the demolition of the citadel of the city where the council resides; sixth, upon the tongue and the organs of speech for being silent about things that should be said and for saying things that should be kept silent; seventh,

[a] παράδειγμα.
[b] σεμνὴν σοφίαν.
[c] ἐπὶ τὴν τῆς ἀδικίας νίκην ὁρμῶντες.
[d] ταλαίπωρον νίκην.
[e] βδελύγματος, μιάσματος.
[f] εἰς τὴν αὐτὴν ἀπολογίαν τὴν τῆς ἀγνοίας.
[g] Lit. "through," διά w. gen.
[h] κοινοπραγίας.
[i] κατὰ τὴν τῆς ψυχῆς ὑπέρθεσιν.
[j] κατ' ἰδίαν.

upon the lower belly [a] which with lawless licentiousness sets the senses on fire. This is (the meaning of) what is said (in Scripture), that a sevenfold vengeance is taken on Cain, but on Lamech seventy times seven, for the reasons mentioned, in accordance with which he, being the second sinner and not being chastened [b] by the punishment of the earlier one, wholly [c] received both the latter's punishment, which was the simpler, as is the unit among numbers, and also the more complex punishment, similar to the tens among numbers.

78. (Gen. iv. 25) Why does Adam in begetting Seth say in addition, " God has raised up for me another seed in place of Abel whom Cain killed " ?

Truly Seth is another seed and the beginning [d] of another birth [e] of Abel in accordance with a certain natural principle.[f] For Abel is like one who comes from above to below, wherefore he is injured,[g] but Seth (is like one who comes) from below to above, wherefore he grows.[h] And a confirmation [i] of this is that " Abel " is interpreted as " brought and offered up on high " [j] to God. And it is not fitting to offer up [k] everything, but only what is good, for (God) is not the cause [l] of evil. Wherefore the undefined [m] and unseparated [n] and obscure [o] and confused [p] and perturbed [q] one appropriately also receives a mixture of praise and blame ; praise, because he honours the Cause, and blame, because just as something happens,[r] so it turns out by chance [s] without his taking thought [t] or giving thanks.[u]

[a] ὁ κάτω γαστήρ. [b] σωφρονισθείς, as in the Greek frag.
[c] παντελῶς in the Greek frag. [d] ἀρχή. [e] γενέσεως.
[f] κατά τινα φυσικὸν λόγον. [g] βλάπτεται or ἐπιβουλεύεται.
[h] αὐξάνεται. [i] πίστις.
[j] προσφέρεται ἄνω, as though from Heb. *ybl*, *wbl* " to bring " ; *cf. Quod Deterius* 32.
[k] προσφέρειν, ἀνάγειν. [l] ἀναίτιος.
[m] ὁ ἀόριστος. [n] ὁ ἀχώριστος. [o] ὁ ἄδηλος.
[p] ὁ συγκεχυμένος, ἀμυδρός. [q] ὁ τεθορυβημένος.
[r] συμβαίνει. [s] ὡς ἔτυχε. [t] ἄνευ τοῦ λογίζεσθαι.
[u] τοῦ εὐχαριστεῖν, ἐξομολογεῖσθαι.

Wherefore nature separated from him his twin,[a] and made the good man worthy of immortality,[b] resolving [c] him into a voice interceding [d] with God; but the wicked man it gave over to destruction. But "Seth" is interpreted as "one who drinks water," [e] in accordance with the changes that take place in plants which by watering grow and blossom and bear fruit. And these are symbols of the soul.[f] But no longer may one say that the Deity is the cause of all things, good and evil, but only of the good, which alone properly puts forth live shoots.[g]

*79. (Gen. iv. 26) Why did Seth's son Enosh hope to call the name of the Lord God?

"Enosh" is interpreted as "man." And this is now taken, not as a mixture,[h] but as the logical part of the soul,[i] the mind,[j] to which hope is peculiarly fitting,[k] for irrational animals are bereft of hope.[l] And hope is a certain anticipation of joy [m]; before joy there is an expectation [n] of good.

80. (Gen. v. 1) Why, after (mentioning) hope, does (Scripture) say, "This is the book of the generation of men"?

By these words (Scripture) makes the aforementioned statement trustworthy.[o] What is man? Man is that which more than other kinds of animals has obtained a very large and extraordinary [p] portion of hope. And this

[a] τὸν δίδυμον.
[b] ἀθανασίας.
[c] λύσας.
[d] παρακαλοῦσαν.
[e] As though from Heb. *šth* "to drink"; *cf. De Poster. Caini* 124 (ποτισμός).
[f] τῆς ψυχῆς, or "spirit"—τοῦ πνεύματος.
[g] ζωοφυτεῖν.
[h] μίξις or κρᾶσις.
[i] τὸ τῆς ψυχῆς λογικὸν μέρος.
[j] ὁ νοῦς.
[k] ἰδίως πρέπον ἐστὶ τὸ ἐλπίζειν.
[l] ἀμέτοχα τῆς ἐλπίδος.
[m] προπάθειά τις τῆς χαρᾶς.
[n] προσδοκία.
[o] πιστόν.
[p] θαυμαστόν or παράδοξον.

is celebrated [a] as if inscribed in nature, for the mind of man naturally hopes.

*81. (Gen. v. 3) Why, in the genealogy of Adam, does (Scripture) no longer mention Cain, but Seth, who, it says, was made according to his appearance and form? Whence it begins to count the generations [b] from him (Seth).

Scripture does not associate the foul and violent homicide with the order of either reason or number, for he is to be thrown out [c] like ordure, as someone has said, considering him to be such. Wherefore (Scripture) does not show him to be either the successor [d] of his earthly father or the beginning of later generations, but distinguishing Seth in both respects as guiltless,[e] being a drinker of water, for he is watered by his father, and begetting hope by his growth and progress.[f] Wherefore not casually or idly does (Scripture) say that he was made according to his father's appearance and form, in reprobation of the elder (brother) who because of his foul homicide bears within himself nothing of his father either in body or in soul. Wherefore (Scripture) separated [g] him and divided [h] him from his kin,[i] but to the other apportioned and gave a part of the honour of primogeniture.[j]

82. (Gen. v. 22) What is the meaning of the words, "Enoch was pleasing to God, after he begot Methuselah, two hundred years"? [k]

(Scripture) legislates [l] about the sources of all good

[a] διαφημίζεται. [b] γενεαλογεῖν.
[c] ἐκβαλλετέος. [d] διάδοχον.
[e] The Arm. is obscure but seems to render διαιρῶν Σὴθ ὡς ἀμφοτέρων ἀναίτιον. Aucher renders, "sed utrumque illibato distribuens praestat Seth." The Greek frag. freely paraphrases.
[f] αὐξήσει καὶ προκοπῇ. [g] διεῖλε. [h] διεχώρισε.
[i] ἀπὸ τῆς συγγενείας. [j] τῆς πρεσβείας.
[k] So LXX: Heb. has "And Enoch walked with God after he begot Methuselah three hundred years." [l] νομοθετεῖ.

things at the beginning of Genesis.[a] What I mean is somewhat as follows. It defined[b] mercy[c] and forgiveness[d] a little earlier. This time, however, it defines repentance, not mocking[e] or in any way reproaching[f] those who appear to have sinned. At the same time it presents the descent[g] of the soul from evil to virtue[h] like the return of those who have fled into a snare.[i] For behold, on becoming a man and father, in his very procreation, he made a beginning of probity,[j] being said to have been pleasing to God. For although he did not altogether remain in piety, none the less that period of time was reckoned to him as belonging to the order of the praiseworthy,[k] for he was pleasing (to God) so many years. And so many (years) are symbolically mentioned,[l] not perhaps because of what he was, but as he was believed by another to appear.[m] But (Scripture) reveals the ordering[n] of things. For not very long after the forgiving of Cain it introduces the fact that Enoch repented, informing us that forgiveness is wont to produce repentance.

83. (Gen. v. 21-23) Why is Enoch, who repented, said to have lived one hundred and sixty-five years before his repentance, but after his repentance two hundred?

The hundred and sixty-five consists of the ten (digits) added one by one—1, 2, 3, 4, 5, 6, 7, 8, 9, 10,[o] which make fifty-five, and of the double numbers after one—2, 4, 6, 8, 10, 12, 14, 16, 18, 20, which make one hundred and ten. And the combination[p] of these (two sets of numbers) pro-

[a] τῆς γενέσεως. [b] διώρισε, or "set apart"—διεχώρισε.
[c] ἔλεος. [d] ἄφεσιν. [e] ἐκγελῶν or χλευάζων.
[f] ὀνειδίζων. [g] (*sic*) κατάβασιν. [h] ἀρετήν.
[i] βρόχον. [j] καλοκἀγαθίας. [k] εἰς τὴν τοῦ ἐπαινετοῦ τάξιν.
[l] The Arm. is obscure, but seems to render τοσαῦτα σύμβολα τῶν εἰρημένων ἐστί.
[m] Here too the Arm. is obscure.
[n] ἀκολουθίαν or διοίκησιν.
[o] The Arm. here uses numeral letters = Greek α′, β′, etc.
[p] σύνθεσις.

duces one hundred and sixty-five. And among these the even numbers are double [a] the odd numbers, for the female is more powerful [b] than the male by some inversion,[c] as when the wicked man lords it over the good man, or sense over mind, the body over sense, matter over cause. But two hundred (years) in which there was repentance consists of twice a hundred, of which the first hundred indicates a purification from wrongdoing,[d] while the other indicates the fullness of one who is perfect in virtue.[e] For even from an ailing body one must cut away [f] the sick part, and afterwards introduce health, for the former is first, while the latter comes second. The number two hundred is composed of fours, for it arises, as if from a seed,[g] from four triangles [h] and four tetragons and four pentagons and four hexagons and four heptagons, and it stands, in a certain manner, in the number seven. And these are the four triangles—1, 3, 6, 10, which make 20.[i] The four tetragons are 1, 4, 9, 16, which make thirty. And the four pentagons are 1, 5, 12, 22, which make forty. The five hexagons are 1, 6, 15, 28, which make 50. And the four heptagons are 1, 7, 18, 34, which make sixty. These combined produce two hundred.

[a] διπλάσιοι.

[b] δυνατωτέρα, or "more violent"—βιαιοτέρα.

[c] τροπήν.

[d] κάθαρσιν ἀδικίας.

[e] τὸ πλήρωμα τὸ τοῦ κατ' ἀρετὴν συντετελεσμένου. Aucher renders, "plenitudinem virtutis consummatae."

[f] ἀποτεμεῖν.

[g] ὡς ἐκ σπέρματος.

[h] "Triangles" (τριγώνων) = "triangular numbers," those which can be arranged in triangular form, *e.g.*

```
                              .
               .             . .
     .        . .           . . .
3 = . .   6 = . . .   10 = . . . .
```

etc.; similarly, "tetragons" are "four-sided numbers," etc.

[i] The Arm. here sometimes uses numeral letters, sometimes numeral words.

84. (Gen. v. 23) Why, being repentant,[a] is (Enoch) said to have lived three hundred and sixty-five years?[b]

First of all, the year has three hundred and sixty-five days. Accordingly (Scripture) symbolically indicates the life of this penitent by the revolution[c] of the sun. Second, just as the sun is the cause of day and night, revolving above the earth's hemisphere by day, and under the earth by night, so also the life of the penitent consists of darkness and light—of darkness by the impact[d] of passions and injustices,[e] and of light when the light of virtue[f] shines out, and its splendour is very bright.[g] Third, (Scripture) apportioned to him a full number, in accordance with which the sun, sovereign of heavenly stars, is adorned; and in this number is included also the time before his repentance, in forgetfulness[h] of the sins which he had formerly committed. For as God is good,[i] He liberally bestows great kindnesses,[j] and at the same time through the virtues of those who so desire,[k] He wipes out[l] the old convictions involving punishment.[m]

*85. (Gen. v. 23-24) Why, after Enoch's end,[n] does (Scripture) add, "He was pleasing to[o] God"?

First of all, because it demonstrates that souls are immortal,[p] since when they become incorporeal,[q] they again become pleasing. Second, it praises the penitent since he persevered in the same condition of morals[r] and did not again change until the end of his life. For behold, some men after briefly experiencing uprightness[s] and

[a] μετανοῶν.

[b] LXX and Heb. "And all the days of Enoch were three hundred and sixty-five years."

[c] περιόδῳ, κυκλώσει.

[d] ἐκ βολῆς.

[e] παθῶν καὶ ἀδικιῶν.

[f] ἀρετῆς.

[g] Or "pure"—καθαρώτατος.

[h] εἰς ἀμνηστίαν.

[i] ἀγαθός.

[j] ἀφθόνως χαρίζεται.

[k] τῶν ἐπιθυμούντων.

[l] ἐξαλείφει.

[m] τὰς καταγνώσεις τὰς τιμωρίαν ἐχούσας.

[n] τελευτήσαντος Ἐνώχου.

[o] εὐηρέστησε.

[p] παρίστησι τὰς ψυχὰς ἀθανάτους οὔσας.

[q] ἀσώματοι γενόμεναι.

[r] ἐν τῇ αὐτῇ ἠθῶν διαθέσει.

[s] γευσάμενοι καλοκἀγαθίας.

having been given hope of health, again quickly revert to the same disease.

86. (Gen. v. 24) What is the meaning of the words, "And he was not found, for God had translated [a] him"?

First of all, the end of worthy and holy men [b] is not death but translation [c] and approaching [d] another place. Second, something very marvellous [e] took place. For he seemed to be rapt away [f] and become invisible.[g] For then he was not found. And this is shown by the fact that when he was sought,[h] he was invisible,[i] not merely rapt from their eyes. For the translation to another place is nothing else than another position [j]; but he is said (to have moved) from a sensible and visible place to an incorporeal and intelligible form.[k] This gift the protoprophet [l] also obtained, for no one knew his burial-place. And still another, Elijah, followed him on high from earth to heaven at the appearance of the divine countenance,[m] or, it would be more proper and correct to say, he ascended.[n]

87. (Gen. v. 29) How is it that at the very birth of Noah his father says, "This one will give us rest from our labours and from our sorrows and from the earth which the Lord God has cursed"?

Not idly [o] did the holy fathers [p] prophesy, and although not always nor in all things, still at least for once and in one thing which they knew [q] are they worthy of prophetic

[a] μετέθηκε. [b] ἀξίων καὶ ἁγίων. [c] μετάθεσις, μεταβολή.
[d] τὸ ἐγγίζειν. [e] θαυμασιώτατόν τι. [f] ἁρπασθῆναι.
[g] ἀόρατος. [h] ζητούμενος. [i] ἀφανής, ἀόρατος. [j] θέσις.
[k] εἰς ἀσώματον καὶ νοερὰν μορφήν (or εἶδος, γένος).
[l] ὁ πρωτοπροφήτης (Moses).
[m] κατὰ τὴν ἐπιφάνειαν τὴν τοῦ θείου προσώπου.
[n] ἀνέβη. [o] οὐκ εἰκῇ.
[p] οἱ ἅγιοι πατέρες. I do not know why Aucher renders, "sanctorum patres."
[q] Arm. *canean* = ἔγνωσαν: variant *cnan* = ἐγέννησαν "produced."

praise.[a] And not idly is this too a symbolical example, for " Noah " is a sort of cognomen [b] of justice, by participation [c] in which the mind gives us rest from the evil of labours and will give us rest from sorrows and fears, making us fearless and sorrowless. And it gives us rest from that earthly nature by whose curse the body is afflicted with sickness ; and they are guilty who consume their lives in pursuit of pleasures.[d] But in the realization of the prediction [e] the prophecy spoke falsely, for in the case of this particular man it was not so much a cessation of evils [f] that took place but an intensification of violence and strange and unavoidable disasters and innovations [g] of the great flood. And carefully bear in mind [h] that Noah is the tenth from the earth-born man.[i]

88. (Gen. v. 32) Who are the three sons of Noah—Shem, Ham and Japheth ?

These names are symbols of three things in nature—of the good, the evil and the indifferent.[j] Shem is distinguished [k] for good, Ham for evil, and Japheth for the indifferent.

*89. (Gen. vi. 1) Why, from the time when the great flood drew near, is the human race said to have increased into a multitude ? [l]

[a] The above is a slightly free (in construction) rendering of the obscure Arm. sentence, which has no main verb and an intrusive rel. pron. [b] ἐπώνυμον. [c] κοινωνίᾳ.

[d] ἡδονῶν. [e] κατὰ τὴν τῶν ἀναγγελθέντων ἐνέργειαν.

[f] κατάπαυσις κακῶν. [g] καινουργίαι. [h] ἐπιμελῶς προνόει.

[i] Before the words " carefully bear in mind " the Arm. glossator inserts (in § 89) in cod. A " Some used to say that there were innumerable aeons from Adam to Noah, and others said that Noah was the first beginning, wherefore Scripture says."

[j] Prob. τοῦ ἀδιαφόρου, although Arm. *anoroš* usu.= ἀόριστος. See below, *QG* ii. 71.

[k] διαφέρει. [l] εἰς πολυανθρωπίαν.

Divine favours [a] always precede His judgments,[b] for His activity [c] is first to do good, while destruction [d] comes afterwards. He, however, is loving, and it is usual,[e] when great evils are about to take place, that an abundance of great and numerous good things is first produced.[f] In this same manner, when the seven years' barrenness was about to come, as the prophet says, Egypt became fruitful for the same number of years in succession through the beneficent and saving power of the universe.[g] In the same way as He does good He teaches (men) to refrain and keep themselves from sins, lest they change the good into the opposite. Because of this now too cities grow to excellence [h] through freedom of customs,[i] so that if afterwards corruption [j] arises, they may condemn [k] their own immeasurable and irremediable wrongdoing, and not make the Deity responsible,[l] for He is innocent of evil and evil deeds,[m] since His activity [n] is to bestow [o] only good first of all.

90. (Gen. vi. 3) What is the meaning of the words, " My spirit [p] shall not remain in men forever, because they are flesh " ?

This legislation [q] is an oracle.[r] For the divine spirit is not a movement of air but intelligence [s] and wisdom.[t] Thus also concerning him who artfully constructed the holy

[a] *αἱ θεῖαι χάριτες.* [b] *κρίσεις, κρίματα.* [c] *ἔργον.*
[d] *τὸ διαφθείρειν, ἀναιρεῖν vel sim.*
[e] *εἴωθε, πέφυκε.* [f] *γεννᾶσθαι.*
[g] *διὰ τὴν εὐεργετικὴν καὶ σωτήριαν δύναμιν τὴν τῶν ὅλων.*
[h] *εἰς ἀνδραγαθίαν* (?).
[i] *ἐκ ἐλευθερίας ἐθῶν* (meaning ?). [j] *διαφθορά vel sim.*
[k] *καταγνῶσι.* [l] *αἴτιον.* [m] *κακίας καὶ κακῶν.*
[n] *ἔργον.* [o] *χαρίζεσθαι.* [p] *πνεῦμα.*
[q] *τὸ νομισθετούμενον.*
[r] *χρησμός.* Aucher reverses subj. and pred., " oraculum est velut lex prolatum."
[s] *σύνεσις* or *φρόνησις* or *νοῦς* or *ἐπιστήμη.*
[t] *σοφία.*

tabernacle, namely Bezaleel, (Scripture) reported, saying, "I filled him with the divine spirit of wisdom and knowledge."[a] Accordingly, this spirit comes into men[b] but does not remain or long endure.[c] But (Scripture) adds the reasons therefor, saying, "because they are flesh." For the nature of flesh is alien to wisdom so long as it is familiar with desire.[d] Whence it is clear that incorporeal and unsubstantial[e] spirits do not stumble over anything heavy or meet any obstacle to seeing and understanding nature, since pure understanding[f] is acquired along with stability.[g]

91. (Gen. vi. 3) Why shall "the days of man be a hundred and twenty years"?

By this number (Scripture) seems to define[h] human life, indicating many prerogatives[i] of honour. For in the first place, it is derived from the units by composition[j] of fifteen.[k] And the fifteenth reckoning[l] is a very brilliant one,[m] for the moon becomes full of light on the fifteenth day, receiving its light from the sun at evening and giving it over to him in the morning, so that on that night no darkness appears, but everything is light. Second, a hundred and twenty is a triangular number[n] and consists of fifteen triangles.[o] Third, because it consists of the equal

[a] *Cf.* LXX, Ex. xxxi. 3, καὶ ἐνέπλησα αὐτὸν πνεῦμα θεῖον σοφίας καὶ συνέσεως καὶ ἐπιστήμης.

[b] ἐγγίνεται ἐν ἀνθρώποις.

[c] οὔτε μένει οὔτε διαιωνίζει (or διαχρονίζει).

[d] τὸ γὰρ ἦθος τὸ τῆς σαρκὸς τῇ σοφίᾳ ἀλλότριόν ἐστι ἐφ' ὅσον χρόνον οἰκεῖόν ἐστι τῇ ἐπιθυμίᾳ.

[e] Prob. ἀναφῆ, as Aucher suggests.

[f] ἄκρατος σύνεσις.

[g] στάσει or βεβαιώσει or στηρίγματι.

[h] Or "limit"—ὁρίζειν.

[i] προνομίας.

[j] κατὰ σύνθεσιν.

[k] *i.e.* 120 is the sum of the first fifteen numbers: $1+2+3 \ldots +15=120$.

[l] λόγος.

[m] φωτοειδέστερος.

[n] ἀριθμὸς τρίγωνος.

[o] 120 is 15×8, and 8 is a triangular number $(2 \times 2 \times 2)$.

and unequal,[a] being comprehended by the power of the joining[b] of sixty-four and fifty-six. For sixty-four is an equality[c] consisting of the units of these eight odd numbers: 1, 3, 5, 7, 9, 11, 13, 15, whose parts when added[d] produce squares summed up[e] in sixty-four. And this is a cube, at the same time producing a square. And from seven double units comes the inequality[f] fifty-six, consisting of seven twin even numbers,[g] which produce their other extensions[h]: 2, 4, 6, 8, 10, 12, 14, which add up to fifty-six. Fourth, it (the number 120) consists of four things: of one triangle,[i] namely fifteen; of another number, a square, namely twenty-five; of a third number, a pentagon, namely thirty-five; and of a fourth number, a hexagon, namely forty-five, in the same proportion.[j] For the fifth (number) is always taken in accordance with its several species.[k] For from the unit of triangles fifteen is the fifth number; similarly, from the unit of squares the fifth number is twenty-five; from the unit of pentagons the fifth number is thirty-five; and from the unit of hexagons the fifth number is forty-five. And each of these numbers is divine[l] and sacred; fifteen has been shown (to be such); twenty-five is that of the Levites[m]; and thirty-five is that of the double scale,[n] the arithmetic and geometric and harmonic. But sixteen, 18, 19, 21[o] add up to seventy-four, by which are formed the seven-month

[a] ἐξ ἴσου καὶ ἀνίσου.

[b] τῇ τῆς συζυγίας δυνάμει (or ἐξουσίᾳ).

[c] Or "even number" (?)—ἰσότης, but see note *f*.

[d] ὧν ἡ κατὰ μέρος σύνθεσις.

[e] τετράγωνα κεφαλαιούμενα.

[f] ἀνισότης.

[g] διδύμων ἀρτίων.

[h] Lit. "lengths."

[i] τριγώνου.

[j] κατὰ τὴν αὐτὴν ἀναλογίαν.

[k] κατὰ τὰ ἕκαστα εἴδη.

[l] Perhaps κυριακός, although this word does not appear in Leisegang's Index to the Greek Philo.

[m] *Cf.* Num. viii. 24 "the tribe of Levi from twenty-five years old and upward."

[n] διπλοῦς διαγράμματος.

[o] The first number in the Arm. is written as a word, the following as numeral letters.

(children); and forty-five is that of the triple scale. But sixteen, nineteen, twenty-two and twenty-eight add up to eighty-five, by which are formed the nine-month (children).[a] And fifth, it (the number 120) has fifteen parts and a double composition[b] of its own, inasmuch as twice sixty is the measure of all things; and it is three times forty, (which is) the form[c] of prophecy[d]; and it is four times thirty, (which is) a generation[e]; and it is five times twenty-four, (which is) the measure of day and night,[f] and it is six times twenty, (which is) the beginning[g]; and it is eight times fifteen, most brilliant[h] (of numbers); it is ten times twelve, (which is) the zodiac[i]; it is twelve times ten, (which is) the holy (number)[j]; it is fifteen times eight, (which is) the first cube[k]; it is twenty times six, (which is) genesis[l]; it is twenty-four times five, (which is) the form[m] of the senses[n]; it is thirty times four, (which is) the beginning of solids[o]; it is four times thirty, (which is) fullness,[p] consisting of beginning, middle and end; it is sixty times two, (which is) the feminine[q]; and it is a hundred and twenty times one, (which is) the masculine.[r] And each of these numbers is very natural,[s] as is shown

[a] On this obscure calculation see Staehle, pp. 81-82.
[b] σύνθεσιν διπλασίαν. [c] εἶδος or ἰδέα.
[d] Referring to Moses' forty-day sojourn on Mt. Sinai.
[e] Reckoning 30 years to a generation.
[f] Referring to the 24 hours of a day.
[g] ἀρχή; probably meaning the age when the young man is ready for communal responsibilities, *cf.* Ex. xxxviii. 26 and *QG* iv. 27.
[h] παμφαίνων, referring to the full moon on the 15th day of the lunar month.
[i] ζῳοφόρος κύκλος.
[j] Elsewhere Philo calls 10 the perfect (τέλειος) number, *cf.* Staehle, pp. 53-58. [k] ὁ πρῶτος κύβος.
[l] γένεσις; referring to the six days of Creation.
[m] Or "species"—ἰδέα. [n] τῶν αἰσθήσεων.
[o] ἡ τῆς στερεομετρίας ἀρχή.
[p] πλήρωμα; probably because it is the sum of the first four square numbers: 1, 4, 9, 16, *cf.* *QG* ii. 5.
[q] τὸ θῆλυ. [r] τὸ ἄρρεν. [s] φυσικώτερος.

separately. Moreover, it is a double composition,[a] for it becomes two hundred and forty, which is a sign of becoming worthy of twofold life, for just as the number of years is doubled, so also life is to be thought of as doubled ; there is one (life) with the body, and another without the body, to receive the gift of prophecy,[b] each of them being holy and altogether perfect.[c] Sixth, because the fifth and sixth are produced when three numbers are multiplied,[d] (namely) three times four five times (*sic*) ; for three times four five times makes sixty. Similarly a hundred and twenty (is produced) by the following numbers, four times five six times (*sic*), for four times five six times makes a hundred and twenty. Seventh, taking the number twenty, in which is the beginning of man, his redemption [e]—twenty added to itself two and three times in the following manner, twenty, forty, sixty, makes a hundred and twenty. But perhaps a hundred and twenty years are not the universal limit [f] of human life, but only of the men living at that time, who were later to perish in the flood after so great a number of years, which a benevolent benefactor [g] prolonged, allowing repentance for sins. However, after this limit they lived a more abundant [h] life in later generations.

*92. (Gen. vi. 4) Why were the giants born from angels and women ?

The poets [i] relate that the giants were earthborn, children of the earth. But he (Moses) uses this name analogically [j] and frequently [k] when he wishes to indicate

[a] *σύνθεσις διπλασία*.

[b] Arm. construction difficult, lit. " the gift with respect to the prophet " : Aucher renders, " donum prophetiae."

[c] *παντέλειος*.

[d] *πολλαπλασιασθέντων*.

[e] *λύτρωσις* ; the connexion of the number 20 with " redemption " eludes me, but see note *g*, p. 59.

[f] *ὁ καθολικὸς ὅρος*.

[g] *εὐεργέτης εὐμενής*.

[h] *πλείονα* or *περισσόν*.

[i] *οἱ ποιηταί*.

[j] *καταχρηστικῶς*.

[k] *συνεχῶς*, or perhaps " for the most part "—*ἐπὶ τὸ πολύ*.

excessive size of body, after the likeness of Haik.[a] And he relates that their creation[b] was a mixture of two things, of angels and mortal women. But the substance[c] of angels is spiritual[d]; however, it often happens that they imitate the forms of men and for immediate purposes,[e] as in respect of knowing women for the sake of begetting Haiks.[f] But if children become zealous emulators[g] of maternal depravity,[h] they will draw away from paternal virtue and depart from it through desire of pleasure[i] in a wicked stock,[j] and through contempt[k] and arrogance[l] toward the better[m] they are condemned as guilty[n] of wilful wrongdoing.[o] But sometimes he calls the angels "sons of God" because they are made incorporeal[p] through no mortal man[q] but are spirits[r] without body. But rather does that exhorter,[s] Moses, give to good and excellent men the name of "sons of God," while wicked and evil men (he calls) "bodies."

*93. (Gen. vi. 6) What is the meaning of the words, "He was concerned[t] when reflecting[u] that He had made man upon the earth, and He considered"[v]?

Some believe that the repentance of the Deity[w] is shown by these words,[x] but not rightly do they so believe, for the

[a] The Arm. has probably substituted the name of the legendary Armenian eponymous hero for Greek Heracles, as Aucher remarks. [b] γένεσιν.
[c] οὐσία. [d] πνευματική. [e] πρὸς ὑποκειμένας χρείας.
[f] *i.e.* "giants," see note *a* above.
[g] ζηλωταί. [h] πονηρίας or ἀφροσύνης. [i] ἡδονῆς (?).
[j] γένους. [k] καταφρονήσει. [l] ὑπερηφανίᾳ or ἀλαζονείᾳ.
[m] τοῦ κρείττονος. [n] ἔνοχοι. [o] ἑκουσίων ἀδικιῶν.
[p] ἀσώματοι. [q] θνητόν. [r] πνεύματα.
[s] προτρεπτικός or παραινετικός.
[t] ἐφρόντισε or ἐμερίμνησε. [u] λογιζόμενος.
[v] διενοήθη. LXX has καὶ ἐνεθυμήθη ὁ θεὸς ὅτι ἐποίησεν τὸν ἄνθρωπον ἐπὶ τῆς γῆς καὶ διενοήθη. The Arm. O.T. also differs from the Arm. text of Philo's citation of the verse.
[w] μεταμέλειαν . . . περὶ τὸ θεῖον in John Monachus.
[x] ὀνομάτων.

Deity is without change. Nor are His being concerned when reflecting and His considering signs of repentance but of lucid and certain reflection,[a] which is concerned and considers the reason why He made man upon the earth. And since earth is a place of wretchedness,[b] even that heavenly man[c] is a mixture[d] consisting of soul and body; and from his birth until his end he is nothing else than a corpse-bearer.[e] Accordingly, it does not seem at all very remarkable[f] that the Father should be concerned with, and consider, these things, since indeed many men acquire wickedness rather than virtue,[g] being governed by the two-fold impulse[h] mentioned above, (namely) by the nature of the corruptible body[i] and the horrid position[j] of the earth, which is the last[k] of things.

*94. (Gen. vi. 7) Why, when threatening to wipe out[l] man, does He say that He will also destroy the beasts[m] together with him, "from man to beasts and from reptiles to birds"?[n] For what sin were the beasts committing?

The literal meaning is this: it makes it clearly known that not necessarily[o] and primarily[p] were beasts made but for the sake of men and for their service.[q] And when these were destroyed, the former were rightly[r] destroyed together with them, since there no longer existed those for whose sake they had been made. But as for the allegorical meaning[s]—inasmuch as symbolically[t] man is the mind[u] within us, and beast is sense-perception,[v] when the chief

[a] John Monachus reads more briefly ἀκραιφνοῦς λογισμοῦ.
[b] ταλαιπορίας, ἀτυχίας.
[c] ὁ οὐράνιος ἄνθρωπος.
[d] μίξις.
[e] νεκροφόρος.
[f] παραδοξότερον.
[g] ἀρετῆς.
[h] ὁρμῇ.
[i] φθαρτοῦ σώματος.
[j] φρικτῷ τόπῳ.
[k] τὸ ἔσχατον.
[l] ἀπαλεῖψαι.
[m] τὰ ἄλογα, τὰ κτήνη.
[n] *Cf.* LXX ἕως πετεινῶν τοῦ οὐρανοῦ.
[o] ἀναγκαίως.
[p] προηγουμένως.
[q] ὑπηρεσίας. See below, *QG* ii. 9.
[r] εἰκότως, δικαίως.
[s] τὸ πρὸς νοῦν or καθ' ὑπόνοιαν.
[t] συμβολικῶς.
[u] νοῦς.
[v] αἴσθησις.

ruler[a] is perverted and corrupted by evil, all sense-perception also perishes together with it, because it has no remains[b] of virtue.

*95. (Gen. vi. 7) Why does He say, "I am angry[c] that I have made them"?

In the first place, again as if warning man He relates something extraordinary.[d] However, properly speaking, God does not become angry but is immune (from anger) and is above all passions.[e] Accordingly, He wishes to prove by using exaggeration[f] that the lawless deeds of men have increased to such an extent that they have invited and provoked and incited to anger One who is naturally without anger. Second, He intimates symbolically that those things which have been done confusedly[g] are also blameworthy,[h] but those things which have been done out of wise reflection[i] and determined[j] are praiseworthy.

*96. (Gen. vi. 8) Why is Noah now said to find favour[k] with God?

In the first place the occasion[l] requires a comparison.[m]

[a] τοῦ πρώτου ἀρχηγοῦ, ἡγεμόνος.

[b] λείψανα, ὑπόλειμμα.

[c] Similarly Arm. O.T.; LXX has ἐνεθυμήθην = Heb. *niḥamtî* "I repent."

[d] ἄκρον, κεφάλαιον. [e] πάθη. [f] ὑπερβολῇ.

[g] συγκεχυμένως or "obscurely"—ἀμυδρῶς (?).

[h] ἔνοχα. [i] τῷ τῆς σοφίας λογισμῷ.

[j] διορισθέντα. The sentence is obscure; Aucher renders, "quae vero ex consilio sapientiae procedunt definitive, laudabilia." Procopius briefly paraphrases the section.

[k] χάριν. [l] καιρός or χρόνος (?).

[m] σύγκρισιν. The meaning of the sentence is not clear, but perhaps is that this statement about Noah stands in contrast to the preceding statement about God's anger. Aucher renders, "primum tempus postulat comparationem," which is literal but as obscure as the original.

Inasmuch as all the others were rejected[a] because of ingratitude,[b] He justly puts him in their place, saying that he found favour, not because he alone was deserving of favour, for the entire human race in common had met with (His) beneficence,[c] but because he alone appeared grateful.[d] In the second place, since the generation was given over to destruction,[e] with the exception of one household,[f] it was necessary to say that the remnant was worthy of the divine favour as the seed and spark[g] of the new generation of men that was to be. And what favour is greater than that this same one should be both the end[h] and beginning[i] of mankind?

97. (Gen. vi. 9) Why does (Scripture) give the generations of Noah not by his predecessors but by his virtues?[j]

First, because the men who were of his time were wicked. Second, it lays down the laws of the will,[k] because to the virtuous man virtue is truly a generation.[l] For a generation of men (consists of) men, and (a generation) of souls (consists) of virtues. Wherefore it says, "he was righteous, perfect and pleasing (to God)."[m] But righteousness and perfection and being pleasing to God are the greatest virtues.

98. (Gen. vi. 11) What is the meaning of the words, "The earth was corrupted[n] before God, and the earth was filled with injustice"[o]?

[a] ἀποδοκιμασθέντων, ἀποβληθέντων. Procopius ἀπολωλότων.
[b] ἀχαριστίαν. [c] εὐεργεσίαν, ἀγαθοποιίαν.
[d] εὐχάριστος.
[e] Or "corruption"—φθορᾷ, διαφθορᾷ.
[f] οἴκου. [g] σπινθήρ. [h] τέλος.
[i] ἀρχή. [j] ἀρεταῖς.
[k] θελήματος (?). The sense escapes me.
[l] Aucher renders, less literally, "virtutis studioso pro vera generatione est virtus."
[m] *Cf.* LXX δίκαιος, τέλειος ὢν ἐν τῇ γενεᾷ αὐτοῦ, τῷ θεῷ εὐηρέστησε. [n] ἐφθάρη. [o] ἀδικίας.

He (Moses) himself has given the reason in speaking of injustice (as being) for the sake of the earth's corruption. For deliverance [a] from this in particular is justice [b] both for men and for the parts of the world, (namely) heaven and earth.

*99. (Gen. vi. 12) What is the meaning of the words, "All flesh corrupted his [c] way upon the earth"?

First of all (Scripture) has called the self-loving [d] man "flesh"; therefore having formerly called him "flesh," it adds, not "the same" [e] but "of the same," [f] evidently meaning "in respect of man," [g] for one who misuses [h] an uncultivated life is flesh. Second, it considers flesh as the cause of spiritual corruption,[i] which is indeed the truth, for it is the seat of desires,[j] from which, as from a spring, flow the properties [k] of desires and other passions.[l] Third, the (pronoun) "his" is more natural, being declined as the oblique case [m] or from the nominative case of the pronoun "himself." [n] For when we offer honour to someone we do not venture to call him by any other name than "himself." Hence was derived the Pythagorean principle,[o] "He himself has said it" [p] when they exalted and magnified their honoured teacher, fearing to call him by name. The same custom is found both in cities and in homes; for at the coming of the master, slaves say "Himself is coming

[a] *σωτηρία*. [b] *δικαιοσύνη*.

[c] *αὐτοῦ* as in LXX; Heb. requires *αὑτοῦ* "his own"; Arm. O.T., like Heb., has reflexive pronoun, referring to man.

[d] *φίλαυτον*. [e] *τὴν αὐτὴν* <*σάρκα*>. [f] *τοῦ αὐτοῦ*.

[g] *περὶ* or *ἕνεκα τοῦ ἀνθρώπου*. [h] *παραχρᾶται*.

[i] *πνευματικῆς φθορᾶς*. [j] *τόπος τῶν ἐπιθυμιῶν*.

[k] *αἱ ἰδιότητες*. [l] *παθῶν*. [m] *πλαγία πτῶσις*.

[n] *i.e. αὐτός*. Lit. "from the nominative pronoun"—*ἀπὸ τῆς ὀρθῆς ἀντωνυμίας*. The sense is somewhat obscure to me. Aucher renders, "tertio magis naturaliter *ejus*, casus est partialis declinatus (ab *Is*), vel de recto pronominis (*Ipse*) *ipsius*." For the general meaning see the parallel, *Quod Deus sit Immut*. §§ 140 f. Procopius condenses and paraphrases.

[o] *ἀρχή*. [p] *αὐτὸς ἔφα*.

in." And in the several cities, when the lord has come, they call him by the name "himself." But why have I dwelt at length on such things? Because I wished to show that the Father of the universe [a] is here mentioned, since all good things celebrated for their virtues are His. And out of reverence [b] (Scripture) uses truly admirable names [c] cautiously because it was about to introduce the destruction (of mankind). But the oblique case of the pronoun is taken in an honourable sense in the saying, "All flesh corrupted his [d] way," for truly the way of the Father has been corrupted through the desires and pleasures of the flesh; for these are the adversaries [e] of the laws of continence,[f] frugality,[g] prudence,[h] courage [i] and justice,[j] through which (virtues) the way which leads to God is found and broadened, becoming wholly . . .[k]

*100. (Gen. vi. 13) What is the meaning of the words, "The time of all mankind has come against [l] me, for the earth is filled with injustice"?

Those who reject Fate [m] use (these and) many other arguments, especially when death comes upon very many in a short time, as in the overthrow of houses, in conflagrations, shipwreck, tumult, in war, in combats on horse and combats on foot, in naval battles and plagues. To those who say this we say the same thing that was just said by the prophet (Moses), taking the reasoning [n] from him. For

[a] *πατὴρ τῶν ὅλων.*
[b] *δι' αἰδῶ.*
[c] *θαυμασίοις ὀνόμασι.*
[d] *αὐτοῦ*; see note *n* on p. 65.
[e] *ἀντίμαχοι, ἀντίπαλοι.*
[f] *ἐγκρατείας.*
[g] *ὀλιγαρκίας, ὀλιγοδείας.*
[h] *σωφροσύνης.*
[i] *ἀνδρείας.*
[j] *δικαιοσύνης.*
[k] The word *eriwr* is, as Aucher remarks, unknown; he emends to *diwr* "smooth" or *iwr* "his"; the Arm. glossator gives "open (or "spacious") road."
[l] LXX *ἐναντίον*, lit. "opposite" or "against" here renders Heb. *lipheнê* "before." Philo stresses the literal meaning of the Greek preposition, ignoring the required sense for homiletical purposes.
[m] *εἱμαρμένην* (prob.).
[n] Lit. "reason"—*αἰτίαν.*

the meaning of the words, "The time of all mankind has come against me" is about as follows. The life-time of all mankind has been limited and restricted to one time.[a] In consequence of this they no longer live in accordance with the harmonious principle of Fate.[b] And the reckoning[c] of every single one is gathered[d] into one, and has the same end in accordance with some harmony[e] and revolution of the stars, by which the race of mortals[f] is constantly preserved and destroyed. Accordingly, these things they may accept as they wish, both those who are among the learned[g] and those who contradict them. But this must first be said by us, that there is nothing so contrary and hostile and opposed to the Almighty[h] as is injustice.[i] Wherefore (Scripture) says that "The time of all mankind has come against me," and adds the reason for the opposition,[j] (namely) that the earth was filled with injustice. Second, time is considered a god[k] by the wicked among men, who would conceal[l] the really existing One.[m] For which reason (Scripture) says, "The time of all mankind has come against me," inasmuch as they make a god[n] of human time and oppose it to the true (God). But this is indicated in other places as well, where (Scripture) expresses the same principle as follows, "The time stood far off from them but God is among us,"[o] as if meaning that by wicked

[a] διωρίσθη καί . . . εἰς ἕνα χρόνον.

[b] κατὰ τὸν συμφωνοῦντα (or ὁμονοοῦντα) λόγον τὸν τῆς εἱμαρμένης. The syntax and meaning are rather obscure to me. Professor H. A. Wolfson of Harvard University calls attention to a relevant statement in Aristotle, *De Gen. et Corr.* ii. 10, 336 b, διὸ καὶ οἱ χρόνοι καὶ οἱ βίοι ἑκάστων ἀριθμὸν ἔχουσι καὶ τούτῳ διορίζονται. πάντων γάρ ἐστι τάξις, καὶ πᾶς χρόνος καὶ βίος μετρεῖται περιόδῳ. [c] λόγος. [d] συνάγεται.

[e] ὁμόνοιαν. [f] τὸ φθαρτὸν γένος. [g] τῶν διδακτῶν (?).

[h] Dam. Par. has "to the most holy powers of God."

[i] ἀδικία. [j] τῆς ἐναντιότητος.

[k] θεός. [l] καλύπτειν *vel sim.*

[m] τὸν ὄντως Ὄντα. The Greek frag. has τῷ ἀληθεῖ θεῷ.

[n] θεοπλαστοῦσι.

[o] *Cf.* LXX, Num. xiv. 9, ἀφέστηκε γὰρ ὁ καιρὸς ἀπ' αὐτῶν, ὁ δὲ κύριος ἐν ἡμῖν.

men time is believed to be the cause of the events of the universe [a]; but by wise and cultured men [b] not time but God (is believed to be the cause), from Whom come times and seasons. But He is the cause not of all things but only of the good and of those which are in accordance with virtue.[c] For just as He is unsharing and without portion in evil, so also is He not responsible [d] for it. Third, in respect of the above statement (Scripture) indicates a certain excess of impiety in saying, " The time of all mankind has come " as if it meant that all men everywhere with one accord [e] had agreed upon impiety. And the statement that " the earth was filled with injustice " is as much as to say that no part of it remains empty [f] so as to receive and support righteousness.[g] But the expression " against " is a confirmation of what has been said, for the divine judgment [h] of choice [i] alone is firm.[j]

[a] *τῶν τοῦ κόσμου πραγμάτων.*

[b] The Greek frag. has *εὐσεβέσι.*

[c] *ἀρετήν.* [d] *ἀναίτιος.* [e] *μιᾷ γνώμῃ.*

[f] *κενόν.* [g] *δικαιοσύνην.* [h] *ἡ θεία δίκη.*

[i] *αἱρεσέως, ἐκλογῆς.* Arm. variant = *θέσεως.*

[j] *βεβαία.* The syntax of the last clause is obscure.

BOOK II

1. (Gen. vi. 14) What is the construction [a] of (the ark of) Noah ?

If anyone wishes to examine that ark more physically,[b] he will find the construction of the human body (in it), as we shall discover in detail.

2. (Gen. vi. 14) Why does he (Noah) make the ark out of quadrangular beams ?

First of all, the figure of a quadrangle, wherever placed, keeps its place firmly, making all right angles ; and the nature [c] of the human body is constituted most impeccably [d] and most faultlessly.[e] Second, although our body is an instrument,[f] and each of its parts is rather rounded,[g] nevertheless the limbs constituted by these parts perforce [h] reduce the quadrangular figure to the circular one, as (for example) in the case of the chest, for the lungs are rather quadrangular.[i] Such too is the stomach before it has become swollen with food or through intemperance,[j] for there are certain fat-bellied people whom one may leave out of the argument. However, if anyone will examine the arms and the hands and the back and the thighs and the feet, he will find them all in common having a quadrangular form together with a spherical one. Third, a

[a] κατασκευή.
[b] φυσικώτερον.
[c] φύσις, *v.l.* = ὕλη.
[d] ἀπλανέστατα, ἀσφαλέστατα.
[e] ἀπταιστότατα.
[f] ὄργανον.
[g] κυκλώτερον.
[h] βίᾳ, ἀνάγκῃ.
[i] Aucher similarly renders, " pro exemplo sit pectus quod quadratum potius est quam orbiculare."
[j] ἀμετρίᾳ.

quadrangular beam has almost all its dimensions [a] unequal, since the length is greater than the width, and the width is greater than the height. Similarly constituted is the construction of our bodies, which are separated into a great, a medium and a small dimension [b]: a great one in length, a medium one in width, and a small one in height.

3. (Gen. vi. 14) Why does (Scripture) say, "Nests, nests [c] thou shalt make the ark"?

Very naturally (does Scripture speak), for the human body is altogether perforated [d] like a nest, and every one of its parts is built like a nest,[e] since a respiratory force [f] penetrates them from their very beginnings. So, for example, the eyes are, in a sense, holes and nests, in which visions nestle. Other nests are the ears, in which sounds nestle. A third kind of nest are the nostrils, in which smells make their home. A fourth kind of nest, greater than the preceding, is the mouth, in which, again, tastes make their nest. And this was made large because another great organ of the articulate voice nestles in it, (namely) the tongue, which, as Socrates said, when it strikes and touches now here now there, articulates [g] and forms the voice, making it truly rational.[h] Moreover there

[a] Lit. "differences (or "intervals") of separation," *διαστολαὶ χωρισμῶν* or the like; Aucher renders, "distinctiones in sua extensione."

[b] *χωρισμός*; Aucher "extensione."

[c] The Arm. and Palest. Syriac versions of Scripture repeat the word *νοσσιάς* = Heb. *qinnîm* "nests," *i.e.* "cells" (A.V. "rooms"). LXX MSS. have only a single occurrence of *νοσσιάς* in this verse. Probably the Armenian translator of Philo has added the second occurrence to make Philo agree with his version of Scripture. Philo quotes part of this verse in *De Confus. Ling.* 105 but does not mention the "nests."

[d] *τετρημένον* (?).

[e] *νοσσεύεται*.

[f] *πνευματικὴ δύναμις* (?).

[g] *ἀρθροῖ*.

[h] *ἐργαζομένη τὴν φωνὴν ὄντως λογικήν*, v.l. "becoming a truly rational instrument"—*γενομένη ὄντως λογικὸν ὄργανον*.

is another (nest) inside the skull.[a] And there is a certain nest of the brain [b] which is called the *dura mater*. And the chest (is the nest) of the lungs and the heart. And both of these are the nests of other parts called the inwards [c]; the lungs (are the nest) of the breath, and the heart (is the nest) of the blood and the breath. For it (the heart) has two sacs [d] as if nests nestling in the chest; (one is) the blood, from which the veins are irrigated like receptacles,[e] and the other is the breath, by which, again, being diffused as into receptacles the trachea is irrigated.[f] And both the firmer and the softer parts are, in a certain sense, nests, and nourish their chicks, the bones; the firmer parts are the nests of the marrow, and the softer flesh (is the nest) of pleasures and pains. And if one were to inquire into other parts he would find them to have the same kind [g] of construction.

4. (Gen. vi. 14) Why does He command that the ark be tarred inside and outside?

Bitumen [h] is so called because of its tarry firmness [i] and because it cements what is brought together of detached and disjoined things, being a bond [j] that is indissoluble and untouched and indivisible.[k] For everything that is held together by glue is forcibly held [l] by this in a natural union.[m] But our body, which consists of many parts, is united both outside and inside. And it stands by its own cohesion.[n] And the higher habit of these parts is the soul,[o] which being in the middle, everywhere rushes out to the entire upper surface and from the upper surface returns to the middle, so that one psychic nature is enveloped [p] by a

[a] ἐν τῷ κρανίῳ. [b] ἐγκεφάλου.
[c] τῶν σπλάγχνων. [d] κοιλίαι. [e] δεξαμεναί.
[f] Lit. "filled with breath."
[g] Lit. "nature"—φύσιν. [h] ἄσφαλτος.
[i] ἀσφάλειαν (?). [j] δεσμός.
[k] ἀδιάλυτος καὶ ἄψαυστος καὶ ἄτμητος. [l] βιάζεται.
[m] κατὰ φυσικὴν ἕνωσιν.
[n] ἕξει, *cf.* Colson on *Leg. All.* ii. 22.
[o] ψυχή. [p] περιπλέκεται.

double bond, (thus) being fitted [a] to a firmer consistency [b] and union.[c] Accordingly this ark is overlaid with bitumen inside and out for the beforementioned reason. But that (other ark) in the temple,[d] which is overlaid with gold, is a likeness of the intelligible world,[e] as is shown in the treatise concerning this subject.[f] For the intelligible world, which exists in one place, is, as it were,[g] incorporated [h] in the incorporeal forms,[i] being fitted together [j] and united [k] out of all the forms. For in the measure that gold is more valuable than bitumen, in the same measure is the (ark) which is in the temple more excellent than (Noah's) ark. Wherefore He instructed that the measure of this ark be quadrangular, looking toward its usefulness [l]; but in the case of the other (ark He was looking toward) its imperishability,[m] since the nature of incorporeal and intelligible things [n] is imperishable and incorruptible[o] and permanent.[p] And this ark is carried about here and there, but the other one has its position firmly in the temple. But that which is stable [q] is related to the divine nature, just as this (ark), which turns now in one direction and now in another and changes (is related) to that which is generated.[r] And this ark of the flood is held up [s] as a type of corruptibility.[t] But the other one in the temple follows the condition [u] of the incorruptible.

*5. (Gen. vi. 15-16) Why does (Scripture) hand down the dimensions of the ark in this manner : " the length (shall

[a] ἁρμοζομένη. [b] βεβαιότερον τόνον.
[c] ἕνωσιν. [d] ἐν τῷ ἱερῷ.
[e] τοῦ νοητοῦ κόσμου. [f] *Cf. De Ebrietate* 88-90.
[g] Construction not certain.
[h] σωματοῦται. [i] ἐν ταῖς ἀσωμάτοις ἰδέαις.
[j] ἁρμοζόμενος. [k] ἑνώμενος. [l] τὸ χρήσιμον.
[m] τὸ ἀσαπές (?). [n] ἀσωμάτων καὶ νοητῶν. [o] ἄφθαρτος.
[p] διαμένων. [q] στάσιμον or βέβαιον.
[r] Arm. here seems to have read τὸ γόνιμον or τὸ γεννητικόν " generative " for γενητόν " generated."
[s] Or " cited "—ἀναφέρεται (?).
[t] ὡς τρόπος τῆς φθορᾶς. [u] Or " lot "—τὸν κλῆρον.

be) three hundred cubits, its width fifty (cubits) and its height thirty (cubits). And to a cubit above (it is to be) finished, coming together gradually in the manner of a mound [a] " ?

In a literal sense [b] it was necessary to construct a great work [c] for the reception of so many animals, of which the several genera were to be brought inside together with their food. But symbolically,[d] correctly considered and understood, it points to the knowledge [e] of the make-up [f] of our body, and there was now to be used,[g] not the quantity of cubits but the accurate proportion [h] which subsists in them. And the reckonings [i] which subsist in them are sixfold and tenfold and five thirds. For three hundred is six times fifty and ten times thirty, while fifty is five thirds of thirty. And similar are the proportions of the body. For if anyone wishes to inspect (the matter), he will perceive on reflexion that man has [j] a measure [k] that is not very great and not very small ; and if one takes a cord and stretches it from the head to the feet he will find that the cord is six times (as long) compared with the width of the chest, and ten times (as long) compared with the thickness of the sides (of the body), and that the width is five thirds of the thickness. Similar is the actual proportion,[l] taken from nature, of the human body, which is made with a measure essentially excellent in the case of those who are neither excessive nor deficient. And He most excellently [m] determined the (ark's) being finished to a cubit above,[n] for the upper part of the body imitates unity ; (that is), the head, like the citadel [o] of a king, has as its occupant

[a] This is an expansion of LXX, καὶ εἰς πῆχυν συντελέσεις αὐτὴν ἄνωθεν. " Mound " here is given for Arm. *kot'oł* which usually renders βάσις or σκόπελον ; Aucher renders " instar obelisci."
[b] πρὸς τὸ ῥητόν.
[c] μέγα ἔργον.
[d] συμβολικῶς or πρὸς τὸ σημειωθέν.
[e] γνῶσιν.
[f] τῆς ποιήσεως (?).
[g] χρησθήσεται *vel sim.*
[h] ἡ ἐπ' ἀκριβείας ἀναλογία.
[i] οἱ λόγοι.
[j] χρώμενον.
[k] μέτρῳ, μετρήσει.
[l] ἀναλογία.
[m] παγκάλως.
[n] See note *a*.
[o] ἄκρον, ἀκρόπολις.

the sovereign mind.[a] But those (parts) which are below the neck are divided into several parts, into hands and especially into the lower limbs ; for the thighs and the legs and the feet are separated (from one another). Accordingly the aforementioned proportion [b] of cubits of relation [c] will easily be recognized, as I have pointed out, by anyone who wishes to learn them.[d] However, it is fitting not to ignore the fact that as for the number of cubits, each of them has its own necessary reckoning [e] ; but one must begin at first with the length. Now three hundred is composed of single numbers joined one by one with an increase of one (each time, namely), of these twenty-four [f] : 1, 2, 3, 4, 5, 6, 7, 8, 9, 10, 11, 12, 13, 14, 15, 16, 17, 18, 19, 20, 21, 22, 23, 24. But twenty-four, a very natural [g] number, is apportioned among the hours of day and night and among the letters of written sound.[h] And being composed of three cubes,[i] it is entire,[j] complete and quite full in equality,[k] since the triad steadily exhibits the first equality, having a beginning, middle and end, which are equal. And the number eight is the first cube because it first shows equality again with others.[l] And the number twenty-four has also many other virtues, being the substance [m] of three hundred, as has been shown ; this is the first (virtue).[n] And another virtue is that it is composed of twelve quadrangles, with which the monad is combined through single and double lengths, and of twelve doubles, moreover, which are com-

[a] τὸν ἡγεμονικὸν νοῦν.
[b] μέτρον, μέτρησις. [c] ἀναλογίας.
[d] Construction of Arm. slightly uncertain.
[e] λόγον.
[f] The following numerals are given as numeral letters in Arm.
[g] φυσικώτατος.
[h] The 24 letters of the Greek alphabet.
[i] $1 \times 3 \times 8$. [j] ὅλος. [k] κατ' ἰσότητα.
[l] So literally ; Aucher renders, " quia cum ceteris aequitatem rursus primam declaravit." Probably Philo means the repetition of 2 in the factors of 8 ($= 2 \times 2 \times 2$).
[m] οὐσία. [n] ἀρετή.

posed of twos, to which two is separately added.[a] Now the angular numbers which compose the twelve quadrangles are as follows: 1, 3, 5, 7, 9, 11, 13, 15, 17, 19, 21, 23. And it composes quadrangles as follows: one, four,[b] 9, 16, 25, 36, 49, 64, 81, 100, 121, 144.[c] But the angular (numbers) which compose the other lengths are the following: 2, 4, 6, 8, 10, 12, 14, 16, 18, 20, 22, 24; these make 12 (numbers). But from these are composed 2, 6, 12, 20, 30, 42, 56, 72, 90, 110, 132, 156, and these again are twelve (numbers).[d] If you add the twelve quadrangles (that is), one hundred forty-four and twelve other lengths (that is), one hundred fifty-six, you will find that three hundred is produced. (And you will get) a harmony of the nature of the odd (number), which is completed and goes over to the even (number) and the infinite.[e] For the odd completed (number) is the maker of equality in accordance with the nature of the square.[f] But the even and infinite (number is the maker) of inequality in accordance with the composition of another length.[g] But the whole consists of the equal and the unequal. Whence the Creator of the world [h] also in the corruption of earthly creatures has given judgment with the ark as an example.[i] Now enough has been said concerning (the number) three hundred. But

[a] The Arm. is obscure. Aucher renders, "adhaec ex duplicibus longis, geminis duodecim, compositis nempe ex duobus singillatim auctis per duo."

[b] The first two numerals are given as numbers, the rest as numeral letters.

[c] The preceding are the squares of the numbers 1 to 12.

[d] As my colleague I. J. Gelb has pointed out to me, each of the twelve numbers of this series combines the corresponding number of the earlier series with the numbers preceding the latter; thus $2=2+0$, $6=2+4$, $12=2+4+6$, $20=2+4+6+8$, etc.

[e] τὸ ἄρτιον καὶ τὸ ἄπειρον.

[f] Aucher inadvertently renders, "trianguli."

[g] *Cf. QG* i. 15.

[h] ὁ κοσμοποιός.

[i] So literally; Aucher renders more smoothly, "unde conditor ipse mundi etiam in corruptione terrenorum certum quasi exemplum praebuit in arca."

now we must speak concerning (the number) fifty.[a] In the first place it consists of a rectangular (triangle) of quadrangles,[b] for a rectangular (triangle) consists of three, four, five; but from these (comes) the quadrangle,[c] nine, sixteen, twenty-five, the sum of which is fifty. And in the second place, fifty is completed and filled[d] by the unity of the following triangles: 1, 3, 6, 10, and again by the following four, equal in unity: 1, 4, 9, 16.[e] Now the triangular (numbers), added together, make twenty,[f] and the quadrangular (numbers) make thirty,[g] of which (the sum) is fifty. And if the triangular and quadrangular (numbers) are combined, the septangular (number) is produced, so that potentially it is contained in the divine fiftieth,[h] which the prophet had in view when he designated it as the festival of the fiftieth (year).[i] But the fiftieth year is entirely free[j] and freedom-giving.[k] The third argument[l] is that three squares[m] in succession from unity and three cubes in succession from unity give fifty; the three squares

[a] The measure of the width of the ark in cubits.

[b] ἐξ ὀρθογώνου τετραγώνων; *cf. De Spec. Leg.* ii. 177, where Philo says it is formed from ὀρθογωνίου τριγώνου.

[c] Meaning the square on each side of the triangle.

[d] τελεσθεὶς πληροῦται.

[e] Apparently these four numbers are considered equal in being squares of the first four digits.

[f] $1+3+6+10=20$.   [g] $1+4+9+16=30$.

[h] ἐν τῷ κυριακῷ πεντηκοστῷ. The Arm. adds "the holy trinity," a Christian gloss. Aucher omits "trinity" in his translation but connects "holy" with "fiftieth."

[i] The word "year" is supplied from the context: Aucher renders, "festum Iubilaeum."

[j] In Lev. xxv. 9 f. Heb. *yôbêl* "Jubilee" is rendered by LXX as ἐνιαυτὸς ἀφέσεως, similarly by Arm. O.T. In *De Spec. Leg.* ii. 176 ff. Philo applies the virtues of 50 to Pentecost, not to the Jubilee year. In dealing with the latter, *De Spec. Leg.* ii. 110 ff., he does not indulge in Pythagorean number-mysticism.

[k] ἐλευθεροποιός, used only of God in extant Greek works of Philo.   [l] θεωρία or θεώρημα.

[m] Aucher again inadvertently gives "trianguli."

in succession from unity are the following : 1, 4, 9 (of which the sum) is 14 ; and the cubes are the following : 1, 8, 27 (of which the sum) is 36 ; and their sum is fifty. Moreover thirty is a very natural [a] (number). For as the triad is to unity, so thirty is to the decad, so that the period of the moon is full-orbed by collections of months.[b] Second, it consists of the following four squares in succession from unity : 1, 4, 9, 16, which (added together) make thirty. Wherefore not idly or inappropriately did Heracleitus call this a generation, saying, " From a man thirty years old there can come a grandfather, for he attains manhood in his fourteenth year, when he is able to sow seed, and the (child) sown within a year comes into being and similarly after fifteen years begets one like himself." [c] And from these names of grandfathers, fathers, begotten sons, and of mothers, daughters,[d] and sons of daughters there comes about a complete generation.

6. (Gen. vi. 16) What is the meaning of the words, " a door at the side " ? For (Scripture) says, " Thou shalt make a door at the side."

Not vulgarly [e] does that door at the side (of the ark) represent the human structure,[f] which He decently mentioned, saying it was " at the side," [g] through which the excreta are removed to the outside. (This is) very excel-

[a] *φυσικώτατος*.

[b] Text and meaning obscure ; Aucher renders, " idque lunae cyclus, collectio singulorum mensium plena delineatione." Staehle, following Robbins, cites a partial parallel from John Lydus, p. 55, *ἐπεὶ καὶ ὁ τοῦ μηνὸς κύκλος συνέστηκεν*.

[c] *Cf.* Plutarch, *Def. Orac.* ii. 415 D *ap.* Diels, *Frag. d. Vorsokratiker*, 4th ed., i. 76, also Censorinus 17. 2 and John Lydus, *De Mens.* iii. 14 (the latter " misverstanden " according to Diels).

[d] Variant " sons."

[e] Aucher " obscure," but Arm. *douznakʿeay* means " small," " slight," " cheap."

[f] *κατασκευήν*.

[g] *πλαγίαν*.

lent, for,[a] as Socrates used to say, whether taught by Moses or moved by the things themselves, the Creator, valuing[b] the decency of our body, turned to the rear of the senses the orifices of the passage of the canals,[c] lest we should feel disgust at ourselves,[d] when in purging ourselves of the bile-carrying waste, we see this shameful sight. Wherefore He surrounded and enclosed that passage by the back and hinder parts as by high swelling mounds; and also for other uses have the buttocks been made soft.

7. (Gen. vi. 16) Why does (Scripture) say, "Ground-floor (chambers)[e] and second-storey ones[f] and third-storey ones[g] shall be made"[h]?

Most excellently[i] has (Scripture) alluded to the receptacles[j] of food by calling them "ground-floor chambers," since food is corruptible and the corruptibility is of the lower part, because it (the food) is carried downward.[k] For only a very little food and drink is distributed (through the body),[l] and by this we are nourished, while the greater part is separated and carried outside in the excrement. But the intestines have been made second-storey and third-storey chambers by the providence of the Creator[m] for the preservation of created things.[n] For if He had made

[a] *k*c*anzi* "for" comes before "very excellent" in the Arm., but the sense requires its transposition.

[b] δοκιμάζων.

[c] τὰς τῆς ὁδοῦ ἐξόδους τῆς τῶν ὀχετῶν. For a different allegory of this physiological fact see *De Poster. Caini* 127 f.

[d] βδελυττώμεθα.

[e] καταγεια. [f] διώροφα. [g] τριώροφα.

[h] So LXX and Arm. O.T. (except for the verb which is 2nd p. sing. as in Heb.). The Heb. has for "ground-floor chambers," etc., merely "lower ones, second ones, third ones."

[i] παγκάλως. [j] ἀγγεῖα or σκεύη. [k] κάτω.

[l] ἀναδίδοται in the medical sense; Aucher renders literally, "sursum exhibentur." [m] τῇ τοῦ ζῳοπλάστου προνοίᾳ.

[n] εἰς τὴν τῶν κτισθέντων διαμονήν. Aucher renders, "ad sustentationem confulciendam factorum."

straight[a] receptacles of food from the stomach[b] to the buttocks,[c] something terrible[d] might have happened. In the first place, (there might have been) continual lack,[e] desire[f] and famine; these are the misfortunes which might have occurred in that case, and instantaneous evacuation.[g] Second, a certain insatiate desire[h] (would have resulted). For when the receptacles have been emptied, hunger and thirst must of necessity immediately follow, as in the case of pregnant matrons, and the pleasant desire of food must become insatiate desire and something unphilosophical.[i] For nothing is more uncultured[j] than to give oneself wholly[k] to the belly. And third, death lies in wait[l] at the entrance, for they must be subject to an early death[m] who, when they eat, are immediately hungry, and when they drink, are immediately thirsty, and before they are filled, are emptied and feel hunger. But by the windings and twistings of the intestines we are saved from all hunger and insatiate desire and from being subject to an early death. So long as the food which is taken remains within (us), not that which is in passage but that which is necessary is changed.[n] For the force[o] of the food is first released[p] and squeezed out[q] in the belly.[r] And then it is warmed in the liver and carried out.[s] And then whatever is best flavoured[t] resolves itself[u] into the several parts, into growth for children and into strength for adults, but the rest is separated as excrement and

[a] Or "direct"—ὀρθά.

[b] ἀπὸ τοῦ στομάχου meaning "stomach" as in *De Opif. Mundi* 118; Aucher renders, "visceribus."

[c] τὴν ἕδραν. [d] δεινότατόν τι. [e] ἔνδεια.

[f] ἐπιθυμία (?). [g] κένωσις. [h] ἀπληστία.

[i] ἀφιλόσοφον. [j] ἀμουσότερον. [k] σχολάζεσθαι.

[l] ἐφεδρεύει. [m] ὠκύμοροι.

[n] ἀλλοιοῦται. The meaning is that only useful food is digested. Aucher renders, "non ut transitus exigit sed ut necessarium erat variatio efficitur." [o] δύναμις.

[p] ἀναλύεται. [q] ἐκπιέζεται. [r] γαστρί.

[s] Variant "it is warmed and poured out from the liver."

[t] Or "most wholesome"—εὐχυμώτατον.

[u] ἀναλύεται.

waste, and cast out. Now for such a dispensation [a] much time is consumed, as nature easily performs this forever.[b] But it seems to me that if the ark is taken (to refer) to the human body, nature is wonderfully [c] fond of life.[d] For these reasons, when living beings were destroyed and perished in the flood, He prepared a counterpart [e] to the earth. Wherefore whatever flourished on the earth the ark most generally [f] carried. And He wished that which was to be on the waves should be like the earth, a mother and nurse. And as they were nourished in the manner of pregnant women, (He wished) to show them (who were) within the sun and moon and the multitude of other stars and also the universal whole heaven.[g] For seeing by means of that which he [h] had constructed by art,[i] they learned more clearly the principle [j] and proportions [k] of the human body. For nothing so enslaved [l] man as the

[a] διακονίαν or διοίκησιν. [b] εἰς αἰῶνα. [c] δεινῶς.

[d] φιλόζωος, *cf. De Spec. Leg.* ii. 205 διὰ τὸ προμηθὲς τῆς φιλοζῴου φύσεως. The Arm. variant reads "it is not impossible for nature to make the human body, being fond of life." [e] ἀντικείμενον *vel sim.*

[f] Or "generically"—γενικώτατα.

[g] Sense obscure. Aucher's rendering is not much clearer, "atque educatores ipsos tamquam gravidas ostendere una cum sole ac luna, caeteraque astrorum multitudine et universo toto caelo." The Armenian gloss reads "as an infant, being in the womb, does not see the sun and moon but still lives and grows, so they were in the ark. They say that Noah had in the ark a device that showed the heavens, and through this knew day and night, and the sun and moon reached him." According to the rabbinic legends, "the ark was illuminated by a precious stone, the light of which was more brilliant by night than by day, so enabling Noah to distinguish between day and night," see L. Ginzberg, *Legends of the Jews*, i. 42; v. 183. Possibly Philo's reference to pregnant women is based on the Heb. word *ṣōhar*, which most versions render "window" (in the ark) but the LXX by ἐπισυνάγων.

[h] Apparently Noah is meant. [i] τέχνῃ.

[j] τὸν λόγον. [k] τὴν ἀναλογίαν. [l] κατεδούλωσε.

bodily elements [a] of his being,[b] and those things through which passions [c] come, and especially wicked passions of pleasure [d] and appetites.[e]

8. (Gen. vi. 17) Why does (Scripture) say, " There shall be a flood to destroy all flesh in which there is living breath [f] under heaven " ?

This is almost as if it now reveals [g] what before it had intimated.[h] For there was no other reason for the destruction of man to take place than that having become slaves of pleasures and appetites, they did everything and suffered,[i] wherefore they attained a life of the very utmost misery. However, (Scripture) adds something very natural [j] in saying that the place of the vital spirit [k] is under heaven, since the heavens too are living.[l] For not (alone ?) fortunate is the body made from a heavenly substance,[m] as if it alone had obtained a peculiar wonderful portion [n] better than (that of) creatures endowed with life.[o] But heaven, in the first place, appeared worthy of this benefit [p] in the form [q] of wonderful divine living beings which are altogether intellectual spirits [r] and give also to those who are on earth a portion of participation in vital power,[s] and animate those who can be animated.[t]

[a] στοιχεῖα (?).
[b] Aucher renders, " corporis humores essentiales."
[c] πάθη or " vices "—κακίαι *vel sim.*
[d] ἡδονῆς.
[e] ἐπιθυμίαι.
[f] πνεῦμα ζῶν, so also Arm. O.T. ; LXX πνεῦμα ζωῆς.
[g] ἀποκαλύπτει (?).
[h] ᾐνίξατο.
[i] ἔπασχον or " were ill "—ἐνόσουν.
[j] φυσικώτερον.
[k] τοῦ ζωτικοῦ πνεύματος, *cf. De Opif. Mundi* 30 ζωτικώτατον τὸ πνεῦμα.
[l] Variant " in heaven there are living beings."
[m] ἐξ οὐρανίας οὐσίας.
[n] ἴδιον καὶ θαυμάσιον κλῆρον.
[o] τῶν ὄντων τῶν ζῳογονηθέντων. Aucher renders less literally, " creaturis viventibus."
[p] χάριτος or χαρίσματος.
[q] εἰκόνος or τύπου.
[r] νοερὰ πνεύματα.
[s] μέρος τῆς κοινωνίας τῆς ζωτικῆς δυνάμεως.
[t] ψυχοῖ τοὺς ψυχοῦσθαι δυναμένους.

*9. (Gen. vi. 17) Why does (Scripture) say, "Whatever is on earth shall die," for what sin did the beasts [a] commit?

In the first place, just as when a king is killed in battle, his military forces also are struck down together with him, so He decides now too that when the human race is destroyed like a king, other beasts should be destroyed together with it. For which reason it happens that beasts die before (men) also in a plague, especially those that are brought up with men and live with them,[b] as, for example, dogs and their like, and men die later. Second, just as when the head is cut off, no one blames [c] nature if so many other parts of the body also die together with it, so also no one will now condemn (this). For man is a kind of ruling head,[d] and when he is destroyed, it is not to be wondered at [e] that other living beings should perish together with him. Third, the beasts were made, not for their own sake, as wise men reason,[f] but for the service [g] and needs [h] and honour [i] of man. It is right that when those are taken away for whose sake they (the beasts) were made, they too should be deprived of life. This is the literal meaning. But as for the deeper meaning,[j] we may say the following, that when the soul is deluged [k] by streams of passion,[l] and in a certain sense [m] is submerged,[n] those who are on earth—by which I mean the earthy parts[o] of the body—must die with it. For a life of evil is death. The eyes that see die [p] when they see unjustly.[q] And the ears that hear die when they hear unjustly. Every sense also dies when it perceives unjustly.

[a] τὰ κτήνη or τὰ ἄλογα. A similar question is asked in *QG* i. 94, see above, p. 62.
[b] σύντροφα καὶ σύνοικα.
[c] αἰτιᾶται.
[d] ἀρχική τις κεφαλή.
[e] οὐ θαυμαστόν.
[f] The Arm. seems literally to translate ὥς ἐστι τῶν σοφῶν ὁ λόγος. Aucher renders, " ut a sapientibus dictum est."
[g] εἰς ὑπηρεσίαν.
[h] χρείας.
[i] εὐπρέπειαν or " enjoyment "—ἀπόλαυσιν.
[j] τὸ πρὸς διάνοιαν.
[k] κατακλύζεται.
[l] Or " sin."
[m] τρόπον τινά.
[n] καταποντίζεται.
[o] τὰ χοϊκά or τὰ γεώδη.
[p] τελευτῶσι.
[q] ἀδίκως.

*10. (Gen. vi. 18) What is the meaning of the words, " I will establish my covenant [a] with thee " ?

In the first place He announces [b] that no one will be the heir [c] of the divine substance [d] except only him who is virtuous. Though men have heirs when they are no longer (alive) but are dead, God is eternal and gives participation in inheritance [e] to the wise, and rejoices in their possession.[f] For he who possesses all things is not in need [g] of anything, but those who lack [h] all things possess nothing in truth. Wherefore, being gracious, He benefits those who are worthy,[i] bestowing [j] on them whatever they lack. Second, He bestows a certain additional inheritance on the wise man, for He does not say, " I will establish my covenant for thee " but " with thee," that is to say, " thou art a just and true [k] covenant, which I will establish as a rational class [l] in possession and enjoyment (of that) for which virtue is necessary."

*11. (Gen. vii. 1) Why does (Scripture) say, " Enter thou and all thy household [m] into the ark, for I have seen thee righteous [n] before me in this generation " ?

In the first place, (it is) clear evidence that because of one righteous and worthy man, many men are saved [o] through their relation [p] to him, just as sailors and a (military) force [q] (are saved, the former) when they meet with a good skipper,[r] and the latter with one who is experienced in battle and is a good commander. In the second place, He praises the righteous man who acquires virtue not only for himself but also for his household,[s] wherefore it also becomes worthy of salvation.[t] And most excellently [u] is the following added, " I see thee righteous before me."

[a] διαθήκην. [b] ἀναγγέλλει. [c] κληρονόμον.
[d] τῆς θείας οὐσίας. [e] κοινωνίαν τῆς κληρονομίας.
[f] Dam. Par. περιουσίᾳ. [g] οὐκ ἐνδεής. [h] ἄποροι.
[i] τοὺς ἀξίους. [j] χαριζόμενος.
[k] δικαία καὶ ἀληθής. [l] λογικὸν γένος.
[m] οἰκία. [n] δίκαιον. [o] σώζονται.
[p] συγγένειαν. [q] δύναμις. [r] κυβερνήτῃ.
[s] οἴκῳ. [t] σωτηρίας. [u] παγκάλως.

For in one way do men appraise [a] the manner of life [b] (of someone), and in another way the Deity (judges). For they judge by visible things, but He judges by the invisible thoughts of the soul.[c] And it is remarkable [d] that what follows this is placed first,[e] in that He means, "in this generation thee have I seen righteous," lest He should seem to condemn former (generations) and cut off hope from those who are to come later.[f] This is the literal meaning. But the deeper meaning [g] (is as follows). When God saves the sovereign mind,[h] which is the master [i] of the soul,[j] then He also saves the whole household with it. By this I mean all the parts [k] and those things which are partial,[l] and speech,[m] which is projected outward, and the things of the body. For as the mind is in the soul, so the soul is in the body.[n] Through reflexion [o] all the parts of the soul are well-off,[p] and all its household experiences benefit together with it. And when the whole soul fares well, then its household experiences benefit with it,[q] the body (doing so) through moderation and restraint of habits [r] and by cutting off its insatiable desire, which is the cause of illnesses.

*12. (Gen. vii. 2, 3) Why does He command (Noah) to lead into the ark seven of the clean beasts,[s] male and

[a] δοκιμάζουσι. [b] διαγωγήν.

[c] ἐκ τῶν τῆς ψυχῆς ἀοράτων λογισμῶν. [d] θαυμαστόν.

[e] τὰ τούτων ἐξῆς ἐτέθη πρότερον. Aucher's rendering, "quod interea additur," misses the point, namely that in Scripture the words "in this generation" follow "thee have I seen righteous."

[f] Aucher renders, "neque posteriorem futurorum spem concideret." Procopius μήτε τὰς αὖθις ἀπογινώσκειν.

[g] τὸ πρὸς διάνοιαν. [h] τὸν ἡγεμονικὸν νοῦν.

[i] οἰκοδεσπότης.

[j] I have slightly transposed here; Arm. has "of the soul" after "mind" and before the rel. pr.

[k] τὰ μέρη. [l] τὰ κατὰ μέρη. [m] λόγος.

[n] Or "what the mind is to the soul, so is the soul to the body." [o] λογισμῶν. [p] εὐπαθοῦντα.

[q] Note the repetition. [r] σωφροσύνῃ καὶ ἐγκρατείᾳ ἐθῶν.

[s] τῶν καθαρῶν κτηνῶν.

female, but of the unclean, two, male and female,[a] to nourish seed on all the earth?

In a manner befitting God[b] (Scripture) calls the hebdomad pure[c] but the dyad impure,[d] for by nature the number seven is truly[e] pure, inasmuch as it is virginal[f] and unmixed[g] and unmothered,[h] nor does it give birth[i] nor is it born, as are the several (digits) which are in the decad, because of its likeness to the Eternal,[j] for He[k] is uncreated and unbegotten[l] and nothing is begotten by Him,[m] although He is the causes of generation[n] and things begotten,[o] for He moves[p] all those powers[q] which are naturally well suited to the generation of what is begotten. But the number two is impure. In the first place, because it is empty and not dense[r]; and what is not full is also not pure. Then too it is the beginning of a vast infinity in matter.[s] And it has inequality because of oblongs,[t] for those (numbers) which are multiplied by two are all oblongs.[u] But the unequal[v] is not pure, and neither is the material,[w] but that which comes from it is doubtful[x] and

[a] Philo omits the birds mentioned in Gen. vii. 3.
[b] θεοπρεπῶς. [c] καθαράν. [d] Lit. "not pure."
[e] ὄντως; Aucher omits this word.
[f] παρθένος. [g] ἄκρατος.
[h] ἀμήτωρ. *Cf. Leg. All.* i. 15.
[i] τίκτει. [j] τῷ ὄντι.
[k] That God is meant seems probable from the context, but *cf. Leg. All.* i. 15.
[l] ἀγένητος καὶ ἀγέννητος.
[m] See note *k*. [n] τῆς γενέσεως.
[o] τῶν γεννηθέντων. [p] κινεῖ.
[q] δυνάμεις. [r] κενὸς καὶ οὐ ναστός, as in J. Lydus.
[s] ἀπειρίας διὰ τὴν ὕλην. *Cf. QG* i. 15.
[t] διὰ τοὺς ἑτερομήκεις (ἀριθμούς), meaning numbers "not square" or produced by multiplying unequal factors; *cf.* Colson's Appendix on *Leg. All.* i. 3 (vol. i. p. 477 of Loeb Philo).
[u] Aucher's rendering "caeteros longos (numeros)" misses the point of the Greek behind Arm. *ayl arkaraçn*, lit. "other lengths," as explained in preceding note.
[v] τὸ ἄνισον. [w] τὸ ὑλικόν. [x] σφαλερόν.

incongruous,[a] lacking a reason [b] for purity, (namely) that which brings it to an end.[c] And it is automatically [d] brought to an end by periods [e] of harmony and equality. These are the natural aspects.[f] But the moral aspects [g] are now to be spoken of. The irrational and unintelligent part [h] of our souls [i] is divided into seven parts, into the five senses,[j] the organ of speech [k] and that of reproduction.[l] These are all pure in a virtuous man [m] and by nature are feminine when they belong to the irrational species,[n] but (when they belong to) a good possessor,[o] they are masculine, for the thoughts [p] of a virtuous man bring virtue to them also, since they are not permitted by his better part [q] to come to the external senses rashly and unrestrained and uncurbed but he subdues [r] them and turns them back to right reason.[s] But in a wicked man [t] the evil produces twins,[u] for the foolish man is of two minds and hesitates between two courses, mixing things that are not to be mixed, and confusing and mingling those things which can easily be separated.[v] Such is he who bears a colour in his soul,[w] for he is like one spotted [x] and a leper in his body,

[a] *ἀνάρμοστον.*

[b] *αἰτίας* or " occasion "—*ἀφορμῆς.*

[c] The last clause is obscure ; Aucher renders, " quae illud in desinentiam (*vel*, perfectionem) conducat."

[d] *αὐτονόμως.*

[e] Arm. *nowag* has several different meanings ; two of its common Greek equivalents are *περίοδος* (or *κάθοδος*) and *μέλος*. Aucher chooses the latter meaning here, rendering it by " canticus."

[f] *τὰ φυσικά.* [g] *τὰ ἠθικά.* [h] *τὸ ἄλογον καὶ ἄνουν.*

[i] *τῶν ψυχῶν.* [j] *αἰσθήσεις.* [k] *τὸ φωνητήριον ὄργανον.*

[l] *τὸ σπερματικόν* or, as usually in Philo, *τὸ γόνιμον.*

[m] *τῷ σπουδαίῳ.* [n] *τῷ ἀλόγῳ εἴδει.*

[o] *ἀγαθῷ κτησαμένῳ.* [p] *οἱ λογισμοί.*

[q] Or possibly " for the most part "—*ἐκ τοῦ πλείστου μέρους.*

[r] *ταπεινοῖ.* [s] *πρὸς τὸν ὀρθὸν λόγον ἀναστρέφει.*

[t] *τῷ φαύλῳ.* [u] *διδυμοτοκεῖ.* [v] *διακρίνεσθαι.*

[w] The Arm. seems to be slightly corrupt ; the Greek fragment has *τοιαῦτα ἐν ψυχῇ χρώματα ἐπιφέρων*, " bearing such colours in his soul." [x] *ποικίλος.*

defiling and staining his healthy thoughts[a] by death-bringing and murderous ones.[b] However, in a natural way[c] there is added (by Scripture) the reason for the entry and guarding[d] of the animals, for (Scripture) says this was for the nourishing[e] and preserving[f] of seed.[g] In the literal sense,[h] although particular (animals)[i] may perish,[j] nevertheless the genus[k] is preserved in the seed of others in order that the divine purpose[l] which was formed at the creation of the world[m] might forever remain inextinguishable by the saving of the genus. But in the figurative sense,[n] it is necessary that there be saved[o] the irrational parts of the soul, pure of movement, to be, as it were, seed-bearing principles[p] of non-holy things[q] as well. For man's nature is receptive of contraries,[r] both virtue and vice, each of which (Scripture) has indicated in the account of the Creation[s] by the tree which is called the knowledge[t] of good and evil, since our mind,[u] in which are knowledge and understanding,[v] comprehends both of them, good and evil. However, the good is kin[w] to the hebdomad, while evil is brother to the dyad. Moreover, the Law, abounding in beauty and loving wisdom,[x] says that seed is to be

[a] τοὺς ὑγιεῖς λογισμούς.
[b] ἐκ θανατούντων καὶ φονούντων.
[c] φυσικῶς.
[d] τῆς εἰσόδου καὶ τῆς φυλακῆς.
[e] τοῦ θρέψαι.
[f] τοῦ διατηρεῖν.
[g] τὸ σπέρμα.
[h] τὸ ῥητόν.
[i] τὰ ἐπὶ μέρους.
[j] διαφθείρηται.
[k] τὸ γένος.
[l] ἡ θεία πρόθεσις.
[m] ἐν τῇ κοσμοποιΐᾳ.
[n] τὸ πρὸς διάνοιαν.
[o] The last four words are bracketed by Aucher.
[p] The syntax of the Arm. is obscure ; Aucher construes differently, rendering, " oportet et in irrationalibus (partibus) animi mundos motus esse ut seminalia quaedam principia etsi non sint munda (animalia)."
[q] ἀνοσίων.
[r] ἐναντίων.
[s] ἐν τῇ κοσμοποιΐᾳ.
[t] τὸ γιγνώσκειν.
[u] ὁ ἡμέτερος νοῦς.
[v] The first Arm. term, *gitoutᶜiwn*, usually renders ἐπιστήμη or γνῶσις : the second term, *hanč̣ar*, renders σύνεσις, φρόνησις, ἐπιστήμη, etc., but in the Arm. version of Philo's *De Vita Contemplativa* it regularly renders ἐπιστήμη.
[w] συγγενές.
[x] φιλόσοφος.

nourished not in one place but in all the earth. This is very natural and at the same time very moral,[a] for it is very natural that in all parts and sections of the earth there should again be the seed of living things[b]; and it is very fitting for God again to fill the emptied places with similar things through another (act of) generation. (It is also) very moral that the substance of our body, being earthy, should not be altogether overlooked,[c] destitute and empty[d] of living beings. For if we resort to drunkenness[e] and fine cooking and chasing after women[f] and to altogether lewd and loose behaviour, we shall be corpse-bearers[g] in our body. But if the merciful[h] God turns aside the flood of vices[i] and makes the soul dry,[j] He will proceed to quicken[k] and animate[l] the body with a purer soul, whose guide[m] is wisdom.[n]

*13. (Gen. vii. 4, 10) Why, after (their) entering the ark, did seven days pass, after which (came) the flood?[o]

The benevolent Saviour[p] grants repentance of sins[q] in order that when they see the ark over against them,[r] which had been made as a symbol of time,[s] and the genera of animals placed in it, which the earth bore in itself, in accordance with their several particular species,[t] they may have faith[u] in the announcing[v] of the flood; (and that)

[a] ἠθικώτατον.
[b] The Arm. syntax seems slightly corrupt here.
[c] παροραθῆναι. [d] ἔρημον καὶ κενήν. [e] οἰνοφλυγίᾳ.
[f] θηλομανίᾳ. [g] νεκροφοροῦντες. [h] οἰκτείρων.
[i] Or "passions." [j] ξηράν.
[k] ζῳογονεῖν. [l] ψυχοῦν. [m] κυβερνήτης.
[n] σοφία. Dam. Par. paraphrases. [o] ὁ κατακλυσμός.
[p] ὁ εὐμενὴς (or ἵλεως) σωτήρ, meaning God.
[q] μετάνοιαν ἁμαρτιῶν.
[r] κατεναντίας. Procopius ἀντίμιμον γῆς.
[s] τύπον τοῦ χρόνου (?) : text and meaning doubtful.
[t] Aucher "quae in se ferebat terra juxta partes ad speciem perspectantes." Cod. Barb. reads somewhat more intelligibly τὰ τῶν ζῴων γένη . . . ὧν ἔφερεν ἡ γῆ τὰ κατὰ μέρος εἴδη.
[u] πιστεύωσι. [v] τῷ κηρύγματι.

fearing destruction, they may first of all turn back (from sin), breaking down and destroying all impiety [a] and evil. Second, this passage [b] clearly represents [c] the extraordinary abundance [d] of the seemly kindness [e] of the Saviour and Benefactor [f] in loosing man's evil of many years,[g] extending almost from birth to old age, in those who repent for a few days.[h] For the Deity is void of malice [i] and a lover of virtue.[j] Accordingly, when He sees genuine virtue [k] in the soul, He apportions [l] such [m] honour to it as to be gracious [n] to all those who stand guilty of earlier sins.[o] Third, the number of seven days, during which the (divine) command [p] kept back the flood after their entering the ark, is a reminder of the genesis of the world,[q] of which the birthday [r] is celebrated on the seventh day, clearly exhibiting the Father [s] as though (saying), "I am both the creator of the world [t] and He who brings into being non-existent things, and now I am about to destroy the world by a great flood. But the cause of creating [u] the world was the goodness and kindness [v] in Me, while (the cause) of the destruction that is about to befall them [w] is the ingratitude and impiety [x] of those who have experienced

[a] ἀσέβειαν. [b] λόγος. [c] παρίστησι.
[d] ἐξαισίαν ὑπερβολήν. [e] Cod. Barb. τῆς ἐπιεικείας.
[f] τοῦ σωτῆρος καὶ εὐεργέτου. [g] τὴν πολυετῆ μοχθηρίαν.
[h] Cod. Barb. and Procopius ἡμέραις ὀλίγαις.
[i] Greek equivalent uncertain.
[j] φιλάρετος. [k] γνησίαν ἀρετήν. [l] ἀπονέμει.
[m] Arm. *ayněap*[c] = "such"; variant *aněap*[c] = ἄμετρον *vel sim.*
[n] χαρίσασθαι.
[o] Aucher renders less literally, "ut deleat omnia de primis delicti imminentia damna."
[p] ὁ χρησμός (?). [q] τῆς τοῦ κόσμου γενέσεως.
[r] τὰ γενέθλια.
[s] Aucher more freely renders, "demonstrando patris auctoritatem."
[t] ὁ κοσμοποιός. [u] τῆς γενέσεως.
[v] ἡ ἀγαθότης καὶ ἡ χρηστότης.
[w] τῆς μελλούσης καταλήψεσθαι.
[x] τὸ ἀχαρίστους καὶ ἀσεβεῖς εἶναι.

good." [a] He therefore holds off [b] for seven days in order that those who lack faith and belief [c] may be mindful of the genesis of the world, and coming as suppliants to the Creator of all [d] may ask for the perpetuity of His works,[e] and that they may ask (this) not with mouth or tongue but rather with a chastened mind.[f]

*14. (Gen. vii. 4, 12) Why was there a flooding rain [g] for forty days and as many nights?

First of all, "day" is spoken of in two senses. The first is the time from morning to evening, from the rising of the shining sun to its setting. Thus do they determine [h] who say, "It is day while the sun is above the earth." But the day is spoken of in a second sense and is reckoned with the night. Thus we say that the month is of thirty days, joining and reckoning with them also the night-time. Now with these things determined,[i] I say that the statement (of Scripture) [j] contains in itself [k] forty days and forty nights not vainly or idly but to emphasize the two numbers which are set apart [l] for the birth of man, (namely) forty and eighty, as is reported by many others, by physicians and also by naturalists.[m] And especially is this written in the sacred Law,[n] which was for them [o] also the beginning [p] of being physiologists.[q] Accordingly, since

[a] Aucher more freely renders, "qui beneficiis a me cumulati fuerant." Procopius τῶν εὐεργετηθέντων ἀσέβεια.

[b] ἐπέχει (or κωλύει sc. τὸν κατακλυσμόν).

[c] οἱ ἀπιστοῦντες καὶ ἀπειθοῦντες, probably Arm. doublet.

[d] τὸν τῶν πάντων ποιητήν.

[e] τὴν τῶν ἔργων αὐτοῦ ἀϊδιότητα.

[f] νῷ ἐπανορθώσεως.

[g] Lit. "a rain of flood."

[h] Or "define"—διορίζουσι or "measure"—μετροῦσι.

[i] τούτων ὡρισμένων.

[j] τὸν λόγον.

[k] περιέχει (?).

[l] ὁρισθέντας.

[m] τῶν φυσικῶν. On the number of days required for forming the male and female embryos see *QG* i. 25.

[n] ἐν τῷ ἱερῷ νόμῳ.

[o] Apparently the generation of Noah.

[p] Or "principle"—ἀρχή.

[q] τοῦ εἶναι φυσιολόγους.

destruction was about to come upon all persons everywhere, both men and women, because of their excessive unity [a] in discord [b] and unbridled wrongdoing,[c] the Judge [d] decided to fix [e] a time for their destruction equal to that which [f] He had determined for the creation of nature [g] and the first production of living beings.[h] For the beginning of generation is eternity in the parts of seeds.[i] And it was necessary to honour man with pure and unshadowed light,[j] but woman, since she was a mixture, with night and darkness and a mixed mass.[k] Therefore in the constitution of the universe [l] the (numerical) oddness [m] of the masculine number composed of unity [n] produces squares,[o] but the feminine even number, composed of two, produces oblongs.[p] Now the square numbers are splendour and light, consisting of an equality of sides.[q] But the oblong numbers have [r] night and darkness because of their inequality,

[a] ὑπερβολῆς τῆς συμφωνίας (or ὁμονοίας).

[b] ἐν ἀσυμφωνίᾳ (or διαφωνίᾳ).

[c] Aucher, construing a little differently, renders, "ob unionem in excessu iniquitatum inter dissidia."

[d] ὁ κριτής.

[e] ὁρίζειν or μετρεῖν.

[f] Aucher, taking "people" as the antecedent of the relative pr. instead of "time," renders, "aequale . . . tempus . . . eis quos" instead of " . . . ei quod."

[g] τῇ τῆς φύσεως κτίσει.

[h] τῇ πρώτῃ ζῳογονίᾳ, *cf. QG* i. 25.

[i] ἡ ἀϊδιότης ἡ ἐν τοῖς τῶν σπερμάτων μέρεσι. This means that the species is eternal while the individual is subject to death ; *cf. QG* i. 96 and *De Aeter. Mundi* 35 ff.

[j] καθαρῷ καὶ ἀσκίῳ (?) φωτί. See also the Greek frag.

[k] φυράματι. The above is a literal translation of the obscure and probably incomplete Arm. clause ; Aucher, disregarding some of the syntactical problems, renders, "femina vero mixturam habebat massae cum nocte atque tenebris." The context requires an original something like "to honour woman, since she had a mixed nature, with a mixture of light and darkness."

[l] ἐν τῇ τῶν ὅλων συστάσει.

[m] τὸ περιττόν.

[n] ἐξ ἑνότητος συντεθέν.

[o] One MS. "triangles."

[p] ἑτερομήκεις (Pythagorean terminology).

[q] ἐξ ἰσότητος πλευρῶν.

[r] Lit. "has."

for that which is excessive casts a shadow on that which falls under the excess. In the second place, the number forty is a power [a] producing many things,[b] as has been shown elsewhere,[c] and is often used as an indication of the giving of the Law [d] both in the case of [e] those who have rightly [f] accomplished something (deserving) of praise and honour and also in the case of those who because of transgressions are subject to blame and punishment. And evidently to adduce testimony [g] of these things would mean a lengthy speech.[h]

*15. (Gen. vii. 4) What is the meaning of the words, "I will blot every growth of vegetation [i] which I have made from the face of the earth"?

Would you not indeed jump up at hearing this because of the beauty of the sentiment? [j] It does not say, "blot from the earth" but "from the face of the earth," that is, from the surface,[k] in order that in the depths the vital power [l] of the seeds of all things may be preserved unharmed and not suffer from anything that might be able to injure them. For the Creator does not forget His own purpose [m] but destroys those things which move above and on the very surface while in the depths He leaves the roots for the generation of other impulses.[n] Moreover, divinely [o]

[a] δύναμις.

[b] Aucher, construing differently, renders, "numerus quadraginta plurimarum productor est virtutum."

[c] *QG* i. 91.

[d] τῆς νομοθεσίας. This probably refers to Ex. xxiv. 18 on Moses' sojourn of forty days and nights on Mt. Sinai, though the "often" may refer to other writings beside Philo's.

[e] ἐπί (?). Aucher has "super."

[f] ὀρθῶς. [g] μαρτύρια προφέρειν. [h] μακρολογία.

[i] ἀνάστημα φυτοῦ. LXX has ἐξανάστασιν = Heb. *yᵉqûm*, "growth" (lit. "rising"); Arm. O.T. has *hasak* = ἡλικίαν. Philo treats this passage again in *QG* ii. 24.

[j] διὰ τὸ τῆς ἐννοίας κάλλος. [k] τῆς ἐπιφανείας.

[l] ἡ ζωτικὴ δύναμις, as in Greek frag.

[m] τῆς ἰδίας προθέσεως.

[n] πρὸς γένεσιν ἄλλων ἀφορμῶν. [o] θεοπρεπῶς.

is it written " I will destroy " for it so happens that when something is to be blotted out, the writing is blotted but the writing-tablets [a] survive. Thereby He shows that because of their impiety He will blot out the superficial generation [b] in the manner of writing but will eternally preserve the use and substance [c] of the human race as seed for those to come in the future. In accord with this is what follows, for next to " I will blot " comes " the growth of vegetation." Now " growth " [d] is the dissolution of opposites,[e] and that which is dissolved casts off its quality [f] but keeps its substance and its matter.[g] This is the literal meaning. But the deeper meaning is as follows. The flood is a symbol of spiritual dissolution.[h] And so, when by the grace of the Father [i] we wish to cast off and wash off [j] from the mind [k] all the sensible and corporeal things [l] by which it was stained as if by ulcers,[m] it is inundated [n] like salt-flats [o] by the flow of sweet streams and potable springs.

*16. (Gen. vii. 5) Why does (Scripture) say, " Noah did everything whatsoever the Lord God instructed [p] him " ?

(This is) great praise for the righteous man,[q] first of all

[a] Lit. " the tablets and writing." The Greek fragments have *αἱ δέλτοι*.

[b] Cod. Barb. has *τὴν ἐπιπολάζουσαν γένεσιν*.

[c] *χρῆσιν καὶ οὐσίαν*: Arm. *var* " use " is Aucher's emendation of MSS. *vayr* " place," based on Ambrose's " substantiam et conversationem." The Greek fragments have *τὴν διαδοχὴν τῆς οὐσίας*.

[d] Lit. " rising," see note *i* on p. 92.

[e] *κατάλυσις ἀντικειμένων*. Procopius *ἀντίπαλον καθαίρεσις*.

[f] *ποιότητα*. [g] *τὴν οὐσίαν καὶ τὴν ὕλην*.

[h] *σύμβολον τῆς πνευματικῆς καταλύσεως*.

[i] *χάριτι τοῦ πατρός*. [j] *ἀπορρίπτειν καὶ ἀπολούεσθαι*.

[k] *τὸν νοῦν*. [l] *πάντα τὰ αἰσθητικὰ καὶ τὰ σωματικά*.

[m] Arm. *palar* " ulcer " here probably corresponds to *κήλη*, a corruption of *κηλίς* " stain," which the context demands.

[n] *κατακλύζεται*. [o] *ἁλμυρά*, *cf. De Confus. Ling.* 26.

[p] *ἐνετείλατο*. [q] *τοῦ δικαίου*.

because he carried out, not a part, but all of the orders with a strong conviction and a god-loving mind.[a] And second, because He does not wish to order [b] him so much as to instruct [c] him. For masters [d] command their servants, but loved ones [e] instruct their friends,[f] especially elders their juniors.[g] Thus it is a wonderful gift to be found in the rank [h] of servants and in the rank [i] of ministers [j] of God. But it is a superfluity of beneficence [k] to be also beloved of the praiseworthy uncreated One.[l] Moreover (Scripture) now carefully presents both names [m]; it speaks of the higher powers,[n] the destructive [o] and the beneficent,[p] and it places "Lord" first, and the beneficent "God" second. For, as it was the time of judgment, (Scripture) says that the destroyer came first. However, being a kind and good and benevolent king,[q] He leaves some remains [r]—seminal principles [s] through which the vacant places may again be filled. Wherefore in the beginning of created things the expression "let there be" was not a destructive power but beneficent. And so, in the creation of the world [t] He changed the style of His names.[u] For He is called God as beneficent, and this name He regularly [v] used in constituting the universe.[w] But after all this was completed He was called Lord in the creation of the world, and

[a] *φιλοθέῳ* (Cod. Barb. *θεοφιλεῖ*) *διανοίᾳ*.
[b] *κελεύειν* or *προστάττειν*.
[c] *ἐντέλλεσθαι*.
[d] *δεσπόται*.
[e] *ἀγαπητοί*.
[f] *τοῖς φίλοις*.
[g] Lit. "the greater the less."
[h] *τάξει*.
[i] Arm. here uses different word also = *τάξει*.
[j] Prob. *θεραπόντων*, as in Cod. Barb.
[k] *ὑπερβολὴ τῆς εὐεργεσίας*.
[l] *ὑπὸ τοῦ ἐπαινετοῦ ἀγενήτου*.
[m] *i.e.* the two highest attributes of God, identified with the names "Lord" and "God" respectively.
[n] *τὰς ἀνωτάτω δυνάμεις*.
[o] *τὴν διαφθείρουσαν* (elsewhere in Philo called *κολαστήριον*).
[p] *τὴν εὐεργέτιν*.
[q] *χρηστὸς καὶ ἀγαθὸς καὶ εὐμενὴς βασιλεύς*.
[r] *λείψανα*.
[s] *σπερματικὰς ἀρχάς*.
[t] *ἐν τῇ κοσμοποιΐᾳ*.
[u] *τὰς τῶν ὀνομάτων κλήσεις*.
[v] *συνεχῶς* or *ἐπὶ πολύ*.
[w] *ἐν τῇ τῶν ὅλων συστάσει*.

this is His kingly and destructive name.[a] For where there is coming into being,[b] "God" is placed first in order, but where there is punishment, "Lord" comes before "God."

*17. (Gen. vii. 11) Why (does Scripture say), "In the six-hundredth (year) of Noah's life was the flood, in the seventh[c] month, on the twenty-seventh[d] of the month"?

Perhaps it would have been fitting for[e] the righteous man[f] to be born at the head of the month in the first month, opportunely[g] at the beginning of that year which it is the custom to call in honorary fashion the sacred month.[h] For (otherwise)[i] (Scripture) would not have been so exact in stating the month and day when the flood took place, both the seventh month and the twenty-seventh day. But perhaps in this way it clearly shows the time of the vernal equinox, for this always occurs in the seventh month, on the twenty-seventh.[j] But why does the flood

[a] See note *o* on p. 94. [b] γένεσις.

[c] Heb. and LXX have "second," Arm. O.T. like Philo has "seventh"; Josephus also gives "second month called . . . Marsuan (Heb. *Marḥešwan*=Oct.–Nov.)." Philo also differs from Heb. and LXX of Gen. viii. 14 (*QG* ii. 47), by giving "seventh" for "second" month for the drying up of the flood-waters in the 601st year of Noah's life.

[d] So LXX; Heb. "seventeenth."

[e] Or "might have happened that"; Arm. *dēp* renders συμβαίνει as well as εἰκός, προσῆκον, etc. [f] τὸν δίκαιον.

[g] κατὰ καιρόν (?); Aucher omits this phrase in his rendering.

[h] τὴν ἱερομηνίαν (not "annum sacrum" as Aucher renders). By this word Philo elsewhere (*cf.* Colson's appendix to *De Decalogo* 159 in vol. vii. pp. 613-614) means the period introduced by the 1st of Tishri (autumnal New Year) or the 1st of Nisan (vernal New Year).

[i] I follow Aucher in inserting "otherwise," which is required by the context.

[j] Philo means the seventh month reckoned from the 1st of Tishri, namely Nisan (March–April); *cf. De Opif. Mundi* 116 on the two equinoxes of the two seventh months, Tishri and Nisan. But on what tradition he bases his statement that the equinox occurs on the 27th of the seventh month is not known to me.

occur at the vernal equinox? Because at that time come the increases and births of all things, both animals and plants. Accordingly, the punishment carries a more terrible threat at the time of increase and abundance of all produce,[a] and in time of fertility the evil supervenes to convict[b] of impiety those who are subject[c] to punishment. For, behold, says (Scripture), the nature[d] of all things contains in itself its own fullness sufficiently[e]—grain, barley and all other things as well which are sown and brought to completion, and it begins to bear the fruits of trees. But you, as mortals, corrupt His benefactions[f] and with them corrupt the intention of the divine gift.[g] For if the flood had happened to take place at the autumnal equinox, when there was nothing on the earth but all things were collected in their mass,[h] it would not have seemed a punishment so much as a benefit[i] because of the water purifying fields and mountains. Accordingly at this time there came into being the first earthborn man,[j] whom the divine oracles[k] call Adam; for it was fitting and proper that the progenitor of the human race or forefather or father or however one ought to call that eldest man[l] should be formed at the time of the vernal equinox when all earthly things are full of fruits. And the vernal equinox occurs in the seventh month and this is also called the first in ac-

[a] Lit. "sheaves" or "stalks"—δραγμάτων.

[b] εἰς ἔλεγχος.

[c] Arm. pres. subj. of *krem* "to bear, suffer."

[d] ἡ φύσις.

[e] Meaning doubtful; apparently = τὰ ἑαυτῆς ἀρκούντως πλήρη. Aucher renders, "sua *vel* plenissime."

[f] τὰς εὐεργεσίας αὐτοῦ.

[g] Syntax and meaning uncertain; Aucher renders, "divina simul dona consilia (*vel*, mysteria)." The Arm. construction *pargew zxorhourdsn* seems to be genitival rather than appositional, but the word *xorhourd* has many meanings such as "thought," "intention," "mystery," "type," "symbol."

[h] *i.e.* future plants under the earth.

[i] εὐεργεσία.

[j] γηγενής.

[k] οἱ θεῖοι χρησμοί.

[l] ἐκεῖνον τὸν πρεσβύτατον.

cordance with a varying assumption.[a] Accordingly, since Noah after the destruction (of mankind) by the flood becomes the first beginning of the race,[b] with mankind again being propagated,[c] he is made similar, so far as possible, to the first earthborn man.[d] Now the six hundredth year has as its source the number six, but the world was created with[e] the number six; accordingly, through this again He exposes[f] those who act impiously[g] and shames[h] them, for in no wise would He who brought all things into being through the number six, have destroyed earthly creatures under the form[i] of six, had it not been for the excess of their wrongdoing.[j] For six hundred is a third and lesser six,[k] and the number sixty is the mean of both, for the tens bear a likeness to one, and in a lesser degree, the hundreds.

18. (Gen. vii. 11) What is the meaning of the words, "All the fountains of the abyss broke forth and the cataracts[l] of heaven were opened"?

The literal meaning[m] is clear, for it is stated that earth and heaven are the principles and extremities of the universe,[n] and are joined in the condemnation[o] and destruction of mortals, as the waters met together with one

[a] Arm. *arac* —usu. = λῆμμα; the Greek fragment has ἐπιβολήν. Philo means that the seventh month of the autumnal calendar, Nisan (March–April), is the first month of the vernal calendar.

[b] ἡ πρώτη τοῦ γένους ἀρχή.

[c] Lit. "sown"—σπειρομένων. The Greek fragment has δευτέρας ἀνθρώπων σπορᾶς.

[d] τῷ πρώτῳ γηγενῆ.

[e] In Arm. expressed by instr. case of noun "number"; Aucher renders, "sub numero."

[f] ἐλέγχει.

[g] τοὺς ἀνοσιουργούς.

[h] καταισχύνων.

[i] σχήματι.

[j] ἀδικίας.

[k] In the sequence 6 : 60 : 600.

[l] Arm. *sohank*ᶜ or *sahank*ᶜ "streams" = LXX καταρράκται.

[m] τὸ ῥητόν.

[n] τῶν πάντων αἱ ἀρχαὶ (καὶ) τὰ ἄκρα. Aucher renders, "orbis extrema."

[o] εἰς κατάκρισιν.

another, some rushing up from the earth, some pouring down from heaven. And most clear and evident (is it why) it is said that " the fountains of the abyss broke forth," for when there is a break,[a] the course (of the waters) is unrestrained. But as for the deeper meaning,[b] this is to be said. The heaven is symbolically [c] the human mind,[d] and the earth is sense-perception and body.[e] And great misfortune and doubt[f] are incurred when neither one remains [g] but both together practise deceit.[h] Now what do I mean by this? Many times the mind entertains cunning and evil and shows bitterness[i] toward all things when the sensual pleasures[j] of the body are restrained and suppressed.[k] And many times it happens that it experiences the contrary when the sensual pleasures are fortunate [l] and creep along[m] and grow luxury-loving and prodigal in living. And the senses and the body [n] are the harbours[o] of these things. Now when the mind stands firm [p] in indifference [q] to these things, they decline and are inert.[r] But when they both come together, reason [s] using all kinds of wickedness, and the body flushed [t] with all the senses and indul-

[a] ῥῆγμα.
[b] τὸ πρὸς διάνοιαν.
[c] συμβολικῶς.
[d] ὁ ἀνθρώπειος νοῦς.
[e] αἴσθησις καὶ σῶμα.
[f] Lit. " of doubt "—ἀπορίας *vel sim.*; Aucher renders, " aerumna calamitatum."
[g] Apparently " remains constant " is meant.
[h] ἀπάτας *vel sim.*
[i] πικρίᾳ χρῆται.
[j] αἱ ἡδοναί.
[k] κωλύονται καὶ συστέλλονται.
[l] εὐτυχεῖς or εὐδαίμονες.
[m] ἕρπουσι.
[n] αἱ αἰσθήσεις καὶ τὸ σῶμα.
[o] λιμένες.
[p] Lit. " stands in itself."
[q] ἀμελείᾳ.
[r] Arm. has verbs in sing. (prob. reflecting sing. verb with neut. pl. in Greek) = κατακλίνεται καὶ παραλύεται. The context requires us to take " senses and body " as the subjects of these verbs; Aucher renders, " sed quum intellectus neglectis rebus constet in se, illi inefficaces jacent ut derelicti," and remarks in a footnote, " Hunc sensum tenuit nobiscum Glossarius in serie obscuri huius loci."
[s] τοῦ λογισμοῦ.
[t] Lit. " watered "—ἀρδευομένου *vel sim.*

ging all the passions to satiety, (then) we are flooded.[a] And this is truly a great flood when the streams of the mind are opened by folly,[b] madness,[c] insatiable desire,[d] wrongdoing,[e] senselessness,[f] recklessness[g] and impiety[h]; and when the fountains of the body are opened by sensual pleasure,[i] desire,[j] drunkenness,[k] gourmandism and licentiousness with kin and sisters and by incurable vices.[l]

19. (Gen. vii. 16) What is the meaning of the words, "God closed[m] the ark outside of[n] him"?

Since we have said that the structure[o] of the human body is symbolically[p] indicated by the ark, it is also to be noted that our body is enclosed[q] on the outside by a hard skin which is laid around it as a covering[r] for all parts. For Nature made this as a garment lest cold and heat have power to do harm. The literal meaning[s] is clear. For the ark is carefully[t] closed from the outside by the divine power[u] for the sake of guarding (it)[v] lest the water come in through any part, since it was destined to be storm-tossed for a whole year.

20. (Gen. vii. 18) What is the meaning of the words,

[a] κατακλυζόμεθα.
[b] ἀφροσύνῃ or "baseness"—πονηρίᾳ, φαυλότητι.
[c] Arm. *šaproumn* is glossed here by *yimarout^ciun*=μωρία, ἔκστασις; Aucher renders, "insipientia"; elsewhere *šaproumn*=μανία or εὐήθεια.
[d] ἀκορέστῳ ἐπιθυμίᾳ.
[e] ἀδικίᾳ.
[f] ἀναισθησίᾳ or ἀφροσύνῃ. Aucher omits the word.
[g] τόλμῃ or θράσει.
[h] ἀσεβείᾳ.
[i] ἡδονῇ.
[j] ὀρέξει.
[k] οἰνοφλυγίᾳ.
[l] ἀνιάτοις πάθεσι.
[m] ἔκλεισε.
[n] ἔξωθεν (so LXX)=Heb. *ba^cadô*, here meaning "behind."
[o] κατασκευή.
[p] συμβολικῶς.
[q] περικλῄεται.
[r] σκέπασμα.
[s] τὸ ῥητόν.
[t] ἐπιμελῶς.
[u] θείᾳ δυνάμει.
[v] τῆς φυλακῆς.

" And the water increased and lifted the ark, and it was borne upon the water " [a] ?

The literal meaning is clear. But it is to be allegorized [b] as follows. Our body must in a certain sense [c] cross the sea and be storm-tossed by necessities [d] overcoming hunger and thirst, cold and heat, by which it is thrown up and down,[e] perturbed and moved.

21. (Gen. vii. 20) Why did the water increase fifteen cubits above all the high mountains ? [f]

It should be noted that as for the literal meaning [g] it was not increased fifteen cubits over [h] all the high mountains but over the very longest and highest,[i] and (thus) it was still higher over [j] the lower ones. But one should treat this allegorically.[k] The high mountains indicate the senses [l] in our bodies, for it happens that they have their fixed position in the top of our head. And they are five, each of them severally being viewed as threefold,[m] so that altogether there are fifteen : sight, the thing seen, (the act of) seeing [n] ; hearing, the thing heard, (the act of) hearing [o] ; smell, the thing smelled, (the act of) smelling [p] ; taste, the thing tasted, (the act of) tasting [q] ; touch, the

[a] Philo's text differs slightly from LXX, which reads *καὶ ἐπεκράτει τὸ ὕδωρ καὶ ἐπληθύνετο σφόδρα ἐπὶ τῆς γῆς καὶ ἐπεφέρετο ἡ κιβωτὸς ἐπάνω τοῦ ὕδατος.* The Arm. O.T. agrees with LXX.

[b] *ἀλληγορεῖται.*

[c] *τρόπον τινά.*

[d] *τοῖς ἀναγκαίοις.*

[e] *ἄνω καὶ κάτω κλονεῖται.*

[f] Philo combines two parts of the LXX verse, *δέκα πέντε πήχεις ἐπάνω ὑψώθη τὸ ὕδωρ καὶ ἐπεκάλυψεν πάντα τὰ ὄρη τὰ ὑψηλά.*

[g] *πρὸς τὸ ῥητόν.*

[h] Lit. " more than."

[i] Apparently Philo takes *πάντα τὰ ὑψηλά* in the LXX to indicate the superlative degree of height.

[j] Lit. " more excessive."

[k] *πραγματεύεσθαι πρὸ ἀλληγορίας vel sim.*

[l] *τὰς αἰσθήσεις.*

[m] Lit. " three."

[n] *ἡ ὅρασις, τὸ ὁρατόν, τὸ ὁρᾶν.*

[o] *ἡ ἀκοή, τὸ ἀκουστόν, τὸ ἀκούειν.*

[p] *ἡ ὄσφρησις, τὸ ὀσφραντόν, τὸ ὀσφραίνεσθαι.*

[q] *ἡ γεῦσις, τὸ γευστόν, τὸ γεύεσθαι.*

thing touched, (the act of) touching.[a] These are the fifteen cubits which were over and above (the mountains). For they too are flooded and destroyed by the sudden onrush of never-ending vices and evils.[b]

22. (Gen. vii. 21) What is the meaning of the words, "All flesh that moved died"?

Excellently and naturally has (Scripture) spoken of the destruction of moving flesh, for flesh moves[c] the sensual pleasures[d] and is moved by sensual pleasures. But such movements are the causes[e] of the destruction of souls, just as the rules of self-control[f] and patience[g] (are the causes) of salvation.[h]

23. (Gen. vii. 22) What is the meaning of the words, "Everything that was upon the dry land died"[i]?

The literal meaning is known to all,[j] for in the great flood everything that was upon the earth was utterly destroyed.[k] But the deeper meaning[l] is that just as the wood of trees, when it is altogether dried out,[m] is immediately consumed by fire, so also the soul,[n] when it is not mixed[o] with wisdom, justice and piety[p] and also with the

[a] ἡ ἁφή, τὸ ἁπτόν, τὸ ἅπτεσθαι.

[b] ἀνηνύτων παθῶν καὶ κακῶν.

[c] κινεῖ. [d] τὰς ἡδονάς. [e] αἱ αἰτίαι.

[f] ἐγκρατείας or "endurance"—καρτερίας.

[g] ὑπομονῆς. [h] σωτηρίας.

[i] Philo's text differs slightly from LXX, which reads καὶ πάντα ὅσα ἔχει πνοὴν ζωῆς καὶ πᾶς ὃς ἦν ἐπὶ τῆς ξηρᾶς ἀπέθανεν. Philo applies the neuter gender of the first subject to the second, which is masc. and animate in LXX (the Heb. indef. pron. *kol* "all" may refer to either animate or inanimate subjects). [j] τὸ ῥητὸν γνώριμόν ἐστι.

[k] Lit. "being destroyed was overturned."

[l] τὸ πρὸς διάνοιαν.

[m] Arm. uses three different adjectives all meaning "dry."

[n] ἡ ψυχή. [o] κεκραμένη *vel sim.*

[p] σοφίᾳ καὶ δικαιοσύνῃ καὶ θεοσεβείᾳ.

other fine virtues [a] which alone are able to gladden the mind,[b] dries up and becomes arid like a plant that is barren and sterile, or like an aged tree, and dies when it is given over to the flood of the body.

24. (Gen. vii. 23) What is the meaning of the words, "He blotted out every growth [c] that was on the face of the earth"?

The literal meaning [d] has a clear explanation.[e] But it is to be allegorized [f] as follows. Not idly [g] does (Scripture) speak of "growth," for this is the name of arrogance and pride,[h] through which men despise the Deity and human rights. But arrogance and haughtiness on the surface of our earthly and corporeal nature appear more (clearly) when the face is lifted up and the eyebrows are knitted. For there are some who approach with their legs, but with their breast, neck and head sway backwards and forwards,[i] rearing back [j] and wavering like a balance; with half the body, the legs, they come forward, but from the breast upward [k] they lean backward like those whose backbone [l] or occiput [m] pains them, whereby they are prevented from bending over naturally. But it was reasonable [n] that all

[a] ἀστείοις ἀρεταῖς. Arm. *asti* is twice used in *De Vita Cont.* to render ἀστεῖος because of its similarity in sound to the Greek word, although its meaning is quite different, usu. "firm," "fresh," etc.; Aucher renders, "virtutibus constantibus."

[b] Lit. "thoughts"—λογισμούς.

[c] Lit. "rising," LXX ἀνάστημα; see above, p. 92 note *i* on *QG* ii. 15.

[d] τὸ ῥητόν.

[e] ἐξήγησιν or "narrative"—διήγησιν, as Aucher renders.

[f] ἀλληγορεῖσθαι.

[g] εἰκῇ or ἀπὸ σκοποῦ.

[h] Both Arm. words render ἀλαζονεία, ὑπερηφανία, ὕβρις, etc.

[i] ταλαντεύουσι.

[j] ἀναχαιτίζοντες *vel sim.*

[k] Not "pectore superiori" as Aucher renders.

[l] Arm. gloss "loins," Aucher "musculi."

[m] ἰνίον. Arm. gloss "nerves," similarly Aucher. Probably the original text of Philo referred to the tendons and nerves of the back of the neck.

[n] εἰκός.

men of this sort should be blotted out from the Lord's memory [a] and from the divine narrative of Scripture.

25. (Gen. vii. 23) What is the meaning of the words, " Noah remained alone and those who were with him in the ark " ?

The literal meaning [b] is clear. But the deeper meaning [c] must be somewhat as follows. The mind [d] which is desirous of wisdom and justice,[e] like a tree, cuts off all the harmful growths which grow on it and drain [f] its nourishment.[g] By this is meant immoderateness of the passions [h] and wickedness and the acts (resulting) from these. He is left alone with his own. And peculiar [i] to each are all the thoughts [j] which are ordered [k] in accordance with virtue.[l] Wherefore it is added that " he remained alone and those who were with him " to (give) a clear impression of the truest joy.[m] And he remained in the ark, by which is meant the body, which is pure [n] of all passions and spiritual diseases,[o] not yet having been enabled to become altogether incorporeal.[p] But thanks should be given to the Saviour and Father [q] for this benefaction also, (namely) that he received a yoke-fellow [r] and one bound to him,[s] no longer a ruler [t] over him but under his rule. Therefore his body was not overwhelmed by the flood but (remained) above the flood, not being destroyed by the streams of the

[a] ἐκ τῆς τοῦ κυρίου μνήμης.

[b] τὸ ῥητόν. [c] τὸ πρὸς διάνοιαν.

[d] ὁ νοῦς. [e] σοφίας καὶ δικαιοσύνης.

[f] Lit. " suck " or " drink up."

[g] τροφήν. Aucher renders, " humores nutritionis."

[h] τὴν τῶν παθῶν ἀμετρίαν.

[i] ἴδιοι. [j] οἱ λογισμοί. [k] τάττονται.

[l] κατὰ τὴν ἀρετήν.

[m] εἰς φανερὰν φαντασίαν τῆς ἀληθεστάτης χαρᾶς.

[n] καθαρόν.

[o] πάντων παθῶν καὶ ψυχικῶν (or πνευματικῶν) νόσων.

[p] πάντως ἀσώματον. [q] τῷ σωτῆρι καὶ πατρί.

[r] σύζυγον (*i.e.* the body). [s] συνδέσμιον.

[t] ἄρχοντα *vel sim.*

cataracts which gurgled up, (namely) luxuriousness and intemperance and lewd habits and empty desires.

*26. (Gen. viii. 1) Why does (Scripture) say, "God remembered Noah and the beasts and the cattle,"[a] but does not mention his wife and children?

When a man is united[b] and associated[c] with his wife, and a father with his sons, there is no need for several[d] names, but only of the first one. And so, having mentioned Noah, (Scripture) potentially[e] mentions those who were in his household.[f] For when a man and woman quarrel, and their children and relatives, the household no longer bears (the name of household),[g] but in place of one there are many. But when there is concord,[h] one household is described[i] after one eldest person,[j] and all (the others) depend[k] on him like the branches which grow out of a tree or like the fruits of a plant which do not fall off. And the prophet has said somewhere,[l] "Look at Abraham your father and at Sarah who travailed with you," which shows very clearly that there was (only) one root[m] in respect of concord with the woman.[n]

27. (Gen. viii. 1) Why does (Scripture) first make mention of the wild beasts[o] and afterwards of the cattle,[p] saying

[a] LXX has "all the beasts (θηρίων) and all the cattle (κτηνῶν) and all the birds and all the reptiles, etc."
[b] ἑνοῦται.
[c] κοινωνεῖται (?).
[d] Lit. "many."
[e] δυνάμει.
[f] ἐν τῇ οἰκίᾳ.
[g] The last phrase must be supplied to make sense; cf. Aucher's rendering, "nec ultra patitur domus (una dici)."
[h] ὁμόνοια. Procopius συμφωνία.
[i] Arm. *grem* usu. = γράφειν. Aucher renders, "exhibetur."
[j] ἀφ' ἑνὸς πρεσβυτάτου.
[k] κρέμανται. Procopius συνυπακούεσθαι.
[l] Isaiah li. 2.
[m] ῥίζα.
[n] The syntax is somewhat obscure; Aucher renders, "quod nempe una erat stirps ad mulierem versus concordiam patefacit."
[o] τῶν θηρίων.
[p] τῶν κτηνῶν.

that "He remembered Noah and the beasts and the cattle"?

In the first place, this poetic saying [a] is not inaptly quoted, (namely) that "he drove the base ones into the middle." [b] For He stationed [c] the wild beasts in the midst of the domestic ones,[d] (that is) men and cattle, in order that they might become tamed and domesticated by acquiring familiarity [e] with both. Second, it did not seem right to the Overseer [f] to bestow a benefaction on the wild beasts at the same time. For (Scripture) was immediately about to [g] mention further the beginning of the diminution of the flood. This is the literal meaning.[h] As for the deeper meaning [i]—the righteous mind,[j] living in the body as in an ark, also has wild beasts and cattle [k] but not those particular ones [l] which bite and are harmful, but, as I might say, the generic ones [m] having the status [n] of seed and principle [o]; for without these the soul [p] is not able to appear in the body. Accordingly, (the soul) of the wicked man [q] uses all things poisonous and lethal, but that of the virtuous [r] those things which transform the nature of wild beasts into that of domestic ones.

*28. (Gen. viii. 1) What is the meaning of the words,

[a] τόδε τὸ ποιητικόν.

[b] κακοὺς δ' ἐς μέσσον ἔλασσεν, *Iliad* iv. 299.

[c] ἔταξεν. [d] τῶν οἰκείων. [e] οἰκειότητος.

[f] τῷ ἐπόπτῃ or ἐπισκόπῳ (God). Perhaps, however, one should take Arm. *tesouč* "overseer" as having adjectival force here, *i.e.* meaning "providential" and agreeing with "benefaction"; so Aucher renders, "providum beneficium."

[g] ἔμελλε.

[h] τὸ ῥητόν. [i] τὸ πρὸς διάνοιαν.

[j] ὁ δίκαιος νοῦς.

[k] Or "animals"; Arm. *anasoun* (lit. "irrational") = both κτῆνος and ἄλογον (ζῷον). [l] τὰ μερικά.

[m] τὰ γενικά. [n] τὸν λόγον.

[o] σπέρματος καὶ ἀρχῆς.

[p] ἡ ψυχή although Arm. *ogi* (*hogi*) also = τὸ πνεῦμα.

[q] τοῦ πονηροῦ (or φαύλου). [r] τοῦ σπουδαίου.

"He [a] brought a spirit [b] over the earth and the water ceased"?

Some would say that by "spirit" is meant the wind [c] through which the flood ceased. But I myself do not know of water being diminished by a wind. Rather is it disturbed and seethes.[d] Otherwise vast expanses [e] of the sea would long ago have been consumed.[f] Accordingly, (Scripture) now seems to speak of the spirit of the Deity,[g] by which all things are made secure,[h] and of the terrible condition of the world, and of those things which are in the air and are in all mixtures [i] of plants and animals. For this time the flood was not a trifling outpouring [j] of water but a limitless and immense one, which almost flowed out beyond the Pillars of Heracles and the Great Sea.[k] Therefore the whole earth and the mountainous regions were flooded. That such (an amount of water) should be cleared out by the wind is not fitting, likely or right; but, as I said, (it must have been done) by the invisible power of God.[l]

*29. (Gen. viii. 2) What is the meaning of the words, "the fountains of the abyss were covered up,[m] and the cataracts of heaven"?

In the first place, it is clear that the downpour [n] was

[a] LXX (and Heb.) "God."

[b] πνεῦμα.

[c] ὁ ἄνεμος.

[d] κυμαίνει, as in Procopius.

[e] Procopius τὰ μέγιστα.

[f] *i.e.* dried up by the action of the winds.

[g] τὸ τοῦ θείου πνεῦμα. Procopius πνεῦμα τὸ θεῖον.

[h] Or "freed (of danger from the flood)"; Arm. *yapahov* = both ἀσφαλής and ἀπηλλαγμένος. Aucher renders, "securitatem assequitur."

[i] So lit., apparently meaning "varied forms."

[j] Lit. "blow," "incidence."

[k] The Atlantic.

[l] ὑπὸ τῆς ἀοράτου δυνάμεως τῆς τοῦ θεοῦ.

[m] ἐπεκαλύφθησαν (as in LXX) or ἐκρύφθησαν. Arm. O.T. "were closed."

[n] Lit. "streams of falling"; Aucher renders, "fluenta poenosa."

incessant during the first forty days when from the earth below the fountains broke forth, and from the heaven above the cataracts were opened[a] until all the regions of plain and mountain were flooded. And for another full hundred and fifty days the streams did not cease from pouring down nor the fountains from welling up, but they were more gentle, no longer for increase[b] but for the continuation[c] of the outpouring[d] of water. And from on high there was assistance.[e] This is indicated by what is now said, " after a hundred and fifty days the fountains and cataracts were covered up." Thus, so long as they were still not kept back, it is clear that they were active.[f] Second, it was necessary that what (Scripture) adduces (as) streams of the flood, (namely) the twofold reservoir[g] of water, one being the fountains in the earth, the other the streams in the heaven, should be closed ; for in proportion as the additional supplies[h] of material give out, so is this consumed by expending itself,[i] especially when the divine power[j] has commanded it. This is the literal meaning.[k] As for the deeper meaning[l]—since the flood of the soul[m] wells up from two (sources), from reason[n] as though from heaven, and also from the body and the senses as though from the earth, evil entering it[o] through the passions, and passions through evil at the same time, it

[a] *Cf.* above, *QG* ii. 18 on Gen. vii. 11.

[b] οὐκέτι πρὸς αὔξησιν.

[c] πρὸς διαμονήν.

[d] Arm. *taraçank*[c] = both κατάχυσις and ἐκτένεια. Aucher "extensionis." John Monachus reads differently.

[e] This seems to mean that at God's command the outpouring of the waters of heaven and earth ceased, *cf.* below.

[f] ἐνήργουν.

[g] ταμεῖον or ἀποθήκην.

[h] Lit. " assistances " or " means."

[i] Aucher more freely renders, " quo magis enim deficiunt praebitiones materiae, ista consumitur a se."

[j] ἡ θεία δύναμις.

[k] τὸ ῥητόν.

[l] τὸ πρὸς διάνοιαν.

[m] ὁ τῆς ψυχῆς κατακλυσμός.

[n] ἐκ τοῦ λογισμοῦ.

[o] *i.e.* the soul.

was necessary for the word [a] of the divine physician [b] to enter into the soul for a visit of healing [c] in order to heal its illness and to keep back [d] both streams. For the beginning of healing is to keep back the causes of the illness and not to leave any more material for the effects of illness.[e] (Scripture) has indicated this also in the case of the leper [f]; for when (the spot) stays and no longer spreads, then in respect of its staying and remaining in the same place, (Scripture) has legislated [g] that it [h] is clean, for that which moves against [i] nature is unclean.

30. (Gen. viii. 3) What is the meaning of the words, "The water went down, diminishing [j] after a hundred and fifty days"?

We must inquire [k] whether indeed these hundred and fifty days of subsiding and diminishing are other than (the period) which lasted five months [l] or else allude to this

[a] τὸν λόγον.

[b] Or "the healing word of God." On the Logos as healer of ills see *Leg. All.* iii. 177 τὸν δὲ ἄγγελον ὅς ἐστι λόγος ὥσπερ ἰατρὸν κακῶν.

[c] πρὸς ἐπισκοπὴν ἰάσεως.

[d] κωλύειν or εἴργειν or ἐπισχεῖν.

[e] Lit. "the making of illness."

[f] *Cf.* Lev. xiii. 6 ff.

[g] ἐνομοθέτησε.

[h] Or "he," the suspected leper.

[i] Lit. "not in accordance with."

[j] Philo's text differs slightly from the LXX, which in turn differs slightly from Heb. (the Arm. O.T. differs slightly from both LXX and Philo). Heb. has "And the waters returned from the earth, continuously returning, and the waters disappeared at the end of a hundred and fifty days"; LXX has καὶ ἐνεδίδου τὸ ὕδωρ πορευόμενον ἀπὸ τῆς γῆς, ἐνεδίδου καὶ ἠλαττονοῦτο τὸ ὕδωρ μετὰ πεντήκοντα καὶ ἑκατὸν ἡμέρας.

[k] ζητητέον.

[l] *Cf.* Gen. vii. 24, not cited by Philo, "and the waters were high upon the earth a hundred and fifty days." Aucher, construing and interpreting differently, renders, "an distincti sint isti centum quinquaginta dies minuendae aquae per quinque menses."

former (period) [a] when the flood was unsubsiding,[b] that is, was still increasing.

31. (Gen. viii. 4) Why does (Scripture) say, "The ark rested [c] in the seventh month [d] on the twenty-seventh day of the month"?

It is fitting to consider how the beginning of the flood fell in the seventh month [e] on the twenty-seventh, and the diminution (of the flood), when the ark rested upon the summits of the mountains, also [f] (fell) in the seventh month on the twenty-seventh of the month. It must therefore be said that there is a homonymity [g] of months and days, for the beginning of the flood fell in the seventh month on the birthday [h] of the righteous man [i] at the vernal equinox, but the diminution (of the flood began) in the seventh month, taking its beginning from the flood, at the autumnal equinox.[j] For the equinoxes are separated and divided from each other by seven months, having five (months) in the middle.[k] For the seventh month of the equinox is potentially [l] also the first, since the creation of the world took place in this (month) because all things were full at

[a] See the verse cited in the preceding note.

[b] Arm. *anznsteli*, not found in the large Arm. dictionary, is composed of the privative particle *an* and a derivative of *znestel* "to subside"; Aucher renders, "indesinens."

[c] ἐκάθισεν (as in LXX).

[d] See notes on *QG* ii. 17.

[e] Philo here means Nisan (March–April), the seventh month in the civil calendar beginning with Tishri (Sept.–Oct.).

[f] Lit. "again."

[g] ὁμωνυμία.

[h] ἐν τῇ γενεθλίᾳ.

[i] τοῦ δικαίου = Noah. Philo takes Gen. vii. 11 and viii. 4 to mean that the beginning of the flood in Noah's 600th year and its subsidence in his 601st year coincided with his birthday.

[j] *i.e.* the flood subsided in Tishri, the seventh month in the festival calendar beginning with Nisan.

[k] Or "an interval of five months," as Aucher renders. Actually there are five months between Tishri and Nisan in both calendars.

[l] δυνάμει.

this time. Similarly the (month of the) autumnal equinox, (which) is the seventh in time,[a] is the first in honour,[b] the seventh having its beginning from the air.[c] Accordingly, the flood takes place in the seventh month, not in time but in nature,[d] having (as) its beginning the vernal equinox.

32. (Gen. viii. 5) Why does (Scripture) say, "In the tenth[e] month, on the first (day of the month), the summits of the mountains appeared"?

Just as among numbers the decad is the limit of the ones[f] (and is) the complete and perfect number, being the cycle and end[g] of the ones and the beginning and cycle of the tens and of an infinity[h] of numbers, so the Creator thought it good[i] that when the flood had ceased, the summits of the mountains should appear through the perfect and complete number ten.

33. (Gen. viii. 6) Why did the righteous man (Noah) open the window of the ark after forty days?

Note carefully that the theologian[j] uses the same num-

[a] κατὰ χρόνον. [b] κατὰ τιμήν.

[c] Or "climate." The original probably was τοῦ ἑβδόμου ἐξ ἀέρος ἔχοντος τὴν ἀρχήν. Three explanations of this puzzling statement occur to me: (1) The Arm. translator read ἀέρος for Philo's ἔαρος (as in the last sentence of the section); (2) Philo is alluding to the etymology of the first Heb. month *Nisan*, as though from *nissa'* (*niphal* ptc. of *ns'*) meaning "lifted up," "exalted"; (3) Philo connects the seventh month Tishri with the beginning of the rainy season in Palestine. Aucher, construing less accurately, renders, "septimi ex aere habens principium." See my note in *Classical Philology* 39 (1945), 257-258.

[d] κατὰ φύσιν.

[e] So Heb.; LXX and Arm. O.T. have "eleventh."

[f] *Cf. De Congressu* 90 ὥσπερ δεκὰς ἀριθμῶν τῶν ἀπὸ μονάδος ἐστὶ πέρας τελειότατον.

[g] κύκλος καὶ τέλος. [h] ἀπειρίας. [i] ἠξίωσε.

[j] ὁ θεολόγος (Moses, *cf. De Vita Mos.* ii. 115).

ber of the course of the flood [a] as of its cessation and the complete remedying of the disaster.[b] And so, in the seventh month on the twenty-seventh (day) in the six hundredth year of Noah's life, that is, on his birthday, the flood began in the spring. Moreover, in the seventh month on the twenty-seventh (day) the ark rested upon the summits of the mountains at the autumnal equinox. And from three things it is clear that the flood became invisible [c] in the six hundred and first year, also in the seventh month on the twenty-seventh (day); for just [d] a year afterwards it was to subside,[e] establishing the earth as it was at (the time of) destruction,[f] blossoming and flourishing in the spring and being full of all (kinds of) fruit. Moreover, it was in forty days that the streams of the flood came, when the cataracts were opened in heaven and the fountains broke forth from beneath the earth. And again, the hope of stability returned [g] in forty days after a long cessation,[h] when he (Noah) opened the window. Again, the duration of the remaining [i] of the flood was a hundred and fifty days, while its diminution was (also) a hundred and fifty days, so that one must wonder at the equality,[j] for the disaster [k] increased and ceased in an equal number (of days), as (does) the moon. For in the same number (of days) it takes its increase from its conjunction [l] until it becomes full, and its waning when it returns to its conjunction after first having been full. Similarly, in divine visitations[m] the

[a] *Cf. QG* ii. 14 on Gen. vii. 12.

[b] *κατὰ τὴν πᾶσαν θεραπείαν τὴν τοῦ κακοῦ.*

[c] *ἀόρατος* or *ἀφανής.* [d] *εὐθύς* (?).

[e] *ἡμερωθήσεται.*

[f] *i.e.* restoring the earth to the condition it was in before the flood.

[g] Syntax and meaning slightly uncertain.

[h] *κατάπαυσιν.*

[i] Lit. = *ἡ διαμονὴ ἡ τοῦ μένειν vel sim.* Probably the original had merely *ἡ διαμονή.*

[j] Or "exact correspondence"—*τὴν ἰσότητα.*

[k] *τὸ κακόν.*

[l] *ἀπὸ συνόδου, i.e.* the new moon.

[m] *ἐν τοῖς θεηλάτοις <κακοῖς>.*

Creator preserves due order [a] and drives out disorder [b] from the divine borders.[c]

*34. (Gen. viii. 6) What is the " window of the ark " which the righteous man (Noah) opened ?

The literal meaning [d] does not admit difficulty or doubt, for it is clear. But as for the deeper meaning,[e] the following is to be said. The several parts of the senses [f] are likened to the windows of the body.[g] For through them as through a window there enters into the mind [h] the apprehension of sense-perceptible things,[i] and, again, the mind stretches out to seize these through them. And a part of the windows, by which I mean the senses, is sight,[j] because it is especially related to the soul [k] and also is familiar [l] with light, the most beautiful of existing things, and a ministrant of things divine.[m] And this same (sense) first cut and made [n] the road to philosophy.[o] For when it sees the movements of the sun and moon, and the wanderings of the other planets,[p] and the inerrant revolution of the entire heaven,[q] and the order which is above all description,[r] and the harmony,[s] and the one true certain Creator

[a] τάξιν.

[b] Probably ἀταξίαν, *cf. De Plantatione* 3 εἰς τάξιν ἐξ ἀταξίας . . . ἄγων ὁ κοσμοπλάστης.

[c] ἐκ τῶν θείων ὅρων.

[d] τὸ ῥητόν.

[e] τὸ πρὸς διάνοιαν.

[f] τὰ τῶν αἰσθήσεων μέρη.

[g] ταῖς τοῦ σώματος θυρίσιν ἐξομοιοῦται.

[h] εἰς τὸν νοῦν.

[i] ἡ τῶν αἰσθητῶν κατάληψις.

[j] ἡ ὅρασις.

[k] τῆς ψυχῆς μάλιστα συγγενής.

[l] οἰκεία.

[m] ὑπηρέτης τῶν θείων.

[n] τεμοῦσα ἀπηργάσατο. Greek frag. has simply ἔτεμε.

[o] τὴν εἰς φιλοσοφίαν ὁδόν.

[p] τὰς τῶν ἄλλων πλανητῶν περιφοράς. Greek frag. has τὰς τῶν ἀστέρων περιόδους.

[q] τὴν ἀπλανῆ περιφορὰν τὴν τοῦ σύμπαντος οὐρανοῦ.

[r] τὴν παντὸς τοῦ λόγου κρείττονα τάξιν.

[s] τὴν ἁρμονίαν.

of the world,[a] it reports to its only[b] sovereign, reason,[c] what it has seen. And this (reason), seeing with a sharp eye both these (celestial phenomena) and through them the higher paradigmatic forms[d] and the cause of all things, immediately apprehends[e] them and genesis and providence,[f] for it reasons[g] that visible nature[h] did not come into being by itself[i]; for it would be impossible for harmony and order[j] and measure[k] and proportions of truth[l] and such concord[m] and real prosperity[n] and happiness to come about by themselves.[o] But it is necessary that there be some Creator and Father,[p] a pilot and charioteer,[q] who both begat[r] and wholly[s] preserves and guards[t] the things begotten.

[a] τὸν τοῦ κόσμου μόνον ἀληθῆ καὶ ἀψευδῆ κοσμοποιόν. Greek frag. has τόν . . . μόνον ἀψευδέστατον κοσμοποιόν.

[b] Aucher, taking Arm. *miayn*=μόνῳ to refer to the subject, renders, "retulit solus"; the Greek frag. omits the word.

[c] Aucher, construing differently, renders, "uni principi consiliorum"; the Greek frag. has ἡγεμόνι λογισμῷ, which is probably correct.

[d] τὰ ἀνώτερα παραδειγματικὰ εἴδη. This text is preferable to that of the Greek frag. παραδείγματι καὶ εἴδει διὰ τούτων; Mangey correctly emended to παραδειγματικὰ εἴδη but wrongly deleted διά.

[e] καταλαμβάνει or perhaps εἰς ἔννοιαν ἦλθε, as in Greek frag.

[f] γένεσιν καὶ πρόνοιαν.

[g] λογισάμενος. Aucher here punctuates wrongly.

[h] ἡ ὁρατὴ φύσις. Greek frag. has ὅλη φύσις.

[i] Probably αὐτοματισθεῖσα, as in Greek frag.

[j] ἁρμονίαν καὶ τάξιν.

[k] λόγους. Greek frag. has λόγον.

[l] ἀναλογίαν ἀληθείας (or ἀκριβείας). Greek frag. has only ἀναλογίαν.

[m] συμφωνίαν.

[n] τὴν τῷ ὄντι εὐοδίαν (?) εὐδαιμονίας. Greek frag. has τῷ ὄντι εὐδαιμονίαν.

[o] See note *i*.

[p] ποιητήν τινα καὶ πατέρα.

[q] κυβερνήτην τε καὶ ἡνίοχον.

[r] ἐγέννησε or γεγέννηκε. The latter is found in Greek frag. p. 70 Harris; Greek frag. p. 22 Harris has πεποίηκε.

[s] ὁλόκληρα; Greek frag. omits.

[t] σώζων φυλάττει; Greek frag. has only σώζει.

35. (Gen. viii. 7) Why did (Noah) first send the raven?

As for the literal meaning,[a] the raven is said to be a sort of heralding [b] and fulfilling [c] creature. Wherefore down to our own time many observantly attend to its flight and its voice when it caws [d] (as though) indicating something hidden.[e] But as for the deeper meaning,[f] the raven is a blackish and reckless [g] and swift creature, which is a symbol of evil,[h] for it brings night and darkness upon the soul, and it is very swift, going out to meet all things in the world at one time. In the second place, (it leads) [i] to the destruction of those who would seize it,[j] and is very reckless, for it produces arrogance [k] and shameless impudence. And [l] to this is opposed virtue,[m] (which is) luminous [n] and steady [o] and modest and reverent by nature. And so it was right to expel beyond the borders whatever residue of darkness there was in the mind which might have led to folly.[p]

36. (Gen. viii. 7) Why, after going out, did the raven

[a] τὸ ῥητόν.
[b] ἀγγελικόν τι.
[c] Arm. *včarem*=συντελεῖν, πληροῦν, περαίνειν, λύειν, etc.; Aucher renders, "functioni addictum."
[d] Var. "calls."
[e] Aucher, punctuating differently, renders, "volatum atque garritum suum (*sic*) multi expectant, dijudicantes aliquid significare de incognitis rebus."
[f] τὸ πρὸς διάνοιαν.
[g] θρασύ or τολμηρόν.
[h] σύμβολον τῆς κακίας.
[i] The Arm. is probably incomplete, and the Greek original can only be guessed.
[j] Meaning doubtful; Arm. *ounołaçn* is *nomen agentis* of verb *ounim*=ἔχειν, κρατεῖν, etc.; Aucher renders, "in exitium aucupantium."
[k] ἀλαζονίαν *vel sim.*; Aucher's "superbia" should be "superbiam."
[l] Arm. has a superfluous "for" after "and."
[m] ἀρετή.
[n] φωτοειδής.
[o] βέβαιος.
[p] ἀφροσύνην or "wickedness"—πονηρίαν or φαυλότητα.

not return again, for not yet was any part of the earth dried ? [a]

The passage is to be interpreted allegorically,[b] for unrighteousness [c] is the adversary [d] of the light of righteousness [e] so that it considers being very merry [f] with its relative,[g] the flood, more desirable than the good works of the virtuous man.[h] For unrighteousness is a lover of confusion and corruption.[i]

37. (Gen. viii. 7) Why has (Scripture) used enallage,[j] saying, " until the water was dried from the earth," for water is not dried from the earth, but the earth is dried of water ?

It allegorizes [k] in these words, indicating by the instance of the water the immeasurableness of the passions.[l] When stuffed and swollen with these, the soul is corrupted.[m] And it is saved [n] when these (passions) are dried up.[o] For then they are not able to injure the soul in any way, being in a certain sense [p] weakened and dead.

38. (Gen. viii. 8) Why does (Noah) a second time send a dove both " from himself " [q] and to see whether the

[a] Philo here slightly alters the LXX, which reads *οὐχ ὑπέστρεψεν ἕως τοῦ ξηρανθῆναι τὸ ὕδωρ ἀπὸ τῆς γῆς*, though in the next section he follows the LXX literally ; Heb. has " and it went out, going and returning, until, etc."

[b] *ἀλληγορίαν δέχεται ὁ τόπος.* [c] *ἀδικία.*

[d] *ἀντίπαλος* or *ἀντίμαχος.* [e] *τῆς δικαιοσύνης.*

[f] *περιχαρής.* [g] *σὺν τῷ συγγενεῖ.*

[h] *τὰ ἀγαθὰ ἔργα τὰ τοῦ σπουδαίου.*

[i] *συγχύσεως καὶ φθορᾶς.* [j] *ἐνήλλαξε.*

[k] *ἀλληγορεῖ.* [l] *τὴν τῶν παθῶν ἀμετρίαν.*

[m] Or " destroyed "—*διαφθείρεται.* [n] *σώζεται.*

[o] Arm. uses two synonyms for " dried." [p] *τρόπον τινά.*

[q] LXX says that Noah sent the dove *ὀπίσω αὐτοῦ*, *i.e.* after the raven ; so the Arm. O.T. Philo here seems to follow the Heb., which has *mē'ittô* " from him(self)." Less plausible is Aucher's suggestion that the reflexive pronoun is based on Gen. viii. 9 (see below, § 40), which says that Noah brought the dove " to himself " into the ark.

water had ceased, which is not said in the case of the raven?

First of all, the dove is a clean creature,[a] and then it is tame and manageable [b] and a fellow-inhabitant [c] of man. Therefore it received the honour of being offered on the altar among the sacrifices.[d] Therefore (Scripture) said in a definite and positive manner,[e] " he sent it from himself," making it appear (that it was) a fellow-inhabitant. But by seeing " whether the water had ceased," (he made it appear that it was) sociable and like-minded.[f] And these (birds), the raven and the dove, are symbols of vice and virtue.[g] For the one is homeless, hearthless, stateless,[h] wild,[i] implacable [j] and unsociable.[k] But virtue is a matter of[l] humaneness[m] and sociability, and it is helpful.[n] This the virtuous man[o] sends (as) a messenger of healthful and salutary things,[p] wishing to learn through this whence to know.[q] But this (dove) like a messenger renders a true service,[r] in order that he may be careful of injurious things and may receive helpful things with great zeal and willingness.

[a] *καθαρὸν ζῷον.* [b] *οἰκεία καὶ χειροήθης.*
[c] *σύνοικος.* [d] *ἐν ταῖς θυσίαις.*
[e] Lit. " sealing and affirming."
[f] *κοινὴν καὶ ὁμογνώμονα vel sim.*
[g] *σύμβολα κακίας καὶ ἀρετῆς.*
[h] *ἄοικος καὶ ἀνέστιος καὶ ἄπολις, cf. De Virtutibus* 190 *ἄοικος . . . καὶ ἄπολις ὁ φαῦλος.*
[i] *ἀνήμερος* or *ἄγριος.*
[j] *ἀκατάλλακτος* or *ἄσπονδος.* [k] *ἀκοινώνητος.*
[l] Aucher more freely renders, " colit."
[m] *φιλανθρωπίας.* [n] *ὠφέλιμος* or *συμφέρων.*
[o] *ὁ σπουδαῖος.*
[p] *ὑγιεινῶν καὶ σωτηρίων.* Aucher renders, " pro rebus sanis ac salutaribus."
[q] This seems to be the literal meaning of the obscure and probably corrupt Arm. (unless the corruption lies in the lost Greek original). Aucher's rendering makes better sense but takes liberties with the Arm. text, " volens per ipsam edoceri condignum."
[r] Lit. " reports a true favour "—*ἀληθῆ ἀναγγέλλει χάριν.*

*39. (Gen. viii. 9) Why did the dove, not finding a resting-place [a] for its feet, return to him (Noah) ?

Is not this, then, clear evidence that through the symbols [b] of the raven and the dove vice and virtue [c] are shown ? For, behold, the dove, after being sent out, does not find a resting-place. How, then, could the raven, which went out first while there was still an excessive flood,[d] find a place to rest ? For the raven was neither an *artawaza-hawd* [e] nor an ibis nor yet one of those (birds) that dwell in the water. But it signifies [f] that vice, going out to the risen streams of passions and desires,[g] which inundate and destroy both souls and (human) lives, welcomes [h] them and consorts with them as with intimates and relatives [i] with whom it dwells. But virtue, being vexed [j] at the first sight (of these things), immediately springs away without returning again, and does not find a resting-place for its feet, that is to say, it does not find any standing-place worthy of it. For what greater evil could there be than that virtue should not find any place in the soul, even the smallest, as a place to rest and remain ?

40. (Gen. viii. 9) What is the meaning of the words, " Stretching forth his hand, he took it and brought it in to himself " ?

The literal meaning [k] is plain. But the deeper meaning [l] is to be exactly determined.[m] The wise man [n] uses virtue [o] as an inspector [p] and messenger [q] of affairs. And when

[a] ἀνάπαυσιν, as in LXX.

[b] διὰ τῶν συμβόλων.

[c] κακία καὶ ἀρετή.

[d] Arm. *aweli arkaçk^c jrheḷeḷin* almost certainly renders ὑπερβολὴ τοῦ κατακλυσμοῦ. Aucher less accurately renders, " aerumna diluvii."

[e] Some sort of water-bird, according to the Arm. gloss ; Aucher renders, " cygnus." Procopius omits.

[f] αἰνίττεται.

[g] παθῶν καὶ ἐπιθυμιῶν.

[h] ἀσπάζεται.

[i] ὡς μετ' οἰκείων καὶ συγγενῶν.

[j] δυσχεραίνουσα *vel sim.*

[k] τὸ ῥητόν.

[l] τὸ πρὸς διάνοιαν.

[m] ἀκριβωτέον.

[n] ὁ σοφός or ἀστεῖος.

[o] ἀρετῇ.

[p] ἐφόρῳ.

[q] ἀγγέλῳ.

he sees them to be natures worthy of himself,[a] he remains and dwells with them, correcting them and making them better. For wisdom [b] is most common, most equal and most helpful.[c] But when it sees them perversely increase in the opposite direction and being altogether uncontrolled and wilful, it returns to its own place. And virtue admits it, stretching forth its hand in word,[d] and in deed [e] opening the whole mind and unfolding [f] and expanding it through the perfect and even and full number [g] with all willingness.[h] Nor then when he sent it forth from himself did he separate it from himself in order to survey the natures of others [i] but in the manner in which the sun sends its rays to earth, making all things bright. For in the great strength of its light there is no separation or division.[j]

*41. (Gen. viii. 10) Why, after holding back [k] still another seven days, did he (Noah) again send out the dove ?

(This was) an excellent manner of life. For although at first he sees that their natures are hard,[l] he does not give up [m] hope of their changing for the better. But just as a good physician does not immediately apply treatment to

[a] *φύσεις ἀξίας ἑαυτοῦ.* [b] *σοφία.*

[c] *κοινοτάτη καὶ ἰσοτάτη καὶ ὠφελιμωτάτη.* [d] *λόγῳ.*

[e] *ἔργῳ.* [f] Or " resolving," " explaining."

[g] *διὰ τοῦ τελείου καὶ ἀρτίου καὶ πλήρους ἀριθμοῦ*, *i.e.* the decad. The same three adjectives are applied to human nature (*φύσις*) in *De Ebrietate* 135.

[h] *μετὰ προθυμίας πάσης.*

[i] *κατασκοπεῖν τὰς τῶν ἄλλων φύσεις.*

[j] Text and meaning uncertain. Arm. *sastkoutᶜiun* usually means " strength " but may also render *ἀποτομή* ; in one MS. it is nominative, in another, genitive. Arm. *yoyž*, here translated " great," normally means " very " ; it may possibly be an anomalous locative of the noun *oyž* " strength." Aucher renders, " quia universae ejus lucis est minime disjungi."

[k] Probably *ἐπισχών*, as in LXX. [l] *φύσεις σκληράς.*

[m] Lit. " cut off " ; *cf.* Greek parallel *προανατέμνῃ τὴν ὁδόν.*

reach the disease all at once but allows nature first to open the way to recovery,[a] and then uses health-giving and salutary drugs (as) a physician, so the virtuous man[b] uses principles[c] which are in accordance with the laws[d] of philosophy.[e] And the hebdomad[f] is holy and sacred[g]; and it was in accordance with this[h] that the Father of the universe, when He created the world, is said to have seen His work. But the seeing of the world and the things in it is nothing else than philosophy, a most glorious and choice part,[i] which is attained by scientific wisdom,[j] which contains in itself an activity most necessary for seeing.

42. (Gen. viii. 11) What is the meaning of the words, "The dove returned again to him at evening, holding an olive-leaf, a dry branch[k] in its mouth"?

All (these) are chosen symbols and tests[l]—the "returning again," the "at evening," the "holding an olive-leaf," the "dry branch," the "oil"[m] and the "in its mouth." But the several symbols must be studied in detail.[n] Now the return is distinguished[o] from the earlier (flight). For

[a] εἰς σωτηρίαν.

[b] ὁ σπουδαῖος.

[c] Or "words"—λόγοις.

[d] νόμοις or "doctrines"—δόγμασι.

[e] τῆς φιλοσοφίας. The Greek parallel has λόγοις κατὰ φιλοσοφίαν καὶ δόγμασιν.

[f] Here meaning both the number seven and the week.

[g] ἱερὰ καὶ ἁγία.

[h] Or "at this (interval of time)"—κατ' αὐτήν.

[i] εὐκλεέστατον καὶ δοκιμώτατον μέρος.

[j] The Arm. literally = ἐπιστήμη σοφίας; Aucher renders, "sapientia."

[k] LXX has φύλλον ἐλαίας κάρφος translating Heb. "olive-leaf freshly plucked"; Arm. O.T. has šiļ "dry-stick" (= LXX κάρφος); Aucher's rendering "ramum gracilem" somewhat obscures the point.

[l] Perhaps the original had "approved symbols," as Aucher conjectures.

[m] Implied by the olive-leaf.

[n] ἀκριβωτέα.

[o] διαφέρει.

the latter brought [a] the report [b] of a nature altogether corrupt and rebellious, and one destroyed by the flood, (that is) by great ignorance and lack of education.[c] But the other [d] repents of its beginning. And to find repentance [e] is not easy but is a very difficult and laborious task. For these reasons it comes at evening, having passed the whole day from early morning until evening in inspection,[f] in word [g] by passing over various places but in deed [h] by looking over and inspecting the parts of its nature [i] and in seeing them clearly from beginning to end,[j] for the evening is a symbol of the end.[k] And the third symbol is the "bearing a leaf." The leaf is a small part of the plant. And similar to this is the beginning to repent.[l] For the beginning of improvement [m] gives a slight indication, as if it were a leaf, that it is to be guarded and also can be shaken off. But [n] there is great hope withal that it will attain correction of its ways.[o] The fourth symbol is that the leaf was of no other tree than the olive. And oil is the material [p] of light. For evil, as I have said, is profound darkness, but virtue [q] is a most radiant splendour; and repentance [r] is the beginning of light. But do not think that the beginning of repentance is already in blossoming and growing things; only while they are still dry and arid do they have a seminal principle.[s] Wherefore the fifth symbol is that when it (the dove) came it bore a "dry branch." And the sixth symbol is that the dry branch

[a] Lit. "held." [b] Or "announcement."

[c] ὑπὸ μεγάλης ἀμαθίας καὶ ἀπαιδευσίας.

[d] *i.e.* the returning dove. [e] μετάνοιαν.

[f] ἐπισκοπῇ or ἐπισκέψει. [g] λόγῳ μέν. [h] ἔργῳ δέ.

[i] τὰ τῆς ἐκείνου φύσεως μέρη. What Arm. *aynorik* = ἐκείνου refers to is not clear. [j] ἀπ' ἀρχῆς εἰς τέλος.

[k] Arm. here uses a different word for "end" which also = τέλος. [l] μετανοεῖν.

[m] Lit. "becoming good" (or "better").

[n] Why Aucher here renders the adversative conjunction *bayç* as "quominus" I do not understand.

[o] κατόρθωσιν τῶν ἐπιτηδευμάτων. [p] ὕλη.

[q] ἀρετή. [r] ἡ μετάνοια. [s] σπερματικὸν λόγον.

was " in its mouth," since six is the first perfect number[a]; for virtue bears in its mouth, that is, in its speech,[b] the seeds of wisdom and justice[c] and generally of goodness of soul.[d] And not only does it bear these but it also gives a share in them[e] to outsiders,[f] offering water to their souls and watering with repentance their desire for sin.

43. (Gen. viii. 11) Why (does Scripture say that) Noah knew that the water had ceased from the earth ?

The literal meaning[g] is clear. For if the leaf had been taken from the water, it would have been still damp and moist. But now it was dry ; and (Scripture) says that it was a " dry stick,"[h] as though it had been dried above a dried earth. But as for the deeper meaning[i]—the wise man[j] takes it as a symbol of repentance,[k] and the bringing of the leaf as preventing the occurrence[l] of great ignorance,[m] even though it was no longer flourishing and blossoming but, on the contrary, was a " dry stick," for the reasons previously stated. And at the same time one must admire the Father for His great goodness and kindness.[n] For though destruction had overtaken earthly creatures through their excess of injustice and impiety,[o] nevertheless there remained a residue of antiquity[p] and of that which had been in the beginning[q] and a small and light seed of ancient virtues.[r] And no less is it a symbol of the fact

[a] τέλειος ἀριθμός (in the Pythagorean sense).
[b] ἐν τῷ λόγῳ.
[c] σοφίας (or φρονήσεως) καὶ δικαιοσύνης.
[d] ἀγαθότητος τῆς ψυχῆς.
[e] κοινωνίαν.
[f] Or " laymen "—τοῖς ἰδιώταις.
[g] τὸ ῥητόν.
[h] κάρφος, see note *k* on p. 119.
[i] τὸ πρὸς διάνοιαν.
[j] ὁ σοφός or ἀστεῖος.
[k] σύμβολον τῆς μετανοίας.
[l] Or " blows "—βολάς.
[m] ἀμαθίας.
[n] τῆς λίαν ἀγαθότητος καὶ χρηστότητος.
[o] ἀδικίας καὶ ἀσεβείας.
[p] ὑπόλειμμα τοῦ ἀρχαίου.
[q] ἐν τῇ ἀρχῇ.
[r] μικρὸν καὶ λεπτὸν σπέρμα ἀρχαίων ἀρετῶν ; Aucher renders, " virtutum majorum semen exile," omitting *azazoun* = λεπτόν, which refers to the " dry stick."

that the memory of the good persons [a] who were created in the beginning is not altogether destroyed. Wherefore the following statement was given as law [b] by some prophet [c] who was a disciple and friend of Moses: "If Almighty God [d] had not left us a seed, we should have become like the blind and barren," [e] so as not to know the good and not be able to beget offspring. And blindness and barrenness are called in the ancestral language [f] of the Chaldaeans "Sodom" and "Gomorrah." [g]

44. (Gen. viii. 12) Why did he (Noah) a third time send out the dove after another seven days, and why did it not again return to him?

The not returning to him applies in word to the dove but in deed [h] to virtue.[i] This is not a symbol of alienation,[j] for it did not at that time,[k] as I have said, separate itself, but in the manner of a ray of light it was sent to see the natures of others. But at that time, not finding any who were receiving discipline,[l] it again returned and hastened straight to him alone. But now it is no longer the possession [m] of one alone but is the common good of all those who wish to take the outpouring of wisdom as if from the earth and from a very early time have thirsted for the knowledge of wisdom.

[a] Or "good things"—τῶν ἀγαθῶν.

[b] ὅδε ὁ λόγος ἐνομοθετέθη.

[c] Isaiah i. 9.

[d] Heb., LXX and Arm. O.T. have "Lord of hosts."

[e] Heb., LXX and Arm. O.T. have "like Sodom and Gomorrah."

[f] τῇ πατρίᾳ γλώττῃ.

[g] *Cf. De Somniis* ii. 192, where "Sodom" alone is etymologized as τύφλωσις or στείρωσις, and "Gomorrah" as μέτρον.

[h] λόγῳ μέν . . . ἔργῳ δέ.

[i] τῆς ἀρετῆς.

[j] σύμβολον τῆς ἀλλοτριώσεως.

[k] *i.e.* the second flight, *cf.* § 42.

[l] Arm. *xrat*= παιδεία, νουθέτησις, ἐπιστήμη, etc.

[m] κτῆμα.

45. (Gen. viii. 13) Why did the water cease [a] from the earth in the six hundred and first year of Noah's life [b] in the first (month) on the first [c] of the month ?

This "first" in connexion with cessation [d] can be said either of the month or of man, and it takes account [e] of both. For though the cessation of the water is to be understood [f] (as taking place) in the first month, we are to suppose that the seventh month is to be understood as meant, namely that (which is first) in respect of the equinox, for the same month is both the first and the seventh [g]; this amounts to saying that the first in nature and power [h] is the seventh in time. Accordingly, in another place [i] (Scripture) says, "This month [j] is for you the beginning of months; it is first in the months of the year." Thus it calls "first" that (month) which is first in nature and power but is seventh in temporal number, for the equinox has first and highest rank among the annual seasons.[k] But if "first" is said of the man it will be said most properly,[l] for the righteous man [m] is truly and particularly first, as the skipper [n] is first in the ship, and the ruler [o] is first in the state.[p] But he [q] is first not only in virtue [r] but also in order,[s] for he himself was the beginning and first in the regeneration [t] of the second human seed. Moreover, it is

[a] So LXX, ἐξέλιπεν. Heb. has "dried up."

[b] "Of Noah's life" is in LXX but not in Heb.

[c] Lit. "on the one," as in LXX and Heb.

[d] κατὰ ἔκλειψιν.

[e] λόγον.

[f] ἀκουστέον.

[g] Depending on whether one uses the vernal or autumnal calendar, *cf.* above, § 17 on Gen. vii. 11 and § 31 on Gen. viii. 4.

[h] Or "rank"—δύναμιν.

[i] Ex. xii. 2.

[j] *i.e.* Nisan (March–April).

[k] The Greek original seems to be τὴν πρώτην καὶ ἀρίστην τάξιν δι' ἔτους ἐν τοῖς χρόνοις, but the meaning is not quite clear.

[l] κυριώτατα.

[m] ὁ δίκαιος.

[n] ὁ κυβερνήτης.

[o] ὁ ἄρχων or δυνάστης or ἡγεμών.

[p] ἐν τῇ πόλει.

[q] *i.e.* Noah.

[r] ἀρετῇ.

[s] τάξει.

[t] κατὰ τὴν παλιγγενεσίαν, *i.e.* of the human race after the flood.

excellently stated in this passage that the flood came in the lifetime of the righteous man and again subsided and returned to its former state. Wherefore, when the flood came, he alone was destined to live with all his household, and when the evil had passed, he alone was destined to be found on earth before the regeneration—his later life.[a] And both then and now this has been not inaptly [b] attested. For whereas he desires only true life, one that is in accord with virtue, others eagerly pursue death because of deathly evils. Accordingly, it was necessarily [c] in the six hundred and first year that the evil ceased, for in the number six there was corruption [d] and in the number one there was salvation,[e] for the number one is most soul-begetting [f] and most able to form life.[g] Wherefore the receding of the water took place at the new moon in order that the monad might have pre-eminence in being honoured above both months and years,[h] when God would save those who were upon the earth. For one who is outstanding in character [i] the Hebrews call " Noah " in their ancestral tongue, while the Greeks say " righteous."[j] But he is not removed from and freed of bodily necessities,[k] for although he is not under (another's) authority [l] and has authority [m] himself, nevertheless he is obliged to die,[n] and so the number six is associated with the monad. For the flood re-

[a] Variant " their later life " ; as Aucher observes, both readings are obscure ; " life " is in apposition with " regeneration," but seems to have the force of a genitive.

[b] *οὐκ ἀπὸ σκοποῦ.*

[c] *ἀνάγκῃ.*

[d] Or " destruction."

[e] *σωτηρία.*

[f] *ψυχογονιμώτατος*, *cf. De Vita Mos.* i. 97.

[g] *ζωοπλαστεῖν.*

[h] Aucher renders, " in mensibus et annis," but Arm. *k'an* has comparative force.

[i] *ἐκλεκτὸν ἦθος vel sim.*

[j] *δίκαιον*, *cf. De Abrahamo* 27. Philo professes to etymologize the Hebrew name " Noah " but really renders the adjective applied to Noah in Scripture.

[k] *οὐκ ἐξαιρεῖται οὐδ' ἐλευθεροῦται σωματικῶν ἀναγκῶν.*

[l] *ἀρχῇ* or *ἐξουσίᾳ.*

[m] Lit. " is a ruler."

[n] Lit. " mixed with dying."

ceded not in one (year) viewed separately by itself, but in six, that (number) proper to the body and inequality,[a] since the number six is the first oblong number.[b] For this reason (Scripture) says "in the six hundred and first (year)" and "righteous in his generation."[c] Not in that (generation) which is universal[d] nor in that which was to be destroyed was he righteous, but in respect of a certain one. For the comparison is with his own generation. But praiseworthy also is that (generation) which God singled out and deemed worthy of life above every generation, setting a limit[e] to it by which it was to be as the end[f] of generations and ages,[g] that is, of those which must perish, and as the beginning of those which were to come afterward. Most of all, however, is it proper to praise him who stretched up with his whole body and looked (upward) because of his kinship[h] with God.

46. (Gen. viii. 13) What is the meaning of the words, "Noah opened the covering[i] of the ark"?

The literal meaning[j] needs no exposition. But as for the deeper meaning,[k] since the ark is symbolically[l] the body, the covering of the body must be thought of as whatever protects[m] and preserves it and closely guards[n] its power,[o] (namely) pleasure.[p] For by pleasure it is truly[q] preserved and sustained in measure[r] and in accordance

[a] τῇ ἑξάδι τῇ τῷ σώματι οἰκείᾳ καὶ τῇ ἀνισότητι, *cf. Leg. All.* i. 4 on the six movements of animals.

[b] ἑτερομήκης, *i.e.* produced by the multiplying of unequal factors, see above, § 12 notes, and below, *QG* iii. 38.

[c] On this phrase, occurring in Gen. vi. 9, Philo does not comment above.

[d] καθολική.

[e] ὅρον.

[f] τὸ τέλος.

[g] γενεῶν καὶ αἰώνων.

[h] οἰκειώσεως.

[i] τὴν στέγην (so LXX).

[j] τὸ ῥητόν.

[k] τὸ πρὸς διάνοιαν.

[l] συμβολικῶς.

[m] σκεπάζει or καλύπτει.

[n] Lit. "long guards" but Arm. *yerkar* here probably reflects the preverbal particle δια- in διαφυλάττει; Aucher renders more literally, "diu conservat."

[o] τὴν δύναμιν.

[p] ἡ ἡδονή.

[q] ὄντως.

[r] μέτροις.

with nature,[a] just as it is disintegrated[b] by pain.[c] Accordingly, when the mind[d] is smitten by heavenly pleasure,[e] it desires to leap upward and cut off all forms of (sensual) pleasure, in order that it may remove from its midst that which covers it with a veil and darkens it like a shadow, and that it may be able to bring sense-perception[f] to naked and incorporeal natures.[g]

*47. (Gen. viii. 14) Why was the earth dried up in the seventh month,[h] on the twenty-seventh (day)?

Do you see that a little before[i] (Scripture) spoke of the first month, and now of the seventh? For the seventh is the same in time, as I have said,[j] but in nature[k] is first in so far as it is connected with the equinox. Moreover, excellently[l] did the advent of the flood fall in the seventh month, on the twenty-seventh (day), and the letting up and subsiding of the flood a year later in the same seventh month and on the same day.[m] For it was at the equinox that the flood came, and at the very same time[n] (came) the return of life. Concerning the causes of this we have already written. But the seventh month is homonymous[o] with such months and days. And again it was on the twenty-seventh day that the ark rested upon the mountains. This is the month which is seventh in nature but first in time, which is at the equinox. So that it is at the equinoxes that distinctions[p] (are made) through the seventh months and twenty-seventh days.[q] For the flood

[a] κατὰ φύσιν. [b] λύεται. [c] ὑπ' ἀλγηδόνων.
[d] ὁ νοῦς. [e] ὑπ' οὐρανίας ἡδονῆς. [f] αἴσθησιν.
[g] γυμναῖς καὶ ἀσωμάτοις φύσεσι.
[h] Heb. and most LXX MSS. "second."
[i] See § 45 on Gen. viii. 13.
[j] See above, §§ 17, 45. [k] φύσει. [l] παγκάλως.
[m] See § 17 on Gen. vii. 11.
[n] Arm. *andren* usu. = εὐθύς or αὐτίκα but here seems to have the meaning given above. [o] ὁμώνυμος.
[p] διαιρέσεις or διακρίσεις, or perhaps "choices"—αἱρέσεις or ἐκλογαί.
[q] Meaning not quite clear to me.

(occurred) in the seventh month, in which the vernal equinox falls, and which is the seventh in time and the first in nature.[a] But with the same number [b] was the return and retreat (of the water) when the ark came to rest on the summits of the mountains ; this, again, was in the seventh month, not in the same one, but in that which falls at the autumnal equinox, which is seventh in nature but first in time.[c] Moreover, the complete remedying of the evil,[d] when the evil was dried up, similarly (took place) in the seventh month, on the twenty-seventh (day), at the vernal equinox. For both the beginning of the flood and its end had previously [e] received a limit-fixing [f] at the same time, but the middle of his later life was the middle time.[g] And more exactly [h] is to be explained what is said (in Scripture) : the flood together with its remedying was a —— [i] year. For its beginning was in the six hundredth year, in the seventh month, on the twenty-seventh day, so that the interval of time was a complete year, taking its beginning from the vernal equinox and similarly ending at the same time, at the vernal equinox. For, as I have said, as they had corrupted earthly things when filled with fruits, so, when those who had used these fruits had perished, and (the survivors) were released and delivered from evil, the earth was again found to be full of seed-bearing things and trees which bore such fruit as spring calls forth. For He thought it right that just as the earth was when it was flooded, so, when it was dried, it should

[a] When the calendar year begins in Tishri (Sept.–Oct.).

[b] Lit. " measure."

[c] See note *a*.

[d] *i.e.* the flood.

[e] πρότερον.

[f] Arm. *sahmanadrout'iun* = ὁροθεσία, but this word seems not to be used elsewhere in Philo's works.

[g] Arm. text is obscure to me ; Aucher renders, " medietas autem vitae reparatae, medii temporis." The Arm. glossator explains that " in this interval a year of Noah's life was completed."

[h] ἀκριβέστερον.

[i] Arm. *ōrabanak* " sojourning a day " may possibly reflect Gr. ἐφ' ἡμέραν " to a day," *i.e.* " exact," as Prof. L. A. Post suggests.

again show itself and yield (its produce). And do not wonder that the earth, given one day, grew all things through the power of God,[a] (such as) seeds, trees, an abundance of grass, ears, plants and fruits, and was unexpectedly full of all kinds. For also in the creation of the world, in one day out of the six He completed the production of plants. But these (later plants) were complete in themselves to start with and bore such fruits as were appropriate to the fertility of the spring season. For all things are possible[b] to God, who does not need time at all[c] in order to create.[d]

*48. (Gen. viii. 15-16). Why, after the drying up of the earth, did Noah not go out of the ark before hearing the word[e] (of God), for "The Lord God[f] said to Noah, Go out, thou and thy wife and thy sons[g] and the wives of thy sons and the other living creatures"[h]?

Righteousness[i] is reverent[j] just as, on the other hand, injustice,[k] which is its opposite, is boastful and self-satisfied.[l] And it is an evidence of reverence not to acquiesce and believe in reason[m] more than in God. And especially for him who saw the whole earth suddenly become a boundless sea was it natural and proper to think that, as was natural and possible, the evil might return again. And he also believed what was consistent[n] with this, (namely) that as he had entered the ark at God's command, so also he

[a] θείᾳ δυνάμει.

[b] Lit. "a power"—δύναμις or ἐξουσία.

[c] πάντως.

[d] ποιῆσαι.

[e] τὸν λόγον (sc. τοῦ θεοῦ).

[f] So LXX; Heb. has only "God." Aucher omits "Lord" in his rendering.

[g] So Heb. and most MSS. of LXX; some LXX MSS. and the Bohairic version have "thy sons" before "thy wife." See § 49.

[h] Here Scripture specifies beasts, birds and reptiles.

[i] δικαιοσύνη.

[j] εὐλαβής.

[k] ἀδικία.

[l] ἀλαζὼν καὶ αὐτάρεσκος.

[m] συγχωρεῖν καὶ πείθεσθαι τῷ λόγῳ.

[n] τὸ ἀκόλουθον.

should go out at God's command, for one cannot have complete power over anything if God does not guide him and first give him a command.

49. (Gen. viii. 18) Why, when they entered the ark, was the order (of words) "he and his sons" and then "and his sons' wives,"[a] but when they went out, was it changed? For (Scripture) says, "Noah went out and his wife" and then "his sons and his sons' wives."[b]

In the literal sense,[c] by "going in" (Scripture) indicates the non-begetting[d] of seed, but by "going out" it indicates generation.[e] For when they went in, the sons are mentioned together with their father, and the daughters-in-law together with their mother-in-law. But when they went out, it was as married couples, the father together with his wife, and then the several sons, each with his wife. For He[f] wishes through deeds rather than through words to teach His disciples[g] what is right for them to do. Accordingly, He said nothing by way of vocal explanation[h] to the effect that those who went in should abstain from intercourse with their wives, and that when they went out, they should sow seed in accordance with nature. This (He indicated) by the order (of words)[i] but not[j] by exclaiming and crying aloud, "After so great a destruction

[a] So Heb. and LXX in Gen. vii. 7 (not separately discussed by Philo).

[b] Here Philo's text agrees with LXX against Heb. in making Noah's wife precede his sons.

[c] τὸ ῥητόν.

[d] ἀγονίαν.

[e] Lit. "begetting of generation"; both Arm. words usu. = γένεσις.

[f] Perhaps not God but Moses is meant. Philo, like the Palestinian rabbis, sometimes treats Scripture as the word of God, sometimes as the word of Moses, God's spokesman.

[g] τοὺς γνωρίμους.

[h] φωνῇ διασαφῶν *vel sim.*

[i] *i.e.* by pairing off Noah with his wife, Noah's sons with their wives.

[j] Lit. "not only"; what the Greek construction was is not clear from the Arm.

of all those who were on earth, do not indulge in luxury, for this is not fitting or lawful. It is enough for you to receive the honour of life.[a] But to go to bed with your wives [b] is the part of those seeking and desiring sensual satisfaction." [c] For these it was fitting to sympathize with wretched humanity, as being kin to it. And at the same time they were watching for something unseen that might be impending, lest evil might overtake [d] them at some time. But in addition to this it would have been inept [e] for them now, while the living were perishing, to beget those who were not (yet) in existence and to be snared and surfeited at an unseasonable hour with sensual pleasure.[f] But after (the flood) had ceased and come to an end, and they had been saved from the evil, He again instructed them through the order (of their leaving the ark) to hasten to procreate, by specifying [g] not that men (should go out) with men nor women with women but females with males. But as for the deeper meaning,[h] this must be said. When the soul [i] is about to wash off and cleanse its sins, man should join with man, (that is) the sovereign mind [j] like a father should join with its particular thoughts [k] as with its sons, but (not join) any of the female sex, (that is) what belongs to sense.[l] For it is a time of war, in which one must separate one's ranks [m] and watch out lest they be mixed up and bring about defeat instead of victory. But when just the right time has come for the

[a] So lit., perhaps meaning "to be thought worthy of life."
[b] *i.e.* while in the ark.
[c] ἡδονῆς.
[d] φθάνῃ.
[e] ἀνοίκειον.
[f] ἡδονῆς.
[g] Lit. "writing," as though God's command were a written order, or as if Moses were here acting God's rôle.
[h] τὸ πρὸς διάνοιαν.
[i] ἡ ψυχή or, less probably, "spirit"—τὸ πνεῦμα; Aucher has "animus."
[j] τὸν ἡγεμόνα νοῦν.
[k] τοῖς κατὰ μέρη λογισμοῖς.
[l] πρὸς αἴσθησιν.
[m] τὰς τάξεις διαιρεῖν *vel sim.*

cleansing,[a] and there is a drying up of all ignorance[b] and of all that which is able to do harm, then it is fitting and proper for it[c] to bring together[d] those (elements) which have been divided and separated, not that the masculine thoughts may be made womanish[e] and relaxed by softness, but that the female element, the senses, may be made manly[f] by following masculine thoughts and by receiving from them seed for procreation, that it may perceive (things) with wisdom, prudence, justice and courage,[g] in sum, with virtue.[h] But in the second place, in addition to this, it is proper to note also that when confusion comes upon the mind, and, like a flood, in the life of the world mounds of affairs are erected at one time,[i] it is impossible to sow or conceive or give birth to anything good. But when discords and attacks and the gradual invasions of monstrous[j] thoughts are kept off, then being dried, like the fertile and productive places of the earth, it produces virtues and excellent things.[k]

50. (Gen. viii. 20) Why did he build an altar, not having been ordered (to do so)?

It was proper that acts of gratitude[l] to God should be (performed) without an order and without deliberate delay, to show a soul free of passions. For it was fitting that he

[a] τῆς καθάρσεως. Because of the double meaning of Arm. *hamōrēn* (=σύμπας and ἅμα) and *dēp linel* (=συμβαίνει and ἐπιτήδειόν ἐστι), one may also accept Aucher's rendering, "quando vero integra fiat purgatio."

[b] ἀμαθίας.

[c] The soul.

[d] συναγαγεῖν.

[e] ἐκθηλύνωνται οἱ ἄρρενες λογισμοί.

[f] ἀρρενικαὶ γίγνωνται αἱ αἰσθήσεις.

[g] σοφίᾳ καὶ σωφροσύνῃ καὶ δικαιοσύνῃ καὶ ἀνδρείᾳ.

[h] ἀρετῇ.

[i] Meaning not quite clear to me; Aucher renders, more freely, "quando confusio pervaserit intellectum ad similitudinem diluvii atque negotiis hujus mundi tamquam aggeribus contra erectis altercari inter se coeperint"; he omits the words "in life" and adds "altercari inter se coeperint."

[j] Or "arrogant."

[k] Lit. "works"—ἔργα.

[l] εὐχαριστήρια.

who had received good by the grace of God should give thanks with a willing disposition. But one who waits for a command [a] is ungrateful,[b] being compelled by necessity [c] to honour his benefactor.

51. (Gen. viii. 20) Why is he said to build an altar to "God," not to "the Lord" [d]?

Because in benefactions and on the occasion [e] of regeneration,[f] as at the creation of the world,[g] He assumes only His beneficent power,[h] by which He makes all things, and causes His kingly power [i] to be put aside, preferring (the former).[j] Similarly, also now there is the beginning of a regeneration [k] and He changes to His beneficent power, which is called "God." For He had set up [l] His kingly and sovereign power, which is called "Lord," when he brought down retribution in the form of water.

52. (Gen. viii. 20) What is the meaning of the words, "He took of the clean beasts and birds and offered whole burnt-offerings" [m]?

[a] Arm. *aṛ karg* = πρὸς τάξιν, an obvious error for πρόσταξιν: Aucher, not seeing this, renders, "ordinem."

[b] ἀχάριστος.

[c] ἀνάγκῃ.

[d] Most uncial MSS. of LXX have θεῷ "God" (so also Arm. O.T.), but a good many cursives and the Coptic versions have κυρίῳ "Lord," rendering *YHWH*, as the Heb. here reads.

[e] Lit. "place."

[f] παλιγγενεσίας.

[g] ἐν τῇ κοσμοποιίᾳ.

[h] τῇ εὐεργέτιδι δυνάμει, one of the two chief divine attributes (also called ποιητική), symbolized by the name θεός.

[i] τὴν βασιλικὴν δύναμιν, the other chief divine attribute (also called κολαστήριος), symbolized by the name κύριος.

[j] Meaning not quite clear to me; Aucher renders, less accurately, I think, "facit autem nomine regio dissimilato tamquam summam auctoritatem praeferente."

[k] Lit. "second genesis."

[l] Lit. "ordered"—ἔταξε *vel sim.*

[m] Arm. *boḷorartouḷ* = both ὁλοκάρπωμα (or ὁλοκάρπωσις) and ὁλοκαύτωμα, both of which words elsewhere in LXX render Heb. *'ôlāh*, used here; most LXX MSS. here have ὁλοκάρπωσιν.

All this is said in a deeper meaning,[a] both because he had received everything from God as a kindness and gift and that that which was of the genus of clean (animals) and unblemished in kind, and of the tame ones the most gentle and unblemished he might completely burn as whole burnt-offerings. For they are sacrifices[b] of good things and are whole and full of wholeness,[c] and they have the status[d] of fruit; and the fruit is the end[e] for the sake of which the plant exists. This is the literal meaning.[f] But as for the deeper meaning,[g] the clean beasts and birds are the senses and the mind of the wise man,[h] (for) in the mind the thoughts[i] rove about. And it is proper to bring all these, when they have altogether become fruits, as a thank-offering[j] to the Father, and to offer them as immaculate and unblemished offerings[k] for sacrifices.[l]

53. (Gen. viii. 21) Why does he sacrifice to the beneficent power[m] of God, when the reception (of the sacrifice) is through both powers, (namely those of) Lord and God, for (Scripture) says, "the Lord God[n] smelled a sweet odour"?

(This is) because we who, when hope wavers, are unexpectedly saved from the evil that comes upon us, consider only the benefactions (of God), and in our joy ascribe this to the Benefactor[o] rather than to the Lord. But the

[a] *πρὸς διάνοιαν.*
[b] *θυσίαι* or *προσφοραί.*
[c] Meaning uncertain; Aucher renders, "integritate plenae."
[d] *τὸν λόγον.*
[e] *τὸ τέλος.*
[f] *τὸ ῥητόν*; but which is the literal, and which the deeper meaning is not clear.
[g] *τὸ πρὸς διάνοιαν.*
[h] *τοῦ σοφοῦ* (or *ἀστείου*) *αἱ αἰσθήσεις καὶ ὁ νοῦς.* Philo apparently means that the beasts symbolize the senses, and the birds, the mind.
[i] *οἱ λογισμοί.*
[j] *εὐχαριστίαν.*
[k] *προσφοράς.*
[l] *πρὸς θυσίας.*
[m] *τῇ εὐεργέτιδι δυνάμει*; see above, § 51.
[n] So LXX and Arm. O.T.; Heb. has only "The Lord" (*YHWH*).
[o] Symbolized by the name "God."

Benefactor inclines to us[a] with either power, Himself accepting (our sacrifice) and honouring the gratitude of the good man[b] lest He seem to make a halting return.[c] But it greatly pleases the Eternal[d] (to make use) of both His powers.[e]

*54. (Gen. viii. 21) What is the meaning of the words, "And the Lord God said, reflecting,[f] Never again will I curse[g] the earth because of the deeds of men, for the thought of man is resolutely turned toward evils from his youth. Therefore never again will I smite all living flesh as I did on another occasion"[h]?

The proposition[i] indicates repentance,[j] which is a passion alien to the divine power. For the dispositions of men are weak and unstable, just as their affairs are full of great uncertainty. But to God nothing is uncertain and nothing is unattainable,[k] for He is most firm of opinion and most stable. How then (did it happen) that with the same cause present and with His knowing from the beginning that the thought of man is resolutely turned toward evils from his youth, He first destroyed the human

[a] κατανεύει *vel sim.*

[b] The Arm. construction is not clear; the above rendering is probably closer to the original than Aucher's rendering, "honorabiliter acceptans gratos animos."

[c] χωλὴν ἀπόδοσιν.

[d] τῷ Ὄντι.

[e] Aucher renders, "sed utrique virtuti Entis gratissimum esse declarabit," and in his footnote, "*vel*, per utramque virtutem agere Enti valde placet."

[f] διανοηθείς, as in LXX; Heb. "said to his heart (= mind)."

[g] Lit. "not again will I add to curse," a Hebrew idiom taken over by the LXX.

[h] ἔτι, found in some LXX MSS. and Syr. and Arm. O.T., is joined to the following verse in our biblical texts.

[i] Or "premiss"; Arm. *patčaṙ* (elsewhere = πρόφασις, αἴτιον, ὁρμή, etc.) here prob. = πρότασις as in the Greek frag.

[j] Or "regret"—μετάνοιαν or μεταμέλειαν; the latter is found in the Greek frag.

[k] Or "incomprehensible"; the Greek frag. has ἀκατάληπτον.

race through the flood, but after this said that He would not again destroy (them), even though the same evils remained in their souls? Now it should be said that all such forms of words (in Scripture) are generally used [a] in the Law rather for learning and aid in teaching than for the nature of truth. For as there are two texts [b] which are found in the Legislation, one in which it is said, "Not like man (is God)," [c] and another in which the Eternal [d] is said to chastise as a man (chastises) his son,[e] the former (text) is the truth. For in reality God is not like man nor yet like the sun nor like heaven nor like the sense-perceptible world but (only) like God, if it is right to say even this. For that blessed and most happy One [f] does not admit any likeness or comparison or parable [g]; nay, rather He is beyond blessedness itself and happiness and whatever is more excellent and better than these.[h] But the second (text pertains) to teaching and exposition,[i] (namely) "like a man (He chastises)," for the sake of chastising us earth-born creatures in order that we may not be eternally requited with His wrath and retribution through His implacable enmity without peace. For it is enough to be resentful [j] and embittered this one time and to exact punish-

[a] So rendered on the basis of περιέχεται in the Greek frag.; Arm. *əmbŗneal p'akin* means "are circumscribed" or "confined."

[b] Lit. "heads"; Greek frag. κεφαλαίων.

[c] Arm. omits "is God," found in Greek frag. The quotation is from Num. xxiii. 19.

[d] ὁ Ὤν, omitted in Greek frag.

[e] Deut. viii. 5.

[f] The Greek frag. has only μακάριον ἐκεῖνο.

[g] παραβολήν as in the Greek frag.

[h] The Greek frag. has only μᾶλλον δὲ μακαριότητος αὐτῆς ὑπεράνω.

[i] Arm. *arajnordout'ean patmout'ean* lit. = "guidance-narration" prob. renders ὑφήγησιν as in the Greek frag.

[j] This appears to be the meaning of Arm. *anazdakel* in this context, with God as implied subject; usu. the verb means "be stubborn" or "disobedient"; Aucher renders, "commoveri."

ment of sinners. But (to punish others) many times for the same cause is the act of a savage and bestial spirit. "For in requiting one who is to be punished as is possible, I will make a fitting recollection of each proposition."[a]

And so, "reflecting" is properly[b] used of God, since (His) mind and intention are most firm, whereas our wills[c] are unsettled and inconstant and vacillating. Wherefore we do not properly reflect in thinking,[d] for reflection is the issue of the mind.[e] But it is impossible for the human mind to be extended and disseminated[f] as it is too weak[g] to pass very completely and effortlessly among all things.

But the words "not again will I curse the earth" are most excellently used. For it is not proper to add new curses to those already given, inasmuch as it is filled with evils. Nevertheless, though they[h] are endless,[i] inasmuch as the Father is good and kind and a lover of mankind,[j] He

[a] The literal retranslation in Greek of this obscure sentence would be something like the following: *ἀνταποδοὺς γὰρ τοῖς ἐξεταζομένοις, ὡς δυνατόν ἐστιν, ἑκάστης προθέσεως ποιήσω τὴν πρέπουσαν μνήμην* (or *ἀνάμνησιν*); the Arm. glossator paraphrases it as follows: "God says, whatever my judgment exacted of the several sinners, this they paid, and so now, in accordance with my first proposal, I consider mercy fitting." Possibly the original Greek read *καθ' ὅσον δυνατόν ἐστιν ἑκάστῳ πρόθεσιν ποιήσω τῆς πρεπούσης ἀμνηστείας*.

[b] The Greek frag. has *οὐ κυριολογεῖται*; either this is a rhetorical question or the *οὐ* is a dittography of the case-ending of *θεοῦ* or *οὐ* was interpolated by a scribe who misunderstood Philo's meaning, which is that God's "reflecting" indicates His sureness of purpose.

[c] *προαιρέσεις* or *βουλαί*.

[d] *οὐ κυρίως διανοοῦντες λογιζόμεθα*.

[e] *ἡ γὰρ διανόησις ἡ τοῦ νοῦ διέξοδός ἐστι*, *cf. Quod Deus Immut.* 34. Without this parallel it would be difficult to render the obscure Arm. clause.

[f] *ἐκτείνεσθαι καὶ διασπείρεσθαι*.

[g] *ἀσθενοῦντι*, or "unable"—*ἀδυνατοῦντι*.

[h] *i.e.* the evils of earth.

[i] Prob. *ἀτελῆ*; Aucher renders, "imperfecta."

[j] *φιλάνθρωπος*.

lightens these evils rather than adds to their misfortunes. But, as the proverb says, it is the same as " washing brick " or " carrying water in a net " to remove evil from the soul of man, which is stamped with its mark.

For if (the evil) exists from the beginning,[a] says (Scripture), it does not exist incidentally [b] but is engraved in (the soul) and closely fitted [c] to it. Moreover, since the mind [d] is the sovereign and ruling part of the soul,[e] (Scripture) adds " resolutely," [f] and that which is reflected upon with resolution and care [g] is investigated [h] with accuracy.[i] But resolution is (turned) not toward one evil (only) but, as is clear, toward all " evils," and this (state) exists not momentarily [j] but " from his youth," which is all but from his very swaddling bands, as if he were to a certain extent united, and at the same time, nourished and grown, with sins.

However, He says, " Not again will I smite all living flesh," showing that He will not again destroy the whole of mankind in common [k] but (only) the greater part of those individuals who commit indescribable wrongs. For He does not leave evil unpunished nor does He grant it unrestraint or security,[l] but while showing consideration [m]

[a] Lit. " first " ; the Arm. differs considerably from the Greek frag. in this sentence.

[b] παρέργως ; the Arm. words *gorç ar gorçou* (lit. = ἔργον πρὸς ἔργῳ) are prob. a gloss to explain *varkaparazi* = παρέργως, or an alternate rendering.

[c] Prob. προσήρμοσται as in the Greek frag.

[d] ὁ νοῦς.

[e] τὸ ἡγεμονικὸν καὶ κυριώτατον μέρος τῆς ψυχῆς.

[f] ἐπιμελῶς.

[g] σὺν ἐπιμελείᾳ καὶ φροντίδι, as in the Greek frag.

[h] διηρευνημένον ; the Greek frag. has διηγορευμένον.

[i] εἰς ἀκρίβειαν, as in the Greek frag., or possibly εἰς ἀλήθειαν.

[j] Lit. " not barely " ; prob. the original was οὐκ ὀψὲ καὶ μόλις as in the Greek frag.

[k] κατὰ κοινόν.

[l] ἀσφάλειαν.

[m] φειδόμενος.

for the (human) race because of His purpose,[a] He specifies [b] punishment by necessity [c] for those who sin.

55. (Gen. viii. 22) What is the meaning of the words, "Seed and harvest, cold and heat, summer and spring, by day and night [d] they shall not cease"?

In the literal meaning [e] this indicates the permanent recurrence [f] of the annual seasons (and that) no longer is there to be a destruction of the earthly climates [g] of animals and plants, for when the seasons are destroyed,[h] they destroy these (creatures) also, and when they are safely preserved, they keep them safe. For in accordance with each of these (seasons) they are kept sound and are not weakened, but are wont to be produced, each in a wonderful way, and to grow with it. But nature was constituted like a harmony of contrary sounds, of low ones and high ones, just as the world (was composed) of contraries. When mortal temperaments [i] fully [j] preserve unmixed the natural order [k] of cold and warmth and of moisture and dryness, they are responsible [l] for the fact that destruction does not fall upon all earthly things. But as for the deeper meaning,[m] seed is the beginning, and harvest is the end.[n] And both [o] the end and the beginning are the

[a] διὰ τὴν πρόθεσιν αὐτοῦ. [b] ὁρίζει. [c] ἀνάγκῃ.

[d] Philo follows the LXX in making "day and night" adverbial rather than part of the compound subject of the verb "cease" as in the Heb. and some ancient versions.

[e] τὸ ῥητόν.

[f] The Arm. lit. = ἀνάστησιν (or ἔγερσιν) τῆς διαμονῆς; Aucher renders, "continuationem durationis."

[g] Lit. "mixtures," prob. κράσεων; Aucher renders, "temperationem."

[h] Or "corrupted"—φθείρονται.

[i] κράσεις.

[j] Lit. "abundantly" or "superfluously": Aucher "apprime."

[k] τὴν κατὰ φύσιν τάξιν. [l] αἴτιαι.

[m] τὸ πρὸς διάνοιαν. [n] ἡ ἀρχὴ . . . καὶ τὸ τέλος.

[o] Aucher, amplifying, renders, "ambo concurrentes."

causes of salvation.[a] For each by itself is imperfect,[b] since the beginning requires an end, and the end looks toward the beginning. But cold and heat motivate [c] winter and autumn. For autumn marks an interval,[d] coming after the annual (crop),[e] and chilling the fiery (summer).[f] But symbolically,[g] in connexion with the soul, cold indicates fear,[h] which causes trembling and shuddering,[i] but heat (indicates) anger, for anger and wrath [j] are flamelike and fiery. For it is necessary for these too to come into being and to endure always with things that come into being and are destroyed.[k] For summer and spring are set apart for fruits; spring is for the ripening [l] of seeds, while summer is for (the ripening) of fruits and foliage.[m] And these are symbolically regarded as pertaining to the mind, as they bear fruits of two kinds, those which are necessary, (such as) those of the vernal season, and those which are by way of superfluity,[n] as in the summer. Thus, necessary are the foods which (are produced) throughout the spring from seeds as for the body,[o] and for the mind (what is produced) through the virtues. But those (which are) in superfluity, such as the corporeal fruits of the trees of

[a] σωτηρίας. [b] ἀτελές.

[c] Or "announce" or "reveal"; Arm. *azdel* = ἐνεργεῖν and ἀναγγέλλειν, δηλοῦν, etc.

[d] For Arm. *bocagoyn* "flamelike" (φλογώδης) we should almost certainly read *bacagoyn* = διάστημα ἔχων; *cf. Quis Heres* 165, where Philo speaks of the divider (τομεύς) of the seasons.

[e] "crop" is supplied from *De Virtutibus* 6, where Philo speaks of τὰς ἐτησίας ὀπώρας.

[f] θέρος is to be supplied, *cf.* Aucher "igneum (aestum)."

[g] συμβολικῶς.

[h] Arm. uses two words both usu. = φόβος.

[i] τρόμον καὶ φρίκην. [j] ὀργὴ καὶ θυμός.

[k] *i.e.* living creatures.

[l] Lit. "perfecting."

[m] Or "buds"—θαλλιῶν. [n] κατὰ περιουσίαν.

[o] The Arm. construction is not clear to me; Aucher renders, "cibus itaque necessarius fere est pro corpore quidquid producitur in vere ex seminibus."

summer, (bring) corporeal and external goods to souls,[a] for the external ones are serviceable to the body. But (the goods) of the body (are serviceable) to the soul, while those of the mind (are serviceable) to God.[b] Moreover,[c] day and night are measures of times and numbers ; and time and number endure long [d] ; and (so) day is a symbol of lucid reason,[e] and night of shadowy folly.[f]

56. (Gen. ix. 1-2) Why does (God) bless Noah and his sons by saying, " Increase and multiply and fill the earth and dominate it.[g] And let the terror and fear of you be upon the beasts and the birds and the reptiles and the fish, which I have given into your hands " [h] ?

This prayer [i] was granted to the man (made) in the image (of God) [j] even at the beginning of creation [k] on the sixth day. For (Scripture) says,[l] " And God made man, in the image of God He made him, male and female He made

[a] This rendering, while literal, is of doubtful correctness, as is the less literal rendering of Aucher, " quotquot autem per excessum veniunt ex arboribus fructus aestate, praeter corpus animo quoque ferunt bona corporalia ut externa."

[b] The distinction between Arm. *ogi* = ψυχή (sometimes πνεῦμα) and *mitk'* = νοῦς is obscured in Aucher's rendering, " haec enim externa serviunt corpori, corpus autem animo, animus Deo."

[c] Arm. *baç* is prob. a printer's error for *bayç*.

[d] Prob. διαμένουσι.

[e] φωτοειδοῦς λογισμοῦ.

[f] σκοταίας ἀφροσύνης ; for the same combination see *De Plantatione* 40.

[g] Prob. κατακυριεύσατε as in LXX ; Heb. omits the last verb, but see below, where Philo quotes Gen. i. 28.

[h] Philo abbreviates the latter part of the biblical verse, which reads, " upon all the beasts of the earth and upon all the birds of heaven and upon all that creeps upon the earth and upon all the fish of the sea, which I have given (Heb. " which have been given ") into your hands."

[i] Or " request " ; Arm. *alōtk'* = εὐχή, δέησις, ἱκετία, etc.

[j] τῷ κατ' εἰκόνα ἀνθρώπῳ.

[k] ἐν τῇ τῆς γενέσεως ἀρχῇ.

[l] Gen. i. 28.

them. And God blessed them, saying, Increase and multiply and fill the earth and dominate it, and rule over the fish and the birds and the reptiles of the earth." [a] But has it not indeed been clearly shown through these words that He considers Noah, who became, as it were, the beginning of a second genesis of man, of equal honour with him who was first made in (His) image? And so He granted rule over earthly creatures in equal measure [b] to the former and the latter. And it should be carefully noted that (Scripture) shows him who in the flood was made righteous king [c] of earthly creatures to have been equal in honour not with the moulded and earthy man [d] but with him who was (made) in the form and likeness of the truly incorporeal Being [e]; and to him (Noah) He also gives authority, appointing as king not the moulded man but him who was (made) in the likeness and form (of God), Who [f] is incorporeal. Wherefore the genesis of him who was incorporeal in form, was shown to be on the sixth day, in accordance with the perfect number [g] six. But the moulded man (was created) after the completion of the world and after the days [h] of the genesis of all creatures, on the seventh day,[i] for then at the very last he was moulded into an earthly statue.[j] And so, after the days of genesis,

[a] Here again Philo slightly abbreviates Scripture.

[b] *κατ' ἰσότητα.* [c] *ὃς καθίστατο ὁ δίκαιος βασιλεύς.*

[d] *τῷ πλαστῷ καὶ γηίνῳ*, *cf.* *QG* i. 4, *Leg. All.* i. 31 *et al.*

[e] *κατὰ τὴν ἰδέαν καὶ τὴν εἰκόνα τοῦ ὄντως ἀσωμάτου Ὄντος.*

[f] The antecedent of " who " is grammatically " him who was made," but ought rather to be " God."

[g] *κατὰ τὸν τέλειον ἀριθμόν.*

[h] Aucher omits " the days of.

[i] *Cf.* Louis Ginzberg, *Legends of the Jews*, vol. v. p. 79, " This does not harmonize with his general view of creation, according to which the former [the ideal man] is of a timeless state (*cf. e.g.* Legum Alleg. 2. 4), and it appears that he tried to fit a Haggadah [homiletic interpretation] into his system but did not succeed."

[j] *εἰς γεώδη ἀνδριάντα*, *cf. e.g.* *De Virtutibus* 203 *χερσὶ μὲν θείαις εἰς ἀνδριάντα τὸν σωματοειδῆ τυπωθείς.*

on the seventh day of the world, (Scripture) says,[a] "For God[b] had not caused it to rain on the earth, and there was no man who should cultivate the earth"; then (it says),[c] "God moulded man, dust from the earth, and breathed into his face the breath of life, and the man became a living soul." And so, by the literal bearing (of Scripture) it has been shown how the beginning of the second genesis of the human race was worthy of the same kingship as the man (made) in the likeness and form (of God).[d] But as for the deeper meaning,[e] it is to be interpreted as follows. He desires that the souls of intelligent men increase in greatness and multitude (and) in the form[f] of virtues, and fill the mind with its form, as though it were the earth, leaving no part empty and void for follies[g]; and that they should dominate and rule over the earthy body and its senses, and strike[h] terror and fear into beasts, which is the exercise[i] of the will against evil, for evil is untamed and savage.[j] And (he wishes that they should rule) over the birds, (that is) those who are lightly lifted up in thought, those who are (filled) with vain and empty arrogance, (and) having been previously armed,[k] cause great harm, not being restrained by fear. Moreover, (He wishes that they should rule over) the reptiles, which are a symbol of poisonous passions[l]; for through

[a] Gen. ii. 5. Philo comments upon the first part of the verse above in *QG* i. 2.

[b] So most MSS. of LXX; Heb. and Arm. O.T. have "the Lord God."

[c] Gen. ii. 7.

[d] Aucher's rendering is less intelligible to me than the Arm.; he gives "quomodo ergo eidem regno dignus efficitur secundum imaginem formati hominis istud principium secundae facturae hominum indicatum fuit juxta litteram referentem."

[e] *τὸ πρὸς διάνοιαν.*

[f] *εἴδει.*

[g] *ἀφροσυνῶν.*

[h] Lit. "make" or "effect."

[i] Prob. *ἐπιτήδευσις.*

[j] *ἀνοικεία καὶ ἀγρία.*

[k] *πρότερον ὡπλισμένοι*; Aucher connects the participle with the preceding phrase, "et inani superbia iam armata." There are syntactical difficulties in both renderings.

[l] *σύμβολον τῶν ἰοβόλων παθῶν.*

every soul sense-pleasures and desires and grief and fear[a] creep, stabbing and piercing and wounding. And by the fish I understand[b] those who eagerly welcome a moist and fluid life[c] but not one that is continent, healthy and lasting.[d]

57. (Gen. ix. 3) Why does (Scripture) say, " Every reptile[e] that lives shall be to you for food " ?

The nature of reptiles is twofold. One is poisonous, and the other is tame.[f] Poisonous are those serpents which in place of feet use the belly and breast to crawl along ; and tame are those which have legs[g] above their feet. This is the literal meaning.[h] But as for the deeper meaning,[i] the passions[j] resemble unclean reptiles, while joy[k] (resembles) clean (reptiles). For alongside sensual pleasures there is the passion of joy.[l] And alongside the desire for sensual pleasure there is reflection.[m] And alongside grief there is remorse and constraint.[n] And alongside desire[o] there is caution.[p] Thus, these passions threaten souls with death and murder, whereas joys are truly living, as He Himself has shown in allegorizing,[q] and are the causes[r] of life for those who possess them.

[a] ἡδοναὶ καὶ ἵμεροι καὶ λύπη καὶ φόβος.
[b] λέγω.
[c] ὑγρὸν καὶ ῥοώδη βίον.
[d] ἐγκρατῆ καὶ ὑγιεινὸν καὶ διαμένοντα.
[e] ἑρπετόν.
[f] ἰοβόλος . . . ἥμερος (or οἰκεῖος).
[g] σκέλος or κνήμην.
[h] τὸ ῥητόν.
[i] τὸ πρὸς διάνοιαν.
[j] τὰ πάθη.
[k] χαρά or εὐφροσύνη.
[l] In each case a good passion is contrasted with an evil one; Arm. *aṙ* here=παρά; Aucher's rendering " apud " here and below is misleading.
[m] Possibly Philo here contrasts ἐνθύμημα and ἐπιθυμία.
[n] Lit. " biting " (or " striking ") and contraction " ; Aucher renders, " punctio et compunctio."
[o] πόθον.
[p] εὐλάβεια.
[q] ἀλληγορῶν.
[r] αἱ αἰτίαι.

58. (Gen. ix. 3) What is the meaning of the words, " As the herbs of fodder [a] I have given you all things " ?

Some say that through this (statement) " as the herbs of fodder I have given you all things " the eating of meat is enjoined.[b] But though this (interpretation) also is admissible, I myself believe that the legislation [c] indicates that above all the use of herbs is necessary, and that it implies other additions [d] in the form of herbs without legislating. But now they [e] are customary not (only) among a chosen race of men nor among those who are desirous of wisdom,[f] by whom continence of habit [g] is honoured, but among all men, all of whom at once [h] it is impossible to keep from eating meat. But perhaps the passage [i] is not about food but about authority [j]; for not everything that is an herb is edible nor is the food of all living creatures [k] sure and safe. For He saw the poisonous and death-bringing (creatures) which are also (found) among all of them. And so it may be that what (Scripture) means is the following, that irrational creatures [l] are to be given over to, and made obedient to man, just as we sow herbs and tend them by agriculture.

*59. (Gen. ix. 4) What is the meaning of the words, " Flesh in the blood of the life you shall not eat " [m] ?

(Scripture) seems to indicate through these (words) that

[a] *ὡς λάχανα χόρτου*, as in LXX ; Heb. " as herbs of grass."
[b] Prob. *χρηματίζεται*, *i.e.* " oracularly spoken."
[c] *τὸ νομοθετεῖν*.
[d] Apparently meaning other kinds of food.
[e] *i.e.* herbs.
[f] *σοφίας*.
[g] *ἐγκράτεια τῶν ἐθῶν*.
[h] *ὁμοῦ* or *κοινῶς*.
[i] *ὁ λόγος*.
[j] *περὶ ἀρχῆς* or *ἐξουσίας* ; this is explained in the last sentence of the section.
[k] *i.e.* food derived from living creatures.
[l] *ἄλογα ζῷα*.
[m] LXX *κρέας ἐν αἵματι ψυχῆς οὐ φάγεσθε* ; Heb. " flesh with its soul (= life), its blood you shall not eat."

the blood is the substance of the soul,[a] but of the sense-perceptive and vital soul,[b] not of that which is called (soul) *katexochen*, (namely) that which is rational and intelligent.[c] For there are three parts of the soul: one is nutritive, another is sense-perceptive, and the third is rational.[d] Now the divine spirit[e] is the substance of the rational (part), according to the theologian,[f] for in (the account of) the creation of the world, he says,[g] "He breathed the breath of life into his face" (as) his cause.[h] But blood is the substance of the sense-perceptive and vital (soul), for he says in another place,[i] "The soul[j] of all flesh is its blood." Very properly does (Scripture) say that the blood is the soul of flesh. And in the flesh are sense-perception and passion but not mind or reflection.[k] Moreover, (the expression) "in the blood of the life"[l] indicates that soul is one thing, and blood another, so that the substance of the soul is truly and infallibly[m] spirit.[n] The spirit,[o] however,

[a] ἡ τῆς ψυχῆς οὐσία, as in Greek frag.

[b] τῆς αἰσθητικῆς καὶ ζωτικῆς ψυχῆς; the second adjective is omitted in the Greek frag.

[c] λογικὴ καὶ νοερά, as in the Greek frag.

[d] θρεπτικόν . . . αἰσθητικόν . . . λογικόν, as in the Greek frag.

[e] τὸ θεῖον πνεῦμα; with the Greek frag. we must emend Arm. *ogouy* = πνεύματος to *ogi* = πνεῦμα.

[f] *i.e.* Moses.

[g] Gen. ii. 7, *cf.* *QG* i. 5.

[h] The last phrase (one word in Arm.) precedes the words "the breath of life," as though it were part of the biblical text.

[i] Lev. xvii. 14.

[j] *i.e.* life.

[k] ἡ αἴσθησις καὶ τὸ πάθος, οὐχ ὁ νοῦς καὶ ὁ λογισμός, as in Greek frag.

[l] ἐν αἵματι ψυχῆς, as in Greek frag. (after LXX); Aucher ineptly renders, "per spiritum sanguinis."

[m] ἀληθῶς καὶ ἀψευδῶς; the Greek frag. has only ἀψευδῶς.

[n] πνεῦμα, as the Greek frag. shows. Arm. *ogi* and *hogi* are phonetic alternants, each of which renders both ψυχή and πνεῦμα; here apparently the Arm. translator artificially equates *ogi* with ψυχή and *hogi* with πνεῦμα.

[o] The Greek frag. does not repeat the word πνεῦμα.

does not occupy any place by itself alone without the blood but is carried along [a] and mixed together [b] with the blood. For the arteries,[c] the vessels of breath, contain not only air by itself, unmixed and pure, but also blood, though perhaps a small amount. For there are two kinds of vessels, veins and arteries [d]; the veins have more blood than breath whereas the arteries have more breath than blood, but the mixture in both kinds of vessel is differentiated by the greater or less (amount of blood and breath). This is the literal meaning.[e] But as for the deeper meaning,[f] (Scripture) calls " blood of the life " its hot and fiery virtue [g] (or) uprightness.[h] And he who is filled with this wisdom despises all food and all sensual pleasure,[i] which are of the belly and of the parts below the belly.[j] For one who is dissolute and sportive [k] like the wind, or hide-bound [l] by sloth and a soft life,[m] does nothing but fall on his belly like a reptile on the ground, and gives himself up to licking what is on the ground, and ends his life without tasting the heavenly food which wisdom-loving souls obtain.

[a] Lit. " woven in and carried," probably a double rendering of *ἐμφέρεσθαι*, found in the Greek frag.

[b] Two Arm. synonyms prob. render the single Greek verb *συγκεκρᾶσθαι*, found in the Greek frag. (which ends at this point).

[c] *αἱ ἀρτηρίαι*, here used in the sense of respiratory vessels, *cf. De Praemiis* 144 *τοῦ μὲν ἐν φλεψὶν αἵματος . . . τοῦ δ' ἐν ἀρτηρίαις πνεύματος.*

[d] *φλέβες καὶ ἀρτηρίαι.*

[e] *τὸ ῥητόν.*

[f] *τὸ πρὸς διάνοιαν.*

[g] *ἀρετήν.*

[h] Or " rising " ; Arm. *kangnout'iun* = *ἀνόρθωσις, ἔγερσις, ἀνάστασις* ; Aucher renders, " fortitudinem " and adds, in a footnote, " vox anceps, *fortitudo* a nobis exposita, poterat etiam verti *vigor* vel *in vigore* aut *rectitudinem.*"

[i] *ἡδονῆς.*

[j] *Cf. QG* i. 12 (above, p. 8).

[k] Lit. " enjoying himself "—prob. *ἡδόμενος.*

[l] Lit. " hardened " or " frozen."

[m] *ὑγρῷ βίῳ, cf. De Vita Cont.* 47 *ὑγρός . . . καὶ ἄσωτος βίος ἅπασιν ἐπίβουλος* ; Aucher's " vitamque humidam " misses the metaphorical sense of the adjective.

60. (Gen. ix. 5) What is the meaning of the words, " I will require your blood of your souls, of all living creatures, and from the hand of man of his brother " [a] ?

There are two classes [b] of preyers,[c] one (consisting) of beasts, and the other of men. But beasts do rather little harm because they have no familiarity [d] with those whom they seek to prey on, and especially because they are not in authority but prey upon those who have authority.[e] And (Scripture) calls " brothers " those men who plot mischief,[f] demonstrating three things. One, that all we men are kinsmen and brothers,[g] being related by the possession of an ancient kinship,[h] since we receive the lot [i] of the rational nature [j] from [k] one mother. The second is that nearly all great quarrels and plots occur between those who are blood-relatives, especially brothers, whether

[a] The above is a literal translation of Philo's abbreviated citation of the biblical verse, which is awkwardly phrased both in Heb. and LXX. The Heb. reads, " and also your blood as to your souls (*i.e.* your life-blood) I will require from the hand of every living creature, I will require it (*sic*), and from the hand of man, from the hand of man his brother (*i.e.* every man's brother) I will require the soul (*i.e.* life) of the man " ; LXX has καὶ γὰρ τὸ ὑμέτερον αἷμα τῶν ψυχῶν ὑμῶν ἐκζητήσω· ἐκ χειρὸς πάντων τῶν θηρίων ἐκζητήσω αὐτό, καὶ ἐκ χειρὸς ἀνθρώπου ἀδελφοῦ ἐκζητήσω τὴν ψυχὴν τοῦ ἀνθρώπου.

[b] τάξεις or τάγματα.

[c] ἐπιβούλων.

[d] οἰκειότητα.

[e] The two verbs are in the sing. but probably reflect Greek usage of sing. verb with neut. pl. subject (θηρία or ζῷα) ; Aucher renders, " maxime quod non sub principatu cadunt sed principes demoliuntur," and remarks in a footnote, " ubi subintelligitur *natura bestiarum*, quamquam Gloss. voluerit intelligi hominem." The Arm. glossator paraphrases, " Man is not under the power (of others ?) but the beasts fear him as their ruler."

[f] Lit. " plotters " or " cheaters " ; Aucher renders, " occisores."

[g] συγγενεῖς καὶ ἀδελφοί.

[h] κατὰ ἄνω συγγενείας σχέσιν ᾠκειωμένοι.

[i] κλῆρον.

[j] τῆς λογικῆς φύσεως.

[k] Lit. " of " (gen. case).

because of inheritance or because of family honour.[a] For family strife is even worse than that of strangers,[b] since (in the former) they quarrel with great knowledge.[c] In truth those are (like ?) genuine brothers [d] who are skilled in knowledge [e] of what attack [f] is to be used in battle.[g]

And third, it seems to me, (Scripture) applies the name of " brothers " to the unrelenting and implacable punishment of homicides in order that they may suffer without mercy for what they have done, for they have slain, not strangers but their own true brothers.[h] And most excellently [i] does (Scripture) say that God is the inspector [j] and overseer [k] of those who are slain by men. For even if (some) men despise and belittle the carrying out of justice,[l] let these men not be carefree and think to escape and be safe though they are impure and savage, but let them know that they have already been apprehended in a great assize,[m] in the divine court of justice set up for the retributive punishment [n] of savage men on behalf of those who have suffered unjust and undeserving attacks.[o] This is the literal meaning.[p] But as for the deeper meaning,[q] (Scripture) says that the beneficent, good, philanthropic and only Saviour [r]

[a] Or " rights of birth " (*i.e.* primogeniture and the like).

[b] *ξένων* or *ἀλλοτρίων*.

[c] *i.e.* of the weaknesses of their opponents.

[d] *γνήσιοι ἀδελφοί* (or *ἀδελφῶν* ?).

[e] *ἔμπειροι*.

[f] *ὁρμῇ*.

[g] The construction of this sentence is not clear to me ; a demonstrative pron. is used as the subject, and the word " brothers " is in the gen.-abl.-dat. case for a reason that escapes me ; Aucher renders, more smoothly but with questionable accuracy, " fratres vere ex natura genuini, satis conscii," etc.

[h] *τοὺς γνησίους ἀδελφούς*.

[i] *παγκάλως*.

[j] Arm. *ayçelou* and *verakaçou* are prob. a double rendering of *ἐπίσκοπος*.

[k] *ἔφορος* ; the meaning is, of course, that God is the observer of the crime.

[l] *δίκην*.

[m] *δικαστήριον*.

[n] *ἐκδίκησιν*.

[o] Lit. " experiences."

[p] *τὸ ῥητόν*.

[q] *τὸ πρὸς διάνοιαν*.

[r] *ὁ εὐμενὴς καὶ ἀγαθὸς καὶ φιλάνθρωπος καὶ μόνος σωτήρ*.

does not overlook [a] the worth of the purity of the soul which can be saved from unending and unbearable corruption, but drives off and scatters all the enemies that surround it, (namely) the beasts and the men (called) brothers. For symbolically those are beasts who act savagely and threaten (others) with wicked murder. But men and brothers (Scripture symbolically calls) the various thoughts [b] and words [c] which are heard when expressed [d] by the tongue and mouth, for they are related [e]; and therefore they bring insurmountable misfortune, omitting no word or deed that results in misery.

61. (Gen. ix. 6) What is the meaning of the words, " He who sheds the blood of a man, in return for his blood he shall be shed " [f]?

There is no error in this text [g] but rather a sign of emphasis,[h] for, says (Scripture), he himself shall be shed like blood who sheds blood; for that which is shed flows out and is absorbed and does not have the power of consistency.[i] And by this (Scripture) indicates [j] that the souls of those who act impiously [k] imitate the mortal body in being corrupted, in so far as each of them is wont to seem

[a] οὐ παρορᾷ.
[b] τοὺς λογισμούς.
[c] τοὺς λόγους.
[d] κατὰ προφορὰν ἀκούονται.
[e] συγγενεῖς.

[f] Philo follows the LXX, which reads ὁ ἐκχέων αἷμα ἀνθρώπου ἀντὶ τοῦ αἵματος αὐτοῦ ἐκχυθήσεται. The Heb. reads more intelligibly " He who sheds the blood of a man, by a man his blood shall be shed." The Arm. O.T. combines the two texts, reading " He who sheds the blood of a man, in return for his blood, his (*i.e.* the slayer's) blood shall be shed."

[g] Prob. ἐξηγήσει, though Arm. *meknout'iun* also renders ἑρμηνεία.

[h] Arm. *erewoyt'* usu. = ἐπιφάνεια or φαντασία, neither of which fits the context; prob. the original had ἐμφάσεως, *cf.* the Ambrosian paraphrase (cited by Aucher), " sed emphasis est." Aucher himself renders, " majoris declarationis."

[i] δύναμιν συστάσεως (or οὐσίας).
[j] αἰνίττεται.
[k] τῶν ἀνοσιουργῶν.

to suffer corruption.[a] For the body is dissolved [b] into those (parts) out of which it was mixed and compounded,[c] and is again resolved into its original elements.[d] But the cruel [e] and labouring [f] soul is tossed about and overwhelmed by its intemperate way of life [g] and by the evils with which it has grown up,[h] (which are) in a certain sense its members [i] and grow together with it.[j]

*62. (Gen. ix. 6) Why does (Scripture) say, as if (speaking) of another God, " in the image of God He made man " and not " in His own image " [k] ?

Most excellently and veraciously [l] this oracle was given by God.[m] For nothing mortal can be made in the likeness of the most high One and Father of the universe but (only) in that of the second God, who is His Logos.[n] For it was

[a] *πέφυκε δοκεῖν* (or *ὁρᾶσθαι*) *φθορὰν ἐνδέχεσθαι*; Aucher renders more freely and with omission of one infinitive, " quatenus singulis soleat corruptia supervenire."

[b] *καταλύεται*.

[c] Prob. *συγχεόμενον πέφυρται*.

[d] *ἀναστοιχειοῦται*.

[e] Or " terrible "; Arm. *džndak* = *δεινός, χαλεπός*, etc.

[f] Apparently the Arm. translator took *μοχθηρά* or *πονηρά* in the sense of " labouring " rather than " wicked."

[g] The Arm. *v.ll.* do not affect the sense.

[h] *συντρόφων κακῶν*, *cf. De Virtutibus* 26 *δειλία . . . ἥ δ' ἐστὶ κακὸν σύντροφον*.

[i] *<τούτων> τρόπον τινὰ μελῶν αὐτῆς ὄντων*; *i.e.* the evils are parts of the soul somewhat as limbs are parts of the body.

[j] Aucher's rendering of this clause is unnecessarily obscure, " una cum illa et ipsa mala connutrita idem pati solita sunt ad modum partium membrorum."

[k] Philo asks the natural question, why does God refer to Himself in the third person? The Arm. here differs from the LXX and the Greek frag. (preserved by Eusebius) as well as from the Arm. O.T. in having the verb " made " in the 3rd pers. instead of the 1st.

[l] *παγκάλως καὶ ἀψευδῶς*; the Greek frag. has *παγκάλως καὶ σοφῶς*.

[m] Prob. *κεχρησμῴδηται*, as in Greek frag.

[n] *πρὸς τὸν δεύτερον θεόν, ὅς ἐστιν ἐκείνου λόγος*, as in Greek frag.

right that the rational (part) of the human soul should be formed as an impression[a] by the divine Logos, since the pre-Logos God[b] is superior to every rational nature.[c] But He who is above the Logos (and) exists in the best and in a special form—what thing that comes into being can rightfully bear His likeness?[d] Moreover, Scripture wishes also to show that God most justly avenges the virtuous and decent men because they have a certain kinship[e] with His Logos, of which the human mind[f] is a likeness and image.[g]

63. (Gen. ix. 11)[h] What is the meaning of the words, "There shall not again[i] be a flood to destroy the whole earth"?

Through this last (statement Scripture) shows us clearly[j] that there may be[k] many floods but not such a one as will be able to inundate the whole earth. This is the literal meaning.[l] But as for the deeper meaning,[m] it is the divine grace[n] which, though it does not aid all the parts of the soul in all the virtues,[o] nevertheless does adorn[p] some (of them) in some respects. For so too, though one may not be able to be vigorous[q] in all his body, nevertheless that which he can do to achieve vigour he should practise with

[a] Prob. σχηματίζεσθαι (or χαραχθῆναι, as in Greek frag.) τύπον.
[b] ὁ πρὸ τοῦ λόγου θεός, as in Greek frag.
[c] One Arm. MS. reads πανλογικὴ φύσις for πᾶσα λογικὴ φύσις; the latter is found in Greek frag.
[d] The Greek frag. (which ends with this sentence) reads slightly differently, having the conclusion in a negative rather than interrogative form.
[e] οἰκειότητα.
[f] ὁ τοῦ ἀνθρώπου νοῦς.
[g] ὁμοίωσις καὶ εἰκών.
[h] Philo prob. omits comment on Gen. ix. 7-10, because these verses are largely repetitions of earlier ones.
[i] Lit. "no longer," as in LXX οὐκ ἔσται ἔτι.
[j] Lit. "face to face."
[k] Or "will be."
[l] τὸ ῥητόν.
[m] τὸ πρὸς διάνοιαν.
[n] ἡ θεία χάρις.
[o] οὐκ ὠφελεῖ πάντα τῆς ψυχῆς μέρη κατὰ πάσας ἀρετάς.
[p] κοσμεῖ.
[q] θάλλειν.

all care (and) diligence. Nor, if one is too weak to correct his way of life completely, should he despair of those things of which he is capable and which he can achieve. For in so far as one does not work in accordance with the power [a] which every one has, he is a slacker [b] and, at the same time, an ingrate. He is a slacker in being sluggish, and an ingrate in that, having received an excellent start,[c] he opposes Being.[d]

*64. (Gen. ix. 13-17) Why, as a sign that there will not be a flood on all the earth, does He speak of placing His bow [e] in the clouds?

Some suppose that this means that bow which by some is called the rainbow,[f] since from its form they take it to be a reliable [g] symbol for the rainbow. I, however, do not find this soundly [h] argued. In the first place, this bow should have its own special nature and substance,[i] since it is called the bow of God, for He says, "my bow I will place." And to belong to God and to be placed (means) that it is not non-existent.[j] But the rainbow does not have a special separate nature by itself but is an appearance [k] of the sun's rays in moist clouds, and all appearances

[a] τὴν δύναμιν.

[b] δειλός or νωθής.

[c] Arm. *patčar* (here used in pl.) usu. = αἰτία, sometimes = πρότασις or πρόφασις. In the present passage it seems to mean a man's natural endowment from God; Aucher renders "mediis."

[d] Apparently God, ὁ Ὤν, is meant.

[e] τόξον, as in LXX.

[f] Lit. "girdle of Aramazd (= Zeus)"; the Greek probably had ἶριν; the following word for "rainbow" also = ἶρις.

[g] Or "accurate" or "true"; Arm. *hastatoun* = βέβαιος, ἀληθής, ἀκριβής, etc.; Aucher renders, "constantem."

[h] ὑγιῶς.

[i] τὴν ἰδίαν φύσιν καὶ οὐσίαν.

[j] Arm. *anē* and *angoy* are prob. a double rendering of ἀνύπαρκτον.

[k] φαντασία or φαινόμενον.

are non-existent and immaterial. And evidence [a] (of this is that) the rainbow never appears at night, although there are clouds (then). In the second place, moreover, it must be said that even by day, when the clouds are overshadowed, the rainbow never appears earlier.[b] But it is necessary to speak without falsehood also of the other things which the legislator [c] (says, namely), "my bow I will place in the clouds." [d] For, behold, while there are clouds there is no appearance of a rainbow. And (Scripture) says that upon the gathering of the clouds the bow will appear in the clouds. For many times when there is a gathering of the clouds, and the air is overshadowed and dense, there is nowhere an appearance of a rainbow. But perhaps the theologian [e] indicates something else by the bow, (namely that) in the laxness and force of earthly things [f] there will not take place a dissolution by their being completely loosened to (the point of) incongruity [g] nor (will there be) force up to (the point of) reaching a break.[h] But either power is determined by fixed measures.[i] For the great flood came about through a break [j] as (Scripture) itself

[a] πίστις.

[b] *i.e.* before the sun comes out.

[c] ὁ νομοθέτης.

[d] In this section the Arm. uses indifferently the sing. and pl. forms of "cloud."

[e] ὁ θεολόγος, *i.e.* Moses.

[f] The Greek frag. reads more intelligibly τούτεστιν ἄνεσιν καὶ ἐπίτασιν τῶν ἐπιγείων; Aucher takes the nouns in a moral sense, rendering, "in ipsa videlicet tum indulgentia tum acerbitate erga terrestres."

[g] This is reasonably close to the text of the Greek frag. μήτε τῆς ἀνέσεως εἰς ἔκλυσιν ὑφιεμένης παντελῆ καὶ ἀναρμοστίαν; Aucher renders the Arm. somewhat freely, "nec ultimam dissolutionem futuram esse ad modum (arcus) nimis mollis et inepti."

[h] This again is close to the text of the Greek frag. μήτε τῆς ἐπιτάσεως ἄχρι ῥήξεως ἐπιτεινομένης.

[i] The Arm. closely agrees with the Greek frag. ἀλλὰ μέτροις ὡρισμένοις ἑκατέρας δυνάμεως σταθμηθείσης.

[j] Arm. *paxmamb pataṙmamb* is a double rendering of ῥήξει.

confesses, saying,[a] "the fountains of the abyss broke forth," [b] but not with any particular (degree of) violence.[c] Second, the bow is not a weapon but an instrument of a weapon, an arrow which pierces; and the arrow released by the bow reaches a long way from a distance,[d] while there is no effect on that which is close-by and remains near.[e] This is a sign that never again will the whole earth be flooded, for no arrow reaches every place but only the place at a distance.[f] Thus the bow is symbolically the invisible power of God,[g] which is in the air. And this (air) is thinned out when it is separated in good weather,[h] and is condensed when there are clouds. It [i] does not permit the clouds to turn wholly into water, taking care that a flood shall not again . . .[j] the earth, for it manages and directs [k] the density of the air, which is likely at that time to be especially

[a] Arm. lit. = *ὁμολογεῖ, λέγων*; Greek frag. has only *φησίν*.

[b] Gen. vii. 11, see above, *QG* ii. 18.

[c] The Arm. corresponds pretty closely with the Greek frag. *οὐκ ἐπιτάσει ποσῇ τινι*; Wendland was perhaps influenced by Aucher's rendering "non tamen vehementia sine mensura" in conjecturing *ἐπιτάσει περιττῇ*.

[d] "A long way" (lit. "part") has no parallel in the Greek frag.; Aucher omits "from a distance," which corresponds to *τοῦ πόρρω* in the Greek frag.; probably the Arm. is merely a double rendering of the latter.

[e] *i.e.* on the bow and the person who uses it.

[f] This differs from the Greek frag., which has *οὕτως οὖν, φησίν, οὐ πάντες κατακλυσθήσονται, κἂν τοῦτό τινας ὑπομένειν συμβῇ*. For some of the remainder of this section there are two Greek parallels, one from Catena Lipsiensis, the other from Procopius.

[g] *θεοῦ δύναμις ἀόρατος*.

[h] This is probably an awkward rendering of some such text as that of Cat. Lips. *ἀνειμένῳ κατὰ τὰς αἰθρίας*.

[i] *i.e.* the divine power.

[j] The Arm. verb *yizdil* (*v.l. yezdil*) is unknown to the Arm. lexicons; the Arm. translator, however, must have had before him a text much like that of Cat. Lips. *τῷ μὴ γενέσθαι καθόλου κατακλυσμόν*.

[k] Prob. *κυβερνᾷ καὶ ἡνιοχεῖ* as in Cat. Lips.

refractory and insolent because of a repletion of satiety,[a] since when there are clouds, it shows itself to be full, dripping and sated.

*65. (Gen. ix. 18-19) Why does (Scripture) in mentioning the sons of the righteous man,[b] Shem, Ham and Japheth, tell of the genealogy of the middle one only, saying, " Ham was the father of Canaan," and after this add, " these (were) the three sons of Noah " ?

After first mentioning four (persons), Noah and his sons, it says that three were . . .[c] Since the offspring[d] was similar in character to the father who begot him, it reckoned both as one (person), so that they are four in number but three in power.[e] But he[f] now speaks of only the middle generation in Scripture because later on the righteous man will speak of his case.[g] For though he was indeed his father,[h] he did not rebuke the father and did not

[a] The Arm. agrees closely with Cat. Lips. (which ends here), ἀπαυχενίζειν καὶ ἐνυβρίζειν διὰ πλησμονῆς κόρου.

[b] Noah.

[c] The word *bnaxratakan* is not found in the Arm. lexicons. It is a compound of *boun* " nature " and *xratakan* " moral," " instructive " from *xrat* = παιδεία, νουθέτησις, ἐπιστήμη (also τάξις). What Greek compound it renders is difficult to say. Possibly it means something like " in a natural moral order." Aucher renders, " morigeratos " and in a footnote adds, " *vel*, pro admonendis morigeratis, *vel*, eos qui morum indicio fuere " : he then quotes the Arm. glossator, who writes, " the three sons were *bnaxrat*, since it [Scripture] has already called Shem good, Ham evil, and Japheth neither good nor evil."

[d] Canaan.

[e] Or " potentially "—δυνάμει ; Aucher has " virtute."

[f] Moses.

[g] *i.e.* Noah will later on (in Gen. ix. 25, *cf.* below, § 75) curse Ham's son Canaan because of Ham's disrespect for him (Noah).

[h] Meaning that Ham was father of Canaan.

give the progenitor a share of that which he thought it right for the son to share.[a] In the second place, it may be that (Scripture) foretells to those who are able to see from afar what is distant with the sharp-sighted eyes of the mind that He will take away the land of the Canaanites after many generations and give it to the chosen and god-beloved race.[b] And so (Scripture) wishes to show that Canaan, the ruler and inhabitant of that country, practised peculiar evils of his own, as well as those of his father, so that from both sides his ignobility and low-born alienness[c] are shown. This is the literal meaning.[d] But as for the deeper meaning,[e] (Scripture) does not say that Canaan was son to Ham but uses a special expression,[f] saying that "Ham was the father of Canaan," for such a character is always the father of such thoughts.[g] This is shown by the interpretations of their names, for when they are rendered from one (language) into the other,[h] "Ham" is "heat" or "hot,"[i] while "Canaan" is "merchant"[j] or "media-

[a] Apparently this means that Noah did not curse Ham as he did curse Ham's son Canaan. The Greek frag. from Procopius has a different sense (the text is given in Appendix A), namely that he (Ham) did not respect (*οὐκ ἐτίμησεν* : Arm. *oč sasteaç* = *οὐκ ἐπετίμησεν*) his father (Noah), and did not give him that portion of respect which he (Noah) thought it right to receive from his son.

[b] *τῷ ἐκλεκτῷ καὶ θεοφιλεῖ γένει.*

[c] The Arm. lit. = *ἀνελευθερία καὶ ἀπαλλοτρίωσις* (or *προγραφὴ*) *τῆς δυσγενείας* ; this last word is perhaps an error for *εὐγενείας*, which seems to be required by the context ; Aucher renders, "mancipatio ac proscriptio ignobilis."

[d] *τὸ ῥητόν.*

[e] *τὸ πρὸς διάνοιαν.*

[f] *ἰδίᾳ προφορᾷ.*

[g] *λογισμῶν.*

[h] *i.e.* from Hebrew into Greek.

[i] Philo gives the same etymology of *ḥam* "to be hot" in *De Sobrietate* 44.

[j] "Canaanite" is sometimes used typologically in the sense of "merchant" in the Old Testament.

tor." [a] But now it is evidently not [b] a matter of kinship [c] or that one is the father or son of the other, but it is now evidently the (kinship of) thought with thought that (Scripture) shows, because of (Canaan's) remoteness from kinship with virtue.[d]

*66. (Gen. ix. 20) What [e] is the meaning of the words, "Noah began to be a husbandman of the earth" [f]?

(Scripture) likens Noah to that first moulded earthy man,[g] for it uses the same expression [h] of him, when he came out of the ark, as of the other,[i] for there was a beginning of agriculture both then and now,[j] both times after a flood. For at the creation of the world the earth was, in a sense,[k] flooded. For (God) would not have said, "Let the waters [l] be gathered into one gathering, and let the dry land appear," if there had not been an inundation in some abyss of the earth. But not ineptly does (Scripture) say "he began to be a husbandman," since in the second genesis of mankind he was the beginning of both seed and agriculture and other (forms of) life. This is the literal

[a] Arm. *aṛit'* = μεσίτης or πρόξενος, also ἀφορμή, ὑπόθεσις; Aucher renders "caussa." What Greek word Philo used it is hard to say. In *De Sobrietate* 44, 48 Philo etymologizes "Canaan" as σάλος "tossing" (seemingly connecting it with Heb. *na'* = "to move (constantly)").

[b] Lit. "not evidently."

[c] συγγενείας.

[d] διὰ τὴν ἀλλοτρίωσιν τὴν τῆς πρὸς ἀρετὴν οἰκειότητος.

[e] We should prob. follow Arm. MS. C in omitting the words "On agriculture" before "what."

[f] Philo closely follows LXX καὶ ἤρξατο Νῶε ἄνθρωπος γεωργὸς γῆς.

[g] τῷ πρώτῳ διαπλασθέντι <καὶ> γεώδει (or γηγενεῖ) ἀνθρώπῳ. The Greek frag. from Procopius omits γεώδει (or γηγενεῖ); perhaps it is a doublet in Arm.

[h] λόγῳ.

[i] *i.e.* Adam when driven from Eden, of Gen. iii. 23.

[j] Both in Adam's time and in Noah's.

[k] τρόπον τινά.

[l] LXX and Heb. have "waters under the heavens."

meaning.[a] But as for the deeper meaning,[b] there is a difference between being a husbandman [c] and a worker of the earth,[d] wherefore, when the fratricide [e] is introduced, it is said of him that he shall work the earth but not that he shall cultivate it. For symbolically the body is called " earth " (since) by nature our [f] (body) is earthy, and it works basely and badly like an unskilled hireling.[g] But the virtuous man cultivates like a skilled and experienced caretaker of plants, and the husbandman is an overseer of the good. For the worker-mind of the body, in accordance with its bodily (nature), pursues bodily pleasures, but the husbandman-mind strives to obtain useful fruits, those which (come) through continence and moderation [h]; and it cuts off the superfluous weaknesses (that grow) around our characters like the branches of wide-spreading trees.

67. (Gen. ix. 20) Why did the righteous man [i] first plant a vineyard ?

It was proper (for him) to fall into perplexity [j] where he should find a plant after the flood, since all those things which were on the earth had wasted away and perished. But what was said a little earlier [k] seemed to be true, (namely) that the earth was dried up at the spring season, for the spring produced a growth of plants ; accordingly,

[a] τὸ ῥητόν.

[b] τὸ πρὸς διάνοιαν.

[c] γεωργός.

[d] ἐργάτης τῆς γῆς ; on this distinction see *De Agricultura* 5 ff.

[e] Cain ; see *De Agricultura* 21 ff. on Gen. iv. 2.

[f] In the Arm. text the pronoun " our " is unaccountably separated by the relative clause from the word " body " in the main clause.

[g] ὡς ἄτεχνος μισθωτός (or ἔμμισθος as in *De Agricultura* 5).

[h] δι' ἐγκρατείας καὶ σωφροσύνης (the latter noun has a double rendering in Arm.).

[i] *i.e.* Noah.

[j] The two Arm. verbs both = ἀπορεῖν.

[k] In *QG* ii. 47 on Gen. viii. 14.

it was natural that both vines and vine-shoots were found that could flourish,[a] and that they were gathered by the righteous man. But it must be shown why he first planted a vineyard and not wheat and barley, since some fruits are necessary and it is impossible to live without them, while others are the material of superfluous luxury.[b] Now those which are necessary to life he consecrated and set apart for God[c] as being useful (to man), not having any co-operation[d] in their production; but superfluous things were assigned to man, for the use of wine is superfluous and not necessary. And so, in the same way that God Himself with His own hand caused fountains of potable water to flow out without the co-operation of men, so also He gave wheat and barley. For both forms of nourishment, food as well as drink, He alone by Himself bestowed (on man). But those (foods) which are for a life of luxury He did not keep for Himself[e] nor grudge that they should fall to man's possession.[f]

*68. (Gen. ix. 21) What is the meaning of the words, "he drank of the wine[g] and became drunken"?

In the first place, the righteous man[h] did not drink the wine but a portion of wine[i] and not all of it. For the incontinent and self-indulgent man[j] does not give up going to drinking-bouts before he has put away inside himself all

[a] Prob. *βλαστοὺς ἀμπέλου ζωοφυτοῦντας.*

[b] *ὕλη πλεοναζούσης τρυφῆς.*

[c] *i.e.* man should not presume to claim credit for producing the necessities of life, for which God alone is responsible.

[d] *συνεργίαν.*

[e] *οὐκ ἐνοσφίσατο.*

[f] Construction of Arm. uncertain; Aucher renders, "quin homines assequerentur per industriam propriam."

[g] *ἔπιεν ἐκ τοῦ οἴνου*, as in LXX.

[h] Noah.

[i] Philo stresses the scriptural wording "drank *of* the wine."

[j] *ὁ ἀκρατὴς καὶ ἀσελγὴς vel sim.*

the unmixed (wine).[a] But the continent and abstemious man measures the things necessary for use. And " becoming drunken " is used in the sense of[b] " making use of wine." For there is a twofold and double way of becoming drunken : one is to drink wine to excess,[c] which is a sin peculiar to the vicious and evil man ; the other is to partake of wine, which always happens to the wise man.[d] Accordingly, it is in the second signification that the virtuous and wise man is said to be drunken, not by drinking wine to excess,[e] but merely by partaking of wine.[f]

69. (Gen. ix. 21) What is the meaning of the words, " he was uncovered in his house " ?[g]

It is a matter of praise for the wise man both literally and in a deeper sense[h] that his nakedness does not (take place) somewhere outside but that he was in his house, concealed by the screen of his house. For the nakedness of his body was concealed by his house, which was built of stone and wood. But the covering and screen of the soul is knowledge.[i] Now there are two kinds of nakedness. One is by chance[j] and comes through involuntary transgressions,[k]

[a] *τὸν ἄκρατον (οἶνον).*

[b] Lit. " instead of."

[c] Lit. " to be excessive in being senseless in drinking wine," probably an awkward rendering of a text like that of the Greek frag. *τὸ παρ' οἶνον ληρεῖν.*

[d] *τὸ οἰνοῦσθαι ὅπερ εἰς σοφὸν πίπτει*, as in the Greek frag.

[e] See note *c* above.

[f] On the theme of " sober drunkenness " (*νηφάλιος μέθη*) in Philo and other Hellenistic writers, see Hans Lewy, *Sobria Ebrietas*, Giessen, 1929.

[g] *ἐγυμνώθη ἐν τῷ οἴκῳ αὐτοῦ*, as in LXX ; for " house " Heb. has " tent." On the theme of Noah's nakedness *cf. Leg. All.* ii. 60 ff.

[h] *καὶ τὸ ῥητὸν καὶ τὸ πρὸς διάνοιαν.*

[i] The compound *xrat hanjaroy* elsewhere in the Arm. translation of Philo = *ἐπιστήμη* ; Aucher here renders, " disciplina sapientiae," which is a perfectly justifiable rendering.

[j] *ἐκ τύχης.*

[k] *δι' ἀκουσίων ἁμαρτημάτων.*

for in a certain sense[a] he who practises rectitude[b] is clothed, and if he stumbles, it is not by his own free will[c] but as is the case of those who are drunken or shakily stagger from one side to the other or fall asleep or are seized by madness. For those who transgress in these ways do not do so with malice aforethought.[d] But it is an obligation[e] to put on, like a covering, good instruction and good training.[f] And there is another nakedness, that of the soul, (which) can very nobly[g] escape the entire burdensome weight[h] of the body, as from a tomb, as if it had been buried in it a long time, as in a tomb,[i] and sense-pleasures and innumerable miseries of other passions and the perturbations of anxieties about evil, and the troubles caused by each of these. For he who has the power to come through[j] so many deeds and wounds, and strip himself of all of them, has obtained a fortunate and blessed lot[k] without false show[l] and deformity. For this I should say is beauty and adornment[m] in those who have proved worthy of living incorporeally.[n]

70. (Gen. ix. 22) Why does (Scripture) not simply say, "Ham saw the nakedness" instead of[o] "Ham, the father of Canaan, saw the nakedness of his father"?

[a] *τρόπον τινά.*

[b] Prob. *κατόρθωσιν*; Aucher suggests *ὄρθωσιν.*

[c] *ἑκουσίᾳ γνώμῃ.*

[d] Prob. *προμηθείᾳ καὶ βουλῇ.*

[e] Lit. "service"—*λειτουργία* or *ὑπηρεσία.*

[f] *εὐμάθειαν καὶ εὐπαίδειαν.*

[g] *πάνυ γενναίως vel sim.*; Aucher "per summam virtutem."

[h] *ὄγκον δυσχερῆ.*

[i] The awkward repetition in the Arm. suggests a scribal error.

[j] *διήκειν.*

[k] *εὐδαίμονα καὶ μακάριον κλῆρον.*

[l] This rendering is based on the Arm. glossator's explanation of *kmayeak* which is not found in the large Arm. lexicon; Aucher renders, "sine labe."

[m] *κάλλος καὶ κόσμος.*

[n] *ἀσωμάτως.*

[o] Lit. "but."

It convicts[a] both the son through the father and the father through the son, for in common and as one they have committed an act of folly, wickedness and impiety[b] and other evils. This is the literal meaning.[c] But as for the deeper meaning,[d] (it is) what has been said before about these things.[e]

*71. (Gen. ix. 22) What is the meaning of the words, "He related it to his two brothers outside"[f]?

(Scripture) increasingly magnifies the accusation.[g] First of all,[h] it was not to one brother alone that he told his father's involuntary transgression but to both. And if there had been many, he would have told them all rather than only those whom he could. And this he did derisively[i] when he spoke to them (of a matter) deserving not of derision and jest[j] but of modesty, awe and reverence.[k] And second, (Scripture) says that he related it not within but outside, which shows clearly that he betrayed it[l] not only to his brothers but also to those who were standing around them outside,[m] men and women alike. This is the literal meaning.[n] But as for the deeper mean-

[a] ἐλέγχει. [b] ἀφροσύνης καὶ ἀδικίας καὶ ἀσεβείας.
[c] τὸ ῥητόν. [d] τὸ πρὸς διάνοιαν.
[e] In § 65 on Gen. ix. 18-19.
[f] LXX καὶ ἐξελθὼν ἀνήγγειλεν τοῖς δυσὶν ἀδελφοῖς αὐτοῦ ἔξω; Heb. has no word corresponding to ἐξελθών.
[g] Lit. "complaint (or "penalty") of accusation," probably an expanded rendering of ἔγκλημα, as in the Greek frag.
[h] The Greek frag. has πρῶτον μὲν ἐκ τοῦ ὑπεριδεῖν, δεύτερον δ' ἐκ τοῦ εἰπεῖν καὶ οὐχ ἑνὶ μόνῳ κτλ.; thus the second charge in the Arm. corresponds to the third charge in the Greek frag., εἶτα οὐκ ἔνδον κτλ.
[i] Prob. διαχλευάζων as in Greek frag.
[j] The Greek frag. has only χλεύης.
[k] The Greek frag. has only αἰδοῦς καὶ εὐλαβείας.
[l] Both Greek fragments (the second ends with this sentence) have ἀκηκοέναι . . . τοὺς ἀδελφούς.
[m] Aucher's translation omits the last word.
[n] τὸ ῥητόν.

ing,[a] the wicked and malevolent character was glad and rejoiced and evilly regarded the misfortunes of others, judging them peculiarly by himself as though (they were) right.[b] Because of this he even now exults at the involuntary behaviour[c] of the lover of wisdom,[d] and celebrates and proclaims[e] his misfortunes, and becomes an adversary and accuser,[f] though it would have been fitting to show tolerance and forgiveness rather than (bring) blame and accusation. And so, because, as I have said before,[g] these three—the good, the bad and the indifferent[h]—are brothers of one another (and) the offspring of one reason,[i] they watch over[j] various things ; some praise the virtues,[k] and some, evils,[l] and others, wealth and honours and other goods which are around the body and outside the body. These watchers and zealots[m] of evil rejoice at the fall[n] of the wise man, and mock, accuse and slander[o] him on the

[a] τὸ πρὸς διάνοιαν.

[b] Text and meaning somewhat uncertain (from " and evilly regarded ") ; Aucher renders, " malum est autem (in note, " *vel*, et male accusat ") aliorum miserias *vel* apud se solum judicare, ut judex corrigens " (in note, " *vel*, sicut correctio ").

[c] Arm. *bark'*, translated above as " character " (=ἦθος or τρόπος), also renders ἀγωγή, the meaning seemingly required by the context here ; Aucher here renders, " casum."

[d] τοῦ τῆς σοφίας ἐραστοῦ, *i.e.* Noah.

[e] Lit. " becoming a singer and announcer."

[f] The Arm. synonyms are probably a double rendering of κατήγορος.

[g] In *QG* i. 88 on Gen. v. 32.

[h] τὸ ἀδιάφορον.

[i] ἑνὸς ἔκγονοι λογισμοῦ.

[j] Arm. *verakaçouk'* lit. = " overseers," " superintendents " and the like, and usu. renders ἐπιστάται, ἐπίσκοποι, etc. ; below it is used as a parallel of *naxanzawork'* = ζηλωταί, which suggests that its Greek original here had the meaning of " jealous observers " or the like ; Aucher renders, " praesides."

[k] τὰς ἀρετάς.

[l] τὰ κακά.

[m] See note *j*.

[n] τῷ πταίσματι.

[o] The two Arm. verbs are prob. a double rendering of διαβάλλουσι.

ground that somehow [a] he does not profit [b] from those parts [c] of which he consists [d] and of which he is zealous, which are good for the soul, nor from those which (are good) for the body and are external—neither in the internal virtues nor in those things which are bodily and external goods.[e] But (they argue) that he alone can achieve his purpose [f] who is practised in wrongdoing,[g] which alone is wont to be of profit to human life. These and similar things are stated by those who are watchers of wicked folly [h] and mock the lovers of virtue [i] and those things by which virtue comes into being and is formed, just as some think that which is bodily and external has the status [j] of instruments of service.[k]

*72. (Gen. ix. 23) What is the meaning of the words, "Shem and Japheth took a garment and laid it upon both their shoulders and went backward and covered the nakedness of their father and did not see it" [l]?

The literal meaning [m] is clear. But as for the deeper meaning,[n] this must be said. The light and hasty man is

[a] τρόπον τινά. [b] οὐκ ὠφελεῖται.

[c] τὰ μέρη: the sense of the phrase is not clear to me.

[d] συνίσταται.

[e] The construction of the Arm. is obscure, as is Aucher's somewhat less literal rendering, "praesides malitiam aemulantes gaudent de sapientis lapsu, irrident et detrahunt, quasi vero ille per partes, quas praefert ac prosequitur sicut meliores pro animo, vel corpore aut externis suis, nihil profecerit nec internis, neque externis virtutibus, quominus et bonis circa et extra corpus," etc.

[f] τὴν πρόθεσιν. [g] ἀδικίαν.

[h] ἀφροσύνης or πονηρίας. [i] τοὺς τῆς ἀρετῆς ἐραστάς.

[j] τὸν λόγον.

[k] ὀργάνων διακονίας (or ὑπηρεσίας or λειτουργίας); the connexion of ideas is far from clear.

[l] Philo abbreviates the biblical verse, which in both LXX and Heb., after "the nakedness of their father," reads "and their faces were backward, and the nakedness of their father they did not see."

[m] τὸ ῥητόν. [n] τὸ πρὸς διάνοιαν.

satisfied to see only what is straight ahead and before his eyes.[a] But the wise man (sees that which is) behind, that is, the future.[b] For just as the things behind come after the things ahead, so the future (comes after) the present,[c] and the constant and wise man [d] obtains sight of this, like the mythical Lynceus,[e] having eyes on all sides. But every wise one, not man but mind,[f] goes backward, that is, looks behind as at a very radiant light [g]; and seeing everything clearly from all sides,[h] and looking around, is found to be hedged about and fortified, so that no part of the soul shall remain naked and unseemly before the blows and attacks that overtake it.[i]

73. (Gen. ix. 24) What is the meaning of the words, " Noah sobered up from the wine " [j]?

[a] The Greek frag. is slightly different: *ὁ εὐχερὴς καὶ ὁ ἀπερίσκεπτος τὸ ἐπ' εὐθείας καὶ πρὸς ὀφθαλμῶν μόνον ὁρᾷ.*

[b] *τὰ μέλλοντα.*

[c] *τῶν ἐνεστώτων.*

[d] Arm. *astin* and *imastoun* are a double rendering of Greek *ἀστεῖος*, as the Greek frag. shows—*astin* " constant " being chosen here as elsewhere in Philo for its phonetic resemblance to *ἀστεῖος*.

[e] For the words " like the mythical Lynceus " the Greek frag. has only *αὐγαίως*, prob. a corruption of *Λυγκέως* <*δίκην*>, as Harris suggests.

[f] The Greek frag. agrees almost literally with the Arm., *πᾶς οὖν σοφὸς οὐκ ἄνθρωπος ἀλλὰ νοῦς*; Aucher, rightly puzzled, somewhat freely renders, " omnis ergo sapiens, qui non ita homo est, quantum intellectus."

[g] The clause " goes backward . . . light " is not found in the Greek frag.

[h] The Greek frag. has only *καταθεώμενος*.

[i] The Greek frag. reads more briefly *περιπέφρακται πρὸς τὰ ἐνεστῶτα καὶ τὰ ἀδοκήτως καταστιλάζοντα.* Apparently the " naked " and " unseemly " are due to the Arm. translator's misunderstanding of *τὰ ἀδοκήτως καταστιλάζοντα* " the things that swoop down unexpectedly " as if *ἄδοξον καὶ καταψιλοῦν* or the like.

[j] So most LXX MSS., *ἐξένηψεν δὲ Νῶε ἀπὸ τοῦ οἴνου*; Heb. has " And Noah awakened from his wine."

The literal meaning is very comprehensible.[a] But the deeper meaning [b] must be rendered. When the mind [c] is strong, it is able to see clearly with soberness [d] both the things before and those behind, that is, the present [e] and the future.[f] But blindness comes upon him who is not able to see clearly either the present or the future.[g] And to him who sees the present and does not guard himself by foreseeing the future, wine-bibbing and drunkenness are (ascribed). But in him who is capable of looking around and comprehending the different natures of things present and future, there are soberness and sobriety.[h]

74. (Gen. ix. 24) Why, after reckoning Ham as the middle child of the three brothers,[i] does (Scripture) call him "the youngest,"[j] saying, "what his youngest son had done to him"?

(Scripture) clearly allegorizes.[k] It takes the youngest to be, not the one who is so in age and time, but the one who is more youthful,[l] for wickedness is unable to receive an aged and elder teaching,[m] and elder are the thoughts of

[a] τὸ ῥητὸν γνωριμώτατόν ἐστι.

[b] τὸ πρὸς διάνοιαν.

[c] ὁ νοῦς.

[d] νήφων.

[e] τὰ ἐνεστῶτα; the Ambrosian paraphrase has "praeterita."

[f] τὰ μέλλοντα.

[g] The Arm. words for "present" and "future" are different from those used in the preceding sentence.

[h] Lit. "soberness of sobriety," prob. rendering τὸ τῆς σωφροσύνης νηφάλιον.

[i] *Cf. QG* i. 88 on Gen. v. 32; Aucher renders less literally, "in medietate prolium, sive medium inter fratres."

[j] νεώτερον, used as superlative, as in LXX; Heb. has "his small son," also indicating the youngest of three.

[k] ἀλληγορεῖ.

[l] νεώτερον; here the Arm. uses a different word from that rendered "youngest" above.

[m] The Arm. lit. = εἰσδέχεσθαι γεροντικὴν καὶ πρεσβυτέραν μάθησιν; Aucher renders more freely, "percipere doctrinam seniori propriam."

wills [a] that are truly hoary [b]—this, moreover, not in body but in mind.[c]

75. (Gen. ix. 26) Why, in praying for Shem, does (Noah) say, " Blessed be the Lord God, God of Shem,[d] and Canaan shall be his servant " ?

" Lord " and " God " is an apposition [e] of the two chief powers, the beneficent and the kingly,[f] through which the world [g] came into being. Now the king made the world in accordance with His beneficence, while after its completion it was put in order [h] by His sovereignty. Accordingly, He deemed the wise man worthy of the common honour [i] which the whole world received in common, for the parts of the world were joined with him by the powers of the Lord and God,[j] and He gave His beneficent grace and largess with peculiarly abundant magnificence. Therefore the name of the beneficent power, " God " is twice used ; once, as has been said, in apposition with the kingly power, and a second time without visible connexion,[k] in order that the wise man may become worthy of both the common and the special gift [l] (of God), being loved both by the world and by God—by the world, because of the common grace ; by God, because of the special (grace).[m]

[a] *οἱ τῶν βουλῶν λογισμοί.*

[b] *πολιαί* ; for the metaphor see *De Sacr. Abelis* 79 *ὡς δέον πολιὸν μὲν μάθημα χρόνῳ μηδὲν ἀρνεῖσθαι.*

[c] *οὐ κατὰ σῶμα ἀλλὰ κατὰ νοῦν.*

[d] So Arm. O.T. ; LXX and Heb. have " The Lord, the God of Shem " (LXX *κύριος* " Lord " renders Heb. *YHWH*).

[e] Or " harmonization."

[f] *τῶν δυεῖν πρώτων δυνάμεων τῆς εὐεργέτιδος καὶ τῆς βασιλικῆς* ; see *QG* ii. 51.

[g] *ὁ κόσμος.*

[h] *ἐτάχθη vel sim.*

[i] *τῆς κοινῆς τιμῆς*, *cf. De Sobrietate* 51-55.

[j] Aucher renders, " junctis itidem partibus quoque mundi cum virtutibus Domini et Dei," but the Arm. requires " junctis cum eo," not " junctis . . . cum virtutibus."

[k] *ἄνευ ὁρατῆς συμπλοκῆς.*

[l] *καὶ τῆς κοινῆς καὶ τῆς ἰδίας δωρεᾶς.*

[m] *διὰ τὴν ἐξαίρετον <χάριν>.*

76. (Gen. ix. 27) Why, in praying for Japheth, does (Noah) say, "God shall enlarge Japheth, and he shall dwell in the house[a] of Shem, and Canaan shall be their[b] servant"?

Leaving aside the literal meaning,[c] since it is clear, the deeper meaning[d] must be examined; according to this, the secondary and tertiary goods[e] receive an enlargement, (such as) health and keenness of perception and beauty and power and wealth, glory, nobility, friends and offices[f] and many other such things. Therefore he says, "shall enlarge." For the full possession of so many things separately and by themselves works harm to many who do not live in accordance with righteousness and wisdom and the other virtues,[g] of which the full possession controls[h] bodily and external things. But the inaccessibility and remoteness (of virtue) leaves it[i] without management and use. And when it is abandoned and left alone by good overseers,[j] it brings harm instead of the profit which it might have brought. Wherefore he prays for him who possesses bodily and external things that "he shall dwell in the houses[k] of the wise man,"[l] in order that he may look toward the example of all good, and seeing this, may set straight his own way.[m]

[a] So Arm. O.T.; LXX has οἴκοις, Heb. "tents"; below the Arm. has "houses" (plural).

[b] Some LXX MSS. and ancient versions have "his."

[c] τὸ ῥητόν.

[d] τὸ πρὸς διάνοιαν.

[e] As the Ambrosian paraphrase explains, Japheth is a symbol of "the indifferent" (τὸ ἀδιάφορον); see above, *QG* i. 88.

[f] ὑγίειαν καὶ εὐαισθησίαν καὶ κάλλος καὶ δύναμιν καὶ πλοῦτον καὶ δόξαν καὶ εὐγένειαν καὶ φίλους καὶ ἀρχάς.

[g] κατὰ δικαιοσύνην καὶ φρόνησιν καὶ τὰς ἄλλας ἀρετάς.

[h] οἰκονομεῖ *vel sim.*; Aucher "optime dispensat."

[i] *i.e.* the possession of worldly goods.

[j] These "overseers" have prob. no connexion with those mentioned above in *QG* ii. 71.

[k] See above, note *a*.

[l] Shem is here the symbol of the wise man, see the preceding section.

[m] εὐθύνῃ τὴν ἑαυτοῦ ὁδόν.

*77. (Gen. ix. 27) Why, when Ham sins, does (Scripture) present his son Canaan as the servant of Shem and Japheth?

In the first place, because both father and son practised the same wickedness, both being mingled without distinction, as if using one body and one soul.[a] And in the second place, because the father too was to be greatly saddened by the cursing of his son, knowing that it was not so much for his own sake as for his father's that he[b] was punished, for the punishment (fell) on the prime mover and teacher of evil thoughts, words and deeds.[c] This is the literal meaning.[d] But as for the deeper meaning,[e] potentially[f] they are two—not so much men as characters.[g] And this is shown by the giving of names, which also clearly indicates the nature of things.[h] For " Ham " is to be interpreted as " heat " or " hot," while " Canaan " means " merchants " or " middle-men."[i]

78. (Gen. ix. 28) Why did Noah, after the flood, live three hundred and fifty years?

The form of the world[j] was represented as founded at the beginning in two heptads of years,[k] and the wise man[l]

[a] ὡς ἑνὶ σώματι καὶ μιᾷ ψυχῇ χρώμενοι.

[b] Canaan.

[c] τὸν ἡγεμόνα (or ἀρχηγέτην) καὶ διδάσκαλον κακῶν λογισμῶν καὶ λόγων καὶ ἔργων.

[d] τὸ ῥητόν.

[e] τὸ πρὸς διάνοιαν.

[f] δυνάμει.

[g] ἤθη or τρόποι.

[h] *i.e.* the etymology of their names is indicative of their characters.

[i] See notes to *QG* ii. 65 near end.

[j] τὸ τοῦ κόσμου εἶδος.

[k] This appears to be the literal meaning of the obscure Arm. sentence which Aucher more freely renders, " bis septenis annis declaratur jam ex principio condita atque renovata (sub Noe) forma mundi " ; he adds in a footnote that, as the Arm. glossator reminds us, the world was created in seven days, and Noah waited seven days before sending out the dove.

[l] ὁ σοφός (or ἀστεῖος), *i.e.* Noah.

lived the same number times twenty-five, for fourteen times twenty-five is seventy times five years, and fifty times seven. Now the reckoning [a] of the seventh and fiftieth year has a special order [b] which is Levitical, for there it is established.[c]

79. (Gen. x. 1) Why, among the three sons of Noah, does Ham always appear in the middle, while the extremes [d] vary? When they are born, Shem is mentioned first, as follows, "Shem, Ham, Japheth," [e] but when they beget children, Japheth is put first in order, and the family begins to be reckoned from Japheth [f]?

Those who investigate the literal nature of Holy Scripture [g] pretend to believe [h] concerning the order of sons that he who is mentioned first, Shem, is the youngest, while the last, Japheth, is the eldest. But such persons may think as they severally please and hold whatever belief they happen to find suitable.[i] By us, however, who investigate the intelligible nature of others [j] it must be said that of these three, the good, the bad and the indifferent, which are called secondary goods,[k] the bad always appears [l] in the middle, in order that it may be caught in the middle and overcome

[a] Or "principle"—*λόγος*.

[b] *ἰδίαν τάξιν*.

[c] This is probably a reference to the passages in the book of Leviticus on the Sabbath and Jubilee year; *cf. De Spec. Leg.* ii. 176.

[d] *τὰ ἄκρα*, *i.e.* the eldest and youngest sons.

[e] In Gen. x. 1; see also *QG* ii. 65 on Gen. ix. 18-19.

[f] In Gen. x. 2.

[g] *τὴν τῶν ἱερῶν γραμμάτων ῥητὴν φύσιν*.

[h] Lit. "make pretences (or "excuses"), believing"; Aucher "ratum habent . . . putantes."

[i] Aucher renders more freely, "opinionis suae ratione ducti."

[j] *τὴν νοερὰν τῶν ἄλλων φύσιν*: Aucher "mentalem in his sensum."

[k] See above, *QG* ii. 76 and *QG* i. 88.

[l] Or "is always reckoned (by Scripture)."

from either side, so that either may seize it, press it closely and crush it. But the good and the indifferent or secondary good exchange their order. So long as the bad is present only virtually but not actually,[a] the good is first and has the rank [b] of governor and ruler.[c] But when an act results from will and intention,[d] and injustice does not merely remain in the mind [e] but is realized in unjust acts, (then) the good, which is first, changes its place to another one in the order, as do the good traits with which it is adorned, and it takes leave of instruction and management,[f] as if not able to understand them, like a physician when he sees an illness that is incurable. However, the eldest good ministers to that virtue [g] which is bodily and external,[h] and carefully watches the extreme ends,[i] confining the beast [j] in a net and showing that it no longer has power to bite and do harm. But when it perceives that this has not been done, it changes to a more secure and stable place, and leaves its former place for [k] a more powerful one, and having obtained one easy to capture [l] lower down, holds it : the barrier [m] and guarding of this is held by a more powerful guard,[n] for there is nothing more powerful than virtue.

[a] δυνάμει μόνον ἀλλ' οὐκ ἐντελεχείᾳ. [b] τὴν τάξιν.
[c] οἰκονόμου καὶ ἄρχοντος *vel sim.*
[d] ἔργον ἐκ τῆς βουλῆς καὶ τοῦ λογισμοῦ γίνεται.
[e] ἐν τῷ νῷ. [f] διδασκαλίαν καὶ οἰκονομίαν.
[g] τῇ ἀρετῇ διακονεῖ.
[h] *i.e.* Shem, the symbol of good, looks after Japheth, the symbol of " the indifferent " ; *cf. QG* ii. 76.
[i] Lit. " the ends of the extremes." [j] τὸ θηρίον.
[k] Or " to " ? As Aucher observes, the whole passage " obscurus est textus."
[l] The Arm. lit. = εὐάλωτον ; Aucher renders, " servatu facilem." The original of the obscure passage (which seems to have no parallel in Philo) would not be easy to reconstruct.
[m] Arm. *çank* means both " barrier " and " always " ; Aucher chooses the latter meaning here and renders, " semper."
[n] This rendering is admittedly obscure but is closer to the Arm. than is Aucher's, " faciliter enim observare semper accidit ei fortiori custodis vi."

80. (Gen. x. 4-5) Why do "the Kittians and Rhodians [a] and the islands of the Gentiles" (spring) from Japheth?

Because (his name) is to be interpreted as "breadth," [b] for he is broadened in growth and progress,[c] and is no longer contained by the other part of those regions which have been granted by Nature for the use of man, (namely) the earth, but he passes over to still another (part), the sea, and to the islands which are in it. This is the literal meaning.[d] But as for the deeper meaning,[e] those things which by nature [f] are external goods, (such as) wealth, honour and authority, are everywhere poured out and extended both to those in whose hands they are, and, at a distance, to those in whose hands they are not. And even more—or not less—do they fence them in round about and keep them close because of those who are filled with desire and are lovers of money and glory, and, since they love authority, nothing is enough for them because of their insatiable desire.

81. (Gen. x. 6) Why is Ham's eldest son Cush?

The theologian [g] has expressed a most natural principle [h] in calling Cush the eldest offspring of evil,[i] (since he is) the sparse [j] nature of earth.[k] For earth that is fertile, well-stocked, well-watered, rich in herbage and in grain, and well-forested is distributed and divided into the products of fruit. But sparse and dusty earth is dry, unfruitful, barren and sterile, and is carried off and lifted up by the wind, and

[a] LXX has Κήτιοι and Ῥόδιοι; Heb. has *Kittîm* and *Dôdānîm* (prob. a scribal error for *Rôdânîm*).

[b] πλάτος; see above, *QG* ii. 76 on Gen. ix. 27.

[c] κατ' αὔξησιν καὶ κατὰ προκοπὴν πλατυνόμενος.

[d] τὸ ῥητόν.

[e] τὸ πρὸς διάνοιαν.

[f] φύσει.

[g] ὁ θεολόγος (Moses).

[h] φυσικώτατον λόγον.

[i] Or "of the evil one."

[j] Lit. "scattered" or "sporadic."

[k] Philo here etymologizes the name "Cush," not as a Hebrew name, but as if from Greek χοῦς "heap of earth," "dust."

causes the salubrious air [a] to suffer from dust. Such are the first buds of evil, for they are barren and unproductive of good practices,[b] and are the causes of barrenness in all the parts of the soul.[c]

82. (Gen. x. 8-9) Why did Cush beget Nimrod [d] who began to be " a giant hunter " [e] before the Lord, wherefore they said, " like Nimrod a giant hunter before God " [f] ?

It is proper that one having a sparse [g] nature, which a spiritual bond does not bring together and hold firmly, and not being the father of constancy either of soul or nature or character, but like a giant valuing and honouring earthly things more than heavenly, should show forth the truth of the story [h] about the giants and Titans. For in truth [i] he who is zealous for earthly and corruptible things always fights against and makes war on heavenly things and praiseworthy and wonderful natures, and builds walls and towers [j] on earth against heaven. But those things which are here [k] are against those things which are there.[l] For this reason it is not ineptly [m] said, " a giant before [n] God," which clearly is opposition to the Deity. For the impious man [o] is none other than the enemy and foe who stands against [p] God. Wherefore it is proverbial that everyone

[a] τὸν ζωτικὸν ἀέρα ; for the same expression see *Leg. ad Gaium* 125.

[b] ἀγαθῶν ἐπιτηδευμάτων.

[c] Aucher more freely renders, " causae sterilitatis animae partiumque ejus omnium."

[d] LXX Νεβρὼ or Νεβρώθ.

[e] LXX γίγας κυνηγός = Heb. *gibbôr-ṣayid* " champion in hunting."

[f] Most LXX MSS. have " before the Lord God " ; Heb. has " before *YHWH* " (= " the Lord ").

[g] See above, *QG* ii. 81, note *k*.

[h] τὸν μῦθον ἀληθεύειν.

[i] ὄντως.

[j] Or " heaps and mounds."

[k] *i.e.* on earth.

[l] *i.e.* in heaven.

[m] οὐκ ἀπὸ σκοποῦ.

[n] ἐναντίον in the biblical sense of " before " is interpreted by Philo in the usual sense of " against."

[o] ὁ ἀσεβής.

[p] Lit. " around."

who is a great sinner should be compared with [a] him as the chief head and fount,[b] as when they say, "like Nimrod." Thus the name is a clear indication of the thing (signified), for it is to be translated as "Ethiopian," [c] and his skill [d] is that of the hunter. Both of these are to be condemned and reprehended, the Ethiopian because pure evil has no participation in light,[e] but follows night and darkness, while hunting is as far removed as possible from the rational nature.[f] But he who is among beasts seeks to equal the bestial habits of animals through evil passions.

[a] Meaning doubtful; lit. "should be exchanged (or "completed"), being brought back"; Aucher renders, "referri."

[b] Lit. "ruler and leader."

[c] Philo confuses the etymology of "Nimrod" with that of his father Cush, elsewhere interpreted as "Ethiopian" (though not above in *QG* ii. 81). In *De Gigantibus* 66 Philo etymologizes "Nimrod" as if from Heb. *mrd* "to rebel" and interprets it as αὐτομόλησις "desertion."

[d] τέχνη.

[e] ἄκρατος κακία οὐδεμίαν ἔχει κοινωνίαν τοῦ φωτός.

[f] τῆς λογικῆς φύσεως.

BOOK III

1. (Gen. xv. 7) What is the meaning of the words, "I am the Lord God[a] who led thee out of the land of the Chaldaeans[b] to give thee this land to inherit"?

The literal meaning[c] is clear. That which must be rendered as the deeper meaning[d] is as follows. The "land of the Chaldaeans" is symbolically mathematical theory,[e] of which astronomy[f] is part. And in this (field) the Chaldaeans labour not unsuccessfully or slothfully. Thus He honours the wise man with two gifts. For one thing He takes him away[g] from Chaldaean doctrine,[h] which in addition to being difficult to seize and grasp, is the cause of great evils and impiety in attributing to that which is created the powers of the Creator, and persuades men to honour and worship the works of the world instead of the

[a] LXX has merely "God," Heb. has merely "Lord" (*YHWH*). In the parallel passage, *Quis Rer. Div. Heres* 96, Philo follows the LXX in reading "God." Possibly the Arm. translator has here inserted "Lord" on the basis of Arm. O.T. which reads, "Lord God."

[b] So LXX; Heb. has "Ur Kasdim" (=Ur of the Chaldaeans).

[c] *τὸ ῥητόν*.

[d] Lit. "to the understanding of its nature"; Aucher more freely renders "ad sensūs essentiam." In the *Quaestiones* the usual antithesis to *τὸ ῥητόν* is *τὸ πρὸς διάνοιαν*.

[e] *συμβολικῶς μαθηματικὴ θεωρία ἐστί.*

[f] *ἀστρονομία* in the sense of astrology.

[g] Or "saves him."

[h] Lit. "doctrine (or "school"—*δόγματος*) of opinions"; Aucher renders *ad hoc*, "de secta astrologorum videlicet de Chaldaeismi hallucinatione."

Creator of the world.[a] And again, He grants him fruitful wisdom which He symbolically calls "land." And the Father shows that wisdom and virtue [b] are immutable and without change or turning, for it is not proper for God to reveal [c] that which is able to admit turning or change, because that which is revealed should be and remain unchangeable and constant. But that which is subject to change and is wont to be always fluid does not admit of true and proper [d] revelation.

2. (Gen. xv. 8) Why does (Abraham) say, "Lord,[e] by what shall I be informed [f] that I shall inherit it"?

He seeks an indication [g] of knowing (His) agreement.[h] But two things worthy of admiration [i] are described. (One), which is an affection of the mind,[j] is to trust in God in accordance with the word which He has earlier spoken. And (the other) is to have an immense [k] desire [l] not to be without a share in certain signs through which one may be sense-perceptibly informed that a promise has been confirmed. And to Him who made the promise (he shows) reverential awe by using the expression "Lord"; "for," he says, "I know that Thou art lord and ruler of all things and that Thou canst do all things and that there is nothing impossible for thee. And though I myself have faith in what Thou hast promised, I now [m] desire and long to

[a] *τὰ τοῦ κόσμου ἔργα ἀντὶ τοῦ κοσμοποιοῦ.*

[b] *σοφία καὶ ἀρετή.*

[c] Lit. "to show."

[d] The Arm. translator seems to have taken *κύριος* in the sense of "divine."

[e] LXX "Lord God," Heb. "Lord *YHWH*" (traditionally read as "Lord God" since *YHWH* by itself is conventionally read "Lord" (*'Adônay*)).

[f] LXX and Heb. "know."

[g] *σημεῖον.*

[h] Or "promise."

[i] Lit. "zeal"—*σπουδῆς.*

[j] *πάθος τοῦ νοῦ.*

[k] Or "inexpressible."

[l] Lit. "desire of yearning."

[m] Aucher may be right in connecting the adverb "now" with the infinitive "to obtain" and in rendering, "citius assequi."

obtain, if not the fulfilment, at least some clear sign by which the fulfilment will be revealed. For I am a mortal,[a] and even though I have attained [b] the highest degree of integrity,[c] I am not always able to contain the impulses of desire,[d] so that when I see or hear something good I go to it slowly and not immediately. Wherefore I pray that Thou wilt show me a way of knowing,[e] so that I may comprehend the future."

*3. (Gen. xv. 9) Why does (God) say, "Take for me a heifer three years old and a she-goat three years old and a ram three years old and a turtle-dove and a dove" [f]?

He mentions five animals which are offered on the sacred altar. And they are divided among these (kinds of) offerings: of terrestrial creatures [g] three—ox, goat and bull,[h] and of birds two—turtle-dove and dove. For (Scripture) celebrates [i] the fact that the eternal offerings take their origin from the patriarch,[j] who was also the founder of the race.[k] But instead of "bring [l] to me" it is said most excellently, "take for me," for to a mortal creature [m] there is nothing properly his own,[n] but all things are the gift and grace [o] of God, to whom it is pleasing that one who has received something should show gratitude with all eagerness.[p] And He commands him to take a three-year old

[a] γενητός.

[b] Or "should attain" (?).

[c] Arm. *k'ajabarout'iun* usu. = καλοκἀγαθία or εὐήθεια; the Arm. variant *k'ajaberout'iun* = εὐφορία.

[d] τὰς τῆς ἐπιθυμίας ὁρμάς.

[e] γνώρισμα or γνῶσιν.

[f] LXX περιστεράν: Heb. *gôzāl* "young pigeon."

[g] τῶν χερσαίων.

[h] Philo here uses the generic names, but the last name, "bull" (Arm. *dowar* usu. = ταῦρος), is puzzling; one expects Arm. *oš̌xar* "sheep," as below. Possibly the Arm. translator read βοῦν for ὄϊν.

[i] Lit. "sings."

[j] τοῦ πατριάρχου.

[k] τοῦ γένους.

[l] Or "offer."

[m] τῷ γενητῷ.

[n] κυρίως ἴδιον.

[o] δῶρον καὶ χάρις.

[p] μετὰ προθυμίας πάσης.

one of each animal, since the number three is full and perfect, consisting of beginning, middle and end. However, it is proper to be in doubt why He adduces two females among the three animals—the heifer and the she-goat, and one male—the ram. May it not be because the ox [a] and goat are offered for sins, and the sheep is not? Sinning comes from weakness,[b] and the female is weak.

So much was it fitting and proper [c] to say first. But I am not unaware that all such things give occasion to idle calumniators [d] to reject the Sacred Writings and to talk nonsense about them. Thus they say that in the present instance nothing else but the sacrificial victim is described and indicated by the dismembering and dividing of the animals and by the inspection of the entrails. And as for what happens to them,[e] they say that this is an indication of chance [f] and of opportunely visible likenesses. But such people, it seems to me, are (in the class) of those who judge and evaluate [g] the whole by only one part, and do not,[h] on the contrary, (judge) the part by the whole. For this is the best test of anything, whether name [i] or object.[j]

Accordingly, the Legislation [k] is in some sense a unified creature,[l] which one should view from all sides in its entirety with open eyes [m] and examine the intention of the

[a] Here again Philo uses the generic name (*βοῦς*).

[b] *ἐξ ἀσθενείας*.

[c] Lit. "harmonious and congruent"; Aucher renders, "apposite."

[d] *τοῖς ἀπὸ σκοποῦ συκοφαντοῦσι*.

[e] Aucher renders, "quod autem adsederit eis"; an ambiguity lies in Arm. *nstim* which means both "sit" and "happen"; the latter meaning is favoured by the use of the noun *anç* "happening," which Aucher omits.

[f] Or "fitness"; Aucher "convenientiae."

[g] The Greek frag., which begins with this sentence, has only one verb, *κρίνουσι*.

[h] The Greek frag. inadvertently omits the negative.

[i] Instead of *ὄνομα* the Greek frag. has *σῶμα*.

[j] *πρᾶγμα*.

[k] *ἡ νομοθεσία* (the Mosaic Law); the Greek frag. has *ἡ θεία νομοθεσία*.

[l] *ζῷον ἡνωμένον*.

[m] *μεγάλοις ὄμμασι*.

entire writing exactly, truly and clearly,[a] not cutting up its harmony or dividing its unity.[b] For when things are deprived of their common element, they appear to be of somewhat different form and species.[c] What, then, is the intention[d] of the Legislation? It is gnostic[e] and describes the various forms of knowledge,[f] since the sacrificial (act) is to be interpreted[g] as conjecture and opportune reasoning[h] and all (kinds of) knowledge,[i] through which not only are the traces of the truth followed out but they are also hidden, as love (is hidden) by flattery, (and as) natural and genuine things are subjected to tests (by comparison with) foreign and untested things.

And the natures of the aforementioned five[j] animals are related to the parts of the universe. The ox (is related) to the earth, for it ploughs and tills the soil. The goat (is related) to water, the animal being so called from its rushing about or leaping,[k] for water is impetuous; this is attested by the currents of rivers and the effusions[l] of the wide sea and the flowing sea. The ram (is related) to air,

[a] The Greek frag. has only ἀκριβῶς καὶ τηλαυγῶς.

[b] Arm. agrees closely with Greek frag., μὴ κατακόπτοντας τὴν ἁρμονίαν, μηδὲ τὴν ἕνωσιν διαρτῶντας.

[c] ἑτερόμορφα καὶ ἑτεροειδῆ, as in Greek frag., which ends with this sentence.

[d] ἡ προαίρεσις.

[e] γνωστική; this seems to be an allusion to the allegorical interpretation of the three animal sacrifices as states of the soul, as given in *Quis Rer. Div. Heres* 125.

[f] τὰ γνωστικὰ εἴδη.

[g] ἀποδέχεται.

[h] στοχασμὸς καὶ καιρολογία (?).

[i] If the above rendering is correct, Aucher's is far off the track, "quoniam convenientiam et coaptatum verbum opinionemque recipit immolatio ac omnis scientia."

[j] The word "five" is inadvertently omitted by Aucher.

[k] Philo plays on the word αἴξ "goat" and ᾄττειν (aor. ᾇξαι) "to dart"; *cf. Quis Rer. Div. Heres* 126 τὴν ᾄττουσαν (Wendland's conj. for MSS. δίττουσαν, διάγουσαν) αἴσθησιν . . . αἶγα.

[l] Arm. *taracoumn* = both κατάχυσις and ἐκτένεια; Aucher here renders, "extensiones."

since it is very violent and lively, whence the ram is a most useful soul [a] and the most helpful of animals to mankind because it provides them with clothing. For these reasons, it seems to me, He commands him to take the females first, (namely) the she-goat and the heifer, because the elements earth and water are material and, as it were, female, while the third animal, the ram, is male because the air or the wind in some sense [b] becomes male.[c] For all nature is divided either into body or earth or water, and these are female by nature ; while the soul-like [d] air (comes under the head) of the more vital spirit.[e] And this, as I have said, is male. It is therefore proper to call the moving and active cause [f] male, and female that which is moved and passive.

But to the birds, such as the dove and the turtle-dove, the whole heaven is equally [g] appropriated,[h] being divided into the circuits of the planets and the fixed stars. And so (Scripture) assigns [i] the dove to the planets, for this is a tame and domesticated creature, and the planets also are rather familiar to us, as though contiguous to terrestrial places, and sympathetic.[j] But the turtle-dove (is related) to the fixed stars, for this animal is something of a lover of solitude,[k] and avoids meeting and mixing with the multitude. (So too) is the inerrant sphere [l] distant (from us) and at the ends of the world,[m] at the very extremes of nature.[n]

[a] So lit. ; Aucher renders, " animal."
[b] *τρόπον τινά.* [c] Prob. *ἀρρενοῦται.*
[d] *ψυχοειδής.*
[e] *ζωτικώτερον πνεῦμα* (or *ζωτικωτέραν πνοήν*).
[f] *τὸ κινοῦν καὶ δρῶν αἴτιον* ; *cf.*, *e.g.*, *De Fuga* 133.
[g] *ἴσως* or " in common "—*κοινῇ* ; Aucher omits the adverb in his rendering.
[h] *οἰκειοῦται* ; Aucher renders, " familiaris reperitur."
[i] *ἀφορίζει vel sim.* [j] *συμπαθεῖς.*
[k] *φιλέρημος* ; *cf.* *Quis Rer. Div. Heres* 126-127.
[l] *ἡ ἀπλανὴς σφαίρα.*
[m] Arm. *tiezerk'* renders both *οἰκουμένη* and *τὸ πᾶν.*
[n] Aucher renders somewhat differently, " sic longinquus et in ultimis orbis extremitatibus est globus inerrans."

And both orders of the two birds[a] are likened to the heavenly forces, wherefore, as the Socratic Plato says,[b] it is likely[c] that "Heaven is a flying chariot" because of its very swift revolution which surpasses in speed even the birds in their course. Moreover, the aforesaid birds are singers, and the prophet[d] is alluding to the music[e] which is perfected in heaven and is produced by the harmony[f] of the movement of the stars. For it is an indication of human skill[g] that all harmonic melody is formed by the voices of animals and living[h] organs through the mechanism[i] of the intelligence. But the heavenly singing does not extend or reach as far as the Creator's earth, as do the rays of the sun, because of His providential care for the human race. For it[j] rouses to madness those who hear it, and produces in the soul an indescribable and unrestrained pleasure. It causes them to despise food and drink and to die an untimely death through hunger[k] in their desire for the song. For did not the singing of the Sirens, as Homer says,[l] so violently summon listeners that they forgot their country, their home, their friends and necessary foods? And would not that most perfect and most harmonious and truly heavenly music, when it strikes the organ of hearing, compel them to go mad and to be frenzied?[m]

Now concerning the fact that these several (animals) were three years old and three in number we have spoken above. But here something must be said in accordance

[a] *Sic*; the "two" is superfluous in English, of course.

[b] *Phaedrus* 246 E ἐν οὐρανῷ Ζεύς, ἐλαύνων πτηνὸν ἅρμα.

[c] Or "fitting."

[d] *i.e.* Moses.

[e] τὴν μουσικήν.

[f] Lit. "is harmonized" (two Arm. verbs being used).

[g] τέχνης.

[h] Or "respiratory"; Aucher renders, "instrumentorum animantium."

[i] Or "contrivance" or "method."

[j] *i.e.* the heavenly singing.

[k] Lit. "to die of early death-bringing hunger."

[l] *Od.* xii. 39-45 (paraphrased).

[m] κορυβαντιᾶν.

with another form of reasoning.[a] For it appears that each of those things which are sublunar, (namely) earth and water and air are triads.[b] For the earth's divisions are vast continents and islands and peniŋsulas. And those of water are sea and rivers and lakes. And of the air the two equinoxes, the summer and winter solstices [c] are reckoned as one, for the equinoxes have one (and the same) interval of night and day and in the same manner are neither hot nor cold. And the summer and winter solstices . . .[d] For the sun is borne through these three cycles,[e] those of summer, winter and the equinox.[f] Now this interpretation is most natural.[g] But a more ethical one [h] must be discussed.

To every one of us there happen to belong [i] these things: body and sense-perception and reason.[j] Accordingly, the heifer is related [k] to bodily substance, for our body is tamed

[a] Or "of the mystery"; Arm. *xorhourd* = both λογισμός and μυστήριον; Aucher here renders, "sub altera specie mysterii."

[b] Aucher more freely renders, "trino gaudere ordine." In *Quis Rer. Div. Heres* 133-136 Philo speaks of the *twofold* division of natural elements to fit his allegory of Abraham's dividing of the sacrificial animals "in the middle"; see below, *QG* iii. 5.

[c] τροπαί. The Arm. text adds in parentheses "like the vernal and autumnal"; the Ambrosian paraphrase has "aer quoque habet divisiones temporum veris, aestatis, autumni, hyberni." Probably the Arm. text is here corrupt; the context seems to require a reference only to the two solstices here; see note *f* below.

[d] There is no verb in the Arm. text; Aucher amplifies in rendering, "quibus adde conversiones aestivam et brumalem."

[e] κύκλους or στροφάς.

[f] τῆς ἰσημερίας (sing.); Philo artificially preserves the threefold division of the climate by counting the two equinoxes as one, and the two solstices separately.

[g] Or "physical"—φυσικωτάτη.

[h] ἠθικωτέρα.

[i] συμβαίνει ὑπάρχειν *vel sim.*

[j] σῶμα καὶ αἴσθησις καὶ λόγος.

[k] Or "likened"—ᾠκείωται.

and driven and made to obey and is yoked to the service of life. And Nature is feminine in a material sense,[a] and proves on investigation[b] to be solely suffering and passive rather than active.[c] And the she-goat is to be likened to the community of senses,[d] whether because the various objects perceived are referred to their (appropriate) sense or because the impulse and movement of the soul come from the impressions made upon the senses.[e] And these are first followed by inclination and aversion,[f] which some call occasion,[g] which is an impulse[h] of any kind. Since sense-perception is feminine, for it is affected by the perceived object, (Scripture) couples it with a female animal, a she-goat. But the ram is kin to reason,[i] first of all, because this is masculine and because it is energetic,[j] and then[k] because it is the cause of the world and its foundation.[l] For the ram (is necessary) because of the clothing (which it yields),[m] while reason (is necessary) in the ordering of life. For whatever is not disordered and unruly, from that very fact[n] has reason. But there are two forms of reason: there is one in nature, by which things in the sense-perceptible world are analysed[o]; and (the other is

[a] καθ' ὕλην.
[b] ἐξετάζεται.
[c] φέρειν καὶ πάσχειν μᾶλλον ἢ ποιεῖν.
[d] τῇ τῶν αἰσθήσεων κοινωνίᾳ.
[e] ἡ τῆς ψυχῆς ὁρμὴ καὶ κίνησις γένονται ἐκ τῶν διὰ τῶν αἰσθήσεων φαντασιῶν. For this formulation see, *e.g.*, *De Opif. Mundi* 166 τὰς διὰ τῶν αἰσθήσεων φαντασίας.
[f] οἰκείωσις καὶ ἀλλοτρίωσις, *cf.* *Quis Rer. Div. Heres* 154.
[g] Prob. ἀφορμήν, see next note.
[h] ὁρμή. It is not clear whether Philo here contrasts ὁρμή with ἀφορμή, as the Stoics sometimes did, or considers ἀφορμή as a special kind of ὁρμή.
[i] τῷ λόγῳ.
[j] ἐνεργός, or "efficient"—δραστήριος.
[k] Aucher's "secundo" and "tertio" are amplifications of the Arm. text.
[l] τοῦ κόσμου καὶ τῆς αὐτοῦ ἱδρύσεως.
[m] Lit. "for the ram is through clothing."
[n] εὐθύς (?).
[o] *Cf.* the parallel passage in *Quis Rer. Div. Heres* 125 λάβε μοι κριόν, λόγον . . . ἱκανὸν μὲν τὰ σοφίσματα . . . λῦσαι.

found) in those forms which are called incorporeal, by which the things of the intelligible world are analysed. With these are compared the dove and the turtle-dove. For the dove (is a symbol) of physical theory,[a] for it is a very tame bird, and sense-perceptible things are familiar to sight. And the soul of the physicist and physiologist [b] leaps up and grows wings and is borne aloft and travels round the heavens, viewing all its parts and their several causes. But the turtle-dove is likened to the intelligible and incorporeal form (of reason); for just as this creature is fond of solitude,[c] so (the reason) by an effort surpasses the forms of sense-perception [d] and is united in essence with the invisible.[e]

4. (Gen. xv. 10) Why does (Scripture) say, "And he took for Him [f] all these things"?

Most excellently does it add the expression, "he took for Him," for it is the act of a god-loving soul [g] which has received any good and precious theories and doctrines, to attribute them not to itself but to God, who gives favours.[h]

5. (Gen. xv. 10) What is the meaning of the words "And he divided them in the middle and placed them one opposite the other" [i]?

[a] φυσικῆς θεωρίας.

[b] τοῦ φυσικοῦ καὶ τοῦ φυσιολόγου. [c] φιλέρημος.

[d] Aucher, wrongly, I think, renders, "excellit violentas sensus species."

[e] For the symbolism of dove and turtle-dove as human and divine reason see *Quis Rer. Div. Heres* 126-127.

[f] LXX ἔλαβεν αὐτῷ renders Heb. *wayyiqaḥ lô*, "he (Abraham) took for himself." In Heb. the reflexive pron. is identical in form with the personal pron. Philo artificially presses the use of αὐτῷ (=God) where LXX should have used ἑαυτῷ (=Abraham). [g] φιλοθέου ψυχῆς. [h] χάριτας.

[i] This phrase provides the text for an extended allegory in *Quis Rer. Div. Heres* 129-229, which is here greatly abridged, though the passage on the bilateral symmetry of the body in our text is longer than the corresponding passage (§ 151) in *Quis Rer. Div. Heres*.

The structure of the body also is somewhat of this sort in make-up. For the kindred [a] parts are as it were divided and separated in opposition, inclining and facing toward one another for the sake of natural co-operation [b]; for the Creator of life [c] so divided it for the sake of use, in order that one (part) might be concerned with [d] another and that they might mutually serve one another by exchanging necessary services. For example, that which is directly seen from the middle of the nose is divided between the two eyes, each of them moving round toward the other. For the pupils inclining toward one side, in a certain sense,[e] look toward each other, not wandering outward or straying from the position of the eyes,[f] but each looking toward the direction of the other, especially when they come across something to be seen. Again, hearing is divided between the two ears, and both of them are turned toward each other, tending to one place and to the same activity. Moreover, smell is divided between the two nostrils, going round to the tubes [g] of each nostril, for these are not turned or bent down to the cheeks [h] or drawn up so that one of them faces toward the right and the other toward the left, but being gathered and brought together inwardly, they admit smells by a common act.[i] Moreover, the hands are made, not interchangeable,[j] (but as) brothers and divided parts facing each other, and by nature prepared beforehand for their appropriate activity and deeds in taking and giving and working. Furthermore, the soles of the feet (co-operate), for each foot is so made that it yields to the other, and walking is achieved by the movement of both but cannot be completed by one alone. And not only the

[a] Lit. "brother."

[b] *ἕνεκα τῆς φυσικῆς συνεργείας.*

[c] *ὁ ζῳοπλάστης.*

[d] *περιεργάζηται* (?).

[e] *τρόπον τινά.*

[f] *μὴ ἔξω πλανούμεναι μηδ' ἐκ τῆς τῶν ὀφθαλμῶν θέσεως ῥεμβόμεναι vel sim.*

[g] *πρὸς τοὺς αὐλούς.*

[h] Or "jaws."

[i] *κοινοπραγίᾳ.*

[j] *οὐκ ἐνηλλαγμέναι.*

feet [a] and the legs but also the thighs and the backbone [b] and the ribs and the breasts and the right and left sides, being divided in the same way, indicate harmony and fitness and, as it were, the natural union of each of the forms considered.

And in general whoever at one and the same time equally considers two divided parts which have been brought together in one place, will find that both constitute one nature.[c] When, for example, the hands are united with, and extended toward, the fingers, they appear to form [d] a harmony with them. And when the feet are brought together, they adhere to the same place.[e] And the ears are gathered in the form of a theatre with circles, and are united across the cavity.[f] So also in the case of each of the forms of those parts that belong to us, nature effects a division and separates the divided parts so that they are opposite and facing, whereby an ornamental effect [g] is obtained, and at the same time that which is of service (is put into) easy operation. And again it unites each of these several forms in one operation and in the same work, bringing together and assembling what is comprehensively viewed.[h]

Now it is not only the parts of the body that one sees

[a] Lit. " steps."

[b] Perhaps Philo means the vertebrae of the spine; Aucher renders, apparently *ad hoc*, " scapulae."

[c] μίαν φύσιν.

[d] Lit. " to admit."

[e] Meaning slightly uncertain; Aucher renders, more freely, " et pedes recollecti in unionem tendere."

[f] Philo compares the ridges of the ear with the circular tiers of an amphitheatre, as in *De Poster. Caini* 104 πρὸς γὰρ τὸ ὤτων σχῆμα ἄκρως ἡ θεάτρων κατασκευὴ μεμίμηται. The " cavity " seems to mean the hollow of the skull, represented as similar to the hollow space enclosed by the tiers of the theatre.

[g] Lit. " ornament "—κόσμος. Aucher rightly remarks in his footnote that Arm. *ašxarh* may be rendered either as " mundus," or " ornamentum." The latter meaning is called for here.

[h] Lit. " what it views moving in a circle "; Aucher renders, " colligens omnia universim considerata."

thus connected and paired, separated in union and united in division, but also those of the soul. For of this too the higher divisions are two, like public squares,[a] that is the rational and irrational,[b] and the parts of either division have their own sections. Thus, for example, the rational (is divided) into mind and speech,[c] while the sensible part [d] (is divided) into the four senses, since the fifth (sense), touch, is common to the (other) four. Two of these, by which we see and hear, are philosophic,[e] and through them a good life is attained by us. But the others, being non-philosophic, (namely) smell and taste, are servants and have been created only for living. Smelling is for the sake of the smell,[f] for they continuously take up one another [g]; and continuous breathing is the food of living beings. And taste is for the sake of [h] food and drink. Thus smell and taste strengthen the mortal body. But sight and hearing help the immortal mind.

Accordingly, these divisions of our limbs in body and soul were made by the Creator. But one should recognize that the parts of the world also are divided into two and are set up one against the other. The earth (is divided) into mountains and plains, and water into sweet and salt; the sweet or potable [i] is that which springs and streams yield, and the salt is from the sea. And the climate (is divided) into winter and summer, and again into spring

[a] Or "colonnades" (possibly double colonnades); Aucher renders "plateae." The point of the comparison escapes me.

[b] λογικὸς καὶ ἄλογος.

[c] εἰς νοῦν καὶ τὸν προφορικὸν λόγον—Stoic terminology often used elsewhere in Philo.

[d] τὸ αἰσθητικόν.

[e] φιλόσοφοι.

[f] ὄσφρησις διὰ τὴν ὀσμήν (?); perhaps Aucher is right in taking the Arm. prep. *i ẓeṛn* in its usual sense of "through" (=διά with gen.), but, if so, the phrase becomes still more obscure.

[g] Meaning uncertain; Aucher renders, "plura continet se se excipientia."

[h] See note *f* above.

[i] Aucher's rendering omits the word "potable."

and autumn. And setting out from this fact, Heracleitus wrote books On Nature, getting his opinions on opposites from our theologian,[a] and adding a great number of laborious arguments to them.[b]

6. (Gen. xv. 10) Why does (Scripture) say, " But the birds he did not divide "[c]?

It indicates[d] the fifth and cyclic nature[e] of which the ancients said the heaven is made.[f] For the four elements,[g] as they are called, are mixtures rather than elements, and by them they divide[h] those divided things into that of which they are mixed.[i] Thus, for example, the earth contains in itself also a watery (element) and an aerial one and what is called a fiery one more by comprehension than by sight. And water is not so pure and unmixed that it does not have some share of wind and earth. And in each of the others there are mixtures. But the fifth substance[j] only is made unmixed and pure, for which reason it is not of a nature to be divided. Wherefore it is well said that " the birds he did not divide," since,

[a] τοῦ θεολόγου (Moses).

[b] That Heracleitus was indebted to Moses for his theory of the harmony of opposites is stated by Philo also in *Quis Rer. Div. Heres* 214.

[c] For another allegory of this half-verse see *Quis Rer. Div. Heres* 230-236.

[d] αἰνίττεται.

[e] *i.e.* the quintessence, *cf. Quis Rer. Div. Heres* 283 πέμπτη . . . οὐσία κυκλοφορητική. Ultimately the term is based on Aristotle, *De Caelo* i. 2 f.

[f] Lit. " is perfected."

[g] στοιχεῖα.

[h] The Arm. verb is 3rd pers. sing., but probably reflects Greek 3rd sing. with neuter pl. subject.

[i] This rendering (like the elements spoken of) is rather mixed up, but so is the Arm. text, as well as Aucher's rendering, " quibus subdividit jam divisa in id (*vel*, ex illo) ex quo commixta sunt."

[j] Or " quintessence," see note *e*.

as in the case of birds, it is the nature of celestial bodies, the planets and fixed (stars), to be elevated and to resemble both (kinds of) clean [a] birds, the turtle-dove and the dove, which do not admit of cutting or division, since they belong to the simpler and unmixed fifth substance,[b] and therefore this nature, more especially resembling unity, is indivisible.

*7. (Gen. xv. 11) What is the meaning of the words, "And the birds came down upon the divided bodies" [c]?

Because the three divided animals, the heifer, the she-goat and the ram, are symbolically,[d] as we have said, earth, water and air. But (we must) harmoniously fit the answer to the question by weighing the truth of the comparison in our reason.[e] May it not be that by the flight of the birds over the divided (bodies, Scripture) alludes to, and warns against, the attack of enemies? For every sublunary nature is full of battles and domestic and foreign disasters.[f] It is for the sake of food and gluttony that birds are seen to fly over divided bodies; and by nature the more powerful rush upon the weaker as if upon dead bodies, often coming at them unexpectedly. But they do not fly over the turtle-dove and dove, for heavenly (beings) are without passion and without guile.

[a] *i.e.* ritually clean—*καθαρῶν*.

[b] *τῇ ἁπλουστέρᾳ καὶ ἀκράτῳ πέμπτῃ οὐσίᾳ.*

[c] LXX (followed by Arm. O.T.) has *κατέβη δὲ ὄρνεα ἐπὶ τὰ σώματα, τὰ διχοτομήματα αὐτῶν*, differing slightly from Heb., which reads "And there came down the birds-of-prey upon the carcases."

[d] *συμβολικῶς.*

[e] By taking Arm. *xndreçeloyn* (here = *ζητήσεως*) to mean "reason," and *xorhrdovk'* (here *λογισμῷ*) to mean "mystery," Aucher has given an inexact rendering, "opus est tamen coaptare redditionem rationis, perpensa veritate sub mysterio similitudinis."

[f] *ἐμφυλίων καὶ ξένων κακῶν*, as in the Greek frag. (which consists of only one sentence).

*8. (Gen. xv. 11) Why does (Scripture) say, "And Abraham stopped and sat over them"[a]?

Now those who believe that a (literal) sacrifice is signified by the present passage say that the virtuous man stops, as it were, and sits in an assembly,[b] examining the entrails and taking them as a reliable indication[c] (and) as that which shows forth the truth. But we disciples[d] of Moses, clearly understanding the intention of our teacher, who turns his face away from every form of prognosis[e] and believes in God alone, say that by these now gathered birds that fly above he[f] represents the virtuous man,[g] and symbolically indicates nothing else than that he restrains wrongdoing and greed, and is hostile to quarrels and fights, but loves stability and peace. And he is really, as it were, the true guardian of peace. For because of evil men no city has quiet and peace,[h] but they remain unmoved[i] through the goodness of one or two inhabitants[j] whose virtue heals these civic diseases,[k] for the virtue-

[a] Philo's "stopped" (or "went over") is an addition to Scripture; his "sat over" is a slight variation of LXX συνεκάθισεν αὐτοῖς, which, in turn, mistakes Heb. *wayyaššēb 'othām* "and he drove them off" for *wayyēšēb 'ittām* "and he sat with them." The half-verse is also allegorized in *Quis Rer. Div. Heres* 243-248 where Philo concludes that the good man sits down in the company of unjust men to restrain them like a presiding officer or judge.

[b] ἐν ἐκκλησίᾳ.

[c] Or "symbol."

[d] γνώριμοι.

[e] ἀπὸ παντὸς γνωστικοῦ (?) εἴδους; Aucher renders, "ab omni specie sophistica vel pronostica."

[f] *i.e.* Moses.

[g] τὸν σπουδαῖον.

[h] The Greek frag., which begins with this sentence, has ἠρέμησεν ἄν.

[i] The Greek frag. has ἀστασίαστοι.

[j] The Greek frag. from Cod. Rup. reads a little differently δι' ἑνὸς ἢ δευτέρου δικαιοσύνην ἀσκοῦντος; the Arm. read οἰκοῦντος (as in John Monachus) for ἀσκοῦντος.

[k] The Arm., like Anton Melissa, read πολιτικὰς νόσους; Cod. Rup. reads πολεμικὰς νόσους.

loving[a] God grants as an honour to excellent men,[b] that they help not only Him[c] but also those who approach (Him).[d]

9. (Gen. xv. 12) What is the meaning of the words, " At sunset an ecstasy[e] fell upon Abram and behold a great dark fear[f] fell upon him "[g]?

A certain divine tranquility[h] came suddenly upon the virtuous man. For ecstasy,[i] as its very name clearly shows, is nothing else than the departing and going out of the understanding.[j] But the race of prophets[k] is wont to suffer this. For when the mind is divinely possessed[l] and becomes filled with God,[m] it is no longer within itself, for it receives the divine spirit[n] to dwell within it. Nay rather, as he[o] himself has said, it fell upon (Abram), for it does not come upon one gently and softly but makes a sudden

[a] φιλαρέτου, as in Anton Melissa; Cod. Rup. has φιλανθρώπου.

[b] Lit. " to excellence "—καλοκἀγαθίᾳ.

[c] God rather than the city seems to be referred to by the pronoun, which has no distinction of gender in Arm.; the Greek frag. has τοῦ μὴ μόνον αὐτὸν ἀλλὰ καὶ τοὺς πλησιάζοντας ὠφελεῖσθαι; Aucher renders differently, " nec eis solum modo sed illis quoque qui (*vel*, quibus) appropinquant ad utilitatem parandam."

[d] The pronoun is supplied from the context.

[e] LXX ἔκστασις; Heb. *tardēmāh* " deep sleep."

[f] LXX φόβος μέγας σκοτεινός.

[g] Philo expounds this verse at length in *Quis Rer. Div. Heres* 249-265, enumerating four kinds of ecstasy, of which the fourth is ἐνθουσιῶντος καὶ θεοφορήτου τὸ πάθος.

[h] Arm. *ẏapahovoumn* usu. = ἀσφάλεια but connotes freedom from anxiety.

[i] Here the Arm. word for " ecstasy," *artakaçout'iun* is different from that used above to render LXX ἔκστασις; the latter, *hiaçoumn* more properly means " astonishment."

[j] λογισμοῦ or διανοίας.

[k] τὸ προφητικὸν γένος.

[l] ἐνθουσιάζει.

[m] θεοφόρητος γίνεται.

[n] τὸ θεῖον πνεῦμα.

[o] Moses.

attack.[a] Excellent, moreover, is that which is added, (namely) that "a great dark fear[b] fell upon him," for all these are ecstasies of the mind, since he who is in fear is not within himself. And darkness is an impediment to sight; and the greater the fear is, so much duller does (the mind) become in seeing and understanding. These things, moreover, are not ineptly[c] spoken of but as evidence of the clear knowledge of prophecy, by which oracles and laws are legislated by God.[d]

10. (Gen. xv. 13-14) Why (does Scripture say), "It was said to him,[e] Thou shalt surely know[f] that thy seed shall be a sojourner[g] in a land not its own, and they[h] will enslave them and oppress them and afflict them[i] for four hundred years"[j]?

Most excellently is it indicated that "it was said to him," for the prophet seems to say something but he does not give his own oracle[k] but is the interpreter[l] of another,[m] who puts things into his mind. However, that which he utters and murmurs in words is all true and divine; first of all, because the human race lives on another's earth, for all that which is under heaven is the possession of God, and those who live on it may properly and legitimately

[a] *ὁρμήν vel sim.*

[b] The Arm. word for "fear" here is different from that used above to render LXX *φόβος*.

[c] *οὐκ ἀπὸ σκοποῦ.*

[d] *χρησμοὶ καὶ νόμοι ὑπὸ τοῦ θεοῦ νομοθετοῦνται.*

[e] Most LXX MSS. and Heb. have "to Abram."

[f] Lit. "knowing thou shalt know." The Arm., like the LXX, reflects the Heb. idiom.

[g] *πάροικος.*

[h] *i.e.* the natives.

[i] *δουλώσουσι καὶ ταπεινώσουσι καὶ κακώσουσι αὐτούς*, as in some LXX MSS.

[j] The verse is discussed also in *Quis Rer. Div. Heres* 266-271.

[k] Or "edict."

[l] *ἑρμηνεύς*, here rendered by two Arm. words.

[m] *i.e.* of God; *cf. Quis Rer. Div. Heres* 266.

be said to be sojourners [a] rather than to inhabit their own territory, (which) they do not [b] hold by nature. Second, because the whole race of mortals [c] is a slave.[d] And no one is free [e] but (everyone) has many masters and gets beatings and ill-treatment both outside and inside himself; outside there is winter, which chills him, and summer, which burns him, and hunger and thirst and many other afflictions; and inside there are sense-pleasures, desires, sorrow and fear. But this slavery is limited to four hundred years after the above-mentioned passions come upon (them).[f] For this reason it was earlier said [g] that "Abram stopped [h] and sat over them," (that is) he was hindering and driving off and turning away, in word [i] the flesh-eating birds which were flying over the divided animals, but in deed [i] the afflictions which come upon men. For he who is by nature zealous for virtue and by practice is a lover of man,[j] is a healer of our race and is a genuine and true apothecary [k] and dispeller of evils. Now all these are allegories of the soul.[l] For the soul of the wise man, when it comes from above [m] from the ether and enters into a mortal and is sown [n] in the field of the body, is truly a sojourner in a land not its own, for the earthy nature of the body is an alien [o] to the pure mind and subjects it to slavery and brings upon it all kinds of suffering until the

[a] παροικεῖν.

[b] The negative seems intrusive here.

[c] Aucher renders less literally, "mortalis quisque in genere."

[d] δοῦλος; *cf. Quis Rer. Div. Heres* 267-271.

[e] ἐλεύθερος.

[f] The point is more clearly made in the parallel, *Quis Rer. Div. Heres* 269, "And the slavery is for 400 years, in accordance with the powers of the four passions."

[g] See *QG* iii. 8 on Gen. xv. 11.

[h] Or "went over."

[i] λόγῳ μέν . . . ἔργῳ δέ.

[j] φιλάνθρωπος.

[k] φαρμακευτής.

[l] περὶ τῆς ψυχῆς ἀλληγορεῖται.

[m] ἄνωθεν. [n] σπείρεται. [o] ξένος.

Saviour [a] brings to judgment the race taken captive [b] by passion, and condemns it; for thus does it once more enter into freedom.[c] Therefore (Scripture) adds [d] "But the nation whom they shall serve I will judge, and after this they shall go out with great possessions," [e] (that is) with the same measure and even better, inasmuch as the mind [f] is released from its evil bond,[g] the body. It [h] goes forth and exchanges its state not only for salvation and freedom but also for possessions, that it may not leave behind for its enemies anything good or useful. For every rational soul [i] bears good fruit or is fruitful.[j] And one who is thought to be very responsible [k] and virtuous [l] in his thoughts is none the less unable to preserve them to the end.[m] Wherefore it is proper that the virtuous man [n] with resolution should attain to that which he has in mind, and for the sake of this it is fitting that he have thoughts of wisdom.[o] For just as some trees enjoy fertility in the first growth of their fruit but are not able to keep nourishing [p] them, so that for some slight cause their entire fruit may

[a] ὁ σωτήρ (God).

[b] Aucher accurately renders Arm. *gerič* by "captivantem" but the context requires a pass. participle in the Greek original.

[c] εἰς ἐλευθερίαν.

[d] Gen. xv. 14.

[e] LXX ἀποσκευῆς.

[f] ὁ νοῦς.

[g] συνδέσμου or "bond-fellow"—συνδεσμίου.

[h] The Arm. pl. verbs undoubtedly refer to the grammatical pl. *mitk'* "mind": Aucher correctly renders the verbs as sing.

[i] πᾶσα λογικὴ ψυχή.

[j] Text obscure and prob. corrupt, as Aucher notes.

[k] This is the best approximation I can give to Arm. *partapan*, which usu. renders ἔνοχος, ὑπόχρεως *vel sim.*; Aucher renders, "onustum."

[l] σπουδαῖος.

[m] εἰς τέλος.

[n] τὸν σπουδαῖον.

[o] This difficult sentence is less literally rendered by Aucher, "id enim decet probum hominem, consequi ultro meditata, sicut etiam eis congruum sapientiae consilium."

[p] τρέφειν.

fall [a] or be shaken off before it reaches maturity, so also the souls of inconstant men [b] understand many things that lead to fertility but are unable to preserve them intact [c] until they are perfected, as is proper for a virtuous man who collects his own possessions.

*11. (Gen. xv. 15) What is the meaning of the words, " But thou shalt go to thy fathers with peace,[d] nourished [e] in a good old age " ?

Clearly this indicates the incorruptibility of the soul, which removes its habitation from the mortal body [f] and returns as if to the mother-city,[g] from which it originally moved its habitation to this place.[h] For when it is said to a dying person, " Thou shalt go to thy fathers," what else is this than to represent another life without the body, which only the soul of the wise man ought to live ? [i] And (Scripture) speaks of " the fathers " of Abraham, meaning not those who begot him, his grandfathers and forefathers, for they were not all worthy of praise [j] so as to be a source of pride and glory to those who reach the same rank,[k] but in the opinion of many it seems that " the fathers " indicate all the elements [l] into which the dissolution (of the

[a] Lit. " flow away."
[b] *αἱ τῶν ἀβεβαίων ψυχαί.*
[c] *ὁλόκληρα.*
[d] So LXX, *μετ' εἰρήνης* ; Heb. " in peace."
[e] So LXX, *τραφείς* ; Heb. has " buried " = *ταφείς*.
[f] *ἐναργῶς ἀφθαρσίαν ψυχῆς αἰνίττεται μετοικιζομένης ἀπὸ τοῦ θνητοῦ σώματος*, as in the paraphrase of Procopius.
[g] *μητρόπολιν.*
[h] *i.e.* this world or the body.
[i] *τί ἕτερον ἢ ζωὴν ἑτέραν παρίστησι τὴν ἄνευ σώματος καθ' ἣν ψυχὴν μόνην τοῦ σοφοῦ συμβαίνει ζῆν*, as in Procopius, except that the latter omits *τοῦ σοφοῦ*.
[j] *ἐπαινετοί*, as in Procopius (which omits the rest of the clause down to " rank ").
[k] *τάξιν.* Meaning uncertain ; Aucher renders, " qui assecutus est successionem ejusdem ordinis."
[l] *πάντα τὰ στοιχεῖα.* Perhaps the original was *τὰ τοῦ παντὸς στοιχεῖα* " the elements of the universe."

body)[a] takes place. To me, however, it seems to indicate the incorporeal Logoi[b] of the divine world, whom elsewhere it is accustomed to call "angels."[c] Moreover, not ineptly does (Scripture) speak of "being nourished with peace" and "in a good old age." For the evil and sinful man is nourished and lives by strife, and ends and grows old in evil.[d] But the virtuous man in both his lives—in that with the body and in that without the body—enjoys peace,[e] and alone is very good[f] while no one of the foolish[g] is (so), even though he should be longer-lived than an elephant. Wherefore (Scripture) has accurately said, "Thou shalt go to thy fathers," nourished not in a long[h] old age but in a "good"[i] old age. For many foolish men linger on[j] to a long life,[k] but to a good and virtuous life only he who is a lover of wisdom.[l]

*12. (Gen. xv. 16) Why does (God) say, "In the fourth generation they shall return hither"?

The number four is the most harmonious[m] with all numbers, as it is the most perfect.[n] And it is the root and base[o] of the most perfect decad. Now in accordance with

[a] Lit. "loosing of the dissolution."

[b] Aucher prefers the reading *bnaks* "inhabitants" to *bans* "Logoi."

[c] The section from "worthy of praise" to "angels" is telescoped in the Greek paraphrase to ἀλλ' ἔοικεν αἰνίττεσθαι πατέρας οὓς ἑτέρωθι καλεῖν ἀγγέλους εἴωθεν.

[d] Perhaps the original was τελευτᾷ ἐν γήρᾳ κακῷ "ends in an evil old age."

[e] εἰρήνῃ χρῆται. [f] Or "very brave."

[g] τῶν ἀφρόνων or πονηρῶν. [h] μακρῷ. [i] καλῷ.

[j] τείνουσι, as in the Greek frag.

[k] The Greek frag. has αἰῶνα.

[l] The Greek frag. has ὁ φρονήσεως ἐραστής.

[m] παναρμόνιος. This adj. is applied to the hebdomad in *De Vita Mosis* ii. 210, *cf. De Opif. Mundi* 48.

[n] For other references to the perfection of the tetrad see Staehle, pp. 26-31.

[o] ῥίζα καὶ θεμέλιον; *cf. De Spec. Leg.* ii. 40 πρὸς τετράδα, τὴν δεκάδος ἀρχήν τε καὶ πηγήν.

the principle [a] of the number four all things being collected return hither, as He himself has said. And as it is perfect in itself,[b] it is filled with perfected beings.[c] Now what do I mean by this? In the generation of living beings the first (stage) is the sowing of seed. The second is when the various organs are modelled [d] by something akin to nature.[e] The third, after the fashioning,[f] is their growth. And the fourth, above all these, is the perfecting of their generation. The same principle [g] applies to plants. The seed is sown in the earth and then it is moved upward and downward, partly into roots, partly into stalks. Then it grows, and in the fourth (stage) bears fruit. Again, trees first of all bear fruit, which then grows. In the third (stage) it changes colour, having become ripe, and in the fourth (stage), which is the last, it becomes full and complete. And thereupon follow the use and enjoyment of it.[h]

13. (Gen. xv. 16) What is the meaning of the words, "Not yet full are the sins of the Amorites until now"?

Some say that by this expression Fate [i] was introduced by Moses into his narrative,[j] as though all things were to be completed in accordance with this time, and times [k] were to be determined by periods.[l]

[a] κατὰ τὸν λόγον. [b] αὐτοτελής.

[c] Aucher renders somewhat differently, "perfectos quoque generat plane." [d] τυποῦσθαι.

[e] Apparently the Arm. = ὑπό τινος τῇ φύσει συγγενοῦς.

[f] μετὰ τὸ πλάττειν. [g] λόγος.

[h] χρῆσις καὶ ἀπόλαυσις.

[i] Arm. *čakatagir* renders εἱμαρμένη, μοῖρα and τύχη.

[j] Arm. *patmout'eamb* is the instr. case of the noun that usu. renders ἱστορία or διήγησις, sometimes ἐξήγησις. Aucher renders, "explicite," and adds in a footnote "notat vox illa . . . *historice*, id est *enarrando explicite*."

[k] The Arm. uses two different words for "time."

[l] περιόδοις. Probably, as Aucher suggests, this section was originally longer and contained Philo's own interpretation in contrast to that of "some" who saw a reference to Fate in this verse. Such a contrasted interpretation is given in *Quis Rer. Div. Heres* 300-306.

14. (Gen. xv. 17) What is the meaning of the words, "When the sun went down there came a flame"[a]?

Either the sun appeared flame-like in its setting, or another flame, not lightning but some kind of fire akin to it, fell[b] from above at evening. This is the plain interpretation of the oracle. But this is to be said by way of conjecture.[c]

15. (Gen. xv. 17) What is the meaning of the words, "Behold, a smoking furnace and torches[d] of fire, which passed through the midst of the half-pieces"[e]?

The literal meaning[f] is clear, for the fountain and root of the divine Logos[g] wishes the victims to be consumed, not by that fire which has been given to us for use,[h] but by that which comes down from above from the ether, in order that the purity of the substance[i] of heaven may be attested by the holiness which is in the victims. But as for the deeper meaning,[j] all sublunary things are likened to the smoking furnace, because of the vapour from earth and water, in which are the divisions of nature. As has been shown above,[k] the several things which are parts of

[a] So LXX, ἐπεὶ δὲ ἐγίνετο ὁ ἥλιος πρὸς δυσμαῖς, φλὸξ ἐγένετο; Heb. reads "when the sun set and it was dark." Apparently LXX read Heb. *lahaṭ* "flame" instead of *ʿalāṭāh* "darkness."

[b] ἔσταξε.

[c] διὰ δοξῶν *vel sim.* Aucher renders, "verum illud quod sensum respicit dicendum est." Evidently the rest of the section is missing or is to be supplied from the following section on the second half of the biblical verse.

[d] So LXX, λαμπάδες; Heb. has sing., "torch."

[e] ἀνὰ μέσον τῶν διχοτομημάτων, as in LXX. For a parallel allegory see *Quis Rer. Div. Heres* 308-312.

[f] τὸ ῥητόν.

[g] *i.e.* God.

[h] *i.e.* for profane use.

[i] τῆς οὐσίας.

[j] τὸ πρὸς διάνοιαν.

[k] *QG* iii. 5.

the world are divided into two. And by these,[a] like torches of fire, are kindled the most swiftly moving and most effective powers,[b] the divine words,[c] burning and aflame. Now they keep the universe intact, one with another together,[d] and now they purify the superfluous fog. The most particular and proper cause[e] is to be explained in the following way. Human life is like a smoking furnace, not having a clear and pure fire and pure[f] light, but abundant smoke (coming) through a smoking and obscuring flame, which produces fog and darkness and veiling of the eyes, not of the body, but of the soul, which prevents them from seeing clearly outwards until the Saviour God[g] lights the heavenly torches. By these I mean the most pure and holy sparks,[h] which unite the two parts divided on the right side and on the left, and at the same time illuminate them and become the causes of harmony and splendour.[i]

16. (Gen. xv. 18) Why does (Scripture) say, " On that

[a] What " these " are is not wholly clear. To judge from the parallel in *Quis Rer. Div. Heres* 311-312 " these " are " the divided things," which are kindled by the divine powers. We should therefore correct the Arm. construction here to read " and these . . . are kindled by the . . . divine words."

[b] *δυνάμεις*.

[c] *οἱ θεῖοι λόγοι*; Aucher renders more freely, " ardentes sane velut ignei sermones divini."

[d] This is the literal meaning of the obscure Arm. text, which Aucher renders, " modo universum totum secum invicem integre servantes." The general idea is the same as that in *Quis Rer. Div. Heres* 312, " the divine powers, as they pass through the midst of objects and bodies, destroy nothing —for the half-pieces remain unharmed—but divide and distinguish very well the nature of each."

[e] *ἡ ἰδιωτάτη καὶ οἰκειοτάτη αἰτία*.

[f] The Arm. uses two different words for " pure."

[g] *ὁ σωτὴρ θεός*.

[h] Prob. *σπινθῆρας*, as in *Quis Rer. Div. Heres* 309; the Arm. word can also mean " rays, beams."

[i] *αἰτίαι γενόμενοι ἁρμονίας καὶ λαμπρότητος*.

day [a] He made a covenant with Abraham, saying, To thy seed will I give this land from the river of Egypt to the great river Euphrates " [b] ?

The literal meaning [c] is that it describes the boundaries of the region between the two rivers, that of Egypt and the Euphrates, for anciently the land and the river were homonymously [d] called " Egypt." A witness to this is the poet,[e] who says, " At the river of Egypt stay the ships which you steer from both sides." But as for the deeper meaning,[f] it indicates felicity,[g] which is the fulfilment of three perfections,[h] of spiritual goods, of corporeal goods and of those which are external. This (doctrine) was praised by some of the philosophers who came afterward, (such as) Aristotle and the Peripatetics. Moreover this is said to have been also the legislation [i] of Pythagoras. For Egypt is the symbol of corporeal and external goods, while the Euphrates (is the symbol) of the spiritual, for through them veritable and true joy [j] comes into being, having as its source wisdom and every virtue. And the boundaries rightly take their beginning from Egypt and they end at the Euphrates. For in the end things happen to the soul which we manage to approach with difficulty. but first one must pass and run through the bodily and

[a] Philo agrees with some LXX MSS. which, like Heb. and the oriental versions, read ἐν τῇ ἡμέρᾳ ἐκείνῃ ; most LXX MSS. read ἐκεῖ.

[b] Arm. *araçani*= " Euphrates " ; the Arm. O.T. transcribes the Greek name.

[c] τὸ ῥητόν.

[d] ὁμωνυμίᾳ.

[e] Homer, *Od.* xiv. 258 στῆσα δ' ἐν Αἰγύπτῳ ποταμῷ νέας ἀμφιελίσσας. The wording is slightly different in the Arm. text.

[f] τὸ πρὸς διάνοιαν.

[g] αἰνίττεται τὴν εὐτυχίαν (or εὐπραγίαν).

[h] So Arm. lit. ; Aucher renders, " perfecta plenitudo tripiclium bonorum." Prob. the original had merely τελειότης τριῶν <ἀγαθῶν>.

[i] ἡ νομοθεσία.

[j] Here, as elsewhere, Philo plays on the similarity of sound between Εὐφράτης and εὐφροσύνη.

external goods,[a] health and keenness of sense [b] and beauty and strength, which are wont to flourish and grow and be attained in youth. And similarly those things which pertain to profit and selling, (such as) piloting and agriculture and trade. For all (this) is proper to youth, especially those things which have rightly been so described.[c]

17. (Gen. xv. 19-21) [d] Who are " the Kenites and the Kenizzites and the Kadmonites and the Hittites and the Perizzites and the Rephaim and the Amorites and the Canaanites and the Girgashites and the Jebusites " ?

These ten nations are reckoned (as) evils which he destroys [e] because of being neighbours,[f] since also a rejected and counterfeit denarius [g] (is a neighbour ?) of acceptable ones.[h] For the all-perfection [i] of the number ten is most

[a] The Arm. text from " in the end " to " external (goods) " is far from clear to me. Aucher's rendering is fairly literal but also obscure, " in ultimis enim occurrunt res animae ; quibus aegre appropinquare succedit nobis, postquam tamen transitum fuerit per corporales et externas." His "postquam" is questionable: *yarajagoyn* means "first" or " formerly," and here is contrasted with *yetoy housk* " in the end " or " finally." The general sense of the passage seems to be that youth is the time for enjoying corporeal and external goods, and later life for spiritual goods. [b] εὐαισθησίαν.

[c] Aucher renders somewhat differently, " juvenem namque omnia decere, maxime praedicta jure dictum est."

[d] These verses are not commented on elsewhere by Philo.

[e] Or " which destroy," assuming that there was a neut. pl. subj. (ἔθνη) in the original ; variant " which (he) likens."

[f] The sentence is obscure and prob. corrupt ; Aucher renders, " decem gentes numerantur malitiae quas destruit ob vicinitatem."

[g] Arm. *dahekan* = " denarius," " drachma," etc.

[h] Lit. " of loved ones." The sentence is very puzzling ; Aucher renders, " quoniam Denarius quoque falsus, et male signatus vicinus est bono ac amabili." The Arm. glossator explains, " The evil which is ten strives to be like the good, just as a rejected denarius, etc."

[i] ἡ παντέλεια, *cf. De Decalogo* 20 τὸν ἀριθμὸν δεκάδι τῇ παντελείᾳ.

completely harmonious [a] and is the measure of an infinity [b] of numbers, by which the world and the mind of the wise man are ordered and ruled. But evil overturns and changes its [c] substance,[d] overlooking the most necessary powers, because of its only being said [e] that that which is good is the pursuit of virtue.[f] For the wicked man is such as to admit opinion rather than truth, in which are those who see.[g]

*18. (Gen. xvi. 1) Why did not Sarah the wife of Abraham bear him children?

As a barren woman is the mother of the race spoken of; first of all, in order that the seed of offspring [h] may appear more wonderful and miraculous.[i] Second, in order that

[a] παναρμονιώτατος (*sic!*).

[b] ἀπειρίας; *cf. De Decalogo* 27 ἡ ἀπειρία τῶν ἀριθμῶν ταύτῃ (*sc.* τῇ δεκάδι) μετρεῖται.

[c] The decad's?

[d] Or "essence"—οὐσίαν.

[e] Variant "heard."

[f] This is a lit. translation of the troublesome Arm. text, which Aucher renders, "hujus tamen substantiam convertit subvertitque malitia, despectis viribus pernecessariis, ut solum restet illud quod dixerit (*vel*, audierit) bonum esse studium virtutis."

[g] The last phrase is unintelligible to me. One MS. adds "The birth of Ishmael"; another MS. prefixes these two words to the following section. Aucher renders—on what basis I do not know—, "in quibus semen prophetarum (*vel*, admittens ad aucupandos videntes)." The Arm. glossator explains, not very helpfully, "the virtuous man with single constancy abides in the truth and sees the good, while the evil man (abides) in opinion, and hearing belongs to him, who has not a credible birth, as seeing belongs to the former one." Here there seems to be an allusion to the symbolism of the names Israel ("seeing God") and Ishmael ("hearing God").

[h] So Arm. lit. = τὸ τῶν ἐκγόνων σπέρμα; prob. the original read, as in the paraphrase of Procopius, ἡ τῶν ἐγγόνων σπορά; Aucher renders awkwardly, "generationibus filius (appareat)."

[i] Prob., as in Procopius, παράδοξος . . . θαυματουργηθεῖσα. The verse is rather differently allegorized in *De Congressu* 1-10.

the conceiving and bearing might be not so much through union with a man as through the providence [a] of God. For when a barren woman gives birth, it is not by way of generation [b] but the work of the divine power.[c] This is the literal meaning.[d] But as for the deeper meaning,[e] first, giving birth is wholly peculiar to woman, just as begetting is to man. (Scripture) therefore wishes the soul of the virtuous man to be likened to the male sex rather than the female, considering that activity rather than passivity is congenial to him.[f] Furthermore, both (kinds of mind) beget—the virtuous mind and the wicked—, but they beget differently and opposites.[g] The virtuous man (begets) good and useful things, while the wicked and evil man (begets) dirty, shameful and useless things. And the third (point) is that he who has progressed [h] even to the very end [i] is near to what is called by some the forgotten and unknown light.[j] This progressive man [k] does not

[a] προνοίᾳ or ἐπιμελείᾳ; the Greek frag. from Cod. Barb. *ap.* Wendland has ἐπιφροσύνῃ, Procopius has ἐπ' εὐφροσύνῃ.

[b] Lit. "not of being in accordance with generation" (or "offspring"); Aucher renders, "non pariendi facultatis est"; the Greek frag. has more simply οὐ γεννήσεως (ἔργον).

[c] τῆς θέας δυνάμεως ἔργον, as in the Greek frag. (omitting the article), which ends here.

[d] τὸ ῥητόν.

[e] τὸ πρὸς διάνοιαν.

[f] τὸ δρᾶν μᾶλλον ἢ τὸ πάσχειν αὐτῷ οἰκεῖον εἶναι.

[g] διαφόρως καὶ ἐναντία.

[h] ὁ προκόψας.

[i] καὶ δὴ εἰς τὰ ἄκρα *vel sim.*

[j] The text is obscure; Aucher, who punctuates and construes differently, renders, "qui est adhuc proficiscens, ad ipsam summitatem invitandus, prope est ad lumen, quod apud aliquos dicitur oblivioni traditum ac incognitum." The Arm. glossator explains it in this way, "He who is alienated from sin has made a beginning of virtue; of this some say that such a man is near the unknown light, which he formerly knew, but strayed from through sin, and now has come back to." Perhaps a partial parallel is to be found in *De Congressu* 5-6, which contrasts the preliminary studies (Hagar) with complete virtue (Sarah).

[k] Reading Arm. *yaṙajatealn* (ptc.) for *yaṙajateln* (inf.).

beget vices nor virtues either, since he is not yet complete, but he is the same as one who is not ill and (yet) not altogether well in body, but is now coming (back) from a long illness to health.

19. (Gen. xvi. 1) What is the meaning of the words, " And she had an Egyptian maidservant, whose name was Hagar " ?

" Hagar " is interpreted as " sojourning," [a] and she is a servant, waiting on a more perfect nature. And she is very naturally an Egyptian by race. For she is the study of school disciplines,[b] and being a lover [c] of wide learning,[d] is in a certain sense [e] a servant waiting on virtue,[f] since school studies [g] are serviceable to him who needs help in receiving it,[h] inasmuch as virtue has the soul as its place, while the school studies need bodily organs ; and Egypt is symbolically the body, (wherefore Scripture) rightly describes the form [i] of the school studies as Egyptian. Moreover, it also named her " sojourning " for the reason that sophistry [j] is a sojourner in comparison with native virtue [k] which alone is at home [l] and which is mistress of

[a] παροίκησις ; *cf. De Congressu* 20.

[b] ἐπιτήδευσις τῶν ἐγκυκλίων ἐπιστημῶν *vel sim.*

[c] Or " friend."

[d] πολυμαθείας.

[e] τρόπον τινά.

[f] ἀρετῆς. Aucher, misled in part by the seemingly erroneous repetition of *bazoumousmnout'iun* (= πολυμάθεια) in the Arm. text, renders, " nam studium encyclicae disciplinae deligit copiam scientiae et copiosa scientia tamquam ministra est virtutis."

[g] τὰ ἐγκύκλια.

[h] This is a slight emendation of the Arm. text which seems to mean lit. " who is of help, etc. " ; Aucher renders freely but more intelligibly, " qui scit proficere acquisitione ejus ad acquirendam virtutem."

[i] εἶδος or ἰδέαν.

[j] τὰ σοφίσματα ; *cf. De Congressu* 18.

[k] κατὰ σύγκρισιν τῆς πατρίας ἀρετῆς.

[l] Lit. " belongs " (= ἐπιτηδεία ?).

intermediate education [a] and provides for us [b] through the school studies.

*20. (Gen. xvi. 2) Why does Sarah say to Abraham,[c] " Behold, the Lord has closed me up so as not to bear. Go into my maidservant that thou mayest beget children [d] from her " ?

In the literal sense [e] it is the same (as) not to be envious and jealous (but) to look out for the wise man and husband and genuine kinsman.[f] At the same time, to make up for her childlessness through the maidservant which she had, she designated her as her husband's concubine. Moreover, the excessiveness of her wifely love is indicated (thereby), for since she seemed to be barren, she did not think it right to let her husband's household suffer from childlessness, for she valued his gain more than her own standing. That is the literal meaning.[g] But as for the deeper meaning,[h] it has somewhat the following argument.[i] Those who are unable by virtue to beget fine and praiseworthy deeds ought to pursue intermediate education,[j] and in a certain sense [k] produce children from the school studies,[l] for wide learning [m] is a sort of whetstone

[a] τῆς μέσης παιδείας, *cf. De Congressu* 12, where Colson translates it as " lower instruction."

[b] χορηγεῖ (?) ; Aucher " choreas agitat " ; *cf. De Congressu* 19.

[c] LXX, Heb. and Arm. O.T. have " Abram." The form " Abraham " is first used in Scripture in Gen. xvii. 5, see below, *QG* iii. 43.

[d] Some LXX MSS. in agreement with Heb. read τεκνοποιήσω(μαι), as do the Oriental versions.

[e] τῷ μὲν ῥητῷ.

[f] The construction and sense are not wholly clear to me ; Aucher renders, " in ipsa littera idem est non invidere et providere de sapiente," etc.

[g] τὸ ῥητόν.

[h] τὸ πρὸς διάνοιαν.

[i] λόγον.

[j] τὴν μέσην παιδείαν.

[k] τρόπον τινά.

[l] ἐκ τῶν ἐγκυκλίων.

[m] πολυμάθεια.

of the mind and reason.[a] But most excellently was it written, " He closed me up," for what is closed is wont to open at a suitable time. So that his [b] wisdom [c] is not resigned [d] to being childless for ever but knows that she will bear children. She will however, not bear now but when the soul [e] shows purity of perfection.[f] But while it is imperfect it is sufficient for it to have a milder and gentler teaching [g] which comes through the school studies. Whence it is not for nothing that in the sacred athletic contests those who cannot take the first prizes in the contest are deserving of the second. For a first and second and third prize are put before the contestants by the officials of the games, who resemble nature, for before him [h] it puts a first prize of virtue and a second of the school studies.

*21. (Gen. xvi. 3) Why does (Scripture) call Sarah the wife of Abraham,[i] for it says, " And Sarah the wife of Abraham, taking her maidservant Hagar the Egyptian, gave her into his hands " ?

The theologian [j] emphasizes [k] the marriage of worthy

[a] ἀκόνη τις τοῦ νοῦ καὶ τοῦ λόγου. In *De Congressu* 25 Rachel, as symbol of the lower education, is called a whetstone.

[b] To what or whom " his " refers is not clear, but prob. is the mind.

[c] σοφία.

[d] *Arm. včarem* has a number of meanings, such as " complete," " discharge," " release," none of which seems to fit here ; Aucher renders freely, " spe destituta erat ac fixa in consilio."

[e] Lit. " souls " ; but in the next sentence the verb is sing.

[f] καθαριότητα τελειότητος (a collocation that sounds un-Philonic).

[g] ἐπιεικεστέρᾳ καὶ γαλακτώδει διδασκαλίᾳ χρῆσθαι ; *cf. De Congressu* 19.

[h] The person referred to is not clear.

[i] *i.e.* why does Scripture repeat the phrase " wife of Abraham ? " ; *cf. De Congressu* 73-80.

[j] ὁ θεολόγος (Moses).

[k] Lit. " seals " or " stamps " ; Aucher renders, " concludit comprobatione."

persons in view of the intemperance of lascivious ones. For these, because of their concubines, whom they madly love, look down upon their wise [a] wives. Wherefore (Scripture) introduces the virtuous man [b] as a more constant [c] husband to his wife when the occasion dictated [d] the use of the maidservant. And (Scripture represents) the wise wife as more sober [e] when he entered another's bed.[f] For with the concubine the embrace was a bodily one for the sake of begetting children. But with the wife the union was one of the soul harmonized to heavenly love.[g] That is the literal meaning.[h] But as for the deeper meaning,[i] he who has truthfully entrusted his thoughts [j] to wisdom and justice and other virtues,[k] when once he has received the thoughts [l] of wisdom and has tasted marriage with her, remains her mate [m] and husband, even though he provides [n] abundantly for the education of the school.[o]

[a] Probably, as Wendland suggests, the Arm. translator read ἀστείων "wise" or "virtuous" (in Philo) for ἀστῶν "lawful." The latter word is used in the frag. from Procopius and in *De Congressu* 77.

[b] τὸν σπουδαῖον, *i.e.* Abraham.

[c] βεβαιότερον, as in Procopius.

[d] ὅτε παρήγγελλον οἱ καιροί, as in Procopius.

[e] Or "temperate." The Procopius frag. has παγιωτέραν "more steadfast"; the point of the reference is clearer in the parallel, *De Congressu* 37, where the name Rebecca is etymologized as ὑπομονή "constancy" or "endurance."

[f] Aucher, construing wrongly, renders, "et sobrium profecto (designat) mulier sapientem quum alium in thalamum ingressus est."

[g] The Arm. agrees literally with the Greek frag. ἕνωσις ψυχῆς ἁρμοζομένης ἔρωτι θείῳ.

[h] τὸ ῥητόν.

[i] τὸ πρὸς διάνοιαν.

[j] Prob. τοὺς λογισμούς; Aucher "secreta sua."

[k] σοφίᾳ καὶ δικαιοσύνῃ καὶ ἄλλαις ἀρεταῖς.

[l] Or perhaps "counsel," as Aucher, renders; the Arm. word is the same as that mentioned in note *j*.

[m] σύνοικος.

[n] Prob. χορηγεῖ; Aucher renders literally, "choreas agitet."

[o] τῇ ἐγκυκλίᾳ παιδείᾳ.

For even if the virtuous man has ready to hand [a] the theories [b] of geometry, arithmetic, grammar, rhetoric and other scientific disciplines, none the less is he mindful of his integrity,[c] and addresses himself to the one as a task, and to the other as to a side-task.[d] But most worthy of praise is it that (Scripture) calls the maidservant "wife,"[e] for he came together with her in bed by the will and at the injunction of his true wife, and not by any means of his own will. For this reason (Scripture) does not (here) call her "maidservant," for the maidservant, having been given to him (as wife), obtains this (status), if not in fact, at any rate in name. However, let us allegorize [f] by saying that the training in intermediate studies has the force [g] of a concubine but the form and rank [h] of a wife. For the several school studies resemble and imitate true virtue.

*22. (Gen. xvi. 4) What is the meaning of the words, "She saw that she was pregnant, and her mistress was dishonoured before her"?

Advisedly [i] does (Scripture) now call Sarah "mistress" when she seems to be eclipsed [j] and subdued by her maidservant—a childless woman by a childbearing one. But this principle of reasoning [k] extends to almost all the matters necessary to life. For more lordly [l] is the wise poor man than the foolish rich man,[m] and the inglorious

[a] πρόχειρα.

[b] τὰ θεωρήματα.

[c] τῆς καλοκἀγαθίας.

[d] ἔργον . . . πάρεργον, as Aucher conjectures.

[e] By implication at least; *cf. De Congressu* 80.

[f] ἀλληγορῶμεν. [g] δύναμιν. [h] τιμήν.

[i] Or "cautiously," "guardedly"; the Greek frag. has κατὰ καιρόν.

[j] Or "made light of"—ἐλαττοῦσθαι.

[k] κεφαλὴ τοῦ λόγου (?); there is nothing corresponding to this phrase in the Greek frag.

[l] κυριώτερος (as in the Greek frag.) is rendered by two Arm. words.

[m] ὁ φρόνιμος πένης ἄφρονος πλουσίου, as in the Greek frag.

man than the glorious one,[a] and the sick man than the healthy one.[b] For whatever is with wisdom [c] is wholly lordly and independent [d] and masterful.[e] But whatever is with folly is a slave and infirm.[f] And well is it said, not that she dishonoured her mistress, but "her mistress was dishonoured." [g] For the former would contain a personal accusation while the latter would be a declaration of things that happened.[h] But (Scripture) does not wish to lay blame and condemnation upon anyone for the sake of praising (another),[i] but to make clear the bare and simple truth of matters. That is the literal meaning.[j] But as for the deeper meaning,[k] those who accept and honour glory more than the science of wisdom,[l] and consider sense-perception [m] more honourable than reason,[n] set themselves apart from familiarity with the facts,[o] thinking that the production of many things and the complacent love [p] of appearances are great and perfect goods and are alone honourable, while barrenness in these is bad and dishonourable. For they do not see that invisible seed [q] and

[a] ἄδοξος ἐνδόξου.

[b] ὁ νοσῶν ὑγιαίνοντος.

[c] σὺν φρονήσει, as in the Greek frag.

[d] Arm. *boun* = φυσικός, γνήσιος, αὐτός, etc.

[e] To these three adjectives the single adj. κύρια corresponds in the Greek frag.

[f] ἄστατον.

[g] A somewhat parallel distinction (between Sarah's seeing Hagar's pregnancy and Hagar's seeing her own pregnancy) is made in *De Congressu* 139-150.

[h] The Greek frag. (which ends here) says more briefly οὐ γὰρ ἐθέλει κατηγορεῖν, δηλῶσαι δὲ τὸ συμβεβηκός.

[i] The context requires the pronoun ; *cf.* Aucher "in alterius laude."

[j] τὸ ῥητόν.

[k] τὸ πρὸς διάνοιαν.

[l] τὴν τῆς σοφίας ἐπιστήμην.

[m] τὴν αἴσθησιν.

[n] τὸν λογισμόν.

[o] ἀπὸ τῆς τῶν πραγμάτων οἰκειότητος *vel sim.*

[p] Lit. "sufficient loving" ; Aucher paraphrases, "magnam generationem . . . produxisse."

[q] Or "sowing" ; *cf.* *De Somniis* i. 199 ἀοράτῳ σπορᾷ φρονήσεως.

the intelligible generations [a] which the mind is wont to produce by itself.

*23. (Gen. xvi. 5) Why does Sarah, as it were, repent, saying to Abraham, " I am wronged by thee. I have given my maidservant into thy bosom, but seeing that she is pregnant, I have been dishonoured before her " [b] ?

This statement contains doubt and indecision. And it is clear that the " since " [c] is the same as " the time when I gave my maidservant." And the other statement refers to a person,[d] that is, when she says, " By thee I am wronged." [e] For this is a reproach. And it is proper (for Scripture) to keep the good, worthy, truthful and unforgetting husband from blame and accusation and always to present him with all honour, calling him " lord." But the first statement is true, for since the time when she gave (him) her maidservant and made her his concubine, she seemed to be disesteemed and dishonoured. That is the literal meaning.[f] But as for the deeper meaning,[g] when

[a] τὰ νοερὰ γένη.

[b] The Arm. closely follows the LXX ἀδικοῦμαι ἐκ σοῦ· ἐγὼ δέδωκα τὴν παιδίσκην μου εἰς τὸν κόλπον σου. ἰδοῦσα δὲ ὅτι ἐν γαστρὶ ἔχει, ἠτιμάσθην ἐναντίον αὐτῆς. Aucher's rendering, " quia vidit," is misleading, since the Arm., like the LXX, makes " seeing " (ptc.) refer to Sarah, whereas the Heb. makes the verb (in its finite form) refer to Hagar. In the parallel, *De Congressu* 139 Philo, following the LXX in reading ἰδοῦσα, makes the point that it was Sarah, not Hagar, who saw Hagar's pregnancy. The concluding part of the verse, Gen. xvi. 5, " let God judge between us," is cited at the end of his comment.

[c] No such conjunction or prep. occurs in the LXX or Arm. O.T. texts of this verse.

[d] Variant " to the opposite."

[e] The argument is unclear but the meaning seems to be that Sarah's doubts about Abraham's feeling are indicated by the interval of time implied ; *cf.* the Greek frag. ἀλλ' ἔστι χρονικὸν τῷ ἑξῆς συναπτόμενον· ἐξ οὗ σοι καὶ ἀφ' οὗ χρόνου ἐγὼ δέδωκα τὴν παιδίσκην μου.

[f] τὸ ῥητόν.

[g] τὸ πρὸς διάνοιαν.

someone gives (to another) the maidservant of wisdom,[a] the latter, being ignorant and through sophistic reasoning,[b] dishonours the mistress. For when he receives and delights in the splendour [c] of the school studies,[d] since each of them is very attractive and seductive and, as it were, has the power of forcibly drawing (others) to itself, he is from then on no longer able to find time to unite with the mistress either in respect of enjoying the image of wisdom or her wonderful appearance [e] until that cutter [f] of things, the divine Logos, supervenes and separates, divides and cuts off the probable from the true,[g] and the means from the ends, and secondary things from those ranged in the first rank. Wherefore she says later, " God will judge between me and thee."

*24. (Gen. xvi. 6) Why does Abraham say, " Behold, thy maidservant is in thy hands. Do with her as is pleasing to thee " ?

The literal text [h] contains praise of the wise man,[i] for it was not " wife " nor " concubine " but " maidservant " of his wife that he called her who was pregnant by him. When he saw that she was growing big, he did not become indignant and provoke [j] the appetite of passion [k] but pacified it. And the passage " in thy hands " contains an allegory [l] in a certain sense,[m] by which I mean that sophistry [n]

[a] τὴν τῆς σοφίας παιδίσκην.

[b] τῷ τῆς σοφιστείας λογισμῷ; Aucher renders, " consilio illa [!] sophismatis ignorans."

[c] Or " clarity."

[d] τῶν ἐγκυκλίων.

[e] Aucher renders a little differently, " sive imagine sapientiae, ac gloriosa ejus mirabilique forma."

[f] τομεύς, a term applied to the Logos in *Quis Rer. Div. Heres* 225; Aucher more freely renders, " acutus judex rerum."

[g] τὰ πιθανὰ ἀπὸ τῶν ἀληθῶν.

[h] τὸ ῥητόν.

[i] τοῦ σοφοῦ.

[j] In the Arm. it is not clear who the subject is.

[k] τὴν τοῦ πάθους ὄρεξιν.

[l] ἀλληγορίαν.

[m] τρόπον τινά.

[n] ἡ σοφιστεία.

is under the authority[a] of wisdom, as if it flowed from the same source but crookedly, not straight, and not keeping its flow whole and pure but carrying filth and many other similar things along with it. And so, since this is in thy hands and thy power, to whom, being wisdom, all the school disciplines belong,[b] do with her as is pleasing to thy heart. For I am confident that thou wilt not judge more severely than is right, for this is very pleasing to thee, (namely) to apportion to each what is in accordance with his deserts,[c] and not to honour or dishonour (anyone) more (than is right).

25. (Gen. xvi. 6) Why does (Scripture) say, "Sarah afflicted her"[d]?

The literal meaning is clear. But as for the deeper meaning,[e] it has something like the following content.[f] Not all afflictions are harmful,[g] but there are times when they are even helpful. This is what sick people experience at the hands of physicians, and children at the hands of teachers, and the foolish at the hands of those who enlighten them. This I would never call an affliction, but salvation[h] and aid to soul and body. This is the part that wisdom gives to the group of school studies,[i] judging that a soul filled with much learning[j] and pregnant with sophistry[k] will not be refractory or haughty, as if it were in possession of a great and excessive good, but will be

[a] Or "power." In *De Congressu* 155 Philo allegorizes the words "in thy hands" as a symbol of the bodily senses used in the school studies.

[b] Aucher, construing differently, renders, "cujus enim sapientia, ejus sunt et omnes encyclicae disciplinae."

[c] τὸ ἄξιον *vel sim.*

[d] ἐκάκωσεν αὐτήν, as in LXX.

[e] τὸ πρὸς διάνοιαν.

[f] λόγον.

[g] οὐ πᾶσαι κακώσεις βλαβεραί εἰσι.

[h] σωτηρίαν.

[i] τῷ τῶν ἐγκυκλίων χορῷ.

[j] πολυμαθείας.

[k] σοφιστείας, here used in a semi-respectable sense.

quiet [a] and show respect for a higher and better nature as its true mistress, to whom belongs stability itself and sovereignty over (all) matters.

*26. (Gen. xvi. 6) [b] Why does Hagar flee from her face? [c]

Not every soul gladly receives discipline,[d] but the friendly and particularly gentle mind [e] loves reproof,[f] and becomes more familiar with [g] those who discipline it, while the hostile and malevolent (mind) [h] hates and avoids and flees from it, and draws near pleasant words [i] rather than those which can profit it, thinking that (the former) are preferable and more valuable.

27. (Gen. xvi. 7) What is the meaning of the words, "There found her an angel of the Lord [j] by a spring of water in the wilderness on the road to Shur" [k]?

All these things that are said are symbols and types,[l] by which (Scripture) represents [m] the widely learned soul,[n] which is the property of virtue [o] but is not yet able to see

[a] Lit. "rest" or "subside."

[b] Gen. xvi. 6-9 forms the subject of *De Fuga et Inventione*, where Philo says (§§ 3-5) that Hagar fled, not out of hatred or fear, but shame.

[c] LXX καὶ ἀπέδρα ἀπὸ προσώπου αὐτῆς.

[d] Variant "receives attention and discipline"; the Greek frag. has merely δέχεται νουθεσίαν.

[e] Aucher renders, "facilis ac suavis proprie (in note: "*vel*, ac constans sibi propria") mens."

[f] ἔλεγχον.

[g] Or "used to"—οἰκειοῦται.

[h] The Greek frag. has only ἡ δὲ ἐχθρὰ <ψυχή>.

[i] τοὺς πρὸς ἡδονὴν λόγους.

[j] Some LXX MSS. have "the Lord God."

[k] In *De Fuga* 1 Philo follows the LXX more closely, in reading ἐπὶ τῆς πηγῆς τοῦ ὕδατος ἐν τῇ ἐρήμῳ, ἐπὶ τῆς πηγῆς ἐν τῇ ὁδῷ Σούρ.

[l] σύμβολα καὶ τύποι.

[m] σχηματίζει.

[n] τὴν πολυμαθῆ ψυχήν.

[o] κτῆμα τῆς ἀρετῆς; *i.e.* Hagar, symbolizing the school studies, is owned by Sarah, symbolizing virtue.

the beauty of its mistress. Now these are the symbols: the "finding," "by the angel," "by the spring," "in the wilderness," "on the road"—none other than (the road) to Shur. However, we must begin with the first one. Now a very deceitful sophist [a] and contentious person [b] is not always [c] found out because of the skill and the sophistical arguments [d] with which he is accustomed to trick and deceive. But he who is without evil habits is zealous only for wide learning,[e] which comes through the group of school studies [f]; and although this is hard to find,[g] still it is not altogether undiscoverable. For perdition [h] is akin to the undiscoverable, while discovery [i] is salvation and life.[j] And especially (is this so) when one is sought and found by a purer and more worthy spirit. But what is purer or more worthy than a divine angel? For it was he who was entrusted with the search for a wandering soul,[k] which because of its learning did not surely know that which it ought to honour.[l] However, it might have [m] obtained correction, for the sake of which the search was made. Now it is not incomplete [n] but is right at hand. For the soul was found fleeing from virtue, not being able to receive discipline.[o] And there is a second symbol after the "finding," namely that the finding by the angel took place "by

[a] σοφιστής. [b] φιλόνεικος.

[c] The Greek prob. had the indef. pr. τι.

[d] Or "proofs," "persuasions."

[e] τῆς πολυμαθείας.

[f] διὰ τοῦ τῶν ἐγκυκλίων χοροῦ.

[g] δυσεύρετος. [h] ἀπώλεια.

[i] Or "discoverability"?

[j] σωτηρία καὶ ζωή. For an extended discussion of the symbolism of other biblical passages on "finding" see *De Fuga* 119-176.

[k] πλανωμένην ψυχήν.

[l] The Arm. seems to make better sense than Aucher's rendering, "et ob praesumptam eruditionem nescientem constanter, quam oportebat venerari."

[m] Or "was able to"—ἐδύνατο.

[n] ἀτελής (?); the noun referred to is prob. "search," as Aucher conjectures. [o] παιδείαν.

a spring."[a] By this I understand nature to be meant. For she offers the sciences of learning in accordance with each one's practices,[b] wiping out and cleansing the wrong kind of learning.[c] And the passage is in praise[d] of the soul which is thirsty for knowledge[e] and is desirous of its laws and is eager to draw up and drink its water, as a fellow-celebrant in the company of those who drink wine. So does it behave with those who are nourished by and luxuriate in the exercises that train the reason,[f] for nature, as from a spring, offers an abundance of instruction and guidance.[g] And the fourth symbol is the finding "in the wilderness,"[h] for the perturbation and anxiety which come upon the various senses, and the floods of the various passions oppress the soul and do not permit it to drink pure water.[i] But when it is able to escape it betakes itself, as it were, to the wilderness, and it has surcease from the thoughts[j] that disturbed it, and recovers its health. And it obtains hope, not only of life, but even of immortal life. The fifth symbol was the finding "on the road," since perverted characters use a trackless route, while he who is able to improve himself goes by the road that leads to virtue. And this road is a wall and a protection to those who are able to save themselves. For "Shur" is

[a] For Philo's extended discussion of the symbolism of the various senses of "spring" in Scripture see *De Fuga* 177-201.

[b] *ἐπιτηδεύματα.*

[c] Lit. "left-handed learning"; variant "lack of learning."

[d] Lit. "is praise."

[e] Prob. *ἐπιστήμης*; Aucher has "ingenium"; *cf. De Fuga* 187 *μαθήσεως διψῶντες . . . ἐπιστήμαις ἱδρύονται.*

[f] *ἐν τοῖς τῆς λογικῆς παιδείας ἐπιτηδεύμασι vel sim.* On this sentence Aucher rightly comments, "totius periodi constructio obscuritatem habet in Arm."

[g] In *De Fuga* 197-198 Philo treats the spring as, among other things, a symbol of the living God, quoting Jer. ii. 13.

[h] Philo omits this symbol in *De Fuga.*

[i] Lit. "drink water purely."

[j] *τῶν λογισμῶν.*

to be translated as "wall."[a] Do you not see that all this is a tropical figure[b] of the soul that progresses?[c] And one who progresses does not become lost like one who is completely foolish. If the divine Logos[d] is to be found, he seeks it. And he who is not pure and good in his habits is put to flight and pursued by the divine Logos; however, he has a spring of water by which he may wash[e] away his passion and evil, and from which he may drink the superabundance[f] of its laws. But he is a lover of the wilderness who flees from passion and evil, and on seeing the road of virtue, turns away from the trackless way of evil. All these are a wall and protection to him, so that he is in no way harmed either in word or deed, and does not suffer evil from those things which rush upon him.

28. (Gen. xvi. 8) Why does the angel say to her, "Hagar, maidservant of Sarah, whence comest thou and whither goest thou"?

The literal meaning[g] does not need any exposition,[h] for it is exceedingly clear. But as for the deeper meaning,[i] forcefulness[j] (is meant), for the divine Logos[k] is a disciplinarian[l] and an excellent healer of the weakness of the soul. He says to her, "Whence comest thou? Dost thou not know what good thou has left? Surely thou art not useless and crippled?[m] For with seeing thou dost not see, and having senses, thou dost not perceive, and though thou

[a] In *De Fuga* 203 Philo etymologizes "Shur" as "wall or straightening."

[b] Prob. τρόπος καὶ σχῆμα; Aucher has "symbolice (*vel*, legitima) figura."

[c] τῆς προκοπτούσης ψυχῆς.

[d] ὁ θεῖος λόγος.

[e] Lit. "he washes."

[f] Lit. "fertility."

[g] τὸ ῥητόν.

[h] ἐξηγήσεως.

[i] τὸ πρὸς διάνοιαν.

[j] Aucher "asperitas"; perhaps the original was ἐπίπληξις, as in *De Fuga* 205.

[k] ὁ θεῖος λόγος.

[l] Perhaps νουθετητής.

[m] Or "blind," as Aucher renders; Arm. *hašm* has both meanings.

seemest to have a portion of mind,[a] thou seemest to me to be altogether without mind. But whither goest thou? From what piety to what misery?[b] Why dost thou wander in such a way as to throw away the good which thou didst have in thy hands, and follow after a more remote good? Do not, do not do this, but subdue this stupid and irrational impulse.[c] Come back and return from there to the same road (as before). Consider wisdom to be thy mistress, whom formerly thou didst have as an overseer and caretaker in those things which thou didst practise."

*29. (Gen. xvi. 8) What is the meaning of the words, "From the face of Sarah my mistress I am fleeing"[d]?

It is proper to praise a sincere nature[e] and consider it a lover of truth. Wherefore it is now also fitting to admit the veracity[f] of a mind that confesses what it has experienced.[g] For "from the face" I take to mean, "I am struck dumb[h] by the appearance of virtue and wisdom."[i] For at the sight of this royal sovereign it[j] shudders and is dismayed, not being able[k] to endure the sight of her greatness and exaltedness, and must flee. For there are some who flee from virtue not because of hate but because of reverential awe,[l] for they believe themselves to be unworthy to live with[m] their mistress.

[a] *νοῦ*: I have omitted an apparently intrusive negative before "to have."

[b] *ἀφ' ὁποίας εὐσεβείας εἰς ὁποῖαν ταλαιπωρίαν.*

[c] *ὁρμήν.*

[d] This scriptural half-verse is not commented on by Philo in *De Fuga.*

[e] *τὸ τοῦ ἤθους ἀνυπόκριτον*, as in the Greek frag. from Procopius.

[f] *ἀψεύδειαν.*

[g] *ὃ πέπονθεν*, as in the Greek frag.

[h] *καταπέπληγμαι*; *cf.* *καταπέπληκται* in the Greek frag.

[i] *ὑπὸ τῆς φαντασίας τῆς ἀρετῆς καὶ σοφίας*, as in the Greek frag.

[j] The mind.

[k] Reading *kareal* (ptc.) for *karel* (inf.).

[l] Prob. *αἰδοῖ*, as in the Greek frag.

[m] *συμβιοῦν*, as in the Greek frag.

*30. (Gen. xvi. 9) Why did the angel say to her, "Return to thy mistress and submit thyself under her hands"?

Since the literal meaning [a] is clear, the deeper meaning [b] must be considered. The divine Logos [c] disciplines and admonishes [d] the soul which is able to receive healing, and turns it back to sovereign wisdom,[e] lest, being left without a mistress,[f] it leap into absurd folly. And he [g] disciplines it,[h] not only that it may turn back to virtue but also submit itself under her hands, by which I mean under her powers.[i] Now submission [j] is of two forms. One is by way of deficiency,[k] arising from the soul's weakness,[l] which it is easy to overcome, arrest and condemn.[m] The other is that which the dominant Logos [n] enjoins, and arises from awe and reverence, such as sons feel toward their parents, and pupils toward their teachers, and youths toward their elders. For it is most expedient to be obedient to, and fall before,[o] one's betters. He who has learned to be ruled, also learns at once how to rule. For not even if one should assume power over all the earth and sea, would he be able to rule in truth if he had not first learned and first been trained to be ruled.

31. (Gen. xvi. 10) Why does the angel say to her, "I will multiply, he says,[p] thy seed and it shall not be numbered for multitude"?

[a] τὸ ῥητόν.
[b] τὸ πρὸς διάνοιαν.
[c] ὁ θεῖος λόγος.
[d] παιδεύει καὶ νουθετεῖ.
[e] πρὸς τὴν ἡγεμονικὴν σοφίαν.
[f] ἀδέσποτος.
[g] The Logos.
[h] The soul.
[i] ταῖς δυνάμεσι.
[j] ταπείνωσις.
[k] κατ' ἔκλειψιν or ἐλάττωσιν; variant "by way of corruption."
[l] ἐκ ψυχικῆς ἀσθενείας.
[m] ὑπερβάλλειν καὶ καταλαμβάνειν καὶ καταγιγνώσκειν.
[n] ὁ κύριος λόγος.
[o] The Greek frag., which begins here, has only τὸ ὑποτάττεσθαι.
[p] Why the Arm. inserts "he says" is not clear; possibly it is a substitute for the Heb. idiom, reproduced in the LXX, "multiplying I will multiply."

The honourable thing for a believing soul [a] is not to revolt and resist because of its progress in learning [b] and the most useful growth [c] which comes from wide learning.[d] For it is no longer like the word-catchers and word-traders [e] who greedily stuff themselves with the various opinions that are (found) in the school studies,[f] but (seeks) that truth which is in the various (studies).[g] When it follows after this, and begins to seek out and search for it, it becomes worthy of beholding the sight of its unbribable, irreprehensible and irreproachable mistress.[h]

32. (Gen. xvi. 11) What is the meaning of the words, "The angel [i] said to her, 'Behold, thou hast conceived and wilt bear a son, and thou shalt call his name Ishmael, for the Lord has heard thy affliction'"?

The literal meaning [j] admits no questioning, but (the verse) is to be allegorized [k] as follows. Wide learning,[l] which is practised and used through the administration [m] of virtue as through a mistress, is not barren but receives the seeds of wisdom.[n] And when it conceives, it bears. However, it bears, not a perfect work,[o] but an imperfect one, like a child that is in need of care and nourishment.[p] And is this not right?[q] For it is clear that the offspring [r]

[a] πιστευούσῃ ψυχῇ.

[b] διὰ τὴν τῆς μαθήσεως προκοπήν.

[c] Lit. "seed."

[d] ἐκ πολυμαθείας.

[e] λογοθῆραι καὶ λογοπῶλαι; these two epithets are coupled in *De Congressu* 53.

[f] ἐν τοῖς ἐγκυκλίοις.

[g] Aucher renders somewhat differently, "non enim ulterius, ut verborum captores venditoresque, ad placitum usurpat omnia encyclopediae argumenta, sed illam quae in singulis continetur veritatem."

[h] τῆς ἀδεκάστου καὶ ἀκαταγνώστου καὶ ἀνεπιτιμήτου κυρίας.

[i] Heb. and LXX "angel of the Lord."

[j] τὸ ῥητόν.

[k] ἀλληγορεῖται.

[l] πολυμάθεια.

[m] οἰκονομίαν *vel sim.*

[n] τὰ τῆς σοφίας σπέρματα.

[o] τέλειον ἔργον.

[p] ἐπιμελείας καὶ τροφῆς.

[q] Aucher, in his rendering, inadvertently omits this sentence.

[r] Lit. "births."

of a perfected soul are perfect, and these are words and deeds.[a] But those of inferior[b] (souls) which are still under service and in bondage are more imperfect. Therefore he was truly[c] named Ishmael, and this is to be interpreted as "hearing God."[d] Now hearing is second in rank to seeing. For as prizes in the contest of the senses[e] Nature has given the first to the eyes, the second to the ears, the third to the nostrils, and the fourth to (the organ) by which we taste.

33. (Gen. xvi. 12) What is the meaning of the words, "He will be a wild man[f]; his hand will be against all, and the hands of all against him, and he will dwell over against[g] all his brothers"?

In the literal sense[h] he has no brothers up to this point, for he was the first who came[i] to his parents. However, Nature indicates[j] something rather unclear, which must be examined, for it gives a picture[k] of those things which are to be. Now this picture clearly represents the sophist,[l] whose mother is wide learning and wisdom.[m] But the sophist is wild in thought,[n] while the wise man is civil[o] and is suited to the state and to civilization[p]; but the man of wild thought is from that very fact[q] a lover of conten-

[a] λόγοι καὶ ἔργα.

[b] δευτερείων.

[c] ἐτύμως.

[d] ἀκοὴ θεοῦ; *cf. De Fuga* 208, where Ishmael and Israel ("seeing God") are contrasted.

[e] ἆθλον ἐν τῷ τῶν αἰσθήσεων ἀγωνίσματι.

[f] LXX ἄγροικος ἄνθρωπος.

[g] LXX κατὰ πρόσωπον.

[h] κατὰ τὸ ῥητόν.

[i] Lit. "began to be."

[j] αἰνίττεται.

[k] σχῆμα (καὶ μορφήν?).

[l] τὸν σοφιστήν; *cf. De Fuga* 209.

[m] πολυμάθεια καὶ σοφία.

[n] In *De Fuga* 209 Philo calls him ἀγροικόσοφον.

[o] πολιτικός.

[p] πόλει καὶ πολιτείᾳ.

[q] Text uncertain; for Arm. *andēn* "thence" Aucher suggests *anden* "infidelis, irreligiosus" [?]; the Arm. glossator explains *andēn* as "crooked," but seems to be guessing.

tion.[a] Therefore (Scripture) adds, "his hands against all, and the hands of all against him," for, being trained in wide learning and much knowledge,[b] he contradicts all men (He is) like those who are now called Academics and Sceptics,[c] who place no foundation [d] under their opinions and doctrines and do not (prefer) one thing to another, for they admit those as philosophers who shoot at (the doctrines) of every school,[e] and these it is customary to call "opinion-fighters."[f] For first they fight and become defenders and champions of their native school [g] lest they be stopped by those who oppose them. For they are all kin and, in a certain sense,[h] uterine brothers,[i] offspring of the same mother, philosophy.[j] Therefore (Scripture) says, "over against all his brothers he will dwell." For in truth [k] the Academics and the Non-committals [l] take opposite stands in their doctrines, and oppose the various opinions which others hold.[m]

34. (Gen. xvi. 13) Why does (Scripture) say, "And she [n] called the name of the Lord, who was speaking to her, Thou art God who seest me, for she said, For indeed I have seen before (me) him who appeared to me" [o]?

[a] *φιλόνεικος*.

[b] *πολλῇ ἐπιστήμῃ* (or *γνώσει*).

[c] Lit. "investigators," but the word evidently reflects Greek *σκεπτικοί*.

[d] Aucher "terminum."

[e] *ἑκάστης αἱρέσεως δόγματα vel sim.*

[f] Perhaps Philo here used *γνωμομαχοῦντες*, though the word is not attested in his writings or elsewhere, it seems; *cf.* *γνωσιμαχοῦντες*, used of sceptics, in *De Congressu* 53; Aucher here renders, "voluntatis oppugnatores (quasi Thelemachos vel Thelemamachos)."

[g] *τῆς πατρίας αἱρέσεως vel sim.*; *cf. De Fuga* 210 *ἀμυνομένων ὡς ὑπὲρ οἰκείων ἐκγόνων ὧν ἔτεκεν αὐτῶν ἡ ψυχὴ δογμάτων*.

[h] *τρόπον τινά*.

[i] *ὁμογάστριοι ἀδελφοί*.

[j] *τῆς φιλοσοφίας*.

[k] *ὄντως*.

[l] Lit. "non-sayers"; Aucher "indicibiles." Prob. the Sceptics are meant, as above.

[m] Lit. "decree"—*νομοθετοῦσι*.

[n] LXX "Hagar."

[o] Philo literally follows the LXX, *ἐνώπιον ἴδον ὀφθέντα μοι*.

Observe the first point carefully, that he [a] was the servant of God in the same way (that Hagar was) the maidservant of wisdom.[b] Hence the angel was called (God) [c] in order that she [d] might harmonize the reality [e] to his appearance.[f]

For it was fitting and proper that God, the Most High One and Lord of all, should appear to wisdom,[g] while he who was his Logos (and) minister [h] (should appear) to the maidservant and attendant of wisdom.[i] But it was not strange [j] (for her) to believe that the angel was God. For those who are unable to see the first cause [k] naturally [l] suffer from an illusion [m]; they believe that the second is the first. (They are like those) who have poor eyesight and are not able to see the corporeal form [n] which is in heaven, (namely) the sun, and believe that the rays which it sends to the earth are this itself. And all those who do not see the Great King ascribe the dignity of the first in sovereignty [o] to his satrap and the one under him. Moreover, wild men,[p] who have never seen cities even from a

[a] That the angel is the implied subject is indicated by the parallel *De Fuga* 212 *ἄγγελοι δ' οἰκέται θεοῦ.*

[b] *τῆς σοφίας.*

[c] So also Aucher and the Arm. glossator understand the elliptical phrase.

[d] Or " it " (Scripture)?

[e] *τὸ πρᾶγμα* (?).

[f] Or " person " ; Aucher renders, " ut personae propriae rem (ipsi) adaptaret." This rendering, like mine, finds no place for the adverb *i veray* " above " ; possibly we should emend the Arm. verb *yarmareçouçē* " might harmonize " to *hamaresçē* " might reckon," and thus fit in the adv. " above," rendering, " in order that she might consider the reality as more important than the appearance."

[g] Apparently Sarah, the symbol of wisdom, is meant.

[h] Aucher " verbum ut ministrum " ; there is no conjunction between the two nouns in the Arm. text.

[i] *i.e.* to Hagar.

[j] *ἄτοπον*, or " inept " —*ἀπὸ σκοποῦ.*

[k] *τὸ πρῶτον αἴτιον.*

[l] *εἰκός.*

[m] Lit. " deceit "—*ἀπάτην vel sim.*

[n] *τὸ σωματοειδές.*

[o] Lit. " first king."

[p] *οἱ ἄγριοι.*

hill-top, believe that a village or a country-estate is a metropolis,[a] and that those who live in them are citizens of a metropolis, because of their ignorance of what a true metropolis really[b] is.

35. (Gen. xvi. 14) What is the meaning of the words, "Therefore she called[c] the well 'the well of him[d] whom I saw before (me)'"[e]?

A well has two things, both depth and a source.[f] Now the teachings of the school studies[g] are not superficial[h] and not without principles,[i] for they have discipline[j] as a source. And so she rightly says that it was before the well that the angel appeared like God. And though the school studies have second rank in learning,[k] they seem to be[l] first, and they are divided and separated from that first wisdom[m] which it is proper for wise men but not for sophists[n] to see.[o]

[a] κώμην ἢ αὐλὴν <εἶναι> μητρόπολιν. [b] ὄντως.

[c] Philo follows the LXX in reading ἐκάλεσεν, rendering Heb. *qārā'* which is here used impersonally, meaning "one called" or "people called."

[d] So the Arm. O.T., taking οὗ as gen. s. masc. of the relative pronoun; the variant in the Arm. text of Philo takes the οὗ as a relative adverb.

[e] Or "face to face" as in the Arm. O.T.; both renderings are based on LXX φρέαρ οὗ ἐνώπιον ἴδον. Heb. reads differently, "the well Beer-lahai-roi," traditionally explained as "the well (*bə'ēr*) of the living one (*laḥay*) who sees me (*rô'î*)." Apparently the LXX translators took Heb. *laḥay* as the noun *leḥî* "cheek" in the sense of "before my face." For a somewhat similar interpretation of this verse see *De Fuga* 213.

[f] πηγήν. [g] τῶν ἐγκυκλίων.

[h] ἐπιπόλαιαι. [i] ἄναρχοι. [j] παιδείαν.

[k] τὰ ἐγκύκλια τῆς πολυμαθείας ἔχει τὴν δευτέραν τάξιν; Aucher renders, "eruditio encyclopediae" although the Arm. construction requires "encyclopedia eruditionis."

[l] πρεσβύτερα. [m] τῆς πρώτης σοφίας.

[n] τοῖς σοφοῖς ἀλλ' οὐ τοῖς σοφισταῖς.

[o] The meaning is unclear in part.

36. (Gen. xvi. 14) Why is the well said to be "between Kadesh and between[a] Pharan"[b]?

"Kadesh" is interpreted as "holy," while "Pharan" is "hail" or "dots."[c]

37. (Gen. xvi. 15) What is the meaning of the words, "Hagar bore to Abraham a son"?

This is very natural,[d] for possession[e] does not bear anything for itself but for him who possesses, as does literature for the literary man,[f] and music for the musician, and mathematics for the mathematician, for he is a part of it and is in need of it. But possession is received[g] as if it were not in need (of anything), as fire is not in need of heat, since it is its own heat and gives a common share[h] of its heat to those who come close or approach it.

*38. (Gen. xvi. 16) Why is Abraham said to be eighty-six[i] years old when Hagar bore him Ishmael?

Because that which follows the "eighty," (namely) the number six, is the first perfect number.[j] It is equal to its parts and is the first even-odd[k] number, having a part in

[a] So the LXX, which retains the Heb. idiom "between and between."

[b] Most LXX MSS. and Arm. O.T. have βαράδ (Heb. *Bered*), as does Philo in *De Fuga* 213.

[c] Or "minute pieces." The etymology "hail" fits the name "Bered" but not "Pharan." In *De Fuga* 213 Philo fancifully etymologizes "Bered" as "in evil" (= Heb. *bəraʿ*).

[d] φυσικώτατον.

[e] Lit. "having of possessions"; perhaps Philo here used ἕξις in the philosophical sense of "condition," "disposition."

[f] ἡ γραμματικὴ τῷ γραμματικῷ.

[g] Or "admitted to be."

[h] Lit. "a part of participation"—μέρος κοινωνίας.

[i] Lit. "six and eighty"; LXX "eighty-six."

[j] ὁ πρῶτος τέλειος ἀριθμός. On the symbolism of the number six see *QG* ii. 45 and Staehle pp. 32-34.

[k] ἀρτιοπέριττος; *cf. De Spec. Leg.* ii. 58.

an active cause through its oddness, and in a material and affective (cause) through its evenness.[a] Therefore among the ancients who were in the beginning,[b] some called it "marriage," others "harmony."[c] And the theologian[d] represented the creation of the world (as taking place) in six (days). And the number eighty is the most harmonious[e] of numbers, consisting of two most excellent scales,[f] (namely) of that which is by doubles and that which is by triples in the scheme[g] of fourths. It includes all[h] progressions,[i] the arithmetic, the geometric and the harmonic; the first is that (consisting) of proportions of two, that is, 6, 8, 9, 12,[j] of which the sum is 35.[k] And the other consists of (proportions of) three, that is, 6, 9, 12, 18,[l] of which the sum is forty-five. And of these two (numbers), thirty-five and forty-five, is made up the number eighty. And when the theologian began to speak of the divine commandments,[m] he was eighty years old.[n] Now the first of our nation who was circumcised by law and was named after

[a] *Cf.* Joh. Lydus, p. 32, 4-8 (cited by Staehle) μετέχων καὶ τῆς δραστικῆς οὐσίας (Arm. = αἰτίας) κατὰ τὸν περιττὸν καὶ τῆς ὑλικῆς κατὰ τὸν ἄρτιον.

[b] Joh. Lydus has only οἱ ἀρχαῖοι.

[c] γάμον . . . ἁρμονίαν, as in the frag. from Joh. Lydus, which ends here.

[d] ὁ θεολόγος, *i.e.* Moses.

[e] ἁρμονικώτατος.

[f] ἐκ δυοῖν ἀρίστων διαγραμμάτων, meaning the numbers 35 and 45, as explained just below.

[g] κατὰ τὸ πλινθίον, the figure of musical intervals; *cf. De Opif. Mundi* 107-110.

[h] Variant "all four."

[i] ἀναλογίας.

[j] Philo explains in *De Opif. Mundi* 107 ff. that 6, 8, 9, 12 form a proportion for 12 : 9 as 8 : 6, making a double proportion of 4 : 3.

[k] The Arm. uses numeral letters here and below.

[l] 18 : 12 = 9 : 6, a double proportion of 3 : 2.

[m] Lit. "commands of precepts"; Aucher "oraculum praeceptorum."

[n] *i.e.* when he appeared before Pharaoh, according to Ex. vii. 7.

the virtue of joy [a] was called Isaac in Chaldaean, which in Armenian [b] is "laughter." (His was) a nature [c] which rejoiced in all things and was not displeased at all with anything in the world, but was pleased with what happened as happening in a good and useful way.

39. (Gen. xvii. 1) [d] Why does (Scripture) say that when Abraham was ninety-nine years old, "the Lord God [e] appeared to him and said, I am the Lord thy God" [f]?

It gives the two appellations [g] of the two highest powers [h] in connexion with [i] the wise man, for by them the world came into being, and having come into being, it is governed [j] by them. By one of them, indicated as [k] "God," it was created and ordered, for "God" is the name of the creative power,[l] while the other, indicated as "the Lord," comes under the head of power and kingship.[m] And so, (Scrip-

[a] Arm. construction obscure; Aucher renders, "virtute praestans ille nomen gerit gaudii." The reference to Isaac properly belongs below, in § 39.

[b] *Sic!* The Arm. translator has substituted "Armenian" for "Greek." Aucher omits "in Armenian" in his translation.

[c] The formerly unidentified Greek frag. in Harris p. 97, recognized by Früchtel as belonging here, has *μακαρία φύσις*.

[d] Gen. xvii. 1-5, 15-22 are commented on in *De Mut. Nom.*, where Philo devotes a long section to the discussion of the second half of verse 1, commented on in the next section.

[e] So also the Arm. O.T.; LXX and Heb. have only "the Lord," as does *De Mut. Nom.*

[f] Heb. "I am El Shaddai"; LXX has *ἐγώ εἰμι ὁ θεός σου*, similarly Arm. O.T. and *De Mut. Nom.* 1.

[g] Prob. = *κλήσεις*.

[h] *τῶν ἀνωτάτω δυνάμεων*, *i.e.* the kingly power, symbolized by the name "Lord," and the creative power, symbolized by the name "God"; see *QG* ii. 51 notes.

[i] Arm. *i veray* prob. here = *ἐπί*; Aucher renders, "super."

[j] *οἰκονομεῖται*.

[k] Lit. "in accordance with"—*κατά*.

[l] *τῆς ποιητικῆς δυνάμεως*.

[m] *ἡγεμονίας* (or *ἐξουσίας vel sim.*) *καὶ βασιλείας*.

ture) wishes to show that the virtuous man [a] is a citizen of the world [b] and of equal honour with the whole world [c] by representing as his overseers and guards [d] the cosmic powers, the divine and kingly, in a unique sense.[e] Now the manifestation [f] took place in his ninety-ninth year, a number rightly (chosen). In the first place, it is next [g] to a hundred, and a hundred is a power [h] of ten when the latter is multiplied by itself, and this the theologian calls "the holy of holies." [i] For the *kor*,[j] the first tenth, is simply called "holy," and this he assigns to the caretakers of the temple.[k] And the tenth of the tenth, which he further commands the caretakers to set aside as an offering [l] to the presiding official,[m] is a tenth reckoned from a hundred, for what else is a tenth of a tenth but a hundredth part? However, the number ninety-nine years is not only distinguished [n] by its kinship and nearness to a hundred but

[a] τὸν σπουδαῖον, *i.e.* Abraham.

[b] κοσμοπολίτην.

[c] ἰσότιμον παντὶ τῷ κόσμῳ.

[d] ἐπιστάτους (*vel sim.*) καὶ φύλακας.

[e] Lit. "by a singularity of word" (or "principle")—κατ' ἰδιότητα λόγου; Aucher renders, "singulari modo." The exact sense is not clear to me.

[f] ἡ ἐπιφάνεια.

[g] Lit. "neighbour."

[h] δύναμις.

[i] Apparently Philo here, as in the parallel, *De Mut. Nom.* 2, refers to the tithe of the Levitical tithe, Num. xviii. 26, though in the biblical passage it is not called "holy of holies"; however, the offerings are generally called τὰ ἅγια in the LXX of Num. xviii. 32.

[j] Arm. *k'oṛ* = Greek κόρος = Heb. *kōr*, a measure = 10 baths, *cf.* Ez. xlv. 14 *et al.*

[k] τοῖς νεωκόροις, a name given by Philo to the Levites, *cf.* *De Fuga* 90, *De Vita Mosis* i. 316.

[l] Prob. ἀπαρχήν, as in *De Mut. Nom.* 2 and LXX Num. xviii. 26.

[m] Prob. τῷ προεστηκότι = the high priest; Aucher supplies "summo sacerdoti."

[n] Lit. "adorned."

it also receives special participation in a remarkable nature,[a] for it consists of fifty and seven heptads.[b] Now the Pentecostal (year) [c] is called " release " [d] in the Legislation,[e] for all are freed,[f] both inanimate and animate beings.

And the Sabbatical [g] years are the power [h] of rest [i] and deep peace in body and soul,[j] for the seventh year is a memorial [k] of the self-grown goods [l] that require no thought or labour, which nature produced by itself at the first establishing of the world. And the number forty-nine, which is made up of seven hebdomads, indicates, not superficial goods,[m] but rather those which have power and wisdom in respect of invincible and most powerful firmness.[n]

*40. (Gen. xvii. 1-2) [o] What is the meaning of the words, " Be well-pleasing before Me [p] and be blameless,[q] and I will place My covenant [r] between Me and between thee, and I will multiply thee greatly greatly " [s] ?

He lays down a law most appropriate [t] to the race of

[a] φύσεως θαυμασίας ἰδίαν (or ἐξαίρετον) κοινωνίαν.

[b] 50 + 49 = 99.

[c] Or Jubilee year, *cf.* Lev. xxv. 10.

[d] ἄφεσις, as in LXX.

[e] ἐν τῇ νομοθεσίᾳ.

[f] *i.e.* of debts and obligations to work.

[g] Lit. " hebdomadal."

[h] δύναμις (?) ; Aucher " mysterium."

[i] ἀναπαύσεως.

[j] κατὰ σῶμα καὶ ψυχήν.

[k] μνημεῖον.

[l] τῶν αὐτομάτων ἀγαθῶν, *cf. De Mut. Nom.* 260.

[m] ἐπιπόλαια ἀγαθά.

[n] βεβαίωσιν or σύστασιν.

[o] This half-verse (1b) and verse 2 are commented on in *De Mut. Nom.* 39-53.

[p] LXX εὐαρέστει ἐναντίον ἐμοῦ; for ἐναντίον some LXX MSS. have ἐνώπιον, as does Philo in *De Mut. Nom.* 39.

[q] ἄμεμπτος.

[r] διαθήκην.

[s] So Heb. ; LXX has only σφόδρα. The last clause is not quoted by Philo in *De Mut. Nom.* 52-53.

[t] οἰκειότατον.

mortals. For he who has no share,[a] and is not involved,[b] in evil [c] is perfectly good and noble—a property of incorporeal natures.[d] But as for those who are in the body, (they are good) to the extent that they reject evil and in accordance with their part in sin. For the life of man appears virtuous not because they are without weaknesses [e] from beginning to end, but when they are inspired (to rise) from weakness to health.[f] For these reasons He said directly and straightly, " Be blameless " because it suffices for the happiness of mortal nature [g] not to incur blame and not to say or do anything deserving of reproach. This is directly pleasing to the Father, wherefore He says, " Be well-pleasing before Me and be blameless." Hence these statements relate and correspond (to each other),[h] for a character which pleases God does not incur blame, while one who is blameless and faultless in all things is altogether pleasing (to God). And He promises to grant a double grace to him who is far from all blame. In the first place, He says that He appoints him the repository and guardian [i] of the divine covenants,[j] and then that He will increase him to an indescribable multitude. For the words, " I will place My covenant between Me and thee " show that the custody and guardianship belong to a truly noble and

[a] Lit. " part of sharing," prob. = κοινωνίαν.

[b] Lit. " is unmixed."

[c] Lit. " in evilness (abstract) and evil (concrete)."

[d] ἰδιότης ἀσωμάτων φύσεων; for a similar idea see *De Mut. Nom.* 50.

[e] Aucher renders, " immunium ab aegritudine."

[f] ὑγίειαν or " wholeness "—ὁλοκληρίαν.

[g] τῇ θνητῇ φύσει πρὸς εὐτυχίαν.

[h] Aucher renders, " ubi mutuam praefert conversionem assertio." The meaning is clearer in the parallel, *De Mut. Nom.* 47, προσεπιλέγει, καὶ γίνου ἄμεμπτος, ἀκολουθίᾳ καὶ εἱρμῷ χρώμενος.

[i] φυλακὴν (or ἀποθήκην) καὶ φύλακα *vel sim.* Aucher renders, " custodem depositi." There is no similar phrase in *De Mut. Nom.*

[j] τῶν θείων διαθηκῶν. The Arm. uses two different words in this section for διαθήκη, namely *ouxt* and *ktakaran.*

virtuous man. Now the divine covenant consists of[a] all the incorporeal principles, forms[b] and measures for the whole of all the things of which this world[c] was made. Moreover that He twice[d] says, "I will multiply thee greatly greatly" clearly shows the indescribability and immensity of the multitude, (that is) the growth of the multitude (of people) and sometimes of human virtues.

*41. (Gen. xvii. 3) What is the meaning of the words, "Abraham fell upon (his) face"[e]?

What is now said is the development of the preceding,[f] for He had said, "be blameless." Now that for which life is blameworthy and reprehensible is nothing else than sense-perception,[g] for this is the head and font of passion.[h] Rightly and properly does he fall upon his face, by which I understand his senses, which (lead) to transgression and sin; and this indicates His beneficence.[i] This is the first (point). And second, it should be said that he is struck[j] by the manifestation[k] of the Existent One,[l] and being

[a] Lit. "are."

[b] οἱ ἀσώματοι λόγοι καὶ τὰ εἴδη (or αἱ ἰδέαι); Aucher less literally renders, "incorporeum est verbum."

[c] οὗτος ὁ κόσμος.

[d] *i.e.* repetitiously.

[e] LXX ἔπεσεν Ἀβραὰμ ἐπὶ πρόσωπον αὐτοῦ. This biblical half-verse is commented upon (in part differently) in *De Mut. Nom.* 54-57, which omits the αὐτοῦ after πρόσωπον, as does the Arm. here.

[f] κατασκευὴ (?) τῶν προτέρων; Aucher "constructio praemissorum."

[g] αἴσθησις.

[h] ἀρχή τε καὶ πηγὴ τῶν παθῶν.

[i] αἰνιττομένης τῆς ἐκείνου εὐεργασίας. In *De Mut. Nom.* 56 Philo more clearly says that God keeps the senses from erring. Aucher's rendering is inaccurate, "sensuum delicta (in unum cecidisse) operibus bonis jam illos deditas (*sic*) fuisse ostendens."

[j] πλήττεται.

[k] Lit. "very manifest appearance," prob. = ἐπιφανείᾳ.

[l] τοῦ ὄντος.

unable to look (at Him) directly, falls down in consternation and kisses the ground, being overawed and abashed by the vision which appeared to him. Third, the manifestation was made by Him who was in the appearance, (namely) the Existent One, who exists, whom he knew in truth by (His) opposition to nature, which comes into being,[a] for the one remains firm and intact,[b] while the other vacillates and falls upon its place, the earth.

42. (Gen. xvii. 3-4) What is the meaning of the words, " And God spoke with him, saying, And I, behold My covenant (is) with thee. And thou shalt become the father of a multitude of peoples " [c] ?

Since He had earlier spoken of the covenant, He says, " Do not seek it in writing,[d] for I Myself am, in the highest sense,[e] the genuine covenant." [f] For after showing Himself and saying, " I," He adds, " behold My covenant," (as if to say, " This is) nothing else but Me, for I am that same covenant by which pacts are made and formed and agreed upon, and, moreover, all things are well distributed and set apart." This is the archetypal form [g] of covenant, composed of ideas and incorporeal measures and principles,[h] through which this world [i] was completed. Was it not

[a] *ὃν οἶδε πρὸς ἀλήθειαν ἐξ ἀντιθέσεως πρὸς τὴν γενομένην φύσιν*; Aucher renders less accurately, " quem novit ut veritatem naturae creatae oppositam."

[b] *ἐν τῷ βεβαίῳ καὶ ἀπταίστῳ vel sim.*

[c] So LXX, *καὶ ἐλάλησεν αὐτῷ ὁ θεὸς λέγων, καὶ ἐγώ, ἰδοὺ ἡ διαθήκη μου μετὰ σοῦ· καὶ ἔσῃ πατὴρ πλήθους ἐθνῶν.* The second half of verse 3 to " with thee " is similarly interpreted in *De Mut. Nom.* 58-59.

[d] *i.e.* in written form.

[e] *κατὰ τὸν ἀνώτατον λόγον*, *cf. De Mut. Nom.* 58 *τὸ δ᾽ ἀνώτατον γένος διαθηκῶν.*

[f] Lit. = *γνησία διαθήκη τῶν διαθηκῶν*; the Arm. here uses two different words for covenant, *ouxt* and *ktakaran*.

[g] *τὸ ἀρχέτυπον εἶδος.*

[h] *ἐξ ἰδεῶν καὶ ἀσωμάτων μέτρων καὶ λόγων συντεθειμένον.*

[i] *οὗτος ὁ κόσμος.*

then indeed a superfluity of beneficence which the Father granted the wise man,[a] that He not only carried him off and brought him up from earth to heaven or from heaven to an incorporeal and intelligible world,[b] but also (brought him) from here to Himself, showing (Himself) clearly,[c] not as He is, for this is impossible,[d] but (in so far) as the eyes of the beholder are able to attain to the genuine and intelligible power itself.[e] Wherefore He says, "No longer shalt thou be a son, but a father." And a father, not of one, but "of a multitude," and of a multitude, not of individuals,[f] but of a numerous group of nations.[g] And of the agreements [h] revealed, two are literal,[i] while the third is more physical.[j] Now of the literal ones, the first is as follows. "Truly [k] thou shalt be a father of nations and shalt beget nations, that is, each of thy sons shall be the founder of a nation." [l] And the other is as follows. "In the manner of a father, thou shalt be invested with the care and supervision of many nations,[m] for a lover of God [n] is by the same token [o] wont to be a lover of mankind,[p] so that he is greatly concerned not only for his countrymen [q] but also for all others at the same time, especially for those who are able to receive the discipline of attention [r] and whose characters are not unpleasant and hard but easily give place to virtue [s] and

[a] τῷ σοφῷ, *i.e.* Abraham.

[b] εἰς ἀσώματον καὶ νοερὸν κόσμον.

[c] Aucher inadvertently omits the adverb. [d] ἀδύνατον.

[e] εἰς αὐτὴν τὴν γνησίαν καὶ νοερὰν δύναμιν.

[f] κατὰ μέρος; Aucher renders literally but not quite to the point, "secundum partes." [g] πολυανθρωπίας γενῶν.

[h] Prob. = τῶν ὁμολογιῶν; Aucher "promissis."

[i] ῥηταί.

[j] φυσικωτέρα, in the sense of physical (or psychic) allegory.

[k] ὄντως. [l] γενάρχης.

[m] πολλῶν γενῶν ἐπιμέλειαν καὶ ἐπιστασίαν ἐνδύσει.

[n] φιλόθεος. [o] εὐθύς.

[p] φιλάνθρωπος. [q] τοῖς ὁμοφύλοις.

[r] τὴν τῆς προσοχῆς (or ἐπιμελείας) παιδείαν; Aucher "disciplinam attentionis"; the exact meaning is not clear to me.

[s] ἀρετῇ.

are submissive to right reason.[a] But the third (promise) is to be allegorized[b] as follows. The multitude of nations is like there being in each of us a variety of inclinations in the soul,[c] both those which it is wont to form[d] by itself, and those which it receives through the senses[e] and which slip[f] into its sight from without.[g] And if the mind[h] assumes sovereignty over these like the father of all,[i] it changes them for the better, nursing[j] the infantile and puerile thoughts, while urging on and helping to advance those which are mature but incomplete, and praising those which persist in the right way but restraining[k] the rebellious and refractory ones through discipline and reproof. For being desirous of imitating the Deity,[l] it receives from His powers, the beneficent and destructive,[m] as if from a fountain, a double stream: beneficence toward those who wish to obey, reproof toward those who are out of hand and refractory, since some profit from praise, others from castigation. For he who is widely versed[n] in virtue can profit from all things in accordance with his power.

43. (Gen. xvii. 5) What is the meaning of the words, "Thy name shall not be called Abram, but Abraham[o] shall be thy name"?

[a] *καὶ ὑποτάττονται τῷ ὀρθῷ λόγῳ.* [b] *ἀλληγορεῖται.*
[c] *ἐν τῇ ψυχῇ πολυτρόπων οὐσῶν γνωμῶν vel sim.*
[d] *πλάττειν.* [e] *διὰ τῶν αἰσθήσεων.*
[f] *παρεισαγόμεναι.*
[g] Lit. "to the sight (or "eyes") of vision inside from without"; Aucher renders more freely, "imaginatione intermediante ab extra intus." [h] *ὁ νοῦς.*
[i] Aucher renders more freely, "communis pater."
[j] *θηλάζων.*
[k] Lit. "putting a bit into the mouth of."
[l] *τῷ Θείῳ.*
[m] On the two divine attributes see *QG* ii. 51 notes.
[n] Lit. "extends everywhere."
[o] Arm. and LXX "Abraam." In *De Mut. Nom.* Philo devotes a long section, §§ 60-120, to the changes of name of various biblical persons beside Abraham.

Some of the uncultivated,[a] or rather, of the uninitiated [b] and of those who do not belong to the divine chorus ridicule and reproach the one who is blameless in nature,[c] and say reproachfully and chidingly, "Oh what a great gift! The Ruler and Lord of all [d] has graciously given one letter,[e] by which He has increased and made greater the name of the patriarch, so that instead of having two syllables it has three." Oh what great devilishness [f] and impiety (it is) that some presume to bring forward slanders against God, being deceived by the superficial aspects of names, whereas it would be proper to thrust their minds into the depths in search of the inner facts for the sake of greatly possessing the truth.[g] And yet these (names) which are ready to hand [h] (and) which someone is said to have granted (in) writing—why do you not believe that (they are the work of) Providence [i] and that this is to be honoured? [j] For the first written element of sound is A, both in order and in power.[k] Second, it is a vowel,[l]

[a] τῶν ἀμούσων, represented by two words in Arm.

[b] τῶν ἀμυήτων.

[c] ἄμωμον φύσει. Apparently Moses is meant.

[d] ὁ ἡγεμὼν καὶ κύριος τῶν ὅλων.

[e] ἐχάρισε ἓν γράμμα (or στοιχεῖον, as in *De Mut. Nom.* 61).

[f] Arm. lit. = μεγαλοδαιμονία (not found in the Greek works of Philo).

[g] Lit. "for the sake of great possessions in truth": Aucher freely renders, "ob veram magnitudinem possessionis."

[h] ἕτοιμα καὶ πρόχειρα.

[i] τὴν πρόνοιαν.

[j] The text is very obscure; Aucher's rendering takes liberties with the syntax, "ad haec et litteram concessam, et si levem et facilem, quare providentiam non reputatis, neque pretium suum ponderatis?" We may well suspect either that the Greek *Vorlage* was corrupt or that the Arm. translator has misunderstood it. In the parallel, *De Mut. Nom.* 64, Philo says that it is impossible to suppose that God took credit for altering Abram's name since "He did not see fit to assign names even in their completed forms, but committed the task to a wise man (Adam)."

[k] καὶ τάξει καὶ δυνάμει.

[l] φωνῆεν (στοιχεῖον).

and the first of the vowels, being fitted on to them like a kind of head. And third, it is not naturally one of the long vowels, and not naturally one of the short ones, but one of those which have both these (quantities). For it is (sometimes) extended in length, and then again it is contracted to the same shortness, easily taking many different forms [a] like wax, and forming the word into various and manifold forms. And the reason is that it is a brother of the number one,[b] with which all things begin and end. And now if someone sees its great beauty and that the letter is exhibited as so necessary, can he pretend [c] that he has not seen it? If he has seen it, he (shows himself) to be captious and a hater of the good.[d] And if he has not seen it, it is very easy to scoff and gleefully make fun of something he knows nothing of, as though he did know it.[e] But these things are, as I have said, mentioned incidentally.[f] Now we must examine the necessary and principle matter.

The addition of A as [g] one letter, by changing the entire position of the forms of the soul,[h] provides it with the knowledge of wisdom [i] instead of the study of astronomy. For skill in the study of astronomy is acquired in one part of the world, (namely) in the heaven and in the revolutions and circlings of the stars, [j] whereas wisdom (pertains) to the nature of all things, both sense-perceptible and intelligible.[k] For wisdom is the science of divine and

[a] Lit. "formed into many things."
[b] *Alpha* as a numeral letter = 1.
[c] σκήπτεται.
[d] φιλόψογος καὶ μισόκαλος.
[e] Aucher, punctuating differently and supplying a verb, renders, "quod si non viderit tam facile negotium, quomodo quod nescit, irridere et despicere praesumit, quasi sciat?"
[f] παρέργως.
[g] Lit. "through."
[h] πάσας τὰς τῶν ψυχῆς εἰδῶν θέσεις *vel sim.*
[i] τὴν τῆς σοφίας ἐπιστήμην.
[j] ἐν ταῖς περιφοραῖς καὶ χορείαις τῶν ἀστέρων.
[k] φύσιν αἰσθητικήν τε καὶ νοεράν.

human things and of their causes.[a] Among these divine things is that which is visible and that which is invisible, and the paradigmatic idea.[b] Among human things there is that which is corporeal and that which is incorporeal; and to obtain knowledge of these is a truly great work of ability and prowess. And not only to see all substances and natures but also to trace and search out their various causes shows a power that is more perfect than is human.[c] For it is necessary for the soul which receives so many good things to be all eyes and to complete its life in the world unsleepingly and wakefully, and with an unshadowed and radiant light all around it, to receive lightning-flashes (of illumination), having God as its teacher and leader in obtaining knowledge of things and attaining to their causes.

Now the dissyllabic name " Abram " is interpreted as " uplifted father "[d] in respect of the nomenclature of astronomy and mathematics.[e] But the trisyllabic (name) " Abraham " is translated as " elect father of sound,"[f] the appellation of a wise man. For what else is an echo in us but an uttered word[g] coming from an organ constructed by nature through the wind-pipe,[h] the mouth and the tongue. And the " father of sound " is our mind,[i] and the elect mind is that of the virtuous man.[j] And that the mind is eminently, properly and naturally the father of the uttered word is clear, for it is the special function

[a] *ἐπιστήμη ἐστὶν ἡ σοφία τῶν θείων καὶ ἀνθρωπίνων καὶ τῶν τούτων αἰτίων.* Exactly the same definition is given in *De Congressu* 79.

[b] *ἡ παραδειγματικὴ ἰδέα.*

[c] *δύναμιν τελειοτέραν ἢ κατὰ ἄνθρωπον.*

[d] *μετέωρος πατήρ*, as in *De Mut. Nom.* 66, *De Cherubim* 4 *et al.*

[e] *μαθηματικῆς* (almost certainly not " astrology " here).

[f] *πατὴρ ἐκλεκτὸς ἠχοῦς*, as in *De Mut. Nom.* 66 *et al.*

[g] *λόγος προφορικός.*

[h] *ἡ τραχεῖα ἀρτηρία.*

[i] *ὁ ἡμέτερος νοῦς.*

[j] *τοῦ σπουδαίου*; the parallel in *De Mut. Nom.* 69 f. has *τοῦ σοφοῦ.*

of a father to beget, and the word is begotten by the mind. And (of this) there is clear evidence, for when it[a] is moved by thoughts, it makes a sound, and when these are lacking, it stops. Witnesses (of this) are the orators and philosophers,[b] who show their tendencies[c] through statements.[d] For so long as the mind produces heads,[e] it begets them in accordance with the various constructions stored up in itself,[f] and the word flows like a fountain into the ears of those who happen to be there as if into cisterns.[g] But when it fails[h] and is no longer able to give out (its thoughts), the sound also stops, since there is no one to cause it to resound.[i]

But now surely it must seem to you, O men who are full of, and overflowing with, all absurd verbosity, and are empty and bereft of wisdom, that this single letter and element is a gift[j] and that through this letter and element he became worthy of the divine power of wisdom, than which there is nothing more precious[k] in our nature, for instead of the knowledge of astronomy He granted (him) that which was entire, full and overflowing in place of a small part. For in wisdom is included astronomy, as is the part in the whole, and mathematics is (also) a part. But it behooves you, O men, to bear this too in mind, that he who is learned and skilled in investigating the nature

[a] Apparently the organ of speech is meant.

[b] *οἱ ῥήτορες καὶ φιλόσοφοι.*

[c] Prob. *τὰς ἕξεις.*

[d] Prob. *διὰ προβλημάτων.*

[e] Arm. *gloux* = *κεφαλή, κεφάλαιον, ἄκρον.*

[f] Aucher renders this obscure sentence a little differently, "in quantum enim mens foras edit capita, singulosque apparatus in se reconditos producit ad modum geniturae."

[g] *δεξαμενάς.*

[h] Prob. "the mind" is the subject (a grammatical pl. with pl. verb in Arm.).

[i] Lit. "to strike it."

[j] Apparently the Arm. translator has interchanged subject and predicate, here reversed; Aucher renders more literally, "videtur ne donum meri unius elementi fuisse."

[k] *τιμιώτερον vel sim.*

of higher things [a] may be [b] of a wicked and impure character. But the wise man [c] is good and fine in all things. Let us then no longer laugh at this gift, for one cannot find anything more perfect. For what is worse than wickedness or better than virtue? [d] Surely it cannot be that good is not opposed to evil? Can it be compared with wealth or honours or freedom or health or anything at all of the body or any abundance of external possessions? For all philosophy comes into our lives like the healing of the soul [e] that it may give freedom from suffering and from sickness.[f] And it is the part of a virtuous man to be a philosopher.[g] That a wonderful skill should be precious is very fine [h] (but) more precious is the end [i] for the sake of which the skill (exists). And this is wisdom and the good, which He called "Abraham" in Chaldaean, and in Armenian,[j] "elect father of sound,"[k] as if giving a definition [l] of the wise man. For just as the definition of man is "rational, mortal animal,"[m] so the definition of the wise man is symbolically [n] "elect father of sound."

[a] *i.e.* heavenly bodies.

[b] Lit. "can be."

[c] ὁ σοφός.

[d] ἀρετή.

[e] ὥσπερ ἰατρεῖον τῆς ψυχῆς.

[f] τὴν ἀπάθειαν καὶ τὸ ἄνοσον.

[g] φιλόσοφος.

[h] The Arm. seems lit. = θαυμασίαν τέχνην τιμίαν <εἶναι> σφόδρα καλόν, but this is not quite certain; Aucher, omitting the word "precious," renders, "et mira ars nobilis veraciter."

[i] τὸ τέλος.

[j] *Sic!* The original, of course, had "Greek"; *cf.* *QG* iii. 38.

[k] Aucher here again mistakenly renders, "pater sonitus electi."

[l] ὅρον or ὁρισμόν.

[m] ζῷον λογικὸν θνητόν; the same definition, common in Greek philosophy, is given by Philo in *De Abrahamo* 32 *et al.*

[n] Arm. *xorhourd* = λογισμός, διάνοια, σύμβολον, τύπος, μυστήριον, etc.; Aucher here renders, "mystica."

44. (Gen xvii. 6) What is the meaning of the words, " I will increase thee greatly [a] and I will make [b] thee into nations, and kings shall come into being [c] from thee " [d] ?

" I will increase thee greatly " is said to the wise man [e] very rightfully,[f] since every wicked and evil man grows and flourishes, not toward increase but toward deficiency,[g] just as those flowers which are (subject to) fading (grow), not into life but death. But he whose life is long is like a cloud which endures and grows exceedingly, and like streams of rivers, for he overflows and broadens out and becomes more ample as he goes out, since he is also the divine wisdom.[h] And the words, " I will make thee into nations " are spoken to show clearly that he does something of worth,[i] as if (to say that) the wise man is the foundation and base and firm support of the nations and of mankind and of those who are of various opinions in soul,[j] as has been said before. For the wise man is the saviour [k] of nations and an intercessor [l] with God and one who seeks forgiveness for his countrymen [m] who have committed sins. Moreover that " kings shall come into being from thee " He very rightfully [n] says, for all that which

[a] So LXX and Arm. O.T. ; Heb. " greatly greatly."
[b] Lit. " place " as in LXX, Heb. and Arm. O.T.
[c] So Old Lat. ; LXX, Heb. and Arm. O.T. " shall go out."
[d] Philo does not comment elsewhere on this verse.
[e] τῷ σοφῷ.
[f] νομιμώτερον.
[g] ἐλάττωσιν or ἔκλειψιν.
[h] ἡ θεία σοφία. It is not wholly clear what the grammatical subject of this sentence is.
[i] The text seems to be in some disorder.
[j] For Arm. *karcik'* " opinion " Aucher suggests *karik'* " needs " ; he renders, " hominibus vario modo egentibus secundum animum." The meaning of the Arm. is far from clear.
[k] σωτήρ.
[l] μεσίτης or παράκλητος. This important passage is overlooked by Nils Johansson, *Parakletoi*, Lund, 1940.
[m] τοῖς ὁμοφύλοις.
[n] νομιμώτερον.

belongs to wisdom is of royal origin, and is sovereign and ruling by nature. And the wise man is unproductive and unfruitful [a] in respect of his own private seed,[b] and is fertile and productive in respect of ruling (seed).[c]

45. (Gen. xvii. 8) What is the meaning of the words, " I will give to thee and to thy seed after thee the land in which thou sojournest,[d] all the land of Canaan as an eternal possession " [e]?

The literal meaning [f] is clear, so that the passage [g] does not require any interpretation. But as for the deeper meaning,[h] it is to be allegorized [i] as follows. The mind of the virtuous man [j] is a sojourner in its corporeal place rather than an inhabitant.[k] For its fatherland [l] is the ether and the heaven, while its temporary abode [m] is the earth and the earthly body, in which it is said to sojourn. But the Father in His benefactions to it,[n] gives it authority [o] over all earthly things as an " eternal possession," as He says, in order that it may never be dominated by the body but may always be the ruler and chief, acquiring it [p] as a servant and follower.

46. (Gen. xvii. 10-11) What is the meaning of the words,

[a] *ἄγονος καὶ ἄκαρπος.*

[b] *τοῦ ἰδίου (?) σπέρματος.*

[c] *τοῦ ἀρχικοῦ (?) <σπέρματος>*; Aucher " semine ab ipso principali."

[d] Lit. " in which thou dwellest in sojourn " = LXX *παροικεῖς*.

[e] *εἰς κατάσχεσιν αἰώνιον*, as in LXX.

[f] *τὸ ῥητόν.*

[g] *ὁ λόγος.*

[h] *τὸ πρὸς διάνοιαν.*

[i] *ἀλληγορεῖται.*

[j] *ὁ τοῦ σπουδαίου νοῦς.*

[k] *πάροικος ἐν τῷ σωματικῷ τόπῳ μᾶλλον ἢ κάτοικος.*

[l] *ἡ πατρίς.*

[m] Arm. *gaḷout'* = *ἀποικία* or *μετάστασις*; here it seems to have the meaning of " exile " as does Heb. *gālûth.*

[n] *εὐεργετῶν αὐτόν.*

[o] *ἀρχήν* or *ἡγεμονίαν vel sim.*

[p] *i.e.* the body.

"There shall be circumcised every male of you, and you shall be circumcised in the flesh of your foreskin"[a]?

I see two circumcisions, one of the male, and the other of the flesh; that of the flesh is by way of the genitals, while that of the male, it seems to me, is by way of the reason.[b] For that which is, one might say,[c] naturally male in us is the mind,[d] whose superfluous growths it is necessary to cut off and throw away in order that it may become pure and naked of every evil and passion, and be a priest of God. Now this is what He indicated[e] by the second circumcision, stating (in) the Law[f] that "you shall circumcise your hardness of heart,"[g] which means your hard and rebellious and refractory thoughts, and by cutting off and removing arrogance, you shall make the sovereign part[h] free and unbound.

47. (Gen. xvii. 10) Why does He command that only the males be circumcised?

In the first place, the Egyptians by the custom of their country circumcise the marriageable youth and maid[i] in the fourteenth (year) of their age, when the male begins to get seed, and the female to have a menstrual flow. But the divine legislator[j] ordained circumcision for males alone for many reasons. The first of these is that the male has more pleasure in, and desire for, mating[k] than does the female, and he is more ready for it.[l] Therefore He rightly

[a] Or "of your uncircumcision," = LXX τῆς ἀκροβυστίας ὑμῶν.
[b] διὰ τοῦ λογισμοῦ or τῆς διανοίας.
[c] σχεδόν.
[d] ὁ νοῦς.
[e] ᾐνίξατο.
[f] Deut. x. 16.
[g] τὴν σκληροκαρδίαν, as in LXX.
[h] τὸ ἡγεμονικόν, *i.e.* the mind.
[i] τὸν νύμφιον καὶ τὴν νύμφην.
[j] ὁ κύριος νομοθέτης. Philo refers to God as a legislator in a few other passages, *e.g. De Fuga* 66; *De Vita Mosis* ii. 48. Usually "the legislator" is Moses.
[k] Arm. *amousnout'iun* = γάμος, ὁμιλία, συνουσία, etc.
[l] Aucher inadvertently omits rendering the last clause.

leaves out the female, and suppresses the undue[a] impulses of the male by the sign of circumcision. The second is that the matter[b] of the female in the remains of the menstrual fluids produces the fetus.[c] But the male (provides) the skill and the cause.[d] And so, since the male provides the greater and more necessary (part) in the process of generation, it was proper that his pride should be checked by the sign of circumcision, but the material element, being inanimate,[e] does not admit of arrogance. So much for that. However, we must note what follows upon it. That which sees in us is the mind,[f] and it is necessary to cut off its superfluous growths.[g] Now these superfluous growths are vain opinions[h] and what is done in accordance with them. And when the mind is circumcised and contains only necessary and useful things, and when at the same time there is cut off whatever causes pride to increase, then with it are circumcised the eyes also, as though they could not (otherwise) see.

*48. (Gen. xvii. 12) Why does He say, " And the child of eight days shall be circumcised, every male " ?

He commands that the foreskin be circumcised. In the first place this is granted because of disease, for it is more difficult and formidable to cure an affliction of the genitals, (which is like) a fire to those on which a covering skin

[a] Lit. " superfluous." [b] ἡ ὕλη.

[c] The text is slightly uncertain as there are variants to three words, but the above rendering is supported by other passages in which Philo follows the common Greek view of the physiology of conception, *e.g. De Opif. Mundi* 132, " just as with women the course of the menstrual fluids (τῶν καταμηνίων), for these are said by physical scientists to be the bodily substance of the fetus (οὐσία σωματικὴ βρεφῶν)."

[d] τὴν τέχνην καὶ τὸ αἴτιον; there is no governing verb in the Arm.

[e] τὸ ὑλικὸν ὡς ἄψυχον.

[f] ὁ νοῦς.

[g] See above, *QG* iii. 46.

[h] κεναὶ δόξαι.

grows,[a] but this does not happen to one who is circumcised. Now if there were some way of avoiding other afflictions and diseases as well by cutting off some member[b] or some part of the body, by the removal of which there would be no obstacle to the functioning of its parts, man would not be known as mortal[c] but would be changed into immortality. And that it has pleased some to circumcise themselves through foresight of soul without any ill effect is plain, for not only the Jews[d] but also the Egyptians, Arabs and Ethiopians and nearly all those who inhabit the southern regions near the torrid zone are circumcised. And what is the particular reason if not that in these places, especially in summer, the foreskin of the genitals, which is the skin that surrounds and covers (them), becomes inflamed and infected.[e] But when this is cut off, by being laid bare (the penis) is restored,[f] and the affliction is resisted and expelled. For this reason the nations which are in the northern regions and all those to whom has been allotted a portion in those regions of the earth which are windy[g] are not circumcised. For in those regions, as the heat of the sun is relaxed and diminished, so too is the disease which is produced by heat in the skin of the parts of the body.[h] And a sure indication of the credibility of this matter one may find in the time (of year) when the disease is especially (strong); it never occurs in winter, and it thrives and flourishes when it comes in summer, for it loves, as it were, to spread in this season[i] like fire.

[a] The Arm. is elliptic; Aucher renders more freely, "igne fere comburens ea quibus membranum supernascitur." The reference is to the disease called anthrax by the Greeks, see *De Spec. Leg.* i. 4.

[b] *μέλος τι.*

[c] Aucher, wrongly, I think, renders, "nesciente mortali homine."

[d] Arm. *hreayk'* (Hebrews).

[e] Lit. "wounded."

[f] Lit. "is revived."

[g] Why Aucher renders, "partium terrae serenae" is a puzzle to me.

[h] Lit. "in the skin of the limbs."

[i] Lit. "in these parts."

In the second place, it was not only for the sake of health that the ancients devoted thought [a] (to this) but also for the sake of populousness,[b] for we see that nature is a living thing and very well disposed toward man.[c] Now as wise men they knew that as the seed often flows into the folds of the foreskin, it is likely that it will be scattered unfruitfully; but if there is no obstacle to prevent, it will succeed in reaching its proper place. For this reason such nations as practise circumcision increase greatly in population. But our legislator,[d] who had in mind, and was familiar with, this result, prohibited the immediate circumcision of infants,[e] having in mind the same thing,[f] that both circumcision and desire were populousness.[g] Wherefore, it seems to me, the Egyptians indicate that for the sake of populousness it is proper to perform circumcision in the fourteenth year when the pleasurable desires for procreation begin. But it is very much better and more far-sighted of us to prescribe circumcision for infants, for perhaps one who is full-grown would hesitate through fear to carry out this ordinance of his own free will.

In the third place, (Scripture) says that it is also for the

[a] Lit. "forethought of soul."

[b] ἕνεκα τῆς πολυανθρωπίας. This is cited as the fourth and "most compelling" reason for circumcision in *De Spec. Leg.* i. 7.

[c] φιλάνθρωπον.

[d] νομοθέτης (here God or Moses).

[e] Apparently Philo means immediately after birth, unless the Arm. is inexact in using "prohibited" for "commanded"; Aucher renders, "citius fieri monuit infantium circumcisionem."

[f] Lit. "seeing in the same mind."

[g] The above is a literal rendering of a clause that is unintelligible to me; Aucher, in disregard of the syntax, renders freely, "eandem intentionem circumcisionis ob populationem attendens." He remarks in a footnote that the passage is obscure, and the punctuation uncertain. Possibly the original Greek meant that Moses (or God) regarded populousness as due to circumcision as well as to sexual desire.

sake of purity in the sacred offerings, for those who enter the courts of the sacred precinct are purified by ablutions and sprinklings. And the Egyptians shave the whole body, (removing) the hair which conceals and overshadows the body, in order that it may appear shining and bare. The circumcision of the skin, moreover, is not a little helpful for one is revolted by this when one sees it as it (really) is.

In the fourth place,[a] there are two generative (organs), in the soul and in the body ; thoughts[b] are the generative (organ) of the soul, and that in the body is the (organ) of the body. Now the ancients[c] were disposed to regard the bodily organ of generation as resembling thought,[d] which is the most generative (force) of the heart.[e] And it is like nothing else so much as the circumcision of the heart. Now these are the widely known facts concerning the problems we are inquiring into. But we must speak about more symbolical things,[f] which have their own status.[g]

They say that the circumcision of the skin is a symbol, as if (to show that) it is proper to cut off superfluous and excessive desires[h] by exercising continence and endurance in matters of the Law.[i] For just as the skin of the foreskin is superfluous in procreation because of the burning affliction which comes upon it, so the excess of desire is

[a] The fourth reason for circumcision given here corresponds to the third reason given in *De Spec. Leg.* i. 6.

[b] τὰ νοήματα. The idea is more clearly expressed in *De Spec. Leg.* i. 6, πρὸς γὰρ γένεσιν ἄμφω παρεσκεύασται, τὸ μὲν ἐγκάρδιον πνεῦμα νοημάτων, τὸ δὲ γόνιμον ὄργανον ζῴων.

[c] οἱ πρῶτοι.

[d] νοήμασι or τῷ νῷ.

[e] τᾶς καρδίας, here regarded as the seat of the mind ; see Colson's note in vol. vii. p. 615.

[f] περὶ συμβολικωτέρων.

[g] τὸν αὐτῶν λόγον ἐχόντων.

[h] τὰς περιττὰς καὶ πλεοναζούσας ἐπιθυμίας, *cf. De Spec. Leg.* i. 9.

[i] Lit. "continence of endurance of the Law"—ἐγκράτειαν ὑπομονῆς τοῦ νόμου (or τῆς θρησκείας) ; Aucher renders, "continentiae religionis." There is no parallel to this phrase in *De Spec. Leg.*

superfluous and at the same time harmful. It is superfluous because it is not necessary, and it is harmful because it is the cause of diseases of body and soul. But through this great desire (Scripture) alludes also to the fact that one ought to cut off other desires as well. And the greatest desire is that of intercourse between man and woman, since it forms the beginning of a great thing, procreation, and brings about in the progenitors a great desire toward their progeny, for it is rather natural [a] to be very fond of, and tender toward, them. And it [b] indicates the cutting off not only of excessive desires but also of arrogance and [c] great evil and such habits.[d] And arrogance, as the saying of the ancients goes, is the excision and impeding of progress,[e] for one who thinks (well of himself) [f] does not admit of betterment,[g] thinking that he is the cause that is involved.[h]

Very naturally does (Scripture) instruct those who think that they are the causes of generation, and do not intently fix their minds on seeing the begetter of all things,[i] for He is the veritable and true [j] Father. But we who are called begetters are used as instruments in the service [k] of generation. For as by a miracle of imitation [l] all those

[a] *φυσικόν τι.*

[b] *i.e.* the symbol of circumcision.

[c] Aucher renders, " ut."

[d] *τῶν συντρόφων.*

[e] The brief Greek frag. printed by Harris, p. 99, was identified by Früchtel as belonging here; it reads *οἴησις, ὡς ὁ τῶν ἀρχαίων λόγος, ἐστὶν ἐκκοπὴ προκοπῆς.*

[f] The Arm. translator either read *οἰόμενος* or mistook the meaning of *κατοιόμενος*, which is found in the Greek frag.

[g] *βελτίωσιν*, as in the Greek frag., which ends here.

[h] Aucher renders, perhaps more aptly, " putans se sufficientem interesse causam."

[i] *τὸν γεννητὴν τῶν συμπάντων.*

[j] The Arm. uses three synonyms, two of which = *ἀψευδής*.

[k] *εἰς χρείαν ὑπηρεσίας* or *διακονίας.*

[l] The Arm. *i hrašs nmanout'ean* is a misunderstanding of *θαύματι*, which here means "puppet-show," as in *Quod Omnis Probus* 5. See also p. 247 note *f*.

things which are visible are inanimate,[a] while that which activates them like puppets[b] is invisible. The cause of this is the cause of the habits[c] and movements of visible things. In the same way the Creator of the world sends out[d] His powers[e] from an eternal and invisible place, but we are wonderfully[f] moved like puppets toward that which pertains to us, (namely) seed and procreation. Otherwise we might think that the shepherd's pipe[g] is played by itself instead of being meant[h] for the production of harmony by the artisan by whom the instrument was devised for this service and necessary use.

49. (Gen. xvii. 12) Why does He command the circumcision (to be) on the eighth day?

The eighth (digit) reveals many beauties.[i] One is, in the first place, that it is a cube. And the second is that everywhere it contains in itself the forms of equality,[j] because the number eight is the first which indicates length and breadth and depth, which are equal to[k] one another. Third, the composition of eight produces agreement, (namely) the number thirty-six, which the Pythagoreans call "homology" since it is the first in which there is an agreement of odd with even,[l] for the four separate odd

[a] ἄψυχα.

[b] νευροσπαστεῖ; Aucher's rendering, "nervos corroborat," misses the point of the implied metaphor.

[c] Prob. σχέσεις in the Aristotelian sense.

[d] Arm. *zgel* = ἐκτείνειν, ἐκπέμπειν, etc.

[e] τὰς δυνάμεις.

[f] Again θαῦμα "puppet-show" has been misunderstood.

[g] Reading, with Aucher, *sring* (σῦριγξ) for *sik'* (πνοή *vel sim.*).

[h] Lit. "set aside" or "apportioned."

[i] κάλλη. For other passages on the properties of the number eight see *QG* i. 75, 91, ii. 5. Staehle, p. 51, also cites parallels from Joh. Lydus.

[j] τὰ τοῦ ἴσου (or τῆς ἰσότητος) εἴδη.

[k] Or "congruent with."

[l] *Cf.* Joh. Lydus, p. 150 ἐν αὐτῷ γὰρ τὰ περιττὰ τοῖς ἀρτίοις ὡμολόγησαν.

(numbers) from one on, and the even ones from two on make a total of thirty-six. The odd ones are 1, 3, 5, 7,[a] making 16 in all; and the even ones are 2, 4, 6, 8, making 20. The sum of both totals amounts to thirty-six, truly a most productive[b] number, for it is quadrangular, having as its side the hexad, which is the first even-odd number[c]; this some accurately[d] call "harmony" or "marriage."[e] By making use of it the Creator of the universe made the world, as the holy and wonderful writing of Moses relates. Fourth, the form[f] of the ogdoad produces sixty-four, which is the first cube and, at the same time, square, the pattern of an incorporeal, intelligible and invisible and (also) corporeal substance[g]; incorporeal in so far as it produces a square plane,[h] but corporeal in so far as it produces a cubic solid.[i] Fifth, it is kin to the ever-virginal hebdomad,[j] for when the parts of eight are added together, they make seven, for a half (of eight) is four, a quarter is two, and an eighth is one; and the sum of these is seven. Sixth, the power[k] of eight is sixty-four, which, as we have said, is the first number that is a cube and a square at the same time. Seventh, from the number one on, the several double (numbers) 1, 2, 4, 8, 16, 32 make 64.[l] The ogdoad

[a] In the Arm. text the two sets of numbers are indicated by numeral letters.

[b] *γεννητικώτατον*. The same adjective is applied to the number six in *De Opif. Mundi* 13.

[c] See *QG* iii. 38, and *cf.* Joh. Lydus, p. 32 (cited by Staehle, p. 33).

[d] *ἐτύμως*.

[e] *Cf.* Joh. Lydus, *loc. cit.* *ὅθεν καὶ ἀρχαῖοι γάμον καὶ ἁρμονίαν αὐτὸν ἐκάλεσαν.*

[f] *εἶδος* in the sense of a numeral base to be raised to a certain power.

[g] *παράδειγμα ἀσωμάτου καὶ νοερᾶς καὶ ἀοράτου καί* <*γε*> *σωματικῆς οὐσίας.*

[h] *τετράγωνον ἐπίπεδον* (or *ἐπιφάνειαν*).

[i] *κυβικὸν στερέωμα.*

[j] *τῇ ἀειπαρθένῳ ἑβδομάδι συγγενής.* *Cf., e.g., De Vita Mosis* ii. 210.

[k] *ἡ δύναμις*, here = exponential power.

[l] In order to get the total 64 we must add the number 1 twice.

has other further powers, about which we have spoken elsewhere.[a] But we must give the reasons which are suitable to, and in harmony with, the present inquiry, and depend upon the facts laid down as fundamental.

However, this is to be said first. That nation to which was given the command to circumcise (children) on the eighth (day) is called " Israel " in Chaldaean, and in Armenian[b] (this means) " seeing God."[c] It wishes to be a part both of naturally righteous ones[d] and of those who are[e] (so) by choice.[f] By the principle of creation[g] (this occurs) through the first hebdomad,[h] which, coming immediately after the creation, the Begetter and Creator clearly showed to be the festival of the creation of the world,[i] for He completed this on the sixth (day). But as to that which is by choice,[j] (it occurs) through the ogdoad, which is the beginning of the second hebdomad. Just as eight is (the sum of) seven and one, so the adorned nation[k] is always a nation, and it receives this lot in addition, being chosen by nature and in accordance with the will and pleasure[l] of the Father. In the second place, the number eight everywhere indicates equality, showing all dimensions equal, as has been said, (namely) length,

[a] See note *i* on p. 247.

[b] Here, as elsewhere, the Arm. translator substitutes " Armenian " for " Greek."

[c] This etymology occurs a good many times throughout Philo's writings.

[d] The Arm. lit. = *μέρος ἔχειν τῶν φυσικῶν* (or *γνησίων*) *δικαίων*; the context seems to show that " righteous " refers to persons rather than things.

[e] Lit. " is."

[f] *καθ' αἵρεσιν.*

[g] *κατὰ τὸν τῆς γενέσεως λόγον.*

[h] Aucher inadvertently renders, " per primum quidem sextum."

[i] *τὴν ἑορτὴν τὴν τῆς τοῦ κόσμου γενέσεως*, cf. *De Opif. Mundi* 89 *ἑορτὴ . . . τοῦ παντός . . . καὶ τοῦ κόσμου γενέθλιον.*

[j] See note *f* above.

[k] *τὸ κεκοσμημένον γένος.*

[l] *κατὰ βούλησιν καὶ γνώμην.*

breadth and depth. Equality produces righteousness,[a] and by this (Scripture) first proves that the god-loving[b] nation is adorned by equality and righteousness, and is brought into possession.[c] In the third place, not only is the (number eight) a measure[d] of complete equality in all dimensions, but also the first, since it is the first cube.[e] For the number eight, which indicates equality, is assigned to the second, but not the first, place in the order of rank.[f] Thus He symbolically indicates[g] that He has adapted[h] this first nation naturally[i] to the highest and utmost equality and righteousness. And it is the foremost of the human race, not through creation[j] or in time, but by the prerogative of virtue,[k] the righteous and equal being cognate[l] and united as if one part.[m] In the fourth place, since there are four elements, earth, water, air and a form of fire,[n] fire has been assigned the homonym of "pyramid,"[o] while air is eight-sided, and water is twenty-sided,[p] and the earth is a cube. It was therefore thought necessary that the earth, which was destined to be the (home) of the worthy and virtuous human race, should have as its share

[a] *δικαιοσύνην*.

[b] *φιλόθεον* or "divinely-favoured"—*θεοφιλές*.

[c] *κατάσχεσιν* or "inheritance"—*κληρονομίαν*.

[d] As Aucher notes, Arm. *ōr* (= *ἡμέρα*) must be a transcription of Greek *ὅρος*.

[e] This fact has been mentioned twice before in the present section.

[f] *i.e.* eight begins a new series after seven.

[g] *συμβολικῶς αἰνίττεται*.

[h] *ἐφήρμοσε*.

[i] Or "genuinely."

[j] Or "generation"—*γενέσεως*.

[k] *προτιμήσει τῆς ἀρετῆς*.

[l] *συμφυῆ*.

[m] Aucher renders differently, "ac si connaturalis pars sit unita justitia cum paritate."

[n] *εἶδος τοῦ πυρός*.

[o] Philo plays on the resemblance between *πυραμίς* and *πῦρ* or *πυροειδές*.

[p] *ὀκτάεδρος . . . εἰκοσάεδρον*.

a cubic number, in accordance with which the whole earth was formed equally,[a] and that it should share in the parts of generation. For the nature [b] of the earth is very productive and fertile, and it brings forth various and distinct species of all animals and plants.

50. (Gen. xvii. 12) Why does one circumcise (both) the home-born and the purchased [c] (child) ?

The literal meaning [d] is clear, for it is right that servants imitate their masters for the sake of the necessary offices of life and service. But as for the deeper meaning,[e] the home-born characters [f] are those which are moved by nature, while the purchased ones are those who are able to improve through reason [g] and teaching. There is need for both of these to be purified and trimmed [h] like plants, both those which are natural and genuine, and those which are able to bear fruit constantly [i]; for well-grown (plants) produce many superfluous (fruits) because of their fertility, which it is useful to cut off. But those who are taught by teachers [j] shave off [k] their ignorance.

51. (Gen. xvii. 13) What is the meaning of the words, " And my covenant shall be upon your flesh " [l] ?

[a] *ἴσως*, or " in common "—*κοινῶς*, or " at the same time " —*ὁμοῦ*.
[b] *ἡ φύσις*.
[c] *οἰκογενῆ καὶ ἀργυρώνητον*, as in LXX.
[d] *τὸ ῥητόν*.
[e] *τὸ πρὸς διάνοιαν*.
[f] *τρόποι* or *ἤθη*. [g] *διὰ λόγου*. [h] Lit. " cut."
[i] *ἐν διαμονῇ vel sim.* Aucher renders somewhat differently, " utraque istarum opus habet ut plantarum more purgetur et putetur, ad propriae ac fructiferae partis constantiam."
[j] *ὑπὸ διδασκάλων*.
[k] So lit. ; Arm. = *ἀποξυροῦσι*.
[l] LXX *καὶ ἔσται ἡ διαθήκη μου ἐπὶ* (Heb. " in ") *τῆς σαρκὸς ὑμῶν*.

He wishes (to point out) that not only does the virtuous man [a] profit (thereby) but that together with the soul the divine word [b] is appointed over the body also, to be, as it were, its physician, to whom it is a matter of concern to circumcise the excessive and harmful impulses [c] of sight, hearing, taste, smell and touch [d] and of the organ of speech and of reproduction and of the whole body, to which taking pleasure in desire (is) to feel pain.[e]

*52. (Gen. xvii. 14) Why does He prescribe a sentence of death for the infant, saying, " The uncircumcised male who shall not circumcise the flesh of his uncircumcision on the eighth day, that soul shall be destroyed from its kind " [f] ?

The law does not declare (anyone) guilty of any involuntary (crime) since it pardons even him who commits involuntary homicide,[g] specifying the cities to which he may flee to find safety. For he becomes sanctified and immune after taking refuge there, and no one has authority to take him away from there and bring him before a court of judgment. But if the child is not circumcised on the eighth day after birth, what sin has he committed that he should be judged deserving of suffering death ? Accord-

[a] τὸν σπουδαῖον.

[b] Or " Logos "—τὸν θεῖον λόγον.

[c] ὁρμάς.

[d] Lit. " of things seen, heard, etc."

[e] The last clause has no verb in Arm. ; Aucher renders freely, " quo peragitur tum delectari in cupiditatibus, tum dolore affici," adding in a footnote, " vel sine puncto sic : cui vel ipsum delectari in cupiditatibus dolore affici est."

[f] The Arm. differs slightly from LXX and Heb., which have " who shall not be circumcised." Moreover, the words " on the eighth day " are not found in the Heb.

[g] So too the Greek fragments in the Catenae and Procopius, οὐδὲν τῶν ἀκουσίων ἔνοχον ἀποφαίνει ὁ νόμος ὁπότε καὶ τῷ φόνον ἀκούσιον δράσαντι συγγινώσκει (the Greek fragments omit the references to cities of refuge, and resume with the sentence beginning, " But if the child ").

ingly, some say that the law of interpretation [a] has in view the parents, for it [b] believes that they show contempt for the commandment of the law. Others, however, say that it has imposed a very excessive penalty on infants, it seems, and that those adults who disregard and violate the law are deserving of punishment without regret or remission.[c] This is the literal meaning.[d] But as for the deeper meaning,[e] that which is excessively male in us is the mind.[f] This He commands to be circumcised in the ogdoad [g] for the reasons which I gave earlier [h]; and (He mentions) no other part but the flesh of the foreskin, symbolizing those sense-pleasures and impulses [i] which afterwards come to the body. Wherefore He adds a principle of law [j] in His statement. For the mind which is not circumcised and purified and sanctified of the body and the passions which come through the body will be corrupted [k] and cannot be saved.[l] And since the argument [m] does not concern man but the mind which has health,[n] He adds, " that soul shall be destroyed " [o]—not the human body or man but the soul [p] and the mind. And from what? " From its

[a] One may also accept Aucher's rendering, " formam edicti."

[b] Apparently the law or Scripture is meant.

[c] The Arm. agrees closely with the Greek frag. printed by Harris from the Catenae, less closely with the recension of Procopius; for these texts see Appendix A.

[d] *τὸ ῥητόν.*

[e] *τὸ πρὸς διάνοιαν.*

[f] *ὁ νοῦς.*

[g] This is Philo's allegorical variation of the scriptural " eighth day."

[h] In § 49.

[i] *ἡδονὰς καὶ ὁρμάς.*

[j] Or, as Aucher renders, " rationem legitimam."

[k] Or " be destroyed."

[l] *σώζεσθαι.*

[m] *ὁ λόγος.*

[n] *ὑγίειαν* or *ὁλοκληρίαν.*

[o] *ἐξολεθρευθήσεται* in LXX.

[p] *ἡ ψυχή* (though sometimes Arm. *ogi* = *πνεῦμα*).

kind," [a] He says. For the whole genus is incorruptible; thus from incorruption the sinner is brought to corruption.

53. (Gen. xvii. 15) Why does He say, "Sara thy wife shall not be called *Sara*, but *Sarra* shall be her name" [b]?

Once more some of the stupid people may laugh [c] at the addition of one letter, *rho*,[d] and ridicule and make fun of it because they are unwilling to apply themselves to the inward facts of things and follow after truth. For that which seems to be the addition of one letter produces all harmony.[e] In place of the small (it gives) the great, and in place of the particular, the general,[f] and in place of the mortal, the immortal. For through the one *rho* she is called Sara, which in translation means "my rule," [g] while with two *rhos* it means "ruler." [h] In what way these are individually distinguished from each other must be investigated. My prudence and temperance and justice and fortitude [i] rule over me only, and are mortal. When I die, they die. But prudence itself is a ruler, and so is justice itself, and each of the other virtues; it is not (merely) sovereign over me but is itself a ruler and queen, an immortal rule and sovereignty. Do you see the greatness of the gift? He has converted the part into the whole, and the species into the genus,[j] and the corruptible into

[a] *γένος* in LXX (Heb. "people").

[b] Philo follows the LXX forms of the Heb. names *Sarai* and *Sarah*; for parallels see *De Congressu* 2, *De Mut. Nom.* 61 *et al.*

[c] See above, § 43 on those who ridicule the change of Abraham's name.

[d] *ἑνὸς στοιχείου ρ′* (the last word is rendered by its numerical equivalent, "hundred," in Arm.).

[e] *πᾶσαν ἁρμονίαν.*

[f] *ἀντὶ τοῦ ἐπὶ μέρους τὸ καθολικόν.*

[g] *ἀρχή μου.*

[h] *ἄρχουσα.*

[i] *φρόνησις καὶ σωφροσύνη καὶ δικαιοσύνη καὶ ἀνδρεία*; *cf. De Congressu* 2 *et al.*

[j] The Arm. misprints *seṙ* (*γνήσιος*) for *ser* (*γένος*); Aucher renders correctly.

the incorruptible. And all these are granted in advance for the sake of the future birth of a more perfect happiness and joy, of which the name is Isaac.[a]

54. (Gen. xvii. 16) Why does He say, " I will give thee from her children,[b] and I will bless him and he shall be for peoples, and the kings of the nations shall come from him "[c]?

It is not in place to inquire why He used the plural " children " in speaking of their only beloved son, for the allusion is to his descendants, from whom (were to come) peoples and kings. This is the literal meaning.[d] But as for the deeper meaning,[e] when the soul has (only) that virtue which is particular,[f] slight and mortal, it is still barren. But when once it receives a portion of the divine and incorruptible (virtue), it begins to conceive and bear a variety of peoples and of all other holy things. For each of the immortal virtues has very many voluntary laws,[g] which bear the likenesses of peoples and kings. For virtues and the generations of virtues are kingly affairs, being taught beforehand[h] by nature what is sovereign and unservile.[i]

[a] Philo etymologizes the name Isaac as γέλως and χαρά in several passages, *e.g. Leg. All.* iii. 218.

[b] LXX, Heb. and Arm. O.T. all have " son " or " child." In the parallel, *De Mut. Nom.* 130-153, Philo not only follows the LXX in reading τέκνον but emphasizes the singular number of the noun.

[c] It is here assumed that the pronouns are masculine, as in the LXX rather than feminine as in the Heb. (referring to Sarah). There is no distinction of gender in Armenian. But Philo follows the Heb. against the LXX in *De Mut. Nom.* 148-151.

[d] τὸ ῥητόν.

[e] τὸ πρὸς διάνοιαν.

[f] Or " partial."

[g] ἑκουσίους νόμους.

[h] προδιδασκόμεναι.

[i] ἀδούλωτον.

55. (Gen. xvii. 17) Why did Abraham fall upon his face and laugh ?

Two things are shown by his falling upon his face.[a] One is his prostration[b] because of an excess of divine ecstasy.[c] And the other is his confession,[d] which is consonant with, and equal to, what has been said. For his mind acknowledged that God stands alone. But those things which[e] are under the generation of birth all fall into periodical change. And they fall with respect to that[f] part through which they are wont to be raised up and be erect, (namely) with respect to the sovereign[g] face. Rightly did he laugh in his joy over the promise, being filled with great hope and in the expectation that it would be fulfilled, and because he had clearly received a vision,[h] through which he knew more certainly Him who always stands firm, and him who[i] naturally bends and falls.

56. (Gen. xvii. 17) Why is he incredulous,[j] as it were, in his confession,[k] for says (Scripture), "He said in his mind,[l] shall a son be born to a centenarian, and shall Sarah[m] bear at ninety years ? "

[a] For parallels in Philo see *Leg. All.* iii. 217 and *De Mut. Nom.* 154 ff.

[b] *προσκύνησις.*

[c] *θείας ἐκστάσεως.*

[d] *ὁμολογία* (in the biblical sense).

[e] The sing. verb in Arm. indicates here that the pronominal subject was neuter plural, not masculine plural, as Aucher renders.

[f] The context requires emendation of the nom. pl. demons. pron. *sok'a* to gen. sing. *sora.* The Arm. letters *k'* and *r* are very similar.

[g] Lit. " first."

[h] *ἐπιφάνειαν.*

[i] Or " that which."

[j] *ἀπιστεῖ.*

[k] *ὁμολογίᾳ.*

[l] LXX *ἐν τῇ διανοίᾳ αὐτοῦ.*

[m] LXX *Sarra.*

Not ineptly or casually [a] are added the words, "He said in his mind." [b] For unworthy words spoken by tongue and mouth fall under transgressions and punishment. But those which are in the mind are not at all guilty.[c] For involuntarily does the mind show arrogance [d] when various desires come upon it from various directions, and there are times when it resists these and disputes with them resentfully, and seeks to avoid their appearances. Perhaps too he is not in a state of doubt [e] but being struck with amazement at the excessiveness of the gift, says, "Behold, our body has passed (its prime) and has gone beyond the age for begetting. But to God all things are possible, even to change old age into youth, and to bring one who has no seed or fruit into the begetting and fruitfulness." And so, if a centenarian and (a woman) of ninety years produce children, the element of ordinary events is removed,[f] and only the divine power and grace clearly appear.

But we must (now) show what virtues [g] the number one hundred has.[h] In the first place, the hundred is a power of the decad. In the second place, the myriad is (a power) of this itself. And the myriad is brother to unity, for just as one times one is one, so ten thousand times one is ten thousand. In the third place, all the parts of the number one hundred are well ordered.[i] In the fourth place, it consists of thirty and of six and of sixty and of four, which is a cube and a square [j] at the same time. In the fifth place, it consists of these several odd numbers, 1, 3,

[a] παρέργως.

[b] See the parallel discussion in *De Mut. Nom.* 177-200.

[c] ἔνοχα. [d] ἀλαζονείαν. [e] οὐκ ἐνδοιάζει.

[f] *i.e.* we are dealing here with something miraculous.

[g] δυνάμεις.

[h] In the parallel, *De Mut. Nom.* 188-192, Philo cites a number of biblical passages involving the number 100, but does not treat them in the fashion of Pythagorean number mysticism as here.

[i] Arm. *parkešt* = σώφρων, κόσμιος, etc.

[j] Aucher inadvertently renders, "triangulum."

5, 7, 9, 11, 13, 15, 17, 19, making 100.[a] In the sixth place, it consists of four (numbers), one and its double, and four and its double, 1, 2, 4, 8, making 15, and of the four numbers,[b] 1, 4, 16, 64, making 85. Now there is a twofold proportion [c] in all things, containing that of four and that of five,[d] but four is twice in all things. In the seventh place, it consists of several fours, each of which has one added (namely), 1, 2, 3, 4, making 10, and of four triangular numbers,[e] 1, 3, 6, 10, making 20, and of four quadrangular numbers, 1, 4, 9, 16, making 30, and of four pentagonal numbers, 1, 5, 12, 22, making 40, and (all) these together make 100. In the eighth place, the number one hundred is completed by the cubes of the four separate numbers beginning with one, for given the numbers from one on, (namely) 1, 2, 3, 4, their cubes, 1, 8, 27, 64, make 100. In the ninth place, it is divided into forty and sixty, both of which are most natural (numbers).[f] And in respect of the several decads in the pentagonal figure up to the number ten thousand, the number one hundred holds the middle place. For the number one hundred is the middle one of (the series) one, ten, a hundred, a thousand and ten thousand.

But it is proper not to pass over in silence the number ninety in respect of its visible [g] (elements). It seems to me that the number ninety takes second place after the hundred, in so far as a tenth part (of the latter) is taken away, which is the decad. For in the Law I find two tenths [h]

[a] These figures are expressed as numeral letters in the Arm. text here and below; other numbers are indicated by name.

[b] Aucher correctly amplifies in rendering, " ex quatuor istis multiplicatis," since the second set of four is that of the squares of the first four.

[c] Or " principle "—λόγος.

[d] " Five " is an error for " two," as Staehle notes, p. 71.

[e] See *QG* i. 83.

[f] φυσικώτατοι <ἀριθμοί>.

[g] Or " conspicuous "; Aucher " quoad notas visibiles."

[h] *i.e.* tithes, the first tithe going to the Levite and the tenth of this Levitical tithe going to the priest (" peace-offering of tithe ").

of first fruits distinguished, one of the whole (produce) and one of the remainder. And when the tenth is taken from the produce of grain or wine or oil, another tenth is taken from the remainder.[a] Now of these two (numbers) the initial and first one is honoured with seniority, and the one that comes after with second place. For the hundred contains the two (kinds of) first fruits of the years of the wise man, by which he is consecrated, (namely) the first and second (offerings), while the number ninety (contains) the second first-fruits of the years of feminine gender, the younger and lesser remainder of the first and greatest among the sacred numbers. The former, therefore, is called " a sown aroura " [b] in the sacred Law, while the latter has a general nature,[c] for the number ninety is generative,[d] wherefore also women are productive in the ninth month. But the decad is sacred and perfect. And when these [e] are multiplied there is formed the sacred and generative power [f] of ninety, which gets its fruitful generation from nine, and its sacredness from the decad.

57. (Gen. xvii. 18) Why does Abraham say to God, " Let this Ishmael [g] live before Thee " ?

[a] *Cf. De Mut. Nom.* 191.

[b] The parallel, *De Mut. Nom.* 190, enables us to correct the unintelligible Arm. text. Arm. *tesouac* renders θεωρία but this is a corruption of ἄρουρα; *əntanaçeal* is the ptc. of the verb which renders σπερματίζειν, not of its homonym which renders οἰκειοῦσθαι. As Colson notes in the passage from *De Mut. Nom.* (L.C.L. Philo, vol. v. p. 239), " Philo interprets ἄρουρα in the technical sense of a piece of land of 100 square cubits."

[c] καθολικὴν φύσιν.

[d] γόνιμος.

[e] The numbers 9 and 10 (9 being unobtrusively substituted for 90).

[f] δύναμις.

[g] So LXX; Heb. has no demonstr. pron. before " Ishmael." Philo comments at length on this verse in *De Mut. Nom.* 201-251.

First of all, (he says), " We[a] do not despair, O Lord, of a better generation, but I have faith in Thy promises. However, it is enough of a gift for me that this one should live who is for the time being a living son, even though he is not a son by genuine descent, being born of a concubine." In the second place, what he now seeks is an additional good, for it is not merely life that he desires for his son but a life " before God,"[b] than which nothing is worthy to be considered more perfect, (a life) before God (being) one of wholeness and salvation,[c] which is on a par with immortality.[d] In the third place, he symbolically[e] indicates that not (only) should the heard laws of God be committed to hearing,[f] but they should (also) pass into the inner (life) and mould and form its most sovereign part,[g] for that (alone) is life in the sight of God whose words are worthy to become deeds.[h]

*58. (Gen. xvii. 19) Why is the divine oracle[i] an agreement,[j] for He says to Abraham, " Yes, behold,[k] Sarah thy wife shall bear thee a son " ?

What is indicated is somewhat as follows. " This agreement,[l] " He says, " is something for Me Myself to

[a] On the 1st pl. for the expected 1st sing. see Colson's note on *De Mut. Nom.* 216 (vol. v. p. 255).

[b] ἐνώπιον τοῦ θεοῦ.

[c] ὑγιείας καὶ σωτηρίας.

[d] ἰσότιμος τῇ ἀθανασίᾳ.

[e] ἐν ὑπονοίαις. Aucher's rendering, " per conjecturam," is not quite right.

[f] In *De Mut. Nom.* 202 *et al.* Philo alludes to the interpretation of the name Ishmael as " hearing God."

[g] τυποῦν καὶ μορφοῦν τὸ ἡγεμονικώτατον μέρος.

[h] Construction and meaning uncertain ; Aucher renders, " vita enim est ista divino conspectui condigna verbum effectum esse."

[i] ὁ θεῖος χρησμός.

[j] Or " assent "—συγχώρησις or ἐπίνευσις.

[k] So LXX, ναί, ἰδού ; Heb. *'abāl* usu. = " but." Philo comments on the expression in *De Mut. Nom.* 253-254.

[l] Arm. has two words, both rendering ὁμολογία, which is also used in the Greek frag.

keep[a] being clearly without denial.[b] And thy faith[c] is not ambiguous but is unhesitating, and partakes of modesty and reverence.[d] Wherefore that which thou didst formerly receive as destined to come about because of thy faith in Me, shall wholly[e] be." For this is shown by the "Yes."

59. (Gen. xvii. 20) Why does He say, "But concerning Ishmael, behold I will hear thee, and I will bless[f] him. Twelve nations he shall beget."

"Both the first and the second good things," He says, "I grant to thee, both that which comes by nature and that which comes by teaching[g]; by nature[h] is that which comes through the genuine[i] Isaac, and by teaching is that which comes through the not-genuine Ishmael, for hearing[j] when compared with seeing is like the not-genuine beside the genuine, and that which comes by teaching does not have the same standing[k] as that which comes by nature. And "he shall beget twelve nations" (means) the train of

[a] Text obscure; Aucher renders, "confessio ac homologiae ista, ait, mea parte admissio est voti." The Greek frag. reads *ἡ ὁμολογία, φησίν, ἡ ἐμὴ κατάφασίς ἐστιν.*

[b] Arm. *ouraxout'enē* "joy" is clearly a scribal error for *ouraçout'enē* = *ἀρνήσεως*, which is also found in the Greek frag. Philo apparently means that the "Yes" of Scripture indicates God's unhesitating willingness to reward Abraham's unhesitating faith.

[c] *πίστις.*

[d] *αἰδοῦς καὶ ἐντροπῆς μετέχουσα*, as in the Greek frag.

[e] Or "absolutely"—*πάντως*, as in the Greek frag.

[f] LXX and Heb. "I have heard thee and I have blessed."

[g] In the parallel, *De Mut. Nom.* 255-264, Philo calls Ishmael *ἔγγονον διδακτόν*, and Isaac *αὐτομαθής.*

[h] *φύσει.*

[i] *γνήσιον.* In *De Mut. Nom.* 261 he is called *γενναῖον.*

[j] Here again, as in *QG* iii. 57, Philo plays on the etymology of the name Ishmael, "hearing God."

[k] *λόγον.*

school studies,[a] for the number twelve is a cyclical number in the cycle of days and years.[b]

60. (Gen. xvii. 21) Why does He say, " And My covenant I will establish with Isaac whom Sarah shall bear [c] at this time [d] in the other year " [e] ?

Just as in human testaments [f] some persons are inscribed as heirs, and some are counted worthy of (receiving) gifts, which they receive from the heirs, so also in the divine testament he is inscribed as heir who is by nature a good disciple [g] of God, adorned with perfect virtues.[h] But he who is introduced [i] through hearing [j] and is subjected to the law of wisdom [k] and participates in the discipline of school studies [l] is not an heir but receives gifts which are bestowed by grace.[m] Most wisely,[n] moreover, is it said that " in the other year " she will bear Isaac, for that birth is not one of the life of the time [o] which now exists but of another great, holy, sacred and

[a] τὸν χορὸν τῶν ἐγκυκλίων. In *De Mut. Nom.* 263 they are called τὸν χορὸν τῶν σοφιστικῶν προπαιδευμάτων.

[b] Since the year consists of 12 months, and day and night of 12 hours each, as Philo explains in *De Fuga* 184.

[c] LXX and Heb. add " to thee."

[d] LXX καιρόν, Heb. *mô'ēd* " set time."

[e] So LXX and Heb., *i.e.* " next year." The verse is differently allegorized in *De Mut. Nom.* 264-269, where the covenant is not mentioned, perhaps because Philo planned to include it in his projected treatise *On Covenants*, which has not come down to us.

[f] διαθήκαις.

[g] μαθητής.

[h] τελείαις ἀρεταῖς.

[i] εἰσάγεται.

[j] *i.e.* Ishmael. See *QG* iii. 59.

[k] ὑποτάττεται τῷ τῆς σοφίας νόμῳ.

[l] τῆς τῶν ἐγκυκλίων παιδείας.

[m] Arm. lit. = χαριστήρια (for χάριτας ?) καὶ δωρεάς.

[n] πανσόφως.

[o] Text slightly emended, following Aucher.

divine one,[a] which has an abundant fullness [b] and is not like that of the gentiles.[c]

*61. (Gen. xvii. 24-25) Why does (Scripture) say that Abraham was ninety-nine years old when he was circumcised, and Ishmael, his son, thirteen years old ?

The number of ninety-nine years is set beside [d] the number one hundred. And in accordance with this number it is destined to be the seed and progeny of a more perfect generation, which is to appear in the hundred.[e] But the number thirteen is composed of the first two squares, of four and nine, of even and odd ; the even one has sides which are a double material form,[f] and the odd one has a practical form.[g] Through all these comes the triad,[h] and this is the greatest [i] and most perfect of festival offerings, which the pillars [j] of the divine scriptures contain. This is one (explanation). But it is proper to mention

[a] Prob. the noun " life " is understood.

[b] πλησμονήν or possibly πλήρωμα.

[c] τῶν ἐθνῶν. Philo does not often use ἔθνη in the biblical sense of " gentiles."

[d] In *QG* iii. 39 (on Gen. xvii. 1) and in *De Mut. Nom.* 1, Philo speaks of 99 as being " neighbour " (γείτων) to 100.

[e] An allusion to the birth of Isaac in Abraham's 100th year.

[f] διπλοῦν ὑλικὸν εἶδος.

[g] πρακτικὸν (?) εἶδος : Aucher " formam operativam." Possibly Philo here refers to the nine months of conception, as above in *QG* iii. 56 ; if so, we might render " productive " (ποιητικόν) rather than " practical."

[h] Apparently Philo means the 3 in 13.

[i] Lit. " greatness."

[j] στῆλαι : Aucher " exarationes." Probably Philo means the tablets of the Law, as elsewhere, or the Law generally. The " festival offerings " are presumably those of Passover, Pentecost and Tabernacles, as the Arm. glossator suggests. It is curious, however, that in *De Somniis* i. 242 (on the pillar at Beth-el, Gen. xxxi. 13), Philo says that a pillar is a symbol of three things, " of standing, of dedication and of inscription."

another as well, (namely) that the age of thirteen years is a neighbour and associate of fourteen [a] years, when [b] the generative movements are brought to their seed.[c] And so, lest alien seed [d] be sown, He takes care that the first generation shall be preserved intact,[e] representing the generative organ by the symbol of generation.[f]

In the third place He instructs him who is about to undertake marriage by all means to circumcise his sense-pleasures [g] and amorous desires, rebuking those who are lascivious and lustful,[h] in order that they may restrain their excessive embraces,[i] which usually come about not for the sake of begetting children but for the sake of unrestrained pleasure.

62. (Gen. xvii. 27) Why does Abraham circumcise those of foreign birth ? [j]

The wise man is helpful and at the same time philanthropic.[k] He saves and calls to himself not only his kinsmen [l] and those of like opinions [m] but also those of foreign birth and of different opinions,[n] giving them of his own goods with patience and ascetic continence,[o] for these are the firm foundations [p] to which all virtue [q] hastens and finds rest.

[a] Lit. " twice seven."
[b] Lit. " behold ! "
[c] The syntax is obscure ; Aucher renders, " quo seminis motus ad generationem fertur."
[d] ἀλλογενὲς σπέρμα.
[e] ὁλόκληρον.
[f] συμβόλῳ τοῦ γένους.
[g] ἡδονάς.
[h] Lit. " woman-loving."
[i] Lit. " minglings."
[j] τοὺς ἀλλογενεῖς.
[k] φιλάνθρωπος.
[l] Or " countrymen."
[m] Text slightly emended by Aucher.
[n] ἑτεροδόξους.
[o] ὑπομονῇ καὶ ἀσκήσει ἐγκρατείας *vel sim.*
[p] θεμέλια.
[q] ἀρετή.

BOOK IV[a]

1. (Gen. xviii. 1-2) Why does (Scripture) say, "And the Lord God[b] appeared to Abraham[c] at the oak of Mambre,[d] when he was sitting in the heat of day[e] at the entrance of his tent; and he lifted up his eyes"[f]?

The literal meaning[g] seems to me quite clear. But it is only necessary to explain the tree allegorically through the Chaldaean[h] speech. According to Heracleitus,[i] our nature [a tree] likes to hide itself.[j] Now, in the first place, it is proper to recognize that the interpretation of *Mambre* is "from sight,"[k] and this means something like the following. Just as being wise comes from wisdom,[l] and being prudent comes from prudence,[m] and having various dispositions comes from these (various dispositions), so

[a] Book IV, which is about as long as the combined first three books of the *Quaestiones in Genesin*, originally comprised Books IV, V and VI, as some ancient MSS. indicate. See the Introduction.

[b] Heb. "*YHWH*"; LXX and Arm. O.T. "God."

[c] LXX and Heb. "to him."

[d] Heb. "Mamre."

[e] So Heb.; LXX and Arm. O.T. "at midday."

[f] So Heb. and Arm. O.T.; LXX "and looking up with his eyes."

[g] τὸ ῥητόν.

[h] *i.e.* Hebrew.

[i] *Cf.* Diels-Kranz, *Fragmenta der Vorsokratiker*, B 123 [10] ἡ φύσις κρύπτεσθαι φιλεῖ (from Porphyry). The Arm. *caṙ* "tree" is out of place here.

[j] Arm. here uses two verbs, both of which render κρύπτεσθαι.

[k] ἀπὸ ὁράσεως (or ὁρωμένων), as if from Heb. *mim-mar'êh*. The same etymology is given in *De Migratione* 165.

[l] σοφίας.

[m] σωφροσύνης.

in the case of the senses[a] the act of touching comes from touch, and tasting from taste, and hearing from the auditory sense, and seeing necessarily comes from sight. This is what enriches the spiritual,[b] clear-sighted and excellent mind, which in Chaldaean is called *Mambre*, and in Armenian,[c] " from sight " by enabling it to see better[d] and to be sharp-sighted[e] and unsleeping, seeing not only the created world,[f] the forms[g] of which it is the part of philosophy to see, but its Father and Creator, the uncreated God.[h] For of what use would it be for Him to come and not be seen ? And since He is incomprehensible,[i] not only to the human race but also to all the purest parts of heaven, He caused to shine forth, as it were, a certain radiance, which we most properly call " form,"[j] and caused this radiance of light to shine around the whole soul, and filled it with an incorporeal and more than heavenly light. And being guided[k] by this, the mind[l] is brought by[m] form to the archetype.[n] For what is said[o] is better fitted to and harmonized with sight than with all the organs,[p] since it is through sight that a vision is apprehended.[q] And

[a] ταῖς αἰσθήσεσι. [b] πνευματικόν.

[c] *Sic !* The original, of course, had " in Greek " or " in our language."

[d] The syntax is not altogether clear. Aucher renders, " Hoc est, quod spirituali perspicacique mente sana, puta Mambre, sive visu ditat animum, praestans ei ut melius videat."

[e] ὀξυδερκής.

[f] τὸν γενητὸν κόσμον.

[g] τὰ εἴδη (or τὰς μορφάς).

[h] τὸν ἀγένητον θεόν.

[i] ἀκατάληπτος, here rendered by two Arm. words.

[j] εἶδος (or μορφήν). [k] ἡγούμενος.

[l] ὁ νοῦς. [m] Or " through."

[n] πρὸς τὸ ἀρχέτυπον.

[o] *i.e.* in Scripture, about God's appearing to Abraham.

[p] *i.e.* the other organs of sense. Aucher's rendering seems to me to miss the point, " siquidem visu potius quam cunctis instrumentis sensus coaptavit symphoniam dictam."

[q] νοεῖται.

in the second place, since the extremes[a] are wonderful—both He who appeared, for He is God, and he to whom He appeared, for he it was who saw, (Scripture) has very symbolically[b] placed between them both an oak-tree, which is most powerful and sovereign. And inasmuch as it is a tree that has been domesticated from a rather wild one,[c] it indicates[d] the wise man who is provided with eyes.[e] And beginning to see the truly existent One,[f] the excellent and powerful and sovereign ruler of all things, he sees a wild (tree) unrestrainedly possessed by density,[g] and the limit of unrestraint which contends, and the radiance which resists until it is reconciled with seeing.[h] For the trunk of the tree[i] is wild, but its fruit is the domesticated acorn,[j] which was given to man as food earlier than wheat; and for this reason they ascribed life to it (as) its principle,[k] considering the oak[l] to be the temple and altar of the only God. For, like the laurel of the sun,[m] it comes to the aid of health. And the turnings[n] of the sun clearly show forth the yearly seasons, of which

[a] Apparently Philo means that God and Abraham were the two end-points in the relation, and the oak of Mambre the mid-point.
[b] *συμβολικώτερον*.
[c] *ἐξ ἀγρίου τι*.
[d] *αἰνίττεται*.
[e] Lit. "eyed." Possibly the original was *ὀφθαλμιζόμενον* "grafted" but there is no other reference here to tree-grafting.
[f] *τὸν ὄντως Ὄντα*.
[g] The Arm. seems literally to render *πυκνότητι κατεχόμενον ἀκωλύτως ἄγριον*, whatever that means.
[h] The above is a literal translation, which is admittedly unintelligible. Aucher very freely renders, or rather paraphrases, "ita tamen ut expedite et libere splendorem obvians renitentem, placidum redderet oculis."
[i] The compound *stełnatounk* is not listed in the great Arm. dictionary. Aucher renders less accurately, "planta ipsa."
[j] *φηγὸς* (or *βάλανος*) *οἰκεῖος*.
[k] *ἀρχήν* (?); Aucher has "ut propriam facultatem."
[l] *τὴν δρῦν*.
[m] Probably a reference to the laurel of Apollo Daphnephoros.
[n] *αἱ τροπαί*, *i.e.* the solstices.

one brings mild temperateness,[a] and the other brings about severe intemperateness (and) sickness. Now the ever-virginal olive-tree[b] is of the purest substance which the inerrant sphere[c] attains, for olive-oil is the material of light, and radiant in form is the heaven in which are the light-giving stars. Wherefore it is customary to call most of them[d] not what they themselves are but after the most sovereign and chief of them, (namely) the oak, in places where trees and groves are especially dense and thick, even though the oak does not seek any payment of tribute.[e] And they are called oak-cutters[f] who cut down fir-trees[g] and cedars and the like, and even others, of the timber of which it is usual to erect what are called *dryphaktoi*.[h] And the fruits of trees of all kinds, both cultivated and wild, are called oak-fruits[i] and olives. And "oak-ripe"[j] is what they call those (fruits) that ripen on the stalk. And the name of oak and olive is given to all (trees) as sovereign and chief. And rightly is He said to have appeared to him when seated, since sitting is a state of tranquillity and[k] peace of body. Now the mind of the virtuous man, when it sits in restful quietness and secure peace, wishing to bear a likeness to the unwearied and unchanging true being of God, which is of an intelligible nature and a thing of non-living life,[l] so far as is possible

[a] *εὐκρασίαν.*

[b] *ἡ ἀειπάρθενος ἐλαιά*, here perhaps considered a variety of *δάφνη*, *cf.* Strabo 16. 3. 6 on the trees of Arabia.

[c] *ἡ ἀπλανὴς σφαίρα*, *i.e.* the sphere of the fixed stars.

[d] *i.e.* trees.

[e] Prob. *τιμὴν φόρου.* Aucher less aptly renders, "ultionem," ignoring Arm. *hark* "tribute."

[f] *δρυηκόποι.*

[g] Arm. *eḷat* is not defined in dictionaries available to me. I have followed Aucher's rendering.

[h] Arm. transliterates *δρύφακτοι* "rails, balconies," etc.

[i] Prob. *βάλανοι*, which includes acorns, dates, etc.

[j] *i.e.* "tree-ripe"—*δρυπεπεῖς.*

[k] Lit. "a state (*ἕξις*) and tranquillity of."

[l] *ἀβιώτου βίου.* Aucher renders the whole clause elliptically, "illam quam secundum intelligibilem vitam laboris nesciam, similitudinem veri Entis Dei volens imitari."

for human nature,[a] describes a form that is very obscure in comparison with the archetype.[b] But the sitting at the entrance of his tent seems to be a symbol,[c] that is, of the body, which the divine and holy Scriptures in another place call a "tunic of skin,"[d] as if of the soul, for (through the body) are the paths of colours, forms, voices, elements[e] and vapours, and everything that is at all sense-perceptible. And it is fitting for the virtuous reason[f] to sit by the senses and be a doorkeeper[g] lest anything harmful slip within and be the cause of harm to the soul, inasmuch as it is able to preserve it unharmed and whole and unaffected by any evil. For the senses of foolish men are left stranded without protection and abandoned to themselves, and there is no one of them at all who stands at the entrance to exclude useless and harmful impressions.[h] Wherefore many desperate misfortunes find their way within, no less voluntary than involuntary, and because of these, which shamelessly and unopposed find their way in, impressions[i] are engraved upon the mind, and by these the soul is shaken and agitated day and night, since the senses are left without protection and abandoned to their own devices.

And excellently is it said that the vision occurred at midday,[j] for this is the most luminous (hour) in the whole length of the day. Thus, symbolically it sets before us[k] the intelligible sun,[l] (which) sends out its incorporeal rays

[a] Aucher wrongly transposes the rendering of "for human life" to the next clause.

[b] Aucher goes astray in rendering, "humana natura similem originali describit obscuram formam."

[c] *σύμβολον.*

[d] *Cf. QG* i. 53 on Gen. iii. 21.

[e] Or "humours."

[f] *τῷ σπουδαίῳ λογισμῷ.*

[g] *θυρωρόν.*

[h] *φαντασίας.*

[i] Aucher amplifies in rendering, "turpes ideae."

[j] Above, in quoting Scripture, Philo writes "in the heat of the day."

[k] *συμβολικῶς ἐναντίον παρίστησι.*

[l] *τὸν νοητὸν ἥλιον.*

most luminously and splendidly upon pure souls,[a] which gaze directly into the rays and behold them ; and piety, after passion is removed,[b] makes the heaven familiar. But they are not able to gaze at it for a long time, since that unmixed, undiluted, holy, pure, diffused and incorporeal light shines too brilliantly, and with its brightness blinds and dulls the eyes. But it seems to me that, since the light is purer and more luminous at midday, when impressions are seen more clearly, it wishes to illumine the mind of the wise man and have the rays shine about him with divine light, and make clearer and firmer the impressions of things that really exist,[c] the rays being without shadow.

2. (Gen. xviii. 2) What is the meaning of the words, " He saw,[d] and behold, three men were standing over him "[e] ?

Most natural things[f] to those who are able to see does (Scripture) present, (namely) that it is reasonable[g] for one to be three and for three to be one, for they were one by a higher principle.[h] But when counted with the chief powers, the creative and kingly,[i] He makes the appearance of three to the human mind. For this cannot be so keen of sight that it can see Him who is above the powers that belong to Him, (namely) God, distinct from anything else. For so soon as one sets eyes upon God, there also appear, together with His being,[j] the ministering powers, so that

[a] In the Arm. text the " and " before " pure souls " seems to be misplaced.

[b] Text uncertain.

[c] τῶν ὄντως ὄντων.

[d] LXX and Heb. " he lifted his eyes and saw."

[e] LXX ἐπάνω αὐτοῦ. The verse is allegorically explained in *De Abrahamo* 119-132 in much the same way as here.

[f] φυσικώτατα.

[g] εἰκός.

[h] κατ' ἀνώτερον λόγον.

[i] σὺν ταῖς πρώταις δυνάμεσι, τῇ ποιητικῇ καὶ τῇ βασιλικῇ. *Cf.* *QG* ii. 51 notes.

[j] Or " essence "—οὐσίᾳ. Aucher renders less accurately, " una cum illo existentes apparent."

in place of one He makes the appearance of a triad. For when the mind begins to have an apprehension of the Existent One,[a] He is known to have arrived there,[b] making (Himself) unique, and appearing as chief and sovereign. But, as I said a little earlier, He cannot be seen in His oneness without something (else), the chief powers that exist immediately[c] with Him, (namely) the creative, which is called God, and the kingly, which is called Lord. For (when Scripture) says, "he lifted up his eyes," (this means) not those of the body, for it is not possible to see God through the senses, but those of the soul. For in the moment of wisdom[d] He is seen with the eyes.[e] But the sight of many ignoble and idle souls is always blocked, since they are in a deep sleep and are never able to leap up and rouse themselves to the things of nature and to the sights and impressions therein. But the spiritual eyes of the virtuous man are awake and see; or rather, he is sleepless because of his desire of seeing, and he spurs himself and leaps up to wakefulness. Wherefore it was well said in the plural that he opened, not one eye, but all the eyes which are in the soul, so that he was altogether an eye.[f] And having become an eye, he begins to see the sovereign, holy and divine[g] vision in such a way that the single appearance appears as a triad, and the triad as a unity.

It is fitting to speak of what follows these words and not omit them. For not idly[h] is it said that "they stood

[a] *κατάληψιν τοῦ Ὄντος.*

[b] Meaning unclear to me.

[c] *εὐθύς.*

[d] *καιρῷ σοφίας.*

[e] One may also render, "For at the (right) time He is seen with the eyes of wisdom."

[f] Aucher amplifies slightly in rendering, "ut totum totaliter oculum esse eum dixeris."

[g] Perhaps in selecting these three adjectives, which render *κυρίαν καὶ ἁγίαν καὶ θείαν*, Philo wishes to suggest that the central being of God is flanked (*παρ᾽ ἑκάτερα* is used in *De Abrahamo* 121) by His kingly and creative powers.

[h] *οὐκ εἰκῇ.*

over him." For God is above and over all generated creatures, and (so are) the divine powers that administer and oversee and govern. Now generally everything necessary has already been said, for concerning the activity of things it is proper to see a vision in no casual manner [a]; with a single turning of the eyes the mind apprehends a double appearance [b]; the one was of God coming with His two highest powers, by which He is served, (namely) the creative, through which He creates and operates the world, and the kingly, through which He rules what has come into being. And the other (appearance) was that of the strange men, not such men as one may happen to meet by chance, but most perfect of body according to human nature, and of venerable holiness. And being struck by either appearance, he was drawn toward seeing, now by one, now by the other. And he was not able to see just which of them was likely to be the true one.[c] For the sake of safety and because of uncertainty and doubt he did not ignore (either of them), nor did he, like some, out of slothfulness forget them but received and apprehended both appearances, thinking it better to accustom [d] his doubt, by truth rather than by falsehood, to the acquisition of two great virtues, (namely) holiness and love of mankind [e]—holiness, in so far as his gaze was fixed upon the one aspect,[f] in which he saw God; and love of mankind, in the other aspect, which is common participation [g] with strangers. And that he was moved by either

[a] Lit. the Arm. seems to render *περὶ γὰρ τῆς τῶν πραγμάτων ἐργασίας πρέπον ἐστὶ οὐ παρέργως ὅρασιν ἰδεῖν*. Aucher renders, "de ipsa vero rerum causa non obiter visionem videre liceat"; in a footnote to "causa" he adds, "ad verb. *opere*, quod accipio sicut *opifice*." The Arm. glossator renders, "concerning the interpretation of things."

[b] Of God with His powers, on the one hand, and of the three angels, on the other.

[c] Aucher renders more freely, "quae ex illis certior credenda sit."

[d] The Arm. verb = *ἐθίζειν, οἰκειοῦν, ἡμεροῦν*.

[e] *ὁσιότητος καὶ φιλανθρωπίας*.

[f] *ἰδέαν*.

[g] *μετοχὴ κοινωνίας vel sim.*

appearance is clear from Scripture, for whatever is said concerning one or to one or by one is brought as evidence of an appearance as God, while whatever is said concerning several or to several is of an appearance as of strange men.

For when it says,[a] " God appeared to him," and " Lord, if indeed I have found favour before Thee," and " Do not pass over thy servant," and, " Thus do as thou hast said," [b] and when it is said to him, " Where is Sarah, thy wife ? ", and " Again I will come to thee at this time," and " God said to him, why did Sarah laugh ? "—all these passages point to His appearance as God. But the following indicate an appearance as of strange men : " And lifting up his eyes, he looked, and three men were standing over him," and " He ran to them," and " Let your feet be washed," and " Refresh yourselves under the tree," and " Eat," [c] and " He stood before them," and " The men got up from there." So that through both piety and love of man [d] (Scripture) guides everyone who is considered civilized.[e] For in such civilized manner [f] did the founder and chief of our race [g] make his way of life an example. Seeing the vision before his eyes, which was not constant, being at one time that of God, at another time that of strangers, he decided to show piety as toward God, and equal oneness and love of man toward the strangers. Some, taking this as a point of departure, have gone astray in their beliefs, for they have been struck by the notion that there are measures and weights of proportion and structure.[h] As the clever and considerably learned Homer

[a] Gen. xviii. 2-15.

[b] This particular phrase does not indicate that one person is speaking.

[c] In the plural.

[d] δι' εὐσεβείας καὶ φιλανθρωπίας.

[e] Lit. " who is written in polity (πολιτείᾳ)."

[f] διὰ τοιαύτης πολιτείας.

[g] *i.e.* Abraham.

[h] Probably we should supply the words " in God," as does Aucher, who renders, " hinc ansa capta, nonnulli mensuram pondusque harmoniae corporeae excogitarunt (in Deo) abnormi opinione."

with beauty of sound describes the conduct of life, it is not right to be harmfully arrogant,[a] for he says that the Deity in the likeness of a beautiful human form is believed to appear many times, (in this) not diverging from the belief of a polytheist. His verses are as follows. "And yet the gods in the likeness of strangers from other lands, in all kinds of form go about unknown, seeing and beholding the many enmities of men and their lawlessness and also their good laws."[b]

3. (Gen. xviii. 2) Why does (Scripture) say, "And when he saw (them), he ran to meet them[c] and prostrated himself upon the ground"[d]?

It gives a warning to those who without reflexion and taking thought rush upon whatever happens to be there, without first thinking and looking, and it teaches them not to rush out before they clearly see and grasp what the matter is. Wherefore (Scripture) says, "Having seen, he ran," in order that when the perception of sight has first taken place, there may afterwards come an act that is irreproachable and pleasing. But excellently is it said that after his seeing, he then "ran forward," for having seen, he did not delay or tarry, but (like) one who has seen something worthy of this, hastened and ran toward them. Moreover, very discriminatingly does (Scripture) say that he made prostration "on the ground," for it would not be to mortal men that he prostrated himself but to Him

[a] This obscure clause is somewhat differently rendered by Aucher, "quem admodum severus ille, et sufficiens in scientia exponit Homerus, decore vitae ut pulchrae harmoniae non licere superbire, ac noxam subire."

[b] *Od.* xvii. 485-488; the same passage is paraphrased by Philo in *De Somniis* i. 233 with the comment, "The report may not be a true one but it is at any rate profitable and beneficial that it is made."

[c] Lit. "ran forward to them." Philo omits the words "from the entrance of the tent."

[d] LXX προσεκύνησεν ἐπὶ τὴν γῆν.

who is above heaven and earth, and is God of the whole world in common.[a]

4. (Gen. xviii. 3) (What is the meaning of the words), "Lord, if I have found favour before Thee, do not pass over [b] Thy servant"?

Now [c] his mind [d] clearly forms an impression with more open eyes and more lucid vision, not roaming about nor wandering off with the triad, and being attracted thereto by quantity and plurality, but running toward the one. And He manifested Himself without the powers [e] that belong to Him, so that he saw His oneness directly before him, as he had known it earlier in the likeness of a triad. But it is something great that he asks, (namely) that God shall not pass by nor remove to a distance and leave his soul desolate and empty.[f] For the limit [g] of happiness is the presence [h] of God, which completely fills the whole soul with His whole incorporeal and eternal light. And (the limit) of misery is (His) passing on the way, for immediately thereafter comes heavy and profound darkness and possesses (the soul). Wherefore also the fratricide Cain says, "Great is the guilt of my punishment that Thou leavest me," [i] indicating that there is no greater punishment for the soul than to be abandoned by God. Moreover, in another place Moses says, "Lest the Lord be

[a] κοινῇ.

[b] So LXX, μὴ παρέλθῃς. Heb. "do not pass from."

[c] *i.e.* on this occasion.

[d] ὁ νοῦς.

[e] ἄνευ τῶν δυνάμεων, *i.e.* the creative and kingly attributes.

[f] The Arm. uses two words to render ἐρήμην and two to render κενήν.

[g] ὁ ὅρος.

[h] The Arm. uses two words to render παρουσία.

[i] Gen. iv. 13, where LXX reads μείζων ἡ αἰτία μου τοῦ ἀφεθῆναί με. *Cf. QG* i. 73 where Philo takes this to mean that Cain is punished by being abandoned by God, not that his guilt is too great to be overlooked.

removed from them," [a] showing that for the soul to be separated from the contemplation of the Existent One [b] is the most complete of evils. For these reasons he [c] attempts to lead the people toward God, not (any men), for this is not possible, but god-loving souls which can (be led), when a heavenly love [d] and desire have come upon them and seized them.

5. (Gen. xviii. 4) Why does he again say, in the plural, "Let water be taken and let them wash [e] your feet, and do you refresh yourselves [f] under the thick [g] tree"?

This again applies to the other appearance, in accordance with which he thought them strangers, having reached a stage of knowledge which was not certain, but again being attracted and strongly drawn by a most excellent and divine countenance.[h] Wherefore he does not give a command like a lord and master, nor does he presume to offer washing of the feet to freemen or servants but (regards) Him who had made Himself directly visible as the one who gives commands, saying, "Let water be taken," and does not add by whom. And again (in saying) "Let them wash (your) feet," he does not make clear whom nor make it known exactly, because, as it seems to me, he did not have confidence and assurance concerning the sense-perceptible appearance as (being one) of men seen, but rather that it was intelligible, as if a divine manifestation had been made. Something like this is clear from Scripture, (namely) that

[a] Probably, as Aucher suggests, a reference to Ex. xix. 22, where LXX reads μήποτε ἀπαλλάξῃ ἀπ' αὐτῶν κύριος.

[b] τοῦ Ὄντος.

[c] Apparently Moses is meant.

[d] ἔρως.

[e] Philo reads νιψάτωσαν, as do some LXX MSS.; most LXX MSS. have νιψάτω. The Masoretic Heb. has 2nd pl. imperative, "wash ye," but the consonantal (*i.e.* unvocalized) Heb. can also be read as 3rd pl. perfect, here meaning "let them wash."

[f] LXX καταψύξατε.

[g] No adjective is used in LXX or Heb.

[h] προσώπου or ὄψεως.

men are sanctified when washed with water, while the water itself (is sanctified) by the divine foot. Now symbolically [a] the foot is the last [b] and lowest (part) of the body, while to the air is allotted the last portion [c] of divine things, for it animates [d] the congregated things that have been created.[e] For if (the air) does not touch and move this (water), it dies; and it becomes alive through nothing else than having air mixed in with it. Wherefore not ineptly [f] is it said at the beginning of the genesis of creatures [g] that "the spirit of God was borne upon the waters," which (Scripture) in allegorizing [h] on this occasion symbolically calls "the foot."

6. (Gen. xviii. 5) Why does he say in this fashion, "I will take bread, and eat ye," [i] and not, "Take ye"?

Here again he shows his doubt and his inclination toward either appearance. For when it is said, "I will take," he imagines it to be God, to Whom he does not dare to say, "Take [j] food." But when (he says), "Eat," [k] he imagines it to be the three strange men. That is the literal meaning.[l] But as for the deeper meaning,[m] when the mind begins to prepare and order itself and to take the divine and holy foods, which are the laws and forms of wisdom,[n] then it is symbolically [o] said to eat also of divine (food); and this is the food that is fitting for the heavenly Olympians,[p]

[a] συμβολικῶς. [b] τὸ ἔσχατον.
[c] ὁ ἔσχατος κλῆρος. [d] ψυχῶν.
[e] τὰ συναχθέντα κτιστά *vel sim.*, *i.e.* the gathering together of the waters, mentioned in Gen. i. 10 (LXX τὰ συστήματα τῶν ὑδάτων).
[f] οὐκ ἀπὸ σκοποῦ.
[g] Gen. i. 2. [h] ἀλληγορῶν.
[i] LXX λήμψομαι ἄρτον, καὶ φάγεσθε.
[j] Imperative sing.
[k] Imperative plural. [l] τὸ ῥητόν.
[m] τὸ πρὸς διάνοιαν.
[n] οἱ νόμοι καὶ αἱ ἰδέαι τῆς σοφίας.
[o] συμβολικῶς.
[p] Aucher renders, "caelestem Olympum."

(namely) the desires and yearnings of the rational soul,[a] which it uses for the apprehension of wisdom and the acquisition of perfect virtue.[b]

7. (Gen. xviii. 5) Why does He say,[c] "So do as thou hast said"?

He reproves those of two minds and two tongues, who say one thing and do the opposite. But the virtuous man[d] He sets apart[e] and determines that he shall be saved[f] through either order,[g] his words first being inclined toward deeds, and his deeds toward words.[h] For just as his words are, so is his life,[i] and as his life is, so do the words of the wise man appear.

*8. (Gen. xviii. 6-7) Why do they all hasten? For (Scripture) says, "Abraham hastened to the tent to Sarah and said to her, Hasten and mix three measures of wheat-flour[j] and make ash-cakes.[k] And he ran to the cattle and took a tender[l] calf and gave it to the boy,[m] and he hastened to do this.[n]"

This is a eulogy of the virtuous man according to either

[a] *τῆς λογικῆς ψυχῆς.*

[b] *τῆς τελείας ἀρετῆς.*

[c] Most LXX MSS. have *εἶπεν*. Some LXX MSS. and ancient versions have *εἶπαν*. Heb. has "they said."

[d] *τὸν σπουδαῖον.*

[e] Or "approves of."

[f] *σώζεσθαι.* Aucher renders less literally, "vivere."

[g] *δι' ἑκατέρας τάξεως.*

[h] *λόγοι* contrasted with *ἔργα*.

[i] *βίος* or *διαγωγή*.

[j] LXX *σεμιδάλεως*.

[k] LXX *ἐγκρυφίας*. Heb. *'ugôth* is rendered in A.V. as "cakes upon the hearth."

[l] LXX and Heb. add "and goodly."

[m] *i.e.* his servant.

[n] LXX *ποιῆσαι αὐτό*, rendering Heb. *la'aśôth 'ôthô*, which here means not "to do this" but "to prepare him" (the calf).

appearance.[a] For if it was the strange men whom he believed to have come to him, he is to be admired for his humanity and hospitality.[b] And if (he thought) that it was God who had come to him together with His chief powers, he was blessed and fortunate. Now, as to what they did for the appearance of the strange men, Abraham and his wife and his boy must be thought hospitable persons. But as to what they did for the powers of God, they must no longer be thought hospitable persons but incorporeal.[c] And the man and woman are (to be considered) ideas,[d] one being that of the most pure mind,[e] which is called Abraham, and the other that of the perfection of virtue,[f] which is called Sarah, while that which is the utterance of thought[g] is[h] named "boy." And without delay or hesitation the mind and the virtues hasten under pressure[i] to please[j] and serve God and His powers. And the mind rules[k] in the manner of an overseer[l] and becomes a helper and stimulator in that which it is proper to do, while virtue shows unhesitating speed in the completion of the three portions and the ash-cakes. Speech,[m] moreover, brings the offering that is commanded.

And most natural[n] is the passage concerning the three measures,[o] for in reality[p] all things are measured by three,

[a] *i.e.* either the three "strange men" or God.
[b] *τῆς φιλανθρωπίας καὶ τῆς φιλοξενίας.*
[c] *ἀσωμάτους.* [d] *ἰδέας.*
[e] *τοῦ καθαρωτάτου νοῦ.*
[f] *τελειότητος τῆς ἀρετῆς.*
[g] The Arm. lit. = *προφορὰ τοῦ λόγου.* Elsewhere in Philo the expressions *ὁ κατὰ προφορὰν λόγος* or *λόγος προφορικός* are used.
[h] There is an intrusive rel. pron. before the verb in the Arm. text.
[i] *ἐπειγόμενοι vel sim.* [j] Or "to attend."
[k] Or "leads (them)."
[l] *ἐπιστάτου vel sim.*
[m] *ὁ λόγος.* [n] *φυσικώτατος.*
[o] For a somewhat different allegorizing of the three measures and ash-cakes see *De Sacr. Abelis* 59-62.
[p] Prob. *ὄντως.*

having a beginning, middle and end. And each of these partial things [a] is empty if it does not have (the others), similarly constituted.[b] Wherefore Homer not ineptly says that "all things are divided into three." [c] And the Pythagoreans assume that the triad among numbers, and the right-angled triangle among figures are the foundation of the knowledge of all things.[d] And so, one measure is that by which the incorporeal and intelligible world was constituted.[e] And the second measure is that by which the perceptible heaven was established in the fifth (element), attaining to a more wonderful and divine essence, unaltered and unchanged in comparison with these (things below),[f] and remaining the same.[g] And the third measure is the way in which sublunary things were made out of the four powers,[h] earth, water, air and fire,[i] admitting generation and corruption.[j] Now the measure of the incorporeal

[a] *ἕκαστον τῶν κατὰ μέρος.*

[b] This sentence is rendered more freely by Aucher, "quorum utrumque inane comperitur absque tertia parte, carens existentia."

[c] *Iliad* xv. 189 *τριχθὰ δὲ πάντα δέδασται.*

[d] Staehle, p. 25, cites Joh. Lydus, p. 25, 12-16, who is probably dependent upon Philo, and quotes the same passage from Homer. Lydus' text continues, *διὰ μὲν τοῦτο οἱ Πυθαγόρειοι τριάδα μὲν ἐν ἀριθμοῖς, ἐν δὲ σχήμασι τὸ ὀρθογώνιον τρίγωνον ὑποτίθενται στοιχεῖον τῆς τῶν ὅλων γενέσεως* (Arm. Philo = *γνώσεως*).

[e] Joh. Lydus has *ἓν μὲν οὖν μέτρον ἐστί, καθ' ὃ συνέστη ὁ ἀσώματος καὶ νοητὸς κόσμος.*

[f] Aucher's rendering, "secundum illud," misses the point of the contrast between the heavenly sphere and the sublunary regions.

[g] Joh. Lydus reads slightly differently *δεύτερον δὲ μέτρον, καθ' ὃ ἐπάγη ὁ αἰσθητὸς οὐρανός, πέμπτην λαχὼν καὶ θειοτέραν οὐσίαν, ἄτρεπτον καὶ ἀμετάβολον.*

[h] So also Joh. Lydus, *τρίτον δὲ καθ' ὃ ἐδημιουργήθη τὰ ὑπὸ σελήνην, ἐκ τῶν τεσσάρων δυνάμεων* (not *στοιχείων*, as one would expect).

[i] The four elements are not named in Lydus' text.

[j] *γένεσιν καὶ φθορὰν ἐπιδεχόμενα*, as in Joh. Lydus, whose parallel text ends here.

forms [a] by which the intelligible world was constituted must be said to be the eldest of causes.[b] And (the cause) of the fifth, perceptible and circular essence,[c] which the heaven has had allotted to it, is the creative power of the Existent One,[d] for it has found an imperishable, pure and unmixed blessing [e] in obtaining an immortal and incorruptible portion. But the kingly (power) [f] (is the cause) of sublunary things, those that (are subject to) change and alteration because they participate in generation and corruption. But (He gives) speech as an aid for guidance in a certain one [g] when something is to be done, for the sake of those who carry out and complete something. And to those who sin in some measure (there is assigned) corrective reformation through deserved punishments and chastisements. But those who commit indescribable and inexpressible wrongs are punished through retributive chastisement and banishment.[h]

So that truly and properly speaking, God alone is the measure of all things, both intelligible and sense-perceptible, and He in His oneness is likened to a triad because of the weakness [i] of the beholders. For the eye of the soul, which is very lucid and bright, is dimmed before it falls upon and gazes at Him who is in His oneness without anyone else at all being seen. For just as the eyes of the body when they are weak, often come upon [j] a double

[a] τῶν ἀσωμάτων ἰδεῶν.

[b] τὸ πρεσβύτατον τῶν αἰτίων.

[c] *i.e.* the sphere of the fixed stars.

[d] ἡ τοῦ Ὄντος ποιητικὴ δύναμις. On the two powers of God see *QG* ii. 51, iv. 2 *et al.*

[e] More literally " benevolence."

[f] ἡ βασιλικὴ (δύναμις).

[g] The Arm. seems lit. to render τὸν λόγον (ὡς) ἐν ἑνί τινι ἡγεμονίας ἀντίληψιν, but the meaning is obscure to me. Aucher renders, " verbum vero certum regiminis auxilium praebet."

[h] Apparently banishment from God's presence is meant.

[i] διὰ τὴν ἀσθένειαν.

[j] The first of the two Arm. verbs used here I cannot translate.

appearance from a single lamp, so also in the case of the soul's vision, it is not able to attain to the One as one but finds it natural to receive an impression of the triad in accordance with the appearances that attend the One like ministers, (namely) the chief powers.

Wherefore Moses, the chief prophet and chief messenger,[a] desired to see the One without His powers, as one in His oneness, to which no one by art or wisdom or anything else that exists [b] hoped to be adequate or to reach the upper regions by advancing upward from below. For he wished to receive the chiefest of all (blessings) [c] and to be granted the mercy of having (Him) appear to the god-loving soul all alone without any other (being present), for he says, "Show Thyself to me that I may see Thee knowingly.[d]"

But most excellently, after the three measures, does (Scripture) speak of the ash-cakes, not only because knowledge and understanding of the wisdom of the Father and His two highest powers are hidden [e] from many, but also because such an inquiry [f] should not be spoken of to all. For to reveal mysteries to uninitiated and unworthy men is the act of one who destroys and sacks and undermines the laws of the mysteries of divine perfection.[g] O thrice happy and thrice fortunate soul, in which God has not disdained to dwell and move and to make it His palace and home, that the giver of joy may have joy, for this is really

[a] ὁ ἀρχιπροφήτης καὶ ὁ ἀρχάγγελος.

[b] Lit. "is in genesis."

[c] τὸ ἀρχικόν.

[d] *Cf.* LXX of Ex. xxxiii. 13 ἐμφάνισόν μοι σεαυτόν, γνωστῶς ἴδω σε, which is quoted by Philo in *Leg. All.* iii. 101 and elsewhere. The Heb. has "Show me Thy ways that I may know Thee."

[e] Philo plays on the word ἐγκρυφίας "ash-cakes," as if meaning "hidden."

[f] ζήτησις.

[g] The Arm. translator has evidently mistaken τελετῆς "initiation" for τελειότητος "perfection"; *cf.* the Greek frag. from Dam. Par. τοῖς ἀμυήτοις ἐκλαλεῖν μυστήρια καταλύοντός ἐστι τοὺς θεσμοὺς τῆς ἱερατικῆς τελετῆς.

genuine and true.[a] For while those who receive men[b] show joy and conviviality, the most pure mind[c] is wholly filled and overflowing with the appearance of God, and it (alone) may properly be said to feast and rejoice lavishly. And may it not be that this is fitting and proper? For the host is in need and in want, while He who came to him is in need of nothing but is most rich and great,[d] and after Him come fountains of ever-flowing good, from which not all men but only those who are well and genuinely purified can drink, being invited to symposia of joy, in which the souls[e] of prophets and messengers rejoice and eat the food of the voluntary laws[f] of imperishable and pure wisdom at the invitation and through the entertainment of God.

9. (Gen. xviii. 8) Why does (Scripture) say, " He placed (it) before them,[g] and they ate "?

It is clear that " they ate " (is said) symbolically[h] and not of food, for these happy and blessed natures do not eat food or drink red wine,[i] but it is (an indication) of their readiness in understanding and assenting to those who appeal to them and put their trust in them.[j] For just as human guests who are hospitably received and are glad-

[a] Apparently the word " joy " is to be understood.

[b] *i.e.* into their homes.

[c] ὁ καθαρώτατος νοῦς.

[d] *Cf. De Abrahamo* 167 ἐν οἷς δοκῶν ἑστιᾶν ὁ ξενοδόχος εἱστιᾶτο.

[e] Or " spirits."

[f] ἑκουσίων νόμων, *cf. De Mut. Nom.* 26 ἑκουσίους ἅπαντας νόμους (Colson conj. μώμους). The text in both passages is suspect.

[g] LXX παρέθηκεν αὐτοῖς.

[h] συμβολικῶς.

[i] *Cf. De Abrahamo* 118 " It is a marvel indeed that though they neither ate nor drank they gave the appearance of both eating and drinking."

[j] Aucher renders more freely, " sed annuendi benignitati fidenter rogantis indicio est."

dened with food rejoice in their host and entertainer, so does the Deity in those whom He finds sincerely and genuinely pleasing to Him. For, more figuratively,[a] the pious and worthy life of a virtuous man is the food of God.

*10. (Gen. xviii. 8) Why is it said, " And he was standing before them [b] under the tree " ?

That he had a multitude of servants is clear from the flock of 318 house-slaves [c] with whom he fought the kings of the gentiles.[d] (But) he himself becomes an attendant and servant [e] to show his hospitality, if he believed them to be men, and his worthy way of life and love of God, if (he believed them to be) the divine powers appearing with the Father, for he thinks it right to perform the service of piety himself.[f]

11. (Gen. xviii. 9) Why does He again say [g] in the singular, " Where is Sarah, thy wife, and he answered, In the tent " ?

The literal meaning [h] is clear from what has been said before. But as for the deeper meaning,[i] (he so answers) because in some sense virtue is the wife and consort of the wise man,[j] and through her are born virtuous thoughts and

[a] *τροπικώτερον*. Aucher has " commodius."

[b] So Arm. O.T.: LXX *παρειστήκει αὐτοῖς*: Heb. " was standing by (or " over ") them." In the Heb. the whole clause precedes the phrase " and they ate," which Philo, following the LXX order of words, has discussed in the preceding section.

[c] *οἰκογενῶν*, *cf.* Gen. xiv. 14. [d] *τῶν ἀλλοφύλων*.

[e] Lit. " attendant of service."

[f] *Cf.* the Greek frag. (paraphrastic) from Procopius, *αὐτουργῶν δὲ τὴν ὑπηρεσίαν*.

[g] Some LXX MSS. and the Heb. have " they said."

[h] *τὸ ῥητόν*. [i] *τὸ πρὸς διάνοιαν*.

[j] *τρόπον τινὰ γυνὴ καὶ σύμβιός ἐστι τοῦ σοφοῦ ἡ ἀρετή*. In the parallel allegory, *Quod Deterius* 59-61, Philo actually substitutes " virtue " for " Sarah " in citing the biblical verse.

fine deeds and praiseworthy words. To this question he replies, " Behold, virtue is not only in my mind [a] but also in an empty and safe tent, in my body, extending itself and spreading as far as the senses [b] and the other functional parts [c] (of the body). For in accordance with virtue I see and hear and smell and taste and touch, and I make other movements in accordance with wisdom, health, fortitude and justice. [d] "

12. (Gen. xviii. 10) Why does He say in the singular, " Returning I will come to thee at this season at hours,[e] and a son will be born to Sarah thy wife " ?

Why (He speaks) in the singular has long ago [f] been said. For in what is now related it is not men but the Father of all whom he imagines [g] to have come with His powers. But His gracious act [h] He postpones in order to give his soul a more certain test of visitation. For He wishes to make his thirst greater by the delay and to give him an unmeasured desire for piety.[i] But " season " [j] is not merely the name of a time [k] (but is found) together with completion,[l] for the season is the time (required) for

[a] ἐν τῷ ἐμῷ νῷ.

[b] τὰς αἰσθήσεις.

[c] τὰ ὀργανικὰ μέρη. The same phrase is used in *De Congressu* 115.

[d] The original prob. had the four Platonic virtues, φρόνησις, σωφροσύνη, ἀνδρεία, δικαιοσύνη.

[e] LXX κατὰ τὸν καιρὸν τοῦτον εἰς ὥρας (Arm. O.T. " at this time in these days "). The Heb. has simply " at the time of living," prob. meaning " at the time of giving birth." This biblical phrase is briefly commented on by Philo in *De Migratione* 126 and *De Abrahamo* 132 ; in the former passage Philo has εἰς ὥρας as here, in the latter, εἰς νέωτα " next year."

[f] πάλαι: Aucher " iam." Prob. the reference is to *QG* iv. 2.

[g] φαντάζεται.

[h] τὴν χάριν.

[i] ἄπειρον πόθον τῆς εὐσεβείας.

[j] καιρός.

[k] χρόνου.

[l] σὺν τῷ περαίνειν (πληροῦν, λύειν, etc.). The sense is not clear. Aucher renders, " sed cum debita solutione rerum."

completing a reformation.[a] And clear evidence of the completion of every reformation [b] is what He has said.[c] For it is peculiar [d] to the divine power to complete something by the reformation of those also to whom He wishes to show favour.[e] And He mentions " hours " not so much (in the sense) of length of time and intervals as for the aptness of order. For it was natural [f] to order and arrange the period of the year by seasons. And these He makes a symbol [g] of the soul which comes from disorder into order and proper arrangement,[h] and to this He says he will grant, if He sees it remaining in order and evenness, a better progeny through a nature that rises [i] by itself.[j]

13. (Gen. xviii. 10) Why does (Scripture) say, " And Sarah heard, for she was by the entrance of the tent behind him " [k] ?

[a] *ἐπανορθώσεως.*

[b] Emending the noun *ullout'iun* from nom. to gen. case.

[c] This obscure sentence is differently punctuated and construed by Aucher, who renders, " persolvendi autem omnem rectitudinem. Manifestam huic facit fidem ille, qui (*vel*, illud quod) dixit."

[d] *ἴδιον.*

[e] Aucher renders differently and, I think, less accurately, " proprium enim ac certum est per divinam virtutem persolvi quidquam recte, sicut et per illos quibus velit concedere."

[f] *εἰκός.* [g] *σύμβολον.*

[h] *εἰς τάξιν καὶ ἄξιον κόσμον.*

[i] Or " proceeds."

[j] The syntax is not clear. Aucher renders, " generationem meliorem natura ipsius per se edocti," but there is no indication of a comparison in the Arm. The " nature that rises by itself " is perhaps an allusion to Isaac who is elsewhere referred to by Philo as a symbol of self-taught virtue.

[k] LXX *Σάρρα δὲ ἤκουσεν πρὸς τῇ θύρᾳ τῆς σκηνῆς οὖσα ὄπισθεν αὐτοῦ.* For " she was behind him " Heb. has " it (or " he ") was behind him," possibly using the masc. pron. *hû'* as a feminine, as occasionally in older Heb., in which case LXX renders correctly.

The literal meaning [a] seems to be clear, but the deeper meaning [b] is perhaps as follows. Virtue [c] stands behind [d] the one who is virtuous by nature, not like a slave-boy but like a perfect administrator and governor,[e] who holds the reins in his hands, directs the entire soul and way of life. For those in front do not see those behind, while those who are behind see those who stand beside them. And the proper place for virtue to stand is at the entrance; and the entrance to reflexion [f] is speech,[g] and each of the senses is (the entrance) to a vital part of the soul. For when this [h] is near at hand, it must necessarily say and perceive what is fitting.

14. (Gen. xviii. 11) Why does (Scripture) say, "Abraham and Sarah were old and advanced in days" [i]?

It tells us of the lawful years,[j] teaching us that the foolish man is a child and a crude person, for even though he may be advanced in age, his folly produces childishness. But the wise man, even though he may be in the prime of youthfulness, is old, and virtue is old and venerable, since it is worthy of old age and higher honour. Wherefore rightly does (Scripture) speak of old age and being "advanced in days," for it is fitting that days and months and years and all intervals and solar lengths (of time) should not be lacking to virtue, which nature has exalted with priority and headship. And in addition to these there is the substance of the light, or rather the mind [k] is luminous in the several disciplines of knowledge. And so this

[a] τὸ ῥητόν.
[b] τὸ πρὸς διάνοιαν.
[c] ἡ ἀρετή, symbolized by Sarah.
[d] Lit. "at the back side of."
[e] ὡς τέλειος οἰκονόμος καὶ κυβερνήτης.
[f] τῷ λογισμῷ.
[g] ὁ λόγος.
[h] *i.e.* virtue.
[i] LXX προβεβηκότες.
[j] ἔτη νόμιμα *vel sim.*, apparently meaning lawfully responsible or law-observant age rather than chronological age. One Arm. MS. has "wishes" for "years."
[k] ὁ νοῦς.

symbol[a] purports to show that virtue is (composed) of all the sciences as light (is) of light.[b]

15. (Gen. xviii. 11) What is the meaning of the words, "There ceased to be to Sarah the ways of women"[c]?

The literal meaning[d] is clear. For (Scripture) by a euphemism calls the monthly purification of women "the ways of women." But as for the deeper meaning,[e] it is to be allegorized[f] as follows. The soul has, as it were, a dwelling, partly men's quarters, partly women's quarters.[g] Now for the men there is a place where properly dwell the masculine thoughts (that are) wise, sound, just, prudent, pious, filled with freedom and boldness,[h] and kin to wisdom. And the women's quarters are a place where womanly opinions go about and dwell, being followers[i] of the female sex. And the female sex is irrational[j] and akin to bestial[k] passions, fear, sorrow, pleasure and desire, from which ensue incurable weaknesses and[l] indescribable diseases. He who is conquered by these is unhappy, while he who controls[m] them is happy. And longing for and

[a] τοῦτο τὸ σύμβολον.

[b] The connexion of the last two sentences with the preceding is not clear. Perhaps Philo refers to a comparison between Sarah (=virtue) being "advanced in days" and the light of day.

[c] LXX ἐξέλειπεν δὲ Σάρρᾳ γίνεσθαι τὰ γυναίκια. Heb. has "there ceased to be to Sarah a way like (that of) women." This half-verse is commented on or referred to by Philo in *De Cherubim* 50, *Quod Deterius* 28, *De Poster. Caini* 134, *De Ebrietate* 60, *De Fuga* 128, 167, *De Somniis* ii. 185. In all of these passages Philo briefly gives about the same allegorical explanation as here.

[d] τὸ ῥητόν.

[e] τὸ πρὸς διάνοιαν.

[f] ἀλληγορεῖται.

[g] γυναικῶν, here connected with LXX τὰ γυναίκια (=τὰ καταμήνια).

[h] ἐλευθερίας καὶ παρρησίας.

[i] ζηλωταί.

[j] ἄλογον.

[k] Or "irrational."

[l] Lit. "of."

[m] Or "repels," "reduces"; Aucher renders, "usus fuit (prudenter)."

desiring this happiness, and seizing a certain time to be able to escape from terrible and unbearable sorrow, which is (what is meant by) "there ceased to be the ways of women"—this clearly belongs to minds full of Law,[a] which resemble the male sex and overcome passions and rise above all sense-pleasure and desire and are without sorrow and fear and, if one must speak the truth, without passion,[b] not zealously[c] practising apathy,[d] for this would be ungrateful[e] and shameless and akin to arrogance and reckless boldness, but that which is consistent with the argument given,[f] (namely) cutting the mind off from disturbing and confusing passions.

16. (Gen. xviii. 12) What is the meaning of the words, "And Sarah laughed within herself, saying, Not yet has anything happened until now,[g] and my lord is old"?

The mind,[h] which was about to be filled with joy and divine laughter, had not yet been freed from sorrow, fear, sense-pleasure and desire, by which it is shaken and compelled to stagger.[i] And when the mind is moved,[j] it does not know laughter, except perhaps for its visible

[a] νόμου or "religion"—θρησκείας.
[b] ἀπαθεῖς.
[c] Variant "shamefully."
[d] ἀπάθειαν.
[e] Arm. *angoy* "non-existent" is clearly a scribal error for *angoh* "ungrateful."
[f] Text and meaning uncertain; Aucher renders, "quae consistit juxta praedictum verbum," adding in a footnote, "ita MS. A, ubi C, D *dicens* vel *prolativum verbum.*"
[g] LXX οὔπω μέν μοι γέγονεν ἕως τοῦ νῦν. The Heb. is different, "After I have become worn, will there be pleasure to me?" The Arm. O.T. has a compromise, "What has not happened to me until now, will it then happen?" This verse is commented on by Philo in *De Mut. Nom.* 166-169; see also *De Spec. Leg.* ii. 54.
[h] ὁ νοῦς or ἡ διάνοια.
[i] καρηβαρεῖν.
[j] *i.e.* by passion.

appearance,[a] until a firm foundation is laid for a very strong and stable position; for, in the fashion of the science of agriculture, virtue[b] does not appear only on the surface and lose its flowers, but it always lasts a long time in a flourishing state, being held together by an invisible bond. Similarly does (Scripture) introduce the high priest[c] rejoicing inwardly and released[d] from all corporeal thoughts and entering into joy,[e] for it says, "And seeing thee he will rejoice within himself." Very reverently does she[f] afterwards say, "Not yet has anything happened until now, and my lord is old," for this shows that having wholly forgotten passion through teaching, she has begun to rejoice, and that she is not yet perfect in attaining the end of perfect joy, whose true and genuine appearance she confesses to have been changed into an elder one.[g]

17. (Gen. xviii. 13-14) Why is Sarah, as it were, rebuked, while Abraham laughed and was not rebuked? For (Scripture) says, "And the Lord said to Abraham, Why is it that[h] Sarah laughed, saying,[i] Shall I then truly bear, and[j] I am old? Can it be that anything is impossible for God?"

That the divine words are deeds and powers is clear from the preceding, for there is no impossibility[k] for the Deity.

[a] *i.e.* merely external laughter, *cf. De Mut. Nom.* 169 κἂν προσποιῆται τῷ προσώπῳ μειδιᾶν.

[b] ἡ ἀρετή.

[c] Aaron, in Ex. iv. 14. The same verse is cited by Philo in the parallel, *De Mut. Nom.* 168.

[d] Lit. "spread out"; Aucher "quod superat."

[e] Aucher omits the last four words.

[f] Sarah.

[g] πρεσβύτερον.

[h] Some LXX MSS. and ancient versions, including Arm., have τί ὅτι, which closely follows Heb. "why then?", but most LXX MSS. have simply ὅτι.

[i] So Heb.; LXX ἐγέλασεν Σάρρα ἐν ἑαυτῇ λέγουσα.

[j] *i.e.* "seeing that."

[k] ἀδυνατία.

But the rebuke would seem to indicate praise rather than personal [a] blame according to natural expectation.[b] For she wonders that when all the necessary and plausible conditions have been removed by which birth can be successfully accomplished, a new act should be sown by God in the whole soul for the birth of joy and great gladness, which in Armenian [c] is called " laughter," and in Chaldaean, " Isaac." [d] But Abraham was delivered and, as it were, escaped rebuke and reprobation, being secured by an unswerving and inflexible conviction of faith,[e] for to him who has faith in God all uncertainty is alien.

18. (Gen. xviii. 14) What is the meaning of the words, " At this season I will return to thee at hours,[f] and a son will be born to Sarah " ?

(Scripture) manifestly and very clearly demonstrates that if God returns to the soul, and the soul returns to Him,[g] He immediately shows it to be filled with joy,[h] the name of which is feminine, while its nature [i] is masculine. For sorrowful and suffering is he from whom God is distant, and full of joy and gladness is he to whom He is near. Joy (consists) in seeming to receive the most lucid radiance that is brought from above.[j]

[a] Or " direct " (?)—ἐκ προσώπου (?).

[b] κατὰ φυσικὴν προσδοκίαν, apparently meaning the expectation of the reader of Scripture.

[c] *i.e.* " Greek."

[d] This is only one of several passages where Philo plays on the meaning of " Isaac," Heb. *yiṣḥaq* = " he laughs."

[e] ἀτρέπτῳ καὶ ἀρρεπεῖ λογισμῷ πίστεως *vel sim.*

[f] LXX εἰς ὥρας. Heb. " at the time of living." See note *e* to *QG* iv. 12 on Gen. xviii. 10.

[g] Aucher inadvertently omits to render the second part of the conditional clause.

[h] χαρᾶς.

[i] φύσις.

[j] Aucher renders somewhat differently, " ita ut pro laetitia lucidiores recepisse se existimabit radios desuper allatos."

19. (Gen. xviii. 15) Why is it that " Sarah made a denial, saying, I did not laugh, for she was afraid. And He said, No, but thou didst laugh " [a] ?

Appropriately this happened to a pious character,[b] who saw the greatness of God and her incapacity to bear (children) and the imminence [c] (of this event). For where does (Scripture) [d] say that she is able to rejoice wholly [e] with most radiant and unmixed joy, when she is involved in sorrow and fear and in many other misfortunes ? But may it not be that rejoicing is peculiar [f] to the divine nature alone, from the territory of Whose kingdom [g] and from its borders are kept out and banished sorrow and fear ? And so, when the soul laughs and seems to rejoice, it takes hold of itself,[h] fearing that perchance through too great ignorance or reckless confidence it may drive away [i] something of the divine, to Whom alone is given the portion [j] of a happy nature. Wherefore, accepting in a gracious, affectionate and benevolent manner the mind's modest humility [k] of prayerfulness and reverence, He says to it, " Do not be afraid, for the matter does not call for [l] fear, that thou shouldst make denial.[m] Accordingly, thou hast laughed and wast filled with joy, for I am about to give thee (cause) for rejoicing, like a stream rushing from a spring, or a form of the archetype,[n] or a mixture of unmixed, pure and whole (wine)—like these (shall be thy joy),[o] for the generation of children is by a double number." [p]

[a] This verse is more briefly allegorized by Philo in *De Abrahamo* 206-207.

[b] θεοσεβεῖ τρόπῳ. Aucher renders, " eventus accidit exempli pietatis opportunus."

[c] τὸ πρόσκαιρον *vel sim.*

[d] Or " she."

[e] ἁπλῶς.

[f] ἴδιον.

[g] βασιλείας.

[h] ἐπιλαμβάνεται ἑαυτῆς.

[i] *i.e.* " alienate."

[j] κλῆρος.

[k] Prob. αἰδῶ καὶ ἐντροπήν.

[l] Lit. " is not worthy of."

[m] *i.e.* of having laughed.

[n] μορφὴν ἐξ ἀρχετύπου.

[o] *i.e.* the soul's joy is an inferior form of its source, the divine joy.

[p] As Aucher notes, this may refer to the double birth, of Isaac and of the soul's joy.

*20. (Gen. xviii. 16) Why did Abraham " go with them, escorting them " [a] ?

Through the literal meaning [b] (Scripture) shows the abundance of the humaneness [c] with which he was endowed,[d] for he had willingly given them whatever was fitting, together with his household, and also he could hardly be separated from them and was so much grieved at parting that he continued and persisted in escorting them ; and in this, it seems to me, he took as his example what the poet [e] fittingly says, " It is proper to welcome a stranger when he comes, and to give him a send-off when he wishes to go," for this shows a most generous and agreeable nature.[f] However, it is not proper to leave unnoticed the deeper meaning.[g] When once the soul of the virtuous man [h] has received a very clear impression [i] of God and His powers,[j] it is filled with longing,[k] and hardly or not at all can it be separated and parted (from Him). If He is with it and remains, it adores Him and holds Him and possesses Him. And if He moves away, it follows Him with longing, having a heavenly desire that clings [l] and

[a] Philo cites only the second half of the verse, the whole of which reads, in the LXX, Ἐξαναστάντες δὲ ἐκεῖθεν οἱ ἄνδρες κατέβλεψαν ἐπὶ πρόσωπον Σοδόμων καὶ Γομόρρας. Ἀβραὰμ δὲ συνεπορεύετο μετ' αὐτῶν συνπροπέμπων αὐτούς. The second half of the verse is commented on also in *De Migratione* 173-175.

[b] διὰ τοῦ ῥητοῦ.

[c] τῆς φιλανθρωπίας.

[d] Construction and meaning uncertain. Aucher omits the participle in his rendering.

[e] ὁ ποιητής, *i.e.* Homer in *Od.* xv. 74, χρὴ ξεῖνον παρέοντα φιλεῖν ἐθέλοντα δὲ πέμπειν (said by Menelaus to Telemachus on the latter's departure).

[f] κοινωνικώτατον καὶ σύμφωνον (*vel sim.*) ἦθος. The Greek frag. from Procopius has simply κοινωνικώτατον ἦθος.

[g] τὸ πρὸς διάνοιαν.

[h] τοῦ σπουδαίου.

[i] φαντασίαν, or " appearance "—ἐπιφάνειαν.

[j] τῶν δυνάμεων, referring to the two angels ; see the preceding sections.

[k] πόθου.

[l] Lit. " that is glued."

adheres closely. For not ineptly [a] is it said that "he went with them," but for a more certain demonstration of the powers of the Father, which he surely [b] knew were not even for a little while far off.

21. (Gen. xviii. 17) Why does He say, "Shall I conceal [c] from my servant Abraham what I do?"?

O happy soul, to which God has shown nature [d] and what is in accordance with [e] nature, when the veil has been removed and various works have been revealed for more effective comprehension! [f] This is the consummation of the contemplative life and all the virtues,[g] (namely) to see nature naked and the coverings of nature by which it is concealed, after the Lord and Father has removed them and clearly shown His works to the mind,[h] than which nothing is to be honoured as a finer sight or more worth seeing and studying. For those who do not philosophize properly [i] with the eyes of the soul are blinded and cannot see either the world [j] or the things that are in it. For all things are deservedly [k] spread out,[l] and concealed from those who cannot see.

22. (Gen. xviii. 19) Why does He say, "I know that he will command his sons and his household after him, and they will observe the ways of the Lord to do righteousness

[a] οὐκ ἀπὸ σκοποῦ. [b] Or "constantly."

[c] LXX μὴ (variant οὐ μὴ) κρύψω here renders a Heb. question, expecting a negative answer.

[d] τὴν φύσιν.

[e] Variant "beyond."

[f] Arm. = εἰς ἐνεργοτέραν κατάληψιν. I suspect that the original adj. was ἐναργεστέραν "clearer."

[g] τοῦ θεωρητικοῦ βίου καὶ πασῶν ἀρετῶν τελείωσις. One Arm. MS. omits "and all the virtues."

[h] τῷ νῷ.

[i] οἰκείως, or "genuinely"—γνησίως.

[j] τὸν κόσμον. [k] ἀξίως.

[l] *i.e.* for the discerning.

and justice,[a] that He[b] may bring upon Abraham that which He said[c] to him"?

(Scripture) clearly shows the prescient power of the Existent One[d] in saying, "For I know[e] that he will command." For it is natural[f] for created beings to know various things from their fulfilment, while for God (it is natural) to know future happenings[g] before their beginning. And the virtuous man[h] is deserving of honour and glory, for he not only himself honours virtue[i] but also produces[j] the desire for it in others. And of honour He spoke before.[k] For sight consists in[l] nakedness and removing the veil of nature, and, with the keen eyes that belong to the mind[m] converting the perception of incorporeal light into a clear apprehension,[n] in finding a more weighty promise,[o] which relegates to a second place[p] the aetiological ideas that belong to philosophy.[q] For it is necessary that the soul which clearly knows and is able

[a] LXX δικαιοσύνην καὶ κρίσιν.

[b] LXX and Heb. "the Lord."

[c] Variant "promised." Philo does not comment here or elsewhere on Gen. xviii. 18, in which God promises that all nations will be blessed in Abraham, unless this is referred to in the obscure passage that follows in this section.

[d] τὴν προγνωστικὴν δύναμιν τὴν τοῦ Ὄντος.

[e] Here and above the Arm. imperfect tense is used to render ᾔδειν, which in the LXX is equivalent to Heb. *yāda'tî*, having the force of the present tense.

[f] οἰκεῖον.

[g] τὰ μέλλοντα (omitted in Aucher's rendering).

[h] ὁ σπουδαῖος.

[i] τὴν ἀρετήν.

[j] ἐνεργῶν.

[k] The subject may be God or Abraham or Scripture.

[l] Lit. "is."

[m] τῷ νῷ.

[n] τὴν τοῦ ἀσωμάτου φωτὸς μετοχὴν εἰς σαφῆ κατάληψιν περιάγοντα.

[o] βαρυτέραν ὁμολογίαν *vel sim.*

[p] ὑποστέλλει.

[q] τὰς κατὰ φιλοσοφίαν αἰτιολογικὰς ἰδέας. The meaning seems to be similar to that found in *De Fuga* 163, "What kind of place is meant (in Ex. iii. 5)? Evidently the aetiological, which He has assigned only to divine natures, deeming no human being capable of dealing with aetiology."

to comprehend should immediately with most lucid reasoning have a notion of the causes through which something has happened.

23. (Gen. xviii. 20) What is the meaning of the words, "And the Lord said, The outcry of the Sodomites and the Gomorrahites [a] has increased, and their sins are very great" [b]?

There are two heads [c] under which the whole Legislation [d] is ordered, (namely) evil and virtue.[e] After treating of virtue [f] and the virtuous character which is adorned by it, it passes over to still another form,[g] that of evil, and to those who are its fond inventors and who practise it. Now he who is truly righteous [h] is a faithful priest [i] of their folly and madness. And God is the common mediator [j] and supporter [k] of all, and His tribunal [l] is unbribable and without deception, but only full of truth with which no falsehood is mixed. Now "Sodom" is to be translated as "blindness" or "sterility," [m] (which are) names of impiety and irrationality, for every unworthy man is blind and sterile. And "Gomorrah" (meaning) "measure"

[a] LXX and Heb. "Sodom and Gomorrah."
[b] So LXX, *αἱ ἁμαρτίαι αὐτῶν μεγάλαι σφόδρα.* Heb. has "their sin is very heavy."
[c] *κεφάλαια.*
[d] *ἡ νομοθεσία*, *i.e.* the Mosaic Law.
[e] *κακία καὶ ἀρετή.*
[f] *i.e.* in the preceding verses.
[g] Or "species"—*εἶδος.*
[h] *δίκαιος.*
[i] *πιστὸς ἱερεύς*, which does not make much sense. Just possibly Arm. *k'ourm* "priest" is here a corruption of *bouṙn*, meaning "lord," "antagonist," "fighter" or the like (Arm. *k'* and *b* look much alike).
[j] *μεσίτης*, a term elsewhere in Philo applied to the Logos.
[k] *ἀντιλαμβανόμενος.*
[l] *βῆμα* or *κριτήριον.*
[m] *τύφλωσις ἢ στείρωσις.* The same fanciful etymologies are given in *De Ebrietate* 222 and *De Somniis* ii. 192.

true and just, is the divine Logos,[a] by which [b] have been measured and are measured all things that are on earth—principles,[c] numbers and proportions in harmony and consonance being included, through which the forms and measures of existing things [d] are seen. But the measure of evil is a spurious thing,[e] a false name without measure and without value. For nothing is measured or numbered or ordered by an evil man, since he is full of all disorder and unmeasuredness.[f]

*24. (Gen. xviii. 21) Why does He speak like a man,[g] saying, "Going down, then, I will see whether it is in accordance with their outcry which has come to Me that they are acting,[h] but if not, that I may know"?

This statement is rightly one of true condescension [i] and accommodation to our nature, for God through His prescient power [j] knows all things, including the future, as I said a little while earlier.[k] And He wishes to instruct those who were to act in accordance with the sacred Legislation [l] not to give orders to anyone lightly and immediately but first to enter into matters and inspect, observe and examine them severally with all care,[m] and

[a] μέτρον . . . ὁ θεῖος λόγος. The same etymology is given in *De Somniis* ii. 192.

[b] Variant "to which" but the dat. reflects Greek dat. of agency with perf. pass. verb.

[c] Or "ratios"—λόγων.

[d] τῶν ὄντων.

[e] νοθεία or κατάχρησις.

[f] ἀμετρίας.

[g] ἀνθρωπίνως *vel sim.*

[h] LXX συντελοῦνται: Heb. "have done (or "do") completely."

[i] Aucher "humiliationis."

[j] προγνωστικῇ δυνάμει. The same phrase occurs in *De Vita Mosis* ii. 190, where it is said to be God's gift to Moses.

[k] In *QG* iv. 22.

[l] κατὰ τὴν ἱερὰν νομοθεσίαν, *i.e.* the Mosaic Law.

[m] πάσῃ ἀκριβείᾳ.

not to be deceived by obvious appearances.[a] For there are some things that appear fair and just, and after they depart and recede, are shameful and unjust. And on the other hand, things which seem evil and deserving of condemnation are found through selective tests to be virtuous and very praiseworthy. It is, therefore, an excellent doctrine of the good life that He announces and legislates,[b] (namely) that one should not lightly and immediately give credence to any appearance before examining it with wise reflexion [c] to see what sort of thing it is in truth. For the first impression [d] is deceptive. And so, no one among men, especially princes, should be ashamed of not knowing, since in the case of an appearance that one encounters one is not able to attain the real truth that is invisible. (And therefore Scripture) represents the ruler and sovereign of the universe as not believing beforehand but as inquiring and examining whether the facts follow rumour or whether they say some things that deserve condemnation, and do other things that are not reprehensible. For many who speak evil act virtuously, and (many) who profess goodness violate the law through their acts. And this must be carefully ascertained by him who is destined to be the champion [e] of human affairs in sincerity.[f]

25. (Gen. xviii. 22) Why does (Scripture) again say in

[a] This sentence is briefly paraphrased by Procopius; see Appendix A.

[b] νομοθετεῖ.

[c] λογισμῷ τῆς σοφίας.

[d] Arm. has *držoumn* (=ἐπιβουλή) which Aucher correctly renders as "fraudatio" (except that he seems to confuse subject and predicate). But ἐπιβουλή is clearly an error for ἐπιβολή, here meaning "first impression," as in *De Vita Mosis* i. 26 τὰς πρώτας τῆς ψυχῆς ἐπιβολάς τε καὶ ὁρμὰς ὡς ἀφηνιαστὴν ἵππον ἐπετήρει.

[e] Lit. "mediator of help."

[f] καθαρῶς: variant "in human fashion."

the singular, "And Abraham was still [a] standing before the Lord" [b]?

Again [c] the soul becomes filled with God,[d] worshipping, admiring and honouring the Cause [e] above His powers, and also standing still in His likeness, for constancy in the truth is immovable and enduring. And so it was now necessary to introduce him in the fashion of a suppliant servant,[f] standing before Him who Was about to inflict punishment upon the impious in order that the human race might not be altogether destroyed but might have some worthy and God-loving [g] example, whose prayers, since He who was entreated was benevolent, He did not disregard. Wherefore He gave him understanding,[h] for not without the assent of divine providence was he about to make entreaty, but He used the wise man [i] as a foundation and base [j] for showing beneficence to those who were worthy of receiving kindness, and for demonstrating two virtues, the power of unconquerable sovereignty and that of righteous judgment,[k] suitably tempered with a familiar gentleness.[l]

26. (Gen. xviii. 23) What is the meaning of the words, "And approaching, Abraham said, Thou wilt not destroy

[a] Some LXX MSS. and ancient versions, like Philo, follow the Heb. in reading "still"; most LXX MSS. omit it.

[b] Philo does not comment on the first half of the verse, which reads "And departing from there, the men went to Sodom." The second half of the verse is briefly alluded to in *De Cherubim* 18, *De Poster. Caini* 27 and *De Somniis* ii. 226.

[c] Or "turning."

[d] ἔνθεος γίνεται or θεοφορεῖται.

[e] τὸ Αἴτιον, *i.e.* God, as elsewhere in Philo.

[f] Aucher renders somewhat differently, "hunc servum supplicantem in exemplum adducere."

[g] Or "God-beloved"—φιλόθεος or θεόφιλος.

[h] διάνοιαν or "mind"—νοῦν.

[i] τῷ σοφῷ.

[j] ὡς θεμελίῳ καὶ βάσει.

[k] δικαιοκρισίας.

[l] Lit. "with a familiarity (οἰκειότητι) of gentleness."

the righteous with the impious, and shall the righteous be as the unrighteous?" [a]?

The literal meaning [b] is clear. But as for the deeper meaning,[c] man is said to be close to [d] God rather figuratively but not in the proper sense.[e] For He is far from, and away from, the body, and never even comes into our mind, for a mortal and dissoluble substance [f] is separated and far removed from an uncreated and undisturbed nature. Nevertheless, the sovereign part of the soul,[g] which is called the mind,[h] and has the dignity and capacity to be close (to God), becomes worthy of travelling [i] with Him who is entreated, and offers Him, together with his entreaties, great praise for His benevolence and kindness and love of man.[j] For he entreats Him not to destroy the righteous together with the impious, nor thought with thought.[k] But it seems to me that the uncorrupted and righteous character, in which there is no admixture of unrighteousness, is removed from the argument that is now put before us. For it is to be firmly believed [l] that such a person is worthy of salvation [m] and will by all means be saved.[n] But he trembles and shudders for the man who is mixed and jumbled up [o] and, as it were, (both) righteous and unrighteous. For he hopes that such a

[a] Philo follows the LXX against the Heb. in including the clause, καὶ ἔσται ὁ δίκαιος ὡς ἀσεβής (except that for ἀσεβής Arm. has ἄδικος). The verse is cited in part in *Leg. All.* iii. 9, *De Cherubim* 18, *De Poster. Caini* 27 and *De Migratione* 132.

[b] τὸ ῥητόν.

[c] τὸ πρὸς διάνοιαν.

[d] Lit. "to be beside" (παρεῖναι) or "to touch" (ἅπτεσθαι).

[e] τροπικώτερον <ἀλλ'> οὐ κυρίως.

[f] οὐσία.

[g] τὸ τῆς ψυχῆς ἡγεμονικόν, a common Stoic term in Philo.

[h] ὁ νοῦς.

[i] τῆς ὁδοιπορίας.

[j] τῆς φιλανθρωπίας.

[k] λογισμὸν σὺν λογισμῷ, *i.e.* the thoughts of the righteous together with those of the impious.

[l] Or "he firmly believes." Aucher's rendering is ambiguous and (or because) ungrammatical, "verum mihi videtur quod purum et justum moribus . . . interim a praesenti sermone seponere, persuasus etc."

[m] ἄξιος τῆς σωτηρίας.

[n] σωθήσεται.

[o] πεφυρμένος.

person, having a revived spark [a] of brightness and a gleam of the fire of righteousness, can be converted to spiritual health.[b] For he believes it to be better and more fitting that through the beneficent powers of God (which are used) for the righteous the punishments awaiting the unrighteous should be lightened and decreased than that on account of the impious the righteous should be involved.

27. (Gen. xviii. 24-32) Why does he [c] begin with fifty and end with ten? And why does he at the beginning subtract five at a time [d] down to forty, and from then on ten at a time down to the end, (namely) the decad? For he says,[e] "If there are fifty righteous men in the city, wilt Thou destroy them? Wilt Thou not spare the place? And what if there are forty-five? And, further, if there are forty? And what if there are 30,[f] or if there are 20? And what if there are ten? [g]"

Two things he seeks: that the righteous be saved, and also others for their sake. And all the numbers are sacred. Fifty (consists) of a rectangular triangle.[h] And in accordance with its power [i] the prophet [j] proclaims the release [k] in the fiftieth (year). But forty-five is a productive number,

[a] Lit. "revivification of a spark." The same figure of speech is used in connexion with the present verse in *De Migratione* 122.

[b] ὑγίειαν ψυχικήν (or πνευματικήν). The phrase ὑγίεια ψυχῆς occurs elsewhere in Philo.

[c] *i.e.* Abraham in pleading with God to spare Sodom.

[d] Lit. "five five."

[e] Here Philo condenses nine verses.

[f] This and the following number in contrast to the rest are indicated by numeral letters in the Arm.

[g] This passage is alluded to in *De Congressu* 109 and *De Mut. Nom.* 228-229, where Philo applies Pythagorean number-mysticism more briefly than here.

[h] See *De Spec. Leg.* ii. 177 and *QG* ii. 5 where Philo explains that the squares of the sides 3, 4, 5 (namely 9, 16, 25) add up to 50.

[i] δύναμιν.

[j] *i.e.* Moses.

[k] ἄφεσιν, *i.e.* from debt-slavery, *cf.* Lev. xxv. 10.

consisting of intervals of three, in accordance with which they first appear as progressions, the arithmetic, the geometric and the harmonic,[a] for the scheme of intervals[b] is 6, 9, 12, 18, the sum of which is 45. And in the same number of odd-numbered days the embryo is formed, rarely in forty, and less (often) in more, for it is productive.[c] And again, in the same number of days is the embryo formed in the womb, in the case of almost (all) nine-month (infants),[d] for in the case of seven-month (infants) it takes thirty-five days, as they say similarly.[e] Thirty (days), moreover, is the lunar interval of separation, the cycle of the moon.[f] And twenty (years is that) of age[g] and of one who has advanced in age and belongs to the elders[h]; and it is the number[i] of military service. And ten is altogether perfect.[j] And through these numbers, which are harmonies in music, all those (numbers)[k] are seen which in all cases[l] are a double ratio, as forty to twenty, or twenty to ten. But through five[m] (they are) the ratio of one and a half to one,[n] (as is) thirty to twenty, while through four[o] (they are) the ratio of four to three,[p] (as

[a] See *QG* iii. 38.

[b] τὸ πλινθίον.

[c] In *QG* i. 25, ii. 14, iv. 154 and *De Vita Mosis* ii. 18 Philo says that the male embryo is formed in 40 days. Which number is here meant as " productive " is not quite certain.

[d] Aucher renders somewhat differently, " fere in paucis novem mensium."

[e] Where the " similarly " belongs is not clear.

[f] Aucher renders less literally but more smoothly, " triginta vero mensuale est spatium circuli lunae."

[g] Philo means that 20 years is the beginning of maturity.

[h] So lit. ; Aucher renders more freely, " et viginti aetatis norma, qua transacta, inter majores computatur."

[i] *i.e.* the age.

[j] παντέλειος. *Cf. De Decalogo* 20 δεκάδι τῇ παντελείᾳ.

[k] What noun is to be supplied is not clear.

[l] Lit. " through all."

[m] Where 5 comes from is not clear. Possibly Philo means the fifth (and below, the fourth) proposal made to God by Abraham.

[n] ἡμιόλιος λόγος.

[o] See note *m*.

[p] ἐπίτριτος λόγος.

is) forty to thirty. But there is an angular interval [a] of separation,[b] (as is) forty to forty. Therefore fittingly and properly,[c] since he makes entreaty on behalf of the salvation [d] of the city, does he use salutary numbers,[e] since they consist of harmony, and harmony is salutary, just as, on the other hand, disharmony is the cause of dissolution and destruction.[f]

28. (Gen. xviii. 27) Why does he say, " Now I have begun [g] to speak with the Lord, and I am earth and ashes " ?

Those who approach God with a pure mind [h] are especially aware of their own weakness in comparison with the greatness of Him whom they approach. For the God-loving mind [i] will tell forth and confess its humility by its deeds. But we should consider his entreaty concerning earth and ashes as noble,[j] and declare the earth and ashes holy as in the holy offerings and holocausts. And either of these is a symbol of the soul.[k] For earth is goodly and fertile, since the mind of the wise man is fruitful.[l] And the ashes [m] are the other (symbol), for whatever mortal remains were mixed in were, under the laws of piety,[n]

[a] γωνιακὸν διάστημα. Did Philo write ἑνωτικόν?

[b] Emending Arm. *makout'iun* (of unknown meaning) to *meknout'ean* as above.

[c] οἰκείως καὶ κυρίως.

[d] τῆς σωτηρίας.

[e] σωτηρίοις ἀριθμοῖς.

[f] Or " corruption."

[g] So LXX, ἠρξάμην, rendering Heb. *hô'altî* " I have presumed."

[h] γνώμῃ or " character "—ἤθει or τρόπῳ.

[i] ὁ φιλόθεος (or θεοφιλὴς) νοῦς.

[j] The two Arm. adjectives used here render σεμνός.

[k] σύμβολον τῆς ψυχῆς.

[l] The Arm. variant is rendered by Aucher, " sapientis mentem fructificat," but this rendering is questionable. Rather does the variant agree in meaning with the accepted reading except that an impersonal construction is used.

[m] The Arm. translator uses three different words for " ashes " in this section.

[n] *i.e.* by the sacrificial laws of the Pentateuch.

tested and examined as is gold by fire. And in his prayers his worthiness remained.[a]

29. (Gen. xviii. 33) What is the meaning of the words, "The Lord went away as He ceased to speak with Abraham. And Abraham returned to his place"[b]?

The one who is begotten and brought into being[c] is not wont to be God-possessed[d] always, but when he has been divinely inspired[e] for some time he then goes and returns to himself. For it is impossible for the soul to remain permanently in the body when nothing slippery or no obstacle strikes its feet. But it is necessary that the most pure and luminous mind[f] should be mixed with the mortal (element)[g] for necessary uses. This is what is indicated by the heavenly ladder,[h] (where) not only an ascent but also a descent of the angels is mentioned. And this is what is said of the prophet,[i] (namely) his descent and ascent reveal the swift turning and change of his thoughts.[j] And thought and change altogether bear a resemblance to those who practise continence[k] for athletic well-being,[l] whom their trainers teach methodically, not in order to do violence to[m] the body but that it may be able to endure necessary labours easily and not

[a] Apparently this means that Abraham's nature was tested and approved by the wording of his prayer.

[b] This verse is more briefly commented on in *De Somniis* i. 70-71.

[c] *i.e.* a mortal.

[d] ἔνθεος or θεόφορος.

[e] ἐνθουσιάσας.

[f] ὁ καθαρώτατος καὶ εἰλικρινέστατος νοῦς.

[g] τῷ θνητῷ.

[h] In Gen. xxviii. 12 ff.

[i] *i.e.* Moses, in Ex. xix. 17 ff. The passage from Exodus is also referred to in the parallel, *De Somniis* i. 71.

[j] τῶν λογισμῶν.

[k] ἐγκρατείᾳ: Aucher "studiosam vitam."

[l] πρὸς ἀθλητικὴν εὐεξίαν, *cf. De Plantatione* 157. Aucher renders, "pro athletica quiete," but though Arm. *hangist* means "rest" as well as "well-being" the context and the parallel seem to support the latter rendering.

[m] ἐξυβρίσωσι.

be worn down and afflicted by continuous and frequent labours. This too is what musicians carefully observe in respect of their instruments, when they loosen the strings lest they snap through unrelieved tension. For these reasons nature too has adjusted the voices of living creatures to sing not with only one intensity but with all kinds of variation, becoming lax and tense (in turn). And so, just as music is by its laws adapted not only to distinct and increased intensities but also to medium ones and to relaxations, so too is it with the mind.[a] For when it is wholly intent upon pleasing[b] the Father and becomes God-possessed,[c] it is rightly said to be fortunate.[d] And when it ceases to be inspired,[e] after its enthusiasm[f] it returns to itself and reflects upon its own affairs and what is proper to it. For piety and love of man are related virtues.[g] And these the wise man[h] uses and observes, taking care to be reverent as a suppliant. While God stays, he remains there, and when He departs, he too departs. And the Father takes His departure because of His providential care and consideration[i] for our race, knowing that it is by nature shackled and involved in its needs.[j] Wherefore he[k] saw fit to retire and be alone, for not everything is to be done by the sons in the sight of the Father.

*30. (Gen. xix. 1) Why, when three had appeared, does (Scripture) say, "The two angels came to Sodom at evening"?

To Abraham three appeared and at midday, while to Lot two (appeared) and at evening. (Scripture) indicates

[a] *ὁ νοῦς.*

[b] Or "being grateful to" or "worshipping."

[c] *ἔνθεος.*

[d] *εὐδαίμων* or *εὐτυχής.*

[e] *κορυβαντιᾶν.*

[f] *τὸν ἐνθουσιασμόν.*

[g] *συγγενεῖς γάρ εἰσι ἀρεταὶ εὐσέβεια καὶ φιλανθρωπία.*

[h] *ὁ σοφός.*

[i] *διὰ τὴν πρόνοιάν τε καὶ φειδώ.*

[j] *ταῖς ἐνδείαις vel sim.*

[k] Apparently Abraham, not God, is meant.

a most natural distinction between the perfect man and the progressive one.[a] For the perfect man has an impression[b] of a triad, a nature that is full, dense,[c] not-empty and overflowing, while the other has the dyad, which is divided and empty. The one perceives the Father between His ministers, the two chief powers,[d] while the other (perceives) the servant-powers[e] without the Father,[f] for he is unequal to seeing and understanding Him who is between and king of the powers. And the one is illumined by a most radiant light at midday without shadow, while the other (is illumined) by a changing (light) between night and day. For evening occupies an intermediate place; it is not[g] the cessation of day, and not[g] the beginning of night.

31. (Gen. xix. 1) Why was Lot sitting at[h] the gate of the Sodomites?[i]

Sodom is to be interpreted as "blindness" or "sterility,"[j] and being seated at the gate is very proper to the progressive man[k] in respect of a symbolical interpretation.[l] The gate is neither within the city nor outside the city; similarly he who wishes to progress is neither within virtue[m] nor outside virtue, but sometimes he is

[a] φυσικωτάτην διαφορὰν τοῦ τελείου καὶ τοῦ προκόπτοντος (the Greek frag. has φυσικώτατα διαφόρον, which may have been the original reading). For the distinction between the τέλειος and the προκόπτων see *Leg. All.* iii. 140.
[b] φαντασιοῦται, as in the Greek frag.
[c] The Greek frag. has διηνεκῆ.
[d] πρώτων δυνάμεων, see *QG* ii. 51.
[e] Lit. "powers of service."
[f] Aucher inaccurately renders, "virtutes ipsas sine cultu Patri exhibito" instead of "virtutes cultus sine patre."
[g] The negatives are surprising.
[h] LXX παρά: Heb. "in."
[i] So Arm. O.T.: LXX and Heb. "of Sodom."
[j] The same etymology is given above in *QG* iv. 23 and elsewhere (see note there).
[k] τῷ προκόπτοντι.
[l] πρὸς συμβολικὴν (or τροπικὴν) ἀπόδοσιν.
[m] ἀρετῇ.

among those who, as if within a city, are involved in the usual passions [a] that belong to the soul and are the work of sterility and unfruitfulness and blindness. And sometimes, as if in a desert, [b] he pursues a pure zeal [c] which is without practical concern, [d] and a truly contemplative way of life. [e]

32. (Gen. xix. 1) What is the meaning of the words, " Seeing (them), he arose (and) hastened toward them and bowed with his face to the ground " [f]?

The face in man is uncovered. Now our —— [g] especially prostrates itself before an appearance [h] and receives it before the truth.[i] Such is everyone who is not perfect.[j] He admires the visible things that are seen rather than the invisible and unseen things, while the mind [k] grasps these before the senses.[l]

*33. (Gen. xix. 2) Why, when they are invited, do they refuse hospitality, saying, " No, but in the street will we spend the night " [m]?

[a] πάθεσι. [b] ἐν ἐρήμῳ. [c] καθαρὸν ζῆλον.

[d] ἄνευ πραγμάτων.

[e] τὴν πρὸς ἀλήθειαν θεωρητικὴν διαγωγήν (or ζωήν). Aucher inaccurately renders, " contemplationem veritatis vitae."

[f] Philo slightly varies the wording of the LXX, ἰδὼν δὲ Λὼτ ἀνέστη εἰς συνάντησιν αὐτοῖς καὶ προσεκύνησεν τῷ προσώπῳ ἐπὶ τὴν γῆν.

[g] Either a word has fallen out after the poss. pronoun, or the text is corrupt.

[h] Aucher renders unintelligibly, " nostro magis itaque modo nunc factam adorat apparitionem."

[i] Or " in preference to the truth "—πρὸ τῆς ἀληθείας: Aucher renders, " ante certificationem."

[j] οὐ τέλειος, *i.e.* Lot in contrast to Abraham.

[k] ὁ νοῦς. [l] αἱ αἰσθήσεις.

[m] So the LXX, οὐχί, ἀλλ' ἢ ἐν τῇ πλατείᾳ καταλύσομεν (the last word is rendered literally in the Arm., " we will break up ").

Him [a] they refuse, being unwilling, but in the case of Abraham, the friend of God,[b] who invited them, they accepted. And the reason is that the divine powers [c] accept the perfect man, while to the imperfect man they hardly ever come.[d] And so the " no " (is the reply) of those who refused to come to him. But (in saying) " in the street will we spend the night " they announced that every foolish man is a narrow one, being constrained by love of money, love of pleasure, love of glory and similar things, which do not permit the mind to move in free space.[e] And so (Scripture) excellently presents a law [f] showing that for the wise man every place in the world is spacious [g] for living with and seeing individual things.[h] But he who is unlike this does not have even his own house or a mind of his own but is confused and is treated contemptuously like those [i] who, as it were, enter an inn only to fill themselves [j] and vomit [k] in their passions.

[a] Lot.

[b] τοῦ φιλοθέου or θεοφιλοῦς (Philo sometimes combines the adjectives in a single phrase).

[c] αἱ θεῖαι δυνάμεις, see the preceding sections and *QG* ii. 51.

[d] Aucher " aegre veniunt."

[e] The Arm. agrees very closely (except for one slight difference in word-order) with the Greek frag. printed by Harris, which ends here. The rest of the section agrees almost as closely with another Greek frag. from the same Catena (Cod. Rupefucaldi) printed by Lewy; see Appendix A.

[f] Or " doctrine " : the Greek frag. has δόγμα.

[g] Here the Arm. differs somewhat from, or freely renders, the Greek τῷ μὲν σοφῷ ἀναπέπταται τὰ ἐν κόσμῳ.

[h] Here the Greek frag., reading τῶν κατὰ μέρος, shows that we must prefer the Arm. reading *i masançn* to the variant *imastnoyn*.

[i] The Greek frag. has ὑπὸ τῶν.

[j] Possibly the Arm. *lçousçen* " fill themselves " is an emendation or corruption of *loucsçen* " spend the night " (καταλύωσι), which the scribe did not understand in its idiomatic Greek sense.

[k] Lewy conjecturally restores κορεσθῶσι.

34. (Gen. xix. 3) What is the meaning of the words, "He forced them, and they turned aside to him"[a]?

Carefully is it said that they did not come in but turned aside. For seldom is there a turning aside[b] of the sacred (and) holy words to those who have progress (but) not wholly perfect acceptance.[c] And the reason for their turning aside was the use of force. For to him who is progressing it is peculiar to attain to a better nature not easily and willingly and with a free and easy letting go,[d] but he is laboriously and arduously forced,[e] whereas the wise man is accustomed to desire wisdom willingly.[f] But the other is disciplined by necessity and unwillingly.

35. (Gen. xix. 3) Why did he[g] alone make for them drink and unleavened bread,[h] whereas Abraham (made) ash-cakes[i] and no drink?

It is said by medical students[j] that the use of drink is not (as) a food but the conveyance[k] of food. And the

[a] LXX *παρεβιάζετο* (*v.l.* *κατεβιάζετο*: Heb. "he pressed") *αὐτοὺς καὶ ἐξέκλιναν πρὸς αὐτόν*. [b] More literally "rolling."

[c] The syntax and meaning are not clear. Aucher, construing differently and, I think, wrongly, renders, "quoniam pauciter tantum declinatio efficitur sacrorum verborum apud proficientes, non vera perfectissima acceptatio." The general meaning is that Lot, the type of the progressive man, could not receive the divine word as easily as Abraham, the type of the perfect man.

[d] *ἀφέσει vel sim.* [e] Or "forces himself."

[f] Construction slightly uncertain.

[g] *i.e.* Lot in distinction from Abraham.

[h] LXX *ἀζύμους*.

[i] *ἐγκρυφίας*, see *QG* iv. 8 on Gen. xviii. 6-7.

[j] *παρὰ τοῖς ἰατρῶν παισί*. *Cf. De Josepho* 160 *ἰατρῶν παῖδες*.

[k] Arm. *kark'* = *ἅρμα*. Apparently the original had *ἄρμα* (with smooth breathing), meaning "conveyance" or "stimulus" or the like (?). According to Liddell-Scott-Jones *ἄρμα* was used by Hippocrates (*ap.* Photius, p. 533 b) in the sense of taking food.

passage shows that it is a superfluous enjoyment [a] and not a necessity.[b] And it was proper and fitting for the wise man [c] to prepare the necessary (foods), in which the greatness of nature is determined and circumscribed,[d] while for him who is still under discipline (it is fitting to prepare) the superfluities of sensual pleasure,[e] which do harm rather than good. But he who is not yet perfectly purified does not have anything hidden [f] but (only) what is in the sight of the multitude, because he has taken hold of what is common.[g] But the wise man has many things that are hidden. For it is not seldom that equality is hardly given to plants and herbs,[h] which exhibit the mysteries [i] of the Deity as if they were intelligible, and a hidden and invisible sense.[j]

36. (Gen. xix. 4) Why did the Sodomites surround his house, from youth up to old man, all the people at once? [k]

All these are causes of their guilt, (namely) their age

[a] *περιττὴ ἀπόλαυσις.*

[b] Lit. " necessary need."

[c] *τὸν σοφόν*, Abraham.

[d] Syntax and meaning are obscure. Aucher renders, " quibus naturae latitudo conclusa est."

[e] *τὰ τῶν ἡδονῶν περιττά.*

[f] *κρυπτόν vel sim.* Philo here makes a punning allusion to the *ἐγκρυφίας* " ash-cakes " of Abraham.

[g] *τοῦ κοινοῦ.*

[h] The above is a literal translation of the obscure Arm., which Aucher renders (with grave doubt expressed in his footnote), " quoniam non desunt neque in plantis res inaequales."

[i] Or " thoughts."

[j] Prob. *διάνοιαν.*

[k] LXX *καὶ οἱ ἄνδρες τῆς πόλεως οἱ Σοδομεῖται περιεκύκλωσαν τὴν οἰκίαν ἀπὸ νεανίσκου ἕως πρεσβυτέρου, ἅπας ὁ λαός ἅμα.* For " at once " Heb. has " from end (to end)." In *De Confus. Ling.* 28 Philo cites the verse a little differently, *πᾶς δ' ὁ λαὸς περιεκύκλωσαν ἅμα τὴν οἰκίαν, νέοι τε καὶ πρεσβῦται*, but in the lines preceding he uses the LXX wording *ἀπὸ νεανίσκου ἕως πρεσβυτέρου.*

and their multitude and that they had neither harmony nor unanimity in their affairs. The literal meaning [a] is very clear. But the literal meaning has a base and foundation in the deeper meaning.[b] For the traits of soul that are blind and unproductive of wisdom, which (Scripture) calls "Sodomites," [c] surround its connatural home,[d] the body. And old men and youths, making up a single chorus with one accord, take care of it and tend it,[e] as if they were offering abundant food and other sensual pleasures to an insatiable, untamed, mad and unclean beast.

37. (Gen. xix. 5) What is the meaning of the words,[f] "Bring them out to us that we may know them" [g]?

The literal meaning [h] indicates servile, lawless and unseemly pederasty.[i] But as for the deeper meaning,[j] lascivious and unrestrainedly impure men, raising a mound of desires,[k] threaten with death those who are self-controlled and desirous of continence.[l] To these they say, "Let them come forth from their own wills and from their choice of a constant, seemly and noble way of life in order that we may know them. For they will be persuaded to change (their ways) and gladly accept ours, learning in the

[a] τὸ ῥητόν.

[b] τὸ πρὸς διάνοιαν.

[c] See above, *QG* iv. 31, for the etymologies of "Sodom" as "blindness" and "sterility."

[d] *Cf. De Somniis* i. 122 τὸν συμφυᾶ τῆς ψυχῆς οἶκον, τὸ σῶμα, similarly *De Praemiis* 120.

[e] *i.e.* the body.

[f] Spoken to Lot by the Sodomites.

[g] The Arm. preposition or preverb *ənd* used here prob. reflects Greek συν- compounded with the verb, as in the LXX συγγενώμεθα αὐτοῖς. Philo, like the Arm. O.T., holds more literally to the Heb. "that we may know them."

[h] τὸ ῥητόν.

[i] Lit. "unseemly and male pederasty."

[j] τὸ πρὸς διάνοιαν.

[k] The "mound," χωμα, is suggested by the picture of the Sodomites surrounding Lot's home as if besieging it.

[l] ἐγκρατείας.

act that souls are not naked and incorporeal[a] so as not to be in want,[b] but have something in common [c] with the body, which lacks many necessities. They should not treat it [d] badly or dismiss it but tame it and domesticate it by offering it the materials that belong to it."

38. (Gen. xix. 7-8) Why does Lot say to them, "Not so, brothers, do not do evil. For I have two daughters, who have not known a man. I will bring them to you, and you shall use them as it pleases you. Only do not do any wrong to these men inasmuch as they have come under the shelter of my roof" [e]?

The literal text [f] very clearly shows that the Sodomites were pederasts. But as for the deeper meaning,[g] in the soul of the progressive man[h] there are some thoughts[i] that are masculine, and some offspring that are feminine. Now he wishes, if it is somehow possible, to save all parts.[j] Otherwise, if his hostile opponents who make war on him overcome him, (he will try) to keep the masculine kind unharmed but will abandon the feminine for the sake of the former. For no one condemns those who for the sake of saving and preserving the better accept the lesser,[k] since, as I have said, they are unable to withstand all

[a] Aucher renders less accurately, "quod non nudae animae incorporeae sunt."

[b] Aucher rightly renders, "immunes a timore," but the context suggests that the Greek had *ἀδεεῖς* which was here rendered by the Arm. translator as "without fear" instead of "without want."

[c] *κοινωνίαν.*

[d] It is not clear whether "it" means the body or the soul.

[e] Philo closely follows the LXX *Μηδαμῶς, ἀδελφοί, μὴ πονηρεύσησθε. εἰσὶν δέ μοι δύο θυγατέρες αἳ οὐκ ἔγνωσαν ἄνδρα· ἐξάγω αὐτὰς πρὸς ὑμᾶς, καὶ χρήσασθε αὐταῖς καθὰ ἀρέσκῃ ὑμῖν. μόνον εἰς τοὺς ἄνδρας τούτους μὴ ποιήσητε μηδὲν ἄδικον οὗ εἵνεκεν εἰσῆλθον ὑπὸ τὴν στέγην* (*v.l.* *σκέπην*) *τῶν δοκῶν μου.*

[f] *τὸ ῥητόν.*

[g] *τὸ πρὸς διάνοιαν.*

[h] *ἐν τῇ τοῦ προκόπτοντος ψυχῇ.*

[i] *λογισμοί.*

[j] *i.e.* of the soul.

[k] Apparently meaning the lesser evil or the like.

things.[a] Which then are the masculine thoughts? Those which are emulous of wisdom and of all virtue in general[b] and of that which is truly good and alone is good. But the feminine kind, having the position of daughters, are under service to bodily needs and under the dominion of the passions.[c]

39. (Gen. xix. 9) What is the meaning of the words, "They said, Go to, stay away.[d] You have come to dwell as a sojourner[e] and not indeed to sit in judgment"?

Those who gather to make war on the soul, workers of evil and impurity, shamelessly choose a leader and teacher, saying, "O thou, dost thou not wish to come to us[f] who are—are we not?—inhabitants and countrymen? Thou art in need of our ways and shouldst emulate the ways of our country. For our territory is licentiousness, and our law and lawful will is sensual pleasure.[g] And now that we have permitted thee to live in freedom as a sojourner, dost thou dare to resist and rebel? And whereas thou shouldst be quiet, dost thou judge and decide matters, saying that these things are bad, and others better, that these are good, virtuous and honourable, and those are evil, disreputable and dishonourable, changing some into virtue,[h] and applying the measure of evil to the nature of[i] others? In every one of the beings who exist there is desire,[j] and to

[a] Aucher curiously renders, "cunctis satisfacere."

[b] ζηλωταὶ τῆς σοφίας καὶ κοινῇ πάσης ἀρετῆς.

[c] τῶν παθῶν.

[d] The Arm. seems to be a double rendering of LXX ἀπόστα ἐκεῖ.

[e] LXX εἰσῆλθες παροικεῖν: Heb. "shall one come to sojourn?"

[f] The text is uncertain, perhaps a conflation of two clauses. Aucher renders, "O tu, qui ingressus es ad nos, an non amas (*vel*, nescis) conversari nobiscum?"

[g] ἡδονή.

[h] ἀρετήν.

[i] Or perhaps "the measure of an evil nature to." Aucher omits "nature" in his rendering.

[j] ἐπιθυμία.

this must we refer all things on earth. This is the ancient law of the Sodomites, which some boys call their helper,[a] like boys in grammar-school[b] who are unable to receive instruction because of weariness."[c]

*40. (Gen. xix. 10-11) What is the meaning of the words, "Stretching out their hands, the men drew Lot to themselves into the house, and closed the door of the house, and the men who were at the door they struck with blindness"[d]?

Three things they did: they saved their host, they closed the door, and they blinded those who were rising up and were using force.[e] In the first place, they passed judgment upon undisciplined and licentious men so that they might not be victorious through the use of force, and having been defeated, might let go the one whom they were mistreating. Second they kept them—in word, from the house, but in deed,[f] from attaining their desire[g] and its end, which remained.[h] For this is the most terrible of evils, (namely) that passion spreads and grows in the suffering soul. For despair of (attaining) the end is like the remainder of a touch of disease.[i] And there is (only) one cure for those who are thirsty and hungry when their need[j] is prolonged, (namely) to drink and eat. And for those who desire something (the only cure) is to attain it. And third, the judgment of blindness overtakes those who

[a] *βοηθόν.* [b] *ἐν τῇ γραμματικῇ.*

[c] Or "labour." Aucher renders, "prae labore." Apparently the meaning is that all work and no play makes for dullness, in the opinion of the "Sodomites."

[d] Philo omits, after "blindness," the words "from small to great."

[e] As stated in the latter part of Gen. xix. 9 which Philo does not comment on in § 39.

[f] *λόγῳ μέν . . . ἔργῳ δέ.* [g] *τὴν ἐπιθυμίαν.*

[h] *i.e.* from completely attaining their desire.

[i] Text and meaning somewhat uncertain; Aucher renders, "velut residuum morbi inurentis."

[j] Lit. "hunger."

have been condemned.[a] This (affliction) would seem to be in the eyes, but in truth (it affects) the soul of those who see, for they are made blind to the appearance of most holy visions. Let the law, therefore, be (invoked)[b] against those who have not seen fit to see nobly and gloriously and in a manner worthy of God[c] that which is noble and pure[d] and divine,[e] and the punishment of being struck with blindness be inflicted (upon them).[f]

41. (Gen. xix. 11) What is the meaning of the words, "And they gave up[g] seeking the door"?

The literal text[h] denotes an excess of licentiousness, for not even when blinded did they lessen in their desire[i] but thought nothing of so great an evil as blindness, and acted madly and wildly in the insanity of desire. But as for the deeper meaning,[j] those who pursue desire[k] as their end while pretending that through this they are seeking virtue,[l] will never find an entrance to it[m] but will soon give up in despair, for nothing fights so hard against another thing as does wisdom[n] against sensual pleasure,[o] and the shameful[p] against the best.[q]

[a] τοὺς κατεγνωσμένους: Aucher "devictos."

[b] Probably νόμος ἔστω, as in the Greek frag., which begins at this point.

[c] The Greek frag. has, more briefly, σεμνῶς καὶ θεοπρεπῶς.

[d] Or "seemly."

[e] Here again the Greek frag. has only two adjectives, σεμνὰ καὶ θεῖα. Aucher's "vultum divinum" is an expansion of the Arm. text.

[f] The Greek frag. has, more briefly, κόλασιν ἐπιφέρειν ἀορασίας.

[g] LXX παρελύθησαν, which, like the Heb., might also be rendered, "they were tired out." The phrase is quoted in *De Fuga* 144.

[h] τὸ ῥητόν.

[i] τῇ ἐπιθυμίᾳ.

[j] τὸ πρὸς διάνοιαν.

[k] τῆς ἐπιθυμίας.

[l] τὴν ἀρετήν.

[m] *i.e.* virtue.

[n] σοφία.

[o] τὴν ἡδονήν.

[p] τὸ αἰσχρόν *vel sim.*

[q] τὸ ἄριστον *vel sim.*

42. (Gen. xix. 12-13) What is the meaning of the words, " The men told Lot to lead out [a] his whole household, for we are about to destroy this place,[b] for," it says,[c] " their outcry has gone up before the Lord, and He has sent us to blot it out " [d] ?

(The phrase) " their outcry has gone up before the Lord " denotes something which is usually found among licentious and intemperate men, and is even greater than impiety.[e] For they do not believe that there is an overseer and inspector [f] of human affairs, nor do they believe that there is a providence [g] over such things as seem good (to Him).[h] And they do nothing else but what is contrary to what He says, and they send forth voices that are hostile to the Father and His truth. But (the phrase) " He has sent us to blot it out " indicates a philosophical law.[i] For He provides the virtues through Himself, but the contraries [j] through His servants.[k] And these are the laws of nature,[l] which He determined from the beginning [m] together with

[a] Aucher supplies " ex urbe." [b] Variant " this city."

[c] Apparently Philo here parenthetically refers to scripture ; Aucher omits the phrase.

[d] Philo here partly paraphrases, partly quotes LXX, which reads εἶπαν δὲ οἱ ἄνδρες πρὸς Λώτ, Ἔστιν τίς σοι ὧδε, γαμβροὶ ἢ υἱοὶ ἢ θυγατέρες ἢ εἴ τίς σοι ἄλλος ἐστὶν ἐν τῇ πόλει, ἐξάγαγε ἐκ τοῦ τόπου τούτου. ὅτι ἀπόλλυμεν ἡμεῖς τὸν τόπον τοῦτον ὅτι ὑψώθη ἡ κραυγὴ αὐτῶν ἐναντίον κυρίου, καὶ ἀπέστειλεν ἡμᾶς κύριος ἐκτρῖψαι αὐτήν. [e] ἀσέβεια.

[f] ἐπίτροπον καὶ ἔφορον *vel sim*. [g] πρόνοιαν.

[h] Construction and meaning uncertain. Aucher renders, " neque existimant ad suum placitum providentiam esse." In a footnote he adds " *Vel*, neque putant quod providentia sit illis, qui existimant ita esse." This second rendering can hardly be right. [i] νόμον φιλόσοφον.

[j] τὰς ἐναντιότητας—a punning allusion to the biblical phrase ἐναντίον κυρίου. Philo here means the contraries of nature, mentioned in the next sentence ; *cf.* also *Quis Rer. Div. Heres* 311 τῶν ἐναντιοτήτων ἐξ ὧν ἅπας ὁ κόσμος συνέστηκε.

[k] *i.e.* the angels, as symbols of natural forces here.

[l] οἱ τῆς φύσεως νόμοι. [m] ἐξ ἀρχῆς.

the things of creation. But (Scripture) clearly represents the beauty of a just judgment [a] in removing from such a destruction one household which had the sparks and seeds of virtue and had become sojourners [b] among sensual pleasures and passions. Not idly,[c] however, but naturally [d] is it written that " we are destroying [e] this place." For it is proper not only to kill venomous creatures but also to destroy and lay waste their holes and caves, in which it may happen that there remains one that has not been destroyed. And now a similar thing is to be applied [f] to the soul, (namely) that not only is that which pertains to sensual pleasure or anger to be removed and destroyed, but also the entire place of desire and anger, where they lurk, in order that the mind [g] may have paths that are broad and free of fear, with nothing to impede its feet and keep it from right conduct.[h]

*43. (Gen. xix. 14) Why does (Scripture) say that when Lot was exhorted by the angels,[i] " he seemed to his sons-in-law to be jesting " [j]?

Those who are in a lavish and unlimited state of wealth and glory and the like, and live in health and strength and vigour of body,[k] and have a store of [l] pleasures (acquired)

[a] τὸ δικαιοκρισίας κάλλος.

[b] πάροικοι. [c] οὐκ εἰκῇ. [d] φυσικῶς.

[e] So LXX, but above in the title-question the Arm. has " we are about to destroy."

[f] Lit. " fitted " or " harmonized."

[g] ὁ νοῦς. [h] ἀπὸ τῆς κατορθώσεως.

[i] Aucher amplifies in rendering, " nunciante Lot ut monitum habuerat ab Angelis."

[j] LXX ἔδοξεν δὲ γελοιάζειν ἐναντίον τῶν γαμβρῶν αὐτοῦ. Philo omits the first part of Gen. xix. 14 containing the angels' warning that Lot and his family must flee to escape destruction.

[k] The Greek frag. differs slightly, reading καὶ ἐν ὑγιείᾳ καὶ εὐαισθησίᾳ σώματος καὶ εὐεξίᾳ ζωῆς.

[l] Lit. " store away " : the Greek frag. has κρατούμενοι, which Harris (p. 110 note) would emend to καρπούμενοι.

through all of the senses,[a] believing themselves to have achieved genuine happiness,[b] do not look for change or variation,[c] but laugh at, and mock, those who say that everything which is in the body and outside contains great harmfulness and is short-lived.[d] For, when the Persians ruled land and sea, who expected that they would fall? And again, when the Macedonians (ruled)? But if anyone had dared to say so, he would most certainly have been laughed at as a fool and simpleton. And no less necessary a change awaits those nations that opposed them, though they have become illustrious and conspicuous in the meantime; so that those at whom (others) laughed are beginning to laugh (at them), while those who laughed are becoming (an object of) laughter for thinking that things which are by nature mobile and changeable are immobile and unalterable.[e]

*44. (Gen. xix. 16) Why did the angels, when they[f] were dazed and confused, take by the hand Lot and his wife and his daughters?[g]

Certainty and clarity not only provided[h] those whom

[a] τὰς διὰ πασῶν τῶν αἰσθήσεων ἡδονάς, as in the Greek frag.

[b] The Greek frag. differs slightly, reading τῆς ἄκρας εὐδαιμονίας.

[c] The Greek frag. has only μεταβολήν.

[d] The Arm. seems to be a double rendering of ἐπικαίρως ἔχει, the reading of the Greek fragment, which ends here.

[e] The Arm. writes "immobile and unalterable" (or "unchangeable") twice, the first time before the ptc. "thinking," where it is out of place. Like Aucher, I have omitted the redundant pair of predicate adjectives.

[f] *i.e.* Lot and his family.

[g] Aucher, following the biblical text, gives "his two daughters." After "daughters" LXX adds ἐν τῷ φείσασθαι κύριον αὐτοῦ, while Heb. continues still farther with the clause, "and they led him out and left him outside the city."

[h] Lit. "(was?) adapted and fitted."

they touched with confidence but also prevented the incidence of evil.[a] For just as living beings[b] (are controlled)[c] by natural reason,[d] so too do inanimate beings[e] reverence and fear the words of the Deity[f]; so that they do not harm those who are touched (by them).[g] This is the literal meaning.[h] But as for the deeper meaning,[i] the souls which are governed and led by the holy scriptures[j] can be saved[k] if only (once) having taken hold, they hold on to them. For if they are separated and cut off from them, they will be condemned to misery along with other things.

45. (Gen. xix. 17) Why did the angels who led (them out) say, " Save thyself. Do not look backward and do not stay in all this region "[l]?

It is the custom of teachers, when they explain some

[a] The syntax is very obscure. Aucher renders somewhat differently and more freely, " certa securitas data eis, quos apprehenderunt, non solum confortare eos debuit, sed etiam impediebat eventum malorum."

[b] Or " animals "—τὰ ζῷα.

[c] What verb is to be supplied is far from clear. Aucher's guess " detinentur " is probably as good as any.

[d] ὑπὸ φυσικοῦ λόγου. Aucher's rendering " verbo naturali " is also acceptable.

[e] Prob. τὰ ἄψυχα rather than οἱ ἄψυχοι, since the following verb is sing., and the Arm. translator usually follows the Greek construction of sing. verb with neuter plural subject. ἄψυχα are contrasted with ζῷα in *De Ebrietate* 183.

[f] Apparently Philo here refers to the (inanimate) evils mentioned in the preceding sentence.

[g] *i.e.* by the angels symbolizing the words of God.

[h] τὸ ῥητόν.

[i] τὸ πρὸς διάνοιαν.

[j] Or " words "—τῶν ἱερῶν λόγων.

[k] σώζεσθαι.

[l] Philo closely follows the LXX, καὶ ἐγένετο ἡνίκα ἐξήγαγον αὐτοὺς ἔξω καὶ εἶπαν (Heb. " and he said "), Σώζων σῶζε τὴν σεαυτοῦ ψυχήν· μὴ περιβλέψῃς εἰς τὰ ὀπίσω μηδὲ στῇς ἐν πάσῃ τῇ περιχώρῳ (Heb. " in the *kikkar*," *i.e.* the land around Sodom).

theory [a] to their pupils, to instruct them to remember it and say it by themselves. And similar to this is what the divine words [b] command, saying, " O thou, behold, on many occasions we have explained worthy things [c] to thee; holding thee by the hand, we have led it [d] on to worthy and useful things. Henceforth, then, do thou move by thyself, having been taught in what manner thou must be saved. Strive to preserve whole [e] all that which is in accord with (our) teaching, willingly and of thine own desire.[f] " This too is what the physician says to the ailing man who has been saved by him, " O thou, I have delivered thee from affliction and I have done everything useful in my art.[g] Now that thou art saved, do not relapse into illness so as again to be in need of another recovery,[h] but keep thyself whole, and enjoy health." Thus, the first command given was, " save thyself," (that is) do not seek [i] salvation elsewhere. And the second was, " do not look backward "—(this being said) philosophically,[j] for the things behind [k] the body are blind and insensitive.[l] And (Scripture) prays that the mind [m] will see and be keen-sighted and avoid those who are licentious and foolish and atheistic, and, after leaving them behind, will hasten with all its might toward continence [n] and holiness.[o] For many men who are, as it were, carried into port, again go back from there and are drawn into the same harm and helplessness [p] because their withdrawal and abandonment (of these) was not carried out with firm resolution (and)

[a] θεώρημά τι.
[b] οἱ θεῖοι λόγοι.
[c] ἄξια *vel sim.*
[d] *i.e.* thy hand.
[e] ὁλόκληρον.
[f] ἑκουσίᾳ γνώμῃ.
[g] τῆς τέχνης μου.
[h] ἄλλης σωτηρίας.
[i] Lit. " hunt " or " catch."
[j] φιλοσοφικῶς.
[k] Or " at the back of."
[l] *Cf. De Somniis* i. 248 on Lot's wife and her backward glance, περιβλέπεται δὲ τὰ ὀπίσω καὶ τὰ νώτια, κωφὴν δόξαν καὶ τυφλὸν πλοῦτον καὶ ἀναίσθητον εὐσαρκίαν κτλ.
[m] τὸν νοῦν.
[n] ἐγκράτειαν, here rendered by two Arm. words.
[o] ὁσιότητα *vel sim.*
[p] ἀπορίαν.

thoughtfulness.[a] And the third divine command was, "do not stay in all this region," (that is) the mind (not staying) in the body, or the mind (not staying) in the soul.[b] Thus it says, "O thou, if thou dost wish to be of pure character, do not stay, not even in any one place of this region, but pass them all by, in order to pass at once from all harm here, by which the mind is harmed (being) in the body and the several senses. But whatever characters remain in these and stand firm, fall of themselves, for they lean on, and trust in, dead things." [c]

46. (Gen. xix. 17) What is the meaning of the words, "Escape to the mountain lest thou be seized among them" [d]?

The literal text [e] reveals the destruction [f] of a plain of low-lying (places).[g] But as for the deeper meaning,[h] it seems to be somewhat as follows. When the mind [i] begins to take the higher road,[j] it becomes better and progresses,[k] leaving behind earth-bound and low things,[l] which those men pursue and admire who are undisciplined.[m] But (the mind), becoming light,[n] is elevated to higher things, and looking around observes what is in the air and in the ether

[a] ἰσχυρᾷ γνώμῃ καὶ λογισμῷ.

[b] The Arm. lit. = τοῦ νοῦ ἐν τῷ σώματι ἢ τοῦ νοῦ ἐν τῇ ψυχῇ. Aucher renders, wrongly, I think, "puta intellectum in carne vel affectibus animi." However, the text is troublesome, and should perhaps be emended from the following sentence.

[c] Aucher "in mortuos," but the neuter ptc. is indicated by the context.

[d] LXX εἰς τὸ ὄρος σώζου μή ποτε συνπαραλημφθῇς.

[e] τὸ ῥητόν.

[f] φθοράν *vel sim.*

[g] Perhaps "people" is to be supplied. Aucher less literally renders, "humilioris campi."

[h] τὸ πρὸς διάνοιαν.

[i] ὁ νοῦς.

[j] τὴν ἀνωτέραν ὁδόν.

[k] προκόπτει.

[l] τὰ χαμαίζηλα καὶ τὰ ταπεινά. The two adjectives are used together of external and bodily things in *Quod Deus Immut. Sit* 167.

[m] ἀπαίδευτοι.

[n] κοῦφος.

and the whole heaven together, its substance [a] and movements and harmonies and affinities [b] and sympathies,[c] by which things are related to one another, and this whole world.[d] This ascent is more figuratively [e] called "mountain," but its true name is "wisdom," [f] for the soul [g] which is truly a lover of wisdom [h] desired a vision of higher and more exalted things, by being in ethereal regions. Accordingly, a divine response and warning was uttered, that those who strive after low and base and earthly things shall die in respect of true life—the soul,[i] wandering about in the manner of the dead. But those who desire heavenly things and are borne on high shall be saved [j] alone, exchanging mortal for immortal life.

*47. (Gen. xix. 18-20) What is the meaning of the words, "Lot said,[k] I shall not be able to escape to the mountain lest perchance evils overtake me, and I die. Behold this city is near to escape to, which is small, and it is not small. Thereto I will escape,[l] and my soul will live " [m] ?

The divine word,[n] extending abundant grace,[o] calls up the soul of the progressive man [p] to perfection.[q] But he is still small and, like those whose health revives after a

[a] οὐσίαν. [b] συγγενείας.

[c] συμπαθείας, in the Stoic sense of cosmic sympathies. Aucher inadvertently omits to render the word.

[d] κόσμον. [e] τροπικώτερον.

[f] σοφία. [g] ἡ ψυχή. [h] φιλόσοφος.

[i] Aucher "moriuntur animā e vera vita."

[j] σωθήσονται.

[k] After "Lot said" Philo omits the last few words of vs. 18 and the first half of vs. 19. In the LXX the phrase which Philo renders "and it is not small" is a question. For a different allegory of the phrase see *De Abrahamo* 166.

[l] In LXX and Heb. the words "thereto I will escape" precede the phrase "and it is not small."

[m] After "will live" many LXX MSS. add "because of thee."

[n] ὁ θεῖος λόγος. [o] ἄφθονον χάριν.

[p] τοῦ προκόπτοντος.

[q] πρὸς τελειότητα, *cf. De Mut. Nom.* 24.

long illness and who, though they are delivered from the danger of death, are not yet well but still maintain a balance between health and illness, confesses his own poverty [a] by saying that he is not able to depart altogether from his city and from civilization [b] and change to the security of quiet that is becoming to wise men.[c] But it is for him to progress and no longer accept the city and civilization as great and honoured, and to restrain his admiration for them, considering them small indeed but somehow necessary and not a little useful.[d] Thus there are three persons who stand in the middle [e]: the wise man, the progressive man and the wicked man; and the extremes are at war. For the wise man (pursues) [f] peace and —— [g] and leisure [h] in order that he may devote himself to following after divine contemplation.[i] But the wicked man (pursues) the city and the excitement of the multitude and the crowding of the city and the stream of men and things as well.[j] For the love of business and greed and zeal to obtain authority [k] are honourable to

[a] Aucher "imbecillitatem." [b] τῆς πολιτείας.

[c] τὴν τοῖς σοφοῖς ἐπιτηδείαν ἀσφάλειαν ἡσυχίας.

[d] The text is suspect. Aucher renders more freely, "flocci faciendo similia, ita tamen ut non parvipendat ceu necessaria utiliaque."

[e] One expects something like "thus he stands in the middle of three persons."

[f] The verb is supplied from the Greek frag., which begins here.

[g] The Arm. here is meaningless; it is either a corruption or misunderstanding of ἀπραγμοσύνην, which is found in the Greek frag. Aucher's rendering, "nescius dimicationis," appears to be a guess.

[h] σχολήν, as in the Greek frag.

[i] The Greek frag. reads ἵνα τοῖς θείοις θεωρήμασιν ἐν ἡσυχίᾳ ἐντύχῃ.

[j] The Greek frag. reads more briefly ὁ φαῦλος πόλιν τε καὶ τὸν κατὰ πόλιν ὄχλον τε καὶ φυρμὸν ἀνθρώπων ὁμοῦ καὶ πραγμάτων μεταδιώκει.

[k] For the last phrase the Greek frag. has δημοκοπίαι τε καὶ δημαρχίαι.

such a man, but quiet is not honourable.[a] But he who is progressive between both [b] moves toward the peacefulness of security; he is not, however, able to get entirely beyond civilization though he no longer, as formerly, admires the city as a great good but restricts his perception [c] and receives the impression that that which formerly seemed great is a slight and small thing. But the statement of contradiction [d] that the same city is small and not small has a most natural reason,[e] which is in order and follows upon the things that were declared earlier. For the life of the city seems great to him who wishes to please the multitude, but small to the progressive man. And this question has a solution something like this. There are three ways of life which are well known: the contemplative, the active [f] and the pleasurable.[g] Great and excellent is the contemplative; slight and unbeautiful is the pleasurable; small and not small is the middle one,[h] which touches on, and adheres to, both of them. It is small by reason of the fact that it is a close neighbour to pleasure; but it is great because of its nearness and also its kinship to contemplation.

48. (Gen. xix. 21) What is the meaning of the words, "Behold, I have admired thy face also concerning this word" [i]?

[a] τὸ δὲ ἡσυχάζειν ἄτιμον (ἀτιμώτατον in the Greek frag., which ends here).

[b] *i.e.* between the perfect man and the wicked man.

[c] Aucher "aviditatem."

[d] Lit. "of quarrelling."

[e] λόγον φυσικώτατον. [f] ὁ θεωρητικὸς καὶ ὁ πρακτικός.

[g] In rendering "condecens" Aucher has chosen the wrong meaning of Arm. *vayelčakan*.

[h] *i.e.* the active or practical life.

[i] Philo follows the LXX rendering, ἐθαύμασά σου τὸ πρόσωπον, of the Heb. idiom which means "I have looked upon thee with favour." Also, LXX ῥῆμα = Heb. *dābār*, meaning both "word" and "matter." Philo omits the rest of the verse, "not to destroy the city of which thou hast spoken."

It is proper to accept [a] those who do not boast and do not promise more than their ability (to perform). Wherefore the divine and sacred word praises the things said.[b] For many men in their desire for the very great things lose even middling things which it is proper to seek.

49. (Gen. xix. 22) What is the meaning of the words, " Hasten to escape [c] there " [d]?

The sweet, good and humane [e] word of God gives a share of salvation [f] to him who is able to save himself, and it accepts his decision [g] as true and inexorable when he promises to progress so far as possible. And so it says, " O thou, although thou art not able to walk upon the mountainous and heavenly road, and the middling things that are worthy [h] still attract thee, nevertheless hasten and bestir thyself, henceforth no longer thinking these the greatest. And now that thou hast most firmly established these opinions, so that no longer may anything soft or dissolute change in thee [i] or emanate (from thee),[j] for thou art most firmly established, the avenger and destroyer of the impious will not bring judgment near to thy borders."

50. (Gen. xix. 22) What is the meaning of the words,

[a] Aucher renders freely, " humaniter recipere."

[b] *i.e.* by Lot.

[c] Or " be saved."

[d] LXX σπεῦσον οὖν τοῦ σωθῆναι ἐκεῖ.

[e] φιλάνθρωπος.

[f] κοινωνίαν σωτηρίας.

[g] γνώμην or " character " (?)—ἦθος, τρόπον.

[h] τὰ μέσα καθήκοντα *vel sim.*

[i] The Arm. = μεταλλάττῃ, perhaps a corruption of μεταλλεύῃ " undermine (thee)." Aucher has " in te haereat," apparently a guess.

[j] Aucher " fluat." The verb is suspect.

"Because of this he[a] called the name of the city 'Zoor'"[b]?

"Zoor" is translated as "mountain,"[c] which is for the salvation of those who progress, and for the destruction of those who are incurable.[d]

*51.[e] (Gen. xix. 23-24) Why (does Scripture say that) "the sun went out over[f] the earth, and Lot entered Zoor,[g] and the Lord rained upon Sodom and Gomorrah sulphur and fire from heaven"[h]?

The same time is given, to those who progress, for salvation, and to those who are incurable, for punishment.[i] And at the very beginning of day, when the sun rose, He immediately brought down punishment,[j] wishing to show that the sun and the day and light and whatever other things in the world are excellent and precious[k] are appor-

[a] The Heb. idiom often has the 3rd sing. pers. pron. (incorporated into the verb) as an impersonal subject = "one" or "people."

[b] LXX (followed by Arm. O.T.) has Σηγώρ for Heb. *Ṣô'ar* (A.V. "Zoar"). In *De Somniis* i. 85 most MSS. of Philo have Σηγώρ or Σιγώρ but two read Σοέρ. Josephus, *Ant.* i. 204, uses the form Ζωώρ.

[c] Philo inaccurately connects Heb. *Ṣô'ar* with *ṣûr* "rock" or "mountain."

[d] For the Greek original of this clause see the following section, where it is repeated.

[e] Two separate Greek fragments, making up the first half of this section, have been preserved in the Catenae, and printed by Harris and Lewy respectively; see Appendix A.

[f] LXX ἐπί.

[g] See the note on the name in the preceding section; the Greek frag. here has Σηγώρ as in the LXX.

[h] LXX and Heb. "from the Lord, from heaven."

[i] The Greek frag. has *ὁ αὐτὸς χρόνος γίνεται καὶ τοῖς προκόπτουσιν εἰς σωτηρίαν, καὶ τοῖς ἀνιάτως ἔχουσι πρὸς κόλασιν.*

[j] Or possibly "he (*i.e.* Moses = Scripture) introduced (the theme of) punishment."

[k] *ὅσα ἄλλα ἐν κόσμῳ καλὰ καὶ τίμια.*

tioned only to the wise [a] and not to any of the wicked whose wickedness is incurable. But from heaven, from which come the annual storms and rains for the growth of plants [b] that are sown and (of) [c] trees for the production of fruits for the food of men and other living creatures, (Scripture) says that sulphur and fire came down [d] for the destruction of all things on earth, in order to show that the cause of the seasons and annual times [e] is not heaven or the sun or the processions and revolutions [f] of the other stars but the power of the Father,[g] who presides over the whole world as over a winged chariot, and guides it as He thinks best and most useful.[h] And this marvellous activity [i] shows, not the established [j] habit of the elements,[k] but a certain autocratic and arbitrary power which trans-

[a] The Greek frag. has *τοῖς ἀστείοις*.

[b] Lit. "of growing things"—*τῶν φυομένων*, as in the Greek frag.

[c] One expects the gen. case of "trees" but both Arm. and the Greek frag. have the nom.

[d] Or "streamed down." The Greek frag. has *καταρραγῆναι*.

[e] The Arm. uses the same word twice for "seasons." The Greek frag. has *τῶν καιρῶν καὶ τῶν ἐτησίων ὡρῶν*.

[f] *χορεῖαι καὶ περιπολήσεις*, as in the Greek frag.

[g] *ἡ τοῦ πατέρος δύναμις*, as in the Greek frag.

[h] Lewy reconstructs the Greek of this clause (not preserved in the Catenae) as *ἐφεδρεύοντος μὲν ὡς ἅρματι πτηνῷ σύμπαντι τῷ κόσμῳ, ἡνιοχοῦντος δ' αὐτὸν ὡς βέλτιστ' ἂν νομίσειεν*. On the concept of the world or heaven as a winged chariot, which Philo in *QG* iii. 3 ascribes to Plato (*cf. Phaedrus* 246 E), see *Quis Rer. Div. Heres* 301 *καὶ τὸν πτηνὸν ἅρμα, τὸν σύμπαντα οὐρανόν, ἡνιοχεῖ χρώμενον αὐτεξουσίῳ καὶ αὐτοκράτορι βασιλείᾳ*.

[i] The Arm. differs slightly in syntax from the Greek frag., which has *ἡ τεθαυματουργημένη πρᾶξις*.

[j] As Lewy notes, the Arm. = *καθεστὸς ἔθος*, while the Greek frag. has *καθ' ἕκαστον ἔθος*.

[k] With Lewy I emend Arm. *tareworsd* "annual (seasons)" to *tareročd* "elements," on the basis of the Greek frag.'s *ἐπὶ τῶν στοιχείων*.

forms the elements of all things as it chooses.[a] For sulphur and fire are light[b] by nature, and for this reason they are borne aloft,[c] but the innovation of the curse[d] changed their movement into the opposite one, from up (to down),[e] and forced the lightest things to be borne like the heaviest.

And it is fitting to enter into the difficult problem why He not only destroyed the inhabitants, for they were unrighteous and impious, but also overturned and burned down cities and homes and all the buildings. In regard to this it should be said that there is a certain principle[f] in the nature of places and sites, and that there are some, on the one hand, that are privileged[g] and honoured, and, on the other, some that are the opposite. For where wise men[h] dwell there are places called venerable and honourable, (such as) council-halls, shrines and temples.[i] But where licentious, intemperate, impious and unrighteous men (dwell), there are defiled, polluted and impure (places), stained by the pollution of those who live there without

[a] Here the Arm. closely follows the wording of the Greek frag., which has τινα δύναμιν αὐτοκρατῆ καὶ αὐτεξούσιον (*cf.* the quotation from *Quis Rer. Div. Heres* in note *h*, p. 327) μεταστοιχειοῦσαν, ὡς ἂν προέληται, τὰ σύμπαντα.

[b] κοῦφα, as in the Greek frag.

[c] ἄνω φορεῖται. The Greek frag. has ἄνω φοιτᾷ.

[d] τὸ δὲ τῆς ἀρᾶς κεκαινουργημένον, as in the Greek frag., except that the Arm. has the ptc. in the accus. instead of the nom. case.

[e] The words "to down" are supplied from the Greek frag., which has κάτω.

[f] λόγος τις. Philo seems to mean "principle of congruence" or the like.

[g] Aucher renders, "ita ut hic praerogativa praevaleant cum utilitate," and adds in a footnote that Arm. *awar* "booty" here seems to mean "utility" or the like. It is more likely, however, that *awar*, which elsewhere = προνομή, is here used merely as a synonym of *haxabašxout'iun*, which = προνομία.

[h] οἱ σοφοί.

[i] Construction uncertain because of the curious word-order.

virtue and in vice.[a] For these reasons that (place) which is honourable flourishes and, in addition, continues to be adorned, while the place of unrestraint is overturned, overthrown and destroyed with its resident[b] men and populace. Moreover, it is also defiled. But the divine word[c] is an example to future generations[d] not to seek to do anything unworthy, (like) those cursed by calamities and burned by fire, in order that they may be admonished by seeing the sufferings of their fellows, and keep them in mind and be fearful lest they suffer their sentence, and that they may be kept from the same impious behaviour. For if men saw this, not with bodily eyes but rather with the mind,[e] they would certainly be converted to virtue.[f] If they cannot be persuaded by reason,[g] at least they may assume moderation[h] through violent and necessary fear. And some will say that there are two examples on earth, (namely) Paradise and the region of the Sodomites, of which one is the immortality of the virtues, and the other, complete destruction through evil.[i] The former (existed) at the beginning and was contemporary with the creation of the world; the other was at the end.[j] For virtue is prior and elder and (is) the activity of nature at the be-

[a] Text slightly emended. The Arm. has the ablative instead of the locative case of the word meaning "vice," probably by attraction to the preceding noun.

[b] Aucher renders, "legitimis" but Arm. *ōrinawor* here translates *ἔννομος* in the sense of "residing in" rather than "lawful."

[c] *ὁ θεῖος λόγος*, *i.e.* Scripture.

[d] The punctuation is uncertain. Aucher, while noting this fact, renders, "imo et ab ipso dominico verbo abominationem subit, ut pote futurae deinde generationes moneantur, etc."

[e] *τῷ νῷ*.

[f] *εἰς ἀρετήν*.

[g] *ὑπὸ τοῦ λόγου*.

[h] *σωφροσύνην*.

[i] Aucher inadvertently omits the rendering of this clause (from "of which one" to "evil").

[j] At the end of what period is not clear.

ginning,[a] while vice is a child and a minor, being born later to a foolish and unjust soul.

*52. (Gen. xix. 26) Why did his [b] wife look backward and become a pillar of salt and not some other material? [c]

The literal meaning [d] is very clear. For the angels had commanded (them) not to turn backward, and she transgressed the command, wherefore she paid the penalty, though it was not the same as that of the Sodomites. For it [e] was destroyed by sulphur and fire, whereas the woman was changed into the nature [f] of salt. All these [g] indicate unproductiveness and unfruitfulness, for when the region was burnt up, the salt-plain was no less unfruitful.[h] Thus, (Scripture) wishes (to admonish) [i] you by producing even more wonderful miracles.[j] Just as in the case of Sodom, that which was light by nature [k] was made to bear downward like those things which are heavy [l] by nature, so did salt, one of those things which were made for well-being and endurance,[m] become a cause of ruin and destruction.

And now [n] the reason must be told why the angels commanded (them) not to turn backward. They knew

[a] The context makes it likely that "activity" is one of the predicates of "virtue" rather than the subject of an independent clause.

[b] *i.e.* Lot's.

[c] This verse is briefly commented on in *Leg. All.* iii. 213 and more fully in *De Fuga* 121-125, but neither passage is a direct parallel to the present one.

[d] τὸ ῥητόν. [e] *i.e.* Sodom. [f] φύσιν.

[g] Exactly what "these" are is not clear.

[h] The meaning of the sentence is somewhat doubtful.

[i] The missing verb is supplied in Aucher's rendering.

[j] θαυματουργῶν.

[k] *i.e.* the sulphur and fire, see *QG* iv. 51.

[l] Aucher inadvertently renders, "levia" instead of "gravia."

[m] εἰς σωτηρίαν καὶ διαμονήν.

[n] To several sentences in the following paragraph there are Greek parallels in Procopius and the Catenae.

that some might perhaps rejoice at seeing these troubles.[a] But to rejoice and exult over the misfortunes of others, while it may be just, is not humane.[b] For the future is unforseeable,[c] and punishment is ——,[d] and suddenly it overtakes (men) everywhere, as do impotence and heaviness. But others might perhaps be soft and weak and might suffer from the misfortune more than they can (bear), being moved to pity and compassion and being overcome (by their feeling) for their friends and acquaintances and those with whom only a short while before they had been living,[e] because it is ——,[f] and they are united by the greatest mutual tenderness and compassion. And so, there were two reasons for their being forbidden (to look backward, namely) that they might not rejoice greatly nor grieve greatly at the punishment inflicted upon those who were suffering deservedly. And there was a third (reason), which I shall at once explain.[g] (Scripture) says, " Do not, O men, look at[h] God when He punishes, for it is enough for you simply to know that they suffered the punishment which they deserved. But to investigate and examine[i] how they suffered is an act of impudence and

[a] *i.e.* of the Sodomites.

[b] Similarly Procopius and the Catenae, *χαίρειν ἐπὶ ταῖς τῶν ἐχθρῶν ἀτυχίαις εἰ καὶ δίκαιον* (+ *ποτε* Catenae), *ἀλλ' οὐκ ἀνθρώπινον*.

[c] *ἄδηλον*, as in the Procopius frag., which lacks the words that follow in Arm., down to " But others."

[d] Arm. *anpatkaṛeli* can mean only " irreverent " or " shameless." Aucher renders, " inexorabile," which fits the context, though it appears to be a guess. Probably the Greek had *ἀπαραίτητος*.

[e] The last part of the sentence reads more briefly in Procopius *ἡττώμενοι φίλων καὶ συνηθείας*.

[f] Arm. *anari* means " unmanly " and also " enormous." Neither meaning fits here. Aucher omits the phrase.

[g] The last clause is missing in the Procopius frag., which resumes here (the Catenae resume with the next sentence).

[h] Procopius and the Catenae have *μὴ κατανοεῖτε*.

[i] Procopius and the Catenae have only one verb, *περιεργάζεσθαι*.

shamelessness [a] and not of reverence,[b] with which it is the part of the rational nature [c] to live most carefully, constantly and familiarly.[d] The above is the literal meaning.[e]

But as for the deeper meaning,[f] the wife of the mind is symbolically sense-perception,[g] which becomes insolent not only in evil men but also in those who progress,[h] and it inclines toward sense-perceptible things which are external rather than the things seen internally by reason.[i] And for this reason it turns back, in appearance to Sodom, but in truth to all the visible possessions, and it returns to those things which are with measure and without measure and to the varieties of their exhalations [j] and to the properties [k] of pleasant odours and tastes and substances,[l] and it changes into an inanimate thing [m] by separating itself from the mind, for the sake of which it was animated.[n]

53. (Gen. xix. 27-28) Why did Abraham "go early in the morning to the place where he had been standing before the Lord and look toward Sodom and Gomorrah [o]

[a] Procopius and the Catenae have *προπετείας καὶ θράσους*.
[b] *εὐλαβείας*, as in the Greek fragments, which end here.
[c] *τῆς λογικῆς φύσεως*.
[d] Aucher renders somewhat differently, " non vero timoris (Dei), quocum conversari diligentius et constantius familiare est naturae rationali."
[e] *τὸ ῥητόν*. [f] *τὸ πρὸς διάνοιαν*.
[g] *ἡ τοῦ νοῦ γυνὴ συμβολικῶς ἐστιν αἴσθησις*.
[h] *τοῖς προκόπτουσι*.
[i] *ὑπὸ τοῦ λόγου*.
[j] *εἰς τὰς τῶν ἀναθυμιάσεων διαφοράς*. Is Philo perhaps thinking of the Heracleitian saying (Diels 4 ed., Frag. 12) *Ζήνων τὴν ψυχὴν λέγει αἰσθητικὴν ἀναθυμίασιν*?
[k] *εἰς τὰς ἰδιότητας*.
[l] Or " humours." [m] *ἄψυχον*.
[n] Aucher mistakes the meaning of the last clauses in rendering, " convertens se ac mutans in res spiritu carentes, reposito intellectu, eo quod jam animalis fere merus erat."
[o] Lit. " Sodomites and Gomorrahites."

and the surrounding region, and behold, a flame went up from the earth like the flame of a furnace " [a] ?

Wonderfully has (Scripture) described piety,[b] for it is the part of the wise man [c] to stand and not to weary but continuously and unceasingly to pray when punishment is inflicted upon undeserving [d] men. O God-worthy example of holiness and humaneness ! [e] For he says, " If thou seest some men going astray,[f] do not be afraid and do not give up." And fearing the authority of the power that punishes and destroys,[g] he made supplication to the Father. And in supplicating Him, without turning backward [h] but with great prayers placating, venerating and worshipping [i] Him, he ran to meet Him with prayer because of the uncertainty of the future. For just as He is kind and gentle, so too He is terrible ; He is kind in so far as He is God, and terrible in so far as He is Lord.[j] That is the literal meaning.[k] But as for the deeper meaning,[l] the mind [m] is firm,[n] as the one God is firm. And behold, when it has become unalterable and unchangeable, all the things which it sees on looking around, which are all sense-perceptible, corporeal and subject to passion—all

[a] So the LXX except that for " flame of a furnace " it has ἀτμὶς καμίνου. Heb. has " smoke " instead of " flame " in both parts of the comparison.

[b] εὐσέβειαν.

[c] τοῦ σοφοῦ.

[d] Or " unworthy " ?—ἀναξίοις.

[e] ὢ θεοπρεποῦς τύπου (*vel sim.*) τῆς ὁσιότητος καὶ τῆς φιλανθρωπίας.

[f] I follow Aucher's rendering, " deviantes," though the Arm. verb regularly means " to scatter."

[g] *i.e.* God's attribute of justice, the δύναμις κολαστήριος or βασιλική, see *QG* ii. 51 notes.

[h] Aucher freely renders, " indesinenter."

[i] Aucher renders the last verb, " de salute anhelando." The original was probably θεραπεύων, in the religious sense.

[j] The two chief divine attributes of mercy and justice correspond to the appellatives θεός and κύριος respectively, see *QG* ii. 51 notes.

[k] τὸ ῥητόν.

[l] τὸ πρὸς διάνοιαν.

[m] ὁ νοῦς.

[n] βέβαιος *vel sim.*

these substances it imagines as exhalation, furnace and smoke. For the feverish body is a furnace, and the exhalation (rising) from the senses is like vapour and smoke (rising) from the earth. And the passions [a] which surround us like a flame [b] and burn us up are fire [c] and wind. And these it is not possible to examine closely and to know and see (that they arise) from vice and evil, for they are certain and clear only to the wise man,[d] especially the appearances of the several parts mentioned.

*54. (Gen. xix. 29) Why is it that "God, after wiping out those inhabiting the environs of Sodom,[e] remembered Abraham, and sent Lot out of the midst of the destruction" [f]?

You see how the literal meaning [g] is. For Lot was saved not for his own sake so much as for the sake of the wise man,[h] Abraham, for the latter had offered prayers for him. But as for the deeper meaning,[i] when the Father remembers a perfect family,[j] He also saves its kinsmen [k] and the progressive man.[l] Excellent and wise, moreover, was it that "He sent Lot out from the midst of the destruction" but not out of all (destruction). For the way of life of the progressive man does not proceed rightly [m] in every respect, but he limps somewhat and falls.[n] And the middle parts are those that guide and are the right ones of those that

[a] τὰ πάθη.

[b] Exact meaning uncertain. Aucher renders, "quae vero flammis circumdant nos."

[c] Variant "odour."

[d] τῷ σοφῷ.

[e] LXX ἐν τῷ ἐκτρίψαι κύριον (Heb. "God") πάσας τὰς πόλεις τῆς περιοίκου.

[f] LXX and Heb. add "when the Lord (Heb. "He") devastated the cities in which Lot dwelt."

[g] τὸ ῥητόν.

[h] τοῦ σοφοῦ.

[i] τὸ πρὸς διάνοιαν.

[j] τελείου γένους.

[k] τοὺς συγγενεῖς.

[l] τὸν προκόπτοντα.

[m] ὀρθῶς.

[n] Aucher, taking the ptc. as transitive, renders, "impingit."

lead.[a] Wherefore he has good hope of moving in the right direction and of being (rightly) ordered toward other things. For when his most proper parts[b] are sound, he is able to give a share of salvation[c] to those that are still ailing.

55. (Gen. xix. 30) Why does Lot, fearing to dwell in Segor,[d] go up to the mountain and dwell in a cave with his two daughters ?[e]

As for the literal meaning,[f] it is fitting to say this, that he did not think it sound or safe to be near cities that had been burned up. But as for the deeper meaning,[g] when the progressive mind[h] becomes still purer, it removes still farther and separates from the guilty and unlivable way of life[i] and, to speak truly and properly, from destruction. And the mind has two connatural daughters,[j] (namely) counsel and consent.[k]

*56. (Gen. xix. 31-32)[l] Why is it that " the elder

[a] The above is a literal translation of the Arm., which makes little sense to me. Aucher, bravely ignoring syntax, renders more smoothly, " partes autem ejus sunt mediocres in principatu conductrices in rectitudine."

[b] τὰ κυριώτατα μέρη. [c] κοινωνίαν σωτηρίας.

[d] So LXX : Heb. *Ṣôʿar* (A.V. " Zoar "). See the note on " Zoor " in *QG* iv. 50.

[e] Philo condenses the verse, which reads " and Lot went out of Segor and dwelt in the mountain, and his two daughters with him, for he was afraid to dwell in Segor, and he dwelt in the cave, he and his two daughters with him."

[f] τὸ ῥητόν. [g] τὸ πρὸς διάνοιαν.

[h] ὁ προκόπτων νοῦς. One might expect ἡ προκόπτουσα ψυχή, " the progressive soul." [i] ἀπὸ τοῦ ἐνόχου καὶ ἀβιώτου βίου.

[j] συμφύτους θυγατέρας.

[k] In *De Poster. Caini* 175 Lot's daughters appear as symbols of βουλή and συγκατάθεσις.

[l] These verses are differently explained in *De Poster. Caini* 175-177. A small portion of this section is paraphrased by Procopius.

(daughter of Lot) said to the younger, Our father is an old man, and there is no one [a] who will come in to us as is proper [b] for the whole earth. Come now [c] and let us give our father wine to drink and let us lie with him and raise up seed from our father " ?

This undertaking [d] against the present custom of marriage is somewhat unlawful and an innovation but it has an excuse.[e] For these virgins, because of their ignorance [f] of external matters and because they saw those cities burned up together with all their inhabitants, supposed that the whole human race (had been destroyed at the same time) [g] and that no one remained anywhere except the three of them. Wherefore, in the belief that (they were showing) foresight (and) that (the earth) [h] might not be devastated and remain desolate and that the human race might not be destroyed, they rushed into an audacious act [i] to overcome their helplessness in this matter and their difficulties. That is the literal meaning.[j] But as for the deeper meaning,[k] this (passage) must be said (to pertain) to counsel and consent,[l] for these are the daughters of the mind,[m] counsel being the elder, and consent being the younger. For it is impossible for anyone to consent before taking counsel. And these are necessarily and naturally born to their father, (namely) the mind. For through counsel the mind sows worthy, fitting

[a] LXX and Heb. " there is no one on earth."

[b] LXX ὡς καθήκει : Heb. " as is the way."

[c] LXX δεῦρο οὖν.

[d] Or " argument "—ἐπιχείρημα.

[e] Aucher renders more freely, " aggressum interim propositum ad morem spectans matrimonii, iniquum est, et novarum rerum molitio enormis ; veniam tamen habere videtur."

[f] Or " inexperience."

[g] This last phrase is included in parentheses in the Arm. text, presumably because it has been supplied by Aucher.

[h] I follow Aucher in supplying the missing noun.

[i] παρρησίαν *vel sim.*

[j] τὸ ῥητόν.

[k] τὸ πρὸς διάνοιαν.

[l] βουλῆς καὶ συγκαταθέσεως. See *QG* iv. 55 last note.

[m] τοῦ νοῦ.

and persuasive things in those who are not discordant in aiming at the truth.[a] But consent is that which in respect of appearances[b] makes way for the several senses.[c] For what can counsel do by itself without the mind, and what (can) consent (do)? For by themselves they are ineffective and unproductive, unless they are moved by the mind to their proper business and activities.[d]

57. (Gen. xix. 37) Why did the elder (daughter) on bearing a son call him Moab, proclaiming aloud[e] what ought to have been concealed, (namely) "he is from my father"[f]?

The literal meaning[g] is (an occasion of) exultation and glorification for those who think rightly. For she did not cease (talking) and remain quiet as if (it were) a reproach but prided herself in thought as if on a great achievement,[h] and with delight said, "I have a deserved honour, which the father, who is the mind in me,[i] sowed. And having been sown,[j] he did not disintegrate[k] and pass away but having been born perfect,[l] he was found worthy of birth

[a] *ἐν τοῖς μὴ ἀσυμφώνοις οὖσιν ἐν τῷ στοχάζεσθαι τῆς ἀληθείας.*

[b] Aucher renders, "juxta propositum."

[c] *ἑκάσταις ταῖς αἰσθήσεσι.*

[d] *εἰς τὰ ἐπιτήδεια πράγματα καὶ ἐνεργείας vel sim.*

[e] Aucher renders, "vocitando super eum."

[f] LXX *ἐκ τοῦ πατρός μου.* Here, as elsewhere (*e.g. Leg. All.* iii. 81), Philo follows the popular, biblical etymology of Moab, as if = *mê-'āb* "from the father."

[g] *τὸ ῥητόν.*

[h] *κατορθώσεως vel sim.* Aucher renders, "de magna probitate."

[i] Perhaps in the original the prepositional phrase "in me" was connected with "sowed" rather than "the mind."

[j] Apparently the unspecified subject is the son born to Lot's daughter (*βουλή*).

[k] Arm. *vižem* has a variety of meanings, including "to miscarry," "to flow," "to be borne," "to be thrown." Aucher renders, "non abortus fuit inaniter."

[l] Or "complete"—*τέλειος.*

and nurture."[a] And what should be the irreprehensible and irreproachable[b] progeny of the mind and counsel if not good and excellent counsel.[c] Wherefore (the child) who was born was a male.

58. (Gen. xix. 37-38) Why does the elder (daughter) call the son born (to her) "from my father," while the younger says, "Ammon,[d] the son of my people"[e]? And of the former (why is it that Scripture) says, "This is the father of the Moabites,[f]" and of the other, "This is the father of the Ammonites unto this day"?

Because that which reflects is called "mind,"[g] and its counsel is directed[h] toward the good, wherefore also counsel[i] naturally exclaims, "from my father." For it is only from the mind that counsel (and) imagination[j] are acquired by me. And consent[k] is nothing (in itself) but gives way to imagination. But to give way and not to retire[l] is a maternal and very feminine thing. For this reason she speaks of the child that is born as "Ammon," as no longer being "from the father" but "from the

[a] τροφῆς.

[b] The two Arm. adjectives probably render the single Greek adj. ἀκατάγνωστος *vel sim.*

[c] The same Arm. word, *xorhourd* (=βουλή, λογισμός etc.), is here used of the offspring of νοῦς and βουλή as of βουλή itself.

[d] Arm. and LXX "Amman."

[e] So LXX, Ἀμμάν, ὁ υἱὸς τοῦ γένους μου. Heb. reads more briefly "The son of my people" (*ben-'ammî*), omitting the ethnic name.

[f] LXX and Heb. add "unto this day."

[g] νοῦς.

[h] Lit. "is thought."

[i] βουλή, symbolized by the elder daughter of Lot, see the preceding sections.

[j] βουλὴ (καὶ) φαντασία: variant "counselling imagination," Aucher renders, "cogitare junctim cum imaginatione," with a query in the footnote.

[k] συγκατάθεσις, see the preceding sections.

[l] Or "to feel shame." Perhaps we should emend *xoršeln* to *xorheln* "to reflect" or "to take counsel."

people." For to give way to imagination, which is consent, is to be close to, and near to, the senses,[a] and sense-perception is in generation and change.[b]

59. (Gen. xx. 1) What is the meaning of the words, "And Abraham moved[c] from there to the land in the south,[d] and he dwelt between Kadesh[e] and between[f] Shur,[g] and he dwelt as a sojourner[h] in Gerar"?

The statement[i] includes the dwelling and the sojourning of the virtuous man,[j] the dwelling being that between Kadesh and Shur, and the sojourning that in Gerar. Naturally does (Scripture) wish to reveal the powers[k] which are in these names, for "Kadesh" is to be interpreted as "sacred,"[l] and "Shur" as "wall."[m] Within the borders of these two is the region of God-loving thoughts.[n] And in this dwell those who are provided with, and surrounded by, virtues[o] as if by an inexpugnable and indestructible wall; and they are nourished by the sacred laws, and rejoice throughout the days of their life with the house-master of wisdom,[p] drinking from ever-flowing

[a] ταῖς αἰσθήσεσι.

[b] Text uncertain; the above is the reading of one MS.

[c] LXX ἐκίνησεν: Heb. "journeyed."

[d] LXX εἰς γῆν πρὸς λίβα: Heb. "to the land of the Negeb" (="dry land" in the south of Palestine).

[e] Arm. and LXX "Kades."

[f] Philo follows the LXX in retaining the Heb. idiom "between . . . and between . . ."

[g] Arm. and LXX "Sur."

[h] Arm. uses two words to render LXX παρῴκησεν. In biblical Greek πάροικος = Heb. *gēr* "resident alien," later "convert."

[i] ἡ πρόθεσις.

[j] τοῦ σπουδαίου.

[k] τὰς δυνάμεις.

[l] Heb. *qādēš* (*qādôš*) "sacred," "holy"; *cf. De Fuga* 213 Κάδης δὲ ἅγια.

[m] See *QG* iii. 27 for the same etymology.

[n] Or "thoughts dear to God"—λογισμῶν θεοφιλῶν.

[o] ἀρεταῖς.

[p] σὺν τῷ οἰκοδεσπότῃ τῆς σοφίας. *Cf. De Somniis* i. 149 where Philo calls God the "house-master of the world."

fountains. And these the divine word [a] has led to one place. And like sojourners they dwell in Gerar,[b] which is the region of God-loving thoughts.

60. (Gen. xx. 2) Why does Abraham again [c] say, concerning his wife, "She is my sister"?

Always and everywhere it was a kind of counsel of homage,[d] that among strangers he called his wife "sister." Wherefore anyone who says that this (was done) through levity of character [e] with unwashed feet [f] and with a changed countenance and with complete practice [g] is deserving of condemnation.[h] For they cannot reflect and bear in mind that [i] no one is so stupid and silly (even) among those who go far in wrongdoing [j] (as to think) that he in whom there is perfection [k] would, as it were, wish

[a] ὁ θεῖος λόγος.

[b] Philo connects the name "Gerar" with Heb. *gēr* "sojourner," "resident alien."

[c] As in Gen. xii. 13 ff., not commented on by Philo in *QG*, but *cf. De Abrahamo* 89 ff. LXX here (Gen. xx. 2) departs from the Heb. in adding that Abraham was afraid to say that Sarah was his wife lest the men of the city kill him on her account.

[d] The Arm. seems to render βουλή τις θεραπείας, but one would expect σωτηρίας "safety."

[e] Syntax and meaning uncertain. The verb "says" is in the 2nd pers. sing., and the phrase "through levity of character" may depend upon it rather than upon the verb here supplied. Aucher renders, "qui levitate morum similia dixerint."

[f] ἀνίπτοις ποσί, *i.e.* "impromptu" or the like.

[g] Arm. lit. = πράγμασι τελείοις but the meaning escapes me (see next note). Aucher renders, "re peracta."

[h] Perhaps we should ignore the conjunction "and" before the phrase "with complete practice" and render, "is completely deserving of condemnation."

[i] Taking Arm. *k'anzi*, which usu. = "for," as here = *zi* "that."

[j] οἳ ἀδικίᾳ προκόπτουσι.

[k] *i.e.* Abraham.

to remain in sinful transgression and to celebrate [a] many times those things which when spoken only once bring shame and disgrace. But let not such a streak of impiety come upon us as that we should think unworthy things of the patriarch, father and founder.[b] For a most noble (occasion of) glorification are those things which are seen by nature.[c] For the virtue-loving mind [d] calls virtue "sister" but not "wife," because it seems to be not only a protector [e] of wisdom [f] as if of a wife but by calling it "sister" it shows that eagerness and zeal for this are common to all who are genuine and sincere in their desire for excellence.[g]

61. (Gen. xx. 2) What is the meaning of the words, "Abimelech, the king of Gerar, sent and took Sarah"?

Passing over the opinion of some who believe that the wise man [h] was a betrayer of the laws of marriage, for the king, being impure and licentious and unrestrainedly lascivious, wished to bring shame upon the laws relating to strangers, and took the wife of another, we say that the question is one of virtue,[i] of which all wicked and evil men claim to be champions [j] so far as appearance is concerned,[k] for few are they who desire it and by labour and great effort succeed in acquiring it.

62. (Gen. xx. 3) What is the meaning of the words, "God went in to Abimelech [l] in his sleep at night, and

[a] Lit. "to sing in speech."
[b] *ἀρχηγέτου*, rendered by two Arm. words.
[c] This sentence is unintelligible to me.
[d] *ὁ φιλάρετος νοῦς* (or *διάνοια*).
[e] *προστάτης vel sim.*
[f] *σοφίας*.
[g] *καλοκἀγαθίας*.
[h] *τὸν σοφόν, i.e.* Abraham.
[i] *ἀρετῆς*, symbolized by Sarah.
[j] *προστάτους vel sim.*
[k] Aucher renders, "quatenus ad vulgi opinionem."
[l] LXX *εἰσῆλθεν ὁ θεὸς πρὸς Ἀβιμέλεχ*.

said, Behold, thou shalt die [a] because of the woman whom thou didst take, and she is living with a man " [b] ?

The literal meaning [c] is clearly signified. But as for the deeper meaning,[d] it presents something like the following. The foolish man who violently insists [e] that he possesses virtue [f] is convicted [g] by the divine Logos,[h] which enters his soul and examines and searches him and forces him to confess that this [i] is the possession of another man and not his. And most excellently is it written, " in his sleep at night." For the foolish soul spends its life carefully shut up [j] in darkness and night and deep sleep, and it has no part at all in wakefulness.[k]

63. (Gen. xx. 4) What is the meaning of the words, " Abimelech did not touch her " [l] ?

The literal meaning [m] indicates holiness and purity. But as for the deeper meaning,[n] this must be said. The foolish soul does not wish to touch or come near virtue, and is unable to do so because of its peculiar nature.[o]

*64. (Gen. xx. 4-5) What is the meaning of the words,

[a] Lit. " thou diest," as in LXX and Heb.

[b] LXX αὕτη δέ ἐστιν συνῳκηκυῖα ἀνδρί : Heb. " she is a married woman."

[c] τὸ ῥητόν.

[d] ἡ διάνοια.

[e] Aucher renders, " falso se persuadet."

[f] ἀρετήν, symbolized by Sarah.

[g] ἐλέγχεται.

[h] ὑπὸ τοῦ θείου λόγου.

[i] *i.e.* virtue.

[j] Aucher, taking, the ptc. as active, renders, " omnino includens."

[k] ἀγρυπνίας.

[l] LXX οὐχ ἥψατο αὐτῆς : Heb. " did not approach her."

[m] τὸ ῥητόν.

[n] τὸ πρὸς διάνοιαν.

[o] διὰ τὴν ἰδίαν φύσιν.

"And Abimelech said, Lord, wilt Thou destroy a nation (that is) in ignorance [a] and righteous?" [b]?

I do not know whether ignorance is compatible with righteousness. However, there are those who say that (this) is not one of the very clear-cut cases [c] so that it is possible to confirm and clearly define the notion and distinguish that which is not germane. For I would say, "My good man, not like a voluntary sin's being unrighteous is an involuntary (sin committed) through ignorance by that very fact righteous,[d] but, it seems to me,[e] it is halfway between both, the righteous and the unrighteous, which by some is called 'indifferent,' for no sin is the effect of righteousness." [f] But this is what he says concerning this, "With a pure heart and with righteous hands [g] have I done this." Of these statements one is true and the other false, for it is true that (it was) with a pure heart, but false that (it was) with righteous hands. For I would say to him, "Is not that which is actually done [h] enough for thee of unrighteousness?" [i]

65. (Gen. xx. 6) What is the meaning of the words,

[a] The LXX has the ptc. ἀγνοοῦν while the Arm. has the noun "ignorance" in the instr. case.

[b] The Heb. reads more briefly "Wilt Thou kill even a righteous nation?"

[c] Lit. "one of the very pure ones"—τῶν λίαν καθαρῶν.

[d] So the Greek frag., οὐχ ὡς τὸ ἑκουσίως ἁμαρτάνειν ἐστὶν ἄδικον, οὕτω τὸ ἀκουσίως καὶ κατ' ἄγνοιαν εὐθὺς δίκαιον.

[e] The Greek frag. has τάχα που.

[f] So the Greek frag. (which ends here), μεθόριον ἀμφοῖν, δικαίου καὶ ἀδίκου, τὸ ὑπό τινων καλούμενον ἀδιάφορον. ἁμάρτημα γὰρ οὐδὲν ἔργον δικαιοσύνης.

[g] Lit. "with hands of righteousness." LXX (Gen. xx. 5) has ἐν δικαιοσύνῃ χειρῶν.

[h] Lit. "that which is through deeds."

[i] In view of Philo's earlier statements about Abimelech's licentiousness, one would expect him here to admit that he had righteous hands, since he had not touched Sarah, but not a pure heart. But see the next section.

" And God said to him in his sleep,[a] Indeed I knew that with a pure heart thou didst this, and I spared thee from sinning against Me. Because of this I did not let thee come near her "[b]?

All the things that stand in these words are truly divine words and commandments.[c] Now to be pure in mind[d] belongs to him who sins unknowingly and in an unwilling manner, not in a willing one. And those are to be spared whom (Scripture) has shown to be grieved,[e] and those are to be held indifferent[f] who have unwillingly done wrong. And, in the third place, those who have acted unlawfully in divine matters, sin not only against these but also against the Deity, to Whom care and overseeing are proper, and to Whom is all grace,[g] and Who reverses the first impulses of the soul and guides it by His providence[h] lest it drop headlong into wrath and anger, and fall into lawlessness.

66. (Gen. xx. 7) What is the meaning of the words, " Now give back his wife to the man, for he is a prophet[i] and will pray for thee.[j] But if thou dost not give (her) back, know that thou wilt die, and all that is thine "?

The literal meaning[k] contains a defence[l] against the event that the betrayer of marriage might suffer retribu-

[a] So LXX: Heb. " in his dream."

[b] Philo here closely follows the LXX.

[c] ὄντως εἰσὶ θεῖοι λόγοι καὶ ἐντολαί.

[d] καθαρὸν τῷ νῷ (or τῇ διανοίᾳ). Aucher omits " mind " in his rendering.

[e] Meaning uncertain. Aucher renders, " parcendum autem esse illis quos monstravit aegre ferendos."

[f] ἀδιαφόρους.

[g] πᾶσα χάρις.

[h] προνοίᾳ. Aucher renders somewhat differently, " quae primos animi impetus rebellantes retrovertit per providentiam."

[i] προφήτης, as in LXX.

[j] LXX and Heb. add " and thou shalt live," as does Philo in the parallel comment *Quis Rer. Div. Heres* 258-259.

[k] τὸ ῥητόν.

[l] ἀπολογίαν (rendered here by two Arm. words).

tion,[a] and especially and peculiarly (a man) of prophecy.[b] Knowing that he[c] would remain without defiling and coming near her, and that his wife would be kept pure, he did not hesitate to call her "sister," (a name that was) sweet, tender, fitting and appropriate among the natives, and not "wife." Altogether excellent also is the manner[d] of speech of the divine command, "Give back his wife," not "sister" or "Sarah," which was as much as to say, "Give back the wife with her body preserved whole, sanctified and holy, not ravished or stripped, and just as she came to her husband from her virgin state, and return her pure and undefiled. If thou dost not return her as a wife, a penal judgment will be set up and increased upon thee and upon all thy house by death." But as for the deeper meaning,[e] those who profess wisdom, righteousness and virtue in general,[f] just as they can live only with a virtuous mate as wife, so they can live an immortal life of soul. But any who drag her[g] off and lacerate her, wishing to shame her, are not able to shame or lacerate her, but out of self-love and in the senselessness of mad impulses are altogether deprived of virtue, and destroy themselves. And, says (Scripture), if thou wert not placated[h] before, and it seemed pleasant to thee to appear to be seized by

[a] Meaning uncertain. Aucher renders, "littera praesefert apologiam juridicam contra eventus, ita ut satisfactio reddatur legi matrimonii," and in a footnote on "legi," adds, "Verba sunt *proditori matrimonii*: quod si ad Abraham referatur, indicat eum per vim sibi factam vel invitus [*sic*] prodidisse alienigenis uxorem suam: si vero ad Abimelech, demonstrat vim ab illo factam, qui tulit Sarram, nolente Abrahamo: sequentia quoque praeferunt ambiguitatem sensus."

[b] Or perhaps "and (this is) special and peculiar to prophecy."

[c] *i.e.* Abimelech. Aucher, rendering somewhat carelessly, has, "quod intacta remansura erat."

[d] Lit. "face"—*πρόσωπον*.

[e] *τὸ πρὸς διάνοιαν*.

[f] *σοφίαν καὶ δικαιοσύνην ὁμοῦ καὶ ἀρετήν*.

[g] *i.e.* virtue.

[h] Variant "pleased."

a mad impulse and passion, at least change, and do not take [a] for thyself what belongs to others. For virtue is a stranger to foolish men if she is thought worthy to be possessed as a wife and not as a sister. For she can indeed be a kinswoman [b] to the progressive man [c] as to a brother, but only to the perfect man [d] as a real wife.[e]

*67. (Gen. xx. 10-11) Why, when Abimelech asked (Abraham), "What was in thy mind [f] that thou didst this?", did he reply, "Because I thought [g] that God [h] was not in this place, and that I should be waylaid and slain" [i]?

Not all the truth is to be told to all men, wherefore also now the wise man manages the whole (affair) with an alteration and change of names.[j] For he knew that as for his wife, she would not be corrupted. This, however, he does not admit but only what it was proper for his interrogators to hear, in order that they might be delighted by the fact that he seemed to be showing that that region had a desire for piety [k] and for respect toward strangers, and that they might be even more mindful of piety and hospitality.[l]

68. (Gen. xx. 12). What is the meaning of the words,

[a] Lit. "cut off."
[b] *συγγενής*.
[c] *τῷ προκόπτοντι*.
[d] *τῷ τελείῳ*.
[e] Lit. "a wife as a wife."
[f] Lit. "seeing what": so LXX, *τί ἐνιδών*, retaining the Heb. idiom.
[g] LXX *εἶπα*, retaining the Heb. idiom "I said" = "I thought."
[h] LXX *θεοσέβεια*, Heb. "fear of God."
[i] LXX and Heb. "that they would kill me because of my wife."
[j] So the Greek frag. (which consists only of this sentence), *οὐ πάντα ἀληθῆ λεκτέον ἅπασιν· ὅθεν καὶ νῦν ὁ ἀστεῖος* (the Arm. word used usu. = *ὁ σοφός*) *ὅλον οἰκονομεῖ τὸ πρᾶγμα μεταθέσει καὶ ἀπαλλαγῇ τῶν ὀνομάτων*.
[k] *τῆς θεοσεβείας*.
[l] *τῆς φιλοξενίας*.

"And in truth she is my sister by the father but not by the mother. And she became my wife" [a]?

The literal meaning [b] is excellently clear. But as for the deeper meaning,[c] (Scripture) says something most natural,[d] for it introduces virtue [e] as in truth being motherless [f] and having no part in the female sex [g] but being sown only by the Father of all,[h] who needs no material substance for His [i] generation. But the virtue of the virtuous man has the rights [j] of both sister and wife, of a sister because there is one Father for both, Who begot all things, and of a wife because everything that comes about through conjugation [k] is called "wife." [l] And so, the righteous man [m] is a consort [n] of righteousness, the ignorant man [o] of ignorance, the sincere man [p] of sincerity, the pious man [q] of piety, and, in a word, the wise man [r] of wisdom.

*69. (Gen. xx. 16) Why does Abimelech say to Sarah, "Behold, I have given a thousand (pieces of) silver [s] to

[a] This verse is allegorized in similar fashion to the first part of this section (down to "generation") in *De Ebrietate* 61 and *Quis Rer. Div. Heres* 62.

[b] τὸ ῥητόν.

[c] τὸ πρὸς διάνοιαν.

[d] φυσικώτατον.

[e] ἀρετήν.

[f] ἀληθῶς ἀμήτορα.

[g] *Cf. De Ebrietate* 61 θήλεος γενεᾶς ἀμέτοχος.

[h] *Cf. Quis Rer. Div. Heres* 62 ἐκ πατρὸς τοῦ πάντων θεοῦ μόνου γεννηθεῖσα.

[i] Or "its" (*i.e.* virtue's). *Cf. De Ebrietate* 61 οὐ γὰρ ἐξ ὕλης τῆς αἰσθητῆς συνισταμένης.

[j] δικαιώματα *vel sim.*

[k] κατὰ συζυγίαν.

[l] So lit. the Arm.

[m] ὁ δίκαιος.

[n] σύμβιος.

[o] Or "foolish man."

[p] Or "sound man."

[q] ὁ εὐσεβής.

[r] ὁ σοφός.

[s] So Heb.: LXX χίλια δίδραχμα (δίδραχμον regularly renders Heb. "shekel," which is here understood).

thy brother. Let this be for the honour [a] of thy face [b] and of all women who are with thee,[c] and speak the truth about everything " [d] ?

He is deserving of approval who has imposed also upon himself a penalty for an involuntary sin [e] for the consolation and assuagement and the honour of the face (of Sarah). But the expression " speak the truth about everything " is the injunction of an unphilosophical and unlearned man.[f] For if human life were properly directed [g] and admitted nothing false, it would be proper to speak the truth to everyone about everything. But since hypocrisy of an evil kind [h] acts with authority as if in a theatre,[i] and arrogance is concealed with the truth,[j] the wise man requires a versatile art from which he may profit in imitating those mockers [k] who say one thing and do another in order to save whom they can.[l] Now it is not right for this to happen in all cases. For it is profitable for a

[a] Or " price "—*τιμήν*.

[b] So LXX: Heb. " covering of the eyes," *i.e.* an " amende honorable."

[c] LXX *καὶ πάσαις ταῖς μετὰ σοῦ*: Heb. " and for all which is with thee."

[d] So LXX: Heb. is somewhat obscure but probably means " and in everything thou hast been justified."

[e] *ὑπὲρ ἀκουσίας ἁμαρτίας*.

[f] *ἀφιλοσόφου καὶ ἰδιώτου παράγγελμα*, as in the Greek frag., which begins with this sentence.

[g] *εὐώδει*, as in the Greek frag.

[h] Lit. " hypocrisy of evil ": the Greek frag. has merely *ὑπόκρισις*.

[i] The Greek frag. has *ὡς ἐν ἑκατέρῳ δυναστεύει*: *ἑκατέρῳ* is evidently a scribal error for *θεάτρῳ*. Whether *δυναστεύει* was the reading of the Arm. translator is less clear.

[j] Variant " with art " or " with artifice ": The Arm. is obscure and is probably an inaccurate rendering of the original. The Greek frag. reads more intelligibly *καὶ τὸ ψεῦδος παραπέτασμα τῆς ἀληθείας ἐστί*.

[k] Prob. an inaccurate rendering of *τοὺς ὑποκριτάς* which the Greek frag. has.

[l] So the Greek frag. (which ends with this sentence).

counsellor of evil to speak falsely about everything to his hearers,[a] while a salutary nature is peculiar to virtue.[b]

70. (Gen. xx. 17-18) Why is it that, after Abraham had prayed, " God healed Abimelech and his wife and his maid-servants, and they bore, for God had closed up [c] every womb in the household of Abimelech because of the wife [d] of Abraham " ?

When the Father wishes to do some kindness to someone, He considers this a special grace to the wise man,[e] as is the case now. For it seems that because the wise man offered up prayers He granted forgiveness [f] of the involuntary sins of the household, even though no one (of them) prayed. Moreover, (Scripture) teaches a doctrine that is beautiful for those who give judgment and for those who are judged, (namely) that the former should not first strike down, or be beforehand in punishing sinners, but should at the very start softly persuade and reconcile the one who seems to have been wronged ; and as for the others, they should supplicate the court not to inflict punishment upon all (of them) for always.

71. (Gen. xxiii. 1) [g] Why was the life of Sarah a hundred and twenty-seven years ?

Each of the numbers which are here contained has a

[a] Aucher, construing differently, renders, " quoniam consultoris malitiae est omnia falso dicere ad aucupandos auditores."
[b] *σωτηρία φύσις ἰδία ἐστὶ τῇ ἀρετῇ.*

[c] Lit. " closing up, closed up," retaining the Heb. idiom. LXX here has only *συνέκλεισεν.*

[d] LXX and Heb. " because of Sarah, the wife."

[e] *ἰδίαν χάριν τῷ σοφῷ* (*i.e.* Abraham).

[f] Lit. " forgetfulness "—*ἀμνηστίαν.*

[g] In the extant text of the *Quaestiones* there are no sections on chaps. xxi and xxii of Genesis. Chap. xxi relates (a second time) the birth of Isaac and the flight of Hagar (see above, §§ 18 ff.) ; chap. xxii tells of the sacrifice of Isaac (see *De Abrahamo* 167-177).

sacred and separate [a] status,[b] (namely) seven, twenty and a hundred. Moreover, it has a wonderful unity and harmony of parts. For the seven after the one [c] by a double proportion produces a hundred and twenty-seven, as follows: 1, 2, 4, 8, 16, 32, 64,[d] which make a hundred and twenty-seven.[e]

72. (Gen. xxiii. 2) Why does (Scripture) specify the place where (Sarah) died, (saying), "She died in the city of Arbok [f] which is in the valley [g]; this is Hebron [h] in the land of Canaan"?

The translation of "Arbok" is "of four," [i] and "Hebron" means "being joined with" or "associating with women" [j] and "Canaan" is, as it were, "their appearance." [k]

*73. (Gen. xxiii. 2-3) Why does (Scripture) say, "Abraham came to bewail Sarah and to mourn, and Abraham arose from his dead"?

Carefully and deliberately [l] does (Scripture) say that he arose, not from Sarah, but "from his dead." And he came there to bewail and mourn, not his dead, but "Sarah." And this is somehow most natural,[m] for it is proper for the virtuous man to separate and dwell far from a body that

[a] Or "consecrated." [b] λόγον.

[c] *i.e.* the digit 7, see *De Opif. Mundi* 91.

[d] The numbers are written as numeral letters in the Arm.

[e] The sum of the seven terms in the geometric progression by 2.

[f] So LXX: Heb. "in Kiriath Arba."

[g] So LXX, ἥ ἐστιν ἐν τῷ κοιλώματι: Heb. omits the clause.

[h] Arm. *K'ebron*: LXX Χεβρών: Heb. *Ḥebrôn*.

[i] Heb. *'arba'* = "four."

[j] *Cf. Quod Deterius* 15 συζυγὴ δὲ καὶ συνεταιρὶς Χεβρὼν καλεῖται συμβολικῶς ἡμῶν τὸ σῶμα.

[k] In *De Sobrietate* 44-48 "Canaan" = σάλος. The present etymology is obscure.

[l] Or "cautiously." [m] φυσικώτατόν τι.

had died naturally by itself,[a] and to mourn for wisdom[b] as though it seemed in actual fact[c] to be separated from virtue.[d] For there is no mourning among incorruptible things,[e] and wisdom is incorruptible, as is all virtue. But in respect of those things which men are able to possess, and which (sometime) fail and are lacking,[f] they must of necessity be grieved. But excellently and carefully does (Scripture) show that the virtuous man did not resort to wailing or mourning but only came there for some such thing. For things that unexpectedly and against his will strike the pusillanimous man[g] weaken, crush and overthrow him, whereas everywhere they merely bow down[h] the man of constancy[i] when they direct their blows against him, and not in such a way as to bring (their work) to completion, since they are strongly repelled by the guiding reason,[j] and retreat. And so it is not fitting for a man devoted to moral excellence[k] to stand (fixed) in prayer when something happens against his will, or to be entirely rapt and moved and drawn toward this, but he should somewhat gradually go toward it, and retire before the end is reached. This holy and consecrated law was written as a warning against those sins that are about to be committed, so that when men are moved by those things which are external, such as the possessions of others, or by the divisions[l] of women or by theft or by plunder or by adultery or by similar evils, they may not perpetrate them but shall think it sufficient[m] to have been struck by these impulses,

[a] Aucher omits the rendering of the reflexive pronoun.
[b] τὴν σοφίαν (symbolized by Sarah). [c] ἔργῳ.
[d] Construction and meaning uncertain. Aucher renders similarly.
[e] ἐν ἀφθάρτοις. [f] *i.e.* material things.
[g] τὸν μικρόψυχον. [h] Or "deflect."
[i] τὸν βέβαιον *vel sim.*
[j] Lit. "by the charioteer, reason." *Cf. Leg. All.* i. 73 τὸν ἡνίοχον, λέγω δὲ τὸν λογισμόν.
[k] καλοκἀγαθίας.
[l] Or "dissensions." The exact meaning is not clear.
[m] Variant "proper."

and shall move away and take their stand upon the immovable and firm mind.[a]

*74. (Gen. xxiii. 4)[b] Why does (Abraham) say, " I am an immigrant and sojourner among you "[c]?

But does not every wise soul[d] live like an immigrant and sojourner in this mortal body, having (as its real) dwelling-place and country[e] the most pure substance[f] of heaven, from which (our) nature migrated to this (place) by a law of necessity?[g] Perhaps this was in order that it might carefully inspect terrestrial things, that even these might not be without a share in wisdom to participate in a better life, or in order that it might be akin[h] to created beings and not be continuously and completely happy. Wherefore in concluding the expression of his thought,[i] he says not ineptly[j] " immigrant and sojourner," but adds, " among you." For truly the lover of wisdom does not dwell, or go about, with any vain or empty things, even though he has grown together with them, (but) is far removed from them in thought. Wherefore the wise man is truly and properly said not to sail, or journey, or be a fellow-citizen, or live, with the foolish man, since the sovereign and ruling mind[k] does not unite, or mix, with anything else.[l]

[a] ὑπὲρ τὸν ἀκίνητον καὶ βέβαιον νοῦν.

[b] This half-verse is briefly commented on in *De Confus. Ling.* 79.

[c] LXX πάροικος καὶ παρεπίδημος ἐγώ εἰμι μεθ' ὑμῶν.

[d] πᾶσα σοφὴ ψυχή. [e] πατρίδα.

[f] καθαρωτάτην οὐσίαν.

[g] Lit. " by a necessary law."

[h] Aucher more freely renders, " sive ut noscat se cognatum."

[i] Lit. " In sealing the thoughts of his opinion" (or " will ").

[j] οὐκ ἀπὸ σκοποῦ *vel sim.* Aucher curiously renders, " non simpliciter." [k] ὁ ἡγεμὼν νοῦς.

[l] The last two sentences are paralleled in somewhat abbreviated form in a Greek frag. from Dam. Par. 754 (Harris, p. 69), identified by Früchtel; see Appendix A.

75. (Gen. xxiii. 4) What is the meaning of the words, "Give me the possession of a grave,[a] and I will bury my dead before me"?

The literal meaning[b] is clear and well known, but as for the deeper meaning,[c] we may explain it allegorically[d]; it is as follows. As it seems, the wise man[e] does not seek a grave, for the body is the grave of the soul,[f] in which it is buried as if in a grave, but "the possession of a grave," that is to say, authority and lordship over it,[g] for,[h] he says, "I shall become master and receive authority, and not be subjected to authority and no longer be, as it were, buried among them as formerly,[i] but rather will I bury (them) far from me."

*76. (Gen. xxiii. 5-6)[j] Why do they say to him, "A king from God[k] art thou among us"?

In the first place, (Scripture) wishes to show that all men, and not merely rational wise men,[l] admire and honour him who is a follower of pure and non-fraudulent wisdom.[m] And not only (is he regarded) as a ruler but as a ruler of rulers and a divine one, and as a king of kings,

[a] Though the Arm. lit. = κλῆρον τάφου, Philo probably read κτῆσιν τάφου, as our text of the LXX reads; similarly Heb. and Arm. O.T. have "possession of a grave." Philo omits "among you" which Heb. and LXX add after "grave."

[b] τὸ ῥητόν.

[c] τὸ πρὸς διάνοιαν.

[d] ἀλληγοροῦντες.

[e] ὁ σοφός or ἀστεῖος.

[f] τὸ σῶμα τάφος τῆς ψυχῆς ἐστι.

[g] *i.e.* the body.

[h] Aucher notes that from here to the middle of § 122 there is a lacuna in Cod. A of the Arm. version.

[i] Aucher renders somewhat differently, "non amplius, sicut illis ante contigebat, dixerim, quasi vero sepeliar."

[j] This passage is briefly commented on by Philo in *De Mut. Nom.* 152, *De Somniis* ii. 244, *De Abrahamo* 261, and is alluded to in *De Virtutibus* 216.

[k] So LXX, βασιλεὺς παρὰ θεοῦ: Heb. "a prince of God."

[l] σοφοὶ λογικοί.

[m] ὃς καθαρᾶς καὶ ἀδόλου ζηλωτής ἐστι σοφίας.

being excellent and virtuous,[a] and as being elected, not by men, but by God.[b] And, in the second place, (Scripture) lays down a most natural law,[c] which some of those who philosophize [d] have rejected. This law is that no one of the foolish [e] (is) a king, even though he should be master of all the land and sea, but only the wise and God-loving man,[f] even if he is without the equipment and resources through which many obtain power with violence and force.[g] For whereas the man ignorant of the art of the pilot or of the physician or of the musician has trouble [h] with the rudders or with the compounding of drugs and ointments [i] or with flutes and lyres, since he is unable to use any of them for its natural purpose, to the pilot, on the other hand, and the physician and the musician they may be said to be fitting and suitable. And this is proper, since there is a certain kingly art,[j] and it is the most noble of the arts.[k] For he who is ignorant and unversed in the needs [l] of men must be considered a layman,[m] while only he (can be considered) a king who is knowing and experienced.[n] In the third place, moreover, (Scripture)

[a] Or " noble " : Aucher " generosus."

[b] *χειροτονηθείς . . . ὑπὸ θεοῦ.* The same phrase is applied to Moses in *De Praemiis* 54, where Philo makes a similar contrast between the ideal and the actual king.

[c] *νόμον φυσικώτατον.*

[d] *τῶν φιλοσοφούντων* : Aucher " nonnulli sophistarum."

[e] *τῶν ἀφρόνων οὐδείς,* as in the Greek frag. (which begins here).

[f] Or " God-beloved "—*θεοφιλής,* as in the Greek frag.

[g] The Greek frag. differs very slightly, *δι' ὧν πολλοὶ κρατύνονται τὰς δυναστείας.*

[h] Following the Greek frag., which has *παρέλκον πρᾶγμα,* misunderstood by the Arm. translator as *παραδειγματικὰ πράγματα* or the like.

[i] The Greek frag. has only *φαρμάκων σύνθεσις.*

[j] *τέχνη τις βασιλική,* as in the Greek frag.

[k] *τεχνῶν ἀρίστη.*

[l] Or " affairs "—*τῶν χρειῶν* or, as in the Greek frag., *χρήσεως.*

[m] The Arm. uses two words to render *ἰδιώτην.*

[n] The Greek frag. (which ends here) has only *τὸν ἐπιστήμονα.*

also tells us this in addition, that the judgments of God are greater than those of men. For men consider him to be their ruler and master who has an abundance of power in respect of corruptible materials,[a] whereas God inspires with all wisdom[b] him for whom no inanimate and irrational materials[c] have any value, when He sees his soul greatly purified and his mind[d] free and unenslaved, and him who has wisdom He inscribes among the greatest rulers and kings. And in the fourth place, there falls under the necessary order of connexion[e] that which pertains to constancy,[f] for the elections[g] of men are inconstant and transitory, changing their direction, now up, now down, in accordance with (changing) customs, events and fortunes, while those of God are constant, and because of their incorruptibility, they make themselves available to law-observant men.[h]

77. (Gen. xxiii. 6) Why do they say, " In our choice monuments[i] bury thy dead " ?

The literal meaning[j] is easy to explain. Because of the honour in which he was held they agreed to give him a choice burial-place. But as for the deeper meaning,[k] in a wicked man the body lives when it is animated by desire

[a] ἐν φθαρταῖς ὕλαις (for this standing expression see Leisegang's *Index Philonis*, p. 794, col. a).

[b] αὐτῷ πᾶσαν σοφίαν ἐμπνεῖ. Arm. *hnčem* means " resound " and also " inspire " (like *šnčem*). Aucher renders, " omnino eum sapientia adornat," which is more nearly correct than his alternate rendering (in his footnote), " sicut sapientiam celebrat."

[c] οὔτινα τῶν ἀψύχων καὶ ἀλόγων ὑλικά.

[d] τὴν ψυχὴν . . . καὶ τὸν νοῦν.

[e] εἰς τὴν κατὰ εἱρμὸν τάξιν ἀναγκαίως.

[f] πρὸς βεβαίωσιν *vel sim.*

[g] αἱ χειροτονίαι.

[h] Aucher renders inaccurately, " exhibentes illis legitimam constantiam."

[i] So LXX, ἐν τοῖς ἐκλεκτοῖς μνημείοις ἡμῶν.

[j] τὸ ῥητόν.

[k] τὸ πρὸς διάνοιαν.

and sensual pleasure [a] and whatever else it delights in, whereas in a virtuous man [b] it is dead, for he is a man of frugality and is self-controlled and endures the hunger of continence,[c] so that it is not wide of the mark to say that the soul of the wise man,[d] having a body that is inanimate and heavy, like a bronze statue, is always carrying a corpse.[e] And so those who are opposite characters say,[f] "Give over to us the care and concern for this,[g] that it may have the choice of everything and be worthy of remembrance [h] through food and drink and clothing and whatever else belongs to a sumptuous, luxurious and enjoyable life. But he is displeased by these words, and biding his time, takes greater care,[i] mollifying them all [j] through prostration,[k] and conciliating and embracing [l] them so far as he thinks it suitable and proper by way of invocation,[m] and that he may not send them away before he has removed [n] his dead, not giving the body into their hands, and taking possession [o] of the burial-place but not the burial-place (itself).[p] Moreover, it is proper to observe also that the characters

[a] *ἐπιθυμίᾳ καὶ ἡδονῇ ψυχωθέν.*

[b] *ἐν τῷ σπουδαίῳ.*

[c] Aucher renders somewhat less literally, "praeferens in se famem mediocritatis et temperatae continentiae."

[d] *ἡ τοῦ σοφοῦ* (or *ἀστείου*) *ψυχή.*

[e] *νεκροφορεῖ.* *Cf. De Agricultura* 25 <*ἡ ψυχὴ*> *οὐκ ἀποτίθεται νεκροφοροῦσα.*

[f] Prob. *οἱ ἐναντίοι τρόποι*, meaning the Hittites as types of materialists. Aucher renders less literally, "porro exempla contraria ponuntur, dicentes."

[g] *i.e.* the body.

[h] Philo plays on the similarity of *μνήμη* and *μνημεῖον*.

[i] The sense is not altogether clear.

[j] Aucher more freely renders, "adversarios."

[k] *διὰ προσκυνήσεως.* *Cf.* LXX of Gen. xxiii. 7 *Ἀβραὰμ προσεκύνησεν τῷ λαῷ τῆς γῆς, τοῖς υἱοῖς Χέτ*, on which Philo comments in *De Somniis* ii. 89-92.

[l] *καταφιλῶν.*

[m] *κατὰ πρόσκλησιν vel sim.* : Aucher "ad alliciendum."

[n] Aucher "deponat."

[o] *κτῆσιν.*

[p] See above, § 75.

who speak [a] call the burial-place a " monument," [b] but the wise man calls it " the possession of a monument " or " the property of a burial-place." Why? Because the former consider only the body and the various (aspects) of the body worthy of remembrance,[c] while he (so considers) not this but lordship over it and possession of it, as was said before.[d]

78. (Gen. xxiii. 8-9) [e] Why does (Abraham) say, " If you have in your mind [f] to bury my dead before me,[g] listen to me and speak of me [h] to Ephron, the son of Sahar,[i] and let him give me the double cave [j] belonging to him, which is in the portion of his field.[k] For as much silver as it is worth [l] let him give it to me and to you [m] as a possession of a monument " [n]?

Having shown his wisdom and presented his case by first prostrating himself,[o] he says, " You who do not use speech [p]

[a] Aucher renders less literally, " quod qui loquuntur sicut exempla."

[b] μνημεῖον.

[c] See note *h*, p. 356.

[d] In § 75.

[e] The " double cave " mentioned in these verses is briefly allegorized in *De Poster. Caini* 62 and *De Somniis* ii. 26.

[f] ἐν τῇ ψυχῇ ὑμῶν, as in LXX.

[g] ἀπὸ προσώπου μου, as in LXX.

[h] So LXX, λαλήσατε περὶ ἐμοῦ: Heb. " intercede for me."

[i] LXX Σάαρ: Heb. *Ṣōhar* (A.V. " Zohar ").

[j] τὸ σπήλαιον τὸ διπλοῦν, as in LXX: Heb. " the cave of Machpelah " (the last word from the root meaning " to double ").

[k] ἐν μερίδι τοῦ ἀγροῦ αὐτοῦ, as in LXX: Heb. " which is in the limit (or " end ") of his field."

[l] LXX ἀργυρίου τοῦ ἀξίου: Heb. " for full silver."

[m] The Arm. " and to you " is prob. an error. LXX has ἐν ὑμῖν: Heb. and Arm. O.T. have " in your midst."

[n] So LXX, εἰς κτῆσιν μνημείου, see above, § 75.

[o] Construction and meaning uncertain. Aucher renders, " sensu rerum usurpato, quem praecedenti adoratione jam intimavit auditoribus."

[p] λόγῳ.

for deception but for the (benefit of the) soul and mind,[a] confess this, (namely) that we are clothed with a dead body and that we should bury this and not permit our passions [b] to arise and be revived and flourish, but keep them out of sight, because [c] they are an obstacle to the impulses [d] which arise from reflexion.[e] Speak, therefore, in the council of the soul [f] on my behalf and for my appearance,[g] and make haste that whatever is the value of the price in silver, that is to say, what has the worth of reason,[h] may be given to me,[i] as I said, not for a burial monument but for the possession of a memorial." [j]

79. (Gen. xxiii. 10) What is " Ephron," and why is it that " he dwelt among the sons of Heth " ?

" Ephron " is to be interpreted as " dust," [k] while " Hittite " [l] means " being out of one's mind." [m] And (Scripture) by " dust " indicates corporeal natures,[n] while by " being out of one's mind " (it indicates) madness and folly.[o] For among foolish and mad men the body has the true and chief rank,[p] receiving the service and attendance

[a] *εἰς ψυχὴν καὶ νοῦν.* [b] *τὰ πάθη.*

[c] Aucher curiously has " ut," introducing a purpose clause.

[d] *ταῖς ὁρμαῖς.* [e] *κατὰ τὸν λογισμόν vel sim.*

[f] Prob. *ἐν τῷ τῆς ψυχῆς βουλευτηρίῳ*, *cf. De Vita Cont.* 27 *ἐν τῷ ἑαυτῆς (sc. τῆς ψυχῆς) συνεδρίῳ καὶ βουλευτηρίῳ.*

[g] Construction and meaning uncertain. Aucher renders, " et apparente mihi (*sic*)." [h] *τοῦ λόγου.*

[i] Philo does not make it as clear as does Scripture that the money is given by Abraham, and the burial-place is given *to* him. [j] See § 77.

[k] *χοῦς* (as if from Heb. *'aphār*). The same etymology is given in *De Confus. Ling.* 79.

[l] *Χετταῖος.*

[m] *ἔκστασις* (as if from Heb. *ḥath* " panic fear "). *Cf. De Somniis* ii. 89 where Philo etymologizes *τοὺς υἱοὺς τοῦ Χέτ* as *ἐξιστάντες.*

[n] *αἰνίττεται σωματικὰς φύσεις.*

[o] *μανίαν καὶ ἀφροσύνην.* [p] *τάξιν.*

of those who know nothing of any proper and genuine good, and do not make an effort to know it.

*80. (Gen. xxiii. 9, 11) [a] What is the "double cave" [b]?

The literal text [c] does not require any exposition, for there are altogether two burial caves under the mountain,[d] one outside and the other inside, or two walls,[e] one, which encloses, and the other, which is enclosed.[f] But as for the deeper meaning,[g] it must be judged as follows. The human body bears a likeness to a double cave. For it insatiably desires that which is external, making insatiable lust [h] its guide and ruler. On the other hand, in respect of internal things it conducts itself with reason,[i] using patient self-control.[j] For he is foolish who gives up internal things for the sake of external things, and psychic things for sense-perceptible ones,[k] and exchanges that which is in accordance with patient self-control for unbridled lust. But the virtuous man [l] makes use of a hedge and a wall, and a screen between [m] psychic things and the forms among phenomena [n] and things that are seen. While the double cave exists in an evil man, the body too is unclean and lewd. But when it dwells within, it changes itself into a god-loving soul,[o] receiving holiness and purity and the

[a] For other Philonic passages on the double cave see § 78.

[b] τὸ σπήλαιον τὸ διπλοῦν: Heb. "the cave of Machpelah" (see § 78 note).

[c] ὁ ῥητὸς λόγος.

[d] The Greek frag. has δύω εἰσὶν ἀντρώδεις ὑπώρειαι.

[e] Arm. *bak* means "colonnade" and "court" or "precinct." The Greek frag. has περίβολοι.

[f] The Greek frag. (which ends here) has ὁ μὲν περιέχων, ὁ δὲ περιεχόμενος.

[g] τὸ πρὸς διάνοιαν.

[h] ἀσελγείᾳ or "profanation"—βεβηλώσει *vel sim.*

[i] κατὰ νοῦν οἰκονομεῖται *vel sim.*

[j] ἐγκρατείᾳ ὑπομονῆς.

[k] ψυχικὰ ἀντὶ αἰσθητῶν.

[l] ὁ σπουδαῖος.

[m] The preposition is supplied.

[n] Meaning uncertain. Aucher renders, "et habentibus visum apparentium."

[o] εἰς ψυχὴν θεοφιλῆ.

possession [a] of a blameless life. Wherefore, I believe, the Creator and Constructor made the tabernacle [b] double, marking off the inner from the outer part by a veil,[c] and calling the inner part the " holy of holies " and the outer part merely " the holy (place)." But all these are entirely psychic and intelligible forms,[d] while the double cave has a share in the body, although they [e] are indeed the possessions of the god-loving mind.[f]

*81. (Gen. xxiii. 11) Why is it that though Abraham sought only the cave, Ephron gave him the field as well? [g]

As for the literal meaning,[h] one would say that out of admiration for the man and for the wisdom which he saw him display,[i] he thought it right to lavish upon him very abundant favours.[j] But as for the deeper meaning,[k] he thought it right to attach [l] the field symbolically [m] to the virtuous man [n] in order that the body might have the things necessary to pleasure [o] and their equipment. And he does not refuse, being of liberal character, as he is rich,[p] but clearly says, " I will give you all the treasures in my possession and everything which has honour and power

[a] Lit. " portion," but here prob. = κτῆσιν as in the LXX, see the preceding sections.

[b] τὴν σκηνήν.

[c] καλύμματι, see *De Vita Mosis* ii. 87.

[d] ψυχικὰ καὶ νοητὰ εἴδη.

[e] What " they " refers to is not clear.

[f] Or " thoughts "—λογισμῶν.

[g] LXX τὸν ἀγρὸν καὶ τὸ σπήλαιον τὸ ἐν αὐτῷ σοὶ δίδωμι.

[h] πρὸς τὸ ῥητόν.

[i] The Greek paraphrase in Procopius reads more briefly, ὁρῶν αὐτοῦ τὴν σοφίαν.

[j] The Arm. here is closer to the Greek frag. (which ends here), οἰόμενος δεῖν ἀφθόνους ἐπιδαψιλεύεσθαι χάριτας.

[k] τὸ πρὸς διάνοιαν.

[l] Meaning somewhat uncertain.

[m] συμβολικῶς.

[n] τῷ σπουδαίῳ.

[o] ταῖς ἡδοναῖς.

[p] Lit. " full."

among men, nor will I be caught by any of those who falsely bear the name of good,[a] but handling them [b] as is proper, I will show everyone what necessary power [c] is in all of them."

82. (Gen. xxiii. 9, 11, 17, 19) Why is it that before his acquiring the burial-place, the cave was said to be " in the field," while after his acquiring it, the field (was said to be) " in the cave " [d]?

(Scripture) says something most natural.[e] For so long as the mind [f] does not rule over the body, the body falls under the power of, and is supported [g] by, external things, by wine and meals and food and other things that grow from the all-bearing earth as if from a field. But when it [h] assumes power, it compels the body, which has long been in servitude, to show its power and not to fall under the power of external things but, on the contrary, to contain [i] them and rule over them, not being a part of them (any longer).

83. (Gen. xxiii. 19) Why does (Scripture) say that the

[a] *τῶν ψευδωνύμων ἀγαθῶν.* But the meaning of the clause is uncertain. Aucher renders, " neque ab ullo falsi nominis bonorum deprehendar."

[b] Apparently the possessions are meant.

[c] *ἀναγκαία δύναμις.*

[d] Although Aucher is correct in distinguishing between the Arm. prepositions *i nerk'oy* = *ὑπό*, and *i nerk's* = *ἐν*, he has completely mistranslated the sentence and missed its point in rendering, " spelunca dicebatur sub agro esse, et post acquisitionem agri, intus in ipso agro." What Philo refers to is the fact that in Gen. xxiii. 9, 11, the cave is said to be in the field, while in vs. 17 (obviously corrupt) the field is said, at the beginning of the verse, to be in the cave, *ὁ ἀγρὸς 'Εφρών, ὃς ἦν ἐν τῷ διπλῷ σπηλαίῳ.*

[e] *φυσικώτατα.*

[f] *ὁ νοῦς.*

[g] Or " overshadowed." Aucher " detentum."

[h] *i.e.* the mind.

[i] *περιέχειν.*

burial-place was "opposite Mambre,"[a] or why does it say that "this is Hebron"[b]?

"Hebron" is to be interpreted as "union"[c] or "the companionship of women,"[d] as has been correctly said. For behold, in some sense,[e] in the case of those who have a double cave, it is possible to join and fit together companionship and sincere liking, and to make the body genuinely (devoted) to the soul,[f] the one as the ruler, and the other as the minister, being persuaded (to do)[g] whatever the queen may announce, in order that she[h] may give a likeness of her power, through which it[i] may have power over external things and rule over sense-perceptible objects.[j]

84. (Gen. xxiv. 1) Why does (Scripture) say, "And Abraham was an old man advanced (in days),[k] and the Lord blessed Abraham in all things"?

[a] LXX ἀπέναντι Μαμβρῆ (Heb. "Mamre").

[b] LXX αὕτη ἐστὶν Χεβρὼν ἐν τῇ γῇ Χανάαν.

[c] συζυγή. The same etymology is given in *Quod Deterius* 15 and *De Poster. Caini* 60, see also *QG* iv. 72.

[d] The alternate etymology συνεταιρίς is given in *Quod Deterius* 15.

[e] τρόπον τινά. Aucher "exempli gratia."

[f] The Arm. lit. = γνήσιον τῇ ψυχῇ. Aucher renders, "fidele . . . cum anima."

[g] This obscure clause apparently refers to the soul as the ruler, and the body as the minister or servant. Aucher renders inaccurately, "uno principem, altera satellitem persuadente."

[h] The fem. pronoun seems to be required by the context, as referring to the soul.

[i] Apparently the body is meant. The Arm. verb is an infinitive but Aucher renders it as a 3rd pers. plural.

[j] τῶν αἰσθητῶν. The passage is obscure, and seems to overlook the reference to Mambre, which in *De Migratione* 165 is allegorized as the contemplative life.

[k] LXX πρεσβύτερος προβεβηκὼς ἡμερῶν. The same phrase is quoted in *De Sobrietate* 17, also with the omission of ἡμερῶν. There too Philo explains that the wise man is figuratively a πρεσβύτερος.

It does not seem that this admits of explanation as chronological age, since one would be at a loss [a] to call him an old man who was more short-lived than all who were before him.[b] He has precedence in virtue who is worthy of old age and honour.[c] Wherefore it says above, "an old man advanced," (meaning) increase in worthiness,[d] of which the consummation is piety,[e] (and) excellent judgment [f] in all aspects of life, in thoughts, deeds and words.[g]

85. (Gen. xxiv. 2) What is the meaning of the words, "The eldest servant of his house and ruler of all his things" [h]?

The literal meaning [i] is clear, for (Scripture) indicates that the man [j] was a sort of steward or manager of his master's possessions.[k] But as for the allegorical and natural meaning,[l] it must, it seems, be considered to be as follows. The status of a servant among us and of a minister and attendant is held by discourse [m] which is an utterance of

[a] ἀπορήσειέ τις ἄν.

[b] Aucher can hardly be blamed for his inaccurate rendering, "qui paucis temporibus superat annos ejus (anteriores)", since the Arm. translator probably misunderstood the Greek original; *cf. De Sobrietate* 17 ὅτι σχεδὸν τῶν προγόνων ἑαυτοῦ πάντων ὁ σοφὸς Ἀβραὰμ ὀλιγοχρονιώτατος εἰσάγεται.

[c] Here again the Arm. translator seems to have misunderstood the Greek; *cf. De Sobrietate* 16 ὡς δὲ καὶ πρεσβύτερον οὐ τὸν γήρᾳ κατεσχημένον ἀλλὰ τὸν γέρως καὶ τιμῆς ἄξιον ὀνομάζει.

[d] καλοκἀγαθίας.

[e] θεοσέβεια, which in *De Congressu* 130 is called ἀγαθὸν τέλειον.

[f] εὐβουλία.

[g] κατὰ λογισμοὺς καὶ ἔργα καὶ λόγους.

[h] LXX τῷ παιδὶ αὐτοῦ, τῷ πρεσβυτέρῳ τῆς οἰκίας αὐτοῦ, τῷ ἄρχοντι πάντων τῶν αὐτοῦ.

[i] τὸ ῥητόν.

[j] Abraham's steward (Eliezer).

[k] οἰκονόμον ἢ ἐπίτροπον τῶν τοῦ κυρίου.

[l] Construction and meaning uncertain.

[m] Philo here refers to the Stoic term λόγος προφορικός.

the mind, which [a] is more perfect [b] than speech, and is the ruler and master. This uttered discourse is the eldest (servant), for (it receives) the authority of natural behaviour over corporeal and invisible objects from the reason as if from a king.[c] For discourse [d] uses and manages all these things with virtue.[e]

*86. (Gen. xxiv. 2) Why does he say, "Place thy hand under my thigh" [f] ?

Being about to bind him by an oath [g] concerning the betrothal,[h] he bids him place his hand close to the place of generation,[i] indicating a pure association and an unpolluted marriage, not having sensual pleasure as its end but the procreation of legitimate children.[j] And allegorizing,[k] we might say that (Scripture) accurately [l] calls "thigh" that place in the soul which does not flow [m] but is firm in solidity and stability. Upon this he bids him with

[a] *i.e.* the mind—ὁ νοῦς.

[b] τελειότερος.

[c] Aucher renders less literally, "principatum habens ex natura tamquam a suo rege, sive ratione super corporalia instrumenta et objecta."

[d] It is not clear whether speech (ὁ προφορικὸς λόγος) or reason (ὁ ἐνδιάθετος λόγος) is meant; probably the former is meant.

[e] Aucher renders less accurately, "haec enim universa per virtute ornatum ministrum disponit ratio."

[f] LXX θὲς τὴν χεῖρά σου ὑπὸ τὸν μηρόν μου.

[g] ἐξορκίσειν.

[h] Of Isaac. *Cf.* the Greek frag. from Procopius ἐπὶ μνηστείαν καὶ γάμον πέμπων.

[i] Procopius κατὰ τῶν γαμικῶν ὀργάνων.

[j] So, almost literally, the Greek frag. (which ends here), καθαρὰν ὁμιλίαν καὶ γάμον ἀνεπίληπτον αἰνιττόμενος οὐχ ἡδονὴν τὸ τέλος ἀλλὰ γνησίους ἔχοντα παῖδας. The last phrase was originally, as Wendland notes, γνησίων παίδων γένεσιν.

[k] ἀλληγοροῦντες.

[l] ἀκριβῶς or ἐτύμως.

[m] μὴ ῥέοντα. Philo here gives a fanciful etymology of μηρός as if from μή and ῥεῖν.

reason [a] place his hand for the sake of reverencing and honouring that place to which nature has given as a special honour undeviating and unchanging forms [b] in order that it may not, so to say, receive lightly what in the same manner has a flow,[c] but may remain unchanged and truthful in its agreements.

87. (Gen. xxiv. 3) Why does he adjure him by heaven, uttering a double invocation, and by earth with a single one,[d] for he says, "I adjure thee by the Lord God of heaven and the God of earth" [e]?

Heaven is the best of the parts of the world,[f] wherefore it has been allotted the highest place, being of the purest substance,[g] and full of stars, each of which is a godlike image.[h] And the last [i] (part) is the earth, to which was allotted the lowest place for the reason that animals and the plants surrounding them are mortal and corruptible. Rightly, therefore, does he give first honour and privilege [j] to the best (part), uttering a double invocation to the powers of the Father, (namely) the creative and kingly.[k] But from the lesser he removed one (appellation) [l] for the

[a] The text seems to be corrupt; the original prob. made the thigh a symbol of reason (ὁ λόγος).

[b] ἄτρεπτα καὶ ἀμετάθετα εἴδη *vel sim.*

[c] The above is an uncertain rendering of what Aucher rightly calls a "locus obscurissimus." He himself renders, "qui itidem ac similiter habet fluxum, non ut dixerit quisquam, pauca receperit." Apparently the λόγος προφορικός is the subject of the last clause.

[d] Philo refers to the expression "Lord God of heaven," contrasted with "God of earth."

[e] LXX ἐξορκίσω σε κύριον τὸν θεὸν τοῦ οὐρανοῦ καὶ τὸν θεὸν (some MSS. omit τὸν θεόν) τῆς γῆς.

[f] τοῦ κόσμου. [g] τῆς καθαρωτάτης οὐσίας.

[h] ἄγαλμα θεοειδές or εἰκὼν θεοειδής.

[i] τὸ ἔσχατον <μέρος>. [j] προτιμίαν καὶ προνομίαν.

[k] ταῖς δυνάμεσι τοῦ πατρός, τῇ ποιητικῇ καὶ τῇ βασιλικῇ. See *QG* ii. 51 notes.

[l] That of "Lord," signifying God's kingly power.

reason that heaven and the natures [a] similar to it, being always undeviating and unchanging, are never sated with, nor fail in, the service of the Father, but serve God as the Creator and obey Him as king,[b] while we earth-born and corruptible creatures cannot deny God, for He who comes to create [c] is necessarily imagined as the efficient cause,[d] but still we do not acknowledge His kingship and government (as) the true Lord,[e] some because of impiety,[f] and others because of perverse and sophistical ingenuity.[g] And so, the whole school of philosophers [h] is not ashamed and does not blush to rule out [i] the providence and care [j] which are given by the Father to His offspring. This was also the opinion and belief [k] of the Egyptian king, who took it upon himself to say, " I do not know the Lord," [l] by which he shows that " I know God, indeed, because of natural necessity," [m] in so far as he perceives and admits that he was made by the Creator, but he denies that he knows the Lord, believing that the world and what is in the world are without providence and care.

*88. (Gen. xxiv. 3) Why does he instruct, not his son,

[a] αἱ φύσεις.

[b] Because the double appellation " Lord God " is associated with heaven in the present verse, Philo argues that heavenly beings worship God as king (" Lord ") and Creator (" God ").

[c] *i.e.* under the name of " God."

[d] ἐξ ἀνάγκης φαντάζεται <ὡς> τὸ ποιητικὸν αἴτιον.

[e] Because Scripture uses only " God of earth " not " Lord God of earth."

[f] δι' ἀσέβειαν.

[g] διὰ κακότεχνον σοφιστείαν καὶ εὑρεσιλογίαν *vel sim.*

[h] Prob. αἵρεσις is rendered by two Arm. words here. Aucher supplies " prava " in rendering, " prava illa sententia sectarum philosophorum."

[i] Lit. " to cut off."

[j] τὴν πρόνοιαν καὶ ἐπιμέλειαν.

[k] Here again Aucher supplies the word " pravus."

[l] Ex. v. 2, on which Philo comments similarly in *De Ebrietate* 19, 77-79.

[m] διὰ φυσικὴν ἀνάγκην.

not to take a Canaanite wife, as later his parents (instructed) Jacob,[a] but the servant ? [b]

Truly the literal meaning [c] contains an anxiety of doubt and the thought of deliberation.[d] For since Isaac was of mature and marriageable age,[e] and was not under the dominion of the servant, one of two things (was bound to happen) : either he would obey or he would oppose (him). Now, in case of his obedience, it would be natural for his father to be his sponsor.[f] And if he did not obey, the ministration of the servant would be superfluous.[g] And to say that because Abraham had migrated from the land of the Chaldaeans on account of a divine oracle, he did not consider it right to send his son (there), is very silly and foolish. In the first place, for this (same) reason it would not have been right (for him) to undertake the matter and be a sponsor at all in a family connexion from which he had been told to depart, nor for Jacob to go there to betroth himself, since he was an imitator of his father, and very well understood the instructions that had been given him.[h]

[a] In Gen. xxviii. 1, on which see *QG* iv. 242.

[b] So the Greek frag. from Procopius, *Διατί δὲ μὴ τῷ υἱῷ παραγγέλλει μὴ λαβεῖν Χανανῖτιν* (LXX *ἀπὸ τῶν θυγατέρων τῶν Χαναναίων*) *ὥσπερ ὕστερον τῷ Ἰακὼβ οἱ γονεῖς, ἀλλὰ τῷ παιδί;*

[c] *τὸ ῥητόν.*

[d] *λογισμὸν ἐπισκέψεως vel sim.* Aucher " consilium consideratione dignum."

[e] So the Greek frag., *καίτοι τελείου τυγχάνοντος Ἰσαὰκ καὶ ἡλικίαν ἔχοντος γάμου.*

[f] The Greek frag. reads less specifically *καὶ εἰ μὲν ἔμελλε πείθεσθαι, εἰκὸς ἦν αὐτῷ μᾶλλον παρεγγυᾶν.* On the meaning of " sponsor " see note below.

[g] So the Greek frag., *εἰ δὲ ἀπειθεῖν, περιττὴ τοῦ παιδὸς ἡ διακονία.*

[h] The Greek frag. (which ends here) reads more briefly *τὸ γὰρ εἰπεῖν ὅτι, χρησμῷ τῆς γῆς ἐξελθών, πέμπειν εἰς αὐτὴν οὐκ ἠξίου τὸν υἱόν [εἰ καὶ εὔλογον, ὅμως ἀπαρέσκει τισί], διὰ τὸ μηδ' ἂν τὸν Ἰακώβ, εἰ τοῦτο ἦν ἀληθές, ὑπὸ τῶν γονέων ἐνταῦθα πεμφθῆναι.* Of the clause in Procopius bracketed by Harris, Wendland rightly remarks (p. 79), " es erinnert wenigstens dem Sinne und dem ganzen Tone nach an Philo."

However, there remain for him [a] not a few questions. For it is not as if (speaking) to a servant-boy [b] that he says, " Be an attendant [c] in going forth, in order that my son may not take a wife from that land," but as if (speaking) to the chief sponsor,[d] for he says, " I adjure thee not to take for my son a Canaanite wife."

And so, necessarily allegorizing, we might most naturally say [e] that Isaac has no need of exhortation,[f] for he had never taken a wife from among the Canaanites. And I say this, not concerning man and woman, but concerning the traits of the soul,[g] to which the symbols of the names here used refer. For Isaac is the mind,[h] the self-teacher and the self-taught,[i] the distinct among the indifferent,[j] rejoicing always and daily in his Father and God and in all His works. And he does not become dissatisfied with anything that happens in the world, but knows that all things happen in accordance with nature through divine providence [k] and are for the wellbeing and eternity of all things.[l] He does not, therefore, take a Canaanite wife, by which I mean that he does not have the traits of the

[a] Or " concerning it," *i.e.* the matter.

[b] The two Arm. words used here prob. render *παιδί*.

[c] *ὑπουργός* or *διάκονος*.

[d] The Arm. lit. = *τῷ κυρίῳ τῆς ἐγγύης*, *i.e.* the guarantor of the marriage-settlement, in this case Abraham's servant acting for the father of the bridegroom.

[e] *ἀναγκαίως οὖν ἀλληγοροῦντες φυσικώτατ' ἂν εἴποιμεν*.

[f] The two Arm. words used here render *παράκλησις* or *παραμυθία*. Aucher renders, " solaminis," but the context calls for " exhortation " rather than " consolation."

[g] *περὶ τῶν κατὰ τὴν ψυχὴν τρόπων*.

[h] *ὁ νοῦς*. Although Philo usually treats Isaac as a symbol of laughter or joy, he sometimes refers to him as *ὁ ἀστεῖος* or *ὁ σοφός*, as in *De Somniis* i. 171, *De Fuga* 200.

[i] *ὁ αὐτομαθὴς καὶ ὁ αὐτοδίδακτος*, *cf. De Somniis* ii. 10.

[j] *ὁ διαφέρων ἐν τοῖς ἀδιαφόροις*, *cf. De Fuga* 152.

[k] *κατὰ φύσιν θείᾳ προνοίᾳ*.

[l] *εἰς τὴν σωτηρίαν καὶ ἀιδιότητα πάντων*.

above-mentioned school,[a] because "Canaanites," when rendered into the Armenian [b] language, means "those out of their mind." [c]

Now it is still to be feared that perhaps the uttered word,[d] which he has called "servant," may use sophistic inventions [e] and so deceive and trick and get the better of [f] him who was by nature well-pleasing (to God).[g] Wherefore he holds him by a horrid and dreadful oath as if placing reins upon him in order to soften and make milder those things which, when spoken, cause consternation [h] and overcome [i] him who is unable to stand upright, as is fitting, and to be firm in speech.[j] He says, "Go there, whence I emigrated" [k]—for it is one family and nation; that is, the migration came about through the command of God.[l] "From there shalt thou take a wife for my son."

[a] τῆς προειρημένης αἱρέσεως, *i.e.* the school of philosophers who deny divine providence, see above, § 87.

[b] Here, as elsewhere, the Arm. translator substitutes "Armenian" for "Greek."

[c] οἱ ἐξιστάντες, see § 79 and *De Somniis* ii. 89 where Philo gives this etymology for "Hittites." Evidently he here equates Hittites and Canaanites, *cf. QG* iv. 242. Elsewhere he etymologizes Χανάαν as σάλος or as "merchants," *cf. QG* ii. 65.

[d] ὁ κατὰ προφορὰν λόγος.

[e] σοφιστικοῖς εὑρήμασι.

[f] Aucher "in delirium vertat."

[g] *i.e.* Isaac, as symbol of the mind.

[h] Or "stupefaction."

[i] Aucher "pervertere." The change of number in the two Arm. verbs in the relative clause is to be disregarded in view of the context which requires a neuter plural (τὰ εἰρημένα or the like) as subject of both verbs.

[j] Aucher, referring to the sentence in a footnote as "locum intricatissimum," renders, "qui nequeat condignam firmitatem tenere in verbo."

[k] The LXX of Gen. xxiv. 4 reads ἀλλὰ εἰς τὴν γῆν μου οὗ ἐγενόμην πορεύσῃ καὶ εἰς τὴν φυλήν μου καὶ λήμψῃ γυναῖκα τῷ υἱῷ μου Ἰσαὰκ ἐκεῖθεν.

[l] This statement seems to be parenthetical.

But he takes from him an admonition (concerning) the character of his spouse,[a] (namely, from) him who was shown to have emigrated, or in accordance with custom and usage, especially as the Chaldaeans practise astronomy, first of all, of invisible and incorporeal nature.[b]

89. (Gen. xxiv. 5-6) Why, when the servant inquired, "Shall I, if the woman is unwilling to migrate here, take thy son there?", does he say, "Look to it (and) take care that thou do not return my son there"[c]?

While the literal meaning[d] is clear, the deeper meaning[e] is in accord with philosophical opinion.[f] For he admonishes the word[g] to look to it and take care not to move the constant character[h] from that worthiness[i] which is in accordance with the laws of good conduct.[j] For what is more worthy than to be pleased with that (which comes) from the Creator of the universe and Father of all, and not to find fault with anything at all, as is the habit of inconstant men and those who do not have a stable character of habit[k] but because of petty things that happen and partake of a

[a] This obscure sentence is somewhat differently rendered by Aucher "alterum monitum ut vitae consortem in moribus accepit."

[b] *ἀοράτου καὶ ἀσωμάτου φύσεως.* The last sentence is also obscure.

[c] LXX *εἶπεν δὲ πρὸς αὐτὸν ὁ παῖς, Μή ποτε οὐ βούλεται ἡ γυνὴ πορευθῆναι μετ' ἐμοῦ ὀπίσω εἰς τὴν γῆν ταύτην· ἀποστρέψω τὸν υἱόν σου εἰς τὴν γῆν ὅθεν ἐξῆλθες ἐκεῖθεν; εἶπεν δὲ πρὸς αὐτὸν Ἀβραάμ, Πρόσεχε σεαυτῷ μὴ ἀποστρέψῃς τὸν υἱόν μου ἐκεῖ.*

[d] *τὸ ῥητόν.* [e] *τὸ πρὸς διάνοιαν.*

[f] *τοῖς φιλοσοφουμένοις.*

[g] *τὸν λόγον* (*i.e. τὸν κατὰ προφορὰν λόγον*), symbolized by the servant of Abraham.

[h] *τὸν βέβαιον τρόπον vel sim.*

[i] *ἀξιώματος vel sim.*

[j] Arm. *hačoyout'iun* usu. = *εὐδοκία* or *θεραπεία*. Here it seems to mean "conduct pleasing (to God)." Aucher renders, "legis gratissimae."

[k] The Arm. translator perhaps confuses *ἔθος* and *ἦθος*.

blameworthy nature,[a] accuse and incriminate that which [b] is not to be accused or incriminated ?

90. (Gen. xxiv. 7) [c] Why does he say, " The Lord God of heaven and God of earth [d] will send His angel before thy face,[e] and thou shalt take a wife for my son Isaac " [f] ?

Thus do I see that he is a prophet and legislates oracularly concerning things that are to come.[g] For law is an invention of nature, not of men.[h] As the god-loving mind [i] changes its residence to another land (away from) every sense-perceptible land,[j] it is immediately seized [k] and prophesies. For whence does he know that the servant will be able to complete his journey through the guidance of the angel if not from [l] some divination and prophecy ? But perhaps someone will say, " What need did the servant have of an angel to go along, since he bore with him the command to complete the marriage with a virgin of their

[a] Or, construing differently, " but play the part of fault-finders concerning the petty things that happen."

[b] Or " Him Who."

[c] Philo briefly comments upon another part of this verse (see next note) in *Leg. All.* iii. 42.

[d] " And God of earth " is found in LXX but not in Heb. In both texts there follows a long clause, here omitted by Philo, reading, " Who took me from the house of my father and from the land where I was born, Who spoke to me and swore to me, saying, ' to thee and [Heb. omits " to thee and "] to thy seed will I give this land.' "

[e] LXX ἔμπροσθέν σου, rendering Heb. *l*ᵉ*phānêkā*, lit. " to thy face."

[f] LXX and Heb. add " from there."

[g] *προφήτης ἐστὶ καὶ νομοθετεῖ ἐπιθειάζων τὰ μέλλοντά τε καὶ τὰ γενησόμενα.*

[h] *νόμος γάρ ἐστι φύσεως εὕρημα ἀλλ' οὐκ ἀνθρώπων.*

[i] *ὁ φιλόθεος νοῦς.*

[j] <*ἀπὸ*> *πάσης αἰσθητῆς γῆς.*

[k] *κατέχεται.* H. A. Wolfson, *Philo* ii. 70, compares Plato, *Ion* 534 B.

[l] Lit. " in accordance with "—*κατά.*

family ?[a]" To this it must be said, "Not ineffectual,[b] Sir,[c] did He wish the human mind to be in nature, but to be active,[d] and the several things that occur to it to be acts,[e] even though it[f] performs everything externally." For this reason the steersman will not abandon the rudder even though the ship may be enjoying a favourable wind, nor will (a soldier)[g] desert the post where he has been stationed by the wisdom of the laws of science and knowledge,[h] nor will the farmer give up[i] the cultivation of the land even though the rains are on time, and the temperature of the air is in accord with the season of the year. And let not any other thing be regarded with astonishment as (happening) automatically,[j] nor anyone choose and hold on to treacherous and evil inactivity. For it is unpleasant that someone who does not wish[k] to do anything or make any effort should get (precious) stones and all kinds of inanimate things for himself.[l] But many wish only to enjoy an increase of sensual pleasure[m] without engaging at all in human affairs. That is the literal meaning.[n] But

[a] Text slightly uncertain. [b] ἀνήνυτον.

[c] Lit. "O Thou." Aucher amplifies this into "benigne lector."

[d] ἐνεργεῖν. [e] *i.e.* to be realized in act.

[f] It is not clear whether the mind or nature is the subject.

[g] Apparently this noun is to be supplied, as is done by Aucher.

[h] Aucher renders, less literally, "a lege sapientiae atque ingenii secundum peritiam."

[i] Arm. *yaytnesçi* "will make clear" is apparently a corruption of *yaresçi* or the like. Aucher renders, "praetermittit."

[j] αὐτομάτως. The sentence is obscure and probably corrupt. Aucher renders differently, "neque alius quisquam oculos figat, ut per se prosperitas adveniat."

[k] Reading *kameal* (ptc.) for *kamel* (inf.).

[l] The sense is not wholly clear to me nor, apparently, to Aucher, who renders, "difficile namque est ut quis nihil facere ac laborare volens, saxum vel quidquid inanimatum sibi acquirere possit (*vel*, imitari velit)."

[m] ἡδονῆς. [n] τὸ ῥητόν.

the passage also contains an allegory [a] in harmony with what has been said before. For inasmuch as the uttered word,[b] which in comparison with [c] the mind has been called "servant," [d] at once was in doubt and gave an appearance [e] of weakness and deceit, the Saviour [f] joined and fitted to it another word,[g] not deceived or defrauded,[h] which He calls "angel," (as) the interpreter of the divine oracles and commands. And when he comes along and teaches man, he compels him not to vacillate in his reasoning [i] or move about and be confused.

91. (Gen. xxiv. 8) What is the meaning of the words, "If the woman does not wish to go with thee,[j] thou shalt be clear of this oath.[k] Only, thou shalt not return my son there"?

Someone may be at a loss and in doubt how it is that after it has been made altogether certain that the woman will come with the angel of God accompanying him on the way,[l] he now says doubtingly, "If the woman does not wish to go with thee, thou shalt be clear of the oath." But may it not be that this (difficulty) is to be solved in the form of an allegory?[m] You need but say [n] that if the angel of God is not there, it would seem that the woman might not wish to go along. Wherefore he says, by way of sealing and confirming the matter, "If she does not go with thee as if perhaps wishing to go with a companion, she may wish to go along with the divine word." [o] And even

[a] ἀλληγορίαν. [b] ὁ κατὰ προφορὰν λόγος.
[c] τοῦ νοῦ. [d] παῖς, see above, § 88.
[e] Or "showed suspicion."
[f] ὁ σωτήρ. [g] ἄλλον λόγον.
[h] Aucher renders, "infallibile ac infallax."
[i] λόγῳ. Aucher "verbis."
[j] Philo agrees with Heb. against LXX in omitting, after "thee," the words "to this land."
[k] LXX καθαρὸς ἔσῃ ἀπὸ τοῦ ὅρκου τούτου (*v.l.* ὅρκου μου, as in Heb.).
[l] συνοδοιπόρου αὐτῷ. [m] τρόπῳ ἀλληγορίας.
[n] *i.e.* the reader need only suppose. [o] σὺν τῷ θείῳ λόγῳ.

though she may not have faith in this youth,[a] she (will have faith) in him who instructs[b] and leads to the elected way and the completion[c] of a great work. And the work is the divine, holy and consecrated marriage of the soul, the harmony of the self-taught reason.[d] Wherefore he will be unchangeable who is wise by nature without teaching.[e]

92. (Gen. xxiv. 10)[f] Why does the servant take with him ten camels of the camels of his master and of all his goods ?[g]

The decad is a most perfect number,[h] and the camel is a symbol of memory,[i] since it ruminates, grinding and chewing its food over and over. And such is the affection[j] of remembering former (experiences), for whatever the mind[k] receives through the activity of thinking,[l] it is moved by these and turns from side to side until it is reduced to order and takes its proper place and is stabilized by the two things[m] being joined and settling together. For this reason he is said to take, not " of the good parts " but " of

[a] *i.e.* Abraham's servant, symbolizing " the uttered word " (see above). The variant " in this honour " makes no sense.

[b] *i.e.* the angel, symbolizing " the divine word " or Logos.

[c] The Arm. has " incompleteness," apparently in error.

[d] *ἁρμονία τοῦ αὐτομαθοῦς* (or *αὐτοδιδάκτου*) *λογισμοῦ*. *Cf. De Somniis* ii. 10.

[e] *ὃς φύσει ἄνευ διδασκαλίας ἐστὶ σοφός.*

[f] In *De Congressu* 111-112 Philo allegorizes this verse similarly ; *cf.* also *De Poster. Caini* 148-149.

[g] LXX *καὶ ἔλαβεν ὁ παῖς δέκα καμήλους ἀπὸ τῶν καμήλων τοῦ κυρίου αὐτοῦ καὶ ἀπὸ πάντων τῶν ἀγαθῶν τοῦ κυρίου αὐτοῦ μεθ' ἑαυτοῦ* (Heb. " in his hand ").

[h] *τελειότατος ἀριθμός.* For parallels in Philo see Staehle, p. 54.

[i] *σύμβολον μνήμης*, as in *De Poster. Caini* 148, or *ἀναμνήσεως*, as in *De Congressu* 111.

[j] *τὸ πάθος.*

[k] *ὁ νοῦς.*

[l] *κατὰ τὸν τῆς διανοίας λογισμόν vel sim.*

[m] Apparently the two things are the mind and sense-impression.

all (his goods)," since the whole life of the virtuous man [a] is completely full of happiness,[b] with no part left vacant and empty for the bringing in and admitting of sins. But it is well that (Scripture) adds, " he took of all his goods with him," for many others make use of good things as of alien possessions without profiting therefrom, such as sophists and word-chasers.[c] For though they have been taught the laws of philosophy, which are beautiful and worthy of zeal and virtue,[d] they do not become any better, but while correcting the lives of others, they leave their own souls uncared for and untended, inasmuch as they do not have in themselves and with themselves a genuine philosophy [e] but one that is on their lips and is superficial. And this is like an ill-favoured woman being dressed in precious purple. The garment is not an ornament to the wearer [f] but a reproach, which very clearly shows her lewdness.[g]

93. (Gen. xxiv. 10) What is " Mesopotamia,[h] " where he goes, and what is " the city of Nahor " [i] ?

In the literal sense [j] " Mesopotamia " is the land of Babylonia, lying between the two rivers Euphrates and Tigris,[k] from which fact it was appropriately [l] named. And as for " Nahor," it is clear that this was first the name of a city in Babylonia, which, as happens in many cases, was changed into another name. But as for the deeper meaning,[m] it is proper to say that " Nahor " is to be trans-

[a] τοῦ σπουδαίου. Aucher renders, less exactly, " sapientis."

[b] εὐδαιμονίας.

[c] ὡς σοφισταὶ καὶ λογοθῆραι.

[d] τοὺς νόμους τῆς φιλοσοφίας τοὺς καλοὺς καὶ σπουδῆς τε καὶ ἀρετῆς ἀξίους.

[e] γνησίαν (rendered by two Arm. words) φιλοσοφίαν.

[f] Lit. " to the one having (it)."

[g] μαχλοσύνην.

[h] The Arm. renders LXX Μεσοποταμία as " between the rivers " : Heb. " Aram Naharaim."

[i] Arm. *Nakʻōr* : LXX Ναχώρ : Heb. *Nāḥôr*.

[j] τῷ ῥητῷ.

[k] Arm. *Aracan* and *Dklatʻ*.

[l] ἐτύμως.

[m] τὸ πρὸς διάνοιαν.

lated as " rest of light." [a] And the light of corporeal eyes is the sun or the moon or the lamp used for fire, while wisdom is the light of the soul.[b] And for this to rest and be quiet and still is not profitable,[c] but movement [d] is profitable for him who possesses (it) and for those who are near him. And he becomes wholly good when moved by wisdom toward those things which are suitable and related to him,[e] while (he becomes) lame and imperfect when he is motionless. For these reasons, though the city of Mesopotamia is confined by its own streams as if by torrents,[f] he proceeds with unimpeded and free steps, while those who oppose the movements that take place in accordance with nature [g] in the soul that becomes knowing and wise when illuminated—in them are many things, some of which are due to us ourselves, others to external causes, which like river-streams flow round the mind [h] and confine it.[i]

94. (Gen. xxiv. 11) Why does (Scripture) say, " He caused the camels to rest outside the city beside a well of water at evening, when the (women-)drawers of water [j] came out " ?

The literal significance [k] is clear, for it is the custom of wayfarers to spend the night by springs in order to rest

[a] *φωτὸς ἀνάπαυσις.* The same fanciful etymology is given in *De Congressu* 45, as if Heb. *Nāḥôr* were a compound of *nāḥ* " to rest " and *'ôr* " light."

[b] *τὸ δὲ τῆς ψυχῆς φῶς σοφία ἐστίν.* *Cf. De Congressu* 47 *φῶς δὲ ψυχῆς ἡλιοειδέστατον ἐπιστήμη.*

[c] Text slightly uncertain.

[d] *κίνησις.*

[e] The Arm. text is obscure but not more so than Aucher's rendering, " namque fit nota familia sua bona per sapientiam mota ad sibi decentia."

[f] This clause too is syntactically unclear in the Arm.

[g] *κατὰ φύσιν.*

[h] *τὸν νοῦν.*

[i] Philo seems to mean that the wise man seeks " the quiet of light " by responding to the right kinds of movement in the soul.

[j] LXX *αἱ ὑδρευόμεναι.*

[k] *τὸ ῥητὸν σύμβολον.*

themselves and their asses for the needs of the journey. But as for the deeper meaning,[a] it is as follows. When the memory [b] rests and is inactive, it turns, as it were, to sleep, and rests outside the city in sleep [c] by nature. For every one of us appears (to be) a city, the body being like a building,[d] and the soul like an inhabitant.[e] When the memory happens to be awake, it wakens the mind by entering the city, that is, by dwelling within us. But when sleep overtakes it—and sleep is forgetfulness [f] of memory—, it necessarily removes its dwelling from that place, namely from us, until it is once again aroused. For what is forgetfulness but the going out (of memory)? And most excellently does (Scripture) say that memory turned to sleep not only " outside the city " but also " beside a well of water," indicating that forgetfulness is not perpetual or daily, since the spring is near by, from which the memory-form [g] is drawn [h] and enters the soul, and sleep, which by another name is called " forgetfulness," is shaken off. And when wakefulness comes in, of which the true name is " memory," it remains by the spring to which the drawers of water come out at evening. Now, who they are (Scripture) does not tell, for the subject of investigation (here) is not women or water but the mind of the God-loving man,[i] which desires a water-course.[j] And the time of its resting is the setting of the sun, when the senses are far gone [k] and there is no longer shadow and shade from its

[a] τὸ πρὸς διάνοιαν.

[b] ἡ μνήμη. On the camels as a symbol of memory see above, *QG* iv. 92.

[c] Variant " at home."

[d] οἰκοδομῇ.

[e] οἰκήτορι. *Cf. De Poster. Caini* 61 ⟨ψυχὴ⟩ σωματικαῖς συζυγίαις ὑποβάλλουσα αὐτὴν οἰκήτορας ἔχει τοὺς λεχθέντας.

[f] λήθη. [g] τὸ μνημονικὸν εἶδος.

[h] Reading Arm. *oroganeal* (ptc.) for *oroganel* (inf.).

[i] περὶ τοῦ νοῦ τοῦ φιλοθέου.

[j] Arm. *vtak* = χειμάρρους, λίμνη, ὑδραγωγός, etc.

[k] Arm. *zarançem* = προβεβηκέναι, ληρεῖν, ἐξιστάναι, etc. Aucher renders, " defatigatis jam sensibus," and adds in a footnote, " *vel*, antiquatis jam sensibilibus."

rays.[a] For then it [b] receives impressions [c] of a more lucid reason [d] from the things seen, and, behold, it arrives at the divine spring, and this is wisdom,[e] which takes the appearance of water by its power.[f] And some persist in drinking with the edges of the lips, some only so much as is sufficient to satisfy their thirst, while still others hasten the more eagerly to rejoice in it, being insatiably impelled to those things which belong to virtue.[g]

95. (Gen. xxiv. 12-14) Why does the servant, beginning with the prospering of the journey, prophesy what is to come? [h]

The literal meaning [i] is that since the angel of God was his companion on the journey and was near by, he was perhaps enthused [j] by him and began to be possessed.[k] But as for the deeper meaning,[l] they [m] are types of God-loving characters, each of which the reason [n] carefully

[a] This last clause is not quite clear.

[b] Apparently the mind is the subject.

[c] *φαντασίας*. [d] Or "Logos"—*λόγου*. [e] *σοφία*.

[f] *πρὸς* (or *κατὰ*) *δύναμιν*. The meaning is not clear, possibly "in accordance with the power (or "capacity") of those who use it." [g] *ἀρετήν*.

[h] This is Philo's somewhat awkward summary of the LXX *καὶ εἶπεν, Κύριε ὁ θεὸς τοῦ κυρίου Ἀβραάμ, εὐόδωσον* (Heb. "cause it to befall") *ἐναντίον ἐμοῦ σήμερον καὶ ποίησον ἔλεος μετὰ τοῦ κυρίου μου Ἀβραάμ. ἰδοὺ ἐγὼ ἕστηκα ἐπὶ τῆς πηγῆς τοῦ ὕδατος, αἱ δὲ θυγατέρες τῶν οἰκούντων τὴν πόλιν ἐκπορεύονται ἀντλῆσαι ὕδωρ καὶ ἔσται ἡ παρθένος ᾗ ἂν ἐγὼ εἴπω, Ἐπίκλινον τὴν ὑδρίαν σου ἵνα πίω, καὶ εἴπῃ μοι, Πίε σύ, καὶ τὰς καμήλας σοῦ ποτιῶ ἕως ἂν παύσωνται πίνουσαι, ταύτην ἡτοίμασας τῷ παιδί σου Ἰσαάκ· καὶ ἐν τούτῳ γνώσομαι ὅτι ἐποίησας ἔλεος τῷ κυρίῳ μου Ἀβραάμ*.

[i] *τὸ ῥητόν*.

[j] Reading *astouacareal* (ptc.) for *astouacarel* (inf.) = *ἐνθουσιάζων* or *ἐπιθειάζων*.

[k] *κατέχεσθαι*. [l] *τὸ πρὸς διάνοιαν*.

[m] *i.e.* the persons and objects mentioned by the servant.

[n] Or "the passage (of Scripture)"—*ὁ λόγος*.

examines and fully investigates.[a] And when it finds that they are united, it rejoices at their being complete, as it hoped. Now, there are three types. One is being a virgin; the second, that she inclines the water-jar; and the third, that she gives (them) to drink. For the sign of a virgin is a pure and sincere intention,[b] which honours the sincere and incorruptible nature without passion. Moreover, the inclining downward of the water-jar (signifies) length of teaching and participation,[c] not for all whomsoever, for death rather than profit.[d] And it is not for those whose custom it is to act like the envious sophists,[e] who with what they have drawn in from things formerly heard take water with the greatest difficulty, being able to draw only a little.[f] For he who in tasting desires to draw [g] the measure of the water-jar is anxious not to spill it altogether on the ground,[h] and lifts up [i] the drink for the sharing (of it) and for love

[a] Aucher renders differently, "ad scrutanda singulorum verba et veraciter adimplenda."

[b] The two Arm. words probably render προαίρεσις.

[c] μῆκος (or μακρότητα) διδασκαλίας καὶ κοινωνίας. Probably τῆς σοφίας or τῆς ἀρετῆς is to be understood. See the parallel in *De Poster. Caini* 146.

[d] The Arm. text is obscure and evidently incomplete or corrupt. Aucher renders, "non cunctis simul, ne mortis, quam utilitatis sit causa." The sense seems to be that wisdom is not for those who prefer death to the help to be obtained from wisdom.

[e] τοῖς φθονεροῖς σοφισταῖς. See the next note.

[f] The text is obscure, partly because of the multiple meanings of the Arm. verb *tanem*, here rendered "to draw." Aucher renders, "qui per auditum anteriorum, quae intus accepere, hauriunt aquam tantam ut paucissimam in se ferre queant." In *De Poster. Caini* 150 Philo speaks of the grudging and mercenary spirit of the sophists, who withold from their pupils much that they ought to tell them.

[g] Here again the Arm. verb *tånem* is ambiguous. Aucher renders, "qui vero post gustum desiderat in mensura hydriae secum dortare" [*l.* "portare"].

[h] Text slightly uncertain.

[i] Variant "opens."

of man,[a] as one might be able to harmonize on a musical instrument, and there would be a most excellent and wonderful harmony.

96. (Gen. xxiv. 15) Why does (Scripture) say, " It came about before he finished speaking in his mind " [b] ?

First, it makes clear that there are two (kinds of) discourse,[c] one which resides within, in the understanding,[d] and (another) which we utter.[e] And each of these has a special sound [f] ; that which we utter has that of nouns and verbs,[g] while that which is in the understanding has that of thoughts, reflection and comprehension,[h] for (Scripture) very emphatically proves this by showing that he spoke what had been decided in his mind. And in the second place, it vividly represents the fact that before every utterance and thought [i] there come the surpassing kindnesses of God,[j] which seem to be swifter than anything in creation.

97. (Gen. xxiv. 15) What is the meaning of the words, " And Rebekah [k] came out, who had been born to Bethuel " [l] ?

[a] εἰς κοινωνίαν καὶ φιλανθρωπίαν.

[b] LXX καὶ ἐγένετο πρὸ τοῦ συντελέσαι αὐτὸν λαλοῦντα ἐν τῇ διανοίᾳ (Heb. lacks the words after " speaking ").

[c] λόγοι. [d] ἐν τῷ λογισμῷ.

[e] προφέρομεν. On the distinction between the λόγος ἐνδιάθετος and the λόγος προφορικός see above, *QG* iv. 85 notes.

[f] ἴδιον φθόγγον or " tone "—τόνον : Aucher " vocem." Although the inner λόγος, strictly speaking, has no " sound," it is articulately expressed, as Philo states in *Quis Rer. Div. Heres* 4.

[g] δι' ὀνομάτων καὶ ῥημάτων, *i.e.* words in general.

[h] διὰ λογισμῶν καὶ ἐννοιῶν καὶ συνέσεως *vel sim.*

[i] Lit. " mind."

[j] αἱ θεῖαι χάριτες αἱ ὑπερβάλλουσαι, *cf. De Abrahamo* 39 αἱ τῶν χαρίτων ὑπερβολαί. Aucher renders, " praecedunt gratiae Dei praevenientes et praetereuntes."

[k] LXX Ῥεβέκκα, Heb. *Ribqāh.*

[l] LXX Βαθουήλ, Heb. *Beᵉthû'ēl.*

Just as in the world the heaven has special honour greater than that of all other things, always being the same in itself,[a] so too the soul of him who philosophizes genuinely [b] is inflexible and unchangeable. And truly equal to the heavenly nature is she whom in their ancestral language the Hebrews and Chaldaeans call " Rebekah," which name is to be translated as " constancy " [c] since she suffers neither diminution nor increase. And (Scripture) tells her lineage, saying that she was born to " Bethuel," which should be interpreted as " daughter of her God." [d] And who is to be considered the daughter of God but Wisdom, who is the first-born mother of all things [e] and most of all of those who are greatly purified in soul?

98. (Gen. xxiv. 15) Why is (Rebekah) said to carry the water-jar " on her shoulders " [f]?

(Scripture) is wont to make a bodily symbol of the shoulders,[g] for they are the beginnings and origins of the

[a] Aucher " semper se suaque aeque habens."

[b] ἡ ψυχὴ ἡ τοῦ ἀνόθως φιλοσοφοῦντος.

[c] As Aucher notes, Arm. *yarout'iun* usually = " resurrection " (ἀνάστασις or ἔγερσις), but here it is evidently a nominal formation from the verb *yarem* " to adhere," as the context and other passages in Philo show. In *De Somniis* i. 46 " Rebekah " is etymologized as ἡ ὑπομονή, in *De Fuga* 45 and *De Cherubim* 41 as ἐπιμονὴ (τῶν καλῶν).

[d] *Cf. De Fuga* 50-51, where the name " Bethuel " is interpreted as θυγάτηρ θεοῦ, *i.e.* σοφία, as if from Heb. *bath* " daughter " and *'el* " God." Here " daughter of *her* God " indicates an etymon *bitto* " his daughter."

[e] *Cf. De Fuga* 109 μητρὸς δὲ σοφίας δι' ἧς τὰ ὅλα ἦλθεν εἰς γένεσιν, and *De Virtutibus* 62 σοφίαν δὲ πρεσβυτέραν οὐ μόνον τῆς ἐμῆς γενέσεως ἀλλὰ καὶ τῆς τοῦ κόσμου παντὸς οὖσαν.

[f] LXX καὶ ἰδοὺ Ῥεβέκκα . . . ἔχουσα τὴν ὑδρίαν ἐπὶ τῶν ὤμων (Heb. " her shoulder ").

[g] *Cf. Quod Deterius* 9 ἐν Συχέμ· ὦμος . . . τλητικοῦ σημεῖον πόνου, *De Mut. Nom.* 193 Συχέμ . . . ἑρμηνευθείς ἐστιν ὦμος, πόνου σύμβολον, *De Vita Mosis* ii. 130 τὸν γὰρ ὦμον ἐνεργείας καὶ πράξεως ποιεῖται σύμβολον.

arms and forearms and also of the hands, through which the works and activities of life are accomplished. And the water-jar is a vessel of water, and this is a symbol of education [a]; and water (is a symbol) of those things which are seen through wisdom.[b] For the water-jar contains water, and knowledge (contains) law, counsel and contemplation.[c] And animals and plants are nourished [d] with water, while the sovereign mind [e] (is nourished) with those things which are seen through wisdom. And so the God-loving soul [f] bears heavy things most lightly, (namely) all things pertaining to knowledge.[g]

*99. (Gen. xxiv. 16) Why does (Scripture) use a double expression in calling her a virgin, saying, "She was a virgin very fair of face. She was a virgin whom no man had known" [h]?

It wishes to show clearly that she had two virginities, one in respect of the body, the other in respect of the incorruptible soul.[i] And she was fair to see and to know.[j] Do not, however, think that it now presents to us fairness of body in respect of that which is called beauty of form,[k]

[a] σύμβολον τῆς παιδείας.

[b] κατὰ σοφίαν. *Cf. De Poster. Caini* 146 ἐπαινετέον οὖν καὶ Ῥεβέκκαν, . . . ἀφ᾽ ὑψηλοτέρου χωρίου καθελοῦσα τὸ σοφίας ἀγγεῖον ἐπὶ τὸν βραχίονα, τὴν ὑδρίαν ὀρέγει τῷ μαθητῇ ἃς ἱκανὸς ἐκεῖνός ἐστι δέξασθαι διδασκαλίας.

[c] ἡ ἐπιστήμη <περιέχει> τὸν νόμον καὶ τὰς βουλὰς καὶ τὰς θεωρίας *vel sim.*

[d] ποτίζονται.

[e] ὁ ἡγεμονικὸς νοῦς.

[f] ἡ φιλόθεος ψυχή.

[g] πάντα τὰ ἐπιστημονικά.

[h] LXX ἡ δὲ παρθένος (Heb. "young woman") ἦν καλὴ τῇ ὄψει σφόδρα. παρθένος ἦν, ἀνὴρ οὐκ ἔγνω αὐτήν.

[i] ἡ μὲν κατὰ τὸ σῶμα, ἡ δὲ κατὰ τὴν ἄφθαρτον ψυχήν.

[j] Or perhaps, as Aucher renders, "erat enim tam visu, quam intellectu pulchra."

[k] κατὰ τὴν λεγομένην εὐμορφίαν.

which consists of the symmetry of parts and beauty of form[a] such as even harlots have. These I would never call fair, but on the contrary, foul,[b] for this is their proper name. And, it seems to me, just as bodily properties are seen in mirrors, so those of the soul (are seen) in the face and countenance. But a shameless look and an elevated neck and a continuous movement of the eyebrows and a womanish walk[c] and not blushing at, or being ashamed of,[d] any evil at all is the sign of a lewd soul,[e] which clearly pictures and describes the forms of its invisible disgraces on its visible body.[f] But he in whom the divine words[g] of wisdom and virtue[h] dwell, even though he may be more deformed of body than Silenus, is necessarily fair.[i] Since it is good for him to be revered through his own modesty, it follows that he will conform to that which is acceptable to those who look at him.[j] Wherefore (Scripture) adds to her virginity[k] what some may think superfluous but is (in fact) necessary, namely " a man had not known her," for, it says, what is she whom a man has known ? But may it not be that by " man " it does not present one who is such in body and soul but a model character,[l] who does not

[a] *Sic.*

[b] Or " lewd."

[c] The Greek frag. has *βάδισμα σεσοβημένον.*

[d] The Greek frag. has only *ἐρυθριᾶν.*

[e] Greek frag. *ψυχῆς αἰσχίστης.*

[f] This is close to the wording of the Greek frag. (which ends here), *τοὺς ἀφανεῖς τῶν οἰκείων ὀνειδῶν τύπους ἐγγραφούσης τῷ φανερῷ σώματι.*

[g] Or " oracles."

[h] *σοφίας καὶ ἀρετῆς.* The syntax is not clear. Aucher renders, " sapientiae studio atque virtutis."

[i] *καλός ἐστι ἐξ ἀνάγκης.*

[j] The text is obscure. Aucher renders, " bonum est enim ei proprio pudore venerabiliter conformari acceptationi videntium."

[k] *τῇ παρθενίᾳ αὐτῆς, i.e.* to the (second) reference to Rebekah's virginity.

[l] *τρόπον ὑποδείγματος vel sim.* ; Aucher " morem exemplarem."

permit himself to corrupt the uncorrupted, or to defile the undefiled, soul but has the courage to think it impious to sow the corrupt seeds of sensual pleasure in the mind,[a] and, instead, receives the unadulterated seeds of divinity which the Father of all is wont to sow in us from above, (namely) those that are incorporeal and intelligible.[b]

*100. (Gen. xxiv. 16) What is the meaning of the words, "Going down to the spring, she filled her water-jar and went up"[c]?

(Scripture) gives the intention of the Law[d] symbolically.[e] For whatever soul is shown to descend from its own beliefs (is shown) to ascend from there quite soon, just as, on the contrary, whoever is haughty, boastful, puffed up and swollen descends and is destroyed[f]; so that it is most natural to enter into the practices of education.[g] For the descent of the soul is its ascent through belief,[h] and its ascent and elevation are the ebbing of arrogance.[i] But it is impossible for one to fly upward to the heavenly place of virtue[j] who has not filled his whole soul like a water-jar[k]

[a] τὰ τῆς ἡδονῆς φθαρτὰ σπέρματα εἰς τὸν νοῦν σπείρειν.

[b] τὰ ἀσώματα καὶ νοερά.

[c] This sentence is more fully commented on in *De Poster. Caini* 136-138 and more briefly in *De Fuga* 195.

[d] τὴν τοῦ νόμου γνώμην. Aucher renders, "legem voluntatis," adding in a footnote, "*ad verb.* voluntatem legis (fortasse ut legitimam)."

[e] συμβολικῶς.

[f] Or "is dissolved" (or, perhaps, "is deflated").

[g] The Arm. lit. = ὥστε εἶναι φυσικώτατόν τι καὶ εἰς τὰ τῆς παιδείας ἐπιτηδεύματα εἰσερχόμενον. The Greek frag. (Harris, p. 100, identified by Früchtel) has merely φυσικώτατα ταῦτα δέδεικται.

[h] Similarly the Greek frag., κατάβασιν μὲν ψυχῆς τὴν δι' οἰήσεως ἀνάβασιν.

[i] The Greek frag. (which ends here) has similarly ἄνοδον δὲ καὶ ὕψος τὴν ἀλαζονείας ὑπονόστησιν.

[j] πρὸς τὸν οὐράνιον ἀρετῆς τόπον.

[k] ὑδρίαν.

from the divine spring, which we declare to be the eternal wisdom of knowledge.[a]

101. (Gen. xxiv. 17) Why did the servant run to meet her[b]?

There are two praises[c] of the servant: one is his running toward her, and the other is his meeting (her). For (thus) is clearly shown, in the first place, the eagerness of the progressive man[d] and the learned man's attainment of the good,[e] and, in the second place, that it is considered a pleasure and delight and joyfulness of mind by those whose (desire) God has entirely approved[f] and whom He has made perfect in the knowledge of wisdom[g] by His wisdom, which like a spring He has opened up and poured out with lavish generosity. For there are those who are slothful in respect of good deeds and voluntarily hold back from them. And there are those who are seized with envy so as not to rejoice (in the good) and even turn their faces away from those who are (held) in honour and are in a state of prosperity. Such men does sacred Scripture[h] rebuke by praising the opposite way of life.

*102. (Gen. xxiv. 17) Why does he ask for a little water, saying, "Give me a little water to drink from thy water-jar"[i]?

[a] The text is perhaps in disorder. *Cf. De Poster. Caini* 138 <Ῥεβέκκαν> *ὑδρευσαμένην οὖν ἀπὸ σοφίας, τῆς θείας πηγῆς, τὰς ἐπιστήμας*.

[b] Lit. "run toward her," as in the Arm. O.T., rendering LXX *εἰς συνάντησιν αὐτῆς*. The sentence is commented on in passing in *De Poster. Caini* 138.

[c] One expects "descriptions" or the like.

[d] *τοῦ προκόπτοντος*.

[e] Aucher renders somewhat differently, "et peritia [abl. case] perveniendi ad bonum."

[f] The text is defective, since the noun-object is lacking. Aucher renders, "quorum Deus votum integerrime acceptans adimplevit."

[g] *κατ' ἐπιστήμην σοφίας*.

[h] *ὁ ἱερὸς λόγος*.

[i] Philo indirectly comments on this phrase in *De Poster. Caini* 139-147.

It is proper to interpret (this as meaning) that one should not desire anything that is beyond one's capacity,[a] for everything that has measure is praiseworthy.[b] Wherefore in another passage sacred Scripture[c] (orders)[d] the measuring of the spiritual food that came forth from the ether and heaven like a spring and was called "manna"[e] by the Hebrews, that it might not be too much for anyone or too little. For it is necessary that teaching should be more abundant for the intelligent man, and less for the foolish man because of the fine equality of proportion.[f] In another place[g] (Scripture) also says that one should offer sacrifices in accordance with the power of the hands,[h] alluding to what has been said, lest there be too little or too much, the little being suited to little men and the great to great men; this is that equality which is most useful to life.[i] And so, he appropriately asks for "a little water," thereby measuring[j] his own nature, for this is little, being that of a servant. And to kindle the spirit of uttered discourse[k] with a more perfect nature, the Father did not leave any part empty but completely filled the vessel of

[a] So the Greek frag., *ἄξιον ἀποδέχεσθαι τὸ μηδενὸς ὀρέγεσθαι τῶν ὑπὲρ δύναμιν.* Aucher renders inexactly, "oportet non desiderare ut recipiantur ampliora suis viribus."

[b] *πᾶν γὰρ τὸ συμμετρίαν ἔχον, ἐπαινετόν* is the reading of the Greek frag., which breaks off here and is resumed below, "For it is necessary, etc."

[c] *ὁ ἱερὸς λόγος.*

[d] There is no main verb in the Arm.

[e] Arm. *mananay.* *Cf. De Sacr. Abelis* 86, *Quis Rer. Div. Heres* 79 *et al.* on manna as spiritual food.

[f] For *ἐν ταῖς ἀναλογίαις* the Greek frag. (which again breaks off, to be resumed briefly below) has *ἐν ταῖς ἀνάγκαις.*

[g] *Cf.* Lev. xii. 8.

[h] *i.e.* in accordance with one's means.

[i] The Greek frag. (which ends here) has *καὶ τοῦτό γέ ἐστι τὸ βιωφελέστατον ἴσον.*

[j] Reading Arm. *čap'eal* (ptc.) for *čap'el* (inf.); so also Aucher, who renders, "mensurans."

[k] *τῷ προφορικῷ λόγῳ*, symbolized by Abraham's servant; see above, *QG* iv. 85.

spirit, knowing that it naturally does not seek drink from her who has it,[a] but from the water-jar,[b] to teach us that it is not mortal man who pours out blessings[c] but the grace of God,[d] which is too high for man[e] and of which he prays to be thought worthy to partake, and that He give him to drink that which He had earlier put into (the vessel).[f]

103. (Gen. xxiv. 18) Why does she say in addition, "Master," (although she was) almost the mistress of the servant?[g]

This is an indication and proof of theoretical matters,[h] from which one ought to see that the passage[i] is not about mortal man but about the characters[j] of good men, who are zealous for immortality. And so, wisdom[k] rightly

[a] *i.e.* from wisdom or virtue, symbolized by Rebekah.

[b] The passage is obscure, and the correctness of the above rendering is uncertain. Aucher renders, "adhaec vero quia secundum verbum pronuntiativum, quod animam refovet, perfectionis erat naturae, nullam reliquit partem vacuam, sed totum ex toto vas animae implendum pater novit. Naturaliter, non ex habente, sed de hydria potum petit." In a footnote he adds "*Vel*, implevit pater. Quod noscens naturaliter, etc."

[c] Lit. "waters with good things."

[d] *χάρις θεοῦ.*

[e] So Aucher, "quae super hominem apparet." Perhaps the Greek original meant "which appears to man from above."

[f] Meaning uncertain. Aucher renders, "de qua rogat sibi largiri dignare, et illam, quam prius introducit (in os animae) potare facere."

[g] LXX *ἡ δὲ εἶπεν, Πίε, κύριε.* The sentence is briefly allegorized in *De Poster. Caini* 138 to mean that "only the wise man is free and a ruler, though he may have ten thousand masters of his body."

[h] *θεωρητικῶν* (or *ὁρατικῶν*). Aucher renders, "speculativae sententiae."

[i] *ὁ λόγος.*

[j] Or "types."

[k] *ἡ σοφία.*

desires to give to another some of the drink [a] which she has taken. For grudging envy does not touch the god-loving soul. And she calls him " Master," not with regard to the empty dignity of slavery or freedom, but with regard to the eagerness of will of the recipient. For he is not constant in ignorance and indiscipline [b] but truly concerns himself with discipline and knowledge,[c] for he labours on behalf of genuinely noble things.

*104. (Gen. xxiv. 18) Why does she hasten to lower the water-jar upon her arm ? [d]

This is in harmony with the preceding. For (Scripture) wishes to reprove the character of the sophist [e] and to praise the true and genuine seeker of wisdom. For he who is trained in words [f] and uses one after the other, helps (only) one soul in training himself, but does not bring any profit to those who come to him. Because of their speed and their being produced one after the other his words when spoken do not enter their ears but are, as it were, poured away outside. This is what those men do who transfer water or wine all at once into a jar with a narrow mouth, for more is spilled than is put into (the jar). But he who genuinely philosophizes and shares (his wisdom) humanely,[g] gives profit through his words by inclining himself and making allowance for the character of the learner. For the pupil's capacity to learn is not like the teacher's capacity to teach,[h] since the one is perfect, and the other imperfect.[i] Wherefore it is fitting to bear in

[a] *i.e.* drinking-water.

[b] Aucher renders more freely, " non enim doctrinae disciplinaeque odium fert."

[c] παιδείας καὶ ἐπιστήμης.

[d] LXX καὶ ἔσπευσεν καὶ καθεῖλεν τὴν ὑδρίαν ἐπὶ τὸν βραχίονα αὐτῆς. The sentence is allegorized in similar fashion but at greater length in *De Poster. Caini* 140-147.

[e] τὸν σοφιστικὸν τρόπον.

[f] λόγοις.

[g] ὁ ἀνόθως φιλοσοφούμενος καὶ κοινωνῶν φιλανθρώπως.

[h] So the Greek frag. (which begins here).

[i] ἐπειδὴ ὁ μὲν τέλειος, ὁ δὲ ἀτελής ἐστι, as in the Greek frag.

mind and to weigh[a] the capacity of the one who is being educated.[b]

105. (Gen. xxiv. 18-19) What is the meaning of the words, "She gave him to drink until he ceased drinking"[c]?

(Scripture) shows the teacher's amiability and friendliness toward the learner from the fact that she not only gave him to drink but until he ceased drinking. And it is an indication of the fact that one should not superficially[d] take account (of the learner's needs)[e] but should take cognizance of the impulse[f] of the disciple and pupil, and completely satisfy all his zeal.[g] For, as I was saying a little before,[h] one should not take either more or less water than one's capacity (to use). For where there is too much, it is spilled outside, and where there is too little, it does not fill but leaves an empty place in the soul of the learner.

106. (Gen. xxiv. 19) Why does she say, "And for thy camels I will draw water until they have all drunk"?

(Scripture) dwells at length on the benevolence of the teacher who wishes not only to hand over and entrust scientific knowledge[i] (to the pupil) but to put it in order[j] and make it stick to him, since she gives drink to his

[a] The Greek frag. has only one verb, *στοχάζεσθαι*.

[b] *τὴν τοῦ παιδευομένου δύναμιν*, as in the Greek frag. (with change of case).

[c] So the LXX, *καὶ ἐπότισεν αὐτὸν ἕως ἐπαύσατο πίνων*. The Heb. is slightly different, "and she gave him to drink and (*i.e.* until) she ceased giving him to drink." The verse is somewhat differently allegorized in *De Poster. Caini* 147.

[d] *οὐκ ἐπιπολαίως*.

[e] The meaning of the Arm. text is not altogether clear. Aucher renders, "cujus indicium est haud obiter facere enarrationem."

[f] *τὴν ὁρμήν*.

[g] *τὴν σπουδήν*.

[h] In *QG* iv. 102, 104.

[i] *τὰ ἐπιστημονικά*.

[j] *κοσμεῖν vel sim.*

memory,[a] of which the camels are symbols. For genuine teachers and instructors [b] direct their teaching not to display but to the profit of their pupils, and compel them to repeat from memory what has been said by them,[c] thus firmly impressing upon them what they have heard.

107. (Gen. xxiv. 20) Why does (Scripture) say, " She hastened and poured out the water-jar into the drinking-trough " [d] ?

In man the drinking-trough is a symbol of hearing,[e] for it is through hearing that the flow of words comes into the mind and soul.[f] Excellently, moreover, is it said that she poured out the whole water-jar, for thereby (Scripture) clearly shows that the good is far removed from envy and grudgingness, for without storing up and keeping them for itself, it gives up the various kinds of knowledge [g] and hides nothing, as some sophists [h] do. And the reason for this is that some men because of small-mindedness [i] suppose that there are only those things in nature which they alone know. But the good man, on the contrary, knows that he knows little or nothing rather than the illimitable greatness of nature,[j] wherefore he has learned to take water from the divine spring, as though having

[a] τὰς μνήμας, plural as in the parallel, *De Poster. Caini* 148-150.

[b] Aucher amplifies in rendering, " fideles magistri, genuinique doctores."

[c] *i.e.* the teachers.

[d] So LXX, καὶ ἔσπευσεν καὶ ἐξεκένωσεν τὴν ὑδρίαν ἐπὶ τὸ ποτιστήριον. The last word is taken by Philo, in the parallel, *De Poster. Caini* 150-152, as a synonym of δεξαμενή and as a symbol of the learner's soul or understanding.

[e] τοῦ ἀκούειν.

[f] εἰς τὸν νοῦν (or τὴν διάνοιαν) καὶ τὴν ψυχήν.

[g] τὰ τῆς ἐπιστήμης εἴδη.

[h] σοφισταί.

[i] δι' ὀλιγοψυχίαν.

[j] τὸ ἄπειρον τῆς φύσεως μέγεθος. *Cf. De Poster. Caini* 152 πάνυ εὐήθεις ὅσοι πρὸς τὸ πέρας ἡστινοσοῦν ἐπιστήμης ἀφικέσθαι διενοήθησαν.

nothing of his own and receiving (everything) from the pure and unfailing wisdom of God.[a]

108. (Gen. xxiv. 21) Why is he no longer called " boy "[b] but " man," for (Scripture) says, " The man examined and studied her and stood silent so as to know whether the Lord God would bring success to him "[c] ?

Because while he was preparing to learn and was at the beginning[d] of instruction,[e] he was considered to be of the boys and minors,[f] but when he began to progress,[g] he was considered a rational man,[h] who was indeed able to use uttered discourse.[i] And this progressive man is a type of character[j] and sees, as it were, a most beautiful image[k] and the nature of a wise teacher of the wisdom of knowledge.[l] And also because he stood silent a long while,[m] giving place to that which spoke in him without mouth or tongue or instruments or voice, (namely) the divine Logos,[n] understanding and seeing that path which leads to virtue and happiness,[o] and whether he will reach it. For in truth there is no prospering[p] for anyone else (or) for those (engaged) in material things,[q] whether as private citizens or as kings.[r]

[a] ἐκ τῆς ἀκράτου καὶ ἀδιαλείπτου σοφίας θεοῦ.

[b] παῖς.

[c] The LXX reads slightly differently ὁ δὲ ἄνθρωπος κατεμάνθανεν αὐτὴν (Heb. " contemplated her") καὶ παρεσιώπα τοῦ γνῶναι ἢ εὐόδωκεν κύριος τὴν ὁδὸν ἢ οὔ.

[d] Lit. " had a beginning."

[e] διδασκαλίας.

[f] ἐν τοῖς ἀτελέσι.

[g] ὡς ἐγένετο προκόπτων.

[h] ἄνθρωπος λογικός.

[i] τῷ προφορικῷ λόγῳ, see above, QG iv. 85 notes.

[j] τύπος ἠθῶν *vel sim.*

[k] Or " picture."

[l] The Arm. lit. = σοφοῦ διδασκάλου φύσιν σοφίας ἐπιστήμης. This can hardly have been the original.

[m] Or " sufficiently."

[n] τῷ θείῳ λόγῳ.

[o] εἰς ἀρετὴν καὶ εὐδαιμονίαν.

[p] εὐοδεῖν *vel sim.*

[q] ἐν τοῖς ὑλικοῖς.

[r] Aucher renders less accurately, I think, " alias vero prosperitas in nullo constitit eorum, quae in materiis sunt, sive privata sive publica aut regia."

109. (Gen. xxiv. 22) Why, after all the camels ceased drinking, did the man give ear-rings of gold and bracelets [a] to the virgin ?

This is something most natural,[b] for he who learns has also learned by remembering the words, " And do thou drink," [c] which was (the same as) learning.[d] And his seeing the camels watered was the equivalent of revivifying his memory.[e] And he returned thanks and gratitude to his teacher very genuinely and appropriately,[f] for in return for what he had heard he gave the ear-rings as an adornment to her ears, for the word was hers who was teaching, and the ears were his who received the teaching. And in return for what she had done, (he gave) a memorial (consisting of) bracelets, an adornment of memory and deeds.

*110. (Gen. xxiv. 22) Why does (Scripture) speak of ear-rings of a drachma in weight [g] and of bracelets of gold of ten drachmas [h] but not of five and five of gold ? [i]

Altogether excellently has it apportioned the two into

[a] Scripture specifies two bracelets. In *De Congressu* 113, where the verse is briefly allegorized (see also the next section), Philo transfers the number two to the ear-rings.

[b] φυσικώτατόν τι.

[c] *Cf.* Gen. xxiv. 18. Philo does not comment on this phrase in dealing with the verse in *QG* iv. 103-105.

[d] As Aucher remarks in a footnote, the syntax of the whole section is " nimis abstrusa obfuscataque."

[e] ἴσον τῷ ζωπυρεῖν τὴν μνήμην. On the camels as a symbol of memory see above, *QG* iv. 92 notes.

[f] Aucher " cum munere familiarissimo."

[g] LXX ἀνὰ δραχμὴν (*v.l.* δίδραχμον) ὁλκῆς : Heb. " a *beqa'* (half-shekel) its weight " : Arm. O.T. " a *dahekan* (usu. = drachma or denarius) in weight." In *De Congressu* 113 Philo has δύο μὲν ἐνώτια ἀνὰ δραχμὴν ὁλκήν. Here the Arm. translator probably uses *k'ank'ar* " talent " in the sense of a drachma.

[h] LXX δύο ψέλια . . . δέκα χρυσῶν ὁλκὴ αὐτόν, so also Heb. In *De Congressu* 113 Philo has ψέλια δὲ δέκα χρυσῶν.

[i] *i.e.* ear-rings and bracelets of five drachmas each.

one [a] in order to change the bad nature of the dyad and adapt it to that of the good monad. And it has taken the dyad and left it undivided,[b] for ten is divisible into two fives. And the decad is better than the pentad, for the former is a most perfect, complete and superior number and is appropriate to the divine mysteries,[c] while the number five is the measure of the senses,[d] and the senses bear the same relation to the mind [e] as does the traveller to the king.[f] And it would be folly to change the better into the worse. Now, what sort of nature the decad has both in respect of intelligible substance [g] and in respect of sense-perceptible (substance) [h] has already been stated in the book *On Numbers*.[i] Now, however, this much must be said, that both in the world and in man the decad is all.[j] In the world, together with the number seven (of planets) and the eighth sphere of fixed stars and those sublunary things of one species which are changeable among themselves,[k] the divine Logos [l] is the governor and administrator [m] of all things, since it has melodically harmonized

[a] Apparently Philo means that it replaced the equation 5 : 5 by the proportion 1 : 10, where 10 is considered a kind of unity, as in *De Congressu* 105.

[b] *ἀδιαίρετον*.

[c] Or "thoughts."

[d] *τῶν αἰσθήσεων*.

[e] *πρὸς τὸν νοῦν* (or *τὴν διάνοιαν*).

[f] *ὁ ὁδοιπόρος πρὸς τὸν βασιλέα*. On the Philonic concept of the king's highway of spiritual progress see Joseph Pascher, Η ΒΑΣΙΛΙΚΗ ΟΔΟΣ . . . *bei Philon von Alexandreia* (Paderborn, 1931), chap. iii, "Der mystische Wanderer auf dem 'Königsweg.'"

[g] *κατὰ νοερὰν οὐσίαν*.

[h] *κατὰ τὴν αἰσθητικήν*.

[i] *ἐν τῷ Περὶ Ἀριθμῶν*. This lost book of Philo has been reconstructed in outline by Staehle, pp. 1-18.

[j] Apparently in the sense of all-important or the sum total.

[k] Such as earth, water, air.

[l] *ὁ θεῖος λόγος*. In *De Congressu* 103-105 the tenth part of the universe is said to be the alone truly existent God. The other nine parts are, as here, the seven planets, the sphere of fixed stars and the sublunary world ; these constitute the "seeming sense-perceptible God."

[m] *κυβερνήτης καὶ οἰκονόμος vel sim.*

the chorus of the nine musical (intervals).[a] And in our body and soul there are also seven irrational parts [b] and the mind, which is a single part.[c] Now, the divine Logos is concerned with these nine (parts),[d] being the leader and ruler of harmony, and by it the nine parts are harmonized, and melodies and songs sound as one. Therefore Moses admits that the decad is holy, naturally leaving the ennead to creation,[e] and the decad to the divine Logos. And rightly is it holy, for it echoes divine things, trumpeting [f] the theme of forgiveness [g] in concordant and antiphonal chants leading to one and the same mixture of harmony. And necessarily does (Scripture) apportion one to the ears and ten to the hands,[h] for one is the beginning of the numbers,[i] and ten is the end ; and these are symbols of things. For it is proper to hear first and then to act, since we learn not for the sake of learning but for the sake of doing.[j] And one is proportioned and united to hearing, for both of them are a beginning, one of numbers, and the

[a] Philo seems here to liken the ninefold visible world to an harmonic progression or scale of nine notes.

[b] ἑπτὰ ἄλογα μέρη.

[c] *i.e.* body and soul = 2, + seven irrational parts = 9, + the mind = 10.

[d] The meaning of Arm. *daṙnam* (usu. = στρέφεσθαι or ἀνιστρέφεσθαι) is not clear here. Aucher renders, " itidem de istis novem distinctionibus disponit."

[e] *i.e.* to created things.

[f] Or " playing " (a stringed instrument), but the rendering given above is favoured by the context, see the next note.

[g] ἄφεσιν. The Arm. glossator's guess that Philo here refers to the Day of Atonement, ushered in by the blowing of trumpets and falling on the 10th day of Tishri (Lev. xxiii. 24, 27), is confirmed by the parallel in *De Congressu* 107.

[h] Philo refers to the one-drachma weight of the ear-rings and ten-drachma weight of the bracelets.

[i] *i.e.* of the digits.

[j] So the brief Greek frag. printed by Mai, ἀκοῦσαι δεῖ πρῶτον, εἶτα ἐργάσασθαι· μανθάνομεν γὰρ οὐ τοῦ μαθεῖν χάριν ἀλλὰ τοῦ πρᾶξαι. In *De Congressu* 113 Philo allegorizes the two numbers a little differently.

other of learning,[a] while the decad (is the beginning) of doing, for it is the end of the numbers and is the act of teaching, through which we learn. And the monad differs from one as the archetype surpasses and differs from the copy, for the monad is the archetype while one is a likeness of the monad.[b] Why? Because one can admit the completion [c] of many (as in the case of) a herd or chorus or family or nation or army or city, for each of these is one. But the monad does not come from many, for it is unsharing and has no association [d] and is without complexity [e] because of its aloneness, as its very name shows. Now this monad is what Moses writes of in the beginning when he commands that half a didrachmon be brought as first fruits.[f] And this [g] was a very appropriate ornament to be fitted to the ears of Rebekah (who was a symbol of) alertness [h] and perseverance,[i] that she might listen and bear in mind the unity [j] of the divine Logos.

111. (Gen. xxiv. 23) Why does he say, "Whose daughter

[a] *i.e.* one is the beginning of the series of digits, and hearing is the beginning of learning.

[b] This agrees closely with the passage from Joh. Lydus given in the Appendix.

[c] τὴν τελειότητα: Aucher "perfectionem."

[d] κοινωνιάν.

[e] ἄνευ συμπλοκῆς *vel sim.*

[f] *Cf. Quis Rer. Div. Heres* 186-189 on Ex. xxx. 13-15 where a tax of half a didrachmon (Heb. shekel) is prescribed as a "ransom" for souls during the taking of the census. On that biblical passage Philo comments that the half didrachmon "is both a drachma and a monad." First fruits (as tithes) are included in his allegories of the number ten in *De Congressu* 95. Here Philo seems to combine the two allegories.

[g] *i.e.* the ear-ring of one-drachma weight.

[h] Lit. "raising up": Aucher "perseverantiae."

[i] The two Arm. nouns probably represent a single Greek noun, ἐπιμονῆς or ὑπομονῆς, which are the allegorical explanations of the name Rebekah given elsewhere by Philo.

[j] Or "monad," here fancifully connected with ἐπιμονή or ὑπομονή.

art thou? Tell me whether there is to thy father a place for us to stay"[a]?

The literal meaning[b] is very easy to understand. But as for the deeper meaning,[c] he is struck speechless and astonished by the beauty of the veritably true virgin[d] and her unstained, intact and holy soul, which[e] remains constant in doing good and worthy deeds. And he is at a loss to tell whether perhaps it was one not a mortal who begot her, and so he asks, "Whose daughter art thou?" "For," he says, "I see that no one who is created and born is worthy to be thought the father of such fair virtue,"[f] as though saying, "Instruct and correct my ignorance by revealing thy lineage and the source[g] of thy beautiful youth.[h]" Since he[i] was embarrassed by modest shame lest he seem to boast too greatly and freely in believing that her lineage was heavenly and marvellous, he asks again immediately, "Is there indeed a place and space for us with thy Father in the ether and heaven or, still higher, with their governor, the divine Logos?[j] For, being there, we should leave all mortal and corruptible things[k] behind. Or shall we be altogether kept back and shut in, planted and rooted in the earth and with heads bent down as if we were trees on a cliff?"

112. (Gen. xxiv. 25) What is the meaning of the words, "There is straw and much fodder with us and a place to lodge"[l]?

[a] So LXX, εἰ ἔστιν παρὰ τῷ πατρί σου τόπος ἡμῖν καταλῦσαι.
[b] τὸ ῥητόν.
[c] τὸ πρὸς διάνοιαν.
[d] τῆς ὄντως ἀληθοῦς παρθένου.
[e] Or "who" (*i.e.* the virgin).
[f] ἀρετῆς.
[g] Lit. "planting."
[h] Variant "beautiful humanity."
[i] The Arm. glossator, who takes Eleazar to be the implied subject, seems to me to be right as against Aucher who takes Rebekah to be the subject.
[j] τῷ κυβερνήτῃ αὐτῶν, τῷ θείῳ λόγῳ.
[k] πάντα τὰ θνητὰ καὶ φθαρτά.
[l] LXX τοῦ καταλῦσαι.

Since some of the soul is rational and some irrational,[a] she mentions also those things which are fitting for the irrational part and are suitable and necessary,[b] (namely) straw and fodder and whatever is the food of animals.[c] And she gives a special place to the rational part for dissolving and breaking up and destroying[d] the passions,[e] inasmuch as each of them is poisonous.

113. (Gen. xxiv. 26) What is the meaning of the words, "The man, being well pleased, prostrated himself before the Lord[f]"?

When the man who has been disciplined[g] hears that which he has especially desired, (namely) that he is not homeless and not kept outside but has found a place and space and has received the word of virtue,[h] he is very well pleased and receives (it) willingly, and in gratitude for this prostrates himself.

114. (Gen. xxiv. 27) Why does he name, not his Lord or God, but that of Abraham, saying, "Blessed is the Lord God of my lord Abraham"[i]?

First of all, he lays upon servants (the obligation) to love their lords and to honour their lords and hold them in greater esteem than themselves. In the second place, he wishes to show clearly the advantage (that comes) from teaching[j] to him who has been properly and genuinely[k]

[a] τῆς ψυχῆς τὸ μὲν λογικόν, τὸ δὲ ἄλογον.

[b] Aucher renders somewhat more freely, "dicit adesse illa quoque, quae conveniunt bruto ad fruendum cum decore."

[c] τῶν ἀλόγων.

[d] Here, as Aucher notes, Philo plays on the double meaning of καταλῦσαι.

[e] τὰ πάθη: Aucher "cupiditates."

[f] So the LXX, καὶ εὐδοκήσας (Heb. "and bowed") ὁ ἄνθρωπος προσεκύνησεν κυρίῳ.

[g] Prob. ἐπαιδεύθη.

[h] τὸν τῆς ἀρετῆς λόγον.

[i] So LXX, Εὐλογητὸς κύριος ὁ θεὸς τοῦ κυρίου μου Ἀβραάμ.

[j] ἐκ διδασκαλίας.

[k] οἰκείως καὶ γνησίως *vel sim.*: Aucher "familiariter ac fideliter."

taught. And profiting from that great saying, "Know thyself," he chose and thought it best to be called, not a servant of God,[a] but an attendant of the intercessor.[b] And the intercessor is a servant of the Creator of all and Father. But he who transgresses this order,[c] which nature has arranged, perpetrates a great injustice[d] by setting before himself a disorder of confusion.[e]

115. (Gen. xxiv. 27) What is the meaning of the words, "He has not abandoned His righteousness and truth to[f] my lord"[g]?

Very naturally[h] does (Scripture) show that these very same virtues,[i] righteousness and truth,[j] are especially and pre-eminently[k] divine. For among the human race there is nothing pure[l] but (only) what is mixed. For there is mixed with it in slight measure both falseness and unrighteousness. And the righteousness and truth among men are, to speak properly, likenesses and images,[m] while those with God are paradigmatic principles and types[n] and ideas.[o] Deservedly, therefore, does he give thanks that he[p] had both (virtues) and that God gives him both virtues uninterruptedly and daily, and that there grows[q]

[a] In the Arm. the negative directly precedes "of God."
[b] The Arm. uses two words to render παρακλήτου.
[c] τάξιν.
[d] ἀδικίαν.
[e] Aucher renders more freely, "proposita sibi morum dissolutione perturbata."
[f] Lit. "from."
[g] LXX οὐκ ἐγκατέλειπεν τὴν δικαιοσύνην (variant ἔλεος, *cf.* Heb. *ḥasdô* "His kindness") καὶ τὴν ἀλήθειαν ἀπὸ τοῦ κυρίου μου.
[h] φυσικώτερον.
[i] αὐτὰς τὰς ἀρετάς.
[j] Both nouns, here and below, are in the plural.
[k] διαφόρως: variant "symbolically."
[l] ἄκρατον.
[m] ὁμοιότητες (or μιμήματα) καὶ εἰκόνες.
[n] The Arm. lit. =παραδειγματικαὶ ἀρχαὶ καὶ τύποι. Possibly, however, Philo wrote ἀρχέτυποι.
[o] ἰδέαι.
[p] *i.e.* Abraham.
[q] Or "wells up" or "bubbles up."

in his soul an estrangement from falsehood and unrighteousness and a familiarity [a] with truth and righteousness.

116. (Gen. xxiv. 28) What is the meaning of the words, "The young woman, running into the house, told her mother" [b] ?

A virtuous soul is a lover of the good [c] and has a status that is greatly inflexible and unchanging. For when it perceives that someone is not quickly satiated with desire but is constant and genuine,[d] it rejoices and makes haste and does not restrain [e] the swiftness of its joy but tells the whole maternal household of wisdom [f] with a sober and prudent festivity of joy and dance and still other lavish displays of welcome, such as he shows who is not strange and spurious in his desire,[g] in order that those who hear it may rejoice and become joyful.

117. (Gen. xxiv. 29) Who is the brother of Rebekah, whose name is Laban ?

Our soul has a natural brother who is rational and one who is irrational.[h] Now to the rational part is assigned Rebekah the virgin, (who is) constancy [i] and perseverance ; and Laban (is assigned) to the irrational part, for this (name) is to be translated as "whiteness," which is a figure of the honours (shown) to the splendour of sense-

[a] ἀλλοτρίωσις μέν . . . οἰκειότης δέ.

[b] LXX (like Heb.) reads a little differently καὶ δραμοῦσα ἡ παῖς ἀπήγγειλεν εἰς τὸν οἶκον τῆς μητρὸς αὐτῆς κατὰ τὰ ῥήματα ταῦτα.

[c] φιλάγαθός (or φιλόκαλός) ἐστι ἡ σπουδαία ψυχή.

[d] Aucher "fidelis."

[e] Lit. "bear" or "contain."

[f] σοφίας.

[g] Aucher, construing less accurately, I think, renders, "quae omnia illis, qui genuinum habent desiderium, demonstrat."

[h] ὁ μὲν λογικός, ὁ δὲ ἄλογος.

[i] The Arm. lit. = ἀνάστασις or ἔγερσις, but see *QG* iv. 97 note *c*.

perceptible things.[a] For one should know very well that just as there are three different kinds of literal elements of speech,[b] namely vowels, semi-vowels and consonants,[c] so also is it with our nature. For the mind [d] is like the vowel, and the senses [e] like the semi-vowel, and the body like the consonant. However, I shall begin my exposition from the end.[f] For just as the consonant by itself alone has no sound at all but (only) when combined with a vowel achieves a literal sound,[g] so also is the body by itself alone unmoving ; and it is moved by the rational soul [h] through the several organic parts toward that which is suitable and necessary to it. Again, just as the semi-vowels make lame and imperfect sounds, but, if they are combined with vowels, make fully articulated speech,[i] so also is sense-perception (only) half effective [j] and imperfect, and it occupies a position midway between the mind and the body, for it has a part in each of them ; it is not inanimate [k] like the body, and it is not intelligent [l] like reason.[m] But when the mind [n] by extending itself [o] is fused with, and engraved on it,[p] it prepares it to see and hear rationally

[a] Construction and meaning are not clear. Aucher renders, " indicium claritatis rerum secundum sensus." The interpretation of " Laban " as " whiteness " and as a symbol of sense-perception is found in several other passages in Philo, *e.g. De Fuga* 44.

[b] *Cf. De Agricultura* 136 τὰ στοιχεῖα τῆς ἐγγραμμάτου φωνῆς.

[c] φωνήεντα καὶ ἡμίφωνα καὶ ἄφωνα, *cf. De Congressu* 150.

[d] ὁ νοῦς.

[e] ἡ αἴσθησις.

[f] *i.e.* from the last of the three terms.

[g] See above, note *b*.

[h] ὑπὸ τῆς λογικῆς ψυχῆς.

[i] ἔναρθρον φωνήν.

[j] ἡμίεργος. Aucher " semivivus."

[k] ἄψυχος.

[l] νοερά or νοητή.

[m] ὁ λογισμός.

[n] ὁ νοῦς.

[o] ἐκτείνων ἑαυτόν.

[p] *i.e.* sense-perception. Perhaps the original was " when the impression (τύπος) is fused with the senses by the mind."

and at the same time to speak with reason and to perceive rationally. However, in the same way as the vowels by themselves alone and also when combined with other (sounds) produce sound, so also is the mind moved by itself alone without anything else, since intelligible things are received and grasped by themselves alone,[a] and it is also the cause of the movement of other things, giving release[b] like the leader of a chorus.[c] But, as I have said, the senses (are moved) to bodily perception by the rational part and are, as it were, effectively brought to their natural[d] functions by the voices of the organic parts.[e]

118. (Gen. xxiv. 30-31) Why does Laban, after seeing the ear-rings and the bracelets on his sister, say to the youth,[f] " Come, enter,[g] blessed of the Lord.[h] Why dost thou stand without ? " ?

In the first place, this is meant to show clearly that whoever belongs to the characters which measure all

[a] The last clause was probably a gen. absolute construction in the Greek original. Aucher, construing differently, renders, " et mens, tam per se solum sine ullo alio movetur, ab intellectualibus per se adjuta."

[b] The Arm. word and its cognates usu. = ἄφεσις. Aucher renders, " vigorem " and in a footnote suggests " permissionem sive motionem."

[c] Aucher " tamquam dux cohorti."

[d] Variant " logical."

[e] Philo apparently means that the meeting of the senses and external objects, which results in perception, is like the meeting of vowels and consonants, which results in speech.

[f] LXX πρὸς τὸν ἄνθρωπον :_ Heb. " to the man." Philo omits most of vs. 30 on Rebekah's report to Laban and the latter's coming out to Eleazar.

[g] LXX Δεῦρο, εἴσελθε : Heb. " come in."

[h] So Heb. and Arm. O.T. : LXX εὐλογητὸς κύριος. Since Philo has the LXX reading below, it is probable that here the Arm. translator or a copyist has accommodated his text to that of the Arm. O.T.

things by the senses [a] is always of necessity bribed [b] by something sense-perceptible,[c] and is unable to judge [d] in purity and holiness without gifts.[e] But when he sees gold, he calls it to him, and when (it) is called, he becomes more subservient. And this is something most natural.[f] And when he sees the ornament of the ears, (namely) the monad, and the ornament of the hands and deeds, (namely) the decad,[g] he is struck by the holy appearance of lordship,[h] and gives thanks and says in a loud voice, "Blessed (be) the Lord." [i] With Him is good teaching, and (for Him) [j] good works are performed, as is indeed fitting, by offering the first fruits [k]; and the first fruits of words [l] (is) the word in accordance with the monad, for just as the monad is holy among numbers, so also is the word (holy) in teaching. And (the first fruits) of deeds (is the word) [m] in accordance with the decad, for just as the decad is the end [n] of numbers, so also is the deed [o] in learning.

119. (Gen. xxiv. 31) Why does Laban say, "I have prepared the house and a place for the camels," although Rebekah had (earlier) added the "lodging," saying,[p]

[a] Laban is a symbol of the sensual character (τύπος or τρόπος). Aucher renders, "quicumque secundum sensum praefert argumentum aliquod exemplare."

[b] The Arm. = δωροκοπεῖται, a word not elsewhere used by Philo. Possibly the original here had δωροδοκεῖ.

[c] ὑπ' αἰσθητικοῦ τινος.

[d] For *datel* = κρίνειν, two Arm. MSS. have *dasel* = τάττειν.

[e] ἄνευ δώρων.

[f] φυσικώτατόν τι.

[g] See above, *QG* iv. 110.

[h] The Arm. lit. = τῇ ἁγίᾳ (or ἱερᾷ) κυριότητος φαντασίᾳ. Perhaps the original was τῇ ἁγίᾳ καὶ θείᾳ φαντασίᾳ.

[i] See p. 401, note *h*.

[j] The context makes it necessary to supply these words.

[k] τὰ πρωτογεννήματα or τὰς ἀπαρχὰς (τῶν πρώτων καρπῶν).

[l] λόγων.

[m] Here too the context requires a supplement.

[n] τὸ τέλος.

[o] Lit. "the doing."

[p] In Gen. xxiv. 25, see above, *QG* iv. 112.

"And there is much fodder with us and a place to lodge"?

(Scripture) reports a very great difference of superiority [a] between the mind of the virgin, which makes use of nothing sense-perceptible,[b] and the class of the type which receives the sense-perceptible.[c] For the loosing [d] and inactivity of those things which are subject to generation and destruction are to instruct us to prepare a place in the soul in this fashion. But the other says that he is prepared, not for loosing, but for the reception of irrational natures,[e] for he is unable to deny what he experiences.[f]

120. (Gen. xxiv. 34) Why does the elderly man begin in this way, "I am the boy [g] of Abraham"?

The deeper meaning [h] of that which is said is very easy to discover and see.[i] For a young boy has the same position in relation to a mature man as does uttered discourse [j] to the inner (discourse) in the reason.[k] But the literal meaning [l] gives the praise of him who is past old age.[m] For whereas others make the error of declaring themselves to be of (such and such) a family or country, he (declares himself to be) of his lord, whom he considers

[a] διαφορὰν ὑπερβολῆς μεγίστην. [b] αἰσθητικῷ.

[c] Construction and meaning uncertain. Aucher renders, "et inter exemplum ejus qui sensibilia recepit in cognationem." Possibly the original was "the type of those who receive the class (γένος) of sense-perceptible things."

[d] Philo here, as earlier, plays on the double meaning of καταλύειν, *i.e.* "to loose" and "to lodge."

[e] ἀλόγων φύσεων. [f] Or "bears."

[g] LXX παῖς, *i.e.* "servant" (as in Heb.). See above, *QG* iv. 108. [h] τὸ πρὸς διάνοιαν. [i] Or "conjecture."

[j] On Abraham's servant as a symbol of the λόγος προφορικός see above, *QG* iv. 85, 88.

[k] ἐν τῷ λογισμῷ. [l] τὸ ῥητόν.

[m] L. A. Post reconstructs the original as τὸ δὲ ῥητὸν εὐλόγως ἀποδίδωσι Μένανδρος (misread as μὲν ἀνδρὸς) ἐν Ὑπεργήρῳ, "Menander rendered the literal meaning eloquently in his *Superannuated*."

his country and family.[a] Going on with the trimeters from that point, he says fittingly,[b] " To me the lord is a city, a refuge and a law and a judge of every righteous and unrighteous man. It befits me to live with the servant mind." [c]

121. (Gen. xxiv. 35) Why does he say, " The Lord has blessed my lord exceedingly, and he has been exalted. And He has given him sheep [d] and cattle and gold and silver [e] and men-servants and maid-servants and camels and asses " ?

It is fitting and proper to admire the literal meaning [f] inasmuch as among the benefits [g] mentioned the divine wonders fall to the lot of the sovereign ruler,[h] while the human (benefits fall to the lot) of the minister and servant. For wonderful and divine is that benefit which is the bles-

[a] Post suggests that Menander's verses were something like the following:

ἄλλοι μὲν ἀποκρίνοιντ' ἂν εἰπόντες γένους
τίνος εἰσὶ καὶ πατρίδος, ἐγὼ δὲ δεσπότου,
ὡς ὄντος ἀντὶ πατρίδος ἡμῖν καὶ γένους.

The Arm. translator prob. read *ἀποκλίνοιντο* instead of *ἀποκρίνοιντο.*

[b] The Greek original, Post suggests, was *ἐντεῦθεν προβαίνων εἰς τὸ πρόσω τῶν τριμέτρων ἑξῆς ποιεῖ.*

[c] The original passage (Frag. 581 Koch) reads

ἐμοὶ πόλις ἐστὶ καὶ καταφυγὴ καὶ νόμος
καὶ τοῦ δικαίου τοῦ τ' ἀδίκου παντὸς κριτὴς
ὁ δεσπότης. πρὸς τοῦτον ἕνα δεῖ ζῆν ἐμέ.

F. G. Allinson in the Loeb Menander renders the passage, " For me my master is at once a city and a place of refuge and law and judge in everything of what is right and wrong. With eyes on him alone I needs must live."

[d] The Arm. *dowar* usu. = *ταῦρος* but here apparently = *πρόβατον.*

[e] LXX and Heb. have " silver and gold," in reverse order.

[f] *τὸ ῥητόν.*

[g] *τῶν ἀγαθῶν.*

[h] *i.e.* the mind (*τὸ ἡγεμονικόν*), symbolized by Abraham.

sing [a] of God, and this is good counsel,[b] while the mortal and material ones are human. And these it was proper for those to hear who receive bodily and external things. For there are two forms [c]: one is he who is said to be wholly worthy of God [d]; and the other is those hearers who are not yet purified. (God) distributed and gave to each his own good, at the same time teaching (us) which of them should precede the other. But as for the allegorical meaning,[e] to whomever God graciously gives [f] good counsel and prudence,[g] to these He (also) gives authority and rule of power [h] over the senses and all the irrational parts [i] and whatever things are blindly invented in accordance with vain opinions by one who is involved [j] in a blind way of life. Wherefore he adds, " exceedingly " and " was exalted," for the good counsel was not superficial [k] nor yet of little worth.[l] And those who are strong in prudence easily prevail [m] and exalt themselves over secondary and tertiary benefits. But all those who receive mighty power [n] through wisdom and prudence are elevated to heavenly greatness and height. Wherefore they rule in truth over earthly and subterranean things (as if) seizing (their own) possessions.

122. (Gen. xxiv. 36) Why does he say, " Sarah, the wife

[a] εὐλογία. [b] εὐβουλία (or εὐφροσύνη). [c] εἴδη.

[d] Construction and meaning uncertain, but apparently reflecting ὃς ἐλέγετο εἶναι οἴκοθεν τοῦ κυρίου ἄξιος. Aucher renders, " quod dicebatur a domo domini subjecto condigno." Two Arm. mss. lack *i tanē* = οἴκοθεν : one lacks *tearn* = τοῦ κυρίου.

[e] τὸ δ' ἐν ἀλληγορίᾳ.

[f] χαρίζεται. [g] φρόνησιν.

[h] Variant " rule of providing " (προνοίας).

[i] τῶν αἰσθήσεων καὶ πάντων τῶν ἀλόγων μερῶν.

[j] Lit. " mixed." [k] ἐπιπόλαιος.

[l] εὐτελής *vel sim.* : Aucher " humile."

[m] Construction not clear. Aucher, construing differently, renders, " ita ut facile exaltari queat per prudentiam."

[n] δύναμιν ἰσχυράν *vel sim.* : Aucher " virtutem fortissimam."

of my lord, bore a son [a] to my lord after (his) becoming old [b]" but not, "Abraham begot"?

The literal meaning [c] is that the father had another son before the legitimate one, (namely) the illegitimate one from his concubine. But this wife was the mother of his beloved and only son, and afterwards she was called "the ruler." [d] But as for the deeper meaning,[e] (she is) the virtue which is perfected through teaching,[f] and was therefore afterwards called "the ruler," which the Hebrews call "Sarah." [g] She gives birth to the model of character,[h] who is by nature self-taught.[i] For the end and beginning and genesis of teaching is sometimes what is heard from another [j] and is sometimes he who becomes wise by nature.[k] And he is born to no one but to his lord, that is, to him who has in his mind [l] a firm grasp of all those things which pertain to us, and also knows them at the same time. And (Scripture) confirms [m] the perfection in all things of him who is born by saying, not that he was born in the old age, but after the old age, of his father; that is, not in length of time but as if to say that nothing in mortal life is untemporal [n] but only that which comes after mortality and is not corruptible. For it belongs peculiarly to the incorruptible soul [o] which has been removed from its corporeal nature and has been fitted to the incorporeal ruler (and)

[a] Most LXX MSS. have *υἱὸν ἕνα*.

[b] LXX *μετὰ τὸ γηρᾶσαι αὐτόν* (*v.l.* *αὐτήν*): Heb. "after her old age."

[c] *τὸ ῥητόν*.

[d] *ἡ ἄρχουσα*, see above, *QG* iii. 53.

[e] *τὸ πρὸς διάνοιαν*.

[f] *ἡ ἐκ διδασκαλίας τελειουμένη ἀρετή*.

[g] Arm. *Sarra* = LXX Σάρρα (Heb. *Śārāh*).

[h] *τύπον ἠθῶν vel sim.*

[i] *αὐτοδίδακτον*, *i.e.* Isaac; *cf.* *De Somniis* ii. 10 *et al.*

[j] Variants "by oneself from another" and "by oneself" (omitting "from another"). Aucher renders, "per se ab alio."

[k] *ὁ ἐκ φύσεως γενόμενος σοφός*.

[l] *ἐν τῷ λογισμῷ*.

[m] Lit. "seals" or "stamps."

[n] *ἄχρονον*. *Cf.* *De Fuga* 169.

[o] *ἴδιόν ἐστι τῇ ἀφθάρτῳ ψυχῇ*.

sovereign of joys to sow gladness,[a] for the race without sorrow[b] approaches and is near to God.

123. (Gen. xxiv. 36) Why does he say, "And he gave him whatever was his"?

Most excellently does the literal meaning[c] contain a symbol[d] for hearers. For it would be fitting for those who receive external material things[e] to hear that the youth receives from his father whatever was his. But the self-taught[f] has a symbol of the things indicated.[g] For whatever over a long period of time teaching[h] enables one to acquire, this does nature[i] grant as a prepared gift. Now the prophet[j] does something similar to this in respect of the patriarchs,[k] for when he prays for the first (tribe) he says, "May Reuben live and not die, and may he be great in number," and immediately thereafter he mentions[l] the fourth (tribe), passing over the second and third,[m] and speaks as follows, "And this (is the blessing) of Judah."[n] What is here said as a blessing of Reuben stands first, and (then) that of Judah. But it is for him alone, while the other is as a part, for he is placed above with the sole and

[a] On Isaac as a symbol of joy and laughter see above, *QG* iii. 53.

[b] τὸ ἄλυπον γένος.

[c] τὸ ῥητόν.

[d] σύμβολον.

[e] τὰς ἐκτὸς ὕλας, *cf. De Poster. Caini* 116.

[f] ὁ αὐτοδίδακτος, *i.e.* Isaac, see above, *QG* iv. 122.

[g] The Arm. text seems corrupt. Possibly the original read "Symbolically this statement refers to the self-taught" or the like.

[h] ἡ διδασκαλία.

[i] ἡ φύσις.

[j] *i.e.* Moses.

[k] Or "tribe-leaders," *i.e.* the sons of Jacob, in Deut. xxxiii. 6-7.

[l] Lit. "he responds" or "requites": Aucher "inducit."

[m] Philo here, as in *De Mut. Nom.* 200, refers to Simeon and Levi.

[n] Aucher seems to have taken this sentence as a comment of Philo instead of a quotation from Scripture.

elder.[a] But what the principle of these things is will be explained when we inquire into the blessings.[b]

124. (Gen. xxiv. 16, 18, 20, 28, 46) Why does Rebekah hasten in everything, for (Scripture) says, " And hastening to the spring, she drew water," and " hastening, she lowered the water-jar upon her arm," and " running, she announced " [c]?

Excellent and good people perform their good works without delay. Such too was the whole household together of the all-wise Abraham.[d] For when he became the host of the divine natures [e] and was about to entertain them with [f] food of gladness, and in turn on the reverse was to receive the same from them, he did not delay at all, but himself hastened and ordered his wife to make ash-cakes [g] in haste, and his wife also hastened. The servant too resorted to running in carrying out the service that was proper to him. Whereas frivolous people are in doubt about those things which it is proper to delay,[h] those who know how to do things accurately and clearly, when an opportunity is found, do not take a long time.[i] Excel-

[a] This obscure statement may refer to Judah's being associated with Reuben, or to Judah's " entering into his people " (Deut. xxxiii. 7) or to Simeon's being included with Levi (Deut. xxxiii. 8).

[b] These Pentateuchal passages, Gen. ch. xlix and Deut. ch. xxxiii, are not discussed in the extant text of the *Quaestiones*.

[c] Philo here includes five different verses, on some of which he has commented above, in *QG* iv. 100, 104, 107, 116.

[d] τοῦ πανσόφου 'Αβραάμου. The same adjective is applied to Abraham in *De Migratione* 45, and to Isaac, Jacob and Moses elsewhere.

[e] τῶν θείων φύσεων, *i.e.* the three angels, see above, *QG* iv. 1 ff.

[f] Lit. " to receive them into."

[g] See above, *QG* iv. 8.

[h] Aucher renders, " quoniam sicut histriones haesitant, ubi par erit, cunctari."

[i] Aucher renders, more freely, " e contra qui conscius est constanter agendorum, hoc dato, non terit tempus."

lently, however, has (Scripture) said this too, and is to speak in future of a double inactivity.[a]

125. (Gen. xxiv. 48) What is "the way of truth," for he says, "in the way of truth"[b]?

(This means) that truth is a wonderful and divine virtue[c] and a force[d] destructive of falsehood, which[e] is (so) called in reprobation,[f] while truth (is so called) because of unforgetfulness,[g] since virtue is worthy of remembrance. Now the way which leads to it, so far as it rests with us, is knowledge and wisdom,[h] for through these is it found. But by an involuntary principle[i] (it is found) through prophecy.[j] And since that which is proportioned and equal[k] is a safe road,[l] it leads to truth more evenly, briefly and smoothly than[m] the former.[n]

[a] Possibly Philo refers to such passages as those commented on below, *QG* iv. 131.

[b] So the LXX (agreeing with Heb.), according to which Abraham's servant blesses God, *ὃς εὐόδωσέν μοι ἐν ὁδῷ ἀληθείας*.

[c] *θαυμασία καὶ θεία ἀρετή*.

[d] *δύναμις*.

[e] *i.e.* falsehood.

[f] Philo evidently plays on the similarity between *ψεῦδος* and *ψόγος*, not, as Aucher suggests in his footnote, on a double meaning of *παράκρουσις*.

[g] As if *ἀλήθεια* were derived from *ἀ-* and *λήθη*.

[h] *ἐπιστήμη καὶ σοφία*.

[i] The Arm. lit. = *κατ' ἀκούσιον λόγον*.

[j] *διὰ προφητείας*. On Philo's theory of divinely vouchsafed prophecy as opposed to human knowledge see H. A. Wolfson, *Philo*, ii. 22-62.

[k] Arm. *hamemat* = *ἀνάλογος* and *ἴσος*. The second adjective *kšir* also = *ἴσος*.

[l] Aucher, construing differently, renders, "porro haec proportionata aequaque via secura est."

[m] Aucher's "quae" is apparently a misprint for "quam" (comparative particle).

[n] Philo evidently means that the way of prophecy leads to truth more directly than does the way of knowledge.

126. (Gen. xxiv. 49) What is the meaning of the words, "If you act with mercy and justice toward my lord, tell me; but if not, indicate (this), that I may turn to the right or to the left" [a]?

The literal meaning [b] is clear. But as for the deeper meaning,[c] it seems to indicate that the right side (consists of) worthy and completed deeds, while the left side (consists of) things outside worthiness and of errors of transgression.

127. (Gen. xxiv. 50) Why did Rebekah's brothers [d] say to the servant, "From the Lord has this command come.[e] We shall not be able to speak against (it) good for evil" [f]?

Imagining (this) in their minds,[g] and with obedience without any hindrance,[h] they knew that the command of God was true, infallible [i] and unimpeded [j] in undertaking benefactions.[k] And there is a complete harmony between constancy [l] and the self-taught wise man.[m]

[a] LXX *εἰ οὖν ποιεῖτε ὑμεῖς ἔλεος καὶ δικαιοσύνην πρὸς τὸν κύριόν μου, ἀπαγγείλατέ μοι. εἰ δὲ μή, ἀπαγγείλατέ μοι ἵνα ἐπιστρέψω εἰς δεξιὰν ἢ εἰς ἀριστεράν.* The Arm. renders the two occurrences of *ἀπαγγείλατε* by different words.

[b] *τὸ ῥητόν.*

[c] *τὸ πρὸς διάνοιαν.*

[d] Scripture mentions by name Laban and Bethuel (Rebekah's father, as Philo notes in *De Fuga* 48).

[e] LXX *ἐξῆλθεν τὸ πρόσταγμα* (*v.l.* *πρᾶγμα*) *τοῦτο*: Heb. "has this word (or "thing") come forth."

[f] LXX *οὐ δυνησόμεθα οὖν σοι ἀντειπεῖν κακὸν καλῷ* (*v.l.* *κακὸν ἢ καλόν*): Heb. "we shall not be able to speak to thee evil or good."

[g] Aucher renders more freely, "revolventes in mente."

[h] Construction uncertain. Aucher renders, "idque rite, sine ullo obstaculo," and in a footnote adds, "*Vel ita*: et videntes nullum esse obstaculi locum."

[i] *ἀδιάπτωτον vel sim.*: Aucher "illaesus."

[j] Lit. "not stumbling."

[k] *εὐεργεσιῶν.*

[l] *ὑπομονῆς*, symbolized by Rebekah, see above, *QG* iv. 97.

[m] *πρὸς τὸν αὐτοδίδακτον σοφόν*, symbolized by Isaac, see above, *QG* iv. 122.

128. (Gen. xxiv. 50) What is the meaning of the words, which they say, " Against (it) we shall not be able to speak " ?

Since whatever we may say against good proposals will be found evil,[a] it is seemly and fine, as I have already said,[b] that he who has become virtuous without teaching[c] should be the consort of constancy[d] and perseverance,[e] for the opposite, the divorce of knowledge[f] from them, is evil.

129. (Gen. xxiv. 51) What is the meaning of the words, " Behold, Rebekah is before thee[g]; take her and go. And she shall be a wife to the son of thy master, as the Lord promised "[h] ?

What is expressly said[i] is clear. The deeper meaning[j] is to be given as follows. Behold, it says, the eye of thy soul[k] has been instructed[l] (and) sees the form of perseverance[m] face to face[n] without shamelessness.[o] For, behold, it is before thee. Thou seest and understandest. Take it and receive it in thy soul, and having taken it hence with

[a] This rendering follows Aucher's in transposing the words " good proposals," which stand after " evil " in the Arm.
[b] In the preceding section.
[c] ἄνευ διδασκαλίας. This refers to Isaac, " the self-taught."
[d] ὑπομονῆς, see above, *QG* iv. 97 notes.
[e] Prob. διαμονῆς.
[f] ἐπιστήμης.
[g] LXX ἐνώπιόν σου.
[h] LXX ἐλάλησεν : Heb. " spoke."
[i] τὸ εἰρημένον.
[j] ἡ διάνοια.
[k] ὁ τῆς ψυχῆς σου ὀφθαλμός, *cf. De Confus. Ling.* 92 *et al.*
[l] πεπαίδευται, *cf. De Mut. Nom.* 203 (τὸ ψυχῆς ὄμμα) μόνον τὸν θεὸν ὁρᾶν πεπαίδευται.
[m] τὸ τῆς διαμονῆς εἶδος, symbolized by Rebekah, see above, *QG* iv. 117, 128.
[n] ἐνώπιον or κατὰ πρόσωπον *vel sim.* : Aucher " intuitive."
[o] Arm. *lpršout'iun* = ἀναισχυντία. Aucher curiously renders, " sine lippitudine," possibly because he fancies that there is an etymological connexion between the Arm. and Latin words.

an unimpaired and uncorrupted character, pass and go, lest perhaps thou mayest again be seized by the lures of the locality and the body.[a] But while thine impulses[b] are moved as if starting a race,[c] go quickly on a straight course. And be a surety[d] of perseverance (and) endurance to the self-taught man,[e] of whom it is said in Proverbs,[f] " From God is woman suited to man "[g]—not to man so much as is virtue to reason.[h]

*130. (Gen. xxiv. 52-53) Why does the servant, after prostrating himself before the Lord, give vessels of silver and gold, and garments to Rebekah and her mother?[i]

This is praise for the house of the virtuous man who is taught,[j] for it is proper to make thanksgiving and honour to God the beginning of every pure deed.[k] For this reason the servant first prostrates himself before the Lord, and then offers the gifts. But prostration[l] is nothing else than a sign of genuine admiration and true love,[m] which those

[a] ταῖς ἐγχωρίαις (or πατρίαις) καὶ σωματικαῖς ἀπάταις.

[b] ὁρμαί.

[c] ὡς ἐν ἀφετηρίῳ: Aucher " velut in linea hippodromi."

[d] ἔγγυος: Aucher " vadimonio."

[e] τῷ αὐτοδιδάκτῳ, symbolized by Isaac, see above, *QG* iv. 122.

[f] Prov. xix. 14.

[g] LXX παρὰ δὲ θεοῦ ἁρμόζεται γυνὴ ἀνδρί: Heb. " from the Lord (comes) an understanding woman." The Arm. variant, rendered by Aucher, " mulier optima a Deo coaptatur " is clearly an error.

[h] ἀρετὴ λογισμῷ.

[i] Scripture says that he gave the vessels and garments to Rebekah, and gifts to her brother and mother.

[j] τοῦ σπουδαίου τοῦ διδασκομένου, *i.e.* Abraham. Aucher renders, " domui sapientis doctae."

[k] πάσης πράξεως καθαρᾶς, as in the Greek frag. (which ends with this sentence). Aucher renders, less literally, " omnis operae praeclarae."

[l] προσκύνησις.

[m] Aucher renders, more freely, " demonstratio admirationis (*sive*, venerationis) verae, amorisque puri."

men know who sip from that source [a] which cannot be approached or touched [b] but is incorporeal. For being given wings and out of heavenly desire being borne aloft, they move in flight about the Father and Creator of all things, and Him, who truly with His being [c] fills all things with His powers [d] for the salvation of all,[e] they call " holy, blessed Creator,[f] all-mighty,[g] God of truth."

*131. (Gen. xxiv. 55-56) Why did they say, " Let the virgin [h] remain with us (some) days," [i] and why does he press on, saying, " Do not slow me up,[j] and the Lord has prospered [k] my way " ?

These men felt regret, who had said a little before,[l] " Behold, Rebekah is before thee ; take her and go." And this is said in reproof [m] of those who are slippery, and against the ways of unstable [n] men, who imagine things now in one way, now in another, as well as many contradictory and conflicting things. But he who shows zeal with constancy and vigour cries out,[o] " Do not hold me back, for God the saviour [p] has sent (me) on the broad [q] way of virtue,[r] on which I came hither and will go hence."

[a] Lit. " taste."
[b] Lit. " has no approach or touch."
[c] ὄντως τῇ οὐσίᾳ.
[d] τὰς δυνάμεις.
[e] εἰς σωτηρίαν πάντων.
[f] κτίστην.
[g] παντοκράτορα.
[h] So the LXX, ἡ παρθένος : Heb. " the young woman."
[i] LXX and Heb. " some ten days." Both texts add " and afterwards she shall go."
[j] So Heb. : LXX μὴ κατέχετέ με.
[k] Both LXX and Heb. use the past tense here, though we expect a future.
[l] In Gen. xxiv. 51, see above, *QG* iv. 129.
[m] εἰς ἔλεγχος.
[n] Variant " unfaithful."
[o] The Arm. has the participle though the pres. indicative is needed.
[p] θεοῦ τοῦ σωτῆρος.
[q] Aucher omits this word in his rendering.
[r] ἀρετῆς.

132. (Gen. xxiv. 57) Why does (Scripture) say, "Let us call the maid and question her mouth"[a]?

In the first place, it is to be said that this law is written by the holy father[b] concerning a virgin who is to be betrothed[c] when she has no guardian,[d] that they[e] may not be led by force like maid-servants or captives but may go willingly and accept marriage of their own accord and enter into an harmonious union. In the second place, since the mind[f] is always variable and subject to all kinds of change because of the thoughts[g] which frequently and continuously come at it from without and come into it like a torrent with ceaseless blows, they said deliberately, "Let us question"—not "her" but—"her mouth," saying this for the reason that they were voluntarily suffering[h] the changes that come like a flood from those things that supervene from without, and they bring speech[i] into account.[j] Wherefore in another passage of the legislation[k] (Moses) says, "And whatsoever comes forth from thy lips thou shalt do," but does not (say), "Whatsoever thou takest into thy mind," for men hear the voice, while God (hears) thoughts. And so, it is fitting that they do not question the thoughts themselves but their servant, (namely) the speech that is uttered.

[a] So the LXX (retaining the Heb. idiom, which A.V. renders, "inquire at her mouth"), καλέσωμεν τὴν παῖδα καὶ ἐπερωτήσωμεν τὸ στόμα αὐτῆς.

[b] Apparently Moses is meant, or possibly God as the author of Scripture.

[c] See above, *QG* iv. 91 on Gen. xxiv. 8. See also *De Spec. Leg.* iii. 71.

[d] Prob. ἐπιμελητήν, as in *De Spec. Leg.* iii. 81.

[e] *i.e.* betrothed women.

[f] ὁ νοῦς.

[g] τοὺς λογισμούς.

[h] Lit. "receiving."

[i] τὸν λόγον.

[j] Aucher renders a little more freely, "et verbum pro ratione in medium duci voluerunt."

[k] νομοθετῶν. See Num. xxx. 2, where LXX reads πάντα ὅσα ἐὰν ἐξέλθῃ ἐκ τοῦ στόματος αὐτοῦ, ποιήσει.

133. (Gen. xxiv. 58) Why, when they ask her, "Wilt thou go with this man?", does she at once make reply, saying, "I will go"?

It is indeed proper to praise her interrogators for esteeming and honouring the voluntary more than the necessary.[a] For violence is the cause of immediately confessing one's reasons.[b] And the soul that is a lover of good [c] avoids arrogance and impiety, and considers of no worth the intentions of the men of the crowd and of those who stick together,[d] since some of them are in no way distinguishable from beasts in human form.[e] And he who a little while before had been a boy is now a man,[f] no longer in natural power [g] but in perfection,[h] having given many proofs of wisdom and prudence and a disposition worthy of regard and master-loving and, what is much more, virtue-loving and God-loving.[i] And knowing this, Constancy [j] consents and says, "I will go with him," in order that she may remain the more firm. For it does not profit one's thinking [k] at all to receive virtue if it is subsequently to flow away and dissolve instead of being strengthened more firmly and powerfully by a lasting bond.

134. (Gen. xxiv. 59) What is the meaning of the words, "They sent Rebekah and whatever belonged to her" [l]?

[a] τὸ ἑκούσιον μᾶλλον ἢ τὸ ἀναγκαῖον.

[b] The somewhat obscure Arm. sentence is rendered more freely by Aucher, "nam violentia in causis est incunctanter fatendi aliquid per praetextum."

[c] Aucher renders, "laude digna."

[d] The Arm. lit. = τῆς συμφυΐας.

[e] τῶν ἀνθρωπομόρφων θηρίων, *cf. De Abrahamo* 33.

[f] See above, *QG* iv. 108 on Gen. xxiv. 21.

[g] δυνάμει φυσικῇ.

[h] τελειότητι.

[i] σοφίας καὶ φρονήσεως καὶ γνώμης ἀξιοθεάτου τε καὶ φιλοδεσπότου καὶ πολὺ μᾶλλον φιλαρέτου τε καὶ φιλοθέου.

[j] ὑπομονή or διαμονή, symbolized by Rebekah, see above, *QG* iv. 97, 128.

[k] Lit. "thoughts"—λογισμούς.

[l] Philo abbreviates Scripture. LXX reads καὶ εὐλόγησαν Ῥεβέκκαν τὴν ἀδελφὴν αὐτῶν καὶ τὰ ὑπάρχοντα αὐτῆς καὶ τὸν παῖδα τὸν Ἀβραὰμ καὶ τοὺς μετ' αὐτοῦ. Heb. reads similarly.

The literal meaning [a] is clearly expressed,[b] but the symbol indicates that the substance of the virtuous soul [c] is the firm grasp of the good in accordance with the contemplation of virtue and wisdom,[d] which are the only substances in truth. For this reason those things which are bodily and external are ephemeral and transitory and uncertain possessions. Happy are they, therefore, to whom the constant family [e] passes over, while those whom it begins to leave are unhappy.

135. (Gen. xxiv. 60) Why do they bless her in this way: "Our sister, mayest thou become [f] thousands of myriads, and may thy seed inherit the cities [g] of their enemies"?

While Constancy [h] is still near the soul, it is its brother,[i] but so soon as it meditates separation and dissociation, it removes itself and diminishes the blessing, saying, "Become myriads." But what possessed [j] those who prayed that they directed their prayers to those not yet born rather than to her? It was because enemy cities are symbolically the evils in us and various invading passions which have lawlessness as their law, and a harmful form of government.[k]

[a] τὸ ῥητόν.

[b] The Arm. adj. *yaytanšan* lit. = "clear as to sign" (or "symbol"). Aucher renders, "evidentis symboli est," and, in a footnote, "*vel*, evidens est valde."

[c] τὰ ὑπάρχοντα (as in LXX, see p. 415, note *l*) τῆς σπουδαίας ψυχῆς.

[d] ἡ βεβαία κατάληψις τοῦ ἀγαθοῦ κατὰ τὰ τῆς ἀρετῆς τε καὶ σοφίας θεωρήματα.

[e] γένος, *i.e.* Rebekah and her train, symbolizing constancy, ὑπομονή or διαμονή, on which see above, *QG* iv. 97, 128, 133.

[f] LXX and Heb. "Our sister art thou; mayest thou become."

[g] So LXX, τὰς πόλεις: Heb. "the gate."

[h] διαμονή, symbolized by Rebekah, see above, *QG* iv. 97, 128, 133.

[i] Which is the brother and which the sister is not clear; apparently the fem. noun ψυχή is here treated symbolically as masc.

[j] Aucher "impedivit."

[k] βλάπτουσαν (or ἐπιβουλεύουσαν) πολιτείαν.

136. (Gen. xxiv. 61) What is the meaning of " mounting the camels "[a]? Who are the maids[b] with whom Rebekah " rose and mounted the camels "?

The mounting of the camels shows that character and religion[c] are superior to the mnemonic form,[d] for Constancy[e] is related to memory, and the camel, as has been said many times,[f] is a symbol of memory. But " to mount " is nothing else than to stand upon memory and not to imagine the sleep of forgetfulness.[g] But the maids are the servants of Constancy, being tender and delicate and docile[h] natures, prepared and adorned to serve their mistress. And the names of the servants of Constancy are Inflexible, Unbending, Unvacillating, Unrepentant, Unchanging, Indifferent, Firm, Stable, Unconquerable and Upright,[i] and all their brothers who desire lasting perseverance.

137. (Gen. xxiv. 61) What is the meaning of the words, " Taking Rebekah, the boy[j] departed "?

Just as we say that disciples[k] and pupils receive from their instructors theories of knowledge[l] which are genuine,

[a] LXX ἐπέβησαν ἐπὶ τὰς καμήλους. Aucher notes that this first question, missing in Cod. A of the Arm. text, is found in Codd. C and D at the beginning of the Answer, though it seems to belong at the beginning of the Question.

[b] LXX αἱ ἅβραι.

[c] ἦθος καὶ θρησκεία (or " continence "—ἐγκράτεια).

[d] τοῦ μνημονικοῦ εἴδους.

[e] Or " perseverance "—διαμονή, symbolized by Rebekah, see the preceding sections.

[f] *e.g.* in *QG* iv. 92, 106.

[g] The Arm. lit. = ὕπνον λήθης φαντάζεσθαι, perhaps " to dream the sleep of forgetfulness."

[h] Here Philo plays on LXX ἅβραι " maids " and ἁβρός " delicate."

[i] ἀρρεπὴς κ. ἀκλινὴς κ. — (?) κ. ἀμετανόητος κ. ἄτρεπτος κ. ἀδιάφορος (?) κ. βέβαιος κ. ἱδρυμένος κ. ἀήττητος κ. ὀρθός.

[j] LXX ὁ παῖς: Heb. " the servant."

[k] γνωρίμους. Aucher less accurately renders, " proximos."

[l] ἐπιστήμης θεωρήματα.

excellent, well chosen and refined by wise men, so also must it be supposed that the progressive mind [a] takes Constancy [b] as (an object of) contemplation.[c] For the inquiry of the theologian [d] is about characters and types and virtues,[e] and not about persons who were created and born.[f]

138. (Gen. xxiv. 62) Why does (Scripture) say, " Isaac went through the wilderness by the well of Seeing " [g] ?

Oh contemplation [h] fitting to God and worthy intellection [i] and vision,[j] which was deserving of being commemorated in song, and most excellent (vision), which the eyes of the body cannot see ! Therefore, O mind,[k] with thy psychic eyes [l] opened behold him who is within thee (as) an example [m] (of) unsorrowing laughter,[n] Isaac, who without interruption [o] rejoices continually over all those

[a] ὁ προκόπτων νοῦς.

[b] Or " perseverance "—διαμονή, symbolized by Rebekah, see the preceding sections.

[c] ὡς θεώρημα.

[d] ἡ τοῦ θεολόγου (Moses) ζήτησις.

[e] περὶ ἠθῶν καὶ τρόπων (*vel sim.*) καὶ ἀρετῶν.

[f] In general Philo attributes both allegorical (usu. ethical or psychological) and historical meaning to the narratives of Scripture, see H. A. Wolfson, *Philo*, i. 125-127. In a private communication Professor Wolfson suggests that Philo's expression " the inquiry of the theologian " corresponds to the rabbinic expression, " the verse comes to teach you," *bā' hak-kātûb lᵉlammēdkā.*

[g] So the LXX, Ἰσαὰκ δὲ ἐπορεύετο διὰ τῆς ἐρήμου κατὰ τὸ φρέαρ τῆς ὁράσεως. Heb. reads " And Isaac came from the direction (lit. " coming ") of the well Lahai Roi." This proper name was anciently explained as meaning " Verily, my seer lives."

[h] θέαν or θεώρημα.

[i] Arm. *imaçowac* = both νόημα (or ἔννοια) and νοῦς, prob. the former here.

[j] ὅρασιν or θεωρίαν.

[k] ὦ νοῦ.

[l] τῶν ψυχικῶν ὀφθαλμῶν.

[m] τρόπον or τύπον.

[n] ἄλυπον γέλωτα. For other references to Isaac as a symbol of joy or laughter see Leisegang *s.v.* Ἰσαάκ.

[o] ἀδιαστάτως.

things which have been created by God. For thou wilt see him not guarded by confused and precipitate [a] beliefs of thought [b] but with firm steps and with feet making use of wisdom,[c] which is devoid [d] of great evils, of ignorance and lack of discipline.[e] And see him spending his time [f] in the genuine and most proper part of wisdom, at the well, (by which) I understand the wonderful and divine source, which (Scripture) calls " Seeing," giving an appropriate and natural name to the contemplative life [g] in reference to Him Who exists [h] and to the incorporeal ideas [i] in Him, which were made as measures of all things of both worlds.[j] For this [k] is the model and archetype [l] of the intelligible and of the sense-perceptible (world) [m] in which we are mixed with the incorporeal,[n] since our better part soars [o] upward to that (region) which is beyond the ether [p] and above the heaven and above all sense-perceptible things. Similarly every true prophet [q] was called " seer " or " beholder," [r] the name being given in reference to the eye of the soul.

[a] Or " stormy " or " vague " : Aucher " procellosis."

[b] So the Arm. lit. Aucher simplifies to " cogitationibus."

[c] *σοφίᾳ*.

[d] Philo plays on the double meaning of *ἔρημος*, " wilderness " and " devoid."

[e] *ἀπαιδευσίας*.

[f] *ποιούμενον διατριβάς*.

[g] *τῷ θεωρητικῷ βίῳ*.

[h] *τοῦ Ὄντος*.

[i] *ταῖς ἀσωμάτοις ἰδέαις* or *τοῖς . . . εἴδεσι*.

[j] *i.e.* the intelligible and the sense-perceptible world, as explained in what follows.

[k] The demonstrative pron. seems to refer to the word " source," symbolizing the cosmic Logos.

[l] *παράδειγμα καὶ ἀρχέτυπος*.

[m] *τοῦ νοητοῦ καὶ τοῦ αἰσθητοῦ (κόσμου)*.

[n] Lit. " are by an incorporeal mixture."

[o] Lit. " leaps," *cf. De Spec. Leg.* iv. 115 *ἄνω πηδᾶν . . . εἰς αἰθέρα*.

[p] *ἐπέκεινα τοῦ αἰθέρος*.

[q] Aucher renders more freely, " omnis propheta mendacii nesciens."

[r] *ὁρῶν ἢ βλέπων*, *cf. Quod Deus Immut. Sit* 139 and *De Migratione* 38, both based on the LXX of 1 Sam. ix. 9.

139. (Gen. xxiv. 62) Why is he said to dwell in the south ? [a]

This too is in harmony with the preceding. For every one who is desirous of wisdom [b] and is really a lover of God [c] avoids what is visible,[d] (that is) vain opinions, and accounts separation and deficiency [e] as good things.[f]

140. (Gen. xxiv. 63) [g] What is the " meditation " [h] of Isaac, and why did he go out " to meditate in the field toward the turn of day," [i] and why is the one with whom (he conversed) not revealed ?

(This statement) has a connexion and order in harmony [j] with the preceding. For he to whom separation from, and deficiency [k] of, opinions of visible things are precious, begins to seclude himself alone with only the invisible God.[l] Moreover, we are accustomed to call long speeches and conversations " meditations." But (Scripture) shows that

[a] LXX ἐν τῇ γῇ πρὸς λίβα : Heb. " in the land of the Negeb" (the dry region south of Judaea).

[b] σοφίας.

[c] φιλόθεος.

[d] Reading *yerewelic̣* for *yarewelic̣* " the east," because of the context.

[e] διάστημα (*vel sim.*) καὶ ἔκλειψιν. The latter noun seems to have been suggested to Philo by LXX πρὸς λίβα, as though λίβα were cognate with λείπειν and ἔκλειψιν. Note, moreover, that in *Quod Deterius* 26-29, where Philo allegorizes the following verse, Gen. xxiv. 63, he explains the place name Δωθαείμ as meaning ἔκλειψις ἱκανή (so also in *De Fuga* 128).

[f] Lit. " places separation and deficiency in a good part " ; Aucher renders, " in melioris partis ratione collocans."

[g] This verse is briefly treated in *Leg. All.* iii. 43 and *Quod Deterius* 29.

[h] ἀδολεσχία.

[i] LXX καὶ ἐξῆλθεν Ἰσαὰκ ἀδολεσχῆσαι εἰς τὸ πεδίον τὸ πρὸς δείλης. Here ἀδολεσχῆσαι renders Heb. *śûaḥ* " to converse " (A.V. " to meditate ").

[j] εἱρμὸν καὶ τάξιν ἐναρμόνιον.

[k] See notes to preceding section.

[l] *Cf. Leg. All.* iii. 43 ὅταν ἀδολεσχῇ καὶ ἰδιάζῃ θεῷ, *Quod Deterius* 29 μόνον δὲ ἰδιάσαι βουλόμενος καὶ ἰδιολογήσασθαι τῷ . . . θεῷ.

the character of the wise man [a] is not quickly satisfied but is constant and hard to efface and hard to remove from the idea [b] of that which is above the good and above the wise man and above the very best.[c] And various conversations come together, one after the other, so that he never departs from the conversation of speech [d] because of his insatiable and incessant desire and longing, by which [e] the sovereign (mind) [f] is drawn and seized ; and it is led by the attractive force of sovereign existences.[g] Hence they come forth, in word, from the city or the home, but in fact [h] particularly when the mind [i] begins to be filled with God and divinely inspired and possessed by God.[j] And the going out on the way takes place in the field in order that it may exercise and enter contests [k] and practise the divine law for the fitting and proper production of sound fruits, which are the immortal foods of the soul.[l] And the time was the turn of day, when the natural force and strength [m] of the sun's rays, by which I understand visible opinions, are lessened and have their many flames extinguished. And meditation takes place when there is no man present [n] but (one is) in undisturbed peacefulness. What does (Scripture) say ? That you should know that the sacred scriptures are not monuments of knowledge and vision [o] but are the

[a] τοῦ σοφοῦ.

[b] Variant " contemplation."

[c] αὐτὸ τὸ ἄριστον *vel sim.*

[d] ἀπὸ τῆς ὁμιλίας τῶν λόγων *vel sim.*

[e] Text slightly uncertain.

[f] τὸ ἡγεμονικόν.

[g] Construction and meaning not clear. Aucher renders, " quod intense tractum captumque est principali duce (mente) per trahentem vim entium principalium."

[h] λόγῳ μέν . . . ἔργῳ δέ. [i] ὁ νοῦς.

[j] θεοφορεῖσθαι καὶ θειάζειν (or ἐνθουσιάζειν) καὶ θεοληπτεῖσθαι.

[k] γυμνάζεσθαι καὶ ἀγωνίζεσθαι.

[l] αἱ ἀθάνατοι τῶν ψυχῶν τροφαί, *cf. Leg. All.* iii. 162 οὐράνιοι αἱ ψυχῆς τροφαί.

[m] Lit. " force of strength."

[n] Lit. " is in the midst."

[o] μνημεῖα ἐπιστήμης καὶ θεωρίας.

divine commands and the divine words,[a] which make known Him who is quiet, who is near as not there.[b] And He speaks without uttering words [c] and talks with someone without audible voice, and He does not turn away from (other) speakers or from His disciples or pupils,[d] but gives them freedom of speech [e] in incorporeal matters and in conversation of speech about the intelligible things which are with Him, in order that by questioning they may understand what they do not (already) know, and may comprehend what they think they surely know. At the same time testimony is given by the Father of wisdom himself. " See, then, and judge for yourselves this spiritual conversation [f] and (also) those friendships with kings and potentates which are fought over,[g] and their outcome, together with the uprightness of those who achieve them.[h] For many (of the latter kind) fail and meet difficulties, while the other (kind) [i] provides joyous well-being and eternal happiness."

141. (Gen. xxiv. 63) Why does (Scripture) say, " Looking up with his eyes, he saw the camels that were coming " [j] ?

[a] This important statement is mistranslated by E. R. Goodenough in his *By Light, Light*, p. 160 (see my review in *American Journal of Philology*, vol. 57 [1936], 203-205), but is correctly translated by H. A. Wolfson, *Philo*, ii. 10, 189, who remarks, " By ' knowledge and vision ' Philo means rational knowledge which ultimately rests upon sensation."

[b] *i.e.* " although not there." The Arm. glossator explains, " God is near to one who prays, and is quiet (or " ceases ") even though He is not seen." The Arm. verb rendered above as " is quiet " usu. = *παύεσθαι* or *ἀναπαύεσθαι*.

[c] *μηδὲν φθεγγόμενος*.

[d] *μαθητῶν καὶ γνωρίμων*.

[e] *παρρησίαν*.

[f] *ταύτην τὴν ψυχικὴν ὁμιλίαν*.

[g] Aucher " suspectae dilectiones."

[h] Aucher " una cum functorum rectitudine." Apparently Philo is being ironical.

[i] *i.e.* friendship or converse with God.

[j] So LXX, *καὶ ἀναβλέψας τοῖς ὀφθαλμοῖς* (Heb. " and he lifted his eyes ") *ἴδεν καμήλους ἐρχομένας*.

It is proper to have doubts [a] (about this statement), for with what else do we look at things than our eyes? Nor do we hear with anything else than our ears. But may it not be that (Scripture) is not discussing the eyes of the body but those of the mind,[b] which have been educated to look up at higher and ethereal (regions) and others above heaven, and at the nature which is outside the world? [c] Wherefore, from other memories,[d] he perceives [e] the presence of the woman, whom (the camels) easily bear as a burden, (namely) the perseverance of the finest virtues,[f] and also her maidservants, concerning whom I wrote what was fitting a little above.[g]

142. (Gen. xxiv. 64) Why did (Rebekah), when she saw Isaac, leap from the camel? [h]

In the literal sense,[i] it was because of modesty and veneration.[j] But as for the deeper meaning,[k] it was because of the humility and submissiveness and perception of virtue [l] (found) in [m] a genuine and sincere lover.[n] For this [o] is not easily able to ascend to such a height but must

[a] ἀπορεῖν. [b] τοῦ νοῦ.

[c] τὴν φύσιν τὴν ἔξω τοῦ κόσμου.

[d] Symbolized by the camels, see *QG* iv. 92, 106 *et al.*

[e] φαντάζεται.

[f] τὴν τῶν ἀρίστων ἀρετῶν διαμονήν. On Rebekah as the symbol of Perseverance or Constancy see *QG* iv. 97, 128 *et al.*

[g] In *QG* iv. 136.

[h] So LXX, κατεπήδησεν ἀπὸ τῆς καμήλου: Heb. "and she fell from the camel."

[i] τὸ ῥητόν. [j] Lit. "modesty of veneration."

[k] τὸ πρὸς διάνοιαν. [l] ἀρετῆς.

[m] The Arm. prep. *əst* usu. = κατά.

[n] Aucher renders the clause, "propter humiliationem, indulgentiam, gustandamque virtutem secundum genuinum fidelemque amore captum," and remarks in a footnote, "*Vel sic*: indulgentiam ad sensibilem etiam virtutem. Ambiguitas oritur ex variante lectione *ew zgaloy* [=gen. case of substantival infinitive] aut *ew zgalwoy* [=gen. case of adjective]."

[o] The demonstr. pron. apparently refers to "virtue."

by all means descend to become intimate.[a] For it is destined [b] to come into participation [c] of converse and speech, and to receive [d] profit (from this). But what was it not destined to receive,[e] since it did not keep within itself any seed or remnant of jealousy and envy and terrible [f] passion [g] but had expelled from its borders conniving and malicious envy?

143. (Gen. xxiv. 65) Why did (Rebekah) take her scarf [h] and throw it about her?

Not in the same manner as virgins now (are adorned) was that wonderful nature and admirable virgin adorned and beautified, for she had within herself an ornament [i] most adequate, and she was not in need of anything else whatever from outside. And the scarf is a visible symbol of clear-shining virtue,[j] of which the inner part and that which is in its depths and in its inner recesses is uncovered and becomes apparent only to the lover of wisdom,[k] and is clearly seen (by him), but is covered from, and becomes invisible to, the uninitiated and unskilled [l] and those who are not possessed by God.[m]

*144. (Gen. xxiv. 66) Why, when (the servant) had been sent on a mission [n] by one person,[o] did he give a response [p]

[a] διὰ τὸ οἰκειοῦσθαι, apparently meaning intimacy with God.

[b] μέλλει.

[c] Text slightly emended.

[d] Text slightly emended. Aucher renders, "utilitatem datura."

[e] See preceding note.

[f] Or "bitter."

[g] Variant "prayer."

[h] LXX τὸ θέριστρον "a light summer-garment": Heb. *ṣā'īf* "veil."

[i] κόσμον.

[j] σύμβολον φανερὸν αὐγοειδεστάτης (*vel sim.*) ἀρετῆς.

[k] μόνῳ τῷ τῆς σοφίας ἐραστῇ.

[l] τοῖς ἀμυήτοις καὶ τοῖς ἀπείροις.

[m] Aucher "non initiatis."

[n] ἐπὶ πρεσβείαν, as in the Greek frag. from Procopius.

[o] *i.e.* by Abraham.

[p] The Greek frag. has ἀποπρεσβεύει.

to another, for, says (Scripture), " He related to Isaac all the things [a] which he had done " [b] ?

One may say that inasmuch as it was on behalf of the son that he had been sent on the mission by the father, when the mission had been completed, he brought the good news [c] to him on whose behalf he had been sent, especially because he met him first on the road, as he was coming. It is clear that [d] he afterwards related (these things) also to the father, who had sent him, for even though this has not been expressly [e] written, it is to be inferred [f] from the text. However, it is proper to speak of this allegorically,[g] for when Abraham and Isaac are analysed,[h] (they are) one and the same thing, that is, (one is a symbol) of taught virtue, (the other) of natural (virtue).[i] For the end of teaching is the beginning of nature.[j] And so he does not relate the events [k] of the journey to anyone else sooner than to him alone. Consider them, therefore, not as mortal men who question each other now,[l] but as formless types of soul being examined,[m] which wisdom [n] harmonizes and

[a] Lit. " words," see the next note.

[b] LXX καὶ διηγήσατο πάντα τὰ ῥήματα (Heb. *debārîm* = " words " and " things ") ἃ ἐποίησεν.

[c] εὐαγγελίζεται, as in the Greek frag.

[d] The Greek frag. has πάντως " certainly."

[e] Prob. ῥητῶς: Aucher " in historia." The Greek frag., which ends here, has merely γέγραπται.

[f] Lit. " it is persuaded " or " is plausible."

[g] ἀλληγοροῦντα.

[h] Prob. ἀναλυομένου. Aucher, who renders, " resoluti," notes that the meaning of the verb is not clear.

[i] See, *e.g.*, *De Vita Mosis* i. 76 θεὸς Ἀβραὰμ καὶ θεὸς Ἰσαὰκ . . . ὧν ὁ μὲν τῆς διδακτῆς, ὁ δὲ τῆς φυσικῆς . . . σοφίας κανών ἐστιν.

[j] τὸ γὰρ τῆς διδασκαλίας τέλος ἀρχή ἐστι τῆς φύσεως.

[k] Lit. " deeds."

[l] Aucher, preferring the variant reading in the Arm., renders, " non ergo homines putabunt, mortales quasdam esse quaestiones."

[m] Meaning not clear. The Arm. lit. = ἀνειδέους τρόπους ψυχῆς ἐξεταζομένους.

[n] ἡ σοφία.

fits together to bring about partnership [a] and unity. For many have been likened to [b] one, and different ones to unity.[c]

*145. (Gen. xxiv. 67) Why is Isaac said to have entered the house, not of his father but of his mother, for the purpose of marriage,[d] and yet these were dwelling in the same house? [e]

Because those who wish to know and examine the literal meaning [f] will perhaps say that since his father had taken to himself many wives, he virtually [g] had many [h] houses also. For " house " is a name given not only to [i] a building but also to the gathering of husband, wife and children.[j] But he [k] until (her) death remained together with the wife (first taken) as a virgin,[l] wherefore he seems to have had (only) one house.[m] One does not, does one,

[a] κοινωνιάν: Aucher " aequalitatem."

[b] Or " imitate," as Aucher renders.

[c] τῇ μονάδι *vel sim.* The meaning of the last sentence is not clear to me.

[d] LXX εἰσῆλθεν δὲ Ἰσαὰκ εἰς τὸν οἶκον τῆς μητρὸς αὐτοῦ, καὶ ἔλαβεν τὴν Ῥεβέκκαν, καὶ ἐγένετο αὐτοῦ γυνή, καὶ ἠγάπησεν αὐτήν. For a slightly different allegorizing of the verse see *De Poster. Caini* 77-78.

[e] The Greek fragments *ap.* Harris and Wendland do not have the last clause.

[f] τὸ ῥητόν.

[g] δυνάμει, as in the Greek fragments.

[h] One Greek text has πλείστους.

[i] Lit. " is said . . . of."

[j] One Greek text has τὸ ἐξ ἀνδρὸς καὶ γυναικὸς καὶ τέκνων σύστημα: the other has τὸ ἐκ γαμικῆς συζυγίας καὶ τέκνων σύστημα.

[k] The Arm. demonstr. pron. may be either masc. or fem. (as Aucher takes it), but the context indicates that the antecedent is Isaac, not Sarah (or Rebekah or Abraham). One Greek text has ὁ δέ, the other ἡ δέ.

[l] Lit. " with his wife from virginity." The Greek fragments have τῷ κουριδίῳ.

[m] The Greek fragments end here.

see (him) separated and betrothed to another.[a] But someone else more naturally [b] giving the sense of the text, (might) say, in allegorizing,[c] that since the mother of the self-taught person [d] was motherless wisdom,[e] whose right reason [f] is symbolically [g] called "house," it was changed into a bridal-chamber for him so as to be a unity of betrothal and a partnership of the self-taught kind with ever-virginal Constancy,[h] from the love [i] of whom may it never come about that I cease.

146. (Gen. xxiv. 67) Why, when he had taken a wife and loved Rebekah, is (Isaac) said to have been consoled for Sarah, his mother? [j]

Rightly and fittingly (is this said), for he did not drive out wisdom [k] but found (it), not after a time in old age but when flourishing in nonage [l] and youth,[m] and ever blossoming without sense-perceived colour in incorporeal beauty.[n] For consolation [o] belongs to the contemplation-loving soul [p] in its concern for [q] the earliest

[a] Text slightly uncertain. Aucher renders, "Numquid visa est separata, et alium despondens?"

[b] φυσικώτερον, probably in the Stoic sense of "symbolically."

[c] ἀλληγορῶν.

[d] On Isaac as a symbol of the αὐτοδίδακτος see *QG* iv. 122.

[e] ἀμήτωρ σοφία. Sarah appears as a symbol of ἀρετή . . . ἀμήτωρ ἀρχή in *Quis Rer. Div. Heres* 62.

[f] ὀρθὸς λόγος.

[g] συμβολικῶς.

[h] εἰς ἕνωσιν καὶ κοινωνίαν τοῦ αὐτοδιδάκτου γένους σὺν τῇ ἀειπαρθένῳ διαμονῇ. On Rebekah as a symbol of constancy see *QG* iv. 128, 129 *et al.*

[i] ἔρωτος.

[j] LXX . . . καὶ ἔλαβεν τὴν Ῥεβέκκαν καὶ ἐγένετο αὐτοῦ γυνή, καὶ ἠγάπησεν αὐτήν· καὶ παρεκλήθη Ἰσαὰκ περὶ (Heb. "after") τῆς μητρὸς αὐτοῦ.

[k] τὴν σοφίαν.

[l] ἐν ἀγηρασίᾳ.

[m] Aucher, disregarding the Arm. word-order, renders, "non per tempus in senectute vigens, sed insenectute ac juventute."

[n] ἄνευ αἰσθητῆς χρόας ἀσωμάτῳ κάλλει.

[o] παράκλησις.

[p] τῆς φιλοθεάμονος ψυχῆς.

[q] Lit. "concerning" or "about."

and first discipline,[a] which it is accustomed to practise from youth, when it is mated with, and betrothed to, a wife who is constant [b] in virtue and perseverance.[c] For when he bears in mind and remembers his former way of life,[d] which he lived without any discipline, he is consoled. And he was consoled (also) by the fact that he has not spent his time in vain and in an unworthy manner.

147. (Gen. xxv. 1) What is the meaning of the words, "And Abraham added to take a wife,[e] whose name was Keturah" [f]?

That which is added is not the same as that to which it is added but is something else altogether. Now what is it, then, which is added to the good? Is it, indeed, the bad or the contrary and unlike? [g] But it is clear that this is a mixture, which is neither bad nor good. For riches and honours and bodily affections [h] and whatever things are connected with [i] the body and are outside the body are measured for the virtuous man,[j] not, however, as good but as additions to his own goods,[k] and being indifferent,[l] they are mixed and foreign. The addition is therefore called "Keturah," which name is to be translated as

[a] παιδείας.

[b] The instrumental case of the Arm. noun "constancy" is here prob. used predicatively.

[c] κατὰ διαμονήν. See the notes to the preceding section.

[d] Lit. "ways and life," prob. = διαγωγὴν τοῦ βίου.

[e] So LXX, προσθέμενος δὲ Ἀβραὰμ ἔλαβεν γυναῖκα, following the Heb. idiom which means "Abraham took another wife."

[f] Arm. *Kentoura*: LXX Χεττούρα: Heb. *Qᵉṭûrāh*.

[g] τὸ ἐναντίον καὶ ἀνόμοιον.

[h] σωματικὰ πάθη.

[i] Lit. "are around."

[j] The Arm. lit. = τῷ σπουδαίῳ μετρεῖται, and probably is an inexact rendering. Aucher renders, "penes honestum dimensa sunt."

[k] *i.e.* to those of the soul.

[l] ἀδιάφορα, in the technical ethical sense. See H. A. Wolfson, *Philo*, ii. 297-303.

"incense-burning."[a] And the odour is an addition to food but is not food, wherefore some have said, not ineptly, that smell is a foretaster.[b] And to those who are subject to danger of pain physicians present odours when they are unable to give them food. This must be said first. And still another thing must be set beside this, that among the senses[c] there are two which are virtuous and philosophical,[d] (namely) those of sight and hearing; and a third, that of smell, is a mean between the good and the bad; and there are two bad ones belonging to the bad, (namely) taste and touch. And when the four (senses) are arranged in groups of two, smell is the middle one,[e] for it is clearer and purer than taste and touch, and is duller and more short-sighted[f] than sight and hearing. For this reason (Scripture) has attributed the three best forms of sense to Him who is the sovereign of all things. For (it refers) to sight when it says,[g] "And God saw all the things which He had made, and, behold, they were very good"; and to hearing when it says,[h] "The Lord heareth the poor"; and to smell when it says,[i] "And the Lord God smelled a sweet savour." Now since the consummation of a happy life is likeness to God,[j] he who was a true man[k] judged it best to marry three wives, (who were) symbolically some three powers,[l] the most admirable of all (the senses, namely) hearing, sight and smell. For the maidservant in Chaldaean was

[a] *θυμιῶσα*, as in *De Sacr. Abelis* 43-44, which partially parallels this section.

[b] *Cf. De Sacr. Abelis* 44 *ὄσφρησιν . . . καθάπερ βασιλίδος προγευστρίδα.*

[c] *τῶν αἰσθήσεων.*

[d] *σπουδαῖαι καὶ φιλόσοφοι*, *cf. De Spec. Leg.* i. 337-338.

[e] *i.e.* smell, the fifth, is between the two groups of two senses each.

[f] Aucher "tardior."

[g] Gen. i. 31.

[h] Ps. lxix. 33.

[i] Gen. viii. 21.

[j] *τὸ τέλος ἐστὶν εὐδαίμονος ζωῆς ἡ πρὸς θεὸν ὁμοιότης.*

[k] *i.e.* Abraham.

[l] *συμβολικῶς τρεῖς τινας δυνάμεις.*

called "Hagar"[a] and in Armenian[b] "sojourning."[c] And her offspring was "hearing God," who among the Hebrews was called "Ishmael."[d] And (the offspring) of his lady[e] (was called) "laughter,"[f] (being) a psychic eye and light,[g] for light and sight are joyful, just as darkness and blindness are sad. And the third (wife) mentioned was allusively[h] named "incense-burning," which the Chaldaeans call "Keturah."

*148. (Gen. xxv. 5-6) What is the meaning of the words, "And Abraham gave all that was his to Isaac his son, and to the sons of his concubines he gave gifts[i]"?

(Scripture) refers to a difference between possessions and gifts,[j] both in the literal sense and in the deeper meaning.[k] As for the literal meaning, those things that assure a quiet life, and whatever things remain stable and in our possession are called "possessions," while gifts are those things given by hand,[l] the use of which is for a short time.[m] But as for the deeper meaning, it is the virtues founded with firmness and the deeds (performed) with virtue[n] that are

[a] Arm. *Agar*, as in LXX.

[b] As usual, the Arm. translator substitutes "Armenian" for "Greek."

[c] παροίκησις, as in *De Congressu* 20.

[d] Ishmael's name is etymologized as ἀκοὴ θεοῦ in *De Mut. Nom.* 202 *et al.*

[e] *i.e.* Sarah, in contrast to the concubines, Hagar and Keturah.

[f] "Isaac" is etymologized as γέλως and χαρά in many passages of Philo.

[g] *Cf. e.g. De Confus. Ling.* 92 ὁ ψυχῆς ὀφθαλμὸς ὁ διαυγέστατος καὶ καθαρώτατος καὶ πάντων ὀξυωπέστατος.

[h] *αἰνίγματι vel sim.*

[i] LXX ἔδωκεν δὲ Ἀβραὰμ πάντα τὰ ὑπάρχοντα αὐτοῦ Ἰσαὰκ τῷ υἱῷ αὐτοῦ· καὶ τοῖς υἱοῖς τῶν παλλακῶν αὐτοῦ ἔδωκεν Ἀβραὰμ δόματα.

[j] διαφορὰν ὑπαρχόντων καὶ δομάτων, as in the Greek frag. from Procopius.

[k] καὶ πρὸς τὸ ῥητὸν καὶ πρὸς τὴν διάνοιαν.

[l] χειρόδοτα, as in the Greek frag.

[m] The Greek frag., which ends here, has ὧν ἡ χρῆσις ἐφήμερος.

[n] κατ' ἀρετήν.

called " substances " and " possessions." [a] Those things, however, which are indifferent [b] and unstable, being about the body and outside the body, it calls " gifts." And so, it presents (as) the heir of the virtues the legitimate son, laughter,[c] who rejoices at all things in nature,[d] whereas the indifferent and undetermined [e] (sons born) to Abraham by his concubines (rejoice in) indifferent things.[f] So much superior was Isaac to (the sons) of the concubines as are possessions [g] to gifts. Wherefore (Scripture) recently [h] described Isaac as motherless, and it calls those born to the concubines fatherless.[i] Accordingly, those who were harmonious in the father's family are of the male progeny, while the (sons) of the women and those of inferior descent are certainly to be called female and unvirile,[j] for which reason they are little admired as great ones.[k]

[a] *οὐσίαι καὶ κτήματα*, " substances " being rendered by two words in the Arm.

[b] *ἀδιάφορα*.

[c] *τὸν γνήσιον υἱόν, γέλωτα*, symbolized by Isaac.

[d] On Isaac as a symbol of the naturally virtuous or self-taught man see, *e.g.*, *QG* iv. 122, 145.

[e] *ἀορίστους*, *cf. De Praemiis* 36 *πᾶσα ἡ αἰσθητὴ φύσις ἀόριστος*.

[f] Aucher renders somewhat differently, " indifferentes autem Abrahae natos ex concubinis indifferentibus ac indistinctis gaudere bonis."

[g] The Arm. has " possessions " in the gen. case, but the context seems to require us to take it as nom. Aucher too renders it as the subject of the final clause.

[h] See *QG* iv. 145 on Gen. xxiv. 67.

[i] *i.e.* as not being legitimate sons of Abraham.

[j] *ἄνανδροι*, an adjective elsewhere applied by Philo to the senses and sense-perceptible things.

[k] The above is a literal translation of the obscure Arm. text, which Aucher, confessing doubt of its meaning (his footnote reads : " Quamquam uncis aliqua adjeci, nec ita tamen me sensum verum expressisse confido "), renders, " illi ergo, qui concordes erant in patria gente, etiam masculi nati (nomen sortiuntur) ; verum illi (ipsi) quia (alienam participant) femineam lineam pravis prolibus gaudentem, certo certius vocandi sunt feminae vecordes, eoquod ob minora illa tamquam majores (sibi ipsi) admiratione sunt."

149. (Gen. xxv. 6) Why, after giving gifts to his alien [a] offspring, did he send them away from his son Isaac, while he was still living, to the land of the east? [b]

In its literal sense [c] the significance is clear. But as for the deeper meaning,[d] it is the intention of the sacred word [e] to preserve (him) for ever virtuous, perfect, passionless and unstained.[f] And he is (so) preserved if those of opposed and earthy thoughts are removed and settled (elsewhere).[g] For, as they are born alien to virtue,[h] so they wish to pollute the legitimate [i] (son). But it is impossible for such a removal to take place unless (the father) is living and sound in true life and healthy thought.[j] For not ineptly is it said that while he was still living he sent away wrongdoing and passion.[k] And he sent them away, not to the region of the east, but most naturally "to the land of the east," (that is) not to the heavenly and divine light but to earthly and corruptible splendours and appearances [l] of arrogance and vain honours, of which they are emulous. For empty are the strivings of the mind, through which many consider riches and honours and the like to be good.

150. (Gen. xxv. 7) Why, in speaking about the life of

[a] *ἀλλοτρίοις*, *cf.* *De Virtutibus* 207, where Philo speaks of the sons of Abraham's concubines as *ἀλλοτριωθέντες τῆς ἀοιδίμου εὐγενείας.*

[b] LXX *καὶ τοῖς υἱοῖς τῶν παλλακῶν αὐτοῦ ἔδωκεν Ἀβραὰμ δόματα, καὶ ἐξαπέστειλεν αὐτοὺς ἀπὸ Ἰσαὰκ τοῦ υἱοῦ αὐτοῦ ἔτι ζῶντος αὐτοῦ πρὸς ἀνατολὰ εἰς γῆν ἀνατολῶν.*

[c] *τὸ ῥητόν.* [d] *τὸ πρὸς διάνοιαν.*

[e] *γνώμη τοῦ ἱεροῦ λόγου.*

[f] *σπουδαῖον καὶ τέλειον καὶ ἀπαθῆ καὶ ἀκηλίδωτον.* Aucher renders slightly differently, "probum (filium), perfectum, vitioque et ulceribus carentem perpetuo servare." Here, as in *QG* ii. 15, the Arm. translator seems to have confused *κήλη* "ulcer" with *κηλίς* "stain."

[g] Aucher "transmittantur in coloniam."

[h] *ἀρετῆς.* [i] *τὸν γνήσιον.* [j] *ὑγιεῖ λογισμῷ.*

[k] *ἀδικίαν* (*vel sim.*) *καὶ πάθος.*

[l] Aucher "lumina et phantasmata."

Abraham, does (Scripture) say, "These are the years of the days of the life of Abraham"[a]?

Most excellently does it say "days," for it does not wish to bring out the number of years, as do those who write (historical) narratives, but to show that the several ages of the wise man are praiseworthy when he lives his whole life excellently.[b] For a year is a sum of days, but days are not (a sum) of years. For it is proper that for those who live in accordance with virtue[c] there should be an addition of the length of time rather than that the time of an old man (should be) a divine splendour.[d]

151. (Gen. xxv. 7) Why are the years of (his) life "one hundred and seventy-five"?

Because (this number) is seven times twenty-five, and twenty-five is a lunar period,[e] in accordance with which (Scripture) wishes the temple-servants to perform the service of the temple,[f] beginning at twenty-five years, and to be in attendance and serve for the same number (of years), for it makes them retire from active service[g] after reaching fifty, taking care that the priest shall be an imitator and emulator of the heavenly (body). Accord-

[a] So LXX, ταῦτα δὲ τὰ ἔτη ἡμερῶν ζωῆς Ἀβραάμ. Heb. has "These are the days of the years of the life of Abraham."

[b] The Arm. seems to render ἑκάστας τὰς τοῦ σοφοῦ ἡλικίας ἐπαινετὰς εἶναι, αὐτὸν δὲ διαφερόντως διαιωνίζειν. Aucher renders, "singulas sapientis aetates distinctas tam laudabiles fuisse, quam perenniter durasse."

[c] κατ' ἀρετήν.

[d] L. A. Post suggests that the meaning of the original was something like the following, "Old age is marked rather by the measure of time of which light is lord (ᾧ φῶς κύριον μέτρῳ), in place of the addition of a long period" (*i.e.* the year).

[e] In round numbers, of course.

[f] See Num. viii. 24-25, prescribing that Levites shall serve from the age of 25 to 50, and Philo's comments in *Quod Deterius* 64.

[g] Lit. "being quiet cease."

ingly, just as that most useful star [a] which is near the earth, (namely) the moon, serves the whole earth in twenty-five (days), so also (Scripture) has thought it right to ordain an equal length of time of attendance for temple-servants.[b] Now the hebdomad is the most sacred of numbers, as has been especially shown.[c] And these are all the perfect numbers which are contained at once in the life of the wise man,[d] (namely) one hundred, and seventy,[e] and five, so that both their addition and their division are most beautiful. And these things have been noted concerning numbers.

*152. (Gen. xxv. 8) What is the meaning of the words, " failing, he died," and why (did he die) " in a good old age, old and full of days " [f]?

The literal meaning [g] does not raise [h] any question, but this (statement) is to be taken more naturally,[i] and the interpretation to be given is that the death of the body is the life of the soul, since the soul lives an incorporeal life of its own.[j] In regard to this, Heracleitus, like a thief taking law and opinions from Moses,[k] says, " we live their death, and we die their life," [l] intimating [m] that the life

[a] ἀστήρ, here as occasionally elsewhere in Philo, means " planet."

[b] *i.e.* 25 days correspond to 25 years.

[c] For the many passages in Philo see Staehle, pp. 34-50.

[d] τοῦ σοφοῦ, *i.e.* Abraham.

[e] Aucher inadvertently renders, " septenarius."

[f] LXX καὶ ἐκλείπων ἀπέθανεν Ἀβραὰμ ἐν γήρει καλῷ πρεσβύτης καὶ πλήρης ἡμερῶν.

[g] τὸ ῥητόν.

[h] Lit. " have."

[i] φυσικώτερον, *i.e.* " more allegorically."

[j] ἴδιον ἑαυτῇ τῆς ψυχῆς ἀσώματον βίον διαγούσης *vel sim.*

[k] On Philo's charges of plagiarism against Heracleitus and other Greek philosophers see Wolfson, *Philo*, i. 141-142.

[l] ζῶμεν τὸν ἐκείνων θάνατον, τεθνήκαμεν δὲ τὸν ἐκείνων βίον, quoted by Philo in *Leg. All.* i. 108 *et al.* The wording of the quotation is slightly different in other ancient sources, *cf.* Bywater, frag. 67, Diels, frag. 62.

[m] αἰνιττόμενος.

of the body is the death of the soul. And what is called "death" is the most glorious [a] life of the first soul.[b] Moreover, "in a good old age" is a most useful description of law and opinions [c] in so far as a virtuous man [d] is said to be "a fine old man." [e] For all these are good and desirable measures of age,[f] and are more flourishing than contemptible youth in which the sensual pleasures [g] of the body are still growing. For as a youth this young man did not highly esteem any passion in word or deed and did not choose such a life.[h] And as a man he did not always stir up childish outbreaks and quarrels and fights, since he practises manliness.[i] And in middle age, with his virtues seated around him,[j] he is highly esteemed. He does not, therefore, first begin to act prudently [k] and soundly when in the course of time the passions of old age pass away and cease, but because in the way one fits a head to a statue he has fitted a most beautiful and lovable aspect [l] to his former way of life. This the eyes of the body do not see, but the pellucid and pure mind is taught to see.[m]

Moreover, I am greatly puzzled [n] by the addition (in Scripture), for it says that he was "full of days," making him appear densely full,[o] for the Father does not allow the life of the virtuous man [p] to be empty or vacant in any

[a] Or "most blessed."

[b] Aucher renders less accurately, "vita felicissima ac prima animae." Probably we should emend Arm. *arajin* "first" to "*arak'ini* "virtuous."

[c] *i.e.* of moral conduct.

[d] σπουδαῖος.

[e] εὐγήρως.

[f] ἡλικίαι.

[g] αἱ ἡδοναί.

[h] Text and meaning are uncertain. Aucher renders, "quoniam in aetate tyronica nullum hic juvenis nec vitium nec verbum neque opus voluit sibi permittere, et praeeligere vitam."

[i] ἀνδρείαν.

[j] τῶν ἀρετῶν συνεδρευουσῶν.

[k] σωφρονίζεσθαι.

[l] πάγκαλον καὶ ἀξιέραστον πρόσωπον.

[m] ὁ διαυγὴς καὶ καθαρὸς νοῦς ἰδεῖν παιδεύεται. Aucher renders more freely, "nitidae tamen ac limpidae animae edoctae sunt ad videndum."

[n] διαπορῶ.

[o] πυκνόν.

[p] τοῦ σπουδαίου.

place for evil (to enter) his mind [a] or any part of him.[b] For (Scripture) says that the virtuous man is full not of years but of days, always ordering and placing the distinctions of length of time of the virtuous man [c] under the divine light. And again in another way it has determined the several days (to be) worthy of study and care, as those guilty of transgressions (are in need of) orators (and) speakers of truth,[d] when the law of nature testifies against them [e] concerning what each of them has said or done day by day from morning to evening and from evening to morning.

*153. (Gen. xxv. 8) Why is it said that "he was added to his people" [f]?

You see that when (Scripture) spoke a little earlier of his "failing," [g] it did not allude to his corruption [h] but to his more stable endurance.[i] And so it naturally [j] is. For the casting off of that which is mortal and bad is the

[a] τὸν νοῦν.

[b] Aucher renders more freely, "tamquam confertam monstrans veri boni vitam, nullum relinquente Patre situm vacuum in mente ejus, vel in aliqua parte, ad ingressum mali."

[c] Aucher renders, "bene transacti temporis spatii distinctiones."

[d] Aucher renders, "tamquam obligatio causarum apud rhetores et juridicos."

[e] The Arm. text seems to render τοῦ τῆς φύσεως νόμου κατ' αὐτῶν διδόντος λόγον. Aucher renders, "ratione ei (*vel*, eis) concessa legis naturae." L. A. Post queries, "Is there a concealed reference to the sun as all-knowing?"

[f] LXX καὶ προσετέθη πρὸς τὸν λαὸν αὐτοῦ: Heb. "and he was gathered to his kin." In *De Sacr. Abelis* 5 Philo quotes the verse as προστίθεται τῷ θεοῦ λαῷ, explaining that Abraham "enjoyed incorruptibility and became equal to the angels"; see further on in this section.

[g] See the preceding section in which Philo quotes LXX καὶ ἐκλείπων ἀπέθανεν κτλ.

[h] φθοράν.

[i] βεβαιοτέραν διαμονήν.

[j] φυσικῶς *vel sim.*

addition of that which is excellent and more immortal.[a] And the addition to his people is spoken of although there was not yet a people in existence, since he himself was the origin and forefather of the race.[b] But that (people) which was to come into being through him [c] (is represented) as already in existence, and (Scripture) establishes this as being granted to him because of the godlike virtues [d] to which he is said to be added.[e] That is the literal meaning.[f] But let us speak allegorically.[g] The people is truly of God,[h] that is to say and declare that it is a transition which is rational and heavenly.[i] For every soul is rational which [j] flees and is loosed and released from that to which it is bound,[k] and is delivered and freed from confinement. For the ancients used to call a tomb a " naked grave." [l] And (Scripture) in another passage calls him " forefather " [m]

[a] The comparative degree of the adj. ἀθάνατος seems not to occur in Philo's extant Greek writings.

[b] ἀρχὴ καὶ προπάτωρ τοῦ γένους, as in the Greek frag. from Procopius.

[c] The Arm. uses the instrumental case of the pers. pron., while the Greek frag. has δι' αὐτόν " because of him."

[d] διὰ τὰς θεοπρεπεῖς ἀρετάς.

[e] The syntax is not certain. The Greek frag., which ends here, has τὸν οὖν μέλλοντα δι' αὐτὸν γενέσθαι ὡς ἤδη γεγονότα χαριζόμενος αὐτοῦ τῷ θεοπρεπεῖ τῶν ἀρετῶν ἱδρύεται, ᾧ καὶ λέγεσθαι (*l.* λέγεται) προστίθεσθαι.

[f] τὸ ῥητόν.

[g] ἀλληγοροῦντες.

[h] See the first note on this section.

[i] διάβασις λογικὴ καὶ οὐρανία. The syntax and meaning of the sentence are uncertain however. Aucher renders, " etenim populus certe Dei est, ut ita dixerim, et transactus rationalis caelestisque," but in a footnote he proposes an alternative rendering, " . . . Dei est ut dictione locutioneque praeditus, et provectus, is qui est rationalis . . ."

[j] The Arm. has the ablative case of the rel. pron., perhaps because of a misreading of ἀφεῖσα as ἀφ' ἧς.

[k] ἀπὸ τοῦ συνδέτου (*sc.* σώματος), *cf. Leg. All.* iii. 72.

[l] Apparently Philo here alludes not to the conventional equation of σῆμα (= σημεῖον) and σῶμα but to the idea of a dead body being naked of soul.

[m] προπάτορα. There does not seem to be any instance of this epithet applied to Abraham in the LXX.

but not "first-born"[a] inheriting all from his divine Father and being without share in a mother or female line.[b]

154. (Gen. xxv. 20)[c] Why was Isaac forty years old when he took Rebekah to wife?[d]

The fortieth year is the right time for the marriage[e] of the wise man,[f] for it is good (for him) to be trained and directed and abound in the right forms[g] of discipline[h] in youth and to have regard for nothing else whatever and not to wander in any other direction toward things which are not to be liked but thoroughly to enjoy the thoughts and company of those (studies) and be more happy in them. It is necessary to receive enjoyment of love and affection from a wife and to fulfil the law concerning the rearing of children.[i] For the generation of living beings[j] (is accomplished) in forty (days), during which, physicians say, the seed injected into the womb is formed[k] and, especially when it is a male, becomes a formed creature.[l] For at

[a] πρωτόγονον, here apparently reserved for Isaac.

[b] On the allegorical motherlessness of Isaac see above, *QG* iv. 145.

[c] At this point, probably the beginning of Book VI in the original form of Philo's *Quaestiones*, begins the Old Latin version of the *Quaestiones in Genesin*, extending to the end of Book IV. The date of this Old Latin version (hereafter abbreviated as *OL*) will be discussed in Appendix B. In the notes I cite the *OL* text as reprinted by Aucher from the 1538 edition. Here it may be noted that *OL* is often paraphrastic rather than literal, if we assume that the Armenian version is literal.

[d] Philo here abbreviates the biblical verse which gives Rebekah's genealogy.

[e] The Arm. uses two words to render γάμος.

[f] τοῦ σοφοῦ.

[g] ὀρθοῖς εἴδεσι or ὀρθαῖς ἰδέαις. *OL* "spiculis" must be a corruption of "speciebus."

[h] τῆς παιδείας.

[i] τῆς παιδοτροφίας.

[j] ἡ ζῳογονία.

[k] κτίζεσθαι or πλάττεσθαι.

[l] κτίσμα or πλάσμα. On the forty-day duration of the male embryo see *QG* i. 25, ii. 14 and iv. 27.

this time it was not for the sake of irrational sensual pleasure [a] or with eagerness [b] that he had intercourse with his wife but for the sake of begetting legitimate children, (and so) it was wholly appropriate that he should undertake marriage when the number of his years was the same as the number of days of the embryo in the womb.

155. (Gen. xxv. 22) [c] Why does (Rebekah) say, " If so it is to be for me, why is this for me ? " [d] ?

Virtuous and a lover of virtue [e] is the mind [f] which announces this not so much by voice as by being sympathetic, and bears itself in mind.[g] For it says, " What (use) was there for me to weigh contrary and opposed (forces) [h] as if in balanced scales, at one time being drawn by opinion [i] and at another time being pulled in the opposite direction by truth. For the uncertainty of the mind [j] is always imperfect and lame and, if one must use the real and proper name, it is also blind. But it is sometimes better to have eyes and to be sharp-sighted for the certain attainment of the knowledge of good and evil.[k] For when someone has come across the nature of either of them and welcomes it [l] or sees it by chance, he necessarily accepts one of them and dismisses the other.

[a] δι' ἄλογον ἡδονήν.

[b] Variant " foolishness."

[c] The two verses, Gen. xxv. 21-22a, not commented on by Philo (but see *De Sacr. Abelis* 4), tell of Rebekah's pregnancy with Jacob and Esau.

[d] LXX εἰ οὕτως μοι μέλλει γίνεσθαι, ἵνα τί μοι τοῦτο : Heb. " If so, why then I ? "

[e] φιλάρετος. [f] ὁ νοῦς or ἡ διάνοια.

[g] The sense is obscure. For " by voice " *OL* has " fastidio."

[h] Symbolized by the twins struggling in Rebekah's womb.

[i] The Arm. translator takes δόξα in the sense of " glory," so too Aucher renders the Arm.

[j] Apparently Philo means the uncertain mind.

[k] γνώσεως τοῦ ἀγαθοῦ καὶ τοῦ κακοῦ (or τοῦ καλοῦ καὶ τοῦ πονηροῦ).

[l] τῇ ἑκατέρου φύσει ἐπιτυχὼν καὶ ἀσπασάμενος.

156. (Gen. xxv. 22) What is the meaning of the words, "She went to inquire of the Lord" [a] ?

This statement [b] is an argument against [c] arrogant and conceited persons who, though they know nothing, admit [d] that they know everything. And they consider nothing (more) shameful and disgraceful (than) searching and being in doubt and inquiring. Wherefore, being afflicted to the end of life with that great disease ignorance and lack of education,[e] they cannot endure to take a physician, by whom they might perhaps easily be cured. But those who have a desire for education [f] are fond of inquiry and fond of learning everything from every source even though they may be elderly.

157. (Gen. xxv. 23) What is the meaning of the words which (the Lord) spoke when she inquired, (namely) "Two nations are in thy womb, and two peoples will be separated from thy womb, and people will surpass people in excellence, and the elder will serve the younger" [g] ?

This statement [h] shows four things. One is most astonishing,[i] for He does not speak of two children in the womb but instead of children speaks of nations. And it is clear that He alludes [j] not to their names but to the nations which were to come into being from both of them, for they were patriarchs [k] of great nations that were later

[a] LXX ἐπορεύθη δὲ πυθέσθαι παρὰ κυρίου: *OL* "perrexit interrogare a domino eloquium Dei."

[b] λόγος.

[c] ἔλεγχος.

[d] ὁμολογοῦσι, here evidently used in irony.

[e] μεγάλῳ πάθει (or νόσῳ) τῆς ἀμαθίας καὶ ἀπαιδευσίας.

[f] παιδείας.

[g] LXX καὶ εἶπεν κύριος αὐτῇ, Δύο ἔθνη ἐν τῇ γαστρί σού εἰσιν, καὶ δύο λαοὶ ἐκ τῆς κοιλίας σου διασταλήσονται· καὶ λαὸς λαοῦ ὑπερέξει, καὶ ὁ μείζων δουλεύσει τῷ ἐλάσσονι. The verse is briefly allegorized by Philo in *Leg. All.* iii. 89 and *De Congressu* 129-130.

[h] λόγος.

[i] παραδοξότατον: *OL* "gloriose dictum."

[j] αἰνίττεται.

[k] πατριάρχαι.

to appear.[a] And second, what was most useful [b] and help ful, they were not to admit confusion but separation and distinction and division, one people from the other, so far as opinion goes, but in reality, prudence and imprudence.[c] For this reason (Scripture) first mentions " nations " and thereafter speaks of " peoples," (so) naming them with reason and prudence.[d] And this is a most helpful distinction of opposed concepts,[e] since one of them desires wickedness, and the other virtue.[f] And third, what is most just, that equals should not be mixed and put together with unequals,[g] whence it is excellently said, " people will surpass people in excellence," for it is necessary for one of the two to surpass the other and to increase, and for the other to decrease and to diminish. And " to surpass in excellence " again means the following, that the good man shall surpass the bad, and the righteous the unrighteous, and the temperate man the intemperate.[h] For one of them is heavenly and worthy of the divine light, and the other is earthy and corruptible and like darkness.[i] And fourth, what is most truthful, that " the elder will serve the younger," for evil is older in time, since from our earliest age it grows with us, while virtue is younger and is acquired by us with difficulty and at the last belatedly,

[a] Aucher renders less accurately, " quia patriarchae magnarum gentium deinde apparituri erant " : *OL* more briefly " qui postmodum principes magnarum gentium fierent."

[b] *OL* " propheticum," which indicates a confusion between χρήσιμος and χρησμός.

[c] σωφροσύνην καὶ ἀφροσύνην : *OL* " sapientiam et modestiam." In *De Congressu* the two children in Rebekah's womb symbolize ἀρετή and κακία, as in the next sentence of this section.

[d] κατὰ λόγον καὶ φρόνησιν *vel sim.* : *OL* " quia multum interest verbo et rationabilitati."

[e] λογισμῶν ἐναντίων.

[f] κακίας . . . ἀρετῆς : *OL* " uno inertiam, altero justitiam appetente."

[g] *OL* " ne justa injusto aptentur."

[h] The Arm. uses two words for " temperate " and for " intemperate."

[i] ὁ μὲν οὐράνιος καὶ θείου φωτὸς ἄξιος, ὁ δὲ γεώδης καὶ φθαρτὸς καὶ σκότῳ ὅμοιος.

when the immense excesses of passion [a] have extended their strength (to the utmost) and have (then) become lax. For it is then that the mind [b] begins to judge and discriminate and obtain sovereign rule.[c] And these things are said to us,[d] for who does not know that heaven has no share or mixture or part of evil, nor do whatever sense-perceptible gods [e] are borne in a circle around it, for they are all good and altogether most perfect in virtue.[f] But in the world [g] temperance (and) prudence [h] are older than folly and imprudence, and justice [i] is older than injustice, and so are the several other (virtues) older than their opposite dispositions.[j] In the human race, however, the opposite and contrary of this (is true), for the good, as I have said, is more recent and younger, while its opposite, folly,[k] has been established in us almost from youth and continues. Nevertheless, the younger [l] is the ruler and sovereign of the elder by the law of nature.[m]

158. (Gen. xxv. 24) What is the meaning of the words, "Fulfilled were the days for her to give birth" [n]?

The birth of the wise man [o] is not defective as to the month or the day but is full and perfect and consists of

[a] ἄπειροι ἀμετρίαι παθῶν.
[b] ὁ νοῦς.
[c] ἡγεμονικὴν ἀρχήν.
[d] *i.e.* for our benefit. *OL* has "haec tamen pro nobis dicta sunt."
[e] ὅσοι αἰσθητοὶ θεοί, *i.e.* the stars, similarly designated in *De Opif. Mundi* 27 and elsewhere.
[f] πάντως (read πάσαις?) ἀρεταῖς τελειότατοι: *OL* "in omnibus necessariis perfectissimi."
[g] ἐν τῷ κόσμῳ.
[h] σωφροσύνη (καὶ) φρόνησις.
[i] δικαιοσύνη.
[j] τῶν ἐναντίων διαθέσεων.
[k] Or "wickedness."
[l] *i.e.* virtue.
[m] τῷ φύσεως νόμῳ. This phrase probably modifies "the elder" rather than "is ruler and sovereign." *OL* has "pravitas . . . regitur a juveniore non temporis lege sed naturae."
[n] LXX καὶ ἐπληρώθησαν αἱ ἡμέραι τοῦ τεκεῖν αὐτήν.
[o] τοῦ σοφοῦ.

perfect numbers.[a] That is the literal meaning.[b] But as for the deeper meaning,[c] (this) must be said. When the soul of the virtuous man becomes filled with the contemplation of wisdom,[d] which, like the day and the sun,[e] illumines the whole reason and the mind,[f] then it begins to give birth to opposites[g] in the separation of distinction and discrimination between holy and profane.

159. (Gen. xxv. 24) What is the meaning of the words, "There were twins in her womb"[h]?

The literal meaning[i] is easily discerned and clear. But one should not fail to recognize the symbolical meaning,[j] that just as two shoots grow from a single root, (so) in the very same mind[k] (there exists) the form[l] of that which is good and of that which is evil, and by nature they are twin.[m] For the soul[n] flees and withdraws and is unable to act but retreats from the proximity of one and goes over to the other.[o] Moreover, the powers[p] which are in the

[a] *ἐκ τελείων ἀριθμῶν*. See *QG* iv. 154.
[b] *τὸ ῥητόν*.
[c] *τὸ πρὸς διάνοιαν*.
[d] *ὅταν ἡ τοῦ σπουδαίου ψυχὴ πεπλήρωται τῶν τῆς σοφίας θεωριῶν* (or *ἰδεῶν*): Aucher "quum animus virtute pollens sit plenus sapientiae speciebus": *OL* "cum studiosa anima saginata fuerit sapientiae institutis."
[e] *OL* "vice meridiani luminis."
[f] *τὸν νοῦν*.
[g] *ἐναντιότητας*, symbolized by the twins in Rebekah's womb, see the preceding section.
[h] LXX *καὶ τῇδε ἦν δίδυμα ἐν τῇ γαστρὶ* (*v.l.* *κοιλίᾳ*: Heb. "belly") *αὐτῆς*.
[i] *τὸ ῥητόν*.
[j] *τὸ συμβολικόν*.
[k] *ἐν τῷ αὐτῷ νῷ*.
[l] *τὸ εἶδος*.
[m] *φύσει δίδυμα*. A similar notion is expressed in *De Sacr. Abelis* 4 and *De Ebrietate* 8. On the phraseology see notes below.
[n] *ἡ ψυχή*.
[o] *i.e.* vacillates between the opposite courses. *OL* paraphrases, "cunctante anima pro utrorumque obsequio, per absentiam enim unius obsecundat altero."
[p] *αἱ δυνάμεις*: Aucher "virtutes": *OL* "valetudinis" (*l.* "valetudines").

body experience the same thing as this, for desires and sensual pleasures and pains [a] are from the same root, as the poet says,[b] (and) whatever things are divided and separated from the top [c] are both divided at the extremities.[d] But these give place to their opposites in respect to the place of chief authority,[e] for when sensual pleasure is powerful and superior, pain retreats and gives place,[f] but when the latter seizes it, sensual pleasure becomes power-

[a] ὀρέξεις καὶ ἡδοναὶ καὶ ἀλγηδόνες. *OL* has more briefly "libido enim et dolor."

[b] In *De Ebrietate* 8 the same notion is attributed to a παλαιὸς λόγος, which Colson in his note *ad loc.* supposes to be *Phaedo* 60 B, where Socrates in discussing the opposed feelings τὸ ἡδύ and τὸ λυπηρόν says, in part, ἐκ μιᾶς κορυφῆς ἡμμένω δύ' ὄντε. A more probable source, called to my attention by my colleague, Prof. B. Einarson, is Sophocles (*Incert. Frag.* 824 in Nauck², 910 in Pearson),

> χῶρος γὰρ αὐτός ἐστιν ἀνθρώπου φρενῶν
> ὅπου τὸ τέρπον καὶ τὸ πημαῖνον φύει.

Prof. Einarson also informs me that the same idea is expressed by Plutarch, *Consolatio ad Uxorem* 609 B.

[c] ἐκ τῆς κορυφῆς, see the preceding note.

[d] περὶ τὰ ἄκρα *vel sim.*: Aucher renders, "quae ex uno vertice distincta divisaque sunt, utriusque eorum summitates separatae comperiuntur": *OL* omits. The repetition of the idea of division in respect of the top and the extremities (here apparently meaning the root) seems a confusion or textual corruption. The passage in *De Ebrietate* 8 reads more intelligibly ὥσπερ γὰρ ἡδονὴν καὶ ἀλγηδόνα φύσει μαχομένας . . . εἰς μίαν κορυφὴν συνάψας ὁ θεὸς ἑκατέρας αἴσθησιν οὐκ ἐν ταὐτῷ . . . οὕτως ἀπὸ μιᾶς ῥίζης τοῦ ἡγεμονικοῦ τά τε ἀρετῆς καὶ κακίας διττὰ ἀνέδραμεν ἔρνη μήτε βλαστάνοντα μήτε καρποφοροῦντα ἐν ταὐτῷ.

[e] Construction and meaning doubtful. Aucher renders, "atque ita contrariis cedunt a principio partibus principatus." *OL* omits.

[f] Aucher ignores the syntax in rendering, "namque quum fortior ac superior sit voluptate dolor, illa vitans abscedit." *OL* has more briefly "agitante enim libidine dolor, caelatur."

ful.[a] In similar fashion every virtue [b] (is related) to every vice, and conversely. For wisdom [c] gives place to folly, and temperance [d] to unbridled lasciviousness, and injustice [e] to justice, and cowardice [f] to courage, and the other contraries similarly.

160. (Gen. xxv. 25) Why was the first-born ruddy and like a hairy hide? [g]

What is said (here) is clear.[h] The ruddy body and the hairy hide are a sign of a savage man [i] who rages furiously in the manner of a wild beast. For a reddish and sanguine aspect is the same as the colour of those who are angry, and character,[j] truly like a hide [k] and whatever else is very hairy, is found (to be) a covering and outer garment and a protection and guard over cunning and aggression.[l] And through this he is everywhere easily captured, for the wicked man, as much as he schemes and contrives to find (a way of making) himself hard to capture, is so much (the more) easily captured by those who follow wisdom [m] and use it. But a distinction should be made between "first-

[a] The context requires us to suppose that the original read "sensual pleasure loses power" or the like. *OL* reads more intelligibly "porro si is [*i.e.* dolor] tenuerit, illa [*i.e.* libido] subducitur." [b] *ἀρετή*. [c] *σοφία*.

[d] *σωφροσύνη*. In disregard of the syntax of the first two clauses Aucher makes "insipientia" and "intemperantia" the subjects of the verb "give place," whereas in the Arm. text, it is the opposite qualities that form the subjects of the verb. [e] *ἀδικία*. [f] *δειλία*.

[g] LXX *ἐξῆλθεν δὲ ὁ υἱὸς ὁ πρωτότοκος πυρράκης, ὅλος ὡσεὶ δορὰ δασύς* (Heb. "like a mantle of hair").

[h] Following Aucher's emendation of Arm. *erek'* "three" to *erewelik'* "clear."

[i] *ἀγρίου*.

[j] *ἦθος* or *τρόπος*.

[k] *OL* "et moribus insuavis ut pellis." The Arm. word rendered "truly" appears to be a misreading.

[l] *OL* reads differently.

[m] *σοφίαν*.

born " and " first-begotten." [a] For the one is (the offspring) of female and material matter,[b] for the female gives birth; but the first-begotten is a male and (the offspring) of a more responsible power,[c] for it is the property of the male to beget.[d] For the wise and cultivated man [e] comes into being as the portion of the Cause,[f] whereas the wicked man, as the first-born in general,[g] is related to passive matter,[h] which gives birth like a mother.[i] Wherefore among beings [j] some incorporeal powers are rightly said to be first-begotten,[k] and some call them " forms " [l] and " measures " and " types." [m] But sense-perceptible things are not so completed,[n] for the forms without a mother are from the Cause alone, while sense-perceptible things are

[a] Philo seems to be making an artificial distinction between *πρωτότοκος*, used of Esau in the LXX, and *πρωτόγονος*, used by him elsewhere in a laudatory sense.

[b] The Arm. lit. = *ὑλικῶν ὑλῶν*. Aucher renders more smoothly but less literally, " humidae materiae." *OL* omits these last two words.

[c] *αἰτιωτέρας δυνάμεως*: Aucher " potioris causae virtutis ": *OL* " principalis virtutis."

[d] Arm. *cnanel* = both *τίκτειν*, as in the first part of this sentence, and *γεννᾶν*, as here.

[e] *ὁ σοφὸς καὶ ἀστεῖος*.

[f] *i.e.* the active and divine principle in contrast to the female and passive principle or matter. Aucher renders somewhat inaccurately, " siquidem sapiens et generosus sortitus est causam propriam." *OL* condenses and paraphrases, " adeo primogenitus melior."

[g] Arm. *əndhanour* usu. = *καθόλου* or *καθολικός*. Aucher, perhaps rightly, here renders, " in genere."

[h] Prob. *παθητῇ ὕλῃ*: Aucher " vitiosis materiae complicibus ": *OL* " fluxu materiali passibilis."

[i] On Philo's concept of matter as mother see Wolfson, *Philo*, i. 267.

[j] *οὐσίαις*.

[k] *ἀσώματοί τινες δυνάμεις δικαίως λεγόμεναι πρωτόγονοι*.

[l] *εἴδη*, or " ideas "—*ἰδέας*.

[m] *καὶ μέτρα καὶ τύπους*. See *De Opif. Mundi* 34, 130.

[n] *τὰ αἰσθητὰ οὐχ οὕτως τελειωθέντα*. Aucher follows the Arm. order in placing the negative after the word meaning " completed " and renders, " sensibilia vero perfectione praedita, non ita."

completed by matter, which not ineptly might be said to be the mother of created things.[a]

161. (Gen. xxv. 25) Why is the man called Esau ?[b]

" Esau " is interpreted as " a thing made "[c] or as " oak,"[d] both being clearly expressive and indicative of character.[e] For the man of evil character is full of fictions and sugared wisdom,[f] as if trained in these and used to them, but he does not think of anything sound. And foolish ignorance,[g] for so I call characters[h] which are unbending and stiff-necked and unyielding, is similar to an oak, which will be broken sooner than bend or yield.

162. (Gen. xxv. 26) What is the meaning of the words, " After this went out his brother "[i] ?

Virtue and vice[j] are brothers inasmuch as they are the offspring of the same soul.[k] And they are enemies inasmuch as they are opposed to each other and fight. Wherefore, though they come together and are united as by necessity[l] and are connected by some bond, they desire

[a] τῶν γενομένων.

[b] Arm. *Isaw* ; LXX Ἠσαύ: Heb. *'Ēśaw*.

[c] πλάσμα or ποίημα.

[d] δρῦς. The same etymologies are given in *De Congressu* 61, *cf. De Sacr. Abelis* 17. The first etymology is based on Heb. *'āśā(h)* " to make," the second on Heb. *'ēṣ* " tree." *OL*, making the interpretations part of the question instead of the beginning of the answer, renders, " factura vel rubor " (*l.* " robur ").

[e] τρόπου.

[f] Aucher " blandis sapientiis " : *OL*, paraphrasing, " infidus."

[g] Or " wickedness."

[h] Following Aucher in reading Arm. *bars* for *bans* (λόγους).

[i] LXX καὶ μετὰ τοῦτο (*v.l.* τοῦτον : Heb. " afterwards ") ἐξῆλθεν ὁ ἀδελφὸς αὐτοῦ.

[j] ἀρετὴ καὶ κακία.

[k] τῆς αὐτῆς ψυχῆς.

[l] ἀνάγκῃ.

separation. And when they are loosed and drawn apart and freed, they become distinct.[a]

163. (Gen. xxv. 26) Why did the hand of the second (child) seize and hold the sole[b] of the foot of the elder ?

Because[c] the noble understanding[d] is a fighter and contestant[e] and is by nature good in battle,[f] always opposing passion[g] and not allowing it to raise itself and rise up. But to seize and hold the heel shows strength of character in the victor and in him who does not allow passion to be refractory and unbridled,[h] and (it shows) the weakness[i] of him who is seized. And if one receives these things not with his eyes but with his understanding and mind,[j] he will grasp the greatest causes among the virtues.[k] For when the mind gets the upper hand and maintains it, becoming more glorious and proud, it seizes its adversary in its hand and holds him. And passion is lamed when it falls down and is held on the ground. What else, then,

[a] Lit. " they appear clearly."

[b] LXX agrees with Heb. in reading, καὶ ἡ χεὶρ αὐτοῦ ἐπειλημμένη τῆς πτέρνης Ἠσαύ : so too Arm. O.T. Farther on in this section as elsewhere, *e.g.* in *De Mut. Nom.* 81, Philo makes Jacob the symbol of the πτερνιστής on the basis of the resemblance (implied in the Heb. of Gen. xxv. 26) between the name *Ya'aqôb* and the word *'āqēb* " heel." *OL* here has " calcaneum," as does Philo below. We must therefore assume that the Arm. translator is inaccurate here.

[c] Reading, with Aucher, Arm. *k'anzi* for *kam zi*.

[d] ὁ σπουδαῖος λογισμός (or νοῦς) : *OL* " studiosus animus."

[e] ἀγωνιστής or, as Philo elsewhere calls Jacob, ἀσκητής.

[f] *OL* " strenuus." Aucher renders freely, " paratus ad mortem."

[g] πάθει : *OL* " vitium " : Aucher " cupiditatibus."

[h] Similarly *OL*, " luctatoris non admittendis (*l.* " admittentis ") malum exaceruari." Aucher renders less accurately, " victoris, qui vix sinit jugum detrectare."

[i] ἀσθένειαν.

[j] λογισμῷ καὶ νῷ.

[k] *OL* " inveniet facultates virtutis idoneas."

must we consider this than the possession[a] of moral excellence?[b] Whence he received the accurate name of Supplanter,[c] whom the Hebrews call "Jacob."

164. (Gen. xxv. 26) Why is Isaac said to have begotten sons (at the age) of sixty years[d]?

The number sixty[e] is the measure which includes in itself those (bodies) which are the zodiac in the world when the twelve pentagons are numbered together.[f] The same relation[g] which the number six bears to the units the number sixty (bears) to the tens. For through the hexad the entire heaven and world were made,[h] and in his sixtieth (year) the perfect man[i] begat (sons), in accordance with his kinship with the world,[j] for as the number sixty is kin to the number six, so the virtuous man[k] (is kin) to the entire world. Wherefore just as there is in the world something which is a pure substance,[l] which the heaven obtains

[a] Possibly the Arm. translator read *σχέσις* for *ἄσκησις*.

[b] *καλοκἀγαθίας* or *εὐηθείας*.

[c] *πτερνιστής* is here rendered by two Arm. words. Aucher has "Deceptorem et Supplantatorem."

[d] Philo here differs slightly from Scripture, which says that Isaac was sixty years old when Rebekah bore him sons.

[e] This seems to be the only passage in which Philo speculates on the symbolism of 60.

[f] Aucher renders, "quinque angulorum duodecim divisionibus simul sumptis." *OL* has something quite different. What the pentagons are is far from clear to me. But see Plato, *Timaeus* 55 c, on the dodecahedron (of which the twelve sides are pentagons) which God is said to use for the decoration (*διαζωγραφῶν*) of the cosmos. R. G. Bury in the Loeb Plato remarks *ad loc.* "The reference may be to the signs of the zodiac."

[g] *λόγον*: *OL* "elegantiam" (!).

[h] *Cf. De Opif. Mundi* 89 *ὁ σύμπας κόσμος ἐτελειώθη κατὰ τὴν ἑξάδος ἀριθμοῦ τελείου φύσιν.* For similar passages see Staehel, pp. 32-34.

[i] *ὁ τέλειος.*

[j] *κατὰ τὴν πρὸς τὸν κόσμον συγγένειαν*: *OL* "secundum seculi proximitatem."

[k] *ὁ σπουδαῖος*: *OL* "strenuus."

[l] *καθαρὰ οὐσία.*

as its lot, and there is something mixed and corruptible,[a] (namely) whatever is sublunary,[b] so also, says (Scripture), is it fitting that the offspring of the virtuous man be distinguished and separated into a mortal and immortal (son).[c] For of these sons one is heavenly and the other earthly.[d]

*165. (Gen. xxv. 27)[e] Why was Esau a hunter and man of the fields, and Jacob a simple man, living at home[f]?

This passage admits of allegorizing,[g] for the wicked man is (so) in a twofold way, being a hunter and a man of the fields. Wherefore? Because just as a hunter spends his time with dogs and beasts, so does the cruel man[h] with passions and evils, of which some, which are like beasts, make the mind[i] wild and untamed and intractable and ferocious and bestial; and some (are like) dogs because they indulge immoderate impulses[j] and in all things act madly and furiously. In addition to this, being a man of the fields, he is without a city and a fugitive from the laws,[k] unknowing[l] of right behaviour[m] and unbridled and refractory and not having anything in common with righteous and good men, and an enemy of intercourse, humaneness and community,[n] and leading an unsocial life.[o] But the

[a] μικτὸν καὶ φθαρτόν. [b] ὅσα κάτω σελήνης.

[c] Symbolized by Esau and Jacob.

[d] ὁ μὲν οὐράνιος, ὁ δὲ γήινος.

[e] Philo comments on this verse in *Leg. All.* iii. 2-3 and, more briefly, in *De Plantatione* 44 and *De Congressu* 62.

[f] LXX καὶ ἦν Ἠσαὺ ἄνθρωπος εἰδὼς κυνηγεῖν, ἄγροικος· Ἰακὼβ δὲ ἦν ἄνθρωπος ἄπλαστος, οἰκῶν οἰκίαν. [g] ἀλληγορίαν.

[h] Arm. *džneay* usu. = δεινός. Aucher here renders, "nefarius": *OL* "pravus."

[i] τὸν νοῦν or τὴν διάνοιαν.

[j] ἀμέτροις ὁρμαῖς. *OL* curiously renders, "justo plus satiati."

[k] *Leg. All.* iii. 3 reads a little differently ἄπολις . . . καὶ ἄοικος, φυγὰς ἀρετῆς ὤν. [l] Lit. "untasting."

[m] Aucher renders, "rectae vitae gustûs nescius."

[n] οἰκειότητος καὶ φιλανθρωπίας καὶ κοινωνίας.

[o] ἄμικτον βίον.

wise and cultivated man,[a] on the other hand, possesses both of the following (qualities): he is simple and he lives at home. A simple nature shows the truth of simplicity [b] and a lack of flattery and hypocrisy, while hypocrites, flatterers and charlatans [c] contrive to show the opposite. Moreover, the domestic care of the house is an antithesis to living in the fields,[d] for one of these (states) is household-management [e] and is a special instance of statecraft on a small scale,[f] since statecraft and household-management are related virtues,[g] which, it would not be amiss to show, are, as it were, interchangeable, both because statecraft is household-management in the state, and because household-management is statecraft in the home.

*166. (Gen. xxv. 28) Why does (Scripture) say, " Isaac loved Esau, and Rebekah was loving Jacob " [h] ?

Who would not admire the position of the names which stand contrasted and dexterously placed, being aptly and

[a] ὁ σοφὸς καὶ ἀστεῖος. *OL* has simply " urbanus."

[b] τὸ ἄπλαστον ἦθος δηλοῖ τὴν τῆς ἁπλότητος ἀλήθειαν. The Greek frag. from Procopius paraphrases, μηδὲν ἔχων ἐπίπλαστον ἢ ἐπείσακτον κακόν. *OL* renders, " infictum insinuat pro simplicitate."

[c] γόητες or φαρμακεῖς, *cf. Quis Rer. Div. Heres* 302 οἱ γόητες, οἱ κόλακες, οἱ πιθανῶν σοφισμάτων εὑρεταί.

[d] The Greek frag. (which ends here) reads ἴσως δὲ καὶ ἀντιδιαστέλλει τῷ κυνηγέτῃ Ἠσαὺ καὶ ἐν ὑπαίθρῳ διάγοντι. *OL* has " ita ruralitas dissipat statum domesticum."

[e] οἰκονομία.

[f] τῆς ἐλάττονος πολιτείας περιγραφή *vel sim.*: Aucher " et urbanitatis exiguae comprehensio " : *OL* " ut civili albo conscriptus." With the notion expressed here compare *De Josepho* 38 οἰκία τε γὰρ πόλις ἐστὶν ἐσταλμένη καὶ βραχεῖα, καὶ οἰκονομία συνηγμένη τις πολιτεία.

[g] συγγενεῖς ἀρεταί.

[h] LXX ἠγάπησεν δὲ Ἰσαὰκ τὸν Ἠσαύ, ὅτι ἡ θήρα αὐτοῦ βρῶσις αὐτῷ· (this clause is discussed in the following section) Ῥεβέκκα δὲ ἠγάπα τὸν Ἰακώβ. LXX follows Heb. in distinguishing the aorist and imperfect aspects in the two occurrences of ἀγαπᾶν.

fittingly adjusted to the correct writing? [a] For "loved" as a narrative (tense) [b] indicates past time,[c] while "was loving" (indicates) what is always present and is eternally the same without ever admitting an end or termination.[d] And may it not be that this is rightly (said)? [e] For the admission of evil and weakness,[f] if it does sometimes occur, is shortlived and ephemeral,[g] but that of virtue [h] is, in a certain sense, immortal,[i] since it does not admit of regret or change of mind.[j]

*167. (Gen. xxv. 28) Why does he (Isaac) love (Esau) for some (stated) reason, for (Scripture) says, "because his venison was food for him," [k] while his mother loved (Jacob) without a reason? [l]

[a] Similarly *OL*, "quis non miretur nominum positionem, tam recte et aptissime rebus consonantem?" The Greek frag. has more briefly and clearly *τίς δ' ἂν οὐκ ἀγάσαιτο τὸ "ἠγάπησε τὸν Ἠσαύ· ἡ δὲ Ῥεβέκκα ἠγάπα τὸν Ἰακώβ"*;

[b] One Arm. MS. omits "as a narrative (tense)."

[c] The Greek frag. has *παρελήλυθε*.

[d] Similarly *OL*, "quod vero diligitur adest utrique et sempiternatur sine fine defectionis." The Greek frag. has much more briefly *πάρεστιν ἀεί*.

[e] There is no parallel to this sentence in the Greek frag. or *OL*.

[f] The Greek frag. has more briefly *ἀποδοχὴ τοῦ φαύλου*. *OL* has "prava conversatio."

[g] *ὀλιγοχρόνιός ἐστι καὶ ἐφήμερος*, as in the Greek frag.: *OL* "temporalis, utpote diurna, non diuturna est."

[h] *τοῦ σπουδαίου*, as in the Greek frag. *OL* "respui" (*marg.* "reprobi") must be an error for "recti" or the like.

[i] *τρόπον τινὰ ἀθανατίζεται*. The Greek frag. has simply *ἀθανατίζεται*. *OL*, misunderstanding *τρόπον τινά*, has "mores immortales." The sentences following *ἀθανατίζεται* in the Greek frag. (Harris, p. 39) belong to the following section, *QG* iv. 167. [j] *μετάνοιαν ἢ μετάμελος*: *OL* "impoenitibiles."

[k] LXX *ὅτι ἡ θήρα αὐτοῦ βρῶσις αὐτῷ*: Heb. "because venison was in his mouth."

[l] *i.e.* without a reason for Rebekah's love being stated in Scripture.

Most wisely is (this said), for virtue [a] is not loved for any other reason.[b] And concerning this some of the younger (philosophers) and those who are recent,[c] having received their virtue-loving opinions directly from Moses as from a source,[d] (have stated) that the good alone is desired and pleasing for its own sake. But that which is not of this nature (is loved) for its usefulness.[e] And so, (Scripture) adds, " he loved (him) because his venison was food for him." And this is most natural,[f] for it is not the venison that it speaks of as food but his hunting of character itself as of a wild animal. And this indeed is the way it is. The soul of the philosopher [g] is not nourished or fed by anything so much as by being able to hunt down the passions [h] and to keep all vice at bay.

*168. (Gen. xxv. 29) What is the meaning of the words, " And Jacob prepared a preparation " [i] ?

I know that things of this kind provide (occasion for) ridicule and mocking derision to uncultivated men and

[a] The brief Greek frag. has τὸ σπουδαῖον : Aucher, following the *OL* " studiosus," has " virtute praeditus." In Arm. the adjective can be either neuter or masculine.

[b] *i.e.* other than itself. The Greek frag. reads οὐ δι' ἕτερόν τι ἀγαπᾶται : *OL* " ex utraque parte diligitur."

[c] Aucher renders, " nonnulli juniorum novissimorumque": *OL* has simply " nonnulli." There seem to be no other references in Philo to οἱ νεώτεροι which clearly indicate to what school of thought he refers.

[d] εὐθὺς δεχόμενοι ὡς ἀπὸ πηγῆς τινος παρὰ Μωυσέως τὰς φιλαρέτους γνώμας (*vel sim.*) : *OL* has merely " imitantes Mosen."

[e] The Greek frag. (which resumes here) has τὸ δὲ μὴ τοιοῦτον, ἐκ τῶν χρειῶν.

[f] φυσικώτατον. *OL*, misconstruing, reads " esca fuit ei naturalis suumque edictum est."

[g] ἡ τοῦ φιλοσόφου ψυχή. [h] τὰ πάθη.

[i] LXX ἥψησεν δὲ Ἰακὼβ ἕψεμα (similarly Arm. Philo below) : Heb. " And Jacob cooked a cooking " (A.V. " And Jacob sod pottage ").

those who lack consistency of character [a] and do not recognize any form or appearance of virtue [b] and attribute their own uneducatedness and stupidity and perversity [c] and thoughtlessness to the holy Scriptures, which are more truthful than any other thing. And the reason for this is that just as the blind merely touch and approach and come near to bodies by touch but are not able to perceive their colour, shape, form or any other particular property whatever, so also uneducated, untrained and untaught men, blinded in soul [d] and thick-skinned,[e] dwell on the literal meaning only rather than on the (content of the) narrative [f] and touch and deal with only the words and the literal text.[g] But they are unable to look into the inner (meaning) at the intelligible forms.[h] And the literal meaning [i] contains a not insignificant [j] reproof of the intemperate man [k] for the admonition of those who can be cured.[l] For it was not for the sake of a trifling cooked pottage that (Esau) gave up his rights as first-born [m] and yielded to the younger (brother) but because he made himself a slave to the pleasures of the belly.[n] Let him be reproved and con-

[a] *τοῖς ἀμούσοις καὶ τοῖς ἀναρμόστοις τὸ ἦθος.* [b] *ἀρετῆς.*

[c] Text slightly emended by Aucher.

[d] Lit. " in eyes of the soul."

[e] Meaning uncertain : Aucher " caecutientes."

[f] Meaning uncertain : Aucher renders, " supra litteras tantum insidunt." *OL* has " in sermone narrationis occupati." [g] *τοῖς ὀνόμασι καὶ τοῖς ῥητοῖς λόγοις.*

[h] *πρὸς τὰ νοητὰ εἴδη.*

[i] The Greek frag. (which begins here) has *τὸ ῥητὸν τῆς διηγήσεως.*

[j] Lit. " small." The Greek frag. omits the adjective.

[k] *ἔλεγχον τοῦ ἀκολάστου*, as in the Greek frag.

[l] *πρὸς νουθεσίαν τῶν θεραπεύεσθαι δυναμένων*, as in the Greek frag.

[m] *τῶν πρεσβείων*, as in the Greek frag., which, however, does not begin the sentence with *οὐ γάρ*, as does the text followed by the Arm., but with *ὁ γάρ*, and therefore has no contrast between the two clauses.

[n] So the Greek frag., *δοῦλος γαστρὸς ἡδοναῖς* : *OL* " famulus ventris."

demned as one who never was zealous for restraint and continence.[a] (The passage) also contains what is in accordance with the appearance of opinion, (namely) a most natural explanation of the narrative.[b] For everything that is cooked is dissolved, and there is a decrease and loss of the virtue [c] which it formerly had. And to this is passion [d] likened in form (by Scripture). For this is unsalted and unbelieving.[e] And the self-restraint of continence loosens and dissolves it through reason [f] by tearing apart and cutting up its sinews and strength.

*169. (Gen. xxv. 29) Why does (Scripture) say, " Esau came from the field, giving up " [g] ?

In the case of the patriarchs,[h] giving up is said to be adding,[i] for when they give up mortal life, they are added to the other life.[j] But the wicked man has only a deficiency, since he suffers only from an incessant hunger for virtue [k] more than from that for food and drink.

[a] The Greek frag. reads a little differently εἰς ὄνειδος προκείσθω τῶν μήποτε ζῆλον ἐγκρατείας λαβόντων. Originally, perhaps, the Greek was τοῦ μήποτε . . . λαβεῖν, as in the Arm. and *OL* " vituperator (*l.* " vituperatur ") nullum continentiae zelum sectando."

[b] The above is a literal translation of the obscure Arm., which Aucher more freely renders, " habet et opinionis locus naturalem quandam rationem historiae elucidandae." *OL* paraphrases, " ita altiora intellectu hujus dicti veritatis titulos commendat."

[c] τῆς δυνάμεως : *OL* " virtute."

[d] πάθος.

[e] The Arm. lit. = ἄναλον καὶ ἀπειθές, and seems to be corrupt. *OL* reads " quod poterat non coctum (*marg.* " contactum ") nullo subjacere improperio."

[f] λόγῳ. For a parallel to the idea see *De Sacr. Abelis* 81.

[g] LXX ἐκλείπων : Heb. " weary."

[h] The Greek frag. has τῶν σπουδαίων.

[i] So the Greek frag., ἡ ἔκλειψις εἶναι λέγεται πρόσθεσις.

[j] Lit. " to that life." The Greek frag. has ἀθανάτῳ ζωῇ : *OL* " immortalitas."

[k] So the Greek frag., μόνον λιμὸν ἀρετῆς ὑπομένων ἀδιάστατον.

170. (Gen. xxv. 30) Why does (Esau) say, "Give me a taste of that red pottage, for I have given up"[a]?

The passion-loving and unmanly character[b] confesses his hunger for wisdom and prudence[c] and, at the same time, his deficiency in all virtue.[d] For this reason he straightway hastens to taste of passion, not considering this as anything less than his virtue but (as something) cooked[e] and mixed so as to be pleasing for its pleasurable colour.[f] And (Scripture) calls this (pottage) "red," adding (this word) as genuinely related to his passion,[g] for an impulse[h] is more red when passion is reddened[i] or else because it is proper and fitting that those who are in passion should blush and be ashamed of lauding and honouring shameful things as though (they were) good and seemly.

171. (Gen. xxv. 30) Why is his name called "Edom"?

"Edom" translated into the Armenian[j] tongue is called "flame-coloured"[k] or "earthy,"[l] and this name is appropriately given to him who is intemperate and unrestrained in character, and seeks not heavenly and divine things but all that is earthy and corruptible.[m] And not even in sleep

[a] LXX *γεῦσόν με ἀπὸ τοῦ ἑψέματος τοῦ πυρροῦ τούτου ὅτι ἐκλείπω ἐγώ.* In the Heb. the red pottage *'ādōm* is connected with the name *Edom*, descendants of Esau.

[b] *τὸ φιλοπαθὲς καὶ ἄνανδρον ἦθος.*

[c] *λιμὸν σοφίας καὶ φρονήσεως.*

[d] *ὁμοῦ πάσης ἔκλειψιν ἀρετῆς.*

[e] Arm. *amok'eal* means both "cooked" and "tempered." Aucher here renders, "contemperatum." The *OL*, though confused, seems to favour the former rendering.

[f] Variant "to be pleasing as more pleasurable."

[g] Aucher misconstrues, I think, in rendering, "simile vitio suo adjecto."

[h] *ὁρμή.*

[i] Text slightly emended. Aucher renders literally, "quia majorem habet impetum rufa, atque rubicunda cupiditas."

[j] *Sic!* The original, of course, had "Greek."

[k] *φλόγινος vel sim.*

[l] *γήινος*, as in *Quod Deus Immut. Sit* 148.

[m] *οὐ τὰ οὐράνια καὶ θεῖα ἀλλὰ πᾶν γήινον καὶ φθαρτόν.*

does he know the Form that is without quality and shape and form and body,[a] but he is the slave of colours and qualities, by which all the senses [b] are deceived.[c]

*172. (Gen. xxv. 31) Why does his brother say, "Sell me this day thy birthright" [d]?

The literal meaning, it would seem,[e] shows the greed [f] of the younger in wishing to deprive his elder brother of his rights.[g] But the virtuous man is not greedy,[h] inasmuch as he is a companion of frugality and restraint,[i] and is especially helpful in these.[j] He therefore clearly understands that a continuous and unlimited abundance of possessions is the occasion and cause of sin to the wicked man [k] and is necessary to the righteous man alone.[l] And he considers

[a] τὸ ἄποιον καὶ ἀσχημάτιστον καὶ ἄμορφον καὶ ἀσώματον εἶδος. *OL* has merely "in reprehensibilem vitam."

[b] αἱ αἰσθήσεις.

[c] *OL* "quibus per omnem sensum opprimitur," perhaps reading a form of πατεῖσθαι instead of ἀπατᾶσθαι.

[d] LXX Ἀπόδου μοι σήμερον τὰ πρωτοτοκεῖά σου ἐμοί.

[e] τὸ μὲν ῥητόν, οἷα τῷ δοκεῖν, as in the Greek frag. from Cat. Lipsiensis.

[f] The Arm. uses two words to render πλεονεξίαν, which is found in both Greek fragments, Cat. Lips. and Procopius.

[g] So, almost exactly, Cat. Lips., σφετερίζεσθαι ἀδελφοῦ δίκαια ποθοῦντος. The phrase is missing from Procopius.

[h] ὁ δὲ σπουδαῖος οὐ πλεονέκτης, as in Cat. Lips. Procopius has ὅπερ ἀλλότριον σπουδαίου.

[i] So both Greek fragments, ὀλιγοδείας καὶ ἐγκρατείας ἑταῖρος.

[j] The Arm. seems to be a partial misunderstanding of an original text like that in Procopius, καὶ ὠφελητικὸς ἐν τοῖς μάλιστα. Cat. Lips. omits the phrase.

[k] The Greek fragments read slightly differently: Cat. Lips. αἱ ἄφθονοι περιουσίαι τῶν φαύλων χορηγοὶ τῶν ἁμαρτημάτων καὶ ἀδικημάτων αὐτοῖς εἰσιν, Procopius αἱ ἄφθονοι περιουσίαι παντὶ φαύλῳ χορηγοὶ τῶν ἁμαρτημάτων καὶ ἀδικημάτων εἰσίν.

[l] Variant "to righteousness." The Greek fragments omit this last clause.

it most necessary to remove from evil,[a] as from a fire, that matter which is set on fire by heat,[b] for the improvement of character.[c] And this does not harm, but is a great benefit to him who is believed to be harmed.[d] That is the literal meaning.[e] But as for the deeper meaning,[f] it should be understood that the discourse of the wise legislator [g] is not so much about brute animals or possessions or harvested fruits [h] as about the dispositions of souls.[i] For by nature the first-born and elder (brother) is activity in accordance with the several virtues,[j] which [k] the wicked man changes because of the opinions of the multitude. For no one among the imprudent has ever been so mad as to confess that he is evil. Therefore does he say to him,[l] "Do not mistreat [m] all truth as if lying or as if laughing at a stage-performance, but confess at once that virtue [n] is a possession unfamiliar and not genuine or natural [o] to thee, and far removed from it wilt thou pass thy days. But it is familiar and suitable and proper and kin to the cultivated and wise character." [p]

[a] Aucher "improbo," but the Arm. = κακία, as the Greek fragments read.

[b] Aucher renders more freely, "materiam illam, quae ignis magis succendendi causa est."

[c] The Greek fragments read more smoothly τὴν προσαναφλέγουσαν ὕλην, ὡς πυρός, τῆς κακίας ἀφαιρεῖν εἰς βελτίωσιν ἠθῶν.

[d] So the Greek fragments (which end with this sentence), ὅπερ οὐ βλάβην ἀλλὰ μεγίστην ὠφέλειαν περιποιεῖ τῷ ζημιοῦσθαι δοκοῦντι.

[e] τὸ ῥητόν.

[f] τὸ πρὸς διάνοιαν.

[g] ὁ τοῦ σοφοῦ νομοθέτου λόγος, *i.e.* of Moses.

[h] *OL* "pecuniis."

[i] Aucher "de animae statu": *OL* "pro constantia animae."

[j] ἡ κατὰ τὰς ἑκάστας ἀρετὰς ἐνέργεια.

[k] Aucher has "quos," which should be "quas," since "virtutes" is the antecedent of the rel. pron. *OL* has "aquarum," obviously a corruption of "quarum."

[l] *i.e.* Jacob to Esau.

[m] μὴ κακοποιήσῃς *vel sim.* Aucher "noli . . . deturbare."

[n] ἀρετή.

[o] παρὰ φύσιν *vel sim.* Aucher "aliena."

[p] τῷ ἀστείῳ καὶ σοφῷ ἤθει.

*173. (Gen. xxv. 32) Why does he reply as follows, "Behold, I am going to die, and for what is this birthright (to me)?"[a]?

The literal meaning[b] of what is said is a parable,[c] for truly the life of the wicked man hastens to death every day, reflecting on and training for dying.[d] For would he not (otherwise) say,[e] "What is this to me which leads to virtue and happiness?"?[f] "For," he says, "I have something else to choose and to recommend to myself,[g] (namely) to desire sensual pleasure and to seek lasciviousness and to be dissolute and to be greedy and avaricious and whatever else is akin[h] to these things."[i]

*174. (Gen. xxv. 34)[j] What is the meaning of the words, "Esau despised the birthright"[k]?

This legislation[l] is also given by God, agreeing with the earlier one.[m] For just as the virtuous and wise man

[a] LXX ἰδοὺ ἐγὼ πορεύομαι τελευτᾶν, καὶ ἵνα τί μοι ταῦτα τὰ πρωτοτοκεῖα; [b] τὸ ῥητόν.

[c] Arm. *aṙak* = παραβολή, αἴνιγμα, τύπος, etc. Aucher here renders, "aenigma." Procopius has λόγιον, *OL* "eloquium."

[d] Procopius omits the words "every day . . . dying." *OL* has "per singulos dies nec enim meditando."

[e] Variant "for he says."

[f] *OL* reads "adeo non dixit: ad quae mihi primitia, quae dirigunt virtutem et beatitudinem." Procopius reads more smoothly οὐ φησὶ δὲ "ἵνα τί μοι πρωτοτόκια," μετὰ προσθήκης δὲ τοῦ "ταῦτα," ὅ ἐστι τὰ πρὸς ἀρετὴν ἄγοντα καὶ εὐδαιμονίαν. According to this reading, Philo stresses the use of the demonstrative pron. before "birthright."

[g] Aucher "eligere et mihi parare." Procopius has ἐξαίρετα ἕτερα, *OL* "praerogativam." [h] Lit. "brother."

[i] So, almost literally, Procopius. *OL* reads more briefly "libidinis et luxuriae et quaecumque horum similia videntur."

[j] Philo omits comment on Gen. xxv. 33, which tells of Esau's oath and the sale of the birthright to Jacob.

[k] LXX καὶ ἐφαύλισεν Ἠσαῦ τὰ πρωτοτοκεῖα. [l] νομοθεσία.

[m] *OL* reads more briefly "divinum responsum consonat priori."

despises and rejects the things of the wicked man,[a] so the wicked man (despises) the thoughts and deeds and words of the virtuous man.[b] For it is impossible and unviable that concord should ever come into being from harmony and disharmony.[c]

175. (Gen. xxvi. 1) Why does a famine come upon the land beside the earlier famine which came in the time of Abraham ? [d]

It is fitting to inquire why (Scripture) adds, " upon the land," for where else does a famine ever come if not upon the land ? For it is not proper to say " in heaven." But may it not be that the passage contains an allegory ? [e] For the body is an earthy substance [f] about us, and when the virtuous and purified mind [g] dwells in it, it causes a famine not of food and drink but of wrongdoing.[h] And these famines are distinct. The former was a lack of ignorance and uneducatedness [i] in the man who has progressed and become perfect through education and teaching.[j] But superior to this is the destruction of things not in accord

[a] Procopius reads more briefly *κακίζει γὰρ ὥσπερ ὁ ἀστεῖος τὰ τοῦ φαύλου*. *OL* has " solertiam (*l.* " solet enim ") strenuus pravorum spernere facta."

[b] So Procopius, *τὰ τοῦ ἀστείου καὶ βουλεύματα καὶ πράξεις καὶ λόγους*. *OL* has " derogat enim et pravus studiosum."

[c] Procopius reads more briefly *ἀσύμφωνον γὰρ ἁρμονία πρὸς ἀναρμοστίαν*.

[d] LXX *Ἐγένετο δὲ λιμὸς ἐπὶ τῆς γῆς χωρὶς τοῦ λιμοῦ τοῦ πρότερον* (Heb. " the first ") *ὃς ἐγενήθη ἐν τῷ χρόνῳ τοῦ Ἀβραάμ*.

[e] *ἀλληγορίαν*.

[f] *γηίνη οὐσία vel sim.* : *OL* " terrenus sensus " : Aucher " terrenum."

[g] *ὁ σπουδαῖος καὶ καθαρθεὶς νοῦς* : *OL* " pura et sobria mens." [h] *ἀδικιῶν*. [i] *ἔνδεια ἀμαθίας καὶ ἀπαιδευσίας*.

[j] *ἐν τῷ προκόψαντι καὶ τελειωθέντι ἐκ παιδείας καὶ διδασκαλίας*. Here, as often elsewhere in Philo, Abraham is a symbol of virtue acquired through learning in contrast to Isaac as a symbol of natural or self-taught virtue and to Jacob as a symbol of virtue acquired by practice.

with nature [a] in him who possesses virtue by nature, without taking thought or practising but by the power of self-teaching and self-hearing.[b] Both are excellent and agreeable to all happiness and prosperity and sagacity, and are susceptible of joy.[c]

176. (Gen. xxvi. 1) What is the meaning of the words, "Isaac went to Abimelech, king of the Philistines, to Gerara"?

The literal meaning [d] clearly shows his journeying. But as for the deeper meaning,[e] it requires a more exact inquiry and examination, which we shall reveal and make clear through the interpretation of the names. For "Abimelech" is to be interpreted as "father king,"[f] and "Philistines" as "foreigners,"[g] and "Gerara" as "hedge."[h]

177. (Gen. xxvi. 2) Why does the (divine) word [i] say to him, "Do not go down to Egypt"[j]?

[a] Text and meaning uncertain. Aucher renders, "verum his superior est corruptio (vitiorum) praeter naturam." *OL* paraphrases, "novissima <*sc.* "fames"> dissipavit ea quae minus apte videbantur."

[b] αὐτοδιδάκτῳ καὶ αὐτηκόῳ δυνάμει, symbolized by Isaac, *cf. De Plantatione* 168. *OL* renders inaccurately, "naturaliter enim et sine doctrina virtutes acquiruntur obediente fortitudine."

[c] *OL* paraphrases, "ita utraque famis abundantiae et frugalitatis meliores ac laetiores" (*v.l.* "lectiores").

[d] τὸ ῥητόν.

[e] τὸ πρὸς διάνοιαν.

[f] *OL* "paternus rex." The name seems to be etymologized merely as "king" in *De Plantatione* 169.

[g] Philo's etymology is based on the fact that this name is usually rendered in the LXX as ἀλλόφυλοι, though not in this particular verse.

[h] Apparently this fanciful etymology is based on Heb. *gādēr*, *geder*= "wall," "hedge."

[i] Or "oracle," as Aucher renders. *OL* has "eloquium divinum."

[j] LXX ὤφθη δὲ αὐτῷ κύριος καὶ εἶπεν, Μὴ καταβῇς εἰς Αἴγυπτον. The verse is allegorized as here in *Quod Deterius* 46, *De Confus. Ling.* 81, *De Migratione* 29.

The passage [a] is clear, containing in itself nothing dark or unclear. It is to be allegorized [b] as follows. "Egypt" is to be translated as "oppressing," [c] for nothing else so constrains and oppresses the mind [d] as do desire for sensual pleasures [e] and grief and fear. But to the perfected man,[f] who by nature enjoys the happiness of virtue,[g] the sacred and divine word [h] recommends all perfection [i] and not to go down into the passions [j] but to accept impassivity [k] with joy, bidding (the passions) a fond farewell.[l] And to those who are moderate [m] (Scripture) reveals and recommends the middle way [n] because of their weakness, and (this) they accept,[o] not being venturesome or confident and not being able to ascend with him.[p] But those who attain and reach the summit [q] and attain to the very limit of the end do not give any thought [r] at all to that which clings to the ground.[s]

178. (Gen. xxvi. 2-3) Why does He say, "Dwell in the land of which I shall tell thee.[t] And thou shalt dwell sojourning in the land" [u]?

[a] ὁ λόγος. [b] ἀλληγορεῖται.
[c] θλίβων. Philo here plays on the resemblance between Heb. *Miṣrayim* "Egypt" and *mēṣārim* "straits." Elsewhere (*passim*) he makes Egypt a symbol of τὰ κατὰ σῶμα πάθη. Interesting in this connexion is his discussion in *De Migratione* 157-160, where Egypt symbolizes bodily passion, and he remarks, διὰ τὸν ὄγκον μηκέτι χωρεῖν τὸ σῶμα θλιβόμενον κτλ. [d] τὸν νοῦν. [e] ἐπιθυμίαι ἡδονῶν.
[f] τῷ τελειωθέντι, symbolized by Isaac. [g] ἀρετῆς.
[h] ὁ ἱερὸς καὶ θεῖος λόγος. [i] παντέλειαν. [j] κάτω εἰς τὰ πάθη.
[k] ἀπάθειαν, *cf. De Plantatione* 98 ἀπάθειαν ἀντὶ παθῶν.
[l] πολλὰ χαίρειν φράζοντα. [m] τοῖς μετρίοις. [n] μεσότητα.
[o] Aucher punctuates differently and renders, "quia ob infirmitatem id ultro acceptant." *OL* paraphrases freely.
[p] *i.e.* Isaac. [q] πρὸς ἀκρότητα.
[r] Lit. "do not make way." [s] τῷ χαμαιζήλῳ.
[t] LXX κατοίκησον δὲ ἐν τῇ γῇ ᾗ ἄν σοι εἴπω.
[u] The Arm. lit. = παροικίᾳ κατοίκει ἐν τῇ γῇ. LXX has καὶ παροίκει ἐν τῇ γῇ ταύτῃ, as does Philo in *De Confus. Ling.* 81. It is probable that this was the original reading here also.

He indicates a distinction between sojourners and dwellers, for in word [a] men dwell in these cities, but in fact the soul [b] does not show the same dispositions.[c] And He commands the wise man [d] to sojourn [e] in that land which admits of pointing to and touching,[f] but to dwell in that (land) which the divine oracle will command. For the sense-perceptible and earthy [g] is our body. And the soul, which is the principal thing within it, if it is to desire a blessing,[h] should and must (merely) sojourn [i] in it, being mindful of the mother-city,[j] to which it seeks to remove and to dwell there. Wherefore He legislates [k] for the divinely born soul, admonishing and encouraging it to dwell there with constancy. And what other city is a fitting symbol [l] of this character according to the law of allegory [m] if not virtue ? [n]

*179. (Gen. xxvi. 3) What is the meaning of the words, " I will be with thee and I will bless thee " [o] ?

(This) shows the connexion and harmonious order of the things fitted together methodically in the divine oracles.

[a] λόγῳ μέν, contrasted with ἔργῳ δέ in the following clause.

[b] τῆς ψυχῆς.

[c] διαθέσεσι. Aucher renders, " re autem animae in suis dispositionibus vix sese uniformiter habentis."

[d] τῷ σοφῷ.

[e] Lit. " to dwell in sojourning," see note *u* on p. 462.

[f] Aucher renders more freely, " in ea, quam tantummodo videat et tangat, terra." *OL* has " permittitur ergo sapienti incolatus pro spectaculo tantum et actu " (*l.* " tactu "), and adds an explanatory clause. [g] τὸ αἰσθητὸν καὶ γήϊνον.

[h] Arm. *geļeçkabanout'iun* = " beauty of speech " or the like, but here prob. is a too literal rendering of εὐλογίαν, mentioned in the next clause in Scripture and in Philo's next section. Aucher here renders, " pulchrum negotium," *OL* " benivolentiam " (*sic*).

[i] Lit. " dwell in sojourning," see note *u* on p. 462.

[j] τῆς μητροπόλεως. [k] νομοθετεῖ.

[l] αἴνιγμα. [m] κατὰ τὸν τῆς ἀλληγορίας νόμον.

[n] ἀρετή. [o] LXX ἔσομαι μετὰ σοῦ καὶ εὐλογήσω σε.

For God necessarily [a] brings near to man concord and blessing [b] and pleasantness of speech,[c] just as, on the contrary, distance (from God brings) irrationality.[d] For there is no greater evil for the soul than folly and stupidity, when it is deprived of the rational genus, the mind, which is characteristic of it.[e]

*180. (Gen. xxvi. 3) What is the meaning of the words, "I will establish my oath which I swore to thy father" [f]?

First, this must be said, that the words of God do not differ from oaths. And by whom does God swear if not by Himself? [g] And He is said to swear, because of our weakness, for we think that just as in the case of man an oath differs from words, so also is it in the case of God.[h] And since He is blessed and gracious and propitious, He does not judge created beings [i] in accordance with His greatness but in accordance with theirs.[j] And in the

[a] ἐξ ἀνάγκης. [b] ὁμόνοιαν καὶ εὐλογίαν.

[c] Aucher "bonamque eloquentiam": *OL* "complacationem." The Arm. variant seems to be merely an orthographic one.

[d] The Arm. word usu. = ἀλογία. Aucher renders, "privationem verbi (*vel*, rationis)": *OL* "maledictionem." The Arm. variant means "lack of (permanent) dwelling."

[e] Slightly different is the text of the Greek frag., *μεῖζον ἀνθρώπῳ κακὸν ἀφροσύνης οὐδέν ἐστι, τὸ ἴδιον τοῦ λογιστικοῦ γένους, τὸν νοῦν, ζημιωθέντι.*

[f] LXX *καὶ στήσω τὸν ὅρκον μου ὃν ὤμοσα Ἀβραὰμ τῷ πατρί σου.*

[g] So the Greek frag., *ἀδιαφοροῦσιν ὅρκων λόγοι θεοῦ. καὶ κατὰ τίνος ἂν ὤμοσεν ὁ θεός, ὅτι μὴ ἑαυτοῦ;*

[h] So the Greek frag., *λέγεται δὲ ὀμνύναι διὰ τὴν ἡμετέραν ἀσθένειαν τῶν ὑπολαμβανόντων ὡς ἐπ' ἀνθρώπου διαφέρειν λόγων ὅρκους, οὕτως ἐπὶ θεοῦ.* *OL*, taking *διαφέρειν* in the sense of "excel," renders the next to last clause, "juracula hominum fortiora esse verborum."

[i] Lit. "those in generation."

[j] Aucher amplifies in rendering, "juxta eorum (pusillanimitatem)," *OL* "adversus generis possibilitatem." There is no Greek preserved of this sentence.

second place, He wishes to praise the son as one worthy of his father's nobility,[a] for He would not firmly establish the prayers [b] made to the father with an oath, for the sake of the son, if He did not witness the same virtue [c] in him.[d] Cease, therefore, now from praising nobility [e] separately by itself and learn from the divine Scriptures what true (nobility) is, and repent. For this (passage) clearly teaches us to define and judge and discern the well-born (as being) not those who have sprung from good fathers or grandparents and are content with that alone, but those who are themselves emulators of their (fathers') piety.[f] And it is wrong [g] to praise those who are involuntarily good [h] or an involuntary origin,[i] for not by taking thought does each of us come into being,[j] and that which is voluntary is not to be placed in any order,[k] and the voluntary is best and is the acceptance and imitation of the good.[l]

181. (Gen. xxvi. 4a) What is the meaning of the words, "I will multiply thy seed as the stars of heaven" [m] ?

Two things are indicated, in which the nature of all things in general [n] consists, (namely) quantity and quality —quantity in "I will multiply," and quality in "as the stars." So may (thy descendants) be pure and far-shining [o]

[a] εὐγενείας. The Greek frag. has εὐεργίας.

[b] The Greek frag. has εὐλογίας, which makes better sense. *OL* has "foederis."

[c] ἀρετήν, as in the Greek frag. [d] *i.e.* the son.

[e] More lit. "freedom" (of birth)—ἐλευθερίαν: *OL* "generis nobilitatem." [f] εὐσεβείας.

[g] ἄτοπον, apparently rendered here by two Arm. words.

[h] Aucher, taking the adj. as neuter, renders, "involuntaria bona," *OL* "minus ultroneum bonum." [i] γένεσιν.

[j] *OL* "nec enim per cujusdam consilium nascimur."

[k] Meaning not wholly clear. *OL* has "ita enim spontanea bonitas pro nihilo imputatur."

[l] *OL* reads "quoniam spontaneum melius actus testimonium est, et paterna imitatio."

[m] LXX καὶ πληθυνῶ τὸ σπέρμα σου ὡς τοὺς ἀστέρας τοῦ οὐρανοῦ.

[n] κοινῶς (*vel sim.*) ἡ τῶν πάντων φύσις. [o] τηλαυγεῖς.

and always be ranged in order and obey their leader,[a] and may they behave like the luciform (stars) which everywhere with the splendour of ethereal brightness also illumine all other things.

182. (Gen. xxvi. 4b) What is the meaning of the words, "To thy seed I will give all this land" [b]?

The literal text [c] makes clear the special meaning of the Law,[d] in which it is said that only the wise man is rich [e] and that all things belong to the wise man. But as for the deeper meaning,[f] He says, "I will grant to thee all earthly and corporeal substances as if servants subject to a ruler.[g] For I wish thee not to collect revenue [h] and not to exact tribute,[i] which immoderate and insatiable passions determine, but in the manner of a king to be a ruler and leader, and to lead the way rather than be led."

183. (Gen. xxvi. 4c) What is the meaning of the words, "In thy seed [j] will be blessed all the nations of the earth" [k]?

The literal meaning [l] is significant [m] and clear. But as for the deeper meaning,[n] it is to be allegorized [o] as follows.

[a] τῷ ταξιάρχῳ. Probably God is meant as in *De Spec. Leg.* ii. 230 <ψυχαὶ> πειθόμεναι τῷ ταξιάρχῳ.

[b] LXX καὶ δώσω τῷ σπέρματί σου πᾶσαν τὴν γῆν ταύτην (Heb. "all these lands"). In *Quis Rer. Div. Heres* 8 Philo comments on Gen. xxvi. 3-5 as a unit.

[c] τὸ ῥητόν.

[d] τὴν ἰδίαν τοῦ νόμου γνώμην *vel sim.*: *OL* "utpote Dei decreto pronuntiatum."

[e] μόνον ὁ σοφὸς πλούσιος.

[f] τὸ πρὸς διάνοιαν.

[g] *OL* "ut principatum (*l.* "principatui"?) quendam subjectum."

[h] εἰσόδους.

[i] φόρον: *OL* "foenora."

[j] *OL* "in nomine tuo."

[k] LXX καὶ ἐνευλογηθήσονται ἐν τῷ σπέρματί σου πάντα τὰ ἔθνη τῆς γῆς.

[l] τὸ ῥητόν.

[m] Aucher "symbolica." *OL* omits the first sentence.

[n] τὸ πρὸς διάνοιαν.

[o] ἀλληγορεῖται.

All the nations of this earth's soil [a] are in us.[b] And the various senses,[c] such as they may be, consist of the various passions.[d] And these become better when they adhere to a governor and overseer and superintendent, who has power as, according to the poet,[e] "both a goodly king and a warlike spearman." But they undergo a change for the bad when the sovereign mind [f] changes to obedience and submission, and, like a bad and weak charioteer, is unable to restrain the headlong course and wildness of yoked [g] horses, and is carried away by their great speed.

*184. (Gen. xxvi. 5) Why does He say, "Forasmuch as thy father was obedient and kept My precepts and My commandments and My rights and My laws" [h]?

Everything which is Mine, He says, is this.[i] For good and virtuous men are familiar with the powers of God,[j]

[a] Lit. "of this earthy earth."

[b] *OL* renders freely, "omnes gentes figuras esse terreni corporis nostri."

[c] αἰσθήσεις.

[d] The Arm. text seems to be inexact; one would expect "give rise to the various passions." Aucher renders, "in singulas cupiditates coalescunt": *OL* "per singulos sensus singula vitia nascuntur."

[e] Homer, *Iliad* iii. 179 (on Agamemnon) ἀμφότερον βασιλεύς τ' ἀγαθὸς κρατερός τ' αἰχμητής.

[f] ὁ ἡγεμὼν νοῦς.

[g] Aucher and *OL* omit the participle.

[h] Philo here slightly abbreviates the LXX text (which he follows verbatim in *Quis Rer. Div. Heres* 8), ἀνθ' ὧν ὑπήκουσεν Ἀβραὰμ ὁ πατήρ σου τῆς ἐμῆς φωνῆς, καὶ ἐφύλαξεν τὰ προστάγματά μου (Heb. "My observance") καὶ τὰς ἐντολάς μου καὶ τὰ δικαιώματά μου (Heb. "My statutes") καὶ τὰ νόμιμά μου. *OL* renders δικαιώματα as "justificationes," and omits νόμιμα. Philo comments on the verse also in *De Migratione* 130 and *De Abrahamo* 275.

[i] So the Arm. literally. Aucher renders, "omnia Mea, haec sunt, ait." *OL* paraphrases.

[j] οἱ ἀγαθοὶ καὶ σπουδαῖοι ταῖς θεοῦ δυνάμεσιν οἰκεῖοι εἰσιν. *OL* renders loosely, "haec Mea praeclara bona divinae virtutis domestica."

from which, as from a spring, a few men draw,[a] (namely) those who are well provided with a proper education,[b] and genuinely desire wisdom.[c] Now, of the four (things mentioned), the first two are considered to be consecrated to God,[d] (namely) " the precepts and commandments," for He gives precepts as a ruler to those who do not readily obey without fear, and He gives commandments as to His friends [e] to those who pray and have faith.[f] But the other two, (namely) " the rights and laws " are virtues [g] toward men, concerning whom it is fitting and proper to have great care of laws and rights,[h] for rights can somehow exist and consist by nature, while laws (do so) by convention. But those things (existing) by nature are older than those (existing) by convention, and so, rights (are older) than laws.[i]

185. (Gen. xxvi. 6) Why does (Scripture) say that " Isaac dwelt as a sojourner [j] in Gerar " [k] ?

[a] Lit. " take."

[b] ὀρθῇ παιδείᾳ κεχορηγημένοι. Aucher renders, " qui recta disciplina pulchre incedunt." *OL* renders defectively (omitting participle or verb), " plura (*l.* " pura " ?) disciplina."

[c] σοφίας γνησίως ἐφίενται.

[d] *i.e.* they are the laws concerning man's duties toward God as opposed to those concerning his relations toward his fellow-men. See H. A. Wolfson, *Philo*, ii. 200.

[e] *OL* " ut amicus " (*l.* " amicis " ?).

[f] Aucher " credulis."

[g] ἀρεταί.

[h] Construction not quite clear. Aucher renders, " quibus etiam convenire dixeris leges et iura (sancire) aut potius magnam habere curam."

[i] Similarly the brief Greek frag. (from Dam. *Sacra Par.*, identified by Lewy, p. 59), διαφέρει δικαιώματα νομίμων· τὰ μὲν γάρ πως δύνανται συνίσθασθαι (*sic*) φύσει, τὰ δὲ νόμιμα θέσει. πρεσβύτερα δὲ τῶν θέσει τὰ φύσει, ὥστε καὶ τὸ δίκαιον νόμου.

[j] Lit. " in sojourn." LXX has simply κατῴκησεν, Heb. and Arm. O.T. " dwelt." The Arm. Philo seems to reflect a reading παρῴκησεν as in one LXX MS. (E).

[k] Arm. and LXX " Gerara."

"Gerar" is to be interpreted as "hedge,"[a] which we allegorically[b] declare to be that which concerns the body and whatever external things vain, empty and useless opinions blindly invent. For he who dwells within this hedge is wretched, serving many implacable, cruel and inexorable masters. And he endures their threats, being deceived,[c] in the manner of beasts, by what is not good as though it were the best of all. But the sojourner[d] imagines the hope of his entire freedom,[e] being contented with necessities. Wherefore he easily slips away from the hedge[f] and from the snares which are in it.

186. (Gen. xxvi. 7) Who are the men who inquired concerning his wife?[g]

To the various parts of the soul there are thoughts related as inhabitants[h] as follows. To the rational (part)[i] (are related thoughts) pertaining to wisdom and folly[j]; to the irascible[k] (are related thoughts) pertaining to courage and cowardice[l]; to the appetitive[m] (are related

[a] φραγμός, a word which the LXX usually employs to render Heb. *gādēr*. In *QG* iv. 59 (on Gen. xx. 1) Philo explains Gerar as "the region of God-loving thoughts," evidently connecting it with Heb. *gēr* "sojourner" or "resident alien."

[b] ἀλληγοροῦντες.

[c] *OL* "infructuosa spe occupatus."

[d] ὁ πάροικος.

[e] Aucher renders, "at peregrinus spe quadam depicta totalis suae libertatis": *OL* "incola vero spem sibi recondit futurae libertatis."

[f] *OL* "cujus spem facillime effugiet."

[g] *OL* reads differently "qui sunt illi viri quos Scriptura meminit?" Philo here comments only on the first part of the verse, which goes on to say that Isaac reported Rebekah to be his sister, fearing that the men of Gerar might kill him because of her beauty.

[h] ἑκάστοις τοῖς τῆς ψυχῆς μέρεσιν οἰκεῖοί εἰσι λογισμοὶ ὥσπερ οἰκήτορες.

[i] τῷ λογικῷ. *OL* renders, "partem eloquentiae."

[j] σοφίαν καὶ ἀφροσύνην.

[k] τῷ θυμικῷ.

[l] ἀνδρείαν καὶ δειλίαν.

[m] τῷ ἐπιθυμητικῷ.

thoughts) pertaining to moderation [a] and licentiousness; to the nutritive [b] (are related thoughts) pertaining to food and drink; to the sense-perceptible [c] (are related the thoughts) which in accordance with the several senses seek to find enjoyment and new sensual pleasures.[d] But the place of the hedge [e] itself has its own men, (namely) the thoughts which depend upon and are attached to [f] the body and external things. Wherefore they attempt to corrupt and stain its unstained, holy and pure nature.

187. (Gen. xxvi. 8a) What is the meaning of the words, "He was there a long time" [g]?

The retreat [h] of the contemplative and God-loving soul [i] is (considered to be) a dwelling in a place of sojourn [j] for a long time even if (only) for a day. But that which [k] is without place and without time is best.[l] For places [m] and times are brothers, which come into existence together and are moved [n] together.

*188. (Gen. xxvi. 8b) [o] What is the game [p] which Abimelech, looking through the window, saw Isaac playing with his wife? [q]

[a] σωφροσύνην.
[b] τῷ θρεπτικῷ.
[c] τῷ αἰσθητικῷ.
[d] ἡδονάς.
[e] *i.e.* Gerar, see the preceding section.
[f] Aucher renders the two ptcs. by one, "adhaerentes."
[g] LXX ἐγένετο δὲ πολυχρόνιος ἐκεῖ.
[h] ἡ ἀναχώρησις: Arm. variant "distance" or "absence."
[i] τῆς φιλοθεάμονος καὶ φιλοθέου ψυχῆς.
[j] ἐν τόπῳ παροικίας.
[k] The rel. pron. here is evidently neuter, as *OL* correctly renders. Aucher renders it as masc., "qui."
[l] Arm. uses two adjectives.
[m] *i.e.* space.
[n] Aucher "incedentia": *OL* "agitata."
[o] Philo comments similarly on this passage in *De Plantatione* 169-177.
[p] ἡ παιδιά.
[q] LXX παρακύψας δὲ Ἀβίμελεχ . . . διὰ τῆς θυρίδος ἴδεν τὸν Ἰσαὰκ παίζοντα μετὰ Ῥεβέκκας τῆς γυναικὸς αὐτοῦ.

The literal meaning [a] represents lawful commerce [b] with one's wife.[c] But as for the deeper meaning,[d] this must be attributed (to it, namely that) not every game is blameworthy but sometimes it is virtuous and praiseworthy, for it is a sign of the innocence and sincerity of the pure festiveness of the heart.[e] For the age of playfulness is guileless and without cunning, whence "boy"[f] was first named. And from this, in accordance with (our) interpretation, the festive enjoyments of perfect men [g] which are worthy and virtuous are called a "game."[h] And wicked and luxury-loving men have no share or part or taste of this at all but lead sorrowful and painful lives. The virtuous,[i] however, happily enjoy (this) [j] always, (as) men, when their souls are impressed upon [k] the mortal body, or when they are released and separated and removed at death, or else when they have never in any way been bound (to bodies). So also (do) the divine beings [l] which

[a] τὸ ῥητόν.

[b] Arm. *hawasarout'iun* usu. = κοινωνία, but here the original prob. had συνουσίαν. The brief paraphrase in Procopius (of this sentence only) reads Ἑβραῖοι δέ φασιν εὐσχημόνως εἰρῆσθαι τὸ "παίζειν" ἀντὶ τοῦ συνουσιάζειν. *OL* has "coitus."

[c] Aucher, construing differently, renders, "litera conversationem mutuam indicat legitimi viri cum uxore."

[d] τὸ πρὸς διάνοιαν.

[e] σημεῖον τῆς ἀκακίας καὶ ἁπλότητος τῆς καθαρῶς εὐωχουμένης καρδίας.

[f] παῖς, as if from παίζων "playing."

[g] τελείων.

[h] παιδιά. Aucher renders somewhat differently, "ex quo secundum usum receptum et perfectorum jucunditas grata et honesta vocatur paedia (relaxatio animi, ludus, jocus)." *OL* has "superveniente autem perfectorum delectatione facile transiguntur. Est enim in ipsis jocositas."

[i] οἱ σπουδαῖοι.

[j] *OL* adds "in bonis operibus."

[k] Such seems to be the literal meaning of Arm. *ənd arak harealk'* here. Aucher has "conjuncti": *OL* reads quite differently "semoti malorum." Possibly the original Greek had ἐντυμβευόμεναι, which was miscopied as ἐντυπούμεναι.

[l] οἱ δαίμονες.

the sacred word of Moses [a] is wont to call "angels," [b] and the stars.[c] For these [d] are, as it were, intelligible, marvellous and divine natures,[e] having acquired eternal joy unmixed with sorrow. Similar is the universal and whole heaven and world since it is both a rational animal and a virtuous animal and philosophical by nature.[f] And for this reason it is without sorrow or fear, and full of joy. Moreover, it is said that even the Father and Creator of the universe [g] continually rejoices in His life and plays and is joyful, finding pleasure in play which is in keeping with the divine and in joyfulness.[h] And He has no need of anything nor does He lack anything, but with joy He delights in Himself and in His powers [i] and in the worlds [j] made by Him. But in the system of invisible evidence these are measures of all incorporeal forms [k] in the likeness and in the image of the invisible.[l] Rightly, therefore, and properly

[a] ὁ ἱερὸς λόγος Μωυσέως. Aucher renders freely, "sacro Moyses verbo": *OL* "religiosus Moses."

[b] ἀγγέλους, *cf. De Somniis* i. 141.

[c] οἱ ἀστέρες.

[d] *i.e.* the stars or heavenly bodies generally.

[e] ὥσπερ νοεραὶ καὶ θαυμάσιαι καὶ θεῖαι φύσεις τινές εἰσιν.

[f] οὐρανὸς καὶ κόσμος· ζῷον γάρ ἐστι λογικὸν καὶ ζῷον σπουδαῖον καὶ φύσει φιλόσοφον.

[g] καὶ ὁ πατὴρ καὶ ποιητὴς τῶν ὅλων, a common locution in Philo.

[h] Aucher renders somewhat differently, "gaudens condecenti divinum jocum jucunditate." *OL* abbreviates the whole passage after "Creator of the universe," reading "semper digno suo lusu delectari."

[i] ταῖς δυνάμεσι.

[j] Note the plural. *OL* renders the sentence more briefly, "delectatur enim in splendore virtutum et creaturarum suarum universitate."

[k] ἀσωμάτων ἰδεῶν (or εἰδῶν).

[l] Aucher, remarking in a footnote that the sentence is "obscurissima," renders more freely, "invisibilis vero illius ideae, quae indicativa est hujus compaginis, incorporearum specierum mensurae haec sunt, omnes illas esse in similitudine formaque invisibilis (creatoris)." *OL* reads more intelligibly "invisibili ergo exemplari ex incorporalibus figuris constituto, merito mensurae universorum in ipsius (*l.* "ipsis"?) visibiles sunt pro imitaculo verae atque syncerae supernae imaginis."

does the wise man,[a] believing (his) end [b] (to consist in) likeness to God, strive, so far as possible, to unite the created with the uncreated and the mortal with the immortal, and not to be deficient or wanting in gladness and joyfulness in His likeness.[c] For this reason he plays this game of unchangeable and constant virtue [d] with Rebekah, whose name is to be interpreted in the Armenian [e] language as "Constancy."[f] This game and delight of the soul the wicked man does not know, since he has no marriage [g] with wonderful pleasure.[h] But the progressive man,[i] as if looking from a window, sees it but not the whole of it and not the mingling [j] of both alone.[k] For this there is need of the especially sharp-sighted eyes of one accustomed (to seeing) from a distance and of those who are accustomed to see.[l]

[a] ὁ σοφός, here represented by Isaac.

[b] τὸ τέλος.

[c] A different text underlies *OL*, "quapropter sapiens finem perfectum aestimando assimilare deo tunc capit nascibilem innato conjectum, festinat non deesse hujus similitudinis et jucunditatis."

[d] βεβαίας ἀρετῆς.

[e] As usual, the Arm. translator substitutes "Armenian" for "Greek."

[f] διαμονή or ὑπομονή, see *QG* iv. 97, 135 *et al.*

[g] γάμον.

[h] Here Philo uses ἡδονή in an (exceptional) good sense.

[i] ὁ προκόπτων, symbolized by Abimelech. *OL* has "munus," which possibly is based on a misreading of προκόπτων as πρακτικόν.

[j] Lit. "those mingled."

[k] Aucher renders more freely, "sive utriusque (ludum) singulariter purum." In a footnote he gives a literal rendering similar to mine. *OL* has "non tamen purum sentit utrorumque jocum" (*v.l.* "jugum").

[l] Aucher renders, "ad quod acutissimi oculi opus est diu assuefacti, etiam quae in consuetudine cernere." *OL* paraphrases, "cujus mens dubitat acutius (*v.l.* "citius") cernere melioras olet (*l.* "meliora, solet") enim suam consuetudinem pro plenitudine laudis accipere."

*189. (Gen. xxvi. 12) [a] What is the meaning of the words, " He sowed in that year and found hundredfold barley " [b] ?

The year is a completed time [c] and consists of all the times [d] of the year, when it is called " within itself and outside of itself." [e] Now, one hundred is the most sacred of numbers, (being) a power [f] of the all-perfect decad.[g] But the literal text is a sort of testimony [h] that for the virtuous man [i] there is prosperity both in agriculture and in other things pertaining to the life of the world, and that that which comes afterwards is many times greater than that which was in the beginning, and is fullness.[j] But as for the deeper meaning,[k] barley is the food of both men and irrational creatures,[l] but in each of us the mind is a man, and sense-perception is a beast.[m] Accordingly, when barrenness and unproductivity of good things do not follow but the soul [n] presents itself as fertile land like a field which is able to receive the seed of virtue,[o] it becomes

[a] Philo here passes over Gen. xxvi. 9-11, telling of Abimelech's discovery that Rebekah was Isaac's wife and his decree that none of his subjects should molest them on pain of death.

[b] Philo abbreviates the LXX text, which reads *ἔσπειρεν δὲ Ἰσαὰκ ἐν τῇ γῇ ἐκείνῃ καὶ εὗρεν ἐν τῷ ἐνιαυτῷ ἐκείνῳ ἑκατοστεύουσαν κριθήν· εὐλόγησεν δὲ αὐτὸν κύριος.* The word *κριθήν* " barley " is based on Heb. *śᵉʿōrîm* ; our extant Heb. text has *šᵉʿārîm* " gates." Philo comments on the hundredfold yield in *De Mut. Nom.* 268-269.

[c] *OL* " anni (*sic*) tempus perfectum."

[d] *i.e.* seasons.

[e] *V.l.* " and outside within itself " : *OL* " apud se et infra se omnia habere." The meaning of the apparently corrupt Arm. text is clear from *De Spec. Leg.* iv. 235 *τὸν ἐνιαυτόν, ὅς, καθάπερ αὐτὸ μηνύει τοὔνομα, αὐτὸς ἐν ἑαυτῷ πάντα περιέχει συμπεραιούμενος.*

[f] *δύναμις.*

[g] *Cf. QG* iii. 56 and Staehle, pp. 70-71.

[h] *τὸ ῥητὸν μαρτύριόν τι ἐστί.*

[i] *τῷ σπουδαίῳ.*

[j] *OL* paraphrases, " semperque ejus germina amplientur plus quam pridem."

[k] *τὸ πρὸς διάνοιαν.*

[l] *καὶ ἀλόγων ζῴων*, *i.e.* beasts.

[m] *ἄνθρωπος ὁ νοῦς καὶ ἄλογον ἡ αἴσθησις.*

[n] *ἡ ψυχή.*

[o] *τὸ τῆς ἀρετῆς σπέρμα.*

fruitful; and when it is seen to bear in accordance with its several virtues, it finds more than it bore, for God furthers the growth.[a] And from the invisible to the visible and another form He benefits [b] the rational and the irrational [c] with one and the same grace,[d] in accordance with the perfect number, the hundred, which is the most perfect and sacred principle [e] from the sacred principle of the decad.[f]

190. (Gen. xxvi. 13) What is the meaning of the words, "Progressing, he became greater until he was very great" [g]?

Since the literal meaning [h] is clear, it is the deeper meaning that must be ascertained.[i] To [j] the perfect number and that which contains the year within itself [k] (Scripture) clearly likens [l] the progress and growth of the mind,[m] and gives an account of the first stage.[n] And when it reaches

[a] Lit. "furthers and causes to grow."

[b] εὐεργετοῦντος.

[c] The above is a literal translation of the obscure Arm. passage, which Aucher renders, "atque ex invisibili in visibilem, et aliam formam benefice transvehente rationalem partem et irrationalem." *OL* paraphrases, "deo palam proferente certa ex invisibili suo thesauro, ut utraque res beneficia sentiat, persona videlicet atque rationabilis."

[d] τῇ αὐτῇ χάριτι.

[e] ἀρχή.

[f] *OL* abbreviates the text after "grace," reading, "quae est primitiva numeri sanctioris."

[g] LXX καὶ ὑψώθη (Heb. "became great") ὁ ἄνθρωπος καὶ προβαίνων μείζων ἐγένετο ἕως οὗ μέγας ἐγίνετο σφόδρα.

[h] τὸ ῥητόν.

[i] τὸ πρὸς διάνοιαν ἀκριβωτέον.

[j] The Arm. prep. *i* with the ablative case usu. = "from" but the context here requires the meaning "to"; *cf. OL* "secundum similitudinem perfecti numeri."

[k] See the preceding section.

[l] Emending the ending of the Arm. verb, *-el* (inf.) to *-eal* (ptc.).

[m] τὴν τοῦ νοῦ προκοπὴν καὶ αὔξησιν.

[n] *OL* "prudentiam crescere, primo interim gradu provectam."

the first magnitude, why should it examine and inquire into those things which are created sinless ? [a]

*191. (Gen. xxvi. 15) Why did the Philistines stop up and fill (the wells) which the servants of his father had dug ? [b]

The literal text [c] indicates a twofold reason. One of them, the first, is that it is the custom of inconsiderate men [d] not to allow any pillars or monuments of the good, whatever they may be, to remain [e] which redound to their happiness.[f] And the second (reason) is that, bursting with envy and jealousy of the others' continuous [g] prosperity, they are contemptuous of their own profit,[h] thinking it better to suffer harm than to find good in that which they

[a] Variant " which are uncreated." The text is obviously corrupt. *OL* has " jam non pro nascibilibus sed pro incomparabilibus mente occupantur." Perhaps the Arm. translator read *ἀναμαρτήτων* for *ἀμέτρων*, the original meaning being that Scripture does not specify the exact measure of greatness which Isaac reached.

[b] LXX *καὶ πάντα τὰ φρέατα ἃ ὤρυξαν οἱ παῖδες τοῦ πατρὸς αὐτοῦ ἐν τῷ χρόνῳ τοῦ πατρὸς αὐτοῦ* (some LXX MSS. and Heb. add " Abraham ") *ἐνέφραξαν αὐτὰ οἱ Φυλιστιεὶμ καὶ ἔπλησαν αὐτὰ γῆς.*

[c] *τὸ ῥητόν.*

[d] *τοῖς γὰρ ἀβούλοις ἔθος ἐστί*, as in the Greek frag. from Cat. Lips. The second Greek frag., from Procopius, has *οἱ ἐμπαθεῖς.*

[e] Cat. Lips. *μήτε μνημεῖόν τι ἀπολιπεῖν τῶν καλῶν* : Procopius *καὶ τὰ μνημεῖα τῶν ἀγαθῶν ἐξαλείφουσι* : *OL* " nullos titulos insignis memoriae relinquere."

[f] Cat. Lips. omits the rel. clause : Procopius *κἂν τύχωσιν ἐξ αὐτῶν ὠφελούμενοι* : *OL* " quod benevoli pro capessenda gloria student."

[g] Or " exceeding."

[h] So, almost verbatim, Cat. Lips., *ἢ ὅτι ῥηγνύμενοι φθόνῳ καὶ βασκανίᾳ τῆς περὶ ἐκείνους* (*v.l.* *ἐκείνων*) *εὐπραγίας ὀλιγωροῦσι καὶ τῆς αὐτῶν* (*l.* *αὑτῶν*) *ὠφελείας* : Procopius omits : *OL* reads inaccurately " secunda, pro invidia et livore prosperitatis communem despicientibus utilitatem."

do not desire.[a] "For what," one might say, "prevented (you), O most stupid and foolish of all men,[b] from leaving alone the springs which another had found, for the use of those among you who were in need (of them)?"[c] But one might say in reply, "Do not look for an apology of liberality[d] from jealous and envious men, who think it a punishment (to accept) kindnesses extended by the noblest men."[e] That is the literal meaning. But the deeper meaning[f] must be sought. The wells that were dug are symbols of education and knowledge,[g] and each of them is deep, and their final end[h] is (to furnish) drink to the thirsty. But do you seek from among the polymaths the stoppers of ignorance[i] in order that they may get rid of it[j] as a burden and purify the observances of those things formerly

[a] The two Greek fragments differ slightly from the Arm. and from each other; Cat. Lips. ἄμεινον ἡγούμενοι βλάπτεσθαι μᾶλλον ἢ ὑφ' ὧν οὐκ εὖ τι θέλουσιν (*v.l.* οὐκέτι θέλουσιν: Wendland conj. οὐκ ἐθέλουσιν) εὐεργετεῖσθαι: Procopius προτιμῶντες βλάβην μᾶλλον ἢ τὴν ἐξ ὧν μὴ θέλουσιν εὐεργεσίαν: *OL* "mallentes laedi potius quam sentire beneficia." Procopius adds, apparently on his own account, ὠφέλουν γὰρ αἱ πηγαὶ καὶ τῶν Φυλιστιεὶμ τοὺς βουλομένους κεχρῆσθαι. The quotations from this section in Cat. Lips. and Procopius end here, but the next two sentences are preserved in a frag. from Cod. Len. 124 (Lewy, p. 59).

[b] The Greek frag. has ὦ πάντων ἠλιθιώτατοι: *OL* "O stolidissimi hominum."

[c] Slightly emending the Arm. from the Greek frag., which reads τὰς πηγὰς ἐᾶσαι, ἃς ἕτερος εὗρεν πρὸς τὴν τῶν παρ' ὑμῖν αὐτοῖς δεομένων χρῆσιν.

[d] *i.e.* "a frank apology"; the Greek frag. has ἀπολογίαν εὐγνώμονα: *OL* "defensionem rationabilitatis."

[e] τῶν βελτίστων χάριτας *vel sim.*

[f] τὸ πρὸς διάνοιαν.

[g] σύμβολα παιδείας καὶ ἐπιστήμης: *OL* "fossuras puteorum auspicia esse disciplinarum." *Cf. De Somniis* i. 11 ἐπιστήμης φρέαρ.

[h] τὸ τέλος.

[i] ἐκ τῶν πολυμαθῶν τοὺς ἐμφράττοντας τὴν ἀμαθίαν.

[j] Aucher "qui abjiciunt," but the context requires a subjunctive, although the Arm. has the indicative (singular !). *OL* reads "harum (*v.l.* "escarum") ergo amatores injectam obstrusionem, quae pro ignorantia accipitur, expurgant."

determined.[a] For it is not the perfect man [b] who is introduced as digging now, for he has the wells in his soul, which clearly means the springs of education (and) knowledge,[c] but the servants whom he considered worthy of the service of his education.[d] These are they who have recently taken hold of education and, by gradually going farther and deeper, have finally attained their end. And so, by exerting themselves in good labours,[e] they become perfect,[f] not failing of that desire.[g] But foreign characters,[h] whom the Hebrews call "Philistines," [i] being envious of our progress,[j] not only obstruct the free spaces [k] through which doctrines proceed on a firm footing,[l] but also fill them with earth, that is, with earthy desires,[m] which are the pleasures connected with the belly,[n] and they hasten to fill it. By these the mind [o] is weighed down (as by) a burden,[p] and becomes irrational and unphilosophical.[q]

[a] The Arm. lit. = τὰς τῶν πρότερον ὡρισμένων παρατηρήσεις: *OL* "per observantiam institutorum." Aucher renders freely, "obstacula ab aliis injecta." [b] ὁ τέλειος.

[c] *OL* "adeo perfectus hujusmodi fossuras non facit, est enim plenus scientiae."

[d] *OL* "sed pueri quos dignos sui ministerii arbitratur."

[e] ἐν καλοῖς πόνοις ἀγωνιζόμενοι.

[f] Variant "they become able."

[g] Aucher "ne aberrent ab ipso desiderio perfectionis." *OL* renders the whole sentence differently, "hi quidem bonum desiderium prosequentes, dignum inveniunt fructum."

[h] ἀλλόφυλοι (or ἀλλογενεῖς) τρόποι: *OL* "alienigenarum mens." I do not understand why Aucher renders, "alienigenae vocitati."

[i] Heb. *Pᵉlištîm* "Philistines" is usu. rendered ἀλλόφυλοι in the LXX.

[j] προκοπῆς: *OL* "prosperitatis."

[k] τὰς εὐρυχωρίας: *OL* "opportunitatis": Aucher "amplitudines (*vel*, liberos transitus)".

[l] *OL* "pro promptis gressibus."

[m] γηίνων ἐπιθυμιῶν.

[n] αἱ περὶ τὴν κοιλίαν ἡδοναί. [o] ὁ νοῦς.

[p] Arm. lit. = "being weighed down by these, the mind becomes a burden." [q] ἄλογος καὶ ἀφιλόσοφος.

192. (Gen. xxvi. 16) Why does Abimelech say to Isaac, "Go, depart from us because thou hast become much [a] more powerful than we" [b] ?

Cruel and envious and at the same time reprehensible and, moreover, blind is the wicked man.[c] He did not think it enough to banish the trained [d] and wise reason,[e] in word from the city but in reality [f] from his soul,[g] but also with cause shows his jealousy and envy.[h] For he says, "Thou hast become more powerful than we," whereas he ought to have ended [i] his weakness and to have congratulated (the other) on the opportune good fortune which he enjoyed and on the power of his abundance of possessions.[j] For some things were within the body, and some were outside the body, but to him who philosophizes [k] further there should be one food [l] for all.[m]

*193. (Gen. xxvi. 18) [n] Why does he again dig the obstructed wells ? [o]

[a] *OL* omits "much."

[b] LXX Ἄπελθε ἀφ' ἡμῶν ὅτι δυνατώτερος ἡμῶν ἐγένου σφόδρα.

[c] *OL* "pessimum invidiae virus et vituperabile, ita pravus utpote caecus."

[d] Arm. *varž* = ἔμπειρος and ἀσκητής. The latter word is usu. applied to Jacob.

[e] καὶ τὸν σοφὸν λόγον. *OL* translates the whole phrase (after "banish"), "virum prudentem."

[f] λόγῳ μέν . . . ὄντως δέ.

[g] ἀπὸ τῆς ψυχῆς.

[h] *OL* "cum clausula (*l.* "causa") livoris ingestae."

[i] Variant "shown": *OL* "optando" (*l.* "ostendendo"?).

[j] *OL* renders unintelligibly, "utpote infirmitatem optando his qui diriguntur, cum possit congratulari melioribus."

[k] τῷ φιλοσοφοῦντι.

[l] Lit. "grain"—σῖτος.

[m] *OL* "et in utrisque proficere, maxime philosophiae titulis, quorum omnes unanimes esse oportuerat."

[n] A different interpretation of this verse (among others) is given in *De Fuga* 200. The preceding verse, Gen. xxvi. 17, omitted by Philo, tells us that Isaac settled in the valley of Gerar.

[o] Philo abbreviates the text of the LXX καὶ πάλιν Ἰσαὰκ ὤρυξεν τὰ φρέατα τοῦ ὕδατος ἃ ὤρυξαν οἱ παῖδες Ἀβραὰμ τοῦ

In the literal sense [a] because the wise man is by nature humane and benevolent and forgiving [b] and does not bear a grudge to anyone at all but in overcoming his enemies thinks [c] it right to do them good rather than harm.[d] That is the literal meaning.[e] But as for the deeper meaning,[f] it is the task of the contemplative man,[g] even though for a short while the mind [h] may be obstructed [i] when it is bogged down by useless and irrelevant distractions [j] as if by the mud and slime of earth, to get rid of these and become light [k] in order to be able to look upward again [l] and be unhindered and unimpeded in seeing the first rays of the light of wisdom.[m]

πατρὸς αὐτοῦ καὶ ἐνέφραξαν αὐτὰ οἱ Φυλιστιεὶμ μετὰ τὸ ἀποθανεῖν Ἀβραὰμ τὸν πατέρα αὐτοῦ. The rest of the verse is cited in the following section.

[a] *τῷ μὲν ῥητῷ.*

[b] So the Greek fragments from Cat. Burney and Cat. Lips., *ὅτι φύσει φιλάνθρωπος ὁ ἀστεῖος καὶ εὐμενὴς καὶ συγγνώμων*: the parallel fragment from Procopius reads *τινὲς δέ φασιν ὡς . . . πάλιν ὤρυξεν Ἰσαὰκ ὡς πᾶσιν ὢν εὐμενής.*

[c] Reading *hamarē* (3 sing.) for *hamarel* (inf.).

[d] So Cat. Burney and Cat. Lips., *ἀλλὰ νικᾶν τοὺς ἐχθροὺς ἀξιῶν ἐν τῷ ποιεῖν εὖ μᾶλλον ἢ βλάπτειν*: Procopius *καὶ πρὸς τῷ μὴ μνησικακεῖν ἐν τῷ εὐεργετῆσαι σπουδάζων νικᾶν τὴν ἐκείνων κακίαν.* The Greek fragments end here.

[e] *τὸ ῥητόν.* Aucher omits this sentence, perhaps because it is missing in *OL*.

[f] *τὸ πρὸς διάνοιαν.*

[g] *τοῦ φιλοθεάμονος*: *OL* "(mens) deo dedita," reading *φιλοθέου.*

[h] *ὁ νοῦς.*

[i] Adopting Aucher's emendation of *xousesçin* "may withdraw" to *xçesçin* "may be obstructed." *OL* has "decipiatur," possibly reading *ἀπατᾶται* for *ἐπιφράττεται vel sim.*

[j] Aucher renders more freely, "occupationibus ingentibus immensisque": *OL* "supradictis quibusdam molestiarum ponderibus . . . inquietantibus et occupantibus."

[k] *OL* "revelare" (*l.* "relevari").

[l] *OL* (omitting the words "to look upward") "interim" (*l.* "iterum").

[m] *σοφίας.*

*194. (Gen. xxvi. 18) Why does he give the wells the same names as those which his father [a] gave ? [b]

The literal meaning [c] shows (Isaac's) piety toward his father and honourably commends his industry in working.[d] For this reason he himself was zealous in again purifying and cleaning out and digging the wells in order that he might not always incur the envy of the inhabitants of the region.[e] Accordingly, it was consistent [f] that he who submitted [g] to the work should similarly abstain also from names.[h] That is one (interpretation). But a second must be given, (namely) that the wise man is an enemy of self-love,[i] since he loves justice and truth,[j] which are worthy of love. These two he clearly showed in youth [k] ; (he showed) justice since he removed nothing else. Although it had been deliberately perverted,[l] he himself with repeated labour found (it).[m] (He showed) truthfulness by

[a] *OL* " praeter " (*l.* " pater ").

[b] LXX καὶ ἐπωνόμασεν αὐτοῖς ὀνόματα κατὰ τὰ ὀνόματα ἃ ὠνόμασεν Ἀβραὰμ ὁ πατὴρ αὐτοῦ.

[c] τὸ ῥητόν.

[d] Text somewhat uncertain. Aucher renders, " et honorem adhibet opere suo labori ejus " : *OL* " honorem sibi referens per (*marg.* " simul pro ") operis industria."

[e] The brief frag. from Procopius (which contains only this clause) reads defectively μὴ συγχωρῶν (*l.* ἐγχωρίων ?) εἰσάπαν τῷ φθόνῳ νικᾶν : *OL* " ne omnino praevaleat invidia in terram eorum."

[f] ἀκόλουθον *vel sim.*

[g] *OL* reads more appropriately " procedentem."

[h] *OL* " etiam nomina confirmare." Aucher, rendering literally as I have done, suggests an alternative rendering in a footnote, " similiter abstineret se a novis nominibus."

[i] ὁ σοφὸς (or ἀστεῖος) τῇ φιλαυτίᾳ ἐχθρός ἐστι.

[j] δικαιοσύνην καὶ ἀλήθειαν.

[k] *OL* " quas utrasque sectatur amator integritatis."

[l] Apparently justice is referred to : *OL* " licet diu obolita": Aucher amplifies, " etsi consulto erat depravatum (opus patris ab aliis)."

[m] *Cf. OL* " potuit invenire." Aucher, taking " his father's work " as the implied object, renders, " refecit."

making acknowledgment [a] to him who first began the work, and (by indicating) the constructor by the giving of names.[b] This reveals a very precise mind.[c] For those who give names are undeniably wise men [d] since they give (names) significative of things,[e] in which as in a mirror their properties [f] and also their figures appear very clearly.[g] And so, repeating former (statements) I say that since his learned [h] father had named (the wells), he himself was content with the names given originally, for he knew that if he should change the names, he would change the things at the same time. Similar is the case of geometrical figures,[i] for each of them has its own appellation,[j] and if anyone changes this, he changes the nature of the object.[k]

195. (Gen. xxvi. 19) Why was the well in the valley of Gerar? [l]

[a] ὁμολογῶν.

[b] *i.e.* by giving the wells the same names as those first given by his father. Aucher renders slightly differently, "prout per nominum impositionem denotans fabricationem ipsam." *OL* renders freely, "veritatem vero in omnibus imitando et paternam operum constitutionem nominumque firmitatem."

[c] The Arm. seems to reflect δηλοῖ νοῦν ἀκριβέστατον (or διάνοιαν ἀκριβεστάτην). Aucher, construing differently, renders, "id probat et mens egregia": *OL* "quibus etiam mens cautior nuntiatur."

[d] *Cf. Leg. All.* ii. 15 οἱ παρ' Ἕλλησι φιλοσοφοῦντες εἶπον εἶναι σοφοὺς τοὺς πρώτους τοῖς πράγμασι τὰ ὀνόματα θέντας.

[e] δηλωτικὰ πραγμάτων.

[f] ἰδιότητες.

[g] *OL* "tamquam de speculo declarantes suarum formarum conditiones."

[h] Or "eloquent": Aucher "eruditissimus."

[i] τὰ κατὰ γεωμετρίαν σχήματα.

[j] τὴν ἰδίαν κλῆσιν.

[k] τὴν τοῦ ὑποκειμένου φύσιν: *OL* "mutatur sensus natura."

[l] *Cf.* LXX ὤρυξαν δὲ οἱ παῖδες Ἰσαὰκ ἐν τῇ φάραγγι Γεράρων. Heb. omits "of Gerar."

"Gerar" is to be interpreted as "sojourn."[a] But this is symbolical[b] and has a twofold content.[c] For he who dwells in sojourn either yields[d] to those among whom he dwells in sojourn or else is alienated.[e] Now yielding[f] is (signified by) the obstructing of the wells, which foreigners accomplish (by changing) the names of virtuous souls.[g] But the digging and cleansing and purifying are an alienation, for the soul is thereby drawn away from that to which it is accustomed toward the depth of the discipline of knowledge[h] and toward difficult labours, by which they[i] are again found. Therefore the valley is like a sojourn,[j] for he who yields in accordance with the lures of custom is out of place[k] and continually goes about in a low-lying (place) and in a valley-site. But he who is raised above them ascends and is removed to the greatness of virtue.[l] And then, when he represents to himself[m] the number four,[n] of which he is in search and is desirous, he leaves

[a] παροικία: *OL* "incolatus." In *QG* iv. 59 Philo explains Gerar as "the region of God-loving thoughts"; in *QG* iv. 185 he etymologizes it as φραγμός, see below.

[b] συμβολικόν.

[c] λόγον.

[d] Prob. συγχωρεῖ: Aucher "acceptat res": *OL* "consentit."

[e] ἀπαλλοτριοῦται: *OL* "alienatur."

[f] Prob. συγχώρησις.

[g] The Arm. clause is syntactically incomplete. Aucher amplifies similarly in rendering, "quam fecerunt alienigenae, deturbantes proborum animorum nomina." Quite unintelligible is *OL* "pares boni pectoris."

[h] εἰς τὸ βάθος τὸ τῆς ἐπιστήμης παιδείας: *OL* "in altitudinem disciplinarum ministrare."

[i] *i.e.* discipline and knowledge.

[j] *OL* "maceries incolato comparatur," apparently reading φραγμός in place of φάραγξ, but see *QG* iv. 185.

[k] Or "is a fugitive": Aucher "aufugit."

[l] ἀρετῆς. *OL* renders the clause, "demigrare autem cupiens, erigitur ad titulos virtutis."

[m] φαντασιοῦται.

[n] This reference to the number four seems to anticipate the commentary on Gen. xxvi. 19b-35, which has been preserved only in the *OL* version; see the first note on *QG* iv. 196.

behind the valley with the three wells,[a] and departs to proceed farther. One (he leaves) because it is an ambush and a snare and ambiguity.[b] And the others (he leaves) because they contain advances[c] and vilenesses[d] and troubles, and not a nature that is untroubled and free of danger and free of misery.[e]

196. (Gen. xxvii. 1)[f] What is the meaning of the words, "After Isaac became old, his eyes became weak[g] in seeing"[h]?

Those who give a literal explanation[i] say that because of a dispensation[j] the prophet failed in sight, and afterwards was again established and became keen of sight.

[a] These the LXX, translating the Heb. names *'Ēśeq*, *Siṭnāh* and *Reḥôbôth*, calls Ἀδικία, Ἐχθρία and Εὐρυχωρία.

[b] *OL* renders more briefly, "separatus ab insidia et ambiguitate."

[c] Arm. *yaṛajatout'iun* usu. = προκοπή. Possibly the original here was κόπους. Aucher renders, "augmentum (rixae)."

[d] εὐτελείας.

[e] *OL* renders the last clause somewhat differently, "revera enim offendebat erumnis detentus miserrimis, titulo infatigatae et minus laboriosae libertatis."

[f] Our Arm. text of *QG*, Book IV, does not contain Philo's comments on the rest of chap. xxvi of Gen. (vss. 19b-35), but *OL* has eleven *quaestiones et solutiones* following § 195. These contain genuine Philonic interpretations mixed with later ones. Moreover, Procopius and the Greek Catenae have preserved a few bits of the missing sections. For the *OL* version of these eleven sections (hereafter designated as *QG* iv. 195a, 195b, etc.) see Appendix B.

[g] Arm. *vatanam* usu. = ὀκνεῖν or ἀργεῖν.

[h] LXX ἐγένετο δὲ μετὰ τὸ γηρᾶσαι Ἰσαὰκ καὶ ἠμβλύνθησαν οἱ ὀφθαλμοὶ αὐτοῦ τοῦ ὁρᾶν.

[i] Or "account"; Arm. *patmout'iun* has both meanings. Aucher renders, "qui literalem historiam prosequuntur": *OL* "ad videndum oratoriam partem examinantes."

[j] διὰ χορηγίαν or οἰκονομίαν: Aucher "propter dispensationem aliquam": *OL* "pro quadam utilitate."

But the dispensation was a blessing,[a] that not a wicked man but one deserving of blessings might obtain it.[b] To me they seem to give a plausible explanation.[c] Not in this, however, does the beauty of Scripture lie but in the natural meaning,[d] which those who allegorize [e] are accustomed to determine.[f] Now it is written appropriately,[g] not (merely) that his eyes became dim but that (they became dim) " after he became old." And (this is) very natural. For in old age the eyes fail since the whole body (fails) altogether. After he becomes old, that is, when he changes and is transformed,[h] then at last the soul,[i] being invested with the senses,[j] begins to see God obscurely [k] and to become keener of sight toward intelligible things,[l] if, indeed, one may properly [m] say this.[n] For he who is seized (by this vision) and is prepared for prophesying,

[a] εὐλογία.

[b] *OL* " et contigit utiliter ne benedictionis indignus accipiat."

[c] *OL* " siquidem verisimili ratione disserunt."

[d] ἐν τῇ φυσικῇ ὑπονοίᾳ, *i.e.* in the Stoic sense of philosophical allegory.

[e] οἱ ἀλληγοροῦντες.

[f] Aucher, construing differently, renders, " non tamen in hoc stat pulchritudo textus sed sententiam naturale inquirere mos est apud eos qui allegoria utuntur " : *OL* " non tamen hac usque scripturae decus definitur sed altioribus titulis allegoriam cautius extendi."

[g] πρεπόντως : *OL* " congrue."

[h] The exact difference in meaning between the two Arm. verbs used here is not clear. Aucher renders, " mutabit et commutabitur " : *OL* " cum decidendo mutaverit."

[i] ἡ ψυχή.

[j] The Arm. lit. = ἐνδυομένη τὰς αἰσθήσεις, but see the next note.

[k] ἀμυδρῶς. Aucher, construing differently, renders the clause, " tunc demum incipiet anima Deum induens per sensus subobscure videre " : *OL* " tunc enim Dei feratur anima sensibili obscure cernendo."

[l] πρὸς τὰ νοητά.

[m] κυρίως.

[n] Aucher renders freely, " hoc sane dixeris verum visum."

no longer uses his own judgment [a] but that of God, echoing [b] the things spoken by Him.[c] And the prophet becomes an instrument,[d] while God (is) the artist.[e] The sound, moreover, comes when the plectrum, His Logos,[f] melodiously and skilfully strikes a harmony, through which legislation is made known.[g]

197. (Gen. xxvii. 1-3) Why does (Isaac) say to his elder son, " Take thy gear, thy quiver and thy bow " [h] ?

Since the literal meaning [i] is known, (the passage) is to be allegorized [j] as follows. It indicates [k] that the wicked man does not think of anything peaceful but delights in battle and is prepared and equipped with war-gear.[l] And he is by nature rash and bold, and at the same time is by nature timid and cowardly.[m] For fear and rashness [n] are bound together in the same place as brothers and kin.[o] For this reason he does not use the arms of

[a] τῷ ἑαυτοῦ λογισμῷ. [b] ἠχῶν.

[c] *OL* " divino spiritu subsona praesagit."

[d] Though Arm. *anōt'* usu. = σκεῦος, the original here was undoubtedly ὄργανον, *cf. OL* " pro organo " and *Quis Rer. Div. Heres* 259 <ὁ σοφὸς> μόνος ὄργανον θεοῦ ἐστιν ἠχεῖον, κρουόμενον καὶ πληττόμενον ἀοράτως ὑπ' αὐτοῦ.

[e] ὁ τεχνίτης : *OL* " Deus autem propheta."

[f] τὸ πλῆκτρον, ὁ λόγος αὐτοῦ.

[g] τὰ νομοθετηθέντα δηλοῦται.

[h] Philo shortens the LXX text of Gen. xxvii. 1b-3a καὶ ἐκάλεσεν Ἠσαῦ τὸν υἱὸν αὐτοῦ τὸν πρεσβύτερον καὶ εἶπεν αὐτῷ, Υἱέ μου. καὶ εἶπεν αὐτῷ, Ἰδοὺ ἐγώ. καὶ εἶπεν, Ἰδοὺ γεγήρακα, καὶ οὐ γινώσκω τὴν ἡμέραν τῆς τελευτῆς μου. νῦν οὖν λάβε τὸ σκεῦος, τήν τε φαρέτραν καὶ τὸ τόξον.

[i] τὸ ῥητόν.

[j] ἀλληγορητέον.

[k] αἰνίττεται.

[l] *OL* " gaudere praelio et paratura belli."

[m] *OL* reads more briefly " natura quidem audacem et plus timidum."

[n] φόβος καὶ προπέτεια (*vel sim.*).

[o] *OL* " uno enim loco versatur contumatia et timiditas ut sorores."

those [a] who in the thick (of battle) contend with their arms locked together and become one mass, in which their renown and prowess become evident, but (he fights) always by shooting from far away and from a great distance. For archery is a contest proper to the cowardly and unmanly, who cannot endure to remain and stand their ground but flee and fight [b] from a distance.[c]

*198. (Gen. xxvii. 3-4) What is the meaning of the words, "Hunt for me game and prepare for me food [d] as I like it, and bring it to me that I may eat, in order that my soul may bless thee before I die" [e]?

The literal text,[f] it seems to me, indicates the following thought.[g] Though there are two sons, one good and the other blameworthy,[h] he says that he will bless the one who is blameworthy,[i] not because he honours [j] him more than the virtuous one [k] but because he knows that the latter is able by himself to set right and complete his affairs, while the former is held fast and restrained by his

[a] Emending Arm. *aynosik* (loc. pl. of dem. pron.) to *aynoçik* (gen. pl.). Aucher, retaining the latter, renders, "in eos."

[b] ἀμύνονται.

[c] *OL* renders the last two sentences more briefly and freely, "cujus causa non utitur armis aptis constantiae virtuti sed sagittis pro inertia timiditatis: uno enim certamine devitantes longiter ulciscere machinantur."

[d] *OL* "epulas," see following note.

[e] LXX (καὶ ἔξελθε εἰς τὸ πεδίον) καὶ θήρευσόν μοι θήραν. καὶ ποίησόν μοι ἐδέσματα (Heb. "delicacies": A.V. "savoury meat") ὡς φιλῶ ἐγώ, καὶ ἔνεγκόν μοι ἵνα φάγω· ὅπως εὐλογήσῃ σε ἡ ψυχή μου πρὸ τοῦ ἀποθανεῖν μου.

[f] τὸ ῥητόν.

[g] αἰνίττεται τοιαύτην διάνοιαν.

[h] *OL* "noxio," see following note.

[i] So the Greek fragments from the Catenae, δυοῖν ὄντων υἱῶν, τοῦ μὲν ἀγαθοῦ, τοῦ δὲ ὑπαιτίου, τὸν μὲν ὑπαίτιον εὐλογήσειν φησίν.

[j] The Arm. uses two verbs with the same meaning.

[k] So the Greek fragments, οὐκ ἐπειδὴ τοῦ σπουδαίου προκρίνει τοῦτον: *OL* more briefly "non anteponendo alterius."

own character,[a] and has hope of salvation only in the prayers[b] of his father.[c] And if he did not obtain this, he would be the most wretched of men.[d] But as for the deeper meaning,[e] this may properly be said. He admonishes him[f] in the first place not to hunt a brute animal[g] but those which are wild beasts by habit,[h] in accordance with which he desires irrational and savage passions,[i] so that he may avenge himself upon an untamed beast that is not domesticated, and kill it.[j] In the second place, when he becomes capable of this or shall repel (these vices ?), it is not that he himself likes it but his father.[k] And all foods are altogether good for the virtuous man through intelligible things and virtuous words and deeds.[l] And so, he says, if it will be that thou wilt hunt the disposition[m]

[a] The Catenae read only slightly differently ἀλλ' ὅτι ἐκεῖνον οἶδε δι' αὐτοῦ κατορθοῦν δυνάμενον, τοῦτον δὲ τοῖς ἰδίοις τρόποις ἀλισκόμενον: Procopius, omitting the last clause, has ἀλλ' εἰδὼς ὡς ἐκεῖνος μὲν ἐκ τῶν οἰκείων τρόπων ἔχει τὴν εὐμένειαν. *cf.* *OL* " sed qui novit illum etiam per semet benedictionis dignum : pravum vero suis moribus prohibendum."

[b] *OL* " oracula."

[c] So the Catenae, μηδεμίαν δὲ ἔχοντα σωτηρίας ἐλπίδα, εἰ μὴ τὰς εὐχὰς τοῦ πατρός: the Procopius frag. (which ends here) has οὗτος δὲ μίαν ἔχει σωτηρίας ἐλπίδα τὰς εὐχὰς τοῦ πατρός.

[d] So the Catenae fragments (which end here), ὧν εἰ μὴ τύχοι, πάντων ἂν εἴη κακοδαιμονέστατος.

[e] τὸ πρὸς διάνοιαν.

[f] *i.e.* Isaac admonishes Esau.

[g] ζῷον ἄλογον : *OL* " animalia."

[h] ἃ ἕξει εἰσὶ θηρία.

[i] καθ' ἃ ἀλόγων καὶ ἀγρίων παθῶν ὀρέγεται : *OL* has more briefly " pessima et ferocissima vitia."

[j] *OL* " uti more immanissimi animalis ulciscatur illas (*l.* " illa " ?) et perimat."

[k] The Arm. is obscure, though obviously meant to explain Isaac's words " prepare for me food as I like it." Aucher renders, " secundo, quod quando ejus compos fit aut erit, non ut sibi placitum faciat sed sicut patri " : *OL* " secundo, ut praevalere possit, non ut ei mos est sed ut patrem libet."

[l] διὰ νοητῶν καὶ λόγων καὶ ἔργων σπουδαίων : *OL* " per intellectus et sermones et strenuas operas."

[m] διάθεσιν.

of eager,[a] unrestrained and savage passions,[b] and wilt sweeten this for me as food that is sweet, pleasant and likable, and wilt bring it and offer it with thy progress,[c] there will pray for thee not the wise man with me[d] but the sovereign soul in me.[e]

199. (Gen. xxvii. 6)[f] Why does Rebekah, on hearing this, say to Jacob, her son, " Behold, I heard thy father saying to Esau thy brother "[g]?

Well and carefully does (Scripture) call Jacob " her son " and Esau " the brother of Jacob " but does not call him " the son " of anyone.[h] For (Jacob) was adorned with orderliness and a system of decency[i] in the manner of Constancy,[j] whose offspring he is described (as being).[k]

[a] Lit. " open-mouthed."

[b] *OL* reads differently " si ergo coeperit pessimorum vitiorum voraginem."

[c] προκοπαῖς: *OL* " demonstrando istam tuam operam."

[d] The Arm. lit. = ὁ σοφὸς ἄνθρωπος κατ' ἐμέ: Aucher " sapiens homo mihi similis ": *OL* " compositus ego homo."

[e] ἡ ἐν ἐμοὶ ἡγεμονικὴ ψυχή: *OL* " quod est in me augustissima sobrietas animae." Philo frequently speaks of the sovereign part of the soul, *i.e.* the mind (νοῦς), rarely of " the sovereign soul," as, *e.g.*, in *De Spec. Leg.* i. 258.

[f] Philo does not comment on Gen. xxvii. 5 which tells us that Rebekah heard Isaac speaking to Esau, and that Esau went out to hunt game for his father.

[g] LXX Ῥεβέκκα δὲ εἶπεν πρὸς Ἰακὼβ τὸν υἱὸν αὐτῆς τὸν ἐλάσσω (*v.l.* τὸν νεώτερον: Heb., like Philo, has only " her son "), Ἴδε (*v.l.* Ἰδοὺ) ἐγὼ ἤκουσα τοῦ πατρός σου λαλοῦντος πρὸς Ἠσαὺ τὸν ἀδελφόν σου λέγοντος—(vs. 7 repeats vs. 4).

[h] *OL* reads defectively " bene et observantissime hunc quidem Jacob, filium autem suum minime."

[i] τάξει καὶ συστήματι (*vel sim.*) εὐκοσμίας. Aucher renders more freely, " moderatione probitateque morum."

[j] διαμονή or ὑπομονή, symbolized by Rebekah, see *QG* iv. 97, 188 *et al.*

[k] *OL* is corrupt, " constantissimi enim et ornatissimi mores perseverantiae ne post merito vacatur " (*l.* " nepos merito vocatur ").

But the other (being an example) of profligacy and indecency,[a] is no longer (called " her son "), for orderliness belongs to peace.[b] And they are brothers (only) as the odd and the even (are brothers), and similarly the ordered and the disordered.[c] And even though [d] they are brothers, it is possible for them to be opposites and contraries.[e]

*200. (Gen. xxvii. 8-10) What is the meaning of the words, " And now, my son, listen to me and go to the flock, (and) fetch me from there two kids of the flock, tender and good,[f] and I will make [g] this food for thy father, as he likes, and after eating, he will bless thee before he dies " [h] ?

The greatness of his body and the healthiness of the stomach in it are clear from the preparation of the food.[i] For the offering of the fat kids shows a huge and immense body with mighty power, which surpasses all medical power.[j] For if as an old man he succeeded in eating two

[a] *ἀσωτίας καὶ ἀκοσμίας* : Aucher " immodestiae et improbitatis " : *OL* " procax vero et iners."

[b] *OL* adds " hujus vero non ita."

[c] Aucher " modestus et immodestus."

[d] Aucher " quia."

[e] *OL* shortens the last two sentences, " quamvis enim constantissimi et temerarii fratres sint, attamen possunt sibi esse contrarii."

[f] *OL* " molles Aegyptios " (*marg.* " et optimos "), see note *h*.

[g] *OL* " fac cito," see note *h*.

[h] LXX *Νῦν οὖν, υἱέ, ἄκουσόν μου καθὰ ἐγὼ ἐντέλλομαί σοι· καὶ πορευθεὶς εἰς τὰ πρόβατα λάβε μοι ἐκεῖθεν δύο ἐρίφους ἁπαλοὺς καὶ καλούς* (Heb. " two good kids of the goats "), *καὶ ποιήσω αὐτοὺς ἐδέσματα* (Heb. " delicacies " : A.V. " savoury meat ") *τῷ πατρί σου ὡς φιλεῖ· καὶ εἰσοίσεις τῷ πατρί σου καὶ φάγεται ὅπως εὐλογήσῃ σε ὁ πατήρ σου πρὸ τοῦ ἀποθανεῖν αὐτόν.*

[i] Slightly different is the wording of a Greek frag. (in Cat. Lips., from Procopius) *ἐντεῦθέν ἐστι μαθεῖν τὸ τοῦ σώματος μέγεθος καὶ τὴν ἐκ κατασκευῆς φυσικὴν εὐεξίαν* : *OL* " vastitas corporis et insita robustis certa est ex praeparatione epularum."

[j] *OL* " quae omnem palestricosibilitatem (!) superat." This sentence is missing from the Greek frag.

kids, how much more when he was young ! [a] (This he did) not through insatiableness, for he was continent as no one else has ever been found (to be), but because of his wonderful structure.[b] For it was fitting that he who was so great in virtue [c] and the founder [d] of so great a nation should have [e] a formidable and wonderful greatness of body. But this they say in passing,[f] and it is said by the way.[g] More clearly,[h] however, must the following be said. The wishes and characters of the parents [i] do not fight and contend with one another, as some are accustomed,[j] but without division and separation the couple (are) in harmony,[k] for they are eager to reach one end [l] although they are motivated by different thoughts.[m] For the one (parent) [n] wishes him who is good [o] to attain that of which he is deserving,[p]

[a] So *OL* : the Greek frag. reads slightly differently ὁ γὰρ ἐν γήρᾳ δύο πίοσιν ἐρίφοις κεχρημένος προεψήμασι, τίς ἂν ὑπῆρχεν ἐν τῇ νεότητι ;

[b] So *OL* : the Greek frag. (which ends here) reads more briefly καὶ ταῦτα ὢν ἐγκρατὴς καὶ οὐκ ἄπληστος.

[c] ἀρεταῖς. [d] γενάρχην.

[e] *OL* " habitare " (*l.* " habere " ?).

[f] ἐν παρεκβάσει.

[g] παρέργως.

[h] *OL* " praecipue."

[i] *i.e.* Rebekah and Isaac.

[j] The Arm. translator seems to have taken νομίσαντας (here = " believing ") to mean " accustomed." The second Greek frag. from Procopius (which begins here) reads οὐ διαμάχονται δὲ κατὰ τοὺς οὕτω νομίσαντας τῶν γονέων αἱ γνῶμαι. *OL* reads somewhat differently " sententiae solertissimorum non dimicantur inter se, ut quidam putaverunt."

[k] This clause is missing in the Greek frag.

[l] The Greek frag. reads similarly πρὸς ἓν δὲ τέλος ἐπείγονται: *OL* " ad unum enim terminum festinat " (*l.* " festinant ").

[m] διαφόροις λογισμοῖς : *OL* " uno consilio freti." The clause is missing in the Greek frag.

[n] *i.e.* Rebekah. [o] *i.e.* Jacob.

[p] So the Greek frag., τῆς μὲν βουλομένης τὸν ἀγαθὸν τυχεῖν ὧν ἄξιος ἦν : *OL* " ideo desiderat mater sibi similem digna nanciscere."

but the other (says),[a] "I do not hold thee in dishonour who art born of her,[b] but on (thy) justified helplessness I have mercy,[c] that I may set thee right and correct thee [d] so far as is possible." [e] That is the literal meaning.[f] But as for the deeper meaning,[g] the soul that practises virtue [h] has a certain disposition of constancy,[i] which is called Rebekah [j]; and it has a certain asceticism,[k] which has the name of Jacob.[l] Accordingly, Constancy says to the ascetic, as if in an assembly of psychic traits,[m] "Go to the flock," that is, to the familiar, pure and well-formed (virtues) [n] which adorn progress,[o] "and fetch me from

[a] *i.e.* Isaac to Esau.

[b] Or "of me," the pronoun being ambiguous in Arm.: Aucher "ex illa (*vel*, ex me)": *OL* "ex eomet." The clause is missing in the Greek frag.

[c] ἀπορίας δικαίας ἐλεῶ *vel sim.* but the construction is uncertain. Aucher renders, "haesitationis justae misereor"; so the Greek frag. and *OL*, see note *e*.

[d] The Arm. synonyms prob. both render ἐπανορθώσασθαι, as in the Greek frag., see next note.

[e] The Greek frag. (which ends here) reads τοῦ δὲ τοῦ σκαιοῦ, τὴν ἀπορίαν ἐπανορθώσασθαι τῷ ἐλέῳ τῷ εἰς αὐτόν: *OL* "pater vero non vult dehonestari ex eomet natum, egestatem pessimi moris per misericordiam emendando."

[f] τὸ ῥητόν.

[g] τὸ πρὸς διάνοιαν

[h] ἡ ἀρετῶσα ψυχή: *OL* "anima cultrix pietatis."

[i] διάθεσιν τινὰ ὑπομονῆς: *OL* "quendam perseverantiae affectum."

[j] On Rebekah as a symbol of constancy see *QG* iv. 97, 199 *et al.*

[k] ἀσκητικόν τι, in the sense of athletic training: *OL* "habet palestricum suum quomodo natura."

[l] There are many references in Philo to Jacob as the ἀσκητής.

[m] ὡσεὶ ἐν ἐκκλησίᾳ ψυχικῶν τρόπων *vel sim.*: *OL* "ut pote ergo in concilio animae morum suadet perseverantiam (*l.* "perseverantia") palestrico."

[n] *OL* "ad lenes et puras auras" (possibly reading τὰ εὔμορφα as πνεύματα?).

[o] τὰς προκοπάς: *OL* reads curiously "quibus censura laudabilis sua capit augmenta."

there two utterances,"[a] which are called kids,[b] one of them being the desire for piety,[c] the other for humanity[d] in form,[e] "in order that I may show them as pleasant and desirable to thy lovable and thoughtful father,[f] and that, being nourished by them, he may make thee similar to (his) good counsel."[g]

201. (Gen. xxvii. 11-12)[h] Why does Jacob reply, "Behold, Esau my brother is a hairy man, and I am smooth. Perhaps my father will feel me, and I shall be before him as a deceiver[i]"[j]?

The conjectured meaning[k] is right and plausible.[l] But as for the deeper meaning,[m] it has a very natural explanation.[n]

[a] Aucher "oracula": *OL* "electos." What the original Greek word was is not easy to conjecture.

[b] *OL* "hordos" (*l.* "haedos").

[c] εὐσεβείας.

[d] φιλανθρωπίας.

[e] The syntax and meaning of the Arm. word (usu. = μορφή) are not clear. *OL* connects it with the following sentence, rendering it, "secundum figuram."

[f] *OL* "hos ego etiam patri tuo, qui est clementissimi pectoris, titulos libentissimos pronunciabo."

[g] *OL* "quibus refectus, te sibi similem faciat destinatione benedictionis" (apparently reading εὐβουλίᾳ as εὐλογίᾳ).

[h] Vs. 11 is briefly commented on in *Leg. All.* ii. 59.

[i] *OL* "contemptor" (see LXX, next note).

[j] LXX εἶπεν δὲ Ἰακὼβ πρὸς Ῥεβέκκαν τὴν μητέρα αὐτοῦ, Ἔστιν Ἠσαὺ ὁ ἀδελφός μου ἀνὴρ δασύς, ἐγὼ δὲ ἀνὴρ λεῖος. μήποτε ψηλαφήσῃ με ὁ πατήρ μου, καὶ ἔσομαι ἐναντίον αὐτοῦ ὡς καταφρονῶν (Heb. "as a mocker": A.V. "as a deceiver").

[k] Lit. "the conjecture (στοχασμός) of meaning" (or "suspicion"): Aucher "conjectura suspicionis (litteralis)": *OL* "conjectura lectionis." In any case, the literal meaning, τὸ ῥητόν, seems to be meant.

[l] *OL* "rationabilis simul ac verisimilis."

[m] τὸ πρὸς διάνοιαν.

[n] ἀπόδοσις φυσικωτάτη τίς ἐστι, in the Stoic sense of "natural" = philosophical-allegorical.

For if continence and restraint,[a] as in a theatre,[b] wear a covering and garment[c] (of) unrestraint and lecherousness, and wish to trick and deceive and to disregard and despise the truth,[d] the protector and helper[e] is accustomed, like a good physician, to feel and examine their most proper and genuine parts,[f] through which one becomes well or ill, and thus (the situation) is grasped and comes to be known.[g] But everything is directly, accurately and truly made known by its correct name.[h] For the hairy one is the unrestrained, lecherous, impure and unholy man, (who feeds) on uncultivated herbs and things of the field, which is the orbit and resort of untamed and undomesticated beasts.[i] But the smooth one is the restrained and continent friend of frugality.[j] Now the father who feels (with his hands) is he who does not leave any part of the soul[k] unexamined and unfelt but to those who are worthy makes it all altogether known in an accurate and careful way.[l] And, he

[a] Aucher's rendering, "religiosa abstinentia," may be defended on the ground that the first of the two Arm. nouns used here = both θρησκεία and ἐγκράτεια : *OL* has only "continentia." [b] ὡς ἐν θεάτρῳ. [c] σκέπασμα καὶ περίβλημα.

[d] *OL* renders the clause, "nam etsi quasdam vestitus species continentia tanquam in spectalon (*sic*) temperantiae fallere videtur, contemnendo veritatis."

[e] ὁ ὑπερασπιστὴς καὶ βοηθός : *OL* "factorem" (*marg.* "fautorem").

[f] τὰ κυριώτατα καὶ γνησιώτατα μέρη *vel sim.* : *OL* has only "membra."

[g] *OL* renders more briefly, "quibus sanitas et imbecillitas declaratur omnis."

[h] *OL* has only "igitur directis vocabulis summae nuntiantur."

[i] The Arm. text is syntactically incomplete : Aucher renders, at once more briefly and more freely, "et incultis nutritus herbis agri in campo agrestium ferarum" : *OL* "sensus [!] enim luxuriosus incultis sordibus agresti luco (*l.* "loco" ?) similis ut habitaculum ferarum."

[j] ὀλιγοδείας ἑταῖρος. The same phrase is used in *De Ebrietate* 58. [k] Lit. "part in respect of souls."

[l] *OL* "totam planam inveniendo servantissime dignatur."

says, it does not seem right that he [a] should be despised [b]; for no one having intelligence [c] despises or disregards him who uses wisdom,[d] for the wise man does not put him to shame.[e]

*202. (Gen. xxvii. 12-13) Why, when he says, "I will bring [f] upon myself a curse and not a blessing," does the mother say, "Upon me (will be) the curse,[g] my son" [h]?

It is fitting indeed to admire the mother for the thoughtfulness of her goodwill,[i] for she agrees to take upon herself the curse upon him,[j] and (to admire) in the son his honouring of both his parents.[k] For he was drawn in opposite directions by his piety toward both [l] lest he seem to deceive his father and to desire (what belonged) to

[a] Who is referred to is not clear, but prob. it is Jacob, as the symbol of the man who strives for virtue.

[b] Aucher renders, "non videtur, inquit, contemnendus ut contemnes me," adding in a footnote that a more literal rendering would be "non contemptum (*vel*, contemnere) videatur, inquit, illum." *OL* has "eum non uti contemptorem respuere." [c] νοῦν or διάνοιαν. [d] σοφίᾳ.

[e] *OL* renders differently, "nec enim possunt sobrii tali vitio maculari."

[f] *OL* "adducat," see note *h*.

[g] *OL* "maledictio tua."

[h] LXX καὶ ἐπάξω ἐπ' ἐμαυτὸν κατάραν καὶ οὐκ εὐλογίαν. εἶπεν δὲ αὐτῷ ἡ μήτηρ (*v.l.* + αὐτοῦ: Heb. "his mother"), Ἐπ' ἐμὲ ἡ κατάρα σου, τέκνον (Heb. "my son").

[i] The Greek frag. from Cat. Ined. Reg. 1825 reads more briefly τῆς εὐνοίας, as does the frag. from Procopius (which, however, places this sentence at the end of the section): *OL* "favorem."

[j] Similarly the Catena (the clause is missing in Procopius), τὰς κατάρας ὁμολογοῦσαν εἰσδέξασθαι τὰς ὑπὲρ ἐκείνου: *OL* "confitentem excipere maledictum pro eo filio."

[k] So the Catena, καὶ τὸν υἱὸν τῆς εἰς ἀμφοτέρους τοὺς γονεῖς τιμῆς: *OL* "qui utrisque tuetur parentibus pro honore."

[l] So the Catena, ἀνθέλκεται γὰρ ὑπὸ τῆς πρὸς ἑκάτερον εὐσεβείας: Procopius θαυμαστὸς τῆς πρὸς ἄμφω τοὺς γονεῖς εὐσεβείας: *OL* "agitur enim gemina pietate."

another,[a] and as for his mother, lest he seem to disobey and disregard her [b] when she addressed herself to him with supplication and importunity.[c] Wherefore he says very reverently and worthily,[d] not, "My father will rebuke [e] me" but, "I will bring a curse upon myself [f]; for even if he is silent and quiet out of beautiful love toward me,[g] my conscience will none the less seize [h] and reproach (me) as having done something deserving of a curse." [i]

203. (Gen. xxvii. 15) Why did Rebekah, taking the beautiful robe of Esau, which was with her in the house, clothe Jacob (in it)? [j]

[a] The Catena reads more fully τὸν μὲν γὰρ πατέρα ἐδεδίει, μὴ δόξῃ φενακίζειν καὶ ὑφαρπάζειν ἑτέρου γέρας: Procopius paraphrases briefly, τὸν μὲν ἵνα μὴ κινήσῃ: *OL* "ne videatur fallere patrem, usurpando privilegium alterius."

[b] Aucher "neque matrem negligere ac verba ejus nihili facere": the Catena has only τὴν δὲ μητέρα, μὴ καὶ ταύτης νομισθῇ παρακούειν: Procopius τῆς δὲ μὴ παρακούσῃ: *OL* "neve matri minus inveniatur obtemperasse."

[c] The Catena reads more briefly λιπαρῶς ἐγκειμένης: Procopius and *OL* omit the clause.

[d] The Catena has ἄγαν εὐλαβῶς καὶ ὁσίως: Procopius only καλῶς: *OL* "verecunda pietate."

[e] Or "curse," as in the Catena, καταράσεται: *OL*, omitting "my father," has "non quod maledictum aliquod prolaturus est."

[f] So the Catena frag. (which ends here): Procopius reads more briefly τὸ "ἐπ' ἐμαυτὸν ἄξω": *OL* "ait nequando superducat maledictum."

[g] κἂν γὰρ ἡσυχάζῃ φιλοστοργίᾳ τῇ πρὸς ἐμέ: *OL* "quamvis ille pro visceribus piis quiverit" (*i.e.* "quieverit").

[h] Possibly the Arm. translator misread ἐπιμέμψεται (found in Procopius, see next note) as ἐπιλήμψεται.

[i] Procopius τὸ συνειδὸς (*i.e.* συνείδησις) ἐπιμέμψεται ὡς ἄξια κατάρας ἐργασάμενον: *OL* "ne forte conscientia mea pulsata, tale aliquid accipiat incusando memet, tanquam merita maledictio paretur."

[j] LXX καὶ λαβοῦσα Ῥεβέκκα τὴν στολὴν (Heb. "garments") Ἠσαῦ τοῦ υἱοῦ αὐτῆς τοῦ πρεσβυτέρου τὴν καλήν, ἣ ἦν παρ' αὐτῇ τῷ οἴκῳ, καὶ ἐνέδυσεν Ἰακὼβ τὸν υἱὸν αὐτῆς τὸν νεώτερον.

The literal meaning [a] is clear and conspicuous [b]: it seemed that through the robe he who was not there was present. But as for the deeper meaning,[c] the wicked man has another robe [d] and many garments, by which he conceals and covers (himself),[e] inasmuch as he cunningly contrives [f] many matters of wrongdoing.[g] And he has one beautiful robe, that of the senses,[h] and outward adornment and the education [i] which extends to words and which some acquire from school-studies.[j] For there is no one who is perfectly evil,[k] but (man) is a mixture of opposites, of righteousness and unrighteousness, of the ignoble and the noble, and, in general, of the good and the bad.[l] Moreover, very excellently does Epicharmus say,[m] "Whoever transgresses the least is the best man, for no one is sinless and no one is without blame." [n] And Euripides (says),[o]

[a] τὸ ῥητόν.

[b] ἐπίσημον *vel sim.*: *OL* renders the clause more briefly, "scriptura clara est."

[c] τὸ πρὸς διάνοιαν.

[d] *OL* "alias stolas."

[e] The Arm. verbs are active forms, but the context requires the passive or the addition of the reflexive pronoun.

[f] The Arm. verb usu. = πανουργεῖν.

[g] *OL* renders the last two clauses somewhat differently, "quibus ut callidus signa injuriarum occulta habet."

[h] τὴν αἰσθητήν: *OL* "sensibilem."

[i] The Arm. lit. = παιδείαν ἐπιστήμης: *OL* "pro industria."

[j] ἐκ τῆς ἐγκυκλίας παιδείας: *OL* "quam ex musica disciplina imbutus placare festinat."

[k] *OL* "non unam (*marg.* "nomanam") naturam perfecte malus est."

[l] *OL* "sed etiam contrarietatibus temperatus justitiae et iniquitatis documentis infamiae et benevolentiae optimorum et malorum esse virorum" (*marg.* "virum").

[m] The Greek text of this frag. of Epicharmus seems not to have been preserved. In the collection of Diels-Kranz, *F V*, frag. 46 (vol. i. p. 205), it is cited in Aucher's Latin version.

[n] *OL* renders defectively, "qui mediocrius delinquit, dum nullus sine peccato," omitting the reference to Epicharmus' name.

[o] Here, too, the Greek original seems not to have been

"Those who are incontinent and (those in whom) evil (and) enmities and injustices [a] abound are evil. But those who have the opposite (qualities) are virtuous. However, some are such that they have an equal mixture, so that there are none who have all evil without a single good (quality)." [b]

*204. (Gen. xxvii. 16) Why does she put a skin of goats upon his arms and upon his neck? [c]

The literal meaning [d] is clear and apparent, (namely) that it was for the sake of being unknown and that (his father) might not understand and that when he [e] was in his presence he might not seem to be who he (really) was but might seem to be the brother who was absent.[f] And she threw the skins of goats over his arms and naked neck [g] because the latter (Esau) was hairy. But as for the deeper meaning,[h] the arms and the back of the neck [i] are stronger than all of man's (other) limbs, and they are smooth.[j] And

---

preserved. Nauck, *TGF* (2nd ed.), p. 660, cites Aucher's Latin version.

[a] Aucher "malum inimicitiae et injustitiae."

[b] *OL* renders the quotation somewhat confusedly, "Erupides (*marg.* "Euripides") quoque neminem irreprehensibilem dixit, tamen quibusdam abundantur (*marg.* "abundant") malitiarum fomenta turpia, iniqua, adeo pravis adversantur strenui, quibusdam tamen ita altrinsecus inest temperantia ut nonnulli omnia pessima obtineant absque uno bono, nonnulli omnia necessaria sine ullo malo." This is followed by several sentences not found in the Arm. text. See Appendix B.

[c] LXX *καὶ τὰ δέρματα τῶν ἐρίφων* (*v.l.* *αἰγῶν*: Heb. "kids of the goats") *περιέθηκεν ἐπὶ τοὺς βραχίονας αὐτοῦ καὶ ἐπὶ τὰ γυμνὰ* (Heb. "smoothness") *τοῦ τραχήλου αὐτοῦ*: *OL* "quare pelles super brachia et nuditatem colli posuit?"

[d] *τὸ ῥητόν.*

[e] *i.e.* Jacob.

[f] *OL* renders more briefly, "dictum insinuat qua possit latere, assistens patri ne videretur quis sit sed absens frater."

[g] *OL* "alia proxima membra."

[h] *τὸ πρὸς διάνοιαν.*

[i] Prob. *ὁ σφόνδυλος τοῦ αὐχένος*: *OL* "terganea colla": Aucher "humerique circa collum."

[j] *OL* "lenia" (*l.* "levia").

the wise man [a] is gleaming and naked to the truth [b]; and just as in the case of the other virtues, so also does he in pure fashion exhibit and practise and pursue courage.[c] And if it sometimes happens that he conceals this and makes it hairy because of the necessity of the occasion, and uses economy,[d] he still remains in the same state and does not retreat from his original purpose,[e] but because of involuntary occurrences he changes to another kind of form, as in a theatre, for the benefit of the spectators.[f] For this is just what physicians are accustomed to do, for they change the foods of ill persons, and their places (of residence) and the ways (of living) which they had before their illness.[g] And the physician who is skilled in worldly matters does foolish things for a time (but) wisely, and

[a] The Greek frag., which begins here, has ὁ ἀστεῖος: *OL* "strenuus vir" (usu. = ὁ σπουδαῖος; Aucher "virtute valens."

[b] The Greek frag. omits the predicate: *OL* has "aperta ad veritatem habet."

[c] Similarly the Greek frag., ὥσπερ τὰς ἄλλας ἀρετὰς ὁ ἀστεῖος, οὕτως καὶ τὴν ἀνδρείαν καθαρῶς ἐπιτετηδευκώς: *OL* renders more briefly, "sicut alias virtutes, ita fortitudinem sectatur."

[d] The Arm. is clearer than the Greek frag., which reads ἐάν που ταύτην ἐπισκιάζῃ χάριν, καιρῶν οἰκονομίᾳ χρῆται (possibly χάριν is a corruption of καὶ τραχύνῃ): *OL* renders, "cum autem hanc obumbraverit densando pro necessitate temporis et utilitate utitur."

[e] Similarly the Greek frag., μένων μὲν ἐν ὁμοίῳ καὶ τῆς ἐξ ἀρχῆς προθέσεως οὐκ ἀναχωρῶν: *OL* "permanens in eodem statu et praecedentia vota non excedens."

[f] Similarly the Greek frag., διὰ δὲ τῶν ἀβουλήτων συντυχίας ἐναλλάττων ὥσπερ ἐν θεάτρῳ μυρφὴν ἑτέραν ὑπὲρ ὠφελείας τῶν ὁρώντων: *OL* renders defectively, "pro secundis autem casibus formam in alteram pro usitate videntur" (*l.* "utilitate videntium").

[g] This sentence is missing in the Greek frag.: *OL* renders more briefly, "hoc enim etiam medici solent observare, immutantes remedia laborantium quam habuerunt ante languorem."

unlasciviously and moderately does lecherous things, and bravely does cowardly things, and righteously does unrighteous things.[a] And sometimes he will speak falsehoods, not being a liar, and he will deceive, not being a deceiver,[b] and he will insult, not being an insulter.[c]

205. (Gen. xxvii. 17) What is the meaning of the words, "She gave the foods and the bread which she had made into the hand of Jacob" [d]?

(This is said) because for a perfect life it is fitting not only to wish for things worthy of pursuit and virtue [e] but also to do them.[f] And appropriately [g] does the character of constancy and continence,[h] because she is the mother of the law of nature, extend to his hands bread, the symbol of frugality,[i] and the foods of a relaxed, released and pure life.[j]

[a] Similarly the Greek frag., *ἰατρὸς γὰρ τῶν κατὰ τὸν βίον πραγμάτων ὁ ἀστεῖος, ὃς ἕνεκα τῶν καιρῶν φρονίμως ἐνεργεῖ τὰ ἀφροσύνης, καὶ σωφρόνως τὰς ἀκολασίας καὶ τὰς δειλίας ἀνδρείως καὶ δικαίως τὰς ἀδικίας*: *OL* renders defectively, "medicus autem circa vitam rerum pro statu temporum fit, sapienter gubernando insipientiae momenta, et viriliter timiditatem, et jusse (*l.* "juste") iniquitatem."

[b] So *OL*, "et fallat alienus fallaciae." The clause is missing in the Greek frag.

[c] So the Greek frag., *καὶ ὑβρίσει μὴ ὢν ὑβριστής*: *OL* "et detrahebat (*l.* "detrahebit") non derogando."

[d] *OL* reads defectively "quid est: dedit Isaac (*marg.* "Esau") panes quos fecit in manibus Jacob?": LXX *καὶ ἔδωκεν τὰ ἐδέσματα καὶ τοὺς ἄρτους οὓς ἐποίησεν εἰς τὰς χεῖρας Ἰακὼβ τοῦ υἱοῦ αὐτῆς.*

[e] *ἄξια σπουδῆς καὶ ἀρετῆς.*

[f] *OL* paraphrases, "complenti vitam (*l.* "vitae"?) mavult perseverantiam non modo per ambitionem studii sed etiam pro merito certatoris agere."

[g] *πρεπόντως vel sim.*

[h] *τρόπος* (or *ἦθος*) *τῆς διαμονῆς* (or *ὑπομονῆς*) *καὶ τῆς ἐγκρατείας.* On Rebekah as a symbol of constancy see *passim*, *QG* iv. 97-199.

[i] *σύμβολον τῆς ὀλιγοδείας.*

[j] *OL* renders the last sentence more briefly, "est enim naturalium conditionum mater quae porrigit in manibus auspicia, parsimonia quidem panis, pro pura autem et abundantiori refectione caeteras epulas."

*206. (Gen. xxvii. 18-19) Why, when his father asks, "Who art thou, son?", does he reply, "I am Esau, thy first-born. I have done as thou hast told me"[a]?

Again he will seem to be a deceiver, although he is not to be thought (to be connected) with any evil.[b] For calumniators[c] call the dispensation of virtue[d] deceit and fraud.[e] And what dispensation is better than when one does not ascribe good things and virtues to those who wish to live shamefully and disgracefully?[f] But let the spy say, when he is caught, "I am not an enemy but a friend"; and if this is not praised,[g] and his words have no place,[h] let him say these words, "I hastened to you of my own accord,[i] condemning my own (side)."[j] Let the general speak

[a] LXX τίς εἶ σύ, τέκνον (Heb. "my son"); καὶ εἶπεν Ἰακὼβ ὁ υἱὸς αὐτοῦ τῷ πατρὶ αὐτοῦ, Ἐγὼ Ἠσαὺ ὁ πρωτότοκός σου, ἐποίησα (*v.l.* πεποίηκα) καθὰ ἐλάλησάς μοι.

[b] The Arm. text is not altogether clear. Aucher renders, "rursum fallax esse putetur nullo cum malo reputandus": *OL* "item fallax esse videtur a bonis emotis pravitate negotationum." Procopius' paraphrase reads πάλιν ἀπατεὼν εἶναι δόξει τοῖς μὴ τὴν κατ' ἀρετὴν σκοποῦσιν οἰκονομίαν.

[c] οἱ συκοφάνται: *OL* "calumniatores."

[d] τὴν τῆς ἀρετῆς οἰκονομίαν (*cf.* the end of the preceding sentence in the Greek frag. from Procopius): *OL* "pro virtute acquisita."

[e] The Procopius fragment lacks this sentence.

[f] *OL* reads unintelligibly "quid autem dispensabilius utilitati quam optime studiosa turpissimi quoque et scrupulosae vitae homines et optimi viri exquirunt?" Procopius is briefer and clearer, ἡ δὲ οἰκονομία πρὸς τὸ μὴ τοῖς ἀναξίοις δίδοσθαι τὰ καλά. The original probably meant that Esau did not merit the status of first-born.

[g] Aucher "haud probetur."

[h] The Arm. idiom *zteḷi ounel* (lit. "to have place") often means "to stop" but occasionally, as here, it seems, "to make an impression." Aucher renders, "neque locum habeat dictum."

[i] Lit. "of myself": Aucher "ego ex me ipso."

[j] Aucher "improbatis meis (sociis)." *OL* lacks this sentence. Procopius reads more briefly λεγέτω καὶ κατάσκοπος συλληφθείς· οὐκ εἰμὶ πολέμιος ἢ ὡς ηὐτομόληκα. For the

of making war when he is doing the work of peace, or in time of peace when he is thinking of drawing up his line of battle.[a] Let the king also put on the guise of a commoner if he is not able in another way to obtain benefit for his realm and his subjects.[b] And (let) the master (put on the guise) of a slave in order not to be ignorant of anything that is done in the house.[c] These are familiar things [d] and principally of the literal meaning.[e] But as for the deeper meaning,[f] let us say allegorically [g] that the soul [h] of each of us has, as it were, several kinds of man in itself [i] in accordance with the various incidences of similar things.[j]

---

following three sentences we have two Greek texts, one from Procopius, the other from Cod. Vat. 1553.

[a] The Arm. is apparently defective. One expects the latter part of the sentence to read "or in time of peace let him think of drawing up his line of battle." *OL* is also awkward, "dicit enim et magister militiae pacem velle, praelia parando, et pacis tempore arma renovando." The Greek fragments have *λεγέτω καὶ* (*v.l.* *καὶ ὁ*) *στρατηγὸς τὰ πολεμοποιοῦντα εἰρήνην πραγματευόμενος ἢ τὰ εἰρηναῖα* (Cod. Vat. *εἰρήνης*) *πολεμεῖν ἐγνωκώς* (Cod. Vat. *διανοούμενος*).

[b] Similarly Cod. Vat., *ὑποδυέσθω καὶ βασιλεὺς ἰδιώτου σχῆμα εἰ μὴ δύναιτο ἑτέρως τὸ συμφέρον τῇ τε ἀρχῇ καὶ τοῖς ὑπηκόοις λαβεῖν.* Procopius reads slightly differently *οὐδὲν κωλύσει καὶ βασιλέα ἰδιώτου σχῆμα λαβεῖν τοῖς ὑπηκόοις τὸ συμφέρον θηρώμενον.* *OL* has "ita demum etiam rex amictu subornatur privati pro utilitate si aliter non poterit evadere, expedit enim ut subjectis, ita et domesticorum conditionibus" (the last four words seem to belong to the sentence which follows in the Arm. version and is not independently rendered in the *OL*).

[c] So Cod. Vat., *καὶ ὁ δεσπότης δούλου, εἵνεκα τοῦ μηδὲν ἀγνοῆσαι τῶν κατὰ τὴν οἰκίαν δρωμένων*: Procopius *καὶ τὸν δεσπότην οἰκέτου μηδὲν ἀγνοεῖν ἐθέλοντα τῶν κτλ.* The Greek fragments end with this sentence.

[d] *οἰκεῖα.*

[e] *τοῦ ῥητοῦ.* *OL* renders the sentence more briefly, "haec pro partibus orationis."

[f] *τὸ πρὸς διάνοιαν.*

[g] *ἀλληγοροῦντες φήσομεν.*

[h] *ἡ ψυχή.*

[i] *OL* "plurimos habere infra se tamquam homines."

[j] *OL* "pro varietate accedentium rerum."

It is as if Esau were in me, an oak [a] inflexible, unbending and hairy, and a type alien to the thoughts of virtue,[b] and confused [c] in his impulses,[d] and yielding to irrational and inscrutable impulses.[e] In me is also Jacob, smooth and not rough.[f] In me are both an old man and a youth, both a ruler and a non-ruler,[g] both a holy person and a profane one.[h] But when one is virtuous [i] and in a (state) opposite to virtue,[j] it is altogether superficially and merely on a tangent that one deceives, and not [k] by an affinity to every being and in mortal fashion.[l] When, however, one is wicked, one openly says that which is foolish and unjust, but feebly gives the appearance of wisdom and justice.[m]

[a] For other references in Philo to Esau as a symbol of an oak, based on the fanciful etymology of " Esau " as Heb. *'ēṣ* " tree," see *QG* iv. 161.

[b] The Arm. seems lit. to render ἀλλότριος ταῖς τῆς ἀρετῆς γνώμαις : Aucher, construing differently, renders, " alienae virtutis probabile exemplum " : *OL* " obscurus ad captandas virtutum fruges."

[c] Or " impure " : Aucher " intemperatus."

[d] *OL* has merely " procax," omitting reference to " his impulses."

[e] The rendering in *OL*, " in montibus passim procedens," is perhaps based in part on a reading ἀν' ἴχνη ἐν τοῖς ὄρεσι *vel sim.* in place of ἀνιχνεύτοις ὁρμαῖς.

[f] *OL* " nec temere audax."

[g] *OL* " et privatus et magistratus."

[h] *OL* " ne (*l.* " in ") me et religiosus, inquit, et profanus."

[i] σπουδαῖος : *OL* " studiosus."

[j] ἀρετῇ.

[k] Arm. *oč* " not " is printed in parentheses as if supplied by Aucher.

[l] The obscure Arm. seems literally to render οὐ κατὰ συγγένειαν πάσῃ οὐσίᾳ καὶ θνητὸν τρόπον *vel sim.* Aucher renders more freely, " minime vero secundum indolem cognatam, qua reperitur exemplum omnis creaturae ac mortalis." *OL* has nothing to correspond (see the next note).

[m] σοφίας καὶ δικαιοσύνης. *OL* seems to incorporate part of this sentence with the preceding in rendering the passage, " si enim studiosus fuero, differentia virtutis ostentatorie et procaciter ego tantummodo quantum oculis placeres (*sic*), sufficit sapientiae et justitiae merita dissimulando."

But when Jacob says to his father, "I am Esau," he speaks the truth according to the principle of nature,[a] for his soul is moved in accordance with that form.[b]

*207. (Gen. xxvii. 20) Why does his father say, "What is this that thou didst quickly find, son?"[c]?

The literal text[d] has both a fitting answer to the question[e] and also one for the allegory[f] of the literal text.[g] For reckoning the time sufficient for a hunter to hunt, he found it brief and thought it little.[h] But as for the deeper meaning,[i] the wise man[j] wondered that one of the wicked should so unexpectedly become well taught[k] so as to be able to find (what he sought) not only with speed but also with keenness and commendably,[l] since he was thought to be very irrational and foolish[m] and really an oak.[n]

[a] κατὰ τὸν τῆς φύσεως λόγον: *OL* "imploratione naturae."

[b] τῆς αὐτοῦ ψυχῆς κατὰ τὸ ἐκείνου εἶδος κινουμένης: *OL* "dum anima secundum illius speciem mota est."

[c] LXX εἶπεν δὲ Ἰσαὰκ τῷ υἱῷ αὐτοῦ, Τί τοῦτο ὃ ταχὺ εὗρες, ὦ τέκνον.

[d] τὸ ῥητόν.

[e] Variant "answer of reply."

[f] πρὸς τὴν ἀλληγορίαν.

[g] The Arm. text is awkward. Aucher renders more freely, "habet litera tam congruam responsionem quae reddi potest quam allegoriam." *OL* reads "habet oratoria pars rationabilem redditionem, allegoria quoque tanto melius."

[h] *OL* "dementi (*sic*) enim sufficientes moras venationi compendiosiorem invenit et minus quam aestimavit." The brief paraphrase in Procopius reads οὐ γὰρ ἔφθασε χρόνον προσήκοντα κυνηγέτῃ.

[i] τὸ πρὸς διάνοιαν.

[j] ὁ σοφός.

[k] οὕτως εὐμαθῆ γενέσθαι παραδόξως *vel sim.*: Aucher "sic repente progressum fecerit in laudabili studio": *OL* "tam cito . . . eruditus sit repentino studio melioratus."

[l] εὐλόγως *vel sim.*: Aucher "acumine optimae rationis": *OL* omits.

[m] *OL* "ex inertia ingeniosus" (?).

[n] See *QG* iv. 206.

*208. (Gen. xxvii. 20) Why does he reply, "What the Lord gave into my hands"[a]?

This answer is virtuous and suitable to a God-loving mind.[b] "For," he says, "I use no mortal teacher,[c] but the Father gave into my hands the contemplation of wisdom and knowledge,[d] because of which I not only learned but was also able to find." For he who uses God as teacher both profits and is competent to bring profit (to others).[e] He profits by learning, and he brings profit by finding disciples and familiars[f] at first.[g] And afterwards he receives the rank of teacher and leader in order.[h]

209. (Gen. xxvii. 21) Why does he say, "Come near to me, and I will feel thee, son, whether thou art my son Esau or not"[i]?

[a] *OL* "quod tradidit dominus in pectu (*l.* "spectu"?) meo." Philo differs from LXX ὃ παρέδωκεν κύριος ὁ θεὸς (*v.l.* + σου) ἐναντίον μου: Heb. "for the Lord Thy God caused (it) to fall before me." In *De Sacr. Abelis* 64 and *Quod Deus Immut. Sit.* 92 Philo follows the LXX text verbatim; in *De Ebrietate* 120 and *De Fuga* 169 he cites the LXX text incompletely, ὃ παρέδωκεν κύριος ὁ θεός. The interpretation of the half-verse given here (in *QG*) resembles most closely that given in *De Sacr. Abelis* 64-65.

[b] θεοφιλεῖ λογισμῷ *vel sim.*: *OL* "religioso animi" (*l.* "animo"?). Procopius paraphrases the sentence (the only one in this section preserved in his commentary), ὁ δὲ θεοφιλὴς ἐπὶ θεὸν τὴν αἰτίαν ἀνάγει διὰ τῆς ἀποκρίσεως.

[c] *OL* "magistro, asserenti, nulli mortalium auxiliosum esse."

[d] τὰς θεωρίας (*vel sim.*) τὰς τῆς σοφίας καὶ τῆς ἐπιστήμης: *OL* "disciplinarum pignora spectatissima sapientiae."

[e] *OL* "et prodesse alteris."

[f] γνωρίμους (in the sense of "disciples"): *OL* "notos."

[g] *OL* curiously renders, "ac minime dissonantes," possibly taking ἐν ἀρχῇ to mean "under authority" or the like.

[h] *OL* renders more briefly, "postmodum autem doctoris dignitatem assumit."

[i] *OL* omits the last two words. Philo here follows the LXX Ἔγγισόν μοι καὶ ψηλαφήσω σε, τέκνον, εἰ σὺ εἶ ὁ υἱός μου Ἠσαῦ ἢ οὔ.

The virtuous man [a] is justly [b] incredulous [c] and wonders that the wicked man in such wholly unexpected fashion [d] received an increase in virtue.[e] In the first place, because he who had been sickly and lazy and slow [f] became quick, and quick to learn.[g] In the second place, because not only did he receive in memory the things in which he had been instructed and had learned,[h] but he also himself became a rule to many,[i] and like quick-witted men who are easily taught, changed into a receptive, fertile and productive (person) instead of being, as a little before, sterile.[j] And in the third place, because he considers the teachings and traditions [k] and doctrines of divine guidance to be worthy of pursuit, and rightly and fittingly does he consecrate and offer [l] them to God, his leader.[m] For this reason, being astonished, he says, " Come near to me, for I wish to know certainly whether you are he or someone else." Wherefore he is said to feel him, not so much with his hands as with the thoughts of his mind,[n] and by himself he grasps and compares the things now said with those earlier ones, in word and deed. For he finds a great opposition [o] between them.

[a] ὁ σπουδαῖος: *OL* " studiosus." [b] Aucher " statim."

[c] *OL* carelessly renders, " non incredulus."

[d] Aucher " tam subito ": *OL* omits. [e] ἀρετῇ.

[f] Aucher, ignoring the first adjective, renders, " ignavus et deses ": similarly *OL*, " surdus et tardus."

[g] *OL* has only " strenuus."

[h] *OL* " quae dicit (*l.* " didicit ") meminit."

[i] *OL* loosely renders, " plurima acquisivit."

[j] *OL* renders the whole clause very briefly, " utpote de sterilitate foetosus." [k] παραδόσεις.

[l] Aucher renders both verbs by " adscribit."

[m] *OL* renders the sentence very briefly, " tertio, quod titulos divinitus largitos refert, et deum confitetur autorem."

[n] Aucher renders more literally, " mente consilii," but it appears that the Arm. translator had the case-endings of the two nouns reversed. *OL* reads more smoothly " mentis intuitu."

[o] Lit. " warfare ": Aucher " oppugnationem ": *OL* " dissonantiam."

*210. (Gen. xxvii. 22) Why after feeling (Jacob) does he say, " The voice is the voice of Jacob, and the hands are the hands of Esau " [a] ?

The voice now brought into speech is not that which is the sound of air through mouth and tongue [b] but that which had already been said,[c] which was indefinite [d] and indifferent in its own significance.[e] And that which is signified is an indication of piety of will,[f] which is suitable to and in harmony with continent characters of productivity and worthiness.[g] For this reason, repeating himself, he twice uses the (same) expression, " The voice is the voice of Jacob, and the hands are the hands of Esau," indicating that it is not any voice whatsoever that he praises but (only) that in which it has been acknowledged that the inventions [h] of good things are in accordance with God.[i] This (attitude) was foreign and strange to the undisciplined and uncultivated character [j] but familiar and genuine to the continent one which considers strenuous labours

[a] So the LXX, Ἡ φωνὴ φωνὴ Ἰακώβ, αἱ δὲ χεῖρες χεῖρες Ἠσαύ.

[b] *OL* " non oris et linguae pulsantis aerem."

[c] *OL* " pro casum (*v.l.* " casu ") dictum " (*v.l.* " vindictam ").

[d] ἀόριστος : *OL* omits.

[e] ἀδιάφορος ἐν τῷ δι' ἑαυτῆς σημαινομένῳ *vel sim.* : *OL* " et habentem differentiam (*sic*) pro suo indicio " (*v.l.* " judicio ").

[f] *Cf.* Procopius' paraphrase τὴν εὐσεβῆ φωνὴν οὐκ ἂν λεχθεῖσαν ὑπὸ τοῦ Ἠσαῦ . . . οὐ γὰρ ἐν ἰδιότητι προφορᾶς ἀλλ' ἐν τοῖς λεχθεῖσιν ἦν ἡ φωνή.

[g] Aucher renders somewhat more freely, " quae convenit indolis religiosae fertilitatis dignitatisque " : *OL* " congrua exercitoriis (*v.l.* " exercitoris ") moribus continentia quibus benevolentia et sanctitas oriuntur." Perhaps for Arm. *k'ajaberout'iun* " productivity " we should read *k'ajabarout'iun* " rectitude," " simplicity."

[h] τὰς εὑρέσεις.

[i] *OL* " non vocem quamlibet sed eam laudat quae professa est autoris esse emolumenta bonorum."

[j] τῷ ἀπαιδεύτῳ καὶ ἀμούσῳ τρόπῳ : *OL* has only " quod erat alienum pravi."

more valuable and not merely more useful than sensual pleasure.[a]

*211. (Gen. xxvii. 23) What is the meaning of the words, " He did not recognize him, for his hands were hairy [b] like Esau's " [c] ?

(Scripture) seals and confirms still more what was said a little earlier, pointing out and declaring that many times the good man and the wicked man perform good and worthy deeds of this sort and bring profit,[d] but not with the same intention,[e] for the one uses his judgment about what is good while the wicked man acts nobly [f] and makes that appear good which is a matter of avaricious greed.[g] For no one is ever able to find folly doing anything worthy unless it is contriving some scheme or scheming some dodge,[h] as the tragic poet says.[i] On that account it gives a hint,[j] adding that their acts are somewhat similar but

[a] τῆς ἡδονῆς. *OL* renders the clause unintelligibly, " pravum (*sic*) vero continentiam studentis et exercitati pro libidine doloris eligentis hanc vitam utiliorem et preciosam credenti." After this sentence *OL* has an additional section, for which see Appendix B.

[b] *OL* omits this word.

[c] LXX and Heb. " Esau's his brother."

[d] The two Arm. verbs prob. render the single Greek verb εὐεργετοῦσι, a variant or corruption of ἐνεργοῦσι, see next note.

[e] The Greek frag. (Harris, p. 70, identified by Bréhier) from Cod. Vat. 1553 reads more smoothly τὰ αὐτὰ καθήκοντα πολλάκις ἐνεργοῦσιν ὅ τε ἀστεῖος καὶ ὁ φαῦλος, ἀλλ' οὐκ ἀπὸ τῆς αὐτῆς διανοίας.

[f] Possibly the Arm. translator read σεμνυνόμενος for μνώμενος (see next note).

[g] The Greek frag. (which ends with this sentence) reads ὁ μὲν γὰρ κρίνων ὅτι καλόν, ὁ δὲ μοχθηρὸς μνώμενός τι τῶν εἰς πλεονεξίαν.

[h] Aucher " aliqua nova " : *OL* " machinam fraudulentam quae nascitur a Mercurio."

[i] This may be an allusion to Euripides, *Hippolytus* 331 ἐκ τῶν γὰρ αἰσχρῶν ἐσθλὰ μηχανώμεθα.

[j] αἰνίγματι.

not that the two are the same,[a] because each has received a (different) type of will.[b]

212. (Gen. xxvii. 23-24) Why is it that he blessed him and (then) says, " Art thou my son Esau ? " [c] ?

The divine oracle ordains [d] that this word [e] be uttered at once, to make evident the (act of) blessing before (mentioning) the individual blessings.[f] And this demonstrates very clearly and certainly that it was God who did the blessing through the prophet, who speaks.[g] For the one did not say anything at all by opening his mouth, while the other by his power of foreknowing [h] first rendered the blessings to the end with an articulate sound.[i] Wherefore indeed (Scripture) seals the conclusion and confirms it by an utterance of the divine oracle, in accordance with which it has made clear that he blessed him.[j]

[a] *OL* " non tamen eadem qualitate amborum."

[b] Aucher " ob insitos in utroque indoles voluntatis " : *OL* " litigant enim utrorumque consilia."

[c] LXX and Heb. add " and he (Jacob) said, I am."

[d] *ὁ θεῖος χρησμὸς νομοθετεῖ.*

[e] *i.e.* the words *ηὐλόγησεν αὐτόν*, the last words of vs. 23.

[f] *OL* renders freely, " tam resonat vox legis Dei per eloquium sanctum, et ante particulares benedictiones quid sit benedictio."

[g] *OL* " deum fuisse secrete benedicentem ante verba dicentis."

[h] *προγνωστικῇ δυνάμει*, *cf. Vita Mosis* ii. 190, where this power is ascribed to Moses.

[i] *ἐνάρθρῳ φωνῇ.* The meaning of the sentence is obscure. Aucher renders, " quoniam unus neque quidquam dixit oretenus : alter vero virtute prophetica ab initio usque ad finem reddidit benedictiones articulata voce " : *OL* " illo enim necdum ori (*sic*) liniamenta distinguente praescia virtute culminis destinantur benedictiones usque in finem paratissime pronuntiatae."

[j] Aucher " quare et finem concludit divinae vocis oraculo secundum illud quo patefecit nimirum benedixisse ei " : *OL* " unde etiam terminum designat responso divino lex, prius declarando quoniam benedixit eum." Apparently Philo is

213. (Gen. xxvii. 25-27) Why, when he had eaten and drunk [a] and smelled his [b] garments, is he said to have blessed (him)? [c]

The literal text [d] does not require any explanation.[e] But as for the deeper meaning,[f] it has a certain necessary speculation.[g] For symbolically [h] the garments are visible decency [i] and opinion, which to many is seemly, splendid and approved.[j] And this, too, is a praiseworthy part, which those use who are not perfected in virtue.[k] Deservedly is the good man [l] introduced [m] both because he desires this and because he partakes of that food which is intellectual.[n]

---

drawing attention to the significance of the fact that the expression " he blessed him " stands at the end of a verse.

[a] *OL* omits the reference to Isaac's drinking.

[b] Jacob's.

[c] Philo summarizes vss. 25-27a, which read, *καὶ εἶπεν, Προσάγαγέ μοι καὶ φάγομαι ἀπὸ τῆς θήρας σου, τέκνον, ὅπως εὐλογήσῃ σε ἡ ψυχή μου· καὶ προσήνεγκεν αὐτῷ καὶ ἔφαγεν· καὶ εἰσήνεγκεν αὐτῷ οἶνον, καὶ ἔπιεν.* (26) *καὶ εἶπεν αὐτῷ Ἰσαὰκ ὁ πατὴρ αὐτοῦ, Ἔγγισόν μοι καὶ φίλησόν με, τέκνον.* (27) *καὶ ἐγγίσας ἐφίλησεν αὐτόν· καὶ ὠσφράνθη τὴν ὀσμὴν τῶν ἱματίων αὐτοῦ. καὶ ηὐλόγησεν αὐτὸν κτλ.*

[d] *τὸ ῥητόν.* [e] *λόγου*: *OL* " dubitationem."

[f] *τὸ πρὸς διάνοιαν.*

[g] *θεωρίαν τινὰ ἀναγκαίαν*: *OL* " relationem necessariam."

[h] *συμβολικῶς.*

[i] *εὐκοσμία*, *cf. De Mut. Nom.* 246: Aucher " probitas ": *OL* " censuram spectabilem."

[j] Aucher, in disregard of the syntax, renders, " qua apud multos habetur quisquam in bona probataque aestimatione ": *OL* " quae est apud probabilis," and makes " existimatio " (= Arm. *karcik'* = Gr. *δόξα*) the subject of the following sentence.

[k] *οἱ μὴ τελειωθέντες ἀρετῇ* : *OL* " minus perfecti."

[l] *ὁ ἀστεῖος* or *ὁ σπουδαῖος.*

[m] *OL* " utator " (*sic* : *v.l.* " ut autor ").

[n] *τῆς κατὰ λογισμὸν τροφῆς vel sim.*: Aucher " tum id desiderante (patre) tum participanti cibum mysterii ": *OL* " hujus stolae prosequitur ad fructum meliorem."

214. (Gen. xxvii. 27b) Why does he begin the blessings in this way, "Behold, the smell of my son is like the smell of a full field, which the Lord [a] has blessed" [b]?

Full is that place in which are all seeds, trees, flowers and fruits.[c] And deserving of blessings is not that which at one time (only) is fragrant [d] and well provided with grain and fruit [e] but that which continually enjoys fertility. And in the soul is a place full of wisdom [f] and herbage of virtue.[g] And the fruits are its several deeds and the words that accompany them,[h] each of which in some way [i] has its own smell,[j] some accompanied by the prudence of wisdom, some by temperance, and others by justice.[k] For our lives are, as it were, made fragrant by our several virtues, for through their speech they send out breaths and exhalations to those near by, who are greatly gladdened when struck by incorporeal smells which are better than incense or myrrh or any other material (smells).[l] Now

[a] *OL* "deus."

[b] LXX Ἰδοὺ ὀσμὴ τοῦ υἱοῦ μου ὡς ὀσμὴ ἀγροῦ πλήρους (Heb. lacks the adjective "full") ὃν ηὐλόγησεν κύριος.

[c] *OL* "plenus itaque ager serendorum arborumque florentium frugiferis auspiciis."

[d] εὐώδης.

[e] εὔσταχυς καὶ εὔκαρπος: *OL* "quod non tempore segetis (*v.l.* "egestuosus") a fecunditate sit."

[f] σοφίας. Aucher, construing slightly differently, renders, "animae vero campus est plenus sapientia": *OL* "est enim anima plena sapientiae et ager, etc."

[g] ἀρετῆς.

[h] ἕκαστα τὰ ἔργα καὶ οἱ κατ' αὐτὰ λόγοι: *OL* "fruges autem facit laudabiles ipsis operibus veritatis."

[i] τρόπον τινά.

[j] *OL* "quarum singulae proprio (*v.l.* "pro pio") pollentes odore benedicuntur."

[k] ὧν τὰ μὲν κατὰ φρόνησιν σοφίας (prob. originally κατὰ φρόνησιν), τὰ δὲ κατὰ σωφροσύνην, τὰ δὲ κατὰ δικαιοσύνην: *OL* has merely "pro vigilantia pudicitia."

[l] *OL* freely "de singulis enim vitales oriuntur vapores suavitatis in dicendis gerendisque: suos etiam approximantes delectant, quod melius est totius libaminis et hostiarum et odoramentorum jucundius: pulsantes enim mentes incorporaliter exhortantur ampliare charitatem."

that which is said above all things [a] is the seal of confirmation of Him Who is above.[b] For to bless and to be blessed by Him Who holds the foundation of all things and is Lord in truth renders the spiritual field [c] full of virtues.[d] For it is fitting to recognize clearly that wherever God is not present, that (place) is altogether imperfect and is easily taken.[e]

215. (Gen. xxvii. 28) Why does he say, "May the Lord God [f] give to thee of the dew of heaven and of the fatness of earth" [g]?

He receives the most excellent order [h] of blessings, which, according to the same prophet,[i] the creation of the world had. For he gave first place to heaven, and second to earth, wishing to teach us that it befits the virtuous man [j] to turn toward [k] and acquire heavenly and divine things first, and in the second place, earthly and corruptible things. For the former are the heads and higher parts, and the latter are the bases and lower parts. In man the mind [l] is like

[a] This is a literal rendering of the obscure Arm. clause.

[b] Aucher "qui supremus est."

[c] τὸν πνευματικὸν (or ψυχικὸν) ἄγρον.

[d] *OL* paraphrases, "est enim pro integro titulo plenissime dictum, quod siquid benedicitur acceptabile est autori domino universorum, ipsa veritate plenum agrum bonarum virtutum in corde operantis" (*sic*).

[e] *OL* again renders freely, "res autem minus perfectae sunt et fluxidolae quae elongantur a scientia dei."

[f] *OL*, like LXX and Heb., has only "God."

[g] LXX καὶ δῴη σοι ὁ θεὸς ἀπὸ τῆς δρόσου τοῦ οὐρανοῦ ἄνωθεν (Heb. omits "from above") καὶ ἀπὸ τῆς πιότητος τῆς γῆς. Philo omits the concluding phrase, καὶ πλῆθος σίτου καὶ οἴνου, as also in *De Migratione* 101, where he briefly allegorizes this verse in similar fashion.

[h] τάξιν.

[i] *i.e.* Moses. *OL*'s "profectu" is an obvious corruption of "profeta."

[j] τῷ σπουδαίῳ: *OL* "vigilantissimo."

[k] Aucher "morem gerere."

[l] ὁ νοῦς.

heaven, for they are both rational parts, the one of the world, the other of the soul.[a] But sense-perception[b] (is like) the earth, for both are irrational.[c] Fittingly, therefore, does he pray and ask that the progressive man[d] become better in respect of both the rational and irrational (part) by acquiring a "fat" sense-perception and a "dewy" mind. And symbolically[e] "dew" is the divine Logos,[f] which greatly, fittingly, gently and continually brings profit to the sovereign mind.[g] But lavish "fatness" is the abundance of provisioning[h] in accordance with the several senses when they are restrained by continence and temperance.[i] Excellently, moreover,[j] did the ancients say that riches and noble birth[k] and friendships and honours and whatever similar things are external are serviceable to the body,[l] while health and power[m] and keenness of

[a] *λογικὸν μέρος ἑκάτερός ἐστιν, ὁ μὲν τοῦ κόσμου, ὁ δὲ τῆς ψυχῆς.*

[b] *ἡ αἴσθησις.*

[c] *ἄλογοι.*

[d] Arm. has the infinitive but the context requires the participle = *ὁ προκόπτων*. Similarly Aucher renders, "proficiens."

[e] *συμβολικῶς.*

[f] *ὁ θεῖος λόγος.*

[g] *τῷ ἡγεμόνι νῷ.* *OL* alters the order of the preceding sentences and condenses. It also contains a Christian interpolation, "et asserunt ipsum coelum animal esse: unde credo Apollinaristas incarnationis animam negasse, indignam salvatoris existimasse."

[h] *χορηγίας*: Aucher "officii choragi (*vel* regiminis)."

[i] *ἐγκρατείᾳ καὶ σωφροσύνῃ*: Aucher "sub habena religionis et sobrietatis": *OL* renders inaccurately, "pinguedo vero copiosae sumministrationis sensualitatis secundum continentiam gubernantem."

[j] Text and meaning uncertain: Aucher "quoque": *OL* "etiam."

[k] *εὐγένεια*: *OL* "parenteles."

[l] *OL*, omitting the last verb and noun, renders, "et alia hujus modi extra corpus esse."

[m] So *OL*, "fortitudinem": Aucher "virtus."

sense [a] (are serviceable) to the soul, as is the soul to the mind.[b] For the senses are its servants, and the mind is God's.[c] From this it is clear that all things serve God, beginning with that which has the highest position in us, (namely) that allotted to the mind.

216. (Gen. xxvii. 29) Why does he say, "The nations shall serve thee" [d]?

The Law is not an exponent of inequality [e] so as to proclaim servitude to all nations, for it is accustomed to reject also those who have obtained liberty.[f] But it recognizes that it is not profitable for all men to be released and free,[g] for many use this (liberty) unrestrainedly and skittishly, kicking and trampling upon that which is right and useful.[h] For this reason, wishing to bring profit to the multitude,[i] it placed a lord [j] over them as a driver, (namely) the mind,[k] in order that it might rein in that to which it is bound.[l] That is the literal meaning.[m] But as for the allegorical

[a] εὐαισθησία: Aucher "bonus sensus": *OL* "sensibilitatem."

[b] ἡ ψυχὴ τῷ νῷ.

[c] *OL* "animam ergo mens protegit et sensus mente stipatur."

[d] LXX καὶ δουλευσάτωσάν σοι ἔθνη.

[e] *OL* "non sunt iniqua legis instituta."

[f] Aucher "quum libertate quoque praeditos consueverit distinguere," adding in a footnote "*vel*, ejicere (a libertate)": *OL* "cum etiam (*v.l.* "eo") minimos in libertatem vocare consuevit."

[g] *OL* "non omnibus utilem esse securitatem."

[h] *OL* renders unintelligibly, "nec acurentur (*v.l.* "alterentur") jura per requiem divaricantibus gentibus adversus ea quae expedit."

[i] *OL* "vitiis," evidently reading πάθει instead of πλήθει.

[j] κύριον.

[k] ὡς ἡνίοχον, τὸν νοῦν: *OL* "utpote agnatorem (*l.* "aurigam"?), ut mentis, etc." (see next note).

[l] τὸ σύνδετον, *i.e.* the body, *cf. Leg. All.* iii. 72 *et al.* *OL* renders inaccurately, "ut mentis ingenio procax infrenaretur caterva."

[m] τὸ ῥητόν.

meaning,[a] this is to be said. There are many nations in the soul, in its various [b] irrational parts,[c] I mean such as anger and desire,[d] for which nothing is so useful as to be ruled by reason, their natural ruler and lord.[e]

217. (Gen. xxvii. 29b) What is the meaning of the words, "Princes shall bow down to thee" [f]?

He corroborates and extends the argument,[g] for first [h] it subjected commoners [i] to him, and now nobles.[j] And the "princes" are those who preside over and are in charge of heterodox principles,[k] whose concern it is to pride themselves on and glorify whatever is connected with the body and external goods.[l] And they deride and jeeringly mock at discipline, wisdom, continence and endurance [m] and all the other things which preserve the soul [n] without passion and without disease.[o]

[a] ἀλληγορικῶς.

[b] Emending Arm. *erkak'anćiur* "both" to *iurak'anćiur* "each": *OL* "singulis." Aucher follows the Arm. text in rendering "utramque."

[c] τὰ ἄλογα μέρη.

[d] ὀργὴ καὶ ἐπιθυμία.

[e] ὑπὸ τοῦ λόγου τοῦ γνησίου ἄρχοντος αὐτῶν καὶ κυρίου.

[f] LXX καὶ προσκυνήσουσίν σοι ἄρχοντες (Heb. "peoples").

[g] τὸν λόγον.

[h] *i.e.* in the preceding sentence of vs. 29.

[i] ἰδιώτας (so Philo interprets the Scriptural word "nations"): Aucher "rusticos": *OL* "privatos."

[j] εὐγενεῖς *vel sim.*: Aucher "liberos": *OL* "principes."

[k] λόγων ἑτεροδόξων: Aucher "sermonum alienae sententiae": *OL* "sectarum quarundum (*sic*)."

[l] *OL* renders defectively, "quibus sollicitudo est haec curare quae corpori expediunt."

[m] παιδείαν καὶ σοφίαν καὶ ἐγκράτειαν καὶ καρτερίαν: Aucher "disciplinam sapientiam et sobrietatem religiosam": *OL* "industriam, sapientiam, pudicitiam, continentiam, patientiam."

[n] τὴν ψυχήν.

[o] *OL* has (after "patientiam") merely "et horum similia."

218. (Gen. xxvii. 29c) What is the meaning of the words, " Be lord of thy brother " [a] ?

He extends (the argument) still farther, gradually coming nearer and going higher. First he mentioned commoners,[b] then princes, and then the nearest kin.[c] But can he who is the teacher of humaneness and domesticity [d] possibly publish this greatest of wrongs in the sacred scriptures, for what could be a greater wrong than for brother to be lorded over by brother ? Such a thing it is not right either to think or to say. But, as I said a little earlier, he believes that it is more profitable for the foolish man [e] not to be free but rather to have wisdom as a mistress,[f] in order that in the fashion of a good physician she may expel his fever and cure the passions and diseases in his miserable and unhappy life.[g] But those who are wont to allegorize [h] may say that the brothers are parts of the soul, the rational and irrational [i] and that the rational ranks above and is appointed over and is lord of the irrational by the law of a more righteous nature.[j] And so long as the former rules, the latter is in a good way of life.[k] But if it becomes indignant and withdraws as if from

[a] LXX *καὶ γίνου κύριος τοῦ ἀδελφοῦ σου.* Philo omits the rest of the sentence *καὶ προσκυνήσουσίν σε οἱ υἱοὶ τοῦ πατρός σου* (Heb. " of thy mother ").

[b] *ἰδιώτας*, see above, *QG* iv. 216, 217.

[c] *OL* " proximum generis fratrem."

[d] *διδάσκαλος φιλανθρωπίας καὶ οἰκειότητος*, *i.e.* Moses.

[e] *τὸν ἄφρονα*, here symbolized by Esau.

[f] *ὡς κυρίαν ἔχειν τὴν σοφίαν.* *OL* renders freely, " dominum studiosum et prudentem virum."

[g] *ἐν τῷ ταλαιπώρῳ καὶ κακοδαίμονι βίῳ αὐτοῦ.* *OL* seems to run this clause into the following sentence, rendering, " qui eum tamquam medicus bonus ut his arceat infirmitates curando reficiat. Caeteras etiam animae anxietates sanare quamvis solent asseverare nonnulli, etc."

[h] *ἀλληγορεῖν.*

[i] *μέρη τῆς ψυχῆς, τὸ μὲν λογικόν, τὸ δὲ ἄλογον.*

[j] *OL*, construing the Greek differently from the Arm. translator, renders, " per justissimam legis naturam."

[k] *OL* " melior enim (*l.* " meliorem ") statum obtinebit."

(another's) drunkenness, (the latter) will suffer the evils of anarchy.[a] For what (else) can be expected if the pilot does not steer the ship, or the charioteer does not drive the yoked horses, or the army commander does not lead his army, or the steward does not rule the household, or the statesman [b] the state? Are not these things, therefore, to be deprecated, and should one not prayerfully ask that they may not happen? [c] Of all these the worst and most terrible is anarchy in the soul.[d]

219. (Gen. xxvii. 29d) What is the meaning of the words, "He who curses thee is cursed,[e] and he who blesses is blessed [f]" [g]?

This expresses a very natural law and opinion,[h] for he who curses the virtuous and wise man [i] first curses himself, while he who praises him similarly praises himself together with him. For, indeed, he who hates good men is himself hated,[j] while he who loves them is at once [k] loved. For (Scripture) does not say that he who curses will incur [l] a curse, and he who blesses (will obtain) blessings but that the former is cursed by himself, and the latter, on the other hand, is praised.[m]

[a] ἀναρχίας. *OL* renders the sentence freely, "porro si indignatur ut populi rebellantis callositas absente magisterio sentiat poenas seviores." [b] ὁ οἰκονομικός . . . ὁ πολιτικός.

[c] *OL* omits this clause.

[d] *OL* "quorum omnium pejor est anima sine rectore."

[e] *OL* "maledictus erit."

[f] *OL* "benedictionibus repleatur."

[g] LXX ὁ καταρώμενός σε ἐπικατάρατος, ὁ δὲ εὐλογῶν σε εὐλογημένος (Heb. has the subjects in the plural, the predicates in the singular number).

[h] *OL* "naturale arbitrium promit."

[i] τὸν ἀστεῖον (or σπουδαῖον) καὶ σοφόν: *OL* "prudentem."

[j] *OL* reads differently "revera enim laus est benivolis quod ab odiosis odiuntur."

[k] *OL* "semper." [l] *OL* "meretur."

[m] *OL* "sed quod is semel maledictus est, ut est alter similiter laudabilis."

220. (Gen. xxvii. 30) What is the meaning of the words, "When Jacob went out from the presence [a] of his father, Esau his brother came" [b]?

The literal text [c] admits no doubt or ambiguity, for it is very significant [d] and very apt.[e] For when one (of two) contraries goes out, the other follows it in. What I mean is something like this.[f] When poverty and ignominy go out, riches and honour follow them in. And when suffering and infirmity go away, health and strength come in after them. And in the same way, when continence and reason [g] go away, which have subjugated and driven out the passions by their attack,[h] there follows them unrestraint, (which is) both the seducer and protagonist of the passions.[i] And not distant or long is the interval which separates them but, as (Scripture) itself says, "while [j] he went out," (that is) after a certain (small) portion of time.[k] For the good and the bad are related to each other as contraries

[a] Lit. "face."

[b] Philo abbreviates LXX, which reads *καὶ ἐγένετο μετὰ τὸ παύσασθαι Ἰσαὰκ εὐλογοῦντα τὸν Ἰακὼβ τὸν υἱὸν αὐτοῦ* (Heb. omits "his son"), *καὶ ἐγένετο ὡς* (*v.l.* *ὅσον*, see below) *ἐξῆλθεν Ἰακὼβ ἀπὸ προσώπου Ἰσαὰκ τοῦ πατρὸς αὐτοῦ καὶ Ἠσαὺ ὁ ἀδελφὸς αὐτοῦ ἦλθεν ἀπὸ τῆς θήρας αὐτοῦ.* In his brief comment on this verse in *De Ebrietate* 9 Philo uses slightly different wording, *ἐγένετο ὅσον ἐξῆλθεν Ἰακώβ, ἧκεν Ἠσαὺ ὁ ἀδελφὸς αὐτοῦ.*

[c] *τὸ ῥητόν.*

[d] Aucher, choosing the alternative meaning of Arm. *nšanakan*, which renders both *σημαντικός* and *συμβολικός*, translates, "valde manifesta per symbolum."

[e] *OL* "auspicia naturalissima et aptissimi tituli dicentur."

[f] Aucher "exempli gratia": *OL* "ut puta."

[g] *ἐγκρατείας καὶ λόγου*: *OL* "continentiae verbo."

[h] *OL* condenses, "excervicante contumaces."

[i] *OL* "vitiorum intemperantia decurrit cum suo defensore et propugnatore."

[j] Here Philo read *ὅσον* in the LXX (see above, note *b*), as in *De Ebrietate* 9.

[k] *OL* "sed ad quantum duxerit momentum quantum exierit."

by mutual observance,[a] just as one (runner) strives to meet the next one at the starting-point.[b] For not even for a little while is the soul deserted [c] nor does it remain altogether empty even for a short time.[d] For the soul is a place of necessity [e] and is always filled with contraries and is densely [f] occupied by inhabitants.[g]

221. (Gen. xxvii. 31a) What is the meaning of the words, "He too prepared food and brought it to his father" [h] ?

Do you see that the divine oracle [i] testifies for Jacob, saying [j] that he prepared food such as his father loved ? Not so in the case of this one,[k] but it remains silent about a name being pleasing.[l] And may this not be right ? [m] For even though wicked men contrive to do things similar and equal to those done by virtuous men,[n] they are none the less deserving of hatred because they do them with

[a] *OL* "tantum ad invicem sibi praestolatur arte quadam observatissima."

[b] τῷ ἀφετηρίῳ, *i.e.* in a relay race : Aucher "quasi vero ex loco cursus in hippodromo se invicem obviassent." *OL* omits the clause.

[c] ἔρημος (rendered by two Arm. adjectives) ἡ ψυχή.

[d] *OL* renders the sentence more briefly, "ne punctum temporis cessant animae vacuitatem relinquere."

[e] τόπος ἀνάγκης (rendered by two Arm. nouns).

[f] πυκνῶς (rendered by two Arm. adverbs).

[g] *OL* renders the sentence obscurely, "necesse enim capacem contrarietatem plenam esse supervenientium habitaturum" (*l.* "habitatorum").

[h] LXX καὶ ἐποίησεν καὶ αὐτὸς ἐδέσματα καὶ προσήνεγκεν τῷ πατρὶ αὐτοῦ.

[i] ὁ θεῖος χρησμός.

[j] See Rebekah's speech in Gen. xxvii. 9 (*cf.* *QG* iv. 200).

[k] *i.e.* Esau.

[l] Aucher "sed tacetur nomen complacentiae" : *OL* "licet siletur de nomine placentis." Whatever the original, it must have meant that nothing was said (in Scripture) about Esau's food being pleasing to Isaac.

[m] *OL* omits this question.

[n] τῶν σπουδαίων.

impure minds.[a] For who does not know that sophists do the same things as wise men,[b] and perhaps still more effectively, since they are trained and exercised in words.[c] But their (speech) seems contrary and opposed (to that of the wise) and unmelodious and loathsome. And no grace blossoms over them because of the interpreters' indiscipline in character and way of life.[d] But acceptable and pleasant and sweet, as though flowing from a sweet spring, (are the words proceeding) from integrity.[e]

222. (Gen. xxvii. 31b) Why does he say, " Let my father arise and eat of the venison of his son " [f] ?

Dissimilar are the forms of address [g] of this (son) and of the former one.[h] For the latter, on entering, properly called (Isaac) by his right name, saying, " Father," but this one says unfamiliarly [i] and savagely, as though from one (stranger) to another, " Let my father arise and eat." Wherefore unwillingly, being compelled by natural necessity,[j] he utters the truth that the virtuous and wise son had placed the food before the venison of the foolish and stupid son.[k] For that which had been caught as game would perhaps become tame, but that which had been set

[a] Aucher " non ex mundis moribus ": *OL* " non puro consilio."

[b] σοφισταί . . . σοφοῖς : *OL* " commentatores velle sapientium similes titulos prosequi."

[c] λόγοις : *OL* " verborum arte."

[d] τῶν ἑρμηνέων τὴν ἀπαιδευσίαν ἤθεσι καὶ βίῳ.

[e] ἐκ καλοκἀγαθίας.

[f] LXX Ἀναστήτω ὁ πατήρ μου καὶ φαγέτω τῆς θήρας τοῦ υἱοῦ αὐτοῦ. Philo does not comment on the rest of the verse, ὅπως εὐλογήσῃ με ἡ ψυχή σου.

[g] Aucher " vociferationes " : *OL* " sententia."

[h] *i.e.* of Jacob who had appeared earlier.

[i] ἀνοικείως.

[j] φυσικῇ ἀνάγκῃ.

[k] The meaning is not altogether clear. Aucher renders, " quod insipientis filii venatum sapiens ille proponit in cibum ": *OL* has only " quoniam copiosam filii venationem."

free and made subject to savage and bestial passion would be incurable.[a]

223. (Gen. xxvii. 32a) Why, when Isaac asks, " Who art thou ? ",[b] does he not add,[c] " Son," as he had said to the former one ? [d]

These are the pleasant and desirable spices with which the wonderful Logos [e] spices holy and divine Scripture.[f] And it confutes and confounds the foolish man, since he is alien in character and is unable to show any kinship [g] to or any part of that which is worthy of zeal and virtue.[h]

224. (Gen. xxvii. 32b-33a) Why, when Esau said, " I am thy first-born son," did his father start up with a very great withdrawal [i] ? [j]

By adding the " very " (Scripture) shows the pitiable wretchedness of him from whom (Isaac) removed himself

[a] *OL* renders defectively, "scilicet mansuetorum, alioquin gurgite ferocitatis detento, insanabilis languor proveniet."

[b] LXX *καὶ εἶπεν αὐτῷ Ἰσαὰκ ὁ πατὴρ αὐτοῦ, Τίς εἶ σύ;*

[c] *OL* " unum (*l.* " non " ?) adjecit."

[d] *i.e.* to Jacob, in Gen. xxvii. 20-21 (*cf. QG* iv. 207, 209).

[e] *ὁ θαυμάσιος λόγος.*

[f] *OL* renders the sentence more freely, " hae sunt suavitates quas divina scriptura condere dignatur, divino sermone temperatus."

[g] *συγγένειαν.*

[h] *σπουδῆς καὶ ἀρετῆς.* *OL* renders the sentence freely, " corripit enim et tacere monet insipientem alienantem se a recta sententia, nullo liberalitatis indicio institutorum nec aliquo digno sobrietatis titulo."

[i] *OL* " escessu (*l.* " excessu ") mentis detentus est pater valde vehementer " (see next note).

[j] LXX *ὁ δὲ εἶπεν, Ἐγώ εἰμι ὁ υἱός σου ὁ πρωτότοκος Ἠσαύ. ἐξέστη δὲ Ἰσαὰκ ἔκστασιν μεγάλην σφόδρα* (Heb. " was fearful with a great fear " : Arm. O.T. " was astonished with very great astonishment ").

and made an additional withdrawal,[a] for he was insolent and disobedient. In the first place, he dared to present himself as a son although, as a wicked man, he was not to be reckoned in the rank of an attendant servant.[b] And in the second place, (he called himself) "first-born son," although a little while before the wretch had sold his birthright for a little sensual pleasure.[c] "For," he says, "these two things will properly be decreed and assigned only to the former one,[d] (namely) that he should be called by both names, that of 'son' and that of 'first-born,' as one who has been marked by distinction.[e] But to thee shall leave and authority not be given to say similar and identical things in arrogance, pride and insolence, for thou art[f] false to the truth."[g]

225. (Gen. xxvii. 33b) What is the meaning of the words, "I ate of all before thou camest"[h]?

The literal meaning[i] is apparent. But as for the deeper

[a] Aucher renders differently, "nimiam cum commiseratione miseriam indicat ejus, a quo recessionem perfectae renuntiationis facit": *OL* "incremento sermonis extenso, lectio notum fecit quod ultra modum compunctus erat. Indignatur namque, etc."

[b] *OL* "ne quidem famuli ordinem promerendo."

[c] ἡδονῆς.

[d] *i.e.* Jacob.

[e] Or "choice"—Arm. *antrout'iun* = διαίρεσις and ἐκλογή: Aucher "probitate (*vel* electione)": *OL* renders the sentence defectively, "haec utraque sancire libet (*v.l.* "licebit") prophetam secundum merita pignorum, quaeritentem quatenus et filius et primogenitus probaretur."

[f] Variant "they are."

[g] *OL* condenses the sentence, "alter vero ne permittitur similia postulare, pro petulantia et superbia sauciante veritatem."

[h] Philo abbreviates vs. 33b, which reads καὶ εἶπεν, Τίς οὖν ὁ θηρεύσας μοι θήραν καὶ εἰσενέγκας μοι, καὶ ἔφαγον ἀπὸ πάντων πρὸ τοῦ σε εἰσελθεῖν. The rest of the verse is quoted in the following section. Philo quotes the entire verse in *Quis Rer. Div. Heres* 251 without allegorical comment.

[i] τὸ ῥητόν.

meaning,[a] the soul of the virtuous man[b] enjoys all good things before there enters it the thought which is alienated from virtue.[c] For this, when it follows and comes in, is like a drunken ribald fellow[d] who upsets and disturbs a well-behaved and orderly gathering of drinkers of wine.[e]

226. (Gen. xxvii. 33c) What is the meaning of the words, "I blessed him, and he shall be blessed "[f]?

That " he who performs what lies before him[g] carries off that which lies in the future " is properly and appropriately[h] said concerning that which is now taking place.[i] For one[j] is undisciplined and untamed and is slow and hesitant toward all that is right and good.[k] But the other, having all discipline[l] in himself, is zealous and keen, and considers it a disgrace when someone makes more progress[m] than he himself. Wherefore he further seals this (attitude) and confirms the blessing for him, being vexed and displeased by the appearance of the unlearned man.[n] Such

[a] τὸ πρὸς διάνοιαν.
[b] ἡ τοῦ σπουδαίου ψυχή.
[c] ἀρετῆς.
[d] εὐτράπελος *vel sim.*
[e] *OL* " vice vinolenti praeconis placidum scholae convivium conturbat."
[f] LXX καὶ ηὐλόγησα αὐτόν, καὶ εὐλογημένος ἔστω (*v.l.* ἔσται).
[g] τὸ προκείμενον *vid.*
[h] κυρίως.
[i] The Arm. sentence is obscure, as Aucher remarks in a footnote to his rendering, " *qui jam opus peragit futuri praesefert perfectionem,* vere proprie dictum est de nunc factis " : *OL* " sic proverbium cujusdam legimus dicentis, Qui antecessu egerit venturi praemia portando habet (*v.l.* " abit "). Hic proprie dicitur de his qui modo consistunt."
[j] Of the two brothers, *i.e.* Esau.
[k] *OL* " inertissimus enim ille per omnia justa et optima procrastinando, et tardus et hebes revelatur."
[l] παιδείαν.
[m] προκόπτειν.
[n] τοῦ ἀμαθοῦς. *OL* renders differently, " cujus gratia confirmat benedictiones ejus adversus praesumptionem inertis, spernendo difficultatem."

is the way things are wont to be. For so long as nothing terrible or evil has crept in, whether as deed or word, the mind [a] enjoys a blessing first of all and sets forth on the open royal highway.[b] But when some (evil) [c] comes along into it, the entire soul [d] is moved and upset and agitated, and its evil-hating passion [e] swells up,[f] so that, as though in envy, it further opposes benevolence in a firmer state of mind which thereafter remains the same.[g]

*227. (Gen. xxvii. 34) Why, when Esau heard (this), did he cry out in a loud voice and very bitterly, and say, " Bless me also, father " [h] ?

The literal meaning [i] is somewhat as follows. He is vexed and grieved [j] not so much because he failed to obtain the blessings as because his brother was thought worthy

[a] ὁ νοῦς.

[b] τὴν λεωφόρον ὁδόν. *OL* renders the latter part of the sentence somewhat differently, " procedentibus benedictionibus paratur spaciosissima via ad proficiscendum."

[c] The context requires " evil " or the like to be supplied, as Aucher does : *OL* " eo tamen molestante."

[d] ψυχή : Aucher " animus " : *OL* " anima."

[e] τὸ μισοπόνηρον αὐτῆς πάθος.

[f] Syntax and meaning not clear. Aucher renders less literally, " et affectus ejus infensus contra malum intumens indignatur." *OL* has merely " pro odio malignitatis."

[g] The Arm. is very obscure. Aucher renders, " quasi vero prae invidia contrarium se objiciat benevolentiae suae ex illa comprobatione fortiori quae et deinceps in illo statu permanet " : *OL* " lacessitur etiam zelo plus exhortante justitia ad benedicendum pro infirmiori (*v.l.* " firmiori ") arbitrio ut etiam in futuro ibidem ordo perseveret."

[h] LXX ἐγένετο δὲ ἡνίκα ἤκουσεν Ἠσαὺ τὰ ῥήματα Ἰσαὰκ (*v.l.* and Heb. omit " Isaac ") τοῦ πατρὸς αὐτοῦ, ἀνεβόησεν Ἠσαὺ φωνὴν μεγάλην καὶ πικρὰν σφόδρα καὶ εἶπεν, Εὐλόγησον δὴ κἀμέ, πάτερ.

[i] τὸ ῥητόν.

[j] The Greek fragments (see next note) have only one verb.

(of them).[a] For he was envious and jealous,[b] and thought that the other's loss was of more concern and interest than his own profit.[c] For this is shown by his crying " aloud and bitterly " and his saying further, " Bless me also." [d] But as for the deeper meaning,[e] he is ignorant and wanders to and fro and is treacherous and self-contradictory and quarrelsome in deeds,[f] thoughts and words.[g] And so you see that at one and the same time he desires a blessing and is envious. And at the same time he confirms for him whom he envies the prophecy of the blessing.[h] For he who says " Bless also me " grants that the prayed-for blessing had rightly been given to the other. For that which confesses something in word but does not admit it in deed is a character-trait [i] rather than a man.[j]

[a] The Greek fragments (from Procopius, Catena Regia Inedita 1825 *et al.*) read almost identically *οὐκ ἐπὶ τῷ μὴ τυχεῖν* (*v.l.* adds *φασί*) *τῶν εὐλογιῶν οὕτω δυσχεραίνει ὡς ἐπὶ τῷ τὸν ἀδελφὸν αὐτῶν* (*v.l.* *αὐτοῦ*) *ἀξιωθῆναι.* *OL* reads defectively " pro nec dum impetrata benedictione aspernatur pro dignis fratri meritis."

[b] The Greek fragments have only one adjective (see next note).

[c] So the Greek fragments, *βασκανὸς γὰρ ὢν ἐπιμελέστερον προκρίνει* (*v.l.* *ἐπιμελεστέραν κρίνει*) *τῆς ἰδίας ὠφελείας τὴν ἐκείνου ζημίαν.* *OL* renders inaccurately, " ut pote enim fascinator curatissimam judicat plus suam utilitatem pro alterius detrimento."

[d] So the Greek fragments (which end with this sentence), *ταῦτα γὰρ ἐμφαίνεται διὰ τοῦ μέγα καὶ πικρὸν ἐκβοῆσαι* (*v.l.* *ἀνοιμῶξαι*) *καὶ ἐπιλέγειν,* " *Εὐλόγησον δὲ* (*v.l.* *δὴ*) *κἀμέ, πάτερ* " : *OL* " adeo magna et amara exclamatio innotuit, eo dicente : Benedic utique etiam me pater."

[e] *τὸ πρὸς διάνοιαν.*

[f] Reading, with Aucher, Arm. *gorcovk'* instead of *grovk'* (= " writings ") : so too *OL* (see next note).

[g] *OL* " dicetur et altero sensu versutia indocti ex utroque dolosa et sibimet adversa in negociis, sententiis, verbis."

[h] Exact meaning of the last two nouns is uncertain. Aucher renders, " confirmat orationem voto factam " : *OL* " in viso confirmat vota."

[i] *τρόπος vel sim.*

[j] *i.e.* Esau is here the symbol of an attitude rather than an

*228. (Gen. xxvii. 35) Why does he reply in this way, "Thy brother coming with deceit received thy blessing"[a]?

Now if he received it through deceit, perhaps someone may say that he is not praiseworthy; how, then, can he[b] also say, "He shall be blessed"[c]? But he seems to indicate by these statements that not every deceit is blameworthy.[d] Thus it is that night-watchers are unable to seize and overcome robbers without deceit, and army commanders (to defeat) the enemy in war; but by ambushing them they seem to achieve their end.[e] And those (acts) which are called stratagems have a similar principle, and so do the contests of athletes, for in these deceit and trickery are considered honourable, and those who by trickery overcome their adversaries are thought worthy of prizes and wreaths.[f] So that no falsehood and blame[g] attach to "with deceit" but rather praise, as it is equi-

---

historical person. *OL* renders unintelligibly, "quae tamen ore tantummodo confitetur, rem autem ipsam sine compromisso subscripsit suis moribus satisfaciens."

[a] LXX *εἶπεν δὲ αὐτῷ, Ἐλθὼν ὁ ἀδελφός σου μετὰ δόλου ἔλαβεν τὴν εὐλογίαν σου.* Heb. reads less ambiguously "Thy brother came with deceit and received thy blessing."

[b] *i.e.* Isaac. Procopius has *πῶς οὖν ἐπιφέρεις.*

[c] See *QG* iv. 226 on Gen. xxvii 33c.

[d] So Cat. Reg. Ined. 1825, *ἀλλ' ἔοικεν αἰνίττεσθαι διὰ τοῦ λεχθέντος ὅτι οὐ πᾶς δόλος ὑπαίτιός ἐστιν.* Procopius reads more briefly *αἰνίττεται τοίνυν ὡς οὐ πᾶς δόλος ὑπαίτιος.*

[e] Similarly Cat. Reg. Ined., *ἐπεὶ καὶ λῃστὰς νυκτοφύλακες καὶ πολεμίους στρατηγοί, οὓς ἀδόλως συλλαβεῖν οὐκ ἔστιν, ἐνεδρεύοντες κατορθοῦν δοκοῦσι.* Aucher divides the Arm. sentences wrongly.

[f] So Cat. Reg. Ined., *καὶ τὰ λεγόμενα στρατηγήματα τοιοῦτον λόγον ἔχει καὶ τὰ τῶν ἀθλητῶν ἀγωνίσματα· καὶ γὰρ ἐπὶ τούτων ἡ ἀπάτη νενόμισται τίμιον καὶ οἱ δι' ἀπάτης περιγενόμενοι τῶν ἀντιπάλων, βραβείων ἀξιοῦνται καὶ στεφάνων.* Procopius reads more briefly *τοιαῦτα γὰρ καὶ τὰ λεγόμενα στρατηγήματα, καὶ ἐπὶ τῶν ἀθλητῶν ὁμοίως οἱ μετὰ δόλου νικῶντες θαυμάζονται στεφανούμενοι.*

[g] The two Arm. nouns probably reflect the single Greek noun *διαβολή*, as in Cat. Reg. Ined. (see next note).

valent to "with art," for the virtuous man does nothing without art.[a]

229. (Gen. xxvii. 36) What is the meaning of what Esau says, "Rightly is his name called Jacob, for he has tripped me now for the second time. My birthright he took, and now he has taken my blessings"[b]?

Although he believes himself to be speaking the truth about both instances, he falsifies. For he[c] did not "take" either the one thing or the other[d] but kept hold[e] of both, (namely) the birthright and the blessing. For these are the private inheritance[f] of the continent[g] and disciplined man and of him who makes progress.[h] And if some foolish or stupid man seizes these for himself for the sake of appearing to be good and being thought (so) by the multitude, none the less, as though they belonged to another, does he either willingly reject them or else unwillingly disdain them.[i] Thus this is not false.[j] But what is added is

[a] Cat. Reg. Ined. *ὥστε οὐ διαβολὴ τὸ "μετὰ δόλου" ἀλλ' ἐγκώμιον ἰσοδυναμοῦν τῷ "μετὰ τέχνης." οὐδὲν γὰρ ἀτέχνως πράττει ὁ σπουδαῖος.* Procopius reads more briefly *οἷς ἰσοδυναμεῖ τὸ "μετὰ δόλου" τῷ "μετὰ τέχνης." οὐδὲν δὲ ἀτέχνως ὁ σπουδαῖος ποιεῖ.*

[b] LXX *καὶ εἶπεν, Δικαίως ἐκλήθη τὸ ὄνομα αὐτοῦ Ἰακώβ· ἐπτέρνικεν* (Heb. *way-ya'qᵉbēnî*, with a play on the name *Ya'aqōb*) *γάρ με ἤδη δεύτερον τοῦτο· τά τε πρωτοτοκεῖά μου εἴληφεν, καὶ νῦν εἴληφεν τὴν εὐλογίαν μου.* In *Leg. All.* iii. 191 Philo quotes the verse with a slight variation, reading *τότε τὰ* for *τοῦτο· τά τε.* His interpretation there is, in general, similar to that given here.

[c] *i.e.* Jacob.

[d] *OL* "nihil enim tulit."

[e] The exact meaning of the Arm. compound verbal form *i baç ehan* is not clear: Aucher "retinuit": *OL* "recepit."

[f] *ἡ ἰδία κληρονομία*: *OL* "propriae sortes."

[g] Aucher "religiosi."

[h] *OL* "certatoris jam et successibus meliorato (*sic*)."

[i] The text is obscure. *OL* renders, "nihilominus ut alienam aut ultro spernit aut invitus soluit."

[j] The text may be corrupt. *OL* renders, "et haec quidem nam (*l.* "non"?) mendose" (*l.* "mendosa").

wholly false and a lie, (namely) when he says, "And now he has taken my blessing." To this one might rightly reply,[a] "Not *thy* blessing, fellow,[b] has he taken, but one which is suitable to him. For the blessing (given) to thee takes its origin from the earth, but that (given) to him, from heaven. And thou wast inscribed among the slaves, he among the masters.[c] And thy hope is the sword and war, while to him peace is beloved, and (also) the hope of making peace.[d] Since, then, there are such great differences and distinctions between (you), how didst thou dare to say that he took thy blessing?—he who did not take any part of that which is his own."[e]

230. (Gen. xxvii. 36b-37) Why, when asked, "Why did not so great a blessing remain for me?," did the father reply,[f] "If[g] I made him thy lord and I made all his brothers servants, I supported him with threshed grain and trees.[h] But for thee, who hast angered me,[i] what shall I do, O son?"[j]?

Virtually[k] he says, "Not one of the hoped for things

[a] *OL* "ego respondebo."

[b] ὦ οὗτος, as in the rough parallel, *Leg. All.* iii. 192.

[c] δούλοις . . . δεσπόταις.

[d] Lit. "peace-making hope." *OL* renders, "spes vero pacis merito funditur."

[e] Aucher "qui nullam illiusmodi tui partem accepit": *OL* "cujus nulla portio tibi competit."

[f] *OL* "non dereliquisti mihi benedictionem pater? Respondit," etc. See LXX below.

[g] See below on LXX.

[h] *OL* "frumento et vino," so LXX, see below.

[i] This relative clause is lacking in *OL* and Scripture.

[j] LXX καὶ εἶπεν Ἠσαὺ τῷ πατρὶ αὐτοῦ, Οὐχ ὑπελείπου μοι εὐλογίαν πάτερ; ἀποκριθεὶς δὲ Ἰσαὰκ εἶπεν τῷ Ἠσαύ, Εἰ (Heb. *hen* here = "behold" rather than "if") κύριον αὐτὸν ἐποίησα σου, καὶ πάντας τοὺς ἀδελφοὺς αὐτοῦ ἐποίησα αὐτοῦ (*v.l.* αὐτῷ) οἰκέτας, σίτῳ καὶ οἴνῳ ἐστήρισα αὐτόν· σοὶ δὲ τί ποιήσω, τέκνον;

[k] δυνάμει: *OL* "in ipsa substantia": Aucher "virtute (*sive*, in intellectu)."

which it is now right for the good man to put away and acquire as his own property [a] have I left for thee." [b] For by nature [c] the good man is a ruler and lord and rich, while the foolish man is poor and a servant and beggar. But it is proper to examine and inquire what men he speaks of as being brothers of Jacob, for there was (only) one, and he a twin. But he seems to invite us to an allegory,[d] and almost openly invites us. For the present passage is not about men but about types of soul,[e] which consist of several irrational parts [f] (such as) sight, hearing, taste, smell and touch, and desires and sensual pleasures and fear and grief.[g] For the passions [h] are kin and brothers of the soul. But when he calls him "son," he does not testify to his genetic descent as a son [i] but to the silliness of a child.

231. (Gen. xxvii. 38) Why does he say, "Is there one blessing (left) to thee, father? Bless me too, father"? [j]

Even the perfectly untamed and undisciplined man [k]

[a] ἴδιον.

[b] Syntax and meaning not wholly clear. Aucher renders somewhat differently, "nec unum ex votis orationis, quae conveniebat (tibi) nunc colligere et acquirere ut bonum proprium (in footnote he adds, "sed forte etiam *bono*"), reservavi tibi." *OL* reads unintelligibly "nullum votorum titulum quem dignum est carpere vere bonum pater misi (*v.l.* "nisi") enim tibi."

[c] φύσει.

[d] ἐπ' ἀλληγορίαν παρακαλεῖν, *cf. De Opif. Mundi* 157.

[e] περὶ τρόπων (*vel sim.*) ψυχῶν: Aucher "de symbolis animarum": *OL* "de moribus animae."

[f] ἀλόγων μερῶν: *OL* "per partes animae."

[g] ἐπιθυμιῶν καὶ ἡδονῶν καὶ φόβου καὶ λύπης.

[h] τὰ πάθη.

[i] *OL* "non ut filio testimonium parentelae perhibeat."

[j] Aucher brackets the word for "father" in the second sentence, which is missing in *OL* as well. In *De Mut. Nom.* 230 Philo differs slightly from LXX in quoting the verse as Μὴ εὐλογία σοι μία (LXX μία σοι) ἐστί, πάτερ; εὐλόγησον (LXX + δή) κἀμέ, πάτερ.

[k] *OL* "maximus inertiarum cultor": Aucher "perquam ineruditus."

knows that the sources of divine grace are abundant [a] and that the mind and thoughts [b] of the virtuous man [c] overflow with good like a source. For this reason he is condemned [d] even more (severely) because in spite of seeing that which is praiseworthy, he welcomes, chooses and accepts for himself that which is blameworthy and reprehensible.[e] For pardon is (to be granted) to a blind person who stumbles [f] and falls over something, but one would rightly condemn a keen-sighted man who does not avoid or keep away from or watch out for paths that are slippery or, to speak more properly,[g] untrodden paths.[h] But another thing must be said,[i] (namely) that there is one blessing and there are also many—one in genus and many in species,[j] in accordance with differences of circumstances.[k]

232. (Gen. xxvii. 38) What is the meaning of the words, "And Isaac was dismayed, and Esau cried out in a loud [l] voice and wept" [m]?

[a] τῶν θείων χαρίτων ἄφθονοί εἰσιν αἱ πηγαί.

[b] The Arm. lit. = νοῦς (or διάνοια) λογισμῶν.

[c] τοῦ σπουδαίου or ἀστείου: Aucher "sapientis": *OL* "prudentis."

[d] κατακρίνεται: *OL* "efficitur conditionalis."

[e] *OL* renders defectively, "quoniam videndo laudabilia, amabilia, vituperabilia."

[f] Aucher, less accurately, "periclitanti": *OL* "offendenti."

[g] κυριώτερον εἰπεῖν.

[h] *OL* condenses greatly, "tanti autem acuminis virum reprehendat quivis merito pro lapsis."

[i] Aucher "porro alias dicendum erit": *OL* "proprie tamen interpretatur" (*v.l.* "interfatur").

[j] γένει μέν . . . εἴδεσι δέ: *OL* "secundum genus . . . secundum species."

[k] κατὰ τὰς τῶν συμβεβηκότων διαφοράς *vel sim.*: Aucher "juxta illorum diversitatem qui (*sic*) eam consequuntur": *OL* "pro differentia interponendorum."

[l] *OL* omits "loud."

[m] Most LXX MSS. lack this sentence but a few read κατανυχθέντος δὲ Ἰσαάκ, ἀνεβόησεν φωνὴν (*v.l.* φωνῇ μεγάλῃ) Ἠσαὺ καὶ ἔκλαυσεν. Heb. has only "And Esau lifted up his voice and wept."

He was dismayed [a] not because of his old age, for he lived thereafter over fifty years more, but because the untamed and undisciplined man possessed an understanding [b] of good and worthy thoughts [c] but made the opposite use of them.[d] And that he assumed some appearance of virtue [e] is clearly attested by the fact that he desired a blessing [f] —not from someone or other but from a man beloved of God.[g] And that he knew the wealth of blessings to be abundant (is clear) from his saying,[h] " Is there one blessing (left) to thee, father ? " And so, when the wise man [i] sees that the untaught man receives nothing more [j] of all these after so many things have happened,[k] he is, as it were, wounded and grieved at (the other's) indiscipline of character.[l]

[a] Aucher, choosing another meaning of Arm. *zljanam*, renders, " poenituit se " : *OL* " compunctum."
[b] Prob. διάνοιαν.
[c] λογισμῶν.
[d] Aucher renders somewhat differently, " ut ineruditus resipiscens bonum aggrederetur consilium et in usum utilem verteret contraria," adding in a footnote " *vel, fortasse melius ita*: propterea quod ineruditus habens intellectionem bonorum usurpabat contraria " : *OL* " quod tam inertissimus novit optimarum rerum merita, utitur autem illis in adversis."
[e] Arm. lit. = ἀρετῶν : Aucher less literally renders, " sapientis " : *OL* " meliorum."
[f] Arm. *alot'* = both εὐχή (*vel sim.*) and εὐλογία : Aucher " benedictionem " : *OL* " optibilia."
[g] Or " loving God "—Arm. *astouacasēr* = both θεοφιλής and φιλόθεος : Aucher " viro Deum amantissimo (*sic*) " : *OL* " vero (*l.* " viro ") amabili deo."
[h] *OL* " scit bene nunc adventibilem esse thesaurum, dicendo."
[i] The Arm. = ὁ ἀστεῖος (καὶ) σοφός : *OL* " strenuus," see *QG* iv. 233 for a different *OL* rendering of presumably the same Greek original.
[j] One MS. omits " more."
[k] *OL* " inductum (*v.l.* " indutum " : *l.* " indoctum ") haec omnia prosequentem et in nullo prudentiarum conspirantem."
[l] δι' ἀπαιδευσίαν τρόπων (or ἠθῶν) : Aucher renders more freely, " cruciatur animo ob ejus voluntariam ineruditionem ": *OL* " sauciatur non leviter pro spontanea ejus imprudentia " (*OL* here adds several lines of comment on various Scriptural meanings of " compunctum ").

233. (Gen. xxvii. 39) Why, after Esau cried aloud and wept, did his father begin to bless him?

Perhaps someone may say that seeing his tears, (his father) was moved to pity.[a] But whoever says this is in error. For the wise man[b] feels pity for all[c] but prays (only) for the deserving. For the deserving are the unfortunate, and not those who do themselves a wrong.[d] And so, it was not pity that aroused[e] the invoker of blessings[f] but the belief in (the other's) repentance (and turning) toward the better.[g] For he saw him weeping and shedding tears, and he believed, as was natural, that he was groaning and lamenting and bewailing his own unhappy life[h] and his indecent ways. Similar to this was the way in which (God) had pity on those whose souls were afflicted in Egypt —(namely, those of) Israel, a name (meaning) " one who sees."[i] And by groaning and lamenting and crying aloud with his voice no more than in his thoughts,[j] he attained

[a] *OL* amplifies in rendering, " lachrymas intuentem anima passum pio dolore patrem pro filio."

[b] Here, as in the preceding section, the Arm. = ὁ ἀστεῖος (καὶ) σοφός: *OL* " prudens." [c] *OL* omits " for all."

[d] *OL* renders more freely, " digni sunt miseri vel infelices, non superbi vel facinorosi."

[e] *OL* " novit," an obvious scribal error for " movit."

[f] Lit. " the one praying " or " the suppliant ": Aucher " orantem ": *OL* " obtuentem " (*l.* " optantem " ?).

[g] μετάνοιαν πρὸς τὰ κρείττονα.

[h] *OL* " pro suavitate infelicissima, felicitate." Here " suavitate " is an obvious scribal error for " sua vita " but the origin of " felicitate " is not clear. *OL* lacks the final phrase.

[i] The etymology of the name " Israel " as " one who sees (God) " is frequently given by Philo, but the syntax and meaning of this sentence are far from clear. Aucher, who comments in a footnote on its obscurity, renders, " huic similiter et in Aegypto cruciante animum suum ille qui *naturae videns nomine Israel* supplex erat ": *OL* " simile hujus patitur deprimentia Aegypti anima, et Israel mentis intuitu stibrium (*sic*)."

[j] *OL* " non regibili voce sed intelligibili."

to the salvation [a] of God, Who calls distress in difficult matters [b] " appeal " and " invocation " and " petition." [c] For He makes allowances, as is necessary for benevolence, and is indulgent to those who complain.[d]

234. (Gen. xxvii. 39) Why does he begin the blessing as follows, " Behold, from the fatness of the earth shall be thy dwelling, and from the dews of heaven from above " [e] ?

Do you see that it is by one who considers earthly things superior to heavenly things that such a mode (of speech) is introduced ? [f] But let all thanks be given to a gracious and beneficent one [g] who does not permit the mind [h] to be emptied and bereft of an excellent and most divine form [i] when it descends into an earthly body and is burned by the necessities and flames of desire,[j] for these are a true Tartarus,[k] but he permits it to spread its wings [l] sometimes and to behold heaven above and to taste (*sic*) of that sight.[m] For there are some who through gluttony, lechery

[a] *σωτηρίαν.*

[b] The whole phrase prob. = *στενοχωρίαν.*

[c] Aucher renders this obscure clause similarly, " qui angustias rerum appellationem et preces vocat." *OL* renders differently, " qui oportunas obsecrationes tacitis exclamationibus praevenit."

[d] Aucher " pro necessario beneficio remissionem ac libertatem concedens invocantibus." *OL* renders defectively, " pro beneficiis peccantium largiendo."

[e] LXX Ἰδοὺ ἀπὸ τῆς πιότητος τῆς γῆς ἔσται ἡ κατοίκησίς σου, καὶ ἀπὸ τῆς δρόσου τοῦ οὐρανοῦ ἄνωθεν.

[f] *τοιοῦτος τρόπος εἰσάγεται vel sim.* : Aucher " talis modus intervenit " : *OL* " modus iste probatur."

[g] It is not clear whether God or Isaac is meant.

[h] *τὸν νοῦν.*

[i] *OL* " a meliori et beatiori specie."

[j] Aucher " vitiis flammisque comburi cupiditatum " : *OL* " in Acheronte et Pyriphlegethonte concupiscentiarum."

[k] *OL* " hii (*sic*) sunt enim tartarei domini."

[l] *πτερύττεσθαι.*

[m] *OL* " jam deitudinis degustare scintillas."

and over-indulgence [a] are always submerged and sunken,[b] being drowned in passion.[c] And these wicked and wretched men do not wish to raise themselves up.[d]

235. (Gen. xxvii. 40a) What is the meaning of the words, "By thy sword shalt thou live" [e]?

Most naturally [f] has he shown and declared that the life of the foolish man is warfare without peace or friendship [g] but that of the righteous man [h] is deep peace.[i] For the latter rejoices in justice and security and rectitude,[j] while the former (rejoices) in strife and avarice,[k] thinking it the part of zeal to do wrong and thereby to overreach (another).[l] But peace and wrath [m] are enemies to one another.[n] And such things are fitting and proper to the dead, whereas the others are for the living. Among those (dead) I should call him thrice (wretched),[o] not once

[a] *OL* renders more briefly, "ex impuni luxuria."

[b] καταποντοῦνται καὶ καταδύονται, as in *De Agricultura* 89: *OL* "diluvium passi."

[c] Aucher renders less literally, "cupiditatibus dediti."

[d] *OL* renders more briefly, "nequaquam se exinde erigentes."

[e] LXX καὶ ἐπὶ τῇ μαχαίρῃ σου ζήσῃ. Philo allegorizes the phrase similarly in *De Congressu* 176.

[f] φυσικώτατα: *OL* "quam natus aliter" (*l.* "naturaliter").

[g] *OL* "insipientis fortunam praelium esse impraedicabile."

[h] τοῦ δικαίου.

[i] *OL* "justi vero per (*l.* "pax") altissima."

[j] δικαιοσύνῃ καὶ ἀσφαλείᾳ καὶ κατορθώσει *vel sim.*: *OL* "segregatione (*l.* "securitate" ?) et constantia."

[k] πλεονεξίᾳ.

[l] *OL* "quemlibet pati injuriam et facere."

[m] Lit. "heat"; evidently the Arm. translator read θερμός instead of θυμός.

[n] The syntax of this sentence is peculiar. Aucher renders, "pacem et iram (confundens) sibi invicem infensas." *OL* omits the sentence.

[o] The word "wretched" is supplied from *OL*, so, too, in Aucher's rendering.

(wretched), who has to suffer death through sense-perception.[a]

236. (Gen. xxvii. 40b) What is the meaning of the words, "Thou shalt serve thy brother"[b]?

This is a great good for the foolish man,[c] (namely) that he should not be left free,[d] for to be headstrong[e] is very harmful for such a man, whereas servitude is most profitable,[f] especially when he happens to get a master who is virtuous.[g] Similarly, a ship is saved when the sailors carry out the orders of the pilot and listen to him, and a household (is saved) when the slaves in service obey the master,[h] and a state[i] (is saved) when the inhabitants yield and submit to the magistrates,[j] and the young to their elders,[k] and the unskilled to the skilled and informed.[l]

237. (Gen. xxvii. 40c) What is the meaning of the words,

[a] In this sentence, too, the syntax and meaning are not clear. Aucher renders the last clause, "qui cum sensu sustinet mortem": *OL* "qui eum (*l.* "cum") nimia (*v.l.* "minima") sensibilitate mortem sustineat."

[b] LXX καὶ τῷ ἀδελφῷ σου δουλεύσεις. Philo gives slightly different allegories of this passage in *Leg. All.* iii. 193-194 and *De Congressu* 176, and a generally similar allegory in *Quod Omnis Probus* 57.

[c] *OL* renders awkwardly, "hoc (*v.l.* "ob") jam proximo bono prosecutis contumaci dignum."

[d] ἐλεύθερον: *OL* "ne laxamentum capiat."

[e] Aucher "elatio cervicis": *OL* "sine jugo degere."

[f] *OL* "dum servituti (*l.* "servitium") conditio utilissima."

[g] δεσπότου σπουδαίου: *OL* "studiosum dominum."

[h] *OL* renders somewhat differently, "et domus erigitur melius famulis vigilantibus pro imperio domini."

[i] πόλις: *OL* "urbs."

[j] *OL* renders more freely, "erit beatior si plebs subjecta sit administranti."

[k] *OL* "et juvenes veteranis debitum deferentes honorem."

[l] τοῖς ἐμπείροις καὶ ἐπιστήμοσιν: *OL* "felices (*marg.* "vides malim") (=?) et indocti sapientibus obsecundantes."

"And it shall be when thou wilt free thyself,[a] and [b] thou shalt cast off his yoke [c] from thy neck" [d]?

"As for this good, which thou believest to be evil," he says, "(namely) servitude, it comes to thee not ineptly [e] nor by chance [f] but when thou wilt cast off pride and empty vaingloriousness by giving up arrogance, and when thou wilt loosen the yoke of the passions [g] from thee. For so long as thou art under their yoke and because of them arrogantly holdest thy head high, the wise man [h] will hold thee unworthy of servitude to him and to be free. For how will it be (possible) to move about and obtain freedom without him? [i] But in place of one thou wilt acquire many masters and mistresses [j] hidden within thee, who will incessantly and uninterruptedly wear out thy soul." [k]

238. (Gen. xxvii. 41b) [l] What is the meaning of the words, "He said in his mind,[m] 'There will draw near the

[a] See the Scriptural text below.

[b] *i.e.* "then" (a Hebraism, retained in the LXX).

[c] *OL* "jugum tuum."

[d] LXX ἔσται δὲ ἡνίκα ἐὰν καθέλῃς (Heb. *tārîd*, prob. = "move freely" or the like: A.V. "have the dominion") καὶ ἐκλύσεις (*v.l.* ἐκλύσῃς, see below) τὸν ζυγὸν αὐτοῦ ἀπὸ τοῦ τραχήλου σου. In *Leg. All.* iii. 193 (see above, *QG* iv. 236), Philo cites this passage in part, ἐκλύσῃς τὸν ζυγὸν ἀπὸ τοῦ τραχήλου σου, and allegorizes in much the same way as here.

[e] οὐκ ἀπὸ σκοποῦ.

[f] *OL* "non quolibet casu advocavit tibi."

[g] τῶν παθῶν: *OL* "vitiorum."

[h] The Arm. lit. = ὁ ἀστεῖος (καὶ) ὁ σοφός: *OL* "prudens."

[i] *OL* omits this sentence.

[j] *OL* omits "and mistresses."

[k] Aucher "qui animam tuam immediate ac sine recessu deperdant": *OL* "qui tuam animam incessanter expos-cant."

[l] Philo omits the first part of vs. 41 "And Esau hated Jacob because of the blessing with which his father had blessed him."

[m] *OL* "in corde," see the Scriptural text below.

days of the mourning of my father,[a] and [b] I will kill Jacob, my brother ' " [c] ?

Wrath and ill-will are not superficial [d] but they appear from within from the heart, as the poet says.[e] For not to say (something) with the voice but (to say it) without voice, in the mind, is very clear evidence of a wrathful and deep intention.[f] Such is the wicked, maleficent, harsh, pleasant [g] and deceitful man.[h] And in addition to this he is perfectly untaught [i] and proposes to himself plans [j] and things which are impossible.[k] For how is it ever possible that to the impassive genus,[l] which nature has endowed,[m] licentiousness,[n] the disturber of the passions of the soul,

[a] The biblical text refers to the mourning for the death of Isaac, not to Isaac's mourning, as Philo takes it.

[b] *OL* " ut," see below.

[c] LXX εἶπεν δὲ 'Ησαὺ ἐν τῇ διανοίᾳ (Heb. " heart," *i.e.* " mind ") αὐτοῦ, 'Εγγισάτωσαν αἱ ἡμέραι τοῦ πένθους (*v.l.* πάθους : Heb. and Arm. O.T. " mourning," see below) τοῦ πατρός μου ἵνα ἀποκτείνω (*v.l.* καὶ ἀποκτενῶ) 'Ιακὼβ τὸν ἀδελφόν μου. In *Quod Deterius* 46 Philo quotes the last two clauses, ἐγγισάτωσαν αἱ ἡμέραι τοῦ πένθους (*v.l.* πάθους, see below) τοῦ πατρός μου ἵνα ἀποκτείνω 'Ιακὼβ τὸν ἀδελφόν μου.

[d] *OL* " non in propatulo saevit infestus."

[e] Philo is probably thinking of such Homeric phrases as περὶ κῆρι . . . ἐχολώθη and κοτεσσάμενος τό γε θυμῷ.

[f] Aucher " consilium offensi animi subdoli et profundi " : *OL* " consilii est externi et profundi."

[g] *Sic* : Aucher " blandus."

[h] *OL* " talis est pravitas malignantium iracundia suppressa scrupulosa insidiosa."

[i] *OL* omits this clause.

[j] ὑποθέσεις.

[k] *OL* " paraturas sibi inpossibiles reservando."

[l] τῷ ἀπαθεῖ γένει, as in *Quod Deterius* 46. Apparently while reading πένθους, not πάθους, in his copy of the Greek Bible, Philo interpreted πένθος as a specific form of πάθος, *cf. Quod Deterius* 46 ἡδονῆς ἢ λύπης ἤ τινος ἄλλου πάθους.

[m] Isaac is often described by Philo as a type of natural virtue.

[n] Symbolized by Esau.

should draw near and kill his virtuous brother? [a] For [b] he has been disciplined by training, exercise and labour to trip up [c] and to catch off guard and to repel, not to be tripped up and to be caught off guard and to be repelled.[d] For true life lies before him as a prize,[e] just as, on the other hand, before the wicked and evil man (lies) death, which is in sense-perception,[f] because of (his) suffering incurable pain.[g]

239. (Gen. xxvii. 42-43) Why, when his mother heard of his outburst,[h] did she say,[i] "Arise, go off [j] to Laban, my brother, in Haran" [k]?

[a] Aucher renders, less accurately, I think, "nam quomodo umquam fieri poterit ut vitium perturbatae animae adsit nationi vitiis carenti ex dono naturae; et occidere fratrem virtute praeditum?": *OL* reads defectively "nullo enim genere praevalebit laedere congeries vitiorum impassibilitatis titulum, cui permittitur a natura decipientis animam et dissipare et perimere."

[b] Arm. *our* lit. = "where": *OL* "enim."

[c] Elsewhere in Philo Jacob is called ἀσκητής and πτερνιστής, as the symbol of virtue acquired by training.

[d] *OL* "didicit enim ex industria hujusmodi frater plantare et superare, non utique superari."

[e] ἆθλον: Aucher's rendering, "bravium," seems to be a printer's error for "praemium." [f] δι' αἰσθήσεως.

[g] *OL* "dum est (*v.l.* "etiam") vita verissima ante oculos ejus preciosa, ut illi a diverso mors quam excipiat consensualitate nimiam (*v.l.* "minimam") pro pessimo contagio et insanabili cruciatu."

[h] Or "revolt": Aucher "insurgentem eum" (footnote, "Sensus est, *comminationem ejus*"): *OL* "minas."

[i] To Jacob, not to Esau, as one might suppose from Philo's wording.

[j] *OL* "surgens fuge."

[k] Philo condenses vss. 42-43, which read, in the LXX, ἀπηγγέλη δὲ Ῥεβέκκᾳ τὰ ῥήματα Ἠσαὺ τοῦ υἱοῦ αὐτῆς τοῦ πρεσβυτέρου· καὶ πέμψασα ἐκάλεσεν Ἰακὼβ τὸν υἱὸν αὐτῆς τὸν νεώτερον καὶ εἶπεν αὐτῷ, Ἰδοὺ Ἠσαὺ ὁ ἀδελφός σου ἀπειλεῖ (Heb. "seeks revenge") τοῦ ἀποκτεῖναί σε. νῦν οὖν, τέκνον, ἄκουσόν

The literal meaning[a] is clear, for it makes apparent the careful solicitude of the mother, who by causing (him) to change residence, contrives his safety.[b] But as for the deeper meaning,[c] "Laban" is to be interpreted as "whiteness,"[d] a symbol of sense-perceptible light,[e] and "Haran" as "openings,"[f] through which (Scripture) indicates some of the senses, (namely) the eyes, the ears and the nose.[g] Thus, the counsel of the soul[h] says to its fellow-counsellors and advisers,[i] "If you laboriously acquire clear, lucid and genuine endurance of patience and firmness in life, and, while dwelling near the envious man, act with complete independence, you will encounter the greatest danger because of him.[j]

μου τῆς φωνῆς, καὶ ἀναστὰς ἀπόδραθι εἰς τὴν Μεσοποταμίαν (*v.l.* and Heb. omit *εἰς τὴν Μεσ.*) *πρὸς Λαβὰν τὸν ἀδελφόν μου εἰς Χαρράν*. Philo cites vss. 42-45 in *De Fuga* 23, vss. 43-44 in *De Somniis* i. 46, and vss. 43-45 in *De Migratione* 208-211, in these places allegorizing somewhat as here.

[a] *τὸ ῥητόν.*

[b] *OL* "dictum palam designat praesagium matris transmigrationem nuntiantis pro cautela dilecti."

[c] *τὸ πρὸς διάνοιαν.*

[d] The same etymology, based on Heb. *lābān* "white," occurs elsewhere in Philo, *e.g. De Agricultura* 42.

[e] *φωτὸς αἰσθητοῦ*, *cf. Quod Deterius* 4 *τὸ ἐκτὸς αἰσθητόν . . . προσηγόρευται Λαβάν.*

[f] *τρῶγλαι.* The same etymology, based on Heb, *ḥōr* "hole," occurs elsewhere in Philo (see next note).

[g] *Cf. De Fuga* 45 *Χαρράν, ἣ μεταληφθεῖσά εἰσι τρῶγλαι, σύμβολον τῶν αἰσθήσεων.*

[h] The Arm. lit. = *λογισμὸς τῆς ψυχῆς*, here symbolized by Rebekah, who is generally for Philo a symbol of constancy.

[i] *τοῖς συνέδροις καὶ συμβούλοις.* *OL* renders the clause more freely, "suadet ergo secrete anima sobria susceptis suis."

[j] The syntax of this sentence, especially of the latter part, is far from clear. Aucher renders much more freely, I think, "quod si lucidam fidelemque patientiae et constantiae vitam acquirere studetis, in quantum assidetis apud invidiosum, omni libertate invadente eo, vix superiores eritis periculis": *OL* "si obstinatissime verissimam vitam sectando, atrocissi-

But if you take leave [a] of concord [b] and separate yourselves, do not immediately thereafter, as if you had become incorporeal, despise necessary foods or consider them bestial,[c] but at once return on the middle way, neither afflicting your bodies with hunger and want nor offering them a variety of the most splendid delicacies; and live carefully with simple elegance.[d] For what is simpler than the colour white, which is called 'Laban' in Chaldaean? [e] For those who are not firmly in control of themselves go very far wrong and cause (others) to transgress in the opposite direction.[f] But the middle course [g]

---

mum et infestissimum vicinum patimini, enormissimam excipietis cladem." My rendering is, I think, supported by the parallel passage in *De Migratione* 208-211, where Philo advises the seeker of virtue to give up philosophy just long enough to come to terms with sense and passion in order to overcome them by diplomacy. It must be admitted, however, that his various treatments of Gen. xxvii. 42-45 (see the references in note *k* on the preceding pages) are obscure, perhaps because he is embarrassed by having to explain why Rebekah (the symbol of constancy) advised Jacob to flee to Haran (the symbol of sense); see also Colson's notes in the Loeb Philo, vol. iv. p. 566, and vol. v. p. 582.

[a] *πολλὰ χαίρειν φράζοντες.*

[b] Or perhaps "association"—ὁμιλίᾳ: *OL* "ejus colloquiis." Whether Philo means separation from philosophy or from sense and passion is not clear.

[c] Aucher renders more freely, "nolite nec illico tamquam incorporii effecti contemnere corporea neque brutorum more cogitare cibos necessarios": *OL* "penitus separati tanquam incorporales ne victum quidem quotidianum habebitis."

[d] *ἁπλῇ εὐπρεπείᾳ vel sim.*: Aucher "simplici victu": *OL* "simpliciter fruentes tutiores eritis."

[e] Here, as frequently elsewhere, Philo refers to the Hebrew language as "Chaldaean."

[f] Aucher, construing differently, renders, "quoniam summa errant errareque faciunt in contraria eos (*sic*), qui non sunt constantius firmati": *OL* renders defectively, "ultra modum ergo meliora concidere possunt ad pejora."

[g] The Arm. word lit. = *αἱ μεσότητες*: Aucher "mediocritates": *OL* "mediae."

has a way out (in the form) of precaution that nothing unforeseen and irremediable be experienced.[a] "

240. (Gen. xxvii. 45b) What is the meaning of the words " Sending, I will call thee from there to here lest perchance I be bereaved of you both in one day " [b] ?

Since the literal meaning [c] is clear, we shall say allegorically [d] that she does not think that dwelling there for all time is good for the practiser [e] but that it is useful for this time.[f] For she wishes him to depart from his kin and twin, (namely) wickedness,[g] not to a simpler [h] and unlighted place but to one lighted by the senses,[i] and in some way [j] to give himself to all (kinds of) exercise, in order that after

[a] *OL* adds a passage on the symbolism of light and darkness which is evidently from a Christian hand, since it ends with the words " ad maternae ecclesiae viscera revocati."

[b] *OL* renders more briefly, " quid aestimando (*l.* " quid est mandando ") accipiam te inde ne quando orbitabor " : LXX καὶ ἀποστείλασα μεταπέμψομαί σε ἐκεῖθεν μή ποτε ἀτεκνωθῶ ἀπὸ τῶν δύο ὑμῶν ἐν ἡμέρᾳ μιᾷ. In vss. 44-45a, which Philo here omits, Rebekah tells Jacob to remain with Laban " some days " until Esau will have forgotten his anger. Philo quotes the phrase μεταπέμψομαί σε ἐκεῖθεν in *De Fuga* 47, and alludes briefly to Rebekah's ἀτεκνία in *Quod Deterius* 51.

[c] τὸ ῥητόν.

[d] ἀλληγοροῦντες φήσομεν.

[e] τῷ ἀσκητῇ, of which Jacob is a standing symbol in Philo : Aucher " religioso " : *OL* " certatorem."

[f] *OL* amplifies somewhat in rendering, " mediam hanc larem assidue habitare certatorem mater inutile arbitratur, sed ad tempus ei prodesse."

[g] Symbolized by Esau.

[h] ἁπλούστερον (τόπον). Possibly " simpler " is here used in the sense of " more primitive," as applied to Esau, see below.

[i] φωτιζόμενον ταῖς αἰσθήσεσιν : *OL* renders freely, " utpote in lucidiori quadam mentis regione exhibernantem." Possibly " lighted by the senses " has some connexion with the phrase τὰς τῆς κενῆς δόξης λαμπράς . . . εὐπραγίας in *De Fuga* 47.

[j] τρόπον τινά.

the athlete has become an accomplished fighter he may come back from there where he will no longer be cheated or harmed.[a] For he was indeed a half-youth, and as his companion at birth [b] was dead to the life of virtue,[c] she rightly feared that the other (son) too might unite with the simpler senses and gradually go on to further and superfluous senses.[d] For if he should fall in love with that place, he would not be able to return from there and would cause her [e] more serious harm, (namely) bereavement of the classes of virtuous thoughts.[f]

241. (Gen. xxvii. 46a) Why does Rebekah say to Isaac, " I am weary of my life because of the daughters [g] of the Hittites " [h] ?

The literal meaning [i] is apparent, for she seemed to be vexed because of the former [j] women who were from that land.[k] And, as was said before,[l] they were envious of her

[a] *OL* renders the last two clauses more briefly, " inde palestricon perfectum redeuntem jam minime decipiendum."

[b] *i.e.* Esau.

[c] τῷ τῆς ἀρετῆς βίῳ *vel sim.* : *OL* renders the clause more freely, " altero tamen per inopiam sobrietatis pro mortuo imputato."

[d] *OL* " veretur merito paternae quibusdam casibus (apparently reading πατρός τισι ἤθεσι *vel sim.* instead of ἁπλουστέραις αἰσθήσεσι) paulatim cedat simplicitas morum, superfluis et curiosis occupatur."

[e] Arm. *anẓn* here seems to be an indirect reflexive : *OL* " animae."

[f] The Arm. seems lit. = ἀτεκνίαν ἀστείων ἐννοιῶν τάξεων : Aucher " orbatio a filiis solidae sapientiae ordinis " : *OL* " sterilitatem (*v.l.* " stabilitatem ") insignium titulorum sapientiae."

[g] *OL* " filias filiorum " (see next note).

[h] LXX εἶπεν Ῥεβέκκα πρὸς Ἰσαάκ, Προσώχθικα (*v.l.* προσώχθισα) τῇ ζωῇ μου διὰ τὰς θυγατέρας τῶν υἱῶν Χέτ (Heb. " daughters of Heth ").

[i] τὸ ῥητόν.

[j] Variant " first."

[k] *OL* " aspernatur enim pro uxoribus prioris (*sic*) interraneis."

[l] Apparently this is a reference to *QG* iv. 88.

daughter-in-law.[a] But we must examine the more philosophical aspect through allegory.[b] The name "Hittite" (means) "being beside oneself"[c] and senselessness.[d] And the daughters of those thoughts which are beside themselves are the unrestrained impulses.[e] And these the virtue-loving soul[f] hates and very bitterly hates, for they honour that which is contrary to order and decency.[g]

242. (Gen. xxvii. 46b) What is the meaning of the words, "If[h] Jacob takes a wife from the daughters of the Hittites,[i] for what should I live?"[j]?

The philosophical character[k] is fearful and in doubt lest perhaps that part[l] which is able to be saved may not be aware that it is incurring corruption[m] by living with earthly and terrestrial things rather than heavenly ones.[n]

[a] *OL* lacks this sentence and part of the following one.
[b] *τὴν φυσικωτέραν θεωρίαν ἐπισκεπτέον ἐν ἀλληγορίᾳ.*
[c] *OL* "excessus." Aucher in a footnote conjectures *ἀποστάσια* as the original, but it was probably *ἔκστασις* as in *QG* iv. 88.
[d] *OL* "dolorationis" (*l.* "delirationis").
[e] *OL* renders more briefly, "filiae autem hujus intentabiles sunt incursiones."
[f] *ἡ φιλάρετος ψυχή*: *OL* "clementissima anima."
[g] *τάξει καὶ κόσμῳ vel sim.*: *OL* renders the clause unintelligibly, "dignus vitii quae deferendo quaeque ordinem cunctaque censuram."
[h] *OL* "Isaac," apparently a corruption of "si ac."
[i] *OL* "ex hac terra" (see next note).
[j] LXX *εἰ λήμψεται Ἰακὼβ γυναῖκα ἀπὸ τῶν θυγατέρων τῆς γῆς ταύτης* (Heb. "from the daughters of Heth like these from the daughters of the land"), *ἵνα τί μοι ζῆν;*
[k] *ὁ φιλόσοφος τρόπος vel sim.*
[l] *i.e.* of the soul.
[m] *διαφθοράν.*
[n] *OL* renders defectively, "clementissimi pectoris decus ne quando ille delitescat per contagium ejus partis quod salvari praecipue possit, terreno matrimonio ante coelestia copulato."

"If," it says, "he who seems to be a practised character [a] takes a wife from the polluted daughters of this land,[b] that is, the senses,[c] which readily wish to be polluted, or the pleasures [d] connected with the senses, and he passes over the heavenly and ever-virginal understanding,[e] what reason is there for me to live, when I see such an overturn, seizure and capture, as if of a city, and the whole soul being desolated? [f] For by nature he [g] is his brother, though hostile in character, and from the beginning being a hater of virtue,[h] he walked in a trackless path,[i] disregarding that which led right and straight. And being alienated from familiarity with that which has discipline,[j] he gladly welcomed the savagery which knows no discipline, and made his mind completely savage through anger, desire, wrongdoing and cunning." [k]

243. (Gen. xxviii. 2) [l] Why does his father say, "Arise, go off to Mesopotamia to the home of Bethuel, the father

[a] ἀσκητικὸς τρόπος: *OL* "qui jam studiosus est moribus inquinatissimis" (the last word perhaps being all that remains of the rendering of the following phrase).

[b] Aucher, construing slightly differently, renders, "ex filiabus hujus terrae (hominum) immundorum."

[c] τὰς αἰσθήσεις.

[d] τὰς ἡδονάς.

[e] ἐῶν (*vel sim.*) τὴν οὐρανίαν καὶ ἀειπάρθενον διάνοιαν: *OL* "praevaricando (*l.* "praetereundo"?) coelestia copulato, quae semper casta sunt concilia."

[f] *OL* omits this last phrase.

[g] Apparently Esau is meant, although he is not mentioned in this verse.

[h] μισάρετος: *OL* "detentus odio clementiae."

[i] *OL* "perversas vias."

[j] *OL* has merely "mansuetudinis (*sic*) alienatus."

[k] θυμῷ καὶ ἐπιθυμίᾳ καὶ ἀδικίᾳ καὶ πανουργίᾳ: *OL* "desideriorum iniquis venatus (*v.l.* "venenatus") se religavit astutiis."

[l] Gen. xxviii. 1 reads "And Isaac, calling Jacob to him, blessed him and commanded him, saying, Thou shalt not take a wife from the daughters of Canaan."

of thy mother,[a] and take for thyself a wife from the daughters of Laban, the brother of thy mother "[b]?

The literal meaning[c] is easy to understand, (namely that) the father orders his son to make a journey to a foreign (land)[d] (and) to seek in marriage[e] a wife of his (own) race.[f] But as for the deeper meaning,[g] it has a symbolical explanation somewhat as follows.[h] In the council-meeting of the soul, in which the thoughts are gathered, it says to the better part,[i] " Thou seest the wicked man uttering cries of accusation against thee.[j] Why dost thou delay and (why) dost thou not move and leap up? And since thou art still resorting to the weaker labours of war and not yet acting with firm enough force to be able to offer opposition and to gain victory through the pursuit of virtue,[k] go away, flee.[l] For if thou removest thy dwelling somewhere far from such a beast, thou wilt fare better and happily, and his desire and anger will cease,

[a] *OL* " matris meae."

[b] LXX ἀναστὰς ἀπόδραθι (Heb. " go ") εἰς τὴν Μεσοποταμίαν (*v.l.* + Συρίας: Heb. " to Paddan Aram ") εἰς τὸν οἶκον Βαθουὴλ (Heb. *B^ethû'ēl*, see below) τοῦ πατρὸς τῆς μητρός σου καὶ λάβε σεαυτῷ ἐκεῖθεν γυναῖκα ἐκ τῶν θυγατέρων Λαβὰν τοῦ ἀδελφοῦ τῆς μητρός σου. Philo quotes the LXX text verbatim in *De Poster. Caini* 77 (without commentary) and in *De Fuga* 48 with an allegorical commentary similar to but briefer than the one given here.

[c] τὸ ῥητόν.

[d] *OL* renders defectively, " in utroque permittere."

[e] μνηστεύειν: *OL* " ad copulandam."

[f] *OL* " proprii generis."

[g] τὸ πρὸς διάνοιαν.

[h] συμβολικὴν ἀπόδοσιν τοιαύτην τινὰ ἔχει.

[i] *OL* " concilium bonarum cogitationum suarum convocando animas vadat (*l.* " anima suadet ") meliori parti."

[j] *OL* condenses, " videns infestum adversarium."

[k] σπουδῇ ἀρετῆς.

[l] *OL* renders defectively, " sed exurgens dum adhuc firmis (*l.* " infirmis " ?) doloribus uteris nec dum certamine prolatam fortitudinem demonstrantes nec ad retribuentem praevalentes festinanter recede."

and (though they are) wicked and fatal, they will become empty and vain.[a] Therefore go off, flee to Mesopotamia, in word [b] to a land in which Chaldaeans and Babylonians dwell, but in truth to the boundary between the region of virtue and that of wickedness,[c] which is progress and improvement,[d] (that is) a path leading to felicity." [e] For the land which is now called Mesopotamia is between two rivers, the Tigris and Euphrates.[f] And as for its place in the soul, it is the boundary, (consisting) of progress and improvement, between wickedness and virtue, as has been said.[g] Of these, wickedness, being ferocious, is equated with the Tigris,[h] whereas virtue, through which joy is obtained, has a name, "pleasantness," similar to that of the river called Euphrates.[i] And "Bethuel" is to be interpreted as "daughter of God." [j] It is a power [k] honoured with second (place) of lineal descent after the

[a] The text and meaning are not wholly certain. Aucher renders more freely, "et ejus ardor ac indignatio malae indolis exitialesque irritae cessabunt": *OL* "hii quoque (*v.l.* "quotque") furorae (*sic*) et concupiscentiae instinctu malitiarum evanescunt."

[b] λόγῳ μέν, contrasted with ἀληθείᾳ δέ below.

[c] τὸ μεσόριον τῆς ἀρετῆς καὶ τῆς κακίας *vel sim.*: *OL* "os (*sic*) malitiae atque virtutis." Philo's implied etymology of "Mesopotamia" differs from those implied in *De Confus. Ling.* 66 ἐν μεσαιτάτῳ ποταμοῦ βυθῷ τῆς διανοίας and in *De Fuga* 49 μέσον τὸν χειμάρρουν ποταμὸν τοῦ βίου.

[d] προκοπὴ καὶ βελτίωσις, *cf. e.g. De Sacr. Abelis* 113.

[e] εἰς εὐδαιμονίαν: *OL* "aut beatitudine" (*l.* "ad beatitudinem").

[f] In Armenian called *Dklatʻ* and *Araccani*, as in *QG* i. 13 (with a slight difference in spelling) and *QG* iv. 93.

[g] *OL* renders more briefly, "talis enim in anima grumus est malitiae atque virtutis."

[h] The same word-play occurs in *Leg. All.* i. 63 f. and *QG* i. 13.

[i] This word-play on εὐφροσύνη and Εὐφράτης is found in *QG* i. 13, where the Euphrates is a symbol of δικαιοσύνη.

[j] So Philo etymologizes elsewhere, see *QG* iv. 97, notes.

[k] δύναμις.

masculine.[a] And this has a place in the soul which [b] the noble word [c] calls " home " [d] from which (Isaac) commands him to take a wife who loves the wisdom of knowledge.[e] And the wife's name was " continence," [f] (and she was) of the daughters of the brilliant family,[g] which in Chaldaean is called " Laban," and in Armenian,[h] " whiteness." [i] There are some who, looking at the faces of things,[j] either blame them or praise them. But for us, for whom it is natural to allegorize [k] and who seek other things beyond

[a] *OL* " secundo quodam gradu pro maribus sustitutus sicut in haereditatibus : prerogativus titulus et subcisivus." This obscure passage is explained by the parallel, *De Fuga* 51, where Philo says that Bethuel, " daughter of God "= σοφία, " occupies a second place and therefore was termed feminine to express the contrast with the Maker of the universe, who is masculine."

[b] The rel. pron. refers to " place " (as in *OL*), not to " soul," as in Aucher's rendering.

[c] *OL* " sermo divinus." Philo nowhere else describes Scripture as " noble " or the like.

[d] *i.e.* the home of Bethuel.

[e] *σοφίαν τῆς ἐπιστήμης vel sim.* : *OL* has merely " disciplinae."

[f] Arm. *krōnaworout'iun* usually renders ἐγκράτεια, more rarely θρησκεία. Aucher here renders, " continentia," adding in a footnote, " Vel *Sobrietas*, ad verb. *religio*." *OL* has " possessio," which may render a corruption of ἐγκράτεια. Elsewhere in Philo Rachel is a symbol of αἴσθησις, and Leah, etymologized as ἡ κοπιῶσα, is a symbol of δικαιοσύνη and similar virtues. Apparently Leah is meant here.

[g] *OL* " pro filiis generis praeclari."

[h] Here, as elsewhere, the Arm. translator substitutes " Armenian " for " Greek."

[i] *OL* " quod jam diximus Laban, Graece enim διειδής (*sic*)." On the etymology " white " for Laban see *QG* iv. 239.

[j] *OL* " personis," reflecting προσώποις.

[k] Arm. lit.= " to whom through allegory is nature," apparently a misunderstanding of οἷς ἀλληγορεῖν πέφυκε. Aucher renders, " nobis tamen quae (*l.* " qui " ?) allegoricam quaerimus naturam " ; *OL* " nobis tamen, qui per allegoricum examen ista requirimus."

that which is seen,[a] it is fitting and proper to examine and question the names, and not to be deceived or taken in by homonyms.[b] Between these [c] there is a distinction and difference: there is one quality [d] which is perfect and splendid and like light,[e] and there is (another) somewhat sense-perceptible quality [f] which is superficially coloured [g] as in those images painted deceptively by bad men.[h]

244. (Gen. xxviii. 7) [i] What is the meaning of the words, "Jacob heard his father and mother, and went to Mesopotamia" [j]?

As for the literal meaning,[k] praise is given to the journeying of the son who obeyed both parents. For some please only one (parent), showing incomplete virtue.[l] And there

[a] *OL* "quia (*l.* "quae" ?) semota sunt a visibilibus."

[b] ὁμωνυμίαις.

[c] *i.e.* the different qualities of whiteness.

[d] ποιότης: Aucher "creatura" (but he gives "qualitas" below for the Arm. synonym of the word used here).

[e] *OL* renders freely, "sic et modo candor, quem ajunt esse Laban, perfecta translatione lucidus vel splendens."

[f] Laban appears as a symbol of sense-perception (αἴσθησις) in several other passages of Philo, *e.g. Leg. All.* iii. 20.

[g] Apparently "with bright colours" is meant.

[h] *OL* amplifies in rendering, "sin vero secundum visibilia transtuleris, nomen candoris, hoc est, albescentis coloris indicium, ut solent pictores ex candore colorum faciem exprimere interno minio." *OL* adds "ita enim Isaac, qui dicitur risus, perfecta translatione serenus atque lucidus intelligitur."

[i] The four verses, Gen. xxviii. 3-6, passed over by Philo, tell of Isaac's blessing Jacob and sending him to Laban and of Esau's overhearing the blessing and Isaac's charge to Jacob not to take a Canaanite wife.

[j] LXX καὶ ἤκουσεν Ἰακὼβ τοῦ πατρὸς καὶ τῆς μητρὸς ἑαυτοῦ καὶ ἐπορεύθη εἰς τὴν Μεσοποταμίαν. In the citation of this verse in *De Congressu* 70, the MSS. of Philo vary between εἰσήκουσεν and ὑπήκουσεν for LXX ἤκουσεν. Philo's brief commentary there differs from that given in the present passage.

[k] πρὸς τὸ ῥητόν.

[l] ἡμιτελῆ ἀρετήν.

are still others who do not (please) even one (parent). These the legislator [a] has denounced and threatened with death.[b] Whence it is clear that (Scripture) has publicly proclaimed [c] life and immortality [d] for those who offer parents a piety [e] that is sound, full and perfect.[f] And as for the deeper meaning, symbolically [g] it appears that praise is bestowed when the continent type of soul honours the sovereign reason,[h] which has the force of a father, and the knowledge of discipline,[i] which bears the glorious honour of a mother who nourishes and tends and carefully watches over (her child).[j]

245. (Gen. xxviii. 8-9) What is the meaning of the words, " When Esau saw that the daughters of the Canaanites [k] were evil before his father Isaac, he went and took Mahalath,[l] the daughter of Ishmael the son of Abraham,[m] the sister of Nebajoth,[n] in addition to his other [o] wives as a wife " ? [p]

[a] ὁ νομοθέτης, *i.e.* Moses.

[b] *OL* renders the sentence defectively, " quidam autem (*v.l.* " enim ") semiplenam et mancam exhibent devotionem malis, nec ipsam quibus legislator interminatur mortem."

[c] προυκήρυξε : *OL* " praedicari."

[d] ἀθανασίαν.

[e] εὐσέβειαν.

[f] *OL* renders freely, " qui recto corde et integra mente utrorumque parentum pietatem suscipiunt."

[g] τὸ πρὸς διάνοιαν συμβολικῶς.

[h] ὅταν ὁ ἐγκρατὴς ψυχῆς τρόπος τὸν ἡγεμονικὸν λόγον τιμᾷ : *OL* " cum studiosi sobrietas moribus synceri pectoris (*v.l.* " pastori ") ornatur et verbo praedicantis defert."

[i] ἐπιστήμην παιδείας.

[j] *OL* renders the latter part of the sentence freely, " pro paterna virtute et disciplinarum dignitati, favens pro materna quoque clementia, quae nutrit et diligit."

[k] *OL* " Chanaan," see note *p*.

[l] Arm. *Mayelet'*, see note *p*.

[m] *OL* omits this phrase.

[n] Arm. *Nabeōt'*, see note *p*.

[o] Reading, with Aucher, *ailoc* " other " for *aync* " those."

[p] LXX καὶ ἴδεν Ἠσαὺ ὅτι πονηραί εἰσιν αἱ θυγατέρες Χανάαν (*v.l.* τῶν Χαναναίων) ἐναντίον Ἰσαὰκ τοῦ πατρὸς αὐτοῦ καὶ ἐπο-

Here, in the present passage, is to be discerned the difference between the former (son) [a] and the one now in question. For the former pleased both his parents and men in the manner of teachers.[b] But the latter [c] did not please anyone, and wishing to act stealthily and secretly in order to seem to be showing honour, he was not mindful of his mother but only of his father.[d] And the wretch does not make even this dissimulation complete,[e] but knowing exactly [f] that his father was displeased with the inhabitants of the land, he did not send away those (wives) whom he had but took others in addition to them, (thus) adding sin to sin and not being absolved of the former ones. Therefore the prophet,[g] ascribing shamelessness to him, adds that he did not send (his wives) away but took a wife in addition to his other wives. This fact is not to be taken as casual or incidental or by the way, but as proof [h] of the goodwill [i] which he had for the women who were alienated from wisdom [j] and whom his incorruptible and impartial father judged evil. "But why, O miserable man," we might say to him, "wouldst thou join and connect thyself

ρεύθη 'Ησαὺ *πρὸς* 'Ισμαήλ, *καὶ ἔλαβεν τὴν* Μαέλεθ (Heb. *Maḥ*[a]*lath*) *θυγατέρα* 'Ισμαὴλ *τοῦ υἱοῦ* 'Αβραάμ, *ἀδελφὴν* Ναβαιὼθ (Heb. *N*[e]*bāyôth*) *πρὸς ταῖς γυναιξὶν αὐτοῦ γυναῖκα.*

[a] *i.e.* Jacob.

[b] The meaning of the last phrase is uncertain. Aucher renders, "tamquam exemplar (*vel*, "exemplaribus") magistrorum": *OL* "ut censura discipuli magistris." Perhaps Philo means that Jacob obeyed his parents as men regularly obey their teachers.

[c] *i.e.* Esau. *OL* has "hi," an obvious scribal error for "hic."

[d] The text of the last phrase is uncertain. *OL* renders, "patrem vero hucusque."

[e] *ὁλόκληρον ὑπόκρισιν.*

[f] Or "clearly."

[g] *ὁ προφήτης*, *i.e.* Moses. *OL*'s "profecto" is an obvious scribal error for "profeta."

[h] Or "reproof"—*ὡς ἔλεγχος*: Aucher "sicut reprehensionem": *OL* "pro testimonio."

[i] *τῆς εὐνοίας vel sim.*: Aucher "intimae amicitiae": *OL* "favoris."

[j] Or "understanding": *OL* "sapientiae et pudicitiae."

with a third (wife)?" [a] But who indeed can bring into a state of reformation that which is with him? Nothing at all (can be done) but, on the contrary, whether some be taken or, on the other hand, given, an unlivable life (is his).[b] And his wife is called in Hebrew "Mahalath," which is to be interpreted "from the beginning." [c] And potentially [d] this is sensual pleasure,[e] for it is considered to have been congenital [f] to every living creature from the beginning and from the first creation. And sensual pleasure is said to be the cause of many evils, both to those who have it and to those who come near it.[g] And her father is Ishmael, who is "hearing" [h] because of his not participating in vision. For the mind of the pleasure-loving man [i] is blind and unable to see those things which are worth seeing, (namely) the world and that which is in the world—the nature of existing things, the sight of which is wonderful to behold and desirable.[j]

[a] *OL* renders freely, "qualem . . . etiam tertiam illam desponsationem."

[b] ἀβίωτος βίος. The text of these two sentences is difficult. Aucher renders freely (with apologies in his footnotes), "quae enim corrigere potuerit eas quae apud illum sunt? Nullatenus, sed potius in contrarium: tum accepta quam data (pro exemplo) vita est praeter vitam": *OL* "de qua possit etiam priores emendare, absit sed ut rursus acciperet et praemuneraret eam quae vitam sine vita conficiunt."

[c] As if composed of the Heb. preposition *mē* "from" and the verbal root *ḥll* "to begin."

[d] δυνάμει. [e] ἡδονή. [f] σύντροφος.

[g] *OL* "pro subcisiva innumerabilium malorum tam pessimam tam noxiam preparavit etiam approximantibus perniciem."

[h] *Cf. De Fuga* 208 ἑρμηνεύεται γὰρ Ἰσμαὴλ ἀκοὴ θεοῦ: *De Mut. Nom.* 209 τὸ θεῖον ἄκουσμα. [i] ὁ τοῦ φιληδόνου νοῦς.

[j] At the end of this section, which concludes Book IV of the *Quaestiones in Genesin*, the Latin translator remarks, "Secundum consequentiam testimoniorum divinae Scripturae non exposuit Philo titulos allegoriae sed ea captare voluit capitula quae videntur intutui mentis suae succurrisse." See also Appendix B in Suppl. II.